AN
ECONOMIC HISTORY
OF MODERN BRITAIN

THE EARLY RAILWAY AGE
1820–1850

AN ECONOMIC HISTORY OF MODERN BRITAIN

THE EARLY RAILWAY AGE
1820-1850

By

J. H. CLAPHAM

CAMBRIDGE
AT THE UNIVERSITY PRESS
1967

PUBLISHED BY
THE SYNDICS OF THE CAMBRIDGE UNIVERSITY PRESS

Bentley House, 200 Euston Road, London, N.W.1
American Branch: 32 East 57th Street, New York, N.Y. 10022

First Edition	1926
Second Edition	1930
Reprinted with corrections	1939
Reprinted	1950
	1959
	1964
	1967

First printed in Great Britain at the University Press, Cambridge
Reprinted by offset lithography by Billing & Sons Limited
Guildford and London

TO
THE MEMORY
OF
ALFRED MARSHALL
AND
WILLIAM CUNNINGHAM

PREFACE TO THE REPRINT OF 1939

I AM putting in the Preface to this corrected reprint, which at the moment of writing (St Bartholomew's Day, 1939) and in view of my age seems likely to be the last, some extracts from the Prefaces to the first and second editions. All personal acknowledgements are left out, but the explanations of method and a few discussions which may have permanent interest are retained.

(*First Preface*.) British economic evolution during the last hundred years is, in some ways, so familiar that this instalment of a history on a fairly large scale perhaps requires an apology. Firstly, then, it has never been handled on the scale selected.

Secondly, stories assumed to be familiar are apt to become good nesting places for legend. Until very recently, historians' accounts of the dominant event of the nineteenth century, the great and rapid growth of population, were nearly all semi-legendary; sometimes they still are. Statisticians had always known the approximate truth; but historians had too often followed a familiar literary tradition. Again, the legend that everything was getting worse for the working man, down to some unspecified date between the drafting of the People's Charter and the Great Exhibition, dies hard. The fact that, after the price fall of 1820–1, the purchasing power of wages in general—not, of course, of everyone's wages—was definitely greater than it had been just before the revolutionary and Napoleonic wars, fits so ill with the tradition that it is very seldom mentioned, the work of statisticians on wages and prices being constantly ignored by social historians. It is symbolic of the divorce of much social and economic history from figures that, in a recent inquiry into the fortunes of one group of trades, the tradition of decline appears in the text, some corrective wage figures in an appendix, and the correlation nowhere.

Thirdly, it is possible, all along the line, to make the story more nearly quantitative than it has yet been made. Dropped here and there in the sources—in the blue books above all—lie all kinds of exact information, not only about wages and prices, but about the sizes of businesses and farms and steam-engines and social groups. Each Census is better and more illuminating than its predecessor; and that of 1851—the *terminus ad quem* for this volume—throws a strong light backward. In 1838 the *Journal* of the Statistical Society begins. A few years earlier the inspectors had started numbering the factories and the Poor Law Commissioners compiling their melancholy tables. We are not in the full statistical age. There are no mineral statistics before the 'fifties. Even foreign trade statistics—one of the oldest series—are very defective, and civil registration of births, deaths and marriages got going only in the same year as the *Statistical Journal*. Much approximation must be tolerated, and some guessing; but if the dimensions of things are not always clear, at least an attempt has been made to offer dimensions, in place of blurred masses of unspecified size.

Figures are invaluable; but the statistician's world is not the historian's. Nor is the general historian's world that of the monograph writer. As a balance to the unreality of the general-ised statistical statement and the undue influence of mono-graphs on particularly important trades or topics—and nearly all the best work on modern British economic history has been done in monograph—it has seemed wise to quote many scattered individual facts from all up and down the country and all over the economic field. Readers may find the tours from trade to trade and from county to county—tours for which the *Victoria Histories* have been invaluable—a little tiresome; but I do not know how to bring out the diversity of the national economic life otherwise. "We are not cotton-spinners all." Farmer, wage-earner, canal dividend or workhouse, in one part of the country, is seldom quite the same as in any other part. Many generalisations about the workings of the old English poor law would have been modified if historians had found time to study even the Scottish law, let alone county administration. There are links between enclosure and pauperism, such as have often been traced, but the most pauperised English county before 1834 was one in which the amount of recent enclosure was small—Sussex. Cobden's platform division of the island into the half that was interested in corn laws, because it was arable, and the half that was not, because it was in grass, may have been overdone; but its foundation was sound enough.

The scope of the book, as its name implies, is British. I have tried to do justice to Scotland and Wales, but have made no attempt to treat Ireland other than incidentally. Recent events justify this on the political side. Economically, the

United Kingdom was never more of a unit than it was geographically: Ireland always had its own distinctive economic
coastline and horizon. The story starts when the short-period
effects of the wars were easing, with a full analysis of economic
Britain as it was in 1820–30, including some retrospect (Book I).
Motion then begins and continues to various halts, according
to the subject handled, all between 1846 and 1851 (Book II).

(*Second Preface*.) In a..review of the first edition Mr J. L. Hammond pointed out that I had made no reference to the game laws
and some other burdens of the poor. Agreed: the economic historian is a specialist and no specialist tells the whole truth. But I
allow that even an economic specialist might well have referred
to the game laws. In a more sustained criticism in the *Economic
History Review* for January 1930 Mr Hammond deals with my
statistics and seems to imply, though of this I am not quite
sure, that I have formed "a happy impression" of this period.
Because in my Preface I described as a legend the view "that
everything was getting worse for the working-man down to
some unspecified date between the drafting of the People's
Charter and the Great Exhibition," I did not mean that everything was getting better. I only meant that recent historians
have too often, in my opinion, stressed the worsenings and
slurred over or ignored the betterings. To this opinion I hold.
Against my statistics of agricultural wages—or rather Professor
Bowley's—Mr Hammond makes a valid point. I use for dia-
grammatic puposes an average of county averages, so far as
these are known, and this figure ignores the relative wage-
earning populations of the counties. Mr Hammond calculates
that 60 per cent. of the labouring population was in counties
where wages fell below the average so arrived at. But in any
average some 50 per cent. of the figures averaged may be
expected to fall below the line, so that the discrepancy between
the two ways of looking at the matter is not very great. And I
have stated quite clearly on p. 129 the various important
counties in which my average was not reached, and why.

Mr Hammond expresses legitimate doubts about some of
the contemporary wage figures on which these generalisations
rest. But he quotes as more illuminating than my wage curves
passages from Lord Ernle which contain the statement that
agricultural wages "fell lower and lower every year after the
peace"—apparently until 1834. ("The Poor Law of 1834

marks the starting point in the recovery," *English Farming*, p. 407.) This is a curve in words and, if literally interpreted, an inaccurate one. There is no statistical evidence that wages fell "lower and lower every year" from 1815 to 1834, though there was a serious fall between 1814 and about 1822, with which I deal on pp. 125-6. To accept even the approximately accurate part of Lord Ernle's curve, Mr Hammond must also accept the wage-figures of 1823-4, with which when I use them he is somewhat dissatisfied. But as he ends a brief criticism of these and other statistics of mine with a "let us take it that so far as statistics can measure material improvement there was improvement," and passes to higher matters, there is no need to maintain an arithmetical wrangle. I agree most profoundly with his opinion that statistics of material well-being can never measure a people's happiness. As I have written on p. 114 "no comfortable statistics should be allowed to obscure...the hardships, injustices, and undeserved humiliations which the years from 1795 to 1825 had brought upon some of these [agricultural] labouring families." And yet I still submit that excessive concentration on these and other shadows of the historical landscape has led historians to ignore the patches of sunlight. It is very easy to do this unawares. Thirty years ago I read and marked Arthur Young's *Travels in France*, and taught from the marked passages. Five years ago I went through it again, to find that whenever Young spoke of a wretched Frenchman I had marked him, but that many of his references to happy or prosperous Frenchmen remained unmarked. Sympathy with wretchedness is the sign of a generous mind. Let us hope that the attempt to record other things, in their due proportion, does not denote an ageing heart hardened by statistics.

In this reprint I have retained the dedication to the memory of the two men who first taught me Economics and Economic History. To all others who have helped me, by writing criticism or advice, I offer, on a dark day, my thanks.

J. H. CLAPHAM

Cambridge
    24 *August, 1939*

CONTENTS

BOOK I

BRITAIN ON THE EVE OF THE RAILWAY AGE

BOOK II

THE EARLY RAILWAY AGE

Chapter XII. OVERSEAS TRADE AND COMMERCIAL
                POLICY   *page*

Chapter XIII. BANKING, PRICES AND THE MONEY
                 MARKET

Chapter XIV. LIFE AND LABOUR IN INDUSTRIAL
                BRITAIN

PLATES AND DIAGRAMS

BOOK I

BRITAIN
ON THE EVE OF
THE RAILWAY AGE

Grossbritannien...indem es sich an die Spitze dieser
Erfindungen und überhaupt aller anderen ökonomi-
schen Fortschritte stellte...erwuchs...zu einer Höhe von
Nationalkraft und Nationalreichtum, die nicht zu ver-
gleichen ist...mit den Zuständen irgendeiner Nation
der älteren oder neuern Zeit.   FRIEDRICH LIST, 1846

> Men of England, wherefore plough
> For the lords who lay ye low?
> Wherefore weave with toil and care
> The rich robes your tyrants wear?
>
> SHELLEY, 1819

The French Revolution produced a war which doubled
the cost and trebled the difficulty of genteel living.
The Lady's Keepsake and Maternal Monitor, 1835

CHAPTER I

THE FACE OF THE COUNTRY

THE foreigner who visited the England of King George IV, to study this "extraordinary land" in which "the new creations springing into life every year bordered on the fabulous,"[1] as a perhaps over-impressionable German put it, found that access had been eased greatly since 1821, when the first steamer began to run between Dover and Calais. The crossing now took only between three and four hours, "even with a contrary wind,"[2] provided the wind was not too strong. Other routes had similar facilities. Between the old wooden jetties, a hundred feet apart, at the mouth of the Sussex Ouse, a little steamer paddled out regularly from Newhaven to the much better cared-for port of Dieppe[3]. From London, steamers plying to the Low Countries and even to Hamburg and Gothenburg had attracted most of the postal and passenger traffic of the narrow seas before 1828: the old packets which still sailed from Harwich were very much neglected[4]. But it was not by the still rather explosive mail steamers that Britain lived; not even by those steamers "equipped with all possible comforts," and with tables actually laid for a hundred and thirty covers, which now plied between London and Leith—in summer[5].

An informed and discerning traveller, approaching England by the Thames, and watching the ships making for the Nore from all points on the British coasts and from every part of the earth, had before him a pageant of commercial sea-power, and a reminder of the high and sustained predominance of London over what were still sometimes called compendiously the outports. Since the wars the mercantile marine of the British Isles had been almost stationary in numbers and aggregate tonnage. If anything, there was a slight downward movement after 1820. But while the British shipping interest grumbled at the stagnation of a tonnage which fluctuated between 2,400,000 and

---

[1] Meidinger, H., *Reisen durch Grossbritannien und Irland* (1828), I. 100.
[2] Meidinger, *op. cit.* I. 1.
[3] Harcourt, L. F. Vernon, *Harbours and Docks* (1885), I. 343, 143.
[4] Meidinger, *op. cit.* I. 200.
[5] Meidinger, *op. cit.* II. 32.

2,200,000, foreigners saw only the unheard-of aggregate[1]. Of
that aggregate a full quarter (573,000 tons) was owned and
registered in London in 1829. Second to London came Newcastle, with 202,000 tons; third Liverpool, growing fast but
still with only 162,000 tons; fourth Sunderland with 108,000;
and fifth Whitehaven with 73,000. No other port in the country, except Hull (72,000), had as much as 50,000 tons of shipping; though Glasgow, Port Glasgow and Greenock taken
together had 84,000[2].

The average London owned ship was of 215 tons burden,
almost exactly twice the size of the average for the British Isles
including London[3]. The ships of Newcastle, Sunderland and
Whitehaven were principally colliers engaged in the coasting
trade; and a very large part of those from Newcastle and
Sunderland worked on a regular beat between their home port
and the Thames; for London had for centuries been the chief
consumer, and an important distributor, of sea-coal. In the
overseas trade, in spite of the growth of Liverpool, the predominance of London had not been even challenged: of the
coasting trade the major portion existed that Londoners might
be housed warmed and fed.

High among the "creations springing into life every year"
stood the new port and harbour works, which served the nineteen thousand ships of the merchant service and sheltered those
of the King's navy, and the new lighthouses which guided them.
Both in scientific harbour, and in lighthouse, building France
had long preceded England; but she had now been passed.
The few old British harbour works, such as the Cobb at Lyme
Regis, the rough quay at Whitby, or the ancient piers at Leith,
could not compare with the seventeenth-century works at
Havre; and, off the mouth of the Garonne, the light on the great
stone Tour de Cordouan had been burning for nearly ninety
years before even Winstanley's unfortunate timber structure
was finished on the Eddystone[4]. Down to the outbreak of what
men called in 1825 "the late wars," few large or difficult operations had been undertaken except at Liverpool. The first rough

---

[1] *Accounts and Papers*, 1821 (XVII. 285). *Ships and Tonnage belonging to Great
Britain* (with figures for earlier years). J. R. McCulloch, *Dictionary of Commerce*, 1832, *s.v.* "Ships" (the figures for 1829).
[2] Figures from McCulloch, *op. cit. s.v.* "Ships." Bristol's figure was 49,535.
[3] London: 2663 ships of 572,835 tons; the United Kingdom: 19,110 of
2,199,959 tons. McCulloch, *op. cit. s.v.* "Ships."
[4] Smiles, S., *Lives of the Engineers*, I. 283–5. Harcourt, *op. cit.* I. 545.

dock near London, the Howland Great Wet Dock at Rotherhithe, dated from the Restoration; but it was neither improved
nor enlarged. Liverpool's Old Dock of about $3\frac{1}{2}$ acres had been
made out of her pool in the first quarter of the eighteenth century. Before 1775, the Salthouse and George Docks had been
added, followed before the end of the century by the King's
and Queen's docks. At Hull the first dock was begun in 1775
and finished in 1778. At Bristol nothing was done beyond the
digging of one small square dock off the Avon, in 1767–9,
"capable of admitting a seventy-four."[1] Smeaton, who died
the year before the great wars began, was consulted by many
harbour authorities; "but in nearly every case want of money
prevented the improvements suggested by him from being fully
carried out,"[2] although Ramsgate harbour was completed to
his plans during the last years of his working life[3].

The needs of the fleet and of the mercantile navy in war-
time, together with the growing wealth and rapidly growing
engineering resources of the country, had transformed the
coasts and harbours of Britain. Between 1789, when Brunswick
Dock, Blackwall, was begun, and 1828, when St Katharine's
Docks were finished, London had been equipped with a dock
system—East and West India, London, Commercial, Surrey
and St Katharine's Docks—which served her, almost unchanged, until after 1850. Of these all but St Katharine's
Docks—the smallest—were finished before 1816[4]. Hull, between 1807 and 1892, completed the half-circle of docks which
enclosed the old town between the river Hull and the Humber[5].
Liverpool, unlike London, had by no means arrived at a point
of temporary equilibrium between dock-demand and dock-
supply, in the 'twenties of the nineteenth century. North and
south the docks were extending along the banks of the Mersey;
and between 1825 and 1846 the dock area was more than
doubled. In the 'twenties the old dock was filled in, and on its
site customs and administration offices were built, the adjacent

---

[1] Baron Dupin, *The Commercial Power of Great Britain*, II. 341. The English
version (2 vols. 1825) is used, not the French original. For Liverpool, see Defoe's
Tour (1724), II. 104, Webb, S. and B., *The Manor and the Borough*, p. 483,
Dupin, *op. cit.* II. 275: for Hull, Harcourt, *op. cit.* I. 521. [The George Dock at
Liverpool was not added before 1760, as stated in the 1st edn, but in 1771.
Marshall T. H., *E.H.R.* 1927, p. 625.]   [2] Smiles, *op. cit.* II. 64.
[3] Smiles, *op. cit.* II. 69. Harcourt, *op. cit.* I. 229–30.
[4] Harcourt, *op. cit.* I. 489. Broodbank, Sir J. G., *History of the Port of London*
(1921) is fuller.   [5] Harcourt, *op. cit.* I. 521.

docks being at the same time enlarged and added to and fitted with new equipment.

"The more recent the construction of the maritime works of Liverpool is," wrote the Baron Dupin, "the less wood is found in their composition...the capstans, the rollers...the footways across the gates of the locks, the railings along the sides of these footways, etc.; all these things are...in constructions of a more modern date, entirely of iron.... This is not the effect of any particular whim, or of a short-lived fashion; it is the necessary result of a comparison between the small cost of this material and the high price of wood."[1]

Bristol had diverted the Avon into a new channel and made a floating harbour out of the abandoned loops of the river, with connecting locks at both ends and the Cumberland Dock Basin —built of free stone—at the western exit. But although the main works were finished in 1809, they had not recovered for Bristol the ground lost to Liverpool: "of all the towns of Great Britain that I visited," Dupin said, "Bristol was the one where the general stagnation was most visible and most alarming."[2]

Though docks were not built nor needed everywhere, there was hardly a port of any size, or a threatened part of the coast, where improvements had not been recently undertaken or were not in hand during the middle 'twenties. Whitehaven, one of the harbours on which Smeaton had reported to no purpose, began important works in 1824; the tiny port of Grimsby had already dug out its first dock; Leith was engaged on extensions of its piers and breakwaters in 1825-8; for Dundee, Telford, who had planned important works at Aberdeen and Peterhead during the wars, completed the floating dock in 1825; dredging and quay-building on the Clyde kept the river abreast of the growing trade of Glasgow; on the Channel coast, the Lords of the Level of Romney Marsh, for the first time in a thousand years, began to use stone on Dymchurch Wall in 1825; various great works were on foot in Dublin Bay and at Holyhead in connection with the scheme for a closer linking of Dublin with London; and the gigantic operations on Plymouth breakwater, where was achieved in 1821 the feat of laying 373,000 tons of stone in a year, went their slow way over many obstacles[3]. The

[1] Dupin, op. cit. II. 279. Harcourt, op. cit. I. 504.

[2] Dupin, op. cit. I. 344. See also Harcourt, op. cit. I. 529 and Webb, op. cit. pp. 460-1.

[3] Whitehaven, Harcourt, op. cit. I. 327; Grimsby, Meidinger, op. cit. I. 230; Leith, Harcourt, op. cit. I. 545; Dundee, Aberdeen and Peterhead, Harcourt,

London-Dublin connection was completed when, on January
30, 1826, an official procession, followed by "a multitude of
private persons too numerous to mention,"[1] crossed Telford's
Menai Bridge, which had taken near six years to build and had
cost the state £120,000.

That ancient and honourable corporation, the Brethren of
the Trinity House, which according to Dupin "carefully retained all its good and bad qualities,"[2] had almost completed
the task of lighting the English coasts—well, if not economically. It controlled thirty-five lighthouses, from Scilly and the
Eddystone to Flamborough, Farne Islands and St Bees, in 1830,
besides the floating lights of Spurn, the Gull Stream, the
Galloper, Sunk Sand, the Goodwins, the Nore and five other
points. The latest addition to its houses was Beachy Head,
lighted up on October 1, 1828, and to its floating lights the Well
Lightship, in Lynn Deeps, of the same year. Besides the houses
of the Brethren there were a few ancient houses belonging to
the Crown, but leased out to private persons. W. T. Coke, Esq.,
held a twenty-one years' lease, as from 1828, and a right to half
the light-dues at Dungeness; while at Hunstanton S. Lane,
Esq. had all the dues. The North and South Foreland lights
belonged to the Greenwich trustees until February, 1832, when
Trinity House took them over. Newcastle had its own light-
owning Trinity House, Liverpool its light-owning Dock
Trustees; and four or five small houses were literally "in the
hands of private individuals," their proprietors[3].

Far younger, as efficient, and by repute more economical
than the Brethren of Trinity House were the Commissioners
for the Northern Lights, created by Act of Parliament in 1786.
They began by lighting Kinnaird Head in 1787 and had won
for themselves a European fame when, on February 2, 1811,
the lamps were first lighted on the Bell Rock. They had continued their work since, in the less frequented Northern and
North-Western Scottish waters. The Rhinns of Islay were
lighted up on November 15, 1825; Buchanness on May 1, 1827;

op. cit. I. 170, and Smiles, op. cit. II. 393–408; Romney Marsh, Webb, S. and B.,
English Local Government, Statutory Authorities for special purposes, p. 38;
Dublin and Holyhead, Harcourt, op. cit. I. 167, 169 and Dupin, op. cit. II. 314;
Plymouth, Harcourt, op. cit. I. 187.

[1] Smiles, op. cit. II. 459. See also Dupin, op. cit. II. 369.

[2] Dupin, op. cit. II. 158, also II. 76 n.

[3] *Accounts and Papers*, 1833 (XXXIII), 1 (Lighthouse Returns), 125 (Trinity
House Receipts).

Cape Wrath on Christmas Day, 1828, and Tarbetness on January 29, 1829[1]. And so—

From reef and rock and skerry—over headland, ness, and voe—
　The Coastwise Lights of England watched the ships of England go.

To keep in touch with the fleets and direct the convoyed merchantmen during the wars, the Admiralty had erected four lines of telegraph from Whitehall—to Plymouth, Portsmouth, Deal and Yarmouth. The line of posts, with their wooden arms, along the Portsmouth road stood to be reported on and compared with the new "galvanic" telegraph in 1840. At that time their maintenance cost £3300 a year. To save three times that sum the other lines had been abolished, as an act of peace economy, in 1816. The French meanwhile maintained, and in the 'twenties and 'thirties extended, their telegraph system. So far as is known, there were no important economic consequences of either policy; only the French Foreign Office gained some hours on the British with the news of Europe[2].

From works of utility and defence, the new art of coastal engineering had already passed to works of ornament and amusement. The Cobb at Lyme Regis, "in its ancient state composed of vast pieces of rocks," had been so improved in the eighteenth century that it served as a genteel promenade in Jane Austen's day[3]. But such things were rare. Ten years after Miss Austen's death, the Margate Pier and Harbour Company was charging one penny admission to the raised promenade, with its green iron railings, on the seaward side of Margate's long pier of finished masonry[4]. Twopence was the charge for admission to the Brighton Chain Pier, which Captain Brown and the Brighton Chain Pier Company had carried over 1100 feet out to sea and furnished with a camera obscura, a sundial, two small cannon, several green benches and some mineral-water booths, in 1824[5]. These were among the beginnings of seaside amenities. Although from 30,000 to 40,000 people were supposed

[1] *Accounts and Papers*, 1833 (XXXIII), 55 (Report of Commissioners for the Northern Lighthouses). For a contemporary appreciation, Dupin, *op. cit.* II. 158.
[2] For the semaphore telegraph see the *Fourth Report of the Select Committee on Railway Communications*, 1840 (XIII. 129), p. 7; for France, Clapham, J. H., *Economic Development of France and Germany*, 1815–1914 (1923), p. 156. [The semaphore telegraph was used for signalling from Holyhead to Liverpool, 1826–9. Dodd, G. H., *The Industrial Revolution in North Wales* (1933), p. 123.]
[3] *The Beauties of England* (1803), IV. 535. Jane Austen, *Persuasion*, ch. 12.
[4] Meidinger, *op. cit.* I. 88. This pier was built by Rennie in 1810.
[5] Meidinger, *op. cit.* I. 100–1. Dupin, *op. cit.* I. 376. *D.N.B.* Sir Samuel Brown. Brown's chain-pier at Leith was earlier (1821).

to visit Margate every summer[1], many of them going down with
music and by steam from London, and although the population
of Brighton, which had been only 7000 in 1801, grew from about
24,000 to about 40,000 while its patron King George IV
reigned; although "a bathing machine," or bathing machines,
were reported at many points along the coasts; yet the temporary
and permanent migrations of population to the sea for reasons
of health and fashion were on but a small scale. Brighton,
however, had made a beginning in both kinds. "Mark the
process; the town of Brighton, in Sussex, 50 miles from the
Wen...is thought by the stock-jobbers to afford a salubrious
air.... They skip backward and forward on the coaches, and
actually carry on stock-jobbing in Change Alley, though they
reside at Brighton."[2] But where Bournemouth now stands were
some half-dozen houses, in 1830, and a wild heath on which
bustard and hen-harrier bred[3].

Behind its coasts, the face of rural Britain was fast losing the
last traces of primitive conditions and primitive agriculture.
Unlike every continental country, it had been stripped almost
completely of its native woodland. A land of park, copse,
plantation, and—in many parts—of hedgerow timber, it was
a land with singularly little forest, natural or cultivated. There
is no forest note in contemporary English literature; only an
occasional prose comment in Wordsworth's Prefaces. The
ancient royal forests had been so neglected during the eighteenth
century, and so heavily drawn upon for ships' timber and fuel
during the wars that, in all probability, they were emptier of
serviceable trees in 1815 than at any time in their history. The
New Forest had produced little fine timber since early Stuart
times. A survey of 1608 had registered 123,927 trees there fit
for navy use; a survey of 1707 could report only 12,476. In
spite of forest legislation under William III, and again in 1769
and 1770, there had been no recovery by 1793. Further legislation, under the goad of war, in 1808, had produced some
results; so that by 1819 five thousand acres had been planted,
mostly with oak[4]. Sherwood had been almost dissipated into
parks and arable, by grant and enclosure. The two main

---

[1] So Meidinger, *op. cit.* I. 87.
[2] Cobbett, W., *Rural Rides* (1823), ed. Pitt Cobbett, 1885, I. 206.
[3] Malmesbury, *Memories of an ex-minister*, I. 10.
[4] *V.C.H. Hampshire*, II. 454.

stretches of wood still under the Crown, Birklands and Bilhagh, were reported to contain 10,000 serviceable oaks in 1790[1]. As a single ship of the line consumed 4000 well-grown trees this was but a poor reserve. Reserves in Waltham Forest—better known by the names of its two chief constituents, Epping and Hainault Forests—were even poorer. The Crown lands in Hainault Forest had been reduced by alienation and encroachment to the paltry figure of less than 3000 acres. In 1783 there stood on them 11,055 oak trees, of which only 2760 were of navy grade and size. No attempt was made to save the forests. The Act of 1808 was not extended to Essex. Sale of forestal rights continued and encroachments were connived at. A little refuge for gipsies; a place of holiday pilgrimage for Londoners; a precious enough sanctuary for wild things; and twenty more or less sinecure posts of keepers and underkeepers for its ten "walks" were the survivals of Waltham Forest in 1831[2].

The Forest of Dean had been heavily cut over for its own iron industry, but still held considerable stretches of ancient and rather neglected woodland, useful only—so Cobbett thought in 1821—"for furnishing a place of being to labourers' families on the skirts.... Some keep cows," he added, "and all of them have bits of ground, cribbed, of course, at different times from the forest."[3] He had noticed the same things in Hampshire. There was, in fact, a fair amount of good navy oak in the forest, which stood until required for the last of the wooden ships, between 1854 and 1864[4].

That ancient royal forests should be mishandled and dwindle was natural. Planted woods in the parks and the woodland on private estates were at least better guarded and sometimes well managed, as was the King's personal forest of Windsor[5]. Much fine navy oak, remnants of Arden, stood on private land in Warwickshire in 1813: the reporter to the Board of Agriculture believed that a single estate there carried £100,000 worth[6]. Sussex, "still the most thickly wooded of English counties to-day,"[7] had sacrificed during the wars much of that "prodigious" timber which Defoe saw on his way from Tunbridge Wells to Lewes; but much of all sorts remained "in the miry coppices, the wild woods and forests of Sussex and Hamp-

[1] *V.C.H. Nottingham*, I. 374.   [2] *V.C.H. Essex*, II. 615 *sqq.*
[3] *Rural Rides*, I. 34.   [4] *V.C.H. Gloucester*, II. 278.
[5] So Meidinger, *op. cit.* I. 425.   [6] *V.C.H. Warwick*, II. 295.
[7] *V.C.H. Sussex*, II. 291.

shire."[1] Forests some of them were in name, but probably only an Englishman would have used the term. Kent had little "wild wood," except on the Sussex border, but much orderly coppice of chestnut, ash, willow and maple for the hop-poles[2]. West of the Hampshire forests and chases there were woods in fair abundance—though not enough to supply the poor with reasonably cheap firing—but nothing even called a forest except the patch of Savernake, twelve miles in circumference, until you came to the Dean Forest and the considerable adjacent woodlands, on the Gloucestershire, Herefordshire and Monmouthshire sides. Somerset and Devon had their forests of heather moor, with some old timber in the combes and valley bottoms. Cornwall had always been short of woodland because of the wind. The shortage was now extreme: it was a man of Launceston, "a tradesman too," who told Cobbett "that the people in general could not afford to have fire in ordinary, and that he himself paid 3d. for boiling a leg of mutton at another man's fire."[3]

Except for the beechwoods of Buckinghamshire, and some other scraps of old beechwood on the chalk, the whole country north of the Thames and east of a line roughly drawn from Gloucester to Whitby had either never been heavily wooded, or had long since lost its natural woods, except for such remnants as Sherwood and Waltham Forest. Its timber was mainly that of park, hedgerow, farmstead and modern plantation. A good deal of it was ornamental, a dignified setting for country seats, like those extensive plantations laid out at Welbeck—in what had once been Sherwood—"to clothe the landscape," about the year 1726[4]. West of the Gloucester-Whitby line, Hereford and Shropshire had retained rather more woodland; but in the North-West, on the bleak Staffordshire slopes, the flats of Cheshire and Lancashire, on the Pennine sands, limestones and gritstones, and in the Lake District valleys, the eighteenth century had seen an almost complete clearance of the last of the ancient forest, where forest had ever existed.

Riding by Woolmer Forest in 1822 Cobbett came upon some plantations of fir. "What he can plant the *fir* for, God only knows," was his comment, "seeing that the country is already overstocked with that rubbish."[5] If it really was, the over-

---

[1] *Rural Rides*, I. 54.
[2] *V.C.H. Kent*, I. 475.
[3] *Rural Rides*, I. 73.
[4] *V.C.H. Nottingham*, I. 380.
[5] *Rural Rides*, I. 182

stocking had been very quick; for the Scots fir had only been
introduced into Southern England—strictly speaking reintro-
duced; but it had been extinct for ages—about the year 1775[1].
The larch, unknown in Britain until some thirty years before
that date, came with it. Progress was at first slow, but the commission on forests which sat from 1787 to 1793 strongly recommended the planting of these conifers[2]; the growing shortage
and the high price of timber during the wars endorsed their
recommendation; and enough at least was done in the next
twenty years to give a tolerable foundation for Cobbett's grumble.
He was not alone in protest. At the far end of England another
man who preferred the country as it was to the country as it
was becoming joined with him. Larch plantations with their
unpleasing surface texture—"ten thousand of this spiky tree...
stuck in at once upon the side of a hill"—and the "platoons"
of artificially distributed Scots fir seemed to Wordsworth improper substitutes for the scrub of oak, ash, holly and birch
and the self-grouped yews which were the native, but now
scanty, timber of his Cumbrian valleys[3]. Cobbett too was all
for British oak and ash; he hated the soft larches; and when
advocating exotic timber, which he did roundly, he spoke of
nothing but the hard American locust-wood. But in spite of
him, and for very good reasons, sandy heath, waste hillside,
and many less suitable places, from one end of England to the
other, were being sprinkled over with wood—coppice screen
and clump of pine or larch or spruce. No doubt Cobbett's
criticisms of errors in the location and management of
many of the young fir woods were right, for he had a fine
eye for the health of a tree; but in the main the fir planters
were right also. Though they made no attempt to reafforest
England on a great scale, they often reclothed old forest
land with firs, besides laying out their new screens and
coppices.

In North Wales most of the ancient forest had vanished very
long ago, though some districts were still heavily timbered
in the early eighteenth century. "Less than a century ago,'
Davies reported of Montgomery in 1813, that country was so

---

[1] First in the New Forest in 1776: *V.C.H. Hampshire*, II. 454.

[2] *V.C.H. Essex*, II. 621; *Hampshire*, II. 454.

[3] Wordsworth, W., *Guide to the Lake District* (1835), p. 6, 29, etc. Wordsworth noted (p. 28) that at one time the Scots fir "must have grown in great
profusion": no ancient ones had survived to his day.

rich in woods that everyone burnt "the best cleft timber."[1]
About the decade 1730–40, the long arm of the navy reached
the Montgomery oak woods and clearing began. The business
was carried too far; but wood was still abundant in 1813.
Flint, Denbigh, Merioneth and Carnarvon had been pretty
thoroughly cleared at an earlier date. Very little wood was
burnt for fuel. Flint had its coal, which served the east of
Denbigh also: westward into the mountains, peat was the staple
firing[2]. But, as in England, plantation—especially the plantation of fir woods—had begun; and, though its progress was
said to be still slow in 1813, something had been accomplished
on the valley slopes of the Mawddach and the Dee in Merioneth
and, to the north, on those of the Conway, from above Bettws
to the sea[3]. In South Wales, the opener parts of Radnor and
Brecon, on the Herefordshire side, were like Montgomery fairly
well wooded: the higher ground was everywhere bare. The
table-land of Cardigan which includes most of the county, all
along the bay and back to the valley of the Teifi, was woodless
and hedgeless[4]. Pembrokeshire had for centuries been open
ground: it was a "bare champion" country in Queen Elizabeth's
day. So was the coastal plain of Glamorgan, "a champion and
open country without great store of inclosures."[5] There was
woodland in some of the valleys, especially in the Vale of Neath,
but neither there nor in Carmarthen was there anything which
might be called forest. As in the North, fir plantation had
begun; and the rapid development of the South Welsh coalfield—though meeting all fuel demands, beyond that of the
high valleys, where peat served—was giving a new value to
any woods and coppices from which pit wood and pit props
could be cut.

Early eighteenth-century Scotland had been a far barer
country than either Wales or England. The author of the
*Essay on Ways and Means for Inclosing, Fallowing, Planting, etc.
Scotland and that in Sixteen Years at farthest*, in 1729, spoke
of his country as being "intirely destitute of forest, or indeed
any quantity of woods to furnish brushwood."[6] If enclosure
was started, he said, the Scots must get their quicksets from

[1] Davies, W.. *General View of the Agriculture of N. Wales* (1813), p. 239.
[2] *Ibid.* p. 368–70.			[3] *Ibid.* p. 236.
[4] Davies, W., *General View of the Agriculture of S. Wales* (1814), I. 221.
[5] Rice Merrick, 1578, quoted in Rhys and Brynmor-Jones, *The Welsh People*
(1900), p. 247.
[6] *Essay on Ways and Means... By a Lover of his Country* (B. Macintosh), p. 23.

England or Holland; for they had none. More than forty years later, Samuel Johnson's sneer about trees in Scotland was still not undeserved, certainly not in the West and North; though, in 1773 when he travelled with Boswell, considerable progress had been made in plantation by the lairds of the South-East[1]. Ayrshire, for example, was still extraordinarily bare in the 'sixties and 'seventies, but plantation was just beginning. Accurately enough, John Galt selected the year 1765 as that in which the fictitious Mr Kibbock, father of the second Mrs Balwhidder, "planted mounts of fir-trees on the bleak and barren tops of the hills of his farm, the which everybody, and I among the rest, considered as a thrashing of the water and raising of bells." But the Mr Kibbocks were imitated, so that when Mr Balwhidder sat down to write his memories, in 1810, he "had heard travellers say, who had been in foreign countries, that the shire of Ayr, for its bonny round green plantings on the tops of the hills" was "above comparison either with Italy or Switzerland, where the hills are, as it were, in a state of nature."[2] On the other side of the country, Aberdeenshire had also been a bare woodless land. But when Anderson reported on the county to the Board of Agriculture, in 1794, plantation was in full swing[3]. Planting went forward rapidly between 1780 and 1820 in the Highlands. Afforestation on a considerable scale was undertaken by some of the great landowners[4]. In Perthshire "great districts are to be met with under timber, such as the pine woods of Rannoch. However the newer plantations are mostly larch." In Garmouth, at the mouth of the Spey, were a number of sawmills, where the timber floated down the river from the forest of Badenoch, rented by the Duke of Gordon to the London Timber Company, was cut up and shipped, mainly to Deptford and Woolwich. "Everywhere now," added Meidinger who reports these facts, "a rational forest administration is being introduced, and if this goes on Scotland will compete with Norway and Sweden."[5] A sanguine judgment but,

[1] Graham, H. G., *Social Life in Scotland in the Eighteenth Century*, 2nd ed. 1906, p. 220.

[2] Galt, J., *Annals of the Parish* (Ed. Everyman), p. 28.

[3] Anderson, J., *General View of the Agriculture of Aberdeen*, p. 33.

[4] Balfour, Lady Frances, *Life of the Earl of Aberdeen* (1922), I. 52, 196, etc., shows the process at work on one great estate from 1801 onwards.

[5] Meidinger, *op. cit.* II. 50, 66. Badenoch and other central districts still had *Urwald* of fir. On the West, woods of "Birch, Alder and Hazel, with a small intermixture of Oak and Ash" predominated. *Survey of the Coasts of Scotland*, 1803 (IV), p. 34-5.

coming as it does from a man in whose country forests and forest administration were understood, a judgment honourable to the pioneers of scientific arboriculture among the Scottish landlords.

Although Britain had lost at a very early date the greater part of its ancient forests and woodlands, there had survived, far into modern times, considerable stretches of sandy waste heath, fenland, rough mountain pasture, and ordinary village common. But by the end of the first quarter of the nineteenth century the work of enclosure, drawn out through many centuries, which the growth of population during the wars had stimulated into fierce activity, had reduced the waste area—at least in England and Wales—to what, judged by any but English standards, must have seemed insignificant dimensions. It is possible that so much as a quarter of England and Wales was still "common and waste"; but though any estimate is highly conjectural, one-fifth seems more probable and even less might well be correct[1]. Whatever estimate were taken would include all the mountain and heath land used for grazing—mainly in Wales and the North-West—which, even eighty-five years later, when the absolute possible minimum of "common and waste" had certainly been almost reached, covered just over one-tenth of the whole country[2]. In no English county except Westmorland was any really large area of waste land enclosed by Act of Parliament between 1820 and 1870, by which date such enclosure had practically ceased[3]. The figure for Westmorland is 8·6 per cent. of the county. Cumberland comes second with 4·4 per cent. Then Northumberland with 3·5 and the West and North Ridings each with 3·0. The only other counties for which the percentage exceeds 2·0 are Hampshire (2·5) and Surrey (2·6). For Wales no similar calculations have been made; but no doubt most Welsh counties would resemble those of North-Western England in having a

[1] Before the *Select Committee on Commons Inclosure* (1844, v) Richard Jones, tithe commissioner, guessed that 8 out of 37 million acres were still "common and waste." *Report*, p. 1, and *Evidence*, Q 1–181.

[2] *Agricultural Statistics*, 1910 (Cd. 5585), p. 62. Area of England and Wales 37,300,000 acres: mountain, etc., grazing 3,700,000 acres.

[3] See Gonner, E. C. K., *Common Land and Inclosure* (1912), p. 279 *sqq.*, where the figures are set out. Under the Act of 1845 (8 and 9 Vict. c. 118), which followed the inquiry, 619,000 acres of common had been enclosed down to 1870. *Ibid.* p. 93.

relatively high enclosure figure after 1820. Enclosures by Act were not the only form of enclosure. Mountain and other waste not subject to common rights might be enclosed by the owner at will. But this situation, though almost universal in Scotland, was uncommon south of the Tweed; so that the work done by Act after 1820 is a fair, though not a complete, indication of what, at that date, remained to be done before the country attained its present standard of enclosure.

The whole business of enclosing commons slackened abruptly after 1820. In the desperate attempt to get corn, and rents, since 1793 it had in some cases been overdone. Riding over Longwood warren, an ancient down, south-east of Winchester, in 1823, Cobbett noted that "these hills are among the most barren in England; yet a part of them was broken up during the rage for improvements....A man must be mad, or nearly mad, to sow wheat upon such a spot. However, a large part of what was enclosed has been thrown out again already, and the rest will be thrown out in a very few years."[1] Much evidence of the same sort is available from Cobbett's writings and elsewhere. But there is an equal amount relating to these late enclosed commons on the other side. Cobbett himself noted that between Fareham and Titchfield "a large part of the ground is a common enclosed some years ago. It is therefore amongst the worst of the land in the country [or it would have been enclosed sooner, is the argument]. Yet I did not see a bare field of corn along here, and the Swedish turnips were, I think, full as fine as any that I saw upon the South Downs."[2] He added, in explanation, that the Portsmouth manure was answerable for some part of the yield.

Meidinger, a great admirer of England, is a partial witness; but he is worth quoting, on this point also. He travelled here in 1820, 1821, 1824, and 1825–6. "I admit I was often amazed," said he, "when I came back after a year or two into neighbourhoods where formerly were great uncultivated areas, to see them made productive as though by magic and transformed into fine corn-bearing fields: notably in the counties of Lincoln, Suffolk, Wiltshire and Devon."[3] It was in Lincolnshire, and about this time, that the "stubbing of Thornaby waäste" was the greatest achievement in the life of one northern farmer[4].

[1] *Rural Rides*, I. 244.   [2] *Ibid.* I. 237.
[3] *Op. cit.* I. xviii.
[4] Tennyson, *The Northern Farmer: Old Style.*

By 1830 the stubbing was nearly done, and well done. When Cobbett zigzagged through the county for the first time, in that year—from Holbeach to Boston, Horncastle, Spittal near Lincoln, Louth and Grimsby to Barton on Humber—he sang an agricultural (but not a social) *Nunc Dimittis* before crossing into Yorkshire: "here...we arrived at the northern point of this noble county, having never seen one single acre of waste land and not one acre of what could be called bad land in the south of England."[1]

What common or open ground now remained in lowland England—below the 500 foot contour line, to take a rough division—was almost entirely in small patches which hardly affected the general character of the scenery. Some of the sand country of Surrey, especially that of the Surrey-Berkshire border, was still rough and wild, and Bagshot Heath was a synonym for neglected barrenness; there was waste land enough, even where trees were scarce, in the New Forest; a good deal of land in Sherwood too was "heath and fern producing nothing"[2]; but the lantern on Dunstan Pillar which used to guide travellers across Lincoln Heath had not been lighted since 1808[3], and even the impracticable warren-land of North-East Suffolk that stretches across the Little Ouse into Norfolk had been attacked, if not completely mastered. Farm names still serve to date the attack—Waterloo Farm, 6½ miles north-east of Brandon and St Helena Farm, on the edge of the sands, just north of Mildenhall. In North Norfolk, Coke and his tenants and his imitators had brought much light soil, previously waste, under the plough; although some of the blown sands by the coast were beyond even their strength.

West of the Norfolk sand and chalk the Fenland, covering some fourteen hundred square miles, including the clay islands that stand above the great levels, had been half-conquered for a century and more[4]. By 1830 the last stage in the conquest had just begun. In April of that year Cobbett made a raid into the northern fens from Peterborough to Wisbech, and so to Boston. He was amazed at this country all "as *level* as the table at

[1] *Rural Rides*, II. 322.
[2] *Select Committee on Commons Inclosure*, 1844, Q. 3589, referring to the state of the land a few years earlier.
[3] Smiles, *op. cit.* I. 233 n.
[4] J. A. Clarke, "On the Great Level of the Fens," *J.R. Ag. Soc.* VIII. 80, reckons 680,000 acres.

which I am now writing": "the land covered with beautiful grass, with sheep lying about upon it, as fat as hogs": "immense bowling-greens separated by ditches": "what a contrast between these and the heath-covered sandhills of Surrey amongst which I was born": "the same...all the way to Boston: endless grass and endless fat sheep: not a stone, not a weed."[1] But a little to one side of his route Whittlesea Mere, Ramsey Mere and Ugg Mere were still undrained. There were patches of the true ancient reed-fen and sedge-fen and much "rotten ground"—ground where sheep rotted—in other parts of the levels. The great copper butterfly was not yet extinct; neither was the ague, against which the fenmen still took their opium pills[2]. That Cobbett saw so many "bowling-greens" was significant. There were still risks of "drowning," and land liable to be "drowned" is seldom tilled. In spite of Rennie's drainage work on the Boston fens, finished in 1814; in spite of the completion, in 1821, of the Eau Brink Cut at Lynn, by which all the waters of the Ouse basin were given a direct, in place of a serpentine, outlet to the Wash and the fall for the water increased back almost to Cambridge; in spite of the opening, in 1831, of Telford's New Outfall Cut for the river Nene which was so successful that, miles away, the fenmen played truant from church to see the "waters running" in their sluggish lodes[3]; in spite of all this, those wide areas even of the most southerly fens which lie only from five to ten feet above tide water were not yet finally safeguarded by an efficient pumping system against occasional "drowning." "From Ely to Cambridge," notes Meidinger in guide-book style, "16 English miles through a swampy land...but drained more and made more cultivable every year."[4] The "scoop-wheels," like mill wheels reversed, which lifted the water had begun to be driven by steam, and their construction was being improved. It was precisely between Ely and Cambridge, at Bottisham Fen, that Rennie had put the first Watt engine to drive a scoop in 1820. Four years later two steam-driven scoops, with engines of 60 and 80 horse-power, were set up at Podehole, just outside

[1] *Rural Rides*, II. 313–15. Oats were still the chief grain crop in the fens. Porter, *Progress of the Nation*, p. 153.

[2] See Kingsley, C., *Prose Idylls: the Fens.*

[3] Smiles, *op. cit.* II. 163–8, 471–2. Wheeler, W. H., *A History of the Fens of South Lincolnshire* (2nd ed. 1896), p. 112 and *passim.* Clarke, "The Great Level of the Fens," *J.R. Ag. Soc.* VIII. 89.

[4] *Op. cit.* I. 219.

Spalding, to drain Deeping Fen; but the work was not well designed and had to be modified. A few more engines were erected before 1830, but not for many years was the steam drive so generally adopted as to guarantee efficient drainage under all conditions of wind and tide[1].

England in the 'twenties, to the eye of a Continental visitor, was essentially a hedged and fenced land with a "garden-like" agriculture. Entry into the country through Kent, anciently enclosed and meticulously cultivated "right up to the edge of the cliffs,"[2] no doubt coloured the visitor's memories and descriptions; but for purposes of comparison with almost any district of Northern Europe, the impression was not seriously at fault. Taken as a whole British agriculture was undoubtedly the best in Europe, and as a land of enclosure England was unique. The work of rearranging and fencing the ancient common arable fields, with their patchwork of scattered holdings, had, generally speaking, preceded the last desperate attack on the common wastes, the fells and the fens, in the age when the swift growth of population was driving Ricardo's margin of cultivation visibly across the heaths and up the hills. There were, in 1820, only half a dozen English counties of whose area more than three per cent. remained to be enclosed from the open-field state by Act of Parliament; and in these a fair part of the remaining work was done before 1830[3].

Parliamentary enclosure of the open fields had only become the regular method about the end of the first quarter of the eighteenth century. From that time onwards enclosure Acts are a good, if not quite a complete, test of the pace and extent of the movement. The section of England affected by the Acts relating to open fields lay almost entirely between two lines, one drawn straight from Lyme Regis to Gloucester and from Gloucester to the Tees estuary, the second straight from Southampton to Lowestoft passing London a few miles to the west. Of the patches of country appreciably affected by the Acts outside these lines the most important, on the west, are

---

[1] The scoop-wheel, which "resembles a breast water-wheel with reverse action" (Wheeler, *op. cit.* p. 380), was a very ancient device. For Bottisham and Podehole see Wheeler, p. 330, 379, and Glynn, J., in *Trans. of the Royal Soc. of Arts*, LI. 1838. See below, p. 135, 445–6.

[2] Meidinger, *op. cit.* I. 5.

[3] The six counties were Bedford, Buckingham, Cambridge, Huntingdon, Northampton, Oxford. Gonner, *op. cit.* p. 279 *sqq.*

a small one in mid-Somerset and another in the Yorkshire
Dales, and, on the east, two patches in South-West Sussex
and one in North-East Surrey. In the last there was still some
open-field to be enclosed, at the time of Waterloo: "we are
two carriages," said John Knightly to poor Mr Woodhouse
when it came on to snow at the dinner party; "if one is blown
over in the bleak part of the common field, there will be the
other at hand."[1]

The counties and parts of counties outside the boundary
lines of the great central wedge, a wedge which covers rather
more than half England, had for the most part been reckoned
districts of ancient enclosure even in Tudor times. Either the
open-field system had never existed in them, or it had existed
in a form which rendered its transformation easy; in either
case it had vanished at an early date. Within the wedge the
work of field enclosure had been continuous since the sixteenth
century; but in the Midlands, particularly in the East Midlands,
a very great deal still remained to do when Parliamentary
enclosure began. The block of counties most affected by that
movement comprised East Warwick, Oxford, Berkshire, Leicester, Rutland, Northampton, Huntingdon, Buckingham,
Cambridge and Bedford. From this block a strip of country
similarly affected ran North through West Lincoln and the
Eastern side of Nottingham into the East Riding. But, by
1820, in most parts of the block the work was nearly finished;
a countryside where the open-field predominated was hardly to
be found; though all over the central wedge, and here and there
outside of it for that matter, common-field parishes lingered on[2].

The only two English counties of whose common-fields a
really considerable proportion remained to be enclosed in 1820
were, by a coincidence which is perhaps not entirely accidental, Oxford and Cambridge; and South Cambridgeshire
furnished, at that time, the nearest approach to a common-
field country still left in England. Cobbett came into it, in
January, 1822, over the poor, high, chalk land of North Hertfordshire by way of Royston. "It is a common market town.
Not mean, but having nothing of beauty about it; and having
on it, on three of the sides out of the four, those very ugly
things, common-fields, which have all the nakedness without

---

[1] Jane Austen, *Emma*, ch. 15. *Emma* was written between 1811 and 1816:
"Hartfield" was 16 miles from London and 7 from Boxhill.

[2] See the Plate facing this page.

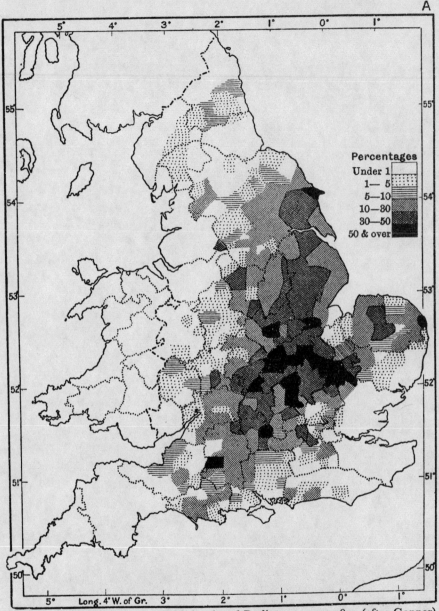

Enclosure of English Common Fields by Act of Parliament, 1700–1870 (after Gonner).
The percentages are those of the total area of each county—or district within a
county—enclosed from common fields in the whole period.

Enclosure of English Common Fields by Acts of Parliament, 1700–1870 (after Gonner). The percentages are those of the total area of each county—or district, within a county—enclosed from common fields in the whole period.

any of the smoothness of Downs."[1] Next day he travelled
north "for a considerable distance with enclosed fields on the
left and open common-fields on the right." All the way along
the Old North Road to Huntingdon "the face of the country
was naked," "generally quite open, or in large fields." Caxton
reminded him of a village in Picardy where he had seen "women
dragging harrows to harrow in the corn." "All was bleak and
comfortless," and Caxton gibbet was fresh painted[2]. Eight
years later, along a different line—from Cambridge to St Ives—
he noted much the same bareness of "open unfenced fields";
but they were no longer predominantly common, for he added
the note "and some common-fields."[3] By that time Oxford
and Cambridge were nearly in line with the rest of England[4].

That the rearrangement of the common-field patchwork into
compact and more or less rectangular areas had not always
been followed by hedging or fencing, this account of the road
from Cambridge to St Ives shows. Cobbett noted similar unfenced fields in some of "the broadest valleys in Wiltshire,"[5]
and no doubt they were to be found on newly divided land
elsewhere. But in most places, actual enclosure was the rule,
whether the land was old common-field or old common pasture
or waste. The Lincoln wolds for instance, once sheep-run, had
been fenced and tilled over their very crests; the fields "not
without fences...from fifteen to forty acres: the hills not downs
as in Wiltshire; but cultivated all over."[6] Cobbett's account of
the two sides of the North Road in Cambridgeshire gives the
contrast between the new England of the Midlands at its best
and that old Midland England which had so nearly vanished
away.

The fields on the left seem to have been enclosed by Act of Parliament; and they certainly are the most beautiful tract of fields that I ever
saw. Their extent may be from ten to thirty acres each. Divided by
quick-set hedges, exceedingly well planted and raised....The cultivation neat, and the stubble heaps, such as remain [it was January], giving
a proof of great crops of straw[7].

He regretted, however, the shortage of swedes and the absence
of drilled wheat. On his right were the open common-fields,

---

[1] *Rural Rides*, I. 98.   [2] *Ibid.* I. 101.   [3] *Ibid.* II. 310.
[4] There were 12 important enclosures of open-field in Oxfordshire, 1820–30:
there were 54 townships remaining in the county with important stretches of
open-field in 1830. Gray, H. L., *English Field Systems* (1915), Ap. IV. p. 536.
[5] *Rural Rides*, II. 321.   [6] *Ibid.* II. 321.
[7] *Ibid.* I. 98–9.

treeless and hedgeless, cut up by balks and mere-stones into furlongs and gores and headlands and the long curving acre or half-acre arable strips: these, however, Cobbett did not describe; he only said "open common-fields on the right." He could still assume in 1822 that all his readers knew what "those very ugly things, common-fields" looked like. Before his death in 1835 such an assumption would already have been dangerous.

The imprint of the latest and most rational enclosure age, that from 1760 to 1820, on the face of England was universally visible only in those central arable counties which it had most affected. Big, efficient, where possible rectangular, fields with fence or quickset were, and are, the design. This design had been partially extended into counties and districts "anciently enclosed," such, for example, as mid and East Suffolk, Kent and the opener parts of Cheshire, Hereford, Somerset and Devon, as a result of the recent cultivation of commons, the enclosure of isolated patches of open-field or the throwing down of old hedges. But areas of ancient enclosure, which were also for the most part areas of broken or forest land with hamlets rather than compact villages, retained everywhere innumerable small irregular fields bounded by the overgrown banks of the West or the stone walls of the North. These fields were the result, generally speaking, not of enclosure of common-fields but of age-long piecemeal encroachment on the forest and the moor. "The multitude of diminutive and awkward inclosures in the North of England, particularly in Yorkshire, Derbyshire, Lancashire, etc. can only be accounted for," a Scottish critic had suggested in 1798, by supposing that owners or secure tenants "threw around them walls built with the stones picked up from their surface."[1] However it may be with the hypothesis, the walls were and are durable. And outside the stone wall country, small old enclosures were the rule in the North-West, "so much so as to cause great loss of ground from their number and the space occupied by hedges, banks, and ditches."[2]

In Scotland nearly all arable land had lain unenclosed so late as 1750–60[3]: the country was as hedgeless as it was, for the

[1] Douglas, R., *General View of the Agriculture in the Counties of Roxburgh and Selkirk* (1798), p. 125.

[2] Holt, J., *General View of the Agriculture...of Lancashire* (1794), p. 52.

[3] Even in Midlothian "so late as thirty years ago (*i.e. c.* 1760–5) there was hardly a farm enclosed in the whole county." *General View...of Midlothian*, p. 34, quoted in Gray, *op. cit.* p. 158.

most part, treeless. Even seventy years later, unhedged and unfenced fields were common enough, though the revolution in the agriculture of the Lowlands had been astonishing. No part of Scotland was a country of large villages and there were many isolated homesteads: the field systems of the big English villages, with their extraordinarily stubborn traditions, had never existed there: property rights were sharply defined and the landlord's power was great; hence change—once it began— had been swift and thorough. The Scottish parallel to the English common-field had been the "run-rig" system, by which the co-tenants of land lying about the little Scottish clachans or hamlets, held intermixed strips (rigs) in open fields[1]. Seeing that the number of such co-tenants rarely exceeded six, reorganisation of the holdings had been easy. Moreover, the old Scottish agriculture had known nothing of the two or three-course rotations of England with their fallows at short intervals. The land nearest the farmstead or clachan was tilled every year: this was the "infield" and it got all the dung. It might or might not be held in run-rig. Beyond it lay the "outfield," on part of which crops of oats were taken year after year until it was tired: this part was "then abandoned for five or six years, during which time it got by degrees a sward of poor grass," and so *da capo*[2]. The outfield might be divided as in Aberdeen-shire into *falds*, which were manured by folding cattle on them before their spell of cropping began, and *faughs* which were tilled in the same way but "never received manure of any sort." In some counties all the outfield was treated as *fald* and in others all as *faugh*; but the system or some variant of it was found everywhere, Lowlands and Highlands[3]. Its very in-efficiency, as compared with the more highly developed English three-field system, had encouraged change, and where co-tenancy had prevailed the great extent of land more or less arable in proportion to population had facilitated division.

The boundary between "Scottish" and "English" agri-culture had never coincided with a political frontier. Perpetual

---

[1] Sinclair, Sir J., *Analysis of the Statistical Account of Scotland* (1825), I. 231. Robson, J., *General View...of Argyll and West Inverness* (1794), p. 57. Fullar-ton, *General View...of Ayr* (1793), p. 9. Douglas, *General View...of Roxburgh and Selkirk*, p. 124, and the *General Views, passim*. A modern discussion in Gray, *op. cit.* p. 164 *sqq*.

[2] Anderson, J., *General View...of Aberdeen*, p. 54. The fullest account in the *General Views*: also Gray, *op. cit.* p. 158–9.

[3] Mr Gray calls it the Celtic System, with doubtful propriety.

cropping of the land nearest the homestead with corn, and some variant of the outfield system, had been common at one time all down the West side of England and in Wales. There were many survivals round about 1800. Cornishmen, in 1810, over-cropped the nearer fields with corn and often took in land from the waste, pulled two or three corn crops out of it, and then let it go to waste again[1]. On the other side of the country, on the wolds of the East Riding, each village late in the eighteenth century had had its infield "portioned into several falls, annually cultivated on a fixed rotation," usually three course. "Beyond this was an outfield cultivated only occasionally." Beyond that again was sheepwalk[2]. This is an almost perfect combination of "English" and "Scottish." But, taking the countries as a whole, the rotation system had been typically English, the infield and outfield system typically Scottish.

Under the working of the Scottish Enclosure Acts of 1695, exact definition of rights over land and the separation of hold-ings had everywhere preceded actual enclosure[3]. In 1798 there were no commons in Selkirk and there "had not been a single common in the whole county" of Roxburgh "these twenty years."[4] By 1814 "almost all common lands in Scotland had been divided": in the whole of Tweeddale, for example, there was only one single scrap, plus a few acres of village green[5]. Similarly, run-rig had been generally abolished south of the Highland line[6]. But at the end of the eighteenth century the most that could be said of enclosure in the most forward Scottish county, Berwickshire, was that "almost the whole or two-thirds, at least of the lands of the lower district...and a considerable part of the arable lands of the higher district" were now enclosed. "One-third" of Dumbarton was "yet open, or but roundly enclosed; that is, the farms are enclosed, but not subdivided," while in Southern Perthshire "three-fifths at least of the whole arable land" was open[7]. Enclosure

---

[1] Worgan, G. B., *General View...of Cornwall* (1811), p. 46, 53.

[2] Strickland, H. E., *General View...of the East Riding of Yorkshire* (1812), p. 91 *sqq.* Young, *Northern Tour*, II. 9.

[3] The Acts only began to be much used from about 1738–40. Douglas, *Roxburgh and Selkirk*, p. 124.

[4] Douglas, *Roxburgh and Selkirk*, p. 125, 287.

[5] Findlater, C., *General View...of Peebles* (1814), p. 126–7.

[6] Fullarton, *Ayr*, p. 9. Findlater, *Peebles*, p. 47. Sinclair, *General Report of the Agricultural State of Scotland* (1814), I. 100, 258.

[7] *General Views*, quoted in Gray, *op. cit.* p. 158.

by stone walls, the natural method in a great part of the country, especially in the uplands, was laborious and expensive and so went forward slowly[1]. Hedges had at first been unpopular[2] and, until plantations had become general and had been allowed some time to grow, fencing was none too easy. By 1800 more rapid movement had become possible. Mr Kibbock of the Gorbyholes in Ayrshire, who first planted "mounts of fir-trees on the...tops of the hills of his farm," had found that "as his rack ran his trees grew, and...supplied him with stabs to make *stake and rice* between his fields, which soon gave them a trig and orderly appearance, such as had never before been seen in the west country."[3] Yet, when summarising the results achieved in 1814, Sir John Sinclair had to admit that "a great proportion of the lands in Scotland still remained open and uninclosed, though divided or appropriated in severalty."[4] The proportion was reduced during the next decade; but as compared with England, above all as compared with those parts of England anciently enclosed, the fields of Scotland remained fenceless and bleak.

Those of Wales had probably changed less in outward aspect than those of either Scotland or England during the two or three generations preceding the decade 1820–30. The greater part of the country, so far as it was cultivated at all, was a land of old enclosures "coeval with the first glimpse of the dawn of Agriculture," as the Reverend William Davies conjectured in 1814, in reporting on South Wales[5]. He believed this to be true of Brecon, Carmarthen, Glamorgan, Radnor and the Eastern parts of Cardigan and Pembroke—Welsh Pembroke, that is, as distinct from "little England beyond Wales." Similarly, from the North the reporter on Flint had inferred "from the appearance of the fences" that "inclosing had been very general many years ago."[6] The "fences" referred to were almost always either dry stone walls or sod banks. Recent improvements in the West had been the sowing of furze on top of the sod banks and the facing of them with stone. Hedging with quickset, in the English fashion, had made headway in Montgomery and Anglesey; and in the vales of Carmarthen the enormous luxuriant "fences"—overgrown sod banks like

---

[1] Findlater, *Peebles*, p. 126–7.   [2] Douglas, *Roxburgh*, p. 63.
[3] Galt, *op. cit.* p. 28.   [4] *General Report*, I. 335.
[5] *South Wales*, I. 219. [And see Thomas, E., *The Economics of Small Holdings* (1927), p. 13.]   [6] Kay, G., *Flintshire*, p. 4, quoted in Gray, *op. cit.* p. 172.

those of the English South-West—had of late years been most admirably plashed[1].

The reporters to the Board of Agriculture had said very little about open-field or run-rig, past or present, except when dealing with Western Cardigan and Pembroke. There were a few open-fields of some sort in Flint, between Flint and St Asaph, at the end of the eighteenth century. As it was "intended to divide and inclose them," no doubt they had vanished quietly before Waterloo. Denbigh had "no common arable lands" to divide, and though Carnarvon was very open, there is no suggestion of open-fields there[2]. It is not much of a field county at best. In the South, the Vale of Glamorgan had certainly not been all enclosed "with the first glimpse of the dawn of agriculture": it was a "champion" country in Elizabethan days. But apparently its character had changed gradually before the eighteenth century, though late in the century there seem to have been still a few traces of the old order. In Western Pembroke the open-field system had been more general and the change later. Though "much altered by inclosures," in 1700, "there be too much champaign" still, it was said[3]. "Between 1750 and 1760 whole parishes were inclosed by common consent,"[4] and the movement went on steadily—as in contemporary England—down to the nineteenth century. Just before 1800 "in the neighbourhood of St David's considerable tracts of open-field land" still remained, "chiefly owing to the possessions of the church being intermixed with private property, and the want of a general law to enable the...clergy to divide, exchange and enclose these lands."[5] This want the General Enclosure Act of 1801 supplied; and under it the medieval tracery had been recently rubbed from the map of Pembrokeshire.

There had been recent change also on the coastal plateau of Cardigan. It was first-rate barley land and so much more arable than most parts of Wales. The lower ground had been much enclosed between 1763 and 1794[6]. "The only tract like a common-field," wrote the reporter, "is an extent of...land reaching on the coast from Aberairon to Llanrhysted. This

[1] Davies, *South Wales*, I. 245, 254; *North Wales*, 125–6, 132.
[2] Quoted in Gray, *op. cit.* p. 171 n., 172.
[3] Quoted in Davies, *South Wales*, I. 221.
[4] *South Wales*, I. 221.
[5] Hassal, *Pembroke*, quoted in Gray, *op. cit.* p. 173.
[6] *South Wales*, I. 221, 357.

quarter is much intermixed and chiefly in small holdings."[1] It was not common-field of the English sort, laid out in strips, but was cut up into irregular blocks called "quillets." Some of it still survived when Davies wrote the General Report on South Wales in 1814. He noted, too, that even in the best enclosed parts of Cardigan there was often one piece of land, always near the church, so cut up into intermixed "quillets."[2] But the bulk of the work was already done, and that without much sudden and abrupt transformation. Just as in Scotland, the smallness of the hamlets and of their appurtenant fields had made enclosure a less formidable proposition in Wales than in the English Midlands.

"Outside some of the northern factory districts and the low quarters of London, one seldom sees rags and tatters in England," wrote Meidinger, "as seldom broken window panes and neglected cottages."[3] Only in Ireland did he note a poverty and backwardness among the rural population comparable with those prevailing "in many parts of Germany, Switzerland, France, Spain and Italy."[4] Meidinger did not visit all the ugliest corners of England; but his impression of relative comfort on the land, and of housing conditions good when compared with average European standards, cannot be rejected. Speaking broadly, the houses of Britain grew worse the farther one went northward and north-westward, reaching the lowest average level in Scotland and Wales; but very ugly corners were to be found almost anywhere. The typical cottage south of the Thames, for example, was a fairly substantial structure, brick built or half-timbered, with glazed windows, and in some districts "usually covered" with a vine[5]. It might have but a single bedroom, for in no part of the country was even the three-room cottage universal, and in places half the cottages were of the one-bedroom, "hay-loft," type; but it was something that could at least be called a house. Yet there were plenty of Dorset cottages with mud walls made of road scrapings, in 1794[6], and on the outskirts of the wastes in Surrey and Hampshire, in the 'twenties, were still to be found

---

[1] Lloyd and Turner, *Cardigan*, quoted in Gray, *op. cit.* p. 172.
[2] *South Wales*, I. 222–3.　　　[3] *Op. cit.* I. 3.　　　[4] *Ibid.* II. 212.
[5] So Hy. Drummond, J.P., speaking of the Hampshire-Surrey boundary. *Select Comm. on Labourers' Wages* (1824, VI. 401), p. 47.
[6] *V.C.H. Dorset*, II. 258. For the prevalence, much later, of "hay-loft" cottages see Loudon, J. C., *An Encyclopædia of Agriculture, Supplement* (1843), p. 1331.

the turf huts of squatters—so long as the farmers tolerated them. Frequently they were pulled down by the Poor Law authorities or, if they were allowed to stand, their owners were refused poor relief as persons of property[1].

Cobbett often dwells with satisfaction on the better cottages of Hampshire, Sussex and Kent, using them as a foil to what he found in the ugly corners. One such, unhappily more than a corner, was in mid-Leicestershire.

Go down into the villages...and then look at the miserable sheds in which the labourers reside! Look at these hovels, made of mud and straw; bits of glass, or of old cast-off windows, without frames or hinges frequently, but merely stuck in the mud-wall. Enter them and look at the bits of chairs or stools; the wretched boards tacked together to serve for a table; the floor of pebble, broken brick or of the bare ground; look at the thing called a bed; and survey the rags on the backs of the wretched inhabitants[2].

Yet the Leicestershire hovel compared not unfavourably with the lower grade houses of Wales and of many parts of Scotland. Of North Wales William Davies had written in 1813 that the labourers' cottages were mostly shameful, with "one smoky hearth, for it should not be styled a kitchen; and one damp litter-cell, for it cannot be called a bedroom." The phrase suggests the absence even of a "thing called a bed." But in Nant Ffrancon, "surrounded by precipices supereminently horrible," Lord Penrhyn had built some excellent cottages[3]. South Wales also, in 1814, had far more so-called "huts" than "handsome modern cottages" such as were to be found near mansions, iron works and the like. Though Glamorgan was said to abound in good old Gothic cottages, neatly thatched with wheat straw, Cardigan, Carmarthen and especially Pembroke were full of "mud" cottages, whose very chimneys were made of wattle and daub[4]. In Pembroke even farm houses were sometimes of "mud." "Mud" generally meant wattle and daub. It might mean, as apparently it did to Cobbett, "cob" building, i.e. earth or chalk mixed with straw. It could hardly include buildings of sun-dried blocks of clay, as found on the Cambridgeshire gault[5].

When reviewing housing conditions for his General Report

[1] Evidence of Hy. Drummond, as above. Compare Cobbett, *Rural Rides*, II. 298.   [2] *Rural Rides*, II. 348.
[3] *North Wales*, p. 82, 84.   [4] *South Wales*, I. 136, 139, 143.
[5] Some of these, called phonetically "clayods," are still in use.

of the Agricultural State of Scotland, published in 1814, Sir John Sinclair referred shamefacedly to those "miserable cottages, built of turf or sod, which are in some districts rapidly, and in others slowly, disappearing." He said that "they did not require any particular description," and hurried on to describe the better sorts[1]. Probably the turf hovel was pretty well extinct in Berwickshire the Lothians and most of the more progressive southern areas ten years later; but it was common in the North-West. There had been still "a few" in Peebles in 1814. In Roxburgh and Selkirk sixteen years earlier the cottages were "mostly" of clay. "Those erected for shepherds were miserable temporary hovels." No doubt many so remained in 1825[2]. In 1814, according to Sinclair, the "clay" cottage prevailed in Dumfries, Perth, Forfar, Kincardine "and elsewhere"[3]; and the ten years after Waterloo were not an age of active housing reform. The clay cottage was reckoned far better than the old Scottish "dry stone'" cottage—five feet of unhewn stone wall, its interstices stuffed with earth; a foot more of turf wall; and a roof of sorts[4]. "Not a few specimens" of a slightly superior variant of this latter type survived in mining districts even beyond the second Reform Bill. Its size was 12 ft. by 15: it had stone walls 4 or 5 ft. high: no ceiling, but a tiled roof: one or two windows 2 ft. square, and an earthen floor. There was no ash-pit and no drain and there was but one room. However, the furniture was so arranged as to make a sort of bed-closet[5].

The one-room cottage, with or without arrangement, was general during the 'twenties—and later—in the Lowlands. It measured about 18 ft. by 16[6]. Sinclair describes it as divided into a living-room and a "store" and as rarely fitted with a loft. A more coloured account from Peebles explains that two "close beds"—the murderous sleeping-boxes of Scottish story —formed the partition, behind which, evidently in Sinclair's "store," "stands the cow, with her tail to the door of the house." "Substantial labourers and tradesmen have generally two apartments, the cow standing in a separate to-fall building."[7]

[1] General Report, I. 127.   [2] Peebles, p. 41. Roxburgh and Selkirk, p. 29.
[3] Op. cit. I. 128.   [4] Ibid. I. 127.
[5] Bremner, D., The Industries of Scotland (1869), p. 27.
[6] Which is of course much larger than any one room in an English cottage. To this day fewer, but larger, rooms differentiate Scottish from English housing, Royal Commission on Housing in Scotland, 1917 (Cd. 8731), p. 44.
[7] Sinclair, op. cit. I. 128. Peebles, p. 41, 45.

In Central Scotland and in the lowlands of the North-East a bigger and better type of built house predominated, though its occupant was probably more often a small farmer than a labourer. It must be thought of in juxtaposition with those turf hovels whose rate of disappearance varied. This was the house of 12 ft. by from 24 to 36 ft., with its two classic divisions, the but and the ben. Each had a fireplace. Each had a bedstead or bedsteads. As a rule, the house had a window in each end. The floor was of earth, the roof of thatch, and there was sometimes a ceiling. "A few of the richer artisans and some of the small farmers" had houses 16 ft. by 36, with side walls 8 ft. high and a loft "the whole length of the house." This being the best Scottish accommodation for families far from the meanest, that of cottars in the Highlands and Islands hardly requires "any particular description."[1] There was much turf there.

Before 1830, the creation of great capitalist farms in the Lothians, and still more in Berwickshire and Northumberland, had brought with it not only farm-buildings of a new sort but a new problem in housing, and its solution. A Scot, writing in 1831, contrasted the well-designed "farmeries and cottages of Northumberland and Berwick" with the "scattered straggling hovels of all shapes and sizes, the monstrous barns and rickety shapeless farmhouses" of Essex and Hertford; and he noted how in Norfolk and Suffolk "setting the dwelling house among dung heaps and urine ponds" was "everywhere conspicuous."[2] The Border farm-builder had no dense villages from which to draw labour: the Scottish and Northumbrian population had been thin and generally grouped in little clusters. In the old days it had been customary, when farms were large enough to employ "married servants," to run up one or two "dry stone cottages" for their accommodation, and for unmarried men to "live in"[3]; but those expedients no longer sufficed. Cobbett first struck the new system about Alnwick, in 1832.

Here we get among the mischief. Here the farms are enormous. Here the thrashing machines are turned by STEAM ENGINES; here the labourers live in a sort of *barracks*: that is to say long sheds with stone walls, and covered with what are called pantiles. They have neither gardens, nor

[1] Sinclair, *op. cit.* I. 128-9.
[2] Loudon, *Encyclopædia of Agriculture* (2nd ed. 1831), p. 453.
[3] Sinclair, *op. cit.* I. 127.

privies, nor back doors....There are no villages, no scattered cottages;
no up-stairs; one little window and one doorway to each dwelling in
the shed or barrack[1].

Farther north, along the fifty odd miles of the "finest land that
I ever saw in my life" from the Tweed to Edinburgh, "there
is neither village, nor church, nor ale-house, nor gardens, nor
cottage, nor flowers, nor pig, nor goose, nor common, nor
green: but the thing is thus"—a square of splendid farm
buildings; "the farmer's house...a house big enough and fine
enough for a gentleman to live in"; the stackyard "as big as
a little town"; the single labourers "put into a shed, quite
away from the farmhouse and out of the farm-yard; which
shed Dr Jamieson, in his dictionary, calls a 'boothie'." Cobbett
went into one—a shed "about sixteen or eighteen feet square"
with a fireplace; "one little window"; "three wooden bedsteads nailed together like the berths in a barrack-room"; and
six men[2].

"But it is the life of the married labourer which will delight
you. Upon a steam-engine farm there are, perhaps, eight or
ten of these."[3] They live in sections of a stone, one-storey
barrack as in Northumberland, each section "having a door
and one little window, all the doors being on one side of the
shed, and there being no *back-doors*; and as to a *privy*, no such
thing, for them, appears ever to be thought of. The ground in
front of the shed is wide or narrow according to circumstances,
but quite smooth; merely a place to walk upon." Each section
was about 17 ft. by 15 "as nearly as his eye could determine."
There was "no ceiling and no floor but the earth. In this place
a man and his wife and family have to live...and...it is quite
surprising to behold how decent the women endeavour to keep
the place."[4] A poor place indeed; but Cobbett probably did
not realise that few of the married women could have been
brought up in bigger places; that one-room dwellings were
normal for the Lowland poor; or that mortared walls and a
pantile roof were new and solid assets to a population sprung
from "dry stone cottages," "clay cottages," or cottages of turf
and sod.

The Scottish one-room cottage, like the Berwickshire barrack, was common enough in Northumberland and southward

---

[1] *Cobbett's Tour in Scotland* (1833), p. 84.
[2] *Tour in Scotland*, p. 103–4, 130.   [3] *Ibid.* p. 104.
[4] *Ibid.* p. 104–5.

beyond Teesdale[1]. So late as 1850 it was reported of Northumberland that "the state of the labourers' cottages" was, "in the majority of cases, most discreditable to the county. It will hardly be believed that the labourers' cow and his pig are still lodged, in too many cases, under the same roof...as himself... the cowhouse being divided only by a slight partition wall from the single apartment which serves...for all the inmates."[2] The opener parts of Cumberland had their "uncouth mud villages" in 1820, such as those which James Graham began to clear from his father's Netherby estate, when he took charge of it in 1821, to make way for the "substantial, extensive, commodious and I might almost say elegant, farmhouses, and farmsteadings" of which his Scottish agent wrote nineteen years later[3]. In the North Riding of Yorkshire in 1800, the two-room cottage had been "very rare," and the cottagers—like the Lowland Scots —slept in "close wainscotted beds."[4] In the East Riding, on the other hand, cottages, though hard to come by, were generally good—two lower rooms and two bedrooms[5]. But neither one-room nor "mud" structure was typical of England generally. Cobbett's horrified "no upstairs" is as South English as the rest of him. When English commissioners report—some years later—on what they describe as the very bad housing conditions of Wiltshire, Dorset, Devon and Somerset, their complaint is, not of one-room cottages, but that the single bedroom cottage is much too common and that three-bedroom cottages are unknown[6]. The Lancashire cottage of the early 'thirties was "most frequently of brick and a roof either of tile or slate."[7] The best Cheshire cottages, at the same date, had a living-room, a larder-scullery, and two "what they call bed-cabins"[8] either on the ground floor or above, a standard which suggests living-room and perhaps one "bed-cabin" for the worst. In the Dudley iron district the normal cottage had "a kitchen, two bedrooms and a brewhouse,"[9] where they no longer brewed; but this, like the stone cottages of the Yorkshire

[1] Reports...on the Employment of Women and Children in Agriculture (1843, XII), p. 298.

[2] Caird, J., English Agriculture in 1850 and 1851, p. 389.

[3] Parker, C. S., Life and Letters of Sir James Graham, I. 58.

[4] Tuke, J., Gen. View of the Agriculture of the North Riding (1800), p. 41.

[5] Strickland, H. E., East Riding (1812), p. 41.

[6] Reports on...Women...in Agriculture, ut sup. p. 20.

[7] Select Comm. on Agriculture (1833, v), Q. 3541.

[8] Ibid. Q. 6149.   [9] Ibid. Q. 9802 sqq.

country weavers, with their well-lighted weaving lofts upstairs, was more of an industrial type. Away in Cornwall, the old cottages were mostly of "mud" and were thatched; but they had two or three rooms and the English "upstairs," or hay-loft[1]. The "mud" cottage, as has been seen, was to be found in the Midlands, and East Anglia had its "straggling hovels of all shapes" and its dwelling-houses among the dunghills[2]. South of the Thames, besides the occasional turf hut of a squatter on the waste, there were places where the labourers' houses were "beggarly in the extreme," and where, like the dwellers in the married quarters of Berwickshire, they had "no place for a pig or a cow to graze, or even to lie down upon," as Cobbett reported from the Isle of Thanet[3]; but throughout England the standard cottage, if the term may be used, was of stone—as in Cotswold—of brick or of half-timber, with generally one room or two upstairs, and with a fair sprinkling of glazed, if unopened, windows. Thatch or tiles the normal roof: here and there a roof of locally quarried stone or slate slabs, or, where the new means of communication allowed it, of Welsh slates shipped coastwise. That too much weight be not given to Cobbett's suggestion of Scottish sanitary back-wardness—he had a feud with the Scots—it should be noted that in England of the 'forties cottages without any kind of privy were still exceedingly common[4].

Between the better cottages of the rural wage-earners and the smaller farmhouses there was not much to choose. Numbers of these better cottages had been, in their day, what Tudor Englishmen called houses of husbandry—houses of the lesser freeholders, copyholders, or tenants at will who lived by hold-ings since absorbed into larger farms. Many cottages still housed cultivators of this class. The census of 1831 showed that nearly one-seventh of all the agricultural families in Great Britain had at their head neither a labourer nor an employing farmer, but a cultivator who employed no labour outside the family, a "husbandman" of the oldest sort[5]. Such holders and such houses were especially numerous in parts of Scotland, in Wales and down the west side of England. The Netherby

---

[1] Worgan, *Cornwall* (1811), p. 26.   [2] Above, p. 30.
[3] *Rural Rides*, i. 322.
[4] Loudon, *Encyclopædia of Agriculture, Supplement* (1843), p. 1333. [Fussell, G. E. and Goodman, C., "The Housing of the Rural Population in the 18th Century," *E.J.* (*Ec. Hist.*), Jan. 1930, confirm the foregoing account of England but omit Scotland.]   [5] Below, p. 113.

estate contained "mud" farmhouses as well as "mud" cottages:
so did Pembrokeshire and so did Cornwall. The old Cornish
mud and thatch farmhouse had a cellar, something that might
be called a dairy, and four mean rooms: the Cornish cottage
might have three[1]. The Lancashire farms, which mostly ran
from fifty to twenty acres, or even less, at the end of the
eighteenth century and had hardly been thrown together at all
since, necessarily carried farmhouses not easily distinguishable
from cottages[2]; and Lancashire conditions were reproduced in
the West Riding, in much of Derbyshire, and at many other
points in the tier of counties from Cheshire to Devon. In the
North Riding the houses on farms of some importance in 1800
often contained only a parlour, usually with a bed in it, a living-
room called "a house," a back kitchen, "and some very ordinary
chambers open to the roof."[3] Not much change occurred in
the next twenty years there either. East of the line from Lyme
Regis, through Gloucester, to the Tees estuary, which marked
the western limit of recent active enclosure of open fields[4],
the cottage farm was less common; but there were few districts,
if any, in which it was not to be found.

Thence upward through every grade of farmhouse—the
"rickety and shapeless" with "monstrous barns" as in Essex
and Hertford; the substantial ancient structures which had once
been manor houses of little manors now absorbed into greater
estates; the new business-like brick buildings on the corn farms
of the East, on a Waterloo farm or a St Helena farm; to the
great "farmeries" of the Berwickshire type, "big enough and
fine enough for a gentleman to live in." Also big enough and
fine enough for a gentleman were not a few of the country
rectories and vicarages, new or completely remodelled since
the middle of the eighteenth century, as the gentleman-parson
of the type "with a considerable independence, besides two
good livings"[5] had become more common.

For the rest, the villages and country towns of England
showed a steadily increasing number of comfortable houses,

---

[1] Parker, *Sir James Graham*, I. 58. Davies, *South Wales*, I. 143. Worgan, *Cornwall*, p. 23.

[2] A tithe survey, of 1794, at King's College, Cambridge, dealing with some 30,000 acres in South Lancashire gives an average holding, excluding cottages and small farms with no arable, of 36 acres. *Cambs. Hist. Journal* (1924), p. 203 *sqq.* See also Holt, *Lancashire* (1794), p. 12.

[3] Tuke, *North Riding*, p. 32.

[4] See above, p. 19.   [5] *Northanger Abbey*, p. 1.

few so much as a hundred years old and most much less than fifty, held neither by labourer, farmer, yeoman, parson nor gentleman of ancient stock. The older were mostly of regular eighteenth-century red brick and tile; the newer inclined towards stucco, low-pitched slate roofs, and verandahs; the newest had often a smack of the Gothic[1]. They housed families "which for the last two or three generations had been rising into gentility and property"[2]—yeomen rising by land purchase; successful doctors and attorneys, corn-merchants and country bankers; scions of "respectable families in the North of England," in danger of forgetting that their fortunes "had been acquired by trade"[3]; city men, functioning or retired, the stockjobbers of Cobbett's *Rides*; and all the unspecified middle-class personages with decent fortunes in the funds who were his "tax-eaters."

The lesser gentlemen's houses differed but little from those of these gentlemen *in posse*, except that among them were more likely to be found buildings with a predominantly Jacobean or even Tudor character. For the most part, however, they too had been built or rebuilt in some one of the styles which had prevailed since the Glorious Revolution. So, for that matter, had those places of the greater gentry and nobility which stood up over the land as the embodiment of the political and social system of the century that was gone, places which every traveller visited and of which everyone still talked. From them the country had been governed and its taste directed. Arthur Young had felt bound to turn from notes on the farming which he understood to pay his debt of deference to the extremely elegant green drawing-room at Woburn, to the execution of the "plaits and folds" of Omphale's flesh in a picture at Duncombe Park, or to the "six magnificent Corinthian pillars" of the portico at Wentworth House[4]. Because the country had been so little fought over, Layer Marney Tower and Sutton Place, Longleat and Burghley House, Audley End, Knole and Hatfield survived to speak for their generations of the governors of England; but the dominant places, as they now stood, were of the eighteenth century or later, with pediment and portico

---

[1] Bowling-Green House, Putney, where Pitt died, is "newer" with traces of "newest." See the sketch in Rose, J. H., *William Pitt and the Great War*, p. 554.
[2] The Westons of Highbury, *Emma*, ch. 2.
[3] The Bingleys, *Pride and Prejudice*, ch. 2.
[4] *Northern Tour*, I. 22; II. 93; I. 278.

and perhaps some flavour of Italy and the Palladian tradition,—from Castle Howard, which Vanbrugh began in 1701, or Blenheim, where he laid such a heavy load on the earth five years later, to Holkham and Woburn and Wentworth House, Harewood and Kedleston Hall, Badminton and Howick. The revival of Gothic, good or bad, had hardly touched the greater houses, few of which had been built or altered since it began to prevail, although Canford Manor was rebuilding on semi-Gothic lines under King George IV; but, helped perhaps by Abbotsford, medievalism was spreading among the lesser places. "The house looks like a sort of church," Cobbett fumed at one of these, "in somewhat of a Gothic style of building, with *crosses* on the tops of different parts of the pile": over its gravel walks were Gothic arches, with crosses atop, "composed of Scotch fir-wood, as rotten as a pear."[1]

Rural labour and town labour, country house and town house, were divided by no clear line. In one sense there was no line at all. Very many of the industrial workpeople were countrymen, though their countryside might be fouling and blackening, their cottages creeping together and adhering into rows, courts, and formless towns. Being, on the whole, better paid than the agricultural labourers, they had usually cottages rather above than below the local standard. Scottish miners, it is true, lived in a very poor type of roughly masoned or "dry-stone" cottage—one- or two-roomed[2]. But Cobbett thought that the Durham miners were well housed. "Their work is terrible to be sure...but, at any rate, they live well, their houses are good and their furniture good."[3] He had the same impression among the cutlers, on the borders of Yorkshire and Derbyshire; though his account is less precise[4]. As has been seen, the best cottages in Wales were those near the iron works: the standard cottage in the Black Country about Dudley was good, and so were the stone cottages of the better class weavers in Yorkshire[5]. The true village artisans—blacksmiths, wheelwrights,

---

[1] *Rural Rides*, I. 4.

[2] For full details see *Report...on Housing in Scotland*, 1917, p. 125.

[3] *Rural Rides*, II. 383. Fully confirmed, for Northumberland in the early 'thirties, in Mrs Haldane's reminiscences—"comfortable well built houses in which they took great pride, an eight day clock and well-polished chest and other furniture...." *Mary Elizabeth Haldane* (1925), p. 70.

[4] *Op. cit.* II. 288.

[5] To be seen in great numbers in the West Riding to-day.

and the rest—were everywhere more prosperous and better housed than their neighbours who worked on the land.

It was natural in a town such as Birmingham, which had grown by mere agglomeration without control or charter, that "every workman" should have "a house of his own."[1] Less natural, and much less generally true, in London, yet it was probably the rule there and certainly the rule in all other English towns. They had never been walled, or had long outgrown their walls, town and country mingling in shabby or in genteel suburbs. Whereas London sprawled out into the country and was now linked up by almost continuous houses with Hammersmith, Kentish town, Deptford, Camberwell and even Highgate and Paddington[2], all the life and activity of Paris stopped at the fortifications. So Parisian houses had grown upwards and the poor normally lived in tenements. The nearest British parallel to the Quartier St Antoine was the old town of Edinburgh, with its stone houses five, six and even ten stories high. Meidinger, who came from Frankfurt, likened the Canongate and the Cowgate to the worst of continental Ghettos. Even in the new town of Edinburgh sewering was defective, and in the old the "nightly emptyings out of window" and the state of the common staircases of the towering tenement houses, staircases which it was no one's business to clean, were purely medieval. The great personal uncleanliness of the tenement dwellers, and something even in their faces, again recalled to Meidinger the *Judengasse*[3]. He spoke of them as Scots, and drew ingenious racial conclusions; but in fact, when he visited Edinburgh, they were mainly Irish[4].

London had terrible slums and abundance of one-room tenements; but old Edinburgh was the only important British town in which tenement dwelling had been normal time out of mind[5]. Seven Dials, Whitechapel, Bethnal Green with its many houses built "en planches mal jointes, ce qui leur donne bientôt l'aspect des plus dégoûtantes étables,"[6] or the Cowgate did not, however, mark the lowest level of human dwelling in

---

[1] *Lords' Committees on the Poor Laws*, 1817, p. 180.

[2] Meidinger, *op. cit.* I. 10, and contemporary maps.

[3] Meidinger, *op. cit.* II. 11.   [4] Below, p. 60.

[5] It was also found in other anciently walled Scottish towns, *e.g.* Stirling, and was being imitated from Edinburgh elsewhere. *Report on Housing in Scotland* (1917), p. 49.

[6] Faucher, L., *Études sur l'Angleterre* (1845); from observations made in the 'thirties.

a British town: that was probably to be found in "the closes and wynds which lie between the Trongate and the Bridge-gate, the Salt Market and Maxwell Street" in Glasgow. The wynds were long lanes

so narrow that a cart could with difficulty pass along them; out of these open the "closes" which are courts about 15 or 20 feet square, round which the houses, mostly of three stories, are built; the centre of the court is the dunghill, which is probably the most lucrative part of the estate to the laird...and which it would consequently be esteemed an invasion of the rights of property to remove. The houses are for the most part in flats.

Many were promiscuous common lodging houses—"as regards dirt, damp and decay, such as no person of common humanity to animals would stable his horse in."[1] These horrible dens, like the worst slums of every town, were not the houses of the ordinary workers, but of the lowest grade of unskilled labourers and of the half-criminal and full criminal classes. Most of the Glasgow wynd population was Highland or Irish. There were no sewers in Glasgow in 1790 and only forty-three in 1816[2].

Every town in the country had its courts and yards no bigger and often not much more sanitary than those of Glasgow, just as each had its half-criminal tenement quarters; but as a rule, courts were surrounded by the two-storied houses of the ordinary workers, built too often back to back, and insanitary horrors were a little less visible[3]. Nowhere in England was tenement dwelling quite normal. "Houses of three or four rooms and a kitchen form throughout England, some parts of London excepted, the general dwellings of the working class."[4] An account of "the streets which have been erected since 1800 in

[1] *Hand Loom Weavers. Assistant Commissioners' Reports*, evidence taken in 1838 (1839, XXII), part I. p. 51–2.

[2] Cleland, J., *Annals of Glasgow* (1816), I. 38, 329.

[3] But see below, p. 537 *sqq.*

[4] Engels, F., *The Condition of the Working Class in England in 1844* (ed. 1888), p. 19: an unexceptionable witness. Mrs George (*London Life in the Eighteenth Century* (1925), ch. 2) has shown how common the one-room tenement was in eighteenth-century London. But it cannot have been representative then, and it certainly was not in 1821–31. In 1831, crowded central parishes averaged over ten persons per inhabited house (*e.g.* Marylebone 10·5); but the figures for the whole of Bethnal Green, St George's-in-the-East and Stepney (including Mile End and Poplar) are 27,856 houses and 168,395 people—6·05 to a house. It might not perhaps be fanciful to suggest a family and "the lodger" as a representative London household. For the varying definitions of a house see below, p. 546–7. In 1831 it was apparently used in its natural sense.

Bethnal Green,"[1] written in 1838, may be taken as typical of the lowest class of new housing run up on the edges of the crawling towns.

Many of them [*i.e.* the streets] are the worst that can be imagined, having no common sewers. The houses generally are of two stories... the foundations...were often laid upon the turf or vegetable mould, and have no ventilation between the floors of the...living rooms and the worst description of undrained soil immediately under such floors. ...The roadway...is of the most wretched kind, often composed of earthy and soft rubbish, and brick dust saturated with moisture.

The water "makes its way under the houses, and, joined by the oozings from the cesspools, frequently passes off in noxious vapour, and that through the sitting rooms....The roofs are covered with pantiles, and but few of them pointed, the pitch very bad, scarcely enough to keep them water tight." Such houses were "erected by speculative builders of the most scampy class," and showed it in their half-burnt bricks, their inferior mortar, and their warping scantlings. But given a sewer—and many streets had sewers, though sometimes they were higher than the cesspools which they drained and some-times they were arranged so as to run uphill[2]; given honest building—and not all builders were scampy—the drab little houses all joined together, two rooms of some kind below and two or three above, could be made into homes.

In London and out of it, the skilled man, like the Durham miner, generally had a tolerable house or section of a house, and tolerable furniture, unless his trade were a dying one and his skill a drug. The slow death of hand-loom weaving, and the consequent misery which was already setting in among certain classes of weavers, with Friedrich Engels' squalid picture of *The Condition of the Working Class in England in 1844*, true in almost all that it paints but not painting all, have perhaps led to some confusion of worst and average housing conditions in the second quarter of the nineteenth century. The worst it is impossible to exaggerate. "In one part of Manchester" in 1843-4—and there is no reason to assume better things of 1830—"the wants of upwards of 7000 inhabitants are supplied by 33 necessaries only....The cellar dwellings are almost of necessity unfurnished with these conveniences."[3] Manchester,

---

[1] *Hand Loom Weavers* (1840, XXIII), part II. p. 239.
[2] Jephson, H., *The sanitary evolution of London* (1907), p. 16.
[3] *Report on the State of Large Towns and Populous Districts* (1845, XVIII), II. 61.

Liverpool, London, and, to a less extent, other towns, such as Leeds, had great cellar populations in the 'thirties and certainly in the 'twenties also. Though full evidence for the latter decade is not available we know of the 20,000 cellar dwellings reported by the Manchester Board of Health in 1832[1]. A quarter of a century after the time now under discussion there were 1132 cellar tenements in Marylebone only[2]. But these were not the houses of the average skilled man and his family. There were far fewer destitute Irish in Britain in 1829 than in 1845, when Engels wrote that "the majority of the families who live in cellars are almost everywhere of Irish origin."[3]

Over against the wretched environment of some Lancashire and Yorkshire cellar weavers may be set the decent comfort of the better class weavers of Spitalfields, Coventry or Yorkshire—representative upper grade skilled men of London, the Midlands, and the North. In Spitalfields, round about 1820, "many of the houses had porticos, with seats at their doors, where the weavers might be seen on summer evenings enjoying their pipes." Unfortunately there was a tendency for these "porticos" "to give way to improvements of the pavements." The weavers were great gardeners, though garden ground was fast being taken up by the scampy builders. Yet even in 1838 the six acres of Saunderson's Gardens, on the east of Bethnal Green, were cut up into nearly two hundred plots: "in almost every garden is a neat summer house, where the weaver and his family may enjoy themselves on Sundays." Nor was it mere gardening for the pot. In June, 1838, the "contest for a silver medal amongst the tulip proprietors" was just over[4].

In the heart of Coventry "the houses of the best class of weavers, as compared with the cottages of agricultural labourers, are good, comfortable dwellings; some of them very well furnished; many have nice clocks, and beds, and drawers; are ornamented with prints; and some have comfortable parlours."[5] Throughout the West Riding of Yorkshire, though some classes of weavers were hard pressed in the 'thirties, "generally speak-

---

[1] Gaskell, *The manufacturing population of England* (1833), p. 138.

[2] Jephson, *op. cit.* p. 30: referring to 1854.

[3] Engels, *op. cit.* p. 61. Fully confirmed by the *Hand Loom Weavers' Commission* for the late 'thirties, *e.g.* III. 572—two-thirds of the weavers in the cellar-quarter of Leeds are Irish, 1838–9.

[4] *Hand Loom Weavers*, II. 217–18. Not all Bethnal Green was so cheerful. See above, p. 37.

[5] *Ibid.* IV. (1840, XXIV), 301.

ing their houses, whilst they bore vestiges of better days, had all the marks of frugal housewifery:—cleanliness, good order and regularity."[1] Of a rather privileged group among them, the Barnsley linen weavers, it was reported,

their cottages are built of stone for the most part, in the airy and dry situations for which the town and neighbourhood afford abundant space. ...The cellars in which they work are not more damp than is desirable for carrying on their trade. Well ventilated, and even when the inhabitants are suffering from extreme poverty, their houses have a look of cleanliness and good order[2].

To set against this there is the gloomy generalisation of Gaskell, based on the facts of the Lancashire cotton industry of 1830–2, who speaks of that "extinction of decent pride in their household establishments, which at present characterizes the mass of the manufacturing population."[3] But cotton was the single industry into which industrial revolution had cut really deep by the 'twenties; Gaskell hated the industrial revolution[4]; and the Lancashire cotton operative was not the representative workman of the Britain of King George IV.

While the shabbier outskirts of London were filling with wage earners and small tradespeople, the genteel suburbs received tradespeople of higher grades who were ceasing to live at their places of business, as John Gilpin, or more recently that "sensible gentlemanlike" merchant, Mr Gardiner of Gracechurch Street, had lived. The greater merchants had gone first. They had long been going westward, or southward to Clapham and Denmark Hill. The lesser followed. Then the shopkeepers began to move. The spell of business activity in 1824–5 was accompanied by wholesale suburban migration.[5] City men, as Cobbett noted, now sometimes lived as far afield as Brighton. From the inner suburbs, where "houses were built by speculators on a uniform plan" with "little terraces and flower gardens," Meidinger saw with intense interest—for to a continental all this was perfectly novel—how men went up daily to the city by horse or coach or gig[6]. Round the commercial and manufacturing towns of the Midlands and North

---

1 *Hand·Loom Weavers*, III. 543.   2 *Ibid.* II. 483.
3 *Op. cit.* p. 114.
4 See Daniels, *The Early English Cotton Industry* (1920), p. 139.
5 Martineau, H., *History of England during the Peace*, I. 353.
6 *Op. cit.* I. 12, 3

this genuine suburbanism was as yet but slightly developed[1]. Few were big enough to require it; though each was beginning to create an inner fringe of "regularly laid out streets," for the "middle bourgeoisie," and an outer fringe of manufacturers' and merchants' houses.

Every traveller in Britain noticed the extraordinary way in which industry and population were being concentrated on or near the coal measures. Apart from its uses in steam-raising and iron smelting, a supply of coal at reasonable prices was essential before population could gather and large scale industry develop at any point; for no other domestic fuel was now available in quantity. If the coal could come by water, as it had for so long come into London, the domestic difficulty and to some extent the steam-raising difficulty might be overcome. So one of the main objects in the construction of the network of canals, now approaching completion, had been the better distribution of coal, particularly in Eastern and South-Eastern England. But important industries in the East, South-East, and South had been losing ground before the age of canals and steam. Decline was not in every case inevitable. The ancient iron industry of Sussex, it is true, could under no circumstances have been kept alive; but the textile industry of East Anglia, whose chief headquarters, Norwich, was well placed for the receipt of sea-borne coal, might well have survived competition from the coal counties had it not shown a certain lack of elasticity and power of adaptation to new conditions[2].

Iron smelting in Sussex died with the eighteenth century. In 1770–4 there were still several charcoal furnaces at work there and in the adjacent Weald of Kent. "Cannon bullets" were made at various places: "kettles and chimney backs" were made at Beckley Furnace and Brede, above Winchelsea[3]. A single Sussex furnace remained in blast in 1796. England and Wales in that year turned out some 125,000 tons of pig iron and Scotland a few thousand tons: in 1788 the total for Great Britain had been about 68,000. In 1806 the whole island

---

[1] The author's mother, daughter of a smallware manufacturer, was born in the heart of Manchester (Ridgefield Flags, where John Dalton Street now is) in 1833. The quotations are from Engels, *op. cit.* p. 32.

[2] Clapham, J. H., "The transference of the Worsted Industry from East Anglia to the West Riding," *E.J.* 1910, p. 203.

[3] Campbell, J., *Political Survey of Great Britain* (1774), I. 374.

turned out about 258,000 and in 1830 about 678,000 tons[1]. By 1830 the concentration of the industry in South Wales and the Black Country was astonishing—278,000 tons coming from South Wales and 286,000 from Staffordshire and Shropshire "I have walked over this country in a dark night," the Baron Dupin wrote a few years earlier; "the horizon about me was bounded by a circle of fire. From all parts, columns of smoke and flame rose in the air, and the whole country around seemed as if lighted by an immense conflagration. Vain would it be ...to attempt to describe the impression of this imposing sight." By day one saw everywhere "heaps of fossil-coal, turned by fire into coke—high furnaces and forges—steam engines used in the extraction of the iron and coals from the mines and in draining those mines, the water of which, conveyed in the smaller canals, becomes useful to navigation."[2] This was the memory of the Black Country before the railway age left in the mind of a sober observer, unaccustomed to the new industry but very appreciative of it. With the extinction of her last iron furnace, at Ashburnham, in 1828, Sussex had slipped back into the peace of her wild woods and her downs, broken only by the dust and jingle of the Brighton Road.

But for a few paper mills[3] and the dockyard and riverside activities of the Medway and the Thames, Kent had none of those industries which catch the traveller's eye or leave their print on the countryside. Nor had Surrey, outside the metropolitan area; though perhaps a few bleach and print works along the Wandle, between Wandsworth and Croydon, should be classed as extra-metropolitan[4]. At one or two places in Hampshire an ancient textile industry was fumbling, in its last decay, at looms for sack-cloth and striped ticking[5]. Southampton was not awake from its long sleep, though its population had begun to grow since the wars, and it owned a few thousand tons of small ships[6]. Peace had stopped the one industry of

---

[1] Scrivenor, H., *History of the Iron Trade* (1854), p. 95–9, with a list of the furnaces in 1796, and p. 135–6, the county outputs in 1830.

[2] Dupin, *op. cit.* I. 317.

[3] Spicer, A. D., *The Paper Trade* (1907), p. 174. Several of the Kentish mills were old fulling mills diverted to paper-making early in the eighteenth century.

[4] *Census of 1831* (1833, xxxvi–viii), xxxvii, 642.

[5] *V.C.H. Hampshire*, v. 488. Some better work, silks and bombazines, had survived till 1813.

[6] Population in 1801, 7913; 1831, 19,324. Ships in 1829, 178 of 8120 tons.

Portsmouth and with it the growth of its population, which only increased from 41,000 to 50,000 between 1811 and 1831 —an abnormally slow rate for an English town at that time. Berkshire was utterly rural, its county capital and only town of any size growing leisurely from 13,000 towards 16,000 in the decade 1821–31.

So early as 1748 the ancient baize manufacture of Essex had, for the most part, been lost to the North and the West, "where provisions are cheaper, the poor more easily satisfied, and coals are very plentiful," as an eighteenth-century historian of Colchester put it[1]. But there were still fourteen baize manufacturers in Colchester in 1793. The great wars really killed these dying wool manufactures of Essex, though there were a couple of baize firms in the county in 1826 and a little cottage-spun worsted yarn was still sold to the Norfolk manufacturers[2]. Suffolk, too, had lost the industry which once made the fortunes of Lavenham, Kersey, Long Melford and of a score more villages and market towns. A little weaving of mixed fabrics of silk and worsted, principally the bombazines so conspicuous in early nineteenth-century romance, lingered at Sudbury, Haverhill, Lavenham, and a few other places; and the Ipswich district span a good deal for Norwich[3]. The Norfolk capital remained the sole important textile manufacturing centre in East Anglia. Its staples were camlets, plain stout materials used for rain cloaks and so on, and the mixed materials of silk and wool, bombazines and crapes. It had done an immense export trade until, as a Norwich man put it in later years, "Buonaparte made his excursions on the continent of Europe."[4] Some of this trade had been recovered since the wars. There was also a good home trade and a heavy export of camlets by the East India Company. There were supposed to be 10,000 looms in Norwich and district in 1818; and although the trade was losing new business to Yorkshire, the available evidence suggests that it did not decline much absolutely in the next ten years[5].

The spread of the silk industry into East Anglia had done something to compensate for the decline in wool. In the eighteenth century silk throwing had been done at various

---

[1] Morant, *History of Colchester* (1748), quoted in *V.C.H. Essex*, II. 400.
[2] *V.C.H. Essex*, II. 401, 403.
[3] *Census of 1831*, XXXVII. 628, and Meidinger, *op. cit.* I. 200.
[4] *Hand Loom Weavers*, II. 302. Narrative of Wm. Stark.
[5] *E.J.* 1910, p. 196.

places in Essex for the Spitalfields industry: since about 1790 weaving also had moved into the country. Besides the mixed weaving, pure silks were now being woven at Braintree, Bocking and Coggeshall and, in small quantities, in Norwich and other worsted towns. The bombazines and crapes had, in fact, been captured by East Anglia from Spitalfields when it lost part of its pure wool business to Yorkshire[1].

Comparable with the concentration of the East Anglian textile manufacture into Norwich, but much less complete, was the growing concentration of the woollen industry of the south-western counties on the Cotswold valleys, and, among the Cotswold valleys, on those of the Gloucestershire escarpment. In the mid-eighteenth century, Eastern and North-Eastern Dorset, along the Wiltshire, Somerset and Devon boundaries, had been a clothing country: it was so no more. The industry had vanished slowly, silently, and without causing marked distress[2]. Devonshire had dropped out much later and much more swiftly. Axminster still made carpets; but as its population remained stationary during the 'twenties at 2700 the business cannot have been active. There were poor remnants of a wool manufacture at Barnstaple and Tiverton; but that was all[3]. Yet so recently as 1800 Exeter itself was "essentially a manufacturing city." It "was the great emporium for the thinner kinds of woollen goods, such as serges, druggets, estamines and long-ells; which being spun and woven in the towns and villages around were dyed and finished in the city, whence they were shipped to Spain, Portugal, Holland, Italy and the East Indies." "From the warehouses within the city the raw materials were distributed into the neighbouring villages, and then returned in the piece. Here it was submitted to a variety of processes...." The merchants "lived in the midst of their business." Twenty years later the business had dwindled to unimportance. (The cause, so it was alleged in 1817, was that the East India Company now bought tea with silver instead of with West Country woollens[4].) Thirty years

---

[1] *V.C.H. Essex*, II. 463. Clapham, J. H., "The Spitalfields Acts," *E.J.* (Dec 1916), p. 462-3.   [2] *V.C.H. Dorset*, II. 360-2.

[3] Tiverton Mills, which were said to have employed 1200 people—no doubt mainly out-weavers—were sold about 1815. The Exeter agent who sold them had 22 other mills to sell in 1817. Evidence of Jas. Dean of Exeter before the *Lords' Committee on the Poor Laws, 1817* (1818, v), p. 127.

[4] Evidence of Jas. Dean, as above. His explanation is not of course a complete one.

later it was gone: "in 1831 this trade may be said to have ceased." "The workshops connected with it had become devoted to other purposes, and the neighbouring fields, previously lined with 'racks,' were given up exclusively to pasturage." Meanwhile Exeter was growing fast in population, in sanitary wisdom, and in health[1].

Serge and fine cloth making were still relatively important industries in several parts of Somerset; but the best of the cloth manufacture was concentrated north of the Mendips in the valleys of the Bristol Avon and its tributaries, and there it was losing ground. The population of Frome, its most important headquarters, actually fell between 1821 and 1831. So did that of Bradford-on-Avon, Great Bradford as it appears in the census of 1831, just over the Wiltshire border. Its neighbour on that side, Trowbridge, grew a little; but in both the fine cloth industry, for which both were famous, was already in a decline. Under the Cotswolds in Gloucestershire the industry showed more life; but only at one point, in the Stroud valley, was it really vigorous, though the excellence of its workmanship in all this region was undoubted. According to the occupation returns of the 1831 census there were 50 per cent. more people connected with the clothing industry in Gloucestershire than in Wiltshire; but for every one in Gloucestershire there were fifteen in the West Riding of Yorkshire. The figures are defective but the proportions were probably as stated[2].

In the East Midlands, Lincolnshire, and the East Riding there were few traces of lost industries of any importance; for the region had never had great industrial significance. Its chalks and clays, the peat soil of its fens and the vales of the oolite and lias formations, formed the heart of rural England. Here, through the centuries, problems not of industry but of agriculture had filled the soiled pages of the economic story. There was a loss of domestic spinning, a specially heavy loss in the districts adjacent to East Anglia which had spun much for Norwich; but this was common to almost all agricultural regions. The iron-stones which occur all along the lias formation had in the past been worked at various points; but at none

---

[1] From the brilliant paper on Exeter by Dr Shapter in *Report on the State of Large Towns* (1845), II. 354–8.

[2] *V.C.H. Gloucester*, II. 193. The Census figures for "clothing" are Wiltshire, 3000; Gloucester, 4500; West Riding, 68,000.

had an important iron industry ever arisen[1]. Industries based on local products, like the chair making of High Wycombe, or not yet dependent on steam and iron, like the bootmaking of Northampton, so far from declining were on the increase[2]. In Oxfordshire the blanket industry of Witney and the horse rugs of Chipping Norton formed the easternmost outliers of the Cotswold textile area; neither was large, but the combined isolation and excellence of the little industry of Witney have always kept it from being overlooked[3].

West of the curved line made by the Trent, the Soar, the Warwickshire Avon and the Severn, a line which corresponds very nearly with the western edge of the new red sandstone, lie all the outcropping coal measures of England and Wales except the small fields of North Somerset. One of the first general accounts of English geology ever put together, that of W. D. Conybeare published in 1822, pictures "an intelligent traveller taking his departure from our metropolis" and going west or north-west towards the coal; whatever line he takes, he will cross clay and chalk and freestone [oolite]; afterwards "a broad zone of red marly sand; and beyond this he will find himself in the midst of coal mines and iron furnaces"[4]—in South Wales; in Dean Forest; in the Black Country proper; in North Warwick and West Leicester and so through Nottingham and Derby to the coal and iron of Yorkshire and the North, the regions of which it was still true that "provisions were cheaper, the poor more easily satisfied, and coals more plentiful" than in the metropolis and the towns of the East; though the greater cheapness of provisions and the greater docility of the poor were now less conspicuous than they had been in 1748[5].

In some of the counties within the coal line, the industries were so young, numerous, strangely named, changing and interlocked, that the attempt which the compilers of the

---

[1] Scrivenor, *op. cit.* p. 95, speaks of two iron furnaces in Lincolnshire in 1796, at Renishaw. But Renishaw is in Derbyshire, six miles north-east by east of Chesterfield.

[2] Chairmakers at Wycombe—"so numerous as to partake of a manufacturing character, but they are entered in the handicraft column," *Census of 1831* (1833), xxxvi. 35. In Northamptonshire over 2000 shoemakers were "deemed manufacturers" because producing "an article consumed elsewhere," *ibid.* xxxvi. 446.

[3] See, for instance, Meidinger, *op. cit.* I. 413.

[4] Quoted in Woodward, H. B., *Geology of England and Wales*, p. 11.

[5] Above, p. 44.

1831 Census made to give a full account of them—based on the defective returns already referred to,—under the two headings of "handicrafts" and "manufactures," several times broke down. Of Lancashire, with its million and a third of inhabitants, they were reduced to the confession that its manufactures could not "be described or even distinctly enumerated."[1] In Staffordshire, after referring to the primary iron industries and enumerating scores of hardware crafts, they explained vaguely that many people were engaged "in producing the more various and complex aid of human industry, which is comprehended under the name of machinery."[2] With the pottery of the Five Towns they felt happier—"a prosperous manufacture, not unfavourable to the health or personal appearance of the potters and their female assistants."[3] In Warwickshire the famous silk ribbon industry of Coventry was easily handled, and it was noted that "watch making had been successfully introduced there"; but the Birmingham trades resisted classification and forced the officials to give all the detail they had collected under innumerable trade headings, such as beer machines, Britannia tea pots, coffin furniture, gas, gilt toys, goldbeaters, to take only a very few from the earlier letters of the alphabet[4]. Sheffield was almost as varied and as difficult as Birmingham, and the returns seem to have been far more defective[5].

Simpler problems in the coal belt industries were presented by Nottingham and Leicester, Shropshire and Cheshire. In the two former counties, and in the adjacent parts of Derbyshire, the staple industries—hosiery and lace-making—had gone through no general technical transformation. They were not dependent on power, though but for the nearness of the coal they could hardly have grown to their present size; stockingers like hand-loom weavers were an old-established and recognised class of domestic outworkers; and their frames were turned out by an equally recognisable class of handicraft framesmiths. But the presence of a few cotton and worsted spinning mills in the district, some of size and importance, marked the approach to the new textile areas. East and North-East Cheshire was industrially a part of Lancashire; but its industrial life was less varied and complex, for beyond the silk and the cotton, the salt of the Northwich area was the sole

---

[1] *Census of 1831*, XXXVI. 308.   [2] *Ibid*. XXXVII. 604.
[3] *Ibid*. XXXVII. 620.   [4] *Ibid*. XXXVII. 680 *sqq*.
[5] *Ibid*. XXXVII. 836.

important manufacture. Shropshire, even on its Staffordshire side, was industrial only in patches, although in those patches there was a considerable variety of industries. Its main manufacturing area was about Coalbrookdale and Madeley, where many men were engaged in "the preparation of iron for the forge," "in iron-castings and at forges, in preparing the weighty apparatus of powerful machinery."[1]

The Baron Dupin had done well to call the attention of the French to the "imposing sight" of the English Black Country. Here even more truly than in Lancashire lay the strength of the new age—those forty years during which the make of iron in Great Britain had increased tenfold. The valleys of Glamorgan and South-West Monmouth were the annexes of the Black Country[2], and Glamorgan was the sole Welsh county where large scale manufactures existed. All the rest, except Flint and a strip across South Carmarthen and Pembroke, lie, like most of Devon and Cornwall, on rocks more ancient than the coal, but rocks in which as Conybeare said "the mines are yet more valuable." He was thinking of the tin and copper mines of Cornwall, at this time at the height of their value, and of the great copper mines in Anglesey, which from 1768 to 1798 had been the most important in the world and were still, though much diminished, employing between 500 and 1000 men[3]. Industrial development in Monmouth and Glamorgan had been swift and revolutionary. The population of Lancashire grew by $98\frac{1}{2}$ per cent. between the first census and the third (1801-31); that of Monmouth (it would all have gone very easily into Manchester at either date) by 117 per cent. Next to Lancashire among English counties came the West Riding with a growth of 74 per cent. in the thirty years; but Glamorgan had grown by 77 per cent. The iron industries of Monmouth and Glamorgan were "extractive": they mined, smelted, cast and rolled but did little finishing work; though already the making of sheets and tinned plates was carried on, if not as yet extensively, in the valleys of Glamorgan, Carmarthen and Monmouth[4].

[1] *Census of 1831*, xxxvi. 528-9.
[2] For the close family connection between South Wales and the Black Country see Ashton, T., *Iron and Steel in the Industrial Revolution* (1924), ch. IX. *The Ironmasters*. The Guests, *e.g.*, came from Broseley.
[3] Davies, *North Wales*, p. 46. Meidinger, *op. cit.* I. 339, and below, p. 186.
[4] *Census of 1831* (1833, xxxvii. 896) reported 2-300 sheet and tinplate workers. Jones, J. H., *The Tinplate Industry* (1914), App. D, gives 18 tinplate-works in Britain in 1825, of which 12 were in the counties mentioned and 4 in Gloucester.

Beyond the green belt of the North Riding, North Lancashire and South Cumberland, the belt between the coal and the coal —"not a country of farmers but a country of graziers," as Cobbett called it[1]—neither Durham nor Northumberland, in 1831, contained as many people as the parish of Manchester[2]. Except in patches, they also were still very green—though in them the farmers outnumbered the graziers. Their industries, but for the coal-mining itself, though varied and important were not extensive. The output of pig iron in the two counties was barely one-sixth of that of the West Riding, and not one-fortieth of that of Staffordshire[3]. The glass and salt and cable and lead and machine manufactures were valuable: the coal-fields had a definitely manufacturing aspect; but there had been no headlong growth anywhere. Newcastle and Gateshead to-gether had been just passed in population by Aberdeen, between 1821 and 1831; South Shields had been stationary for thirty years; and Sunderland, the largest town in Durham, was con-siderably smaller than the stagnant academic Cambridge of the 'twenties, whose "solemn organ pipes" blew "melodious thunders through her vacant courts at morn and even."[4]

In Westmorland the ancient woollen manufacture of Kendal was dying, but had been partly replaced by a small cotton industry. About Carlisle a coarse linen manufacture of the mid-eighteenth century had been replaced first by calico-stamping and, latterly, by a cotton manufacture which at this time was showing considerable activity[5]. The coalfields by the coast had long been worked with almost as much vigour as those of the Tyne and Wear: pits were down to 95, 130 and even 160 fathom when the nineteenth century began, and the shipments through Whitehaven were steadily growing[6]. Since 1820 systematic attempts had also been made to develop the hematite iron ore of Cumberland and Furness—the richest and finest ore in the island—by Antony Hill, a South Wales iron-master. The exploitation was in its infancy and was little noticed outside the circles directly concerned; but it marked a most important stage in British iron-mining and metallurgy[7].

[1] *Rural Rides*, II. 364.
[2] Northumberland, 223,000; Durham, 253,700; Manchester Parish, 270,961.
[3] Scrivenor, *op. cit.* p. 136: figures for 1830.
[4] Tennyson's suppressed *Cambridge* (1833). Sunderland, 17,060; Cambridge, 20,917.
[5] *V.C.H. Cumberland*, II. 345.
[6] *Ibid.* II. 355, 363.
[7] *Ibid.* II. 385. Below, p. 189.

Geological conditions have set peculiarly sharp bounds to the only area of Scotland which can ever be populous and industrial. The two almost parallel north-eastward trending lines, one from near Girvan on the Ayrshire coast to a point on the eastern sea just south of Dunbar, the second from the Clyde near Helensburgh to Stonehaven in Kincardineshire, bound that central belt, geologically speaking that rift valley, which contains all the coal and most of the really open ground of the country, with the political and economic capitals[1]. The Lowland shires, south of this central belt, held in their valleys a few domestic weavers and stockingers and only a single town of more than five thousand inhabitants[2]. North of the belt lay the almost townless Highlands; and beyond them on the east the coastal strip set with occasional towns from Aberdeen round to Wick. Of these Aberdeen held a high place among British seaports being, in 1831, more populous than either Newcastle or Hull, though much inferior to Bristol, Liverpool and London. Besides its maritime occupations it had well-developed textile industries, and all the minor industries necessary to a somewhat isolated urban centre with a vast rural *hinterland*.

Commercially and industrially Dundee, which lies well within the central belt, closely resembled Aberdeen—a town dominated by the sea, with a textile industry spread into the county behind it, based on sailcloth and sacking. Localised textile industries of importance and a fairly dense population occurred also in Fife, which covers the most northerly Scottish coal. But the real and only serious concentration of industry lay where Scottish civilisation had always been concentrated, in the strip of land from Forth to Clyde. The four contiguous counties of Midlothian, Linlithgow, Lanark and Renfrew contained in 1831 between a third and a quarter of the whole Scottish population. In and about Edinburgh were all the industries necessary to the life of a capital city, but not the large scale industries of the new age[3]. These were mainly in the Glasgow area and in Clydesdale, and among them cotton was dominant. All others were represented there: the great Carron ironworks employed over 1500 men: the output of pig iron in Scotland, which had been relatively small down to 1825, received a great impetus from the application of the hot-air blast to the furnaces by Neilson in 1828: Charles Tennant and Co.'s chemical works

[1] Mackinder, H. J., *Britain and the British Seas* (1902). p. 68. The accuracy of the description "rift valley" is disputed.

[2] Dumfries: population 1821, 11,052; 1831, 11,606.   [3] Below, p. 71.

at St Rollox were supposed, in 1830, to be the largest in Europe, and the Census officials—perhaps not quite abreast of the course of industrial development—noted that "even steam engines" were constructed at Greenock; but it was the cotton mills, from Dale and Owen's world-famous establishment at New Lanark to those of Monteith, Bogle and Co., who had been the first in Britain to organise weaving by steam-power on a large scale, at Pollokshaws, to which public attention was mainly directed between 1815 and 1830[1]. Dupin was in Glasgow in 1817. He was enormously interested in the transport developments of the district, especially in the Forth and Clyde Canal, along which he sailed with James Watt himself, then in his eighty-second year; but he treated the fifty-four cotton spinning mills of Glasgow, with their capital of over £1,000,000, as the crown of the economic life of Scotland[2].

Nowhere in Britain had the face of the country seen more changes during the generation preceding the Census of 1831 and the Reform Bill. The population of Lanarkshire had grown appreciably faster even than that of Lancashire since 1801[3]. The "spreading of the hideous town" had grimed a whole countryside. Meidinger, the German, thought that, taken all in all, the Scots were dirtier than the English[4]. Dupin, the Frenchman, was sure that they bred the best educated working class in Europe. "In all the workshops and manufactories that I visited, I found the workmen well informed, appreciating with sagacity the practice of their trade, and judging rationally of the power of their tools and the efficacy of their machinery."[5] The combination of a magnificent geographical endowment, an educated aristocracy of workers, a thick substratum of less educated Highlanders and Irishmen, and a tradition of inferior and not too clean housing, rendered it certain that the Glasgow area would change and change again, with the release and extended action of new economic forces, and that the best and the worst growths of the new industrial civilisation might there continue to sprout side by side.

---

[1] See below, p. 185. Scrivenor, *op. cit.* p. 135–6. *Census of 1831* (1833), XXXVII. 1000–2.

[2] *Op. cit.* II. 222 *sqq.* There were 63 power-loom mills, with 14,127 looms, in 1831. *Census of 1831*, as above. Moreover, the cotton mills of Scotland "however widespread their location...were generally owned in Glasgow." Marwick, W. H., "The Cotton Industry and the Industrial Revolution in Scotland," *Sc. Hist. Rev.* XXI (1924), 212.

[3] Though not quite so fast as that of Monmouth. Above, p. 49.

[4] *Op. cit.* II. 11.   [5] *Ibid.* II. 237.

CHAPTER II

POPULATION

THERE was no place for illusions about the growth of British population in the third decade of the nineteenth century. But men not much beyond middle life could remember when the question whether it was growing or not had been treated as an open one among persons of education. Only in the nineteen years (1798–1817) between the issue of the first edition of Malthus' *Essay* and of the fifth had it been finally decided, by the method of the Census, that population was not merely growing but growing extraordinarily fast. The doubts as to whether there really was growth at all, which had been confidently expressed so late as the decade 1780–90, were unreasonable, in view of the evidence then existing, but they could hardly at that time be proved absurd[1]. Nor, it should be added, was the growth before the great wars very swift. To believe in growth had required some faith. About the year 1750, David Hume had been forced to use all his learning and sane scepticism to support the contention that "it seems impossible to assign any just reason why the world should have been more populous in ancient than in modern times,"[2] so tenacious was the tradition of decline from a greater age. In his day everyone wished to see the population grow, yet few were certain that it was growing. But when the second and third censuses had been taken (1811–21), the flood of life, accompanied as it had been by war, by social changes unprecedently swift, by some unusual sequences of bad harvests, and by mishandled policies for the relief of distress, had popularised the phrase "a redundant population." From perhaps 7,250,000 in 1751, when Hume was writing, and a possible 9,250,000 in 1781, the people of Great Britain had increased to a measured 10,943,000 in 1801, to 12,597,000 in 1811, and

---

[1] The fourth edition of Price's *Reversionary Payments*, arguing for a declining population, appeared in 1783. The anonymous author of *The Uncertainty of the Present Population of the Kingdom* (1781), after summarising the controversy between Price, Eden, Wales and Howlett, left the question open. See Gonner, E. C. K., "The Population of England in the Eighteenth Century," *S.J.* LXXVI. 261 (1913).

[2] *Of the Populousness of Ancient Nations* (1752). *Essays* (ed. 1779), I. 436.

to 14,392,000 in 1821. In 1831 the return was to be 16,539,000[1].
For Ireland a census had been first authorised in 1812. Competent statisticians at that time were discussing whether there
were four or four and a half million Irishmen living[2]. The
measure of their ignorance was shown when the census, at
length taken in 1821, showed 6,803,000: that of 1831 would
show nearly a million more.

Contrary to an opinion still widely held, the flood of life,
which made Malthus and his generation speculate on the causes
and cure of a redundant population, was due far more to life
saving, since the mid-eighteenth century, than to reckless pro-
creation since the great inventions and the start of the Speenhamland policy of adjusting family receipts to the number of
mouths to be fed[3]. Campaigning against the poor law, Malthus
wrote bitterly of the English "population raised by bounties."[4]
The many who have since echoed his bitter cry should at least
have paused to recall that the rate of growth was very nearly
the same in Scotland, where there were no bounties, and may
have been even greater in Ireland, where there was not so much
as a poor law. Some hold that the cotton industry, by its
demand for the labour of women and children, "was chiefly
responsible for the great avalanche of population"[5] in the towns
during the generation and a half preceding the Reform Bill.
But the cotton-mill population of Great Britain, even in 1830,
was perhaps one-eightieth of the total population[6]. The Census
reporters of 1841 noted that "in Lancashire, where the large
manufactories are supposed to include so large a juvenile
population, the numbers between the ages of 15 and 20...are
as nearly as possible the same as in Huntingdon."[7]

That the industrial revolution, with the attendant changes
in agriculture and transport, rendered the maintenance of a
rapidly growing British population possible, without resort to
the cabin-and-potato standard of life, is beyond question; but

[1] For the eighteenth century see Gonner, *ut sup.*; the early census figures are
of course subject to criticism in detail.

[2] Colquhoun, *A Treatise on the Wealth, Power and Resources of the British
Empire* (2nd ed. 1815), p. 10, referring to the year 1811.

[3] See below, p. 122 *sqq.*

[4] *Essay on...Population* (ed. 1826), II. 109.

[5] Hammond, J. L. and B., *The Town Labourer, 1760–1832* (1917), p. 15;
no statistical evidence used.

[6] Total population, 1831, 16,539,000: cotton-mill population, 1831, probably
not above 200,000. See below, p. 72.

[7] 1843, XXII. 18.

the sequence of events should not be misconstrued. First the death rate fell, after 1740, in an age of growing comfort and improved medical knowledge, when as yet invention had brought no true industrial revolution, the age which ended, say, with the first application of steam to cotton spinning in 1790. Meanwhile the crude birth rate for England and Wales—that is the number of births per thousand living—either remained fairly steady or, as some statisticians are disposed to argue, rose slightly. That "the number of births everywhere increased by leaps and bounds,"[1] either before or after 1790, is a statement without statistical foundation, if by "the number of births" is meant the birth rate; but if what is meant is that as there were more people there were more children, it is no doubt true enough.

After 1790 the death rate continued to fall rapidly until 1811–20. The evidence points to a slight rise during the following decade; but it never again got anywhere near the rates of the mid-eighteenth century. Had the birth rate risen appreciably during this, the Speenhamland, age, as is so constantly suggested by historians who neglect quantities, then there would indeed have been an "avalanche of population." There was something like an avalanche as it was, so effective had become the saving of life; though the evidence suggests that the crude birth rate, so far from rising, fell a little, if only a little, during the years 1811–30 from the level reached in 1791–1810[2]. The conquest of small-pox, the curtailment of agueish disorders through drainage, the disappearance of scurvy as a disease of the land, improvements in obstetrics leading to a reduction in the losses both of infant and of maternal life in childbed, the spreading of hospitals, dispensaries and medical schools, all had helped to save life. In the course of the eighteenth century gentlemen had become clean—in the seventeenth kings might not wash, like James I of England, or with Henry of Navarre, on his own confession, might "smell of their armpits."[3] Now cheap cotton shirts and cleanliness were spreading slowly downwards through society, with results beneficial to health. London might be honeycombed with cesspools and rank with city graveyards; but it

---

[1] Webb, S. and B., *English Local Government* (1922), IV. 405.

[2] There is a margin of error in all calculations of vital statistics for the eighteenth century. Those adopted here are Dr Brownlee's, in *Public Health*, June–July 1916. See also Griffith, G. T., *Population Problems of the Age of Malthus* (1926) and Buer, M. C., *Health, Wealth and Population in the Early Years of the Industrial Revolution* (1926).

[3] Not all eighteenth-century kings washed: Frederick the Great did not.

was better to be born a Londoner than a Parisian, better to be born a Londoner of 1820 than a Londoner of 1760, and much better to be born an average Englishman than an average citizen of France, or of the almost completely rural Prussia of the 'twenties, if the goodness of life is to be measured by its probable length[1].

To all of which Parson Malthus may be conceived as replying—"even if population is not raised by bounties, the more need for the preventive check, since medicine and philanthropy have dulled the edge of the positive ones. Let the birth rate fall still faster: but I greatly fear that it will not."

In Ireland, too, as it would seem, the positive checks had lost their power for a time. Irish vital statistics for the eighteenth and early nineteenth century do not exist; so all that can be said about Ireland is conjectural. There is, however, no reason to suppose that improved medical knowledge or progress in cleanliness and sanitation had saved very much Irish life before 1800; though something had been accomplished in Dublin. What seems to have been the main cause of the undoubtedly rapid, though not accurately measurable, growth of population between 1750 and 1820 was not any of the somewhat fantastical special causes often assigned—the Irish, so far as is known, always married young and bred freely—but a gap in the famines. The famine of 1727 had been terrible, the "years of death," 1739–41, more terrible still: after that, although shortages and local famines were chronic, "no famine at all approaching that of 1741 occurred throughout the remainder of the century."[2] Nor were the famines of 1817 and of 1822 comparable with those of 1739–41 or 1846–7. Although thousands died of hunger and hunger typhus in 1822[3], the population of Ireland grew by nearly a million—if the early census figures are to be trusted—between 1821 and 1831. It can hardly be

[1] [The general conclusions here summarised, which are to be found already in outline in Porter's *Progress of the Nation*, ch. I, would be accepted by most students of the subject. For divergent views on some general and many particular questions see Yule, G. U. in *S.J.* 1906; Gonner, E. C. K. in *S.J.* 1913; Beveridge, Sir W. H. in *Economica*, March, 1925; Hammond, J. L. in *History*, July, 1927; Marshall, T. H. in *E.J.* (*Ec. Hist.*), Jan. 1929; Brownlee, *op. cit.*; Griffith, *op. cit.*]

[2] O'Brien, G., *The Economic History of Ireland in the Eighteenth Century* (1915), p. 105. But 1800–1 was a very bad year. See Gill, C., *The Rise of the Irish Linen Industry* (1925), p. 341, and authorities there quoted. Griffith, *op. cit.* ch. III, does not discuss the gap in the famines.

[3] Locker-Lampson, G., *A Consideration of the State of Ireland in the Nineteenth Century* (1907), p. 182.

supposed that the very doubtful prospect of poor relief in a
London slum or of ultimate employment in a Lancashire cotton
mill had much to do with the begetting of this million of
Irishmen. They were just born; and if they all stayed in Ireland
they were in danger of dying[1].

Therefore the Irish of the 'twenties moved towards the English slums and mills with a more definite intention of stopping
there than their fathers and grandfathers had shown. Small
Irish colonies in the towns of Great Britain were of old standing,
that of St Giles-in-the-Fields dating from early in the seventeenth century. All through the eighteenth century the numbers
and social significance of the London Irish had been on the
increase. "Ireland greatly assists in filling up the capital," a
student of population wrote in 1757[2]. These colonies were
mainly recruited, so it seems, from the labourers who—from
early in the eighteenth century at least[3]—crossed over to do
seasonal work in the building trades or in the hay and corn
harvests of the metropolitan area. Hawkers, porters, coal-
heavers, chairmen—such people were often Irish before 1800.
By that time "spalpeen" agricultural labour was an organised
institution. "In many parts of Hertfordshire and other places,"
Bell wrote in 1804[4], "there have been and still are a species of
contractors or spalpeen brokers whose purpose it is to furnish
the farmers with Irish labourers. They would...engage the
miserable labourer at the lowest possible rate, and pocket themselves the difference between it and the wages paid by the
farmers to them on the labourers' behalf." From evidence
given before a parliamentary committee in 1828 it appears that
bargaining with the farmer was originally done by the leader
of a gang, successful leaders often becoming in time professional
brokers or gang masters[5]. A witness from Hertfordshire, where
the Irish were evidently very numerous—because of its near-

---

[1] Carr-Saunders, A. M., *The Population Problem* (1922), p. 308, treats the
whole growth of population as "merely the response to increase in skill." Something turns on the meaning of "response," but I do not see how the formula
can be made to cover Ireland, except by saying that had skill not increased in
England the Irish would have died in Ireland.

[2] Burrington, quoted in George, *op. cit.* p. 111. For a general account of the
eighteenth-century London Irish see p. 113 *sqq.*

[3] O'Brien, *op. cit.* p. 98.

[4] Quoted in O'Brien, p. 98.

[5] *Select Committee on the Laws relating to Irish and Scotch Vagrants* (1828,
IV. 201), p. 9.

ness to London, which acted as a distributing centre—stated
in 1826 that they were not only most useful, but "most ex-
emplary," even when they arrived too early for hay or corn
harvest and walked "about the country almost starved for
perhaps a week or ten days."[1] Outside Hertfordshire, as might
be expected, many were employed on the great hay fields of
Middlesex which supplied the cow houses and mews of
London[2]. In Essex, rather later, it was reported that they
formed a very important element in the supply of agricultural
labour. That at the same time (1833) there were said to be
"not very many" on the land in Lancashire, a fact at first sight
surprising seeing that Liverpool was the main port of entry,
is to be explained no doubt by the small average size of the
Lancashire farms and the abundant supply of casual or
weavers' labour in time of harvest[3]. In the South some got so
far as Sussex, where, as a witness put it in 1826, "we have a
great irruption, I may say, of barbarians...during the time of
harvest, but not peculiarly Irish."[4] The flow of Irishmen thinned
out as the distance from London increased, but it had a wide
radius. In the North they got across to Lincolnshire in 1831;
but "the native labourers assembled in great numbers and
drove them away."[5] In Scotland the true agricultural labourers
did not often get beyond the South-Western counties in the
'twenties: "they remain generally in Wigton and Ayr."[6] By
1833 it was stated that, as temporary agricultural labourers,
they had "nearly cut out Highlanders out of the Lowland
market,"[7] which no doubt includes the Eastern Lowlands; but
such a statement by a single witness for a wide area cannot be
pressed too far.

From agriculture proper the temporary migrants passed
easily to other unskilled country jobs. They were invaluable
in connection with the enclosure of waste land and the drainage
of mosses in South-Western Scotland. "They are employed
almost exclusively in making ditches and cutting drains and in
carrying loads for masons"; and for such work they were driving
out the Scots, J. R. McCulloch said in 1824. He added that

---

[1] S. C. on Emigration (1826–7, v), Q. 1200.
[2] S. C. on Vagrants (1821, IV), p. 94.
[3] S. C. on Agriculture (1833, v), Q. 1566 (Essex), Q. 3713 (Lancashire).
[4] S. C. on Emigration, Q. 1176.
[5] Poor Law Report, 1834 (1834, XXIX. App. A, part II. p. 140).
[6] S. C. on Emigration, Q. 2200.
[7] S. C. on Agriculture, Q. 2674.

they were generally speaking well behaved[1]. In the home counties of England they swelled the working force which, under the high command of McAdam and Telford, was re-making the road surface and even the road bed along the principal highways[2].

So long as the Irishman remained in a country district his chances of becoming permanently domiciled in Britain were small. In every parish overseers of the poor, often conscious of a redundant population of their own, were certain to move him on, the more so as the genuine work-seekers were mixed up with confirmed vagrants and beggars. The former, with characteristic peasant pride, as one who knew them well testified, counted it a disgrace to travel with a poor law pass, even though that meant travel on wheels; so they walked their way resolutely from Connaught to the sea and from Liverpool to London[3]. The latter were an extra and most galling burden to the overstrained English poor law authorities, who had to pass them on towards their native place. "It is only giving them a voyage to Ireland that they may have another back," grumbled a Cumberland poor law official from a seaport town[4]. Inland officials dumped their Irish at the county boundaries, sometimes keeping a regular "contractor for the removal of vagrants" to do the work. The counties quarrelled because they had to handle so many vagrants who did not "originate" within their bounds. In four years, 1823-7, Lancashire passed homewards more than 20,000 Irish and 1600 Scottish vagrants, itself bearing the sea costs[5].

This machinery for moving the vagrant and destitute Irish was expensive and, in its application to London and the other towns where they most congregated, certainly inefficient. In 1828 conveyance alone for a vagrant from London to Liverpool cost £4. 11s. 3d. The price of an inside ticket by mail coach was £4. 4s. 0d.[6] The Middlesex contractor for the removal of vagrants had admitted in 1821 that they often "rode as far as they liked and when they did not want to go any further they

[1] S. C. on Disturbances in Ireland (1825, VIII), p. 824.
[2] S. C. on Labourers' Wages, 1824 (VI. 401), p. 14.
[3] S. C. on Irish and Scotch Vagrants, 1828, p. 9: evidence of J. E. Strickland an Irish agent.
[4] S. C. on Vagrants, 1821, p. 57: evidence from Maryport.
[5] S. C. of 1828, p. 4. These removals were under the Act of 1819 (59 Geo. III, c. 12): before that the Irish were not removed unless they were guilty of an "act of vagrancy." [6] Ibid. p. 4.

came back again."[1] It is not surprising that the London Mendicity Society, founded in 1818 for dealing with beggars and vagrants, had over 8000 Irish applicants in 1826–7[2]. These were the completely destitute and the more or less professional mendicants. Vastly more numerous were the unskilled but industrious Irish who had gradually established themselves in the towns. Bricklayer's labourer, seasonal or permanent, was their chosen trade. They are heard of remitting money home to pay the rent of a Connaught potato patch[3]. St Giles and Whitechapel were their chosen parishes[4]. When hard times came these semi-domiciled Irish, although not strictly entitled to poor law assistance, often got casual relief from the London authorities because, as was reported in 1821, many of them had been resident there for twenty or thirty years[5].

In much the same way, between 1810 and 1830, they became a permanent element in the population of Edinburgh, for capital cities had always drawn the Irish migrant—first Dublin, then London, now Edinburgh. About the year 1810 "all the menial offices of porters, water-carriers, and such like were performed by Highlanders; since then," an Edinburgh witness stated in 1831, "the Irish have been gradually increasing, till now the Westport, Grassmarket and Cowgate and adjoining closes are completely filled with them."[6] "The scavengers and lamplighters and people of that description were almost all Irishmen" in 1826[7]. Leerie the lamplighter, who "with lantern and with ladder" came "posting up the street," more than five and twenty years later, to rejoice the baby Louis Stevenson, "and nod to him good night," may perhaps have been an O'Leary of the second generation[8].

But it was the new industrial accessible west side of Britain, where labour was wanted and the organisation for sifting out its undesirable elements was weak, which drew and held most of the Irish; though they pushed across country not only to London and Edinburgh, but to Dundee and Aberdeen[9]. They

[1] S. C. of 1821, p. 25.

[2] S. C. on Emigration, Third Report, Appendix, p. 590.

[3] S. C. of 1828, p. 7 sqq.: evidence running back some twenty years.

[4] S. C. of 1821, p. 22.

[5] Ibid. p. 59. Till 1819 they had been able to apply without the risk of removal to their native parish. See George, op. cit. p. 125.

[6] S. C. on the Observance of the Sabbath, 1831 (VII. 253), Q. 4143.

[7] S. C. on Emigration, Second Report, Q. 254.

[8] [Leerie, a reviewer in the Scotsman pointed out, is a good Scots name.]

[9] S. C. on Hand Loom Weavers' Petitions, 1834 (X), Q. 3111, 6042.

can be tracked all the way up. Bristol, an old port of arrival, held some. Many were employed at the growing iron works of South Wales[1]. In Lancashire, though not found much on the land, they were numerous in all the great towns and in some of the small ones[2]. There was a considerable and increasing influx into Liverpool and district, especially after the establishment of regular steamboat connection between Ireland and the Mersey in 1824[3]. And although some years earlier it had been maintained that more than half the paupers of Manchester were Irish[4], the Lancashire business world as a whole would probably have agreed with a philanthropic Liverpool witness, an anti-slavery man who had also laboured to improve the social conditions of these same Irish in his own town, when he said that without them "they could not have extended" the cotton trade[5]. They were helping to staff all sections of the trade—spinning, hand-loom weaving, and general labour. Of their numbers in Lancashire at this time there is no trustworthy evidence; but it must have been reckoned in scores of thousands by 1825 and it was always growing. By 1834–5 it was estimated at nearly 150,000; and one-fifth of the population of Manchester was believed to be Irish[6].

For Glasgow, which so nearly reproduced the commercial and industrial conditions of South Lancashire, evidence is more precise. The Scottish officials who collected information for the early censuses had a habit of appending notes on matters of special interest which the headquarters' officials fortunately reproduced. James Cleland, cabinet-maker, statistician, local historian and Doctor of Laws, who took the Glasgow census in 1821 and again in 1831, reported about 25,000 Irish there in the former year and 35,554, out of a total population of just over 200,000, in the latter[7]. It might not be unreasonable to conjecture that there were as many again in the adjacent industrial area; though the West Scottish towns had not been hospitable to the newcomers. "By a sort of moral compulsion," the sort

[1] S. C. on Agriculture, 1833, Q. 180.
[2] S. C. on Emigration, Second Report, Q. 2270 (The Bishop of Chester).
[3] S. C. on Disturbances in Ireland, 1825, p. 691: evidence of Jas. Cropper.
[4] Lords' Comm. on Poor Laws, 1817 (1818, v), p. 154.
[5] Evidence of Jas. Cropper, ut sup.
[6] First Ann. Report of the Poor Law Commissioners, App. XI. 1835 (XXXV. 295). The Manchester estimate is in Wheeler, J., Manchester, its political, social and commercial history (1836), p. 340.
[7] Census of 1831 (1833, XXXVII. 1000 sqq.). For Cleland see D.N.B.

not specified, 1517 Irish were shipped from Paisley in 1827. The witness to this exact figure believed that the same thing "was done in Glasgow to a still greater extent."[1] It was legal, a part of the policy of moving on which was very necessary, if on occasion very brutal, under the old Scottish parochial poor relief system. And, beyond question, J. R. McCulloch the economist was right, if harshly right, when he spoke before a parliamentary committee in 1825 of the infinite harm done during the ten or fifteen years last passed by the Irish immigration, in lowering wages and, what was worse, the standard of life. "I do not know that any such serious mischief was ever inflicted on the West of Scotland."[2]

The Irishman could underlive, perhaps both underlive and overwork, the Highlander, as the record of the two races in "menial tasks" at Edinburgh shows. But as the Highlands, like Ireland, held a population which was, certainly in the existing—and probably in any—conditions, redundant[3], the flow of Highlanders into the Lowlands, which had run since the '45, continued. They shared with the Irish intermittent work on the land. They crowded as casual labourers into the pestilent wynds of Glasgow, and, being but a few generations removed from a hard primitive life which—despite romantic idealisations—was "nasty, brutish and short," they too helped to keep down the standard of life in the new industrial South-West. Highlands and Lowlands were still imperfectly welded and a southern Scot, in 1814, could write of the "natives" of Inverness and Argyle with a touch of the contempt which that word so often carries[4]. To England the raw Highlanders seldom penetrated, though no doubt there would be some among those

---

[1] *S. C. on Emigration, Second Report*, Q. 1813–14.

[2] *S. C. on Disturbances in Ireland*, p. 823. By 1842 the opinion was expressed in the West of Scotland that the lowest grade of Scotsmen were worse than the Irish. Dr Cowan of Glasgow reported to the Poor Law Commission that "the Irish appeared...to exhibit much less of that squalid misery and addiction to the use of ardent spirits than the Scotch of the same grade." Edwin Chadwick's *Report on the Sanitary Condition of the Labouring Population*, p. 132.

[3] Population of Skye, 1772, 13,000; 1831, 22,796; 1845, 29,500; 1911, 13,319. Macleod, R. C., "The Western Highlands in the 18th Century," *Sc. Hist. Rev.* XIX. 31. Population of the Hebrides, 1750, 49,485; 1808–9, 91,049. *Sc. Hist. Rev.* XVII. 85.

[4] Sinclair, Sir J., *General Report of the Agricultural State of Scotland*, I. 181: "A great part of these two counties is let to tacksmen who generally cultivate from 30 to 50 acres, and sublet the rest to the natives."

more than 1600 Scottish vagrants who were "passed" home-
ward from Lancashire by sea between 1823 and 1827. The Scot
who came South in the late eighteenth and early nineteenth
century was generally an educated mechanic, an expert farmer,
gardener, or land agent, a pedlar who found domicile and fortune as a settled English shopkeeper, a merchant's apprentice,
or an already established tradesman seeking better establishment. The guess was hazarded in 1833, by a man whose guess
must carry weight, that "one half of all the mechanics educated
in Scotland" emigrated to England, the Continent or America[1].
There are Grants and Macaulays of the right number of generations on the land in more than one English county. James
McGuffog, the Stamford draper, Robert Owen's first master,
started life in Scotland with half-a-crown and a basket[2]. John
Gladstone served as a lad in his father's Scottish shop, till he
found "the nest too small for him," so went to Liverpool about
1780[3]. Of the first three really great cotton mills in Manchester
one belonged to McConnel and Kennedy and one to George
and Adam Murray[4]. But these were migrants of another
sort than the spalpeens and raw Highland men, the migrants
from a more primitive culture, whose advent exercised Malthus
and McCulloch.

To set against the influx from Ireland and the Highlands into
the economically more developed parts of the Kingdom, there
was an increasing emigration from those parts to America and
to the new colonies of the Southern Hemisphere. Emigration
as a cure for redundancy became fashionable in the 'twenties.
Restrictions on the emigration of skilled artisans were swept
away in 1825, though no one complained of redundant skill.
The first parliamentary inquiry into emigration, "this comparatively unexamined subject"[5] as the inquirers described it,
was made in 1826–7. The tide of emigration from the United
Kingdom was flowing strongly from 1829 to 1833. But even
including the high figures of 1829–30, the average annual out-

[1] *S. C. on the State of Manufactures, Commerce, and Shipping*, 1833 (VI),
Q. 5330. Hy. Houldsworth, who knew both Lanark and Lancashire. [For the
whole subject see Redford, A., *Labour Migration in England, 1800–50* (1926).]
[2] Podmore, F., *Robert Owen*, I. 16, and below, p. 221–2.
[3] Morley, *Gladstone*, I. 9.
[4] These were the two largest in 1815–16. *Report on...Children...in Manufactures*, 1816, p. 374.
[5] *S. C. on Emigration, First Report*, p. 4.

flow from the year of Waterloo to 1830 was only about 25,000[1]; and we happen to know that out of some 36,000 emigrants to North America in 1822-3 nearly 21,000 were Irish and that out of 77,000 in 1829-30, 34,000 were Irish and 7500 Scottish[2]. How many of the latter were redundant Highland crofters and how many Lowland farmers or mechanics is not recorded[3]. The Highlanders would certainly be numerous, for there were many already in Canada, and the flow from the Western Highlands and the Hebrides was continuous because of the clearances and the layings of farm to farm, which had for some time been in progress. It is therefore most unlikely that the outward movement of English, Welsh and Lowland Scots made, so to speak, anything like room enough for the incoming Irish and the few raw Highlanders. Even if it had done so, it did nothing to counteract their influence on the standard of wages and life in those places where they were numerous.

How the whole position struck contemporaries is very clearly shown in the records of the Emigration Inquiry of 1826-7. The select committee who conducted the inquiry were more interested, and rightly, in the evidence for a redundant population in Ireland and the Highlands, and in the movement of the Irish into Britain, than in the migration overseas of British subjects in general. In their report[4] they insisted that no policies or palliatives which left Ireland out of account were of the least use. They testified to the "infinite increase" of would-be permanent Irish migrants, and they called Malthus to witness to the threat to the British standard of life. They reported instances of rural redundance from ten or eleven English counties. There had been put in evidence, for example, a statement from the Weald of Kent that there were more people "in almost every parish" than the needs of agriculture demanded and that, so soon as some of them could be moved away, cottages would be pulled down; from Headcorn parish, Maidstone, a statement that the parish, finding it had 550

---

[1] *Emigration from the United Kingdom*, 1825-32 (1833, XXVI. 279). Johnson, S. C., *Emigration from the United Kingdom to North America* (1913), p. 344. Porter, *Progress of the Nation*, ch. 5. All the figures are a little doubtful.

[2] *S. C. on Emigration, Second Report*, Q. 389, and Porter, *op. cit.* p. 129.

[3] The crofters were really redundant. Highland emigration became necessary when the population ceased to be "reduced...by the sword, the small-pox, or other destructive maladies." *Transac. of the Highland Society*, 1807, in Adam, M. I., "The causes of the Highland Emigration, 1783-1803," *Sc. Hist. Rev.* XVII. 89.

[4] In the *Third Report* (June 1827), p. 1-38.

persons in receipt of poor relief out of 1190 all told, had organised emigration for a considerable group of labourers to Canada;
and from other parishes similar instances of organised migration
though on a smaller scale. Of Scotland the committee reported
that there was no general redundance outside the North-West
Highlands and the Isles. One witness from those parts had
told them how he was trying to "draw" the people "into
villages"; another how there were few crofters now in the
interior—"they had nearly all come down to the shores,"
where they lived by fishing and kelping; a third told how
Maclean of Coll had just emptied the island of Rum into that
of Cape Breton[1]. What the rest of Scotland needed, the committee thought, was an improved poor law and settlement
system plus, if this were in any way possible, a diversion of
the Irish flood.

The problem of redundant hand-loom weavers, which had
been pressed upon them as one which called for special treatment, they handled with the sympathy which it deserved, but
always in connection with the Irish, pointing out that the 40,000
Irish reputed to be found in and about Glasgow were mostly
weavers. Of Ireland they explained how "the present object
of all wise landlords was to increase the size of farms,"[2] as the
Bishop of Limerick made clear to them; how dispossessed
under-tenants of under-tenants "after a season of patient
suffering went into some other district...there they failed not
to find friends...whom they brought back with them at night
to avenge their cause"; how Irish landlords were now almost
unanimously against the under-tenant system, with the results
that clearances were continuous and cabins were springing up
on the bogs; but how, as Sir Henry Parnell had shown them[3],
the clearing of estates must go slowly, because a great part of
Ireland was still under leases which had many years to run,
because on poor land small farms actually paid best, and because
the resistance of the sitting tenants and "the means which they
possessed of deterring landlords"—familiar note!—had to be
taken into account.

Having told all this and much more of the same sort, and
having suggested that if the State were to organise emigration

[1] *Evidence*, Q. 628 (W. F. Campbell, M.P.), Q. 706 (Sir Hugh Innes),
Q. 2907 *sqq.* (Alex. Hunter on Rum).
[2] Q. 1440 *sqq.* (Bishop of Limerick).
[3] Parnell's evidence is Q. 4335 *sqq.*

and provide funds for the purpose so that—in the countries to
be settled—food might precede population, a system which
"had never been fairly acted on by any country," then Irishmen ejected or like-to-be-ejected from their holdings should
have the first claim on these funds, that food, and those colonial
lands, they signed a peroration about Emigration as a National
System and left the matter with no very sanguine hope, apparently, that generation and eviction would go slow enough in
Ireland to render this national system a working possibility.
No system was ever adopted. Individual need and individual
enterprise continued their work of filling the new worlds, at
a price. There was no slackening in Irish generation and there
was a fair deal more eviction, though that was a subordinate
cause. No dam was erected against the Irish flood, and as the
English and Scottish countrysides had all the labour they
needed, and more, except when some big work of construction
was on hand, the Irish who sought permanent settlement went
increasingly into the towns.

The man of the crowded countryside was still the typical
Englishman. The census of 1831 showed that 961,100 families
were employed in agriculture, or 28 per cent. of all the families
in Great Britain. If to these are added the fishing and waterside families outside the towns, the workers on the country
roads and canals, and all those rural handicraftsmen and small
traders who are essential to the most purely agricultural life
under any civilised conditions—the blacksmiths, carpenters,
wheelwrights, cobblers, bricklayers, millers, village shopkeepers—together with the populations of the many little country market towns, there can be very little doubt that some
50 per cent. of the families of Great Britain lived under
conditions which may properly be classed as rural. There
were, for instance, at least 50,000 country cobblers and
at least 25,000 country blacksmiths over twenty years of
age[1]. A purely rural county like Bedfordshire[2], with its
95,000 inhabitants, supported more than 500 adult bricklayers
and 636 "shoe and boot makers or menders," mostly the
cobblers aforesaid.

----

[1] Calculated from the occupational returns of 1831 (1833, XXVII. 1044 *sqq.*)
with allowance for the towns.
[2] Its three towns, Bedford, Luton and Leighton Buzzard, had only 14,000
inhabitants between them.

From the official distinction between urban and rural districts, under modern British conditions, no quite certain conclusion can be drawn about the economic life of either type of area. A coal pit or cotton mill may well be in a rural district. Moreover, the distinction was not adopted until 1851 and then only in England. But the fact that, after twenty more years of rapid urbanisation, nearly 50 per cent. of the English population was still enumerated in rural districts in 1851 is favourable to the view that at least an equal percentage may well have been economically rural in 1831. The town statistics for 1831 point in the same direction[1]. At that time about 25 per cent. of the population of England and Wales and 23 per cent. of that of Scotland lived in towns of 20,000 inhabitants and upwards. It is most unlikely that more than another 25 per cent. lived in what could be properly called towns, if the smaller country market town population be grouped as rural[2].

The representative Englishman, then, was not yet a townsman, though soon he would be[3]. Nor was the representative townsman either a man tied to the wheels of iron of the new industrialism, or even a wage earner in a business of considerable size. The townsmen were no doubt often connected with industries which had been undergoing transformation and becoming, as we say, more capitalistic; but generally such transformations had been neither rapid nor recent. Consider, in the first place, the position of London and the character of the London industries. In 1831 nearly 11 per cent. of the population of England and Wales and more than two-fifths of all the townsmen in towns of over 20,000 inhabitants were Londoners; and, as the census reporters of 1831 observed, "in the appropriate application of the word manufacture, none of importance can be attributed to Middlesex...other than that

[1] See Weber, A. F., *The Growth of Cities in the Nineteenth Century* (Columbia Studies, 1899), p. 47, 58.

[2] An exact calculation would require complete knowledge of every populous area. The word "town" or "borough" as used in the census is not a sufficient guide, nor can populous parishes be treated as "towns." Congleton, with 9352 inhabitants, appears as a chapelry; the purely rural parishes of Soham and Whittlesea, Cambs., both had over 3000 inhabitants, and the borough of Fowey had 1767.

[3] So far as the balance of town and country goes the England of 1831 was in about the same position as the France of 1911, in which 55·9 per cent. of the population was classed as rural, a "rural" commune being one which has a population, living in contiguous houses—"agglomerée"—of less than 2000 people.

of silk."[1] Now the silk workers were hand-loom weavers, as they always had been, working for masters, small or great, as their great-grandfathers had worked. There were of course London firms who made or used the new machinery. One of Boulton and Watt's first engines had gone to a London distillery[2] and *The Times* began to print by steam in 1814. In 1831 twenty-three adult Londoners described themselves as gas-fitters, two hundred and sixty as millwrights; and certainly these figures are incomplete. But in any case such people were not representative. To quote again the exceedingly just appreciation of the state of things by the census reporters of 1831:

a few of the best workmen of every kind are employed in London for combining, fitting, and finishing all the commodities requisite for the consumption and vast commerce of the Metropolis...but workmen so employed are more properly classed...in the detail of Trades and Handicrafts, to the amount of four hundred different kinds,

than under Manufactures.

To this day London is the home of small businesses. More than half the London business firms of all sorts in 1921 had less than twenty workpeople[3]; in 1898 the average number of workpeople in the 8500 businesses classed as factories, *i.e.* which used power, was only 42[4]. For statistical purposes, the businesses which used power in 1831 were negligible, and the large businesses of any kind were very few. Some of the breweries were the biggest. The "eleven great brewers" of London were a recognised group—but there were also seventy-three small ones[5]. More than eighty years earlier Campbell, the author of the *London Tradesman* (1747), had estimated—or shall we say guessed—that more capital was needed to set up as a brewer than as anything else except a banker. By 1777 Thrale, *teste* Dr Johnson, was "not far from the great year of a hundred thousand barrels" and Whitbread at least was ahead of him. Four years later Thrale's business fetched £135,000. By 1814 Barclay, Perkins and Co.—who had bought it—were turning out 262,000 barrels of porter, and five other firms were at, or

[1] XXVI. 382.

[2] The fifth engine, to be exact. Lord, J., *Capital and Steam Power* (1923), p. 152.

[3] Bowley, A. L., "The Survival of Small Firms," *Economica*, May, 1921.

[4] *Ann. Report of the Chief Inspector of Factories*, 1901, Part II, p. 59.

[5] *S. C. on Price of Beer*, 1818 (III. 295), p. 4, and *Brewing Returns*, 1830 (XXII. 167).

above, the 100,000[1]. Employment statistics are not available. There is, however, an estimate from 1825 that in the ancillary trade of the cooper a representative master would employ sixty or seventy men[2]. But such estimates at all times are apt to give as a representative firm one that is not average; so it might be wise to put the average a good deal lower. Another London industry which contained some large, but also some very small, concerns was shipbuilding. Robert Campbell was of opinion that you needed no more capital to start as a shipbuilder than you did to start as a coachbuilder or a "broker of pawns." There had been no revolution in shipbuilding since his day. The largest yard on the river in 1825, Wigram and Green, "when...in full run" employed 400–500 shipwrights and 100–200 other workmen. G. F. Young, the leading, or at least the most vocal London shipbuilder of that generation—he appeared before a whole series of parliamentary committees—reported at the same time that he had nearly 200 men on strike and only "about 30" still at work. These were the shipwrights. Two other first-class firms spoke one of 140 and the other of 150 shipwrights as their normal working staff[3]. If these leaders of the industry employed so few men, there can be no risk in assuming that the average staff of the ship, boat, and barge builders, ship-breakers, repairers, mast and sail makers, and other lesser members of the whole industry—none of whom used power—was comparatively small. It would not be surprising to find that it was well under twenty. In the year of the Reform Bill, 708 ships were built in Great Britain. Of these 389 were of less than 100 tons burthen and only forty of more than 300 tons[4]. It was not in the least necessary for the average shipyard to be of any considerable size.

Even the solitary London industry which was officially described in 1831 as a manufacture was not organised in large units[5]. In 1818 the average number of hand-looms running, in the weavers' homes, for each of fifteen Spitalfields silk manufacturers was only fifty-eight. These fifteen were the big employers. Five years later it was reported that there were many

---

[1] Barnard, A., *The noted breweries of Great Britain and Ireland* (1889), p. xiii.
[2] *S. C. on Combination Laws*, 1825 (IV. 565), p. 32.
[3] *Ibid.* p. 197, 220, 243, 245.
[4] 1833, XXXIII. 501, Shipbuilding return.
[5] Clapham, J. H., "The Spitalfields Acts," *E.J.* XXVI. 459 (1916), and references there given.

manufacturers "that employ 10, 20, 30 and 40 looms" and even a few working weavers who had no master, but bought silk and sold fabrics to warehousemen. Now the typical London skilled workman was neither brewery hand, shipwright nor silk weaver, but either a member of the building trades; or a shoemaker, tailor, cabinet-maker, printer, clockmaker, jeweller, baker—to mention the chief trades each of which had over 2500 adult members in 1831; or he belonged to one of the four hundred or so other occupations of the metropolis. He worked as a rule for a shopkeeper or dealer of some sort, and occasionally in a really big workshop[1]. Very often he worked for several masters, as the working bespoke tailor still does. It is most unlikely that the ratio of wage earners to independent workmen throughout London industry and trade was that ratio of twenty to one which Adam Smith had conjectured for "all Europe" in 1776. When account is taken of all the petty shopkeepers, small dealers and hawkers, the superior craftsmen working direct for consumers, the shopkeepers who were also handicraftsmen with perhaps an apprentice or two, the black-smiths, tinsmiths, locksmiths, butchers, bakers and candle-stick makers, something a good deal less than ten to one is more probable. In 1851 the 87,270 masters in England and Wales who took the trouble to fill up one of the census inquiries employed eight and one-third men each, on an average[2], and a census of "industrial establishments"—the term being used in the very widest sense—taken in France so late as 1896 showed an average number of only five and a half workpeople in each of 575,000 establishments in the whole country[3]. Although these French figures include a vast number of village craftsmen working almost alone, they include also Lille, le Creusot, Havre and modern Paris. The London of 1831 had no thousand-man businesses to keep up the average and plenty of crafts-man-shops to keep it down.

Outside London the small-scale, unrevolutionised, industrial system was widely reproduced: first, in the main seaports—

[1] A few of the largest London tailors employed some scores of men on the premises: Stultzes were credited with 250 in the 'thirties. Thos. Brownlow in *Report on the Sanitary Condition of the Labouring Population*, 1842, p. 98.

[2] *Census of 1851, Population Tables* (1854), I. lxxviii. The number employed was 727,468; but these figures include the industrial areas. See below, p. 448.

[3] Clapham, J. H., *The Economic Development of France and Germany*, p. 258. [The figure for all France in 1851 was 2·4. Sée, H., *La vie écon. de la France sous la monarchie censitaire* (1927), p. 87.]

Hull, Bristol, Newcastle, Liverpool, Plymouth, Portsmouth, Glasgow in so far as it was a seaport, Aberdeen, Dundee. "At Liverpool," the census notes, "340 [adult] men are engaged in various manufactures usual in a large seaport town." The figures must be defective and they exclude the shipwrights, but the average scale of operations along the Mersey was certainly no greater than at Limehouse and in London Pool. For Hull the corresponding figure, also no doubt defective, is 100, with the note appended that "boilers for steam-engines are also made...but on a very limited scale." A second group of towns includes a large number of national or local capitals—Edinburgh, whose industries are definitely reported as many but small; York whose only adult "manufacturers," as distinguished from retail tradesmen and handicraftsmen, were 200 linen weavers and eighteen makers of combs; and most of the county towns. Thirdly: all the definitely manufacturing towns had an important group of small-scale unrevolutionised industries. Fourthly: a large number of the staple manufactures themselves were as yet barely touched by the new power and the factory system. To take but four illustrations: the power-loom had really affected no textile industry but cotton before 1830[1]; the old, highly organised, industry of hand wool-combing was similarly untouched; so were the majority of the hardware and cutlery industries of the Black Country and Sheffield; and machinery was used in "scarcely any branches" of the leather manufacture[2]. In 1833 the business with under five employees was approximately normal in brass founderies, and more than thirty years later the ratio of men to masters in the lock-making industry at Wolverhampton, Walsall and Willenhall was only eleven to one[3].

Neither in London nor anywhere else had there been a revolution—but only a slow development—in perhaps the most important of all industrial groups, the building trades. Iron, cast iron, was certainly coming into new structural uses; it was even used to replace "the cumbrous, unsightly columns which occupy so much space, and so obstruct the view in most old

---

[1] "Should it ever be found practicable to make use of it [the power-loom] extensively in the fabric of Woollens or Silks." *S. C. on Manufacturers' Employment*, 1830 (x. 221), p. 3, and below, p. 145.

[2] Below, p. 170, 323, and *S. C. on the Petitions relating to the duties on Leather* (1813, IV). Evidence of F. Brewin, a Bermondsey tanner.

[3] *S. C. on Manufactures*, 1833, Q. 4330 *sqq*. *Birmingham and the Midland Hardware District* (1866), p. 89.

churches"[1]; but the technique of the trades had not been much affected by that, still less the organisation. The building trades formed not only the most important, but the largest, trade group for men in the country, outside agriculture. They contained some big businesses but a vast majority of small ones[2]. The skilled workpeople were craftsmen, proud of their trades and well known to their neighbours: it is probable therefore that the returns of their numbers in the census of 1831 are reasonably accurate. Taking the bricklayers, masons, carpenters, plasterers, slaters, house-painters, plumbers, and glaziers but omitting the brickmakers and the sawyers, the total is 203,000 men of twenty years old and upwards in Great Britain[3]. To these must be added the young men and lads who were tradesmen apprentices or learners, who can hardly have been fewer than a quarter of the adults, and a large body of bricklayers' labourers carters and the like, many of whom—in London at any rate—were Irish migrants. The total, it may be conjectured, would be between 350,000 and 400,000, all men and boys.

The only trade group in England which could compare with this in size was the great new raw industry of which everyone was talking, for whose reputedly peculiar evils parliament was beginning to legislate—cotton. Three or four years later the cotton mills of Great Britain contained from 210,000 to 230,000 men, women and children, and there were at least 200,000 and possibly 250,000 cotton hand-looms, each presumably with its weaver[4]. But in this great army of perhaps 450,000 cotton workers, in 1833-4, the majority were probably women and girls[5]. The trade was growing so fast that an interval of even three years is of importance. The estimate of power-looms in 1830 was only 55,000–60,000[6] as compared with 100,000 three years later. If 450,000 be the correct employment figure for 1833-4, 375,000–400,000 might be correct for 1831. And, owing to the difference in organisation, if the cotton trades

[1] Lardner, D., *Cabinet Cyclopædia*, "Manufactures in Metal" (1831), I. 67.
[2] See below, p. 162 *sqq.*
[3] From the occupational tables, 1833, XXXVII. 1044 *sqq.*
[4] Baines, E., *History of the Cotton Manufacture* (1835), p. 394, 383. The mill population is calculated from the first inspectors' reports.
[5] More than half were women and girls in the census of 1851, when the figures are not much complicated by hand-loom weavers, and there was generally one female worker, wife or daughter, in a hand-loom weaving family.
[6] *S. C. on Manufacturers' Employment*, 1830, p. 3.

employed more pairs of hands the building trades certainly contained many more heads of families.

Consider again the clothing trades, as yet untouched by machinery. Taking shopkeepers and craftsmen together, there were 133,000 adult male boot and shoe makers and menders in Great Britain, and 74,000 adult male tailors. (What the number of sewing women was, who plied needle and thread to the song of the shirt, no one ever estimated.) On the assumption that tailors and shoemakers were distributed in exact proportion to population, about 63,500 of the tailors and about 114,000 of the shoemakers would be English and Welsh. Compare these trades with that of coal-mining. Round about 1830 so far as is known—the figures are very unsatisfactory—Northumberland and Durham produced about a quarter of the coal raised in England and Wales[1]. The men and boys above and below ground at the collieries of the two counties were estimated, by a good witness, in 1829 at 20,954[2]. The number of adult tailors and bootmakers in London alone, two years later, was 31,051. It can hardly be doubted, when allowance has been made for the tailors' apprentices, that, in the England and Wales of the Reform Bill, there were more tailors, and many more shoemakers, than there were coal-miners. There were some fair-sized businesses in both trades; but in neither was even the moderately large business representative[3].

Lastly attention may be directed to one little-changed calling, occupation group, or industry, about which contemporaries made no inquiry and heard no witnesses, which is not referred to even incidentally in those parliamentary papers from which most of our exact knowledge is derived, whose history no one has ever begun to write. For this group there is a bare figure in the census: for the rest inquiry must be made down Dickens' basement staircases and into his shabbier garrets and closets for Susan Nipper and 'Gusta and the underlings at Todgers's. No notes about wages or dietaries, such as exist in abundance for many classes of labour, occur in the public documents of the age in reference to the 670,491 female domestic servants—who were yet probably more than 50 per cent. more numerous than all the men and women, boys and girls, in the cotton industry

---

[1] Galloway, R. L., *Annals of Coalmining, First Series* (1898), p. 462.

[2] Buddle, Jas. before *Lords' Comm. on Coal Trade*, 1829 (1830, VIII. 405), p. 54.

[3] Below, p. 167, 181.

put together. More figures are not needed to illustrate the fact
that the typical town worker of the decade 1820–30 was very
far indeed from being a person who performed for a self-made
employer in steaming air, with the aid of recently devised
mechanism, operations which would have made his grandfather gape. Nor was he normally attached to a big business.
The figures have been set out for the sake of perspective.
Decade after decade, as the century drove on, more people
came into the sphere of harnessed power, the new mechanism
and bigger businesses. At what point the typical worker may be
pictured as engaged on tasks which would have made earlier
generations gape is a matter for discussion. It may be suggested here that this point will be found some rather long
way down the century.

CHAPTER III

COMMUNICATIONS

NOTHING in England seemed more admirable to the foreign visitor than the perfection of the means of transport and travel. From the ports to the capital a mail coach which "everywhere on the continent would be taken for a princely equipage" swept him along the "magnificent and perfectly level highways, swiftly and without any vibration."[1] Even if he came from France, where scientific road-making was an older art than in England, he was prepared, if candid, to admire "the superior excellence of the roads, as compared with the generality of" those in his own country[2]. Dupin, while allowing that geological conditions and climate had favoured the British road engineers, was not disposed to agree with those continental critics who would have attributed their success primarily to Britain's abundance of good road metal. He was not however dazzled by their achievement as a German, whose country a generation earlier possessed no made roads worth mentioning, might well be. He knew that the best French roads were as good as anything in Britain and he considered that the roads of Sweden—macadamised with broken granite before McAdam—were better. But when he turned from roads to the canal system, though still critically judicious, he could hardly withhold his superlatives from the achievement which "within the short space of half a century" had linked up "opposite seas; river-basins separated by numberless chains of hills and mountains; opulent ports; industrious towns; fertile plains; and inexhaustible mines—a system more than 1000 leagues in length, upon an area not equal to one-fourth of France."[3]

By 1830 the construction of the original—that is, with but few modifications, the existing—British canal system was all but complete[4]. From South Lancashire, where the work began,

---

[1] Meidinger, *op. cit.* I. 4, i.   [2] Dupin, *op. cit.* I. 181.

[3] I. xx. Porter, in 1838, reckoned 2200 miles of canal and 1800 of navigable, and partly canalised, rivers. *S.J.* I. 29.

[4] Priestley, Jos., *Hist. Account of the...rivers, canals and waterways of Great Britain* (1831). Priestley, *Map of Inland Navigation*, 1830. *Commission on Canals and Waterways* (1907). *Hist. and Stat. Returns*, IV. Cd. 3719, 1908.

waterways had been carried across the Pennine chain at three separate points, the summit level of the Leeds and Liverpool Canal being 500 ft., that of the Rochdale Canal 610 ft., and that of the Huddersfield Canal 650 ft., above the sea. By a series of new works, carried out between 1774 and 1826, the old Aire and Calder Navigation—which dated from William and Mary's reign—had become a thoroughly efficient connecting link between these high-level waterways and the Humber. To the north of the Humber basin canals or canalisations were unimportant, but on the south the Trent and its dependent canals opened out the centre of England, and connected the South Yorkshire Nottingham and Derbyshire coal and manufacturing districts with one another and with those of Leicester Warwick and Stafford. Through Stourport and Worcester the close-netted waterways of the Birmingham area articulated with the Severn. Northward, the Trent and Mersey Canal completed the circuit back to Lancashire. In 1826 and 1827 powers were taken for the construction of an additional link farther west, and as a result the Birmingham and Liverpool Junction, the last of the important long canals, was carried through East Staffordshire to join the navigation systems of Cheshire.

Southward and south-eastward from Warwickshire, the Oxford Canal and the long line of the Grand Junction reached, the one the Isis, and the other the lower Thames. Twelve years' work (1793–1805) and five Acts of Parliament had been required to bring the Grand Junction from the edge of Warwickshire to Brentford and the Paddington Canal. From the upper Thames valley the Thames and Severn, and from the middle Thames valley the Kennet and Avon, struck back to the western sea.

The waterways of the Fen District were not very well attached to the general system of the Midlands. By the Witham Navigation and the revived Fossdike a through route existed from Boston to the Trent. From the head of the Nene Navigation at Northampton, in 1831, "a double railway allowing carriages going different ways to pass without interruption"[1] linked a main fenland stream with the Grand Junction Canal; but the Nene is tortuous and the arrangement involved much rehandling of goods. The plan for a direct connection between London and Cambridge, the southern terminus of fenland

_____
[1] Priestley, *op. cit.* p. 371.

navigation, was old. Acts for such a canal were passed in 1812 and 1814; but this was one of a group of schemes which, not having been carried out by 1830, died with the opening of the locomotive age.

A number of such "intended canals" and "parliamentary lines" were shown on the canal maps of the day in the southern and south-western counties—the Weald of Kent, from the Medway to Romney Marsh; the Dorset and Somerset from Bradford-on-Avon to the Dorset Stour; the Grand Western from the Exe to Bridgwater Bay, and above all the English and Bristol Channels Ship Canal, running from Bridgwater Bay across the plain of Somerset and over the low watershed near Chard to Axminster and the sea. The only one of these lines ever completed was that of the—now derelict—Wey and Arun Junction, which runs south from the neighbourhood of Guildford. Possibly the difficulties met with in the construction of the Gloucester and Berkeley Ship Canal, along a perfectly level course for only 16½ miles, helped to discourage the ambitious English and Bristol Channels scheme. The Gloucester and Berkeley for a variety of reasons, mainly financial, was thirty-three years in the making (1794–1827); although when made, with its width of 70 ft. and its depth of 18, it fulfilled the hopes of its promoters—carrying a tonnage of 107,000 in its first year[1]. Much more discouraging were the histories of the Crinan and Caledonian canals, both intended for sea-going vessels, the latter constructed entirely from national funds, the former heavily subsidised by government; neither a commercial success. The Caledonian, it was pathetically complained in 1831, had not "hitherto attracted the attention of seafaring adventurers so much as might have been expected"[2]; the Crinan—opened in 1816—was never able to pay even the interest on the exchequer advances.

The effective Scottish canals were the Forth and Clyde—in its improved form a semi-ship canal with a depth of 10 ft.—the associated Edinburgh and Glasgow Union[3], and the few other waterways of the industrial rift-valley of central Scotland. Here all the conditions were found which had made the successful through canals of industrial England.

Such conditions were also found in parts of Wales, but the contours of the country did not encourage through routes.

---

[1] *V.C.H. Gloucester*, II. 192.
[2] Priestley, *op. cit.* p. 128.   [3] Only begun in 1817.

The North Welsh canals, in Denbigh and Montgomery, though famous as engineering feats, were, from the national point of view, merely not very important feeders of the Cheshire and Severn navigation systems. But those of South Wales and Monmouth, the Monmouthshire with its branch into Ebbw Vale and its continuation the Brecon and Abergavenny, the Neath, the Swansea—all projected and finished during the great wars—were both evidence and cause of that industrial development on and about the South Welsh coalfield which was so marked a feature of the national economic scene in the new century. Like many small unimportant canals and navigations round the coasts, their object was merely to bring an upland district into touch with tide-water; but their upland district was not some agricultural or secondary manufacturing region. It was trenched by the coal and iron valleys of Monmouth and Glamorgan.

From the first, coal transport had been a dominant factor in the canal movement. The fuel famine of the eighteenth century would have stopped the growth not solely of industry but of population, in many districts, had not means been devised for overcoming it[1]. The Duke of Bridgewater was a coal-owner and his canal had halved the price of coal in Manchester. Eight years later the first section of the old Birmingham Canal had done much the same for Birmingham[2]. At the close of the century, the opening of the Hereford and Gloucester reduced the cost of coal at Ledbury from 24s. to 13s. 6d. and it was hoped that a waterway from the sea to Louth, in Lincolnshire, would "induce the inhabitants to desist from their ancient practice...of using the dung of their cattle for fuel."[3] The improved Fossdike was intended mainly for the transport of corn, but it was used "more particularly to import coal to Lincoln and its vicinity."[4] As the monotonous bread and cheese dietary of the agricultural labourers in the South had been in part due to lack of firing[5], it is not surprising that the social benefits of cheap coal are so much heard of in connection with the promotion and working of the Southern canals. Even

[1] Sombart has drawn a picture of the possible collapse of the "early capitalist" age for lack of fuel. *Moderne Kapitalismus*, 3rd ed. II. 1137 *sqq.*
[2] Rees' *Cyclopædia*, 1819, *s.v.* "Canals."
[3] Eden, *State of the Poor*, II. 397.
[4] Priestley, *op. cit.* p. 278.
[5] Eden, *op. cit.* I. 547 and below p. 118.

where a good sea-borne supply was available, much had been hoped from the regulative competition of inland waterways. Complaints of the high prices of north-country coal in London had been met, in 1800, by the suggestion that a perfected canal system would allow midland coals to compete with it effectively. This however they never did. From 1825 to 1830 no coal came to London by canal. Over 8000 tons came in 1831 and nearly 11,000 in 1832; but in 1836–7 the figure was back at zero[1]. The London market for Newcastle and Durham coal was powerfully organised, and the waterways of the Thames basin were used far more to distribute this coal from London than to bring in midland coal to compete with it.

Important as was the movement of fuel along the inland waterways, on the chief through routes it was subordinate to that of general merchandise. There was a huge local coal trade on the Black Country, South Lancashire, and Yorkshire canal systems; but between those areas coal obviously would not move. The manufacturing districts now brought such of their raw materials as were not locally produced, and sent away the bulk of their finished produce, by water. London drew in immense quantities of manufactures, building materials, and agricultural produce by way of the Thames basin navigation systems and the Grand Junction Canal. Owing to her unique commercial position and the undisputed dominance of London shipping[2], she was, relatively, a more important distributing centre than she became later. Not merely her own fine finished goods and imported colonial wares, but such raw materials as wool, tin and cotton were regularly shipped to the manufacturing Midlands and the North along the Grand Junction Canal[3]. Throughout the country, stone for building, paving and road-making; bricks, tiles and timber; limestone for the builder, farmer or blast furnace owner; beasts and cattle; corn, hay and straw; manure from the London mews and the mountainous London dustheaps; the heavy castings which were coming into use for bridge-building and other structural purposes— all these, and whatever other bulky wares there may be, moved along the new waterways over what, half a century earlier, had been impossible routes or impossible distances. Around the more populous canal centres there was an active traffic in passengers and cargo requiring quick transport: on the Grand

---

[1] *Royal Commission on Coal Supplies*, 1871 (XVIII. 863).
[2] Above p. 4.　　　　　[3] Priestley, *op. cit.* p. 312.

Junction Canal "Mr Pickford had a succession of barges day and night"[1], and in the winter, on the Firth and Clyde Canal, ice-breaking boats "set out every morning before the passage-boats, which nothing must delay."[2]

There is no way of measuring the economic gain to Great Britain from the canal system. So far as can be calculated, the cost of carriage by canal was from a half to a quarter of the cost of carriage by road[3]; but that is not the whole story. Shareholders' losses on a commercially unremunerative enterprise, and it will be seen that there were many such among the canals, cannot be set over against the gains of residents and traders along the new lines of traffic. The sum originally raised to make the Louth Canal was lost because the work was ill done: in 1777 a local gentleman[4] made the work good in return for a ninety years' lease of the tolls; the people of the district were saved from cow-dung fires. No balance can be struck here. Yet canal dividends and the market values of canal shares, on the eve of the railway age, do provide a test of the capacity for responding to the stimulus of new means of communication shown by different districts. Further, the commercial position of the canals at this time is of great importance in relation to the subsequent struggle between the canal and the locomotive railway. The main qualifications to be borne in mind in using so rough a test are, first, that legal and other preliminary expenses formed a by no means uniform proportion of the capital sunk in the different canals and, second, that unforeseen engineering difficulties, or mere engineering blunders, might seriously reduce the earning power of the capital expended on any given enterprise[5]. But such considerations do not greatly affect the broad conclusions to be drawn from the relative financial positions of the main groups of canals in the middle of the 'twenties, a decade before the locomotive began to compete with water transport in any general way.

Canal dividends fluctuated a good deal, and a canal might be a paying, or a non-paying, proposition for a series of years and then take a turn for the worse, or the better. But the following dividend figures for important selected canals, in the year 1825

[1] Priestley, *op. cit.* p. 312.   [2] Dupin, *op. cit.* II. 228 n.
[3] See the elaborate calculation in Jackman, W. T., *Transportation in Modern England* (1916), II. App. 8.
[4] Mr Chaplin. Priestley, *op. cit.* p. 428.
[5] There was also some dishonest promotion. Jackman, *op. cit.* I. 427.

—a year of active trade—indicate with tolerable accuracy the general situation at a time when all the canals quoted had had some years in which to settle down to their work[1].

Selected successful canal companies.

	%		%
Forth and Clyde	6¼	Birmingham	70
Mersey and Irwell Navigation	35		plus bonus
Leeds and Liverpool	16	Coventry	44
Trent and Mersey	75		plus bonus
	plus bonus	Stafford and Worcester	28½
Oxford	32	Stourbridge	11⅞
	plus bonus	Warwick and Birmingham	11
Grand Junction	13	Glamorgan	8
Leicester	11½	Monmouthshire	10
Stroudwater (Stroud to Severn)	15⅓	Neath	15
Barnsley	8¾	Swansea	14
	plus bonus		

The dividends of 10 per cent. and upwards are all in the manufacturing districts or on the main routes from the North to the Thames valley. The industrial districts, however, had their unsuccessful enterprises, as appears from the second list.

Selected unsuccessful canal companies.

	%		%
Ashby-de-la-Zouch	Nil	Montgomery	2½
Basingstoke	Nil	Thames and Severn	$1\frac{1}{20}$
Bolton and Bury	2½	Thames and Medway	Nil
Ellesmere and Chester	2⅘	Worcester and Birmingham	2
Grand Western	Nil	Wilts. and Berks.	Nil
Huddersfield	Nil	Wey and Arun	$\frac{9}{10}$
Kennet and Avon	2¼		

Several of the canals in this list had been faced with severe engineering difficulties; the Huddersfield had a famous tunnel, the Ellesmere and Chester a stupendous aqueduct. For many the failure was the more serious because they had been among the most expensive in the country to build: the Kennet and Avon stood alone with the Grand Junction in the group whose share capital was over £1,000,000: thanks to its ambitious lay out, the Ellesmere and Chester had a capital of £500,000, as much as that of the Forth and Clyde: both the Thames and Severn and the Grand Western had paid up capitals of nearly £250,000.

[1] Based on English, H., *A Complete View of the Joint Stock Companies formed during...1824 and 1825...with an Appendix...of Companies formed antecedent to that Period* (1827). Comments and amplifications from *Wettenhall's Commercial List* in Jackman, *op. cit.* I. 416 *sqq.* The dividends are reduced to percentages: a number of the canals had not £100 shares.

On the other hand, several of the very high dividend group had small paid up capitals—the Coventry £50,000; the Stafford and Worcester £98,000; even the Trent and Mersey only £130,000.

It is clear from the second list that canal-building across the watersheds of southern England—it might almost be said, canal-building in the South—had not been a paying enterprise. Most of the works in this region had been completed rather late in the war years or in the years of post-war depression, so that their proprietors had not been able to see towns and factories grow up about their properties, as had some of the proprietors of the older midland and northern navigations. The admission made by the secretary of the Thames and Severn in 1800 that his canal, after ten years' existence, "had not so much trade as the proprietors could wish"[1] is easily explicable. Yet there had been time and fair opportunity for development between 1815 and 1825, had southern England been able to set goods enough on the water.

How far the whole canal system of the country gave a decent reward to those who sank their money in it is open to question. The impression that the canals were immensely lucrative before the railways cut into their monopoly has been supported by the practice, too common among railway controversialists, of quoting only the more luscious dividends. A writer in the *Quarterly Review* calculated in 1825 that eighty canals with an aggregate capital of £13,205,117 "now paid" a total of £782,257, or about 5¾ per cent., in dividends. The ten most successful canals on his list, with capital of £1,127,230, averaged 27·6 per cent.; which means that the remaining £12,077,887 of capital got less than 4 per cent. On £3,734,910 of capital no dividend at all was paid[2].

The average canal investor might have been more generously rewarded had the average canal promoter and engineer employed more system and foresight, or had a little intelligent supervision by government been possible. In the middle of his song of praise over British canal enterprise the Baron Dupin stopped to notice that there were two sorts of canals—those of

---

[1] *Second Report on the State of the Coal Trade*, 1800. *Reports from Committees ..not inserted in the Journals*, x. 645.

[2] *Quarterly Review*, XXXII, 160 *sqq.* An article discussing Joseph Lowe's *Present State of England* (1822). "Now" means to the writer 1824-5. Just under 4 per cent. was the average yield of 3 per cent. Consols 1821-4. Further details are in Jackman, *op. cit.* I. 420.

large and those of small section—and that "all the canals of
the large or small section had not exactly a determined relative
size of locks." "The English," he added, "have never thought
of arranging the two systems into one uniform and perfect
whole. The very nature of English institutions is in opposition
to such a harmony."[1] Examined in detail this lack of harmony
is astonishing. The small section was not confined to minor
navigations and branch canals. It was found, for instance, on
the Oxford Canal which could not be used by boats with more
than 7 ft. beam and 3 ft. 8 in. draft. Seven feet was also the
maximum width on the Grand Trunk, owing to the cost and
difficulty—in early days—of constructing the famous Hare-
castle summit tunnel. When a second tunnel was added after
1823 it was made no wider because the canal had narrow locks[2].
The Thames and Severn had 12 ft. 9 in. locks, but its summit
tunnel at Sapperton was rather more than 1 ft. narrower and
its summit section would not take boats of over 3 ft. 6 in.
draft, whereas the general maximum draft of the English canals
was 4 ft. Even on closely associated canal systems where width
and depth of locks were fairly uniform—there was never perfect
uniformity: in no single case were the dimensions of the locks
on the Bridgewater Canal reproduced—even on such systems
great inequalities in length were to be found. The Leeds and
Liverpool could lock a boat of 76 ft. from Liverpool to Wigan;
from Wigan to Leeds only a 66 ft. boat could travel; at Leeds
the canal met the Aire and Calder Navigation, whose locks
would only take a 53 ft. boat. A little farther South a 73 ft.
boat could get over the watershed on the Rochdale Canal; but
on the Yorkshire side it met at once—on the Calder and Hebble
Navigation—what was, apparently, the fashionable West Riding
lock, which required a boat 20 ft. shorter.

A natural result of this situation and of the absence of competing transport systems was that very little improvement had
taken place, during the canal age, in the type of boat used for
ordinary purposes. Long and very narrow, with vertical sides,
"the head and stem cut like a wedge,"[3] the "flat" was almost
exactly what it always had been—and often still is. Lighter and

---

[1] *Op. cit.* I. 229–30.
[2] Priestley, *op. cit.* p. 645 and Cd. 3719 (1908), p. 203. These, with Fairbairn, W.,
Remarks on Canal Navigation, 1831, are the sources for the whole paragraph.
There was little change between 1831 and 1908.
[3] Dupin, *op. cit.* I. 246.

more attractive vessels had been built latterly for passengers: on a few canals, such as the Forth and Clyde or the Stroudwater, heavy barges or small sea-going craft might navigate; but the unseaworthy flat with its horses or human trackers was the real cargo carrier on British canals. Its pace was rarely more than $2\frac{1}{2}$ miles an hour when travelling freely[1]. The "passage boat" usually travelled at from four to five miles, and in a few cases even faster[2]. Not until the danger of railway competition for passenger traffic began to threaten the canal companies was any real attention given to the possibility of higher rates of speed or to steam traction. Between 1825 and 1831 the matter was receiving attention from canal engineers, but no important modification in canal practice had resulted. It was admitted by the advocates of higher speeds that, on the narrow canals, there was little prospect of improving the pace of ordinary goods traffic; but it was argued in 1831 that

much might be done, even on narrow canals, in the conveyance of passengers, provided light iron boats were employed, and worked by horses in the same manner as the boat [observe the singular number] on the Ardrossan Canal, which is now in regular use, plying between Glasgow and Johnstone, at the rate of from nine to ten miles an hour[3].

More progress had certainly been made in the art of making canals than in that of making canal boats; but, except in one matter, the possibilities of progress were not very great, because mechanical engineering had as yet added but little to the stock of tools and powers available for the canal-builder. The embankment, the tunnel, the aqueduct were all part of the Brindley tradition. Brindley's successors, especially Telford, had become bolder in handling all three. An early visitor to the Barton aqueduct, in 1763, "durst hardly venture to walk on the Terrass of the canal, as he almost trembled to behold the large river Irwell underneath him, across which this navigation is carried by a bridge, which contains upon it the canal of water"[4]: yet the drop was only thirty-eight feet. His terror would have been more extreme had he lived forty years to cross Telford's Pont-Cysylltau aqueduct on the Ellesmere Canal, 127 ft. above the

[1] Fairbairn, *op. cit.* p. 7, 10. The word "flat," still in use in the North of England, dates from the eighteenth century.
[2] Grahame, T., *A letter addressed to Nicholas Wood, Esq.* (1831), p. 10–12. Grahame was a keen advocate of steam on the canals.
[3] Fairbairn, *op. cit.* p. 51.
[4] *Hist. of Inland Navigation, particularly that of the Duke of Bridgewater,* 3rd ed. 1779. Anon. Reference to a visit in 1763.

river Dee in the Vale of Llangollen. But the real significance
of the Welsh aqueduct was not its height but its material—the
whole canal trough was made of iron. It was designed in 1795
and opened in 1805, when iron bridge-building was still a
young and experimental art, and it showed great boldness in
conception and execution[1]. But it was not a representative
piece of canal engineering—fortunately for the dividend-
earning power of the canals, as it cost nearly £50,000—for the
bridging of really deep valleys was seldom undertaken. That
iron age which set in during the last quarter of the eighteenth
century, though it had produced some iron canal boats and
other accessories of inland navigation, together with plenty of
cargo, had not made the canals markedly more efficient when
first the question of canal *versus* railroad stirred "intense anxiety
in the public mind," in the year 1825[2].

The railroad party in that controversy were fond of reminding their opponents that theirs was the older system of transport, at any rate in England. They asserted that the original
"tram road" of plain wooden rails was started at Newcastle
by "Master Beaumont, a gentleman of great ingenuity and
rare parts," who sank—and lost—£30,000 in colliery enterprise
in Charles I's reign: they were able to prove that it was well
known a generation later[3]. By 1738 the absence of such tram-
ways on the Whitehaven coalfield was a matter for adverse
comment[4]. Gradually improvements were introduced: a
second strip of wood was laid on the first so that, when worn
out, it might be renewed without touching the sleepers: the
surface was sometimes protected with a plate of iron: iron-
wheeled waggons were tried about 1750: cast-iron plate rails,
with a vertical flange on the inner side to keep the waggon
wheels in position, were tried experimentally in Staffordshire
and South Yorkshire between 1767 and 1776; and the cast-
iron edge rail, upon which the waggon wheels were kept by
flanges on their own tires, was tried at Loughborough in 1789[5].

---

[1] Dupin, *op. cit.* I. 263, and Smiles, *Lives of the Engineers*, II. 346 *sqq.*
[2] Wood, Nicholas, *A Practical Treatise on Railroads*, 1st ed. 1825, Preface.
[3] Wood, *op. cit.* p. 6–7. Smiles, *op. cit.* III. 5 *sqq.*, follows Wood.
[4] Rees, *Cyclopædia* (1819), *s.v.* "Canal." Smiles' statement (III. 7) that *iron*
rails were supposed to have been in use at Whitehaven as early as 1738 looks
like a mistake based on this reference.
[5] See *inter alia* Wood, *op. cit.* p. 12. *Industrial Resources of the Tyne, Wear and
Tees* (1864), p. 279. Ashton, T. S., *Iron and Steel in the Industrial Revolution*
(1924), p. 135.

Beginning as a coal-pit accessory, the railroad developed fast with the growth of mining and metallurgy after 1790. The longest lines up to that time had been those "great works, carried over all sorts of inequalities of ground, so far as the distance of nine or ten miles," which Arthur Young greatly admired near Newcastle in 1768, on one of which—built about 1720—a branch of the North-Eastern Railway still runs[1]. Young had pointed out that "many other branches of business" besides coal-mining "which have much carriage in a regular track" would do well to use rails. The first to do so extensively was the metallurgical business of South Wales, under the stimulus of the wars. There was not a yard of railway in Monmouth, Glamorgan or Carmarthen in 1791: by September, 1811, there were nearly 150 miles "connected with canals, collieries, iron and copper works."[2] The first important line was the Cardiff and Merthyr, constructed in the late 'nineties, the line on which Trevithick experimented with the locomotive. Started as a rival to the Glamorgan Canal it ended by being a tributary to it. One of the longest was the Sirhowey—over twenty miles in length—built jointly by the Monmouthshire Canal, Sir Charles Morgan of Tredegar and the lessees of the Sirhowey furnaces, under an Act of 1802[3]. In 1802 also the Carmarthenshire railroad company secured powers to build a line running sixteen miles inland from Llanelly. These are only the main lines built before 1825, the year in which four men put up nearly £50,000 to build the second long line of the district, the Rhymney—the metals of which ran from Pye Corner, near Newport, on the Sirhowey line for twenty-one miles through a coal country to the Rhymney forges.

Across the Wye, the coal, iron and timber of the Forest of Dean had stimulated railroad construction early in the century. A parliamentary company, which had considerable difficulty in raising its capital between 1809 and 1822, at length managed to lay the thirteen miles of the Severn and Wye line, running North and South through the Forest. Before it got to work, four private owners had built from Cinderford to the Severn an East and West line, which became a parliamentary company in

---

[1] Young's *Northern Tour*, III. 12. Tomlinson, W. W., *The North-Eastern Railway* (1915), p. 4–10.

[2] Davies, *South Wales*, II. 383. See also Dupin, *op. cit.* I. 207. [There were some waggon-ways and rails laid in the collieries in 1791, but no "great works" as on Tyneside.]

[3] Priestley, *op. cit.* p. 575.

1809. From these lines branches ran to the pits and forges scattered about among the oak woods of His Majesty's Forest[1].

Before the later 'twenties, the railway even in its simplest form, the short private line, was curiously localised. Tyneside was said to have 225 miles of iron roads before the Stockton and Darlington was projected[2] and the South Welsh industrial area certainly had more. South Lancashire had none at all, at least none known to contemporary enumerators of railways and makers of railway maps. Nor had the busy triangle whose corners are at Birmingham, Wolverhampton and Stourbridge. The explanation in both cases is probably the same, the relative excellence of the existing canal systems. Canals had never been used on Tyneside because the drams were already there and the pits were near the river yet well above it. The Birmingham area was particularly well furnished with canal cuts and feeders. A little to the North-West, however, the district about Ironbridge, traversed by the Severn and the Shropshire Canal, used many short railroads to link its pits and ironworks to the waterways.

On the Derbyshire, Nottingham and South Yorkshire coalfield, a few isolated railway lines fed the canals: a rather important double line, eight miles long, from Mansfield to the Cromford Canal at Pinxton, was authorised in 1817[3]: for a few miles south of Leeds ran the colliery line for which Blenkinsop had constructed, in 1811, that rack-and-pinion locomotive to which foreign princes made pilgrimage. But in no one of the three counties was there either a network of line so close as those of the Tyne and the Ironbridge district, or individual undertakings so considerable as those of South Wales.

This is true also of the Scottish industrial area. The rail was early in use at the Carron ironworks and at "Lord Elgin's, Mr Erskine's and Sir J. Hope's coal-mines"[4]: among others, a line very famous in its day was built, under a private Act of 1808, from Kilmarnock to the coast at Troon, ten miles away, to develop the general trade of that part of Ayrshire[5]; but the remaining long iron roads of the pre-locomotive period, such as the Edinburgh and Dalkeith, the Glasgow and Kirkintilloch and the West Lothian, were all planned in the period of transition, between 1823—when the use of the locomotive was first

---

[1] Priestley, *op. cit.* p. 565, 109.   [2] Dupin, *op. cit.* I. 207.
[3] Priestley, *op. cit.* p. 439.   [4] Dupin, *op. cit.* I. 208.
[5] Priestley, *op. cit.* p. 367.

authorised on a public railway, by the second Act of the Stockton and Darlington—and the final victory of the locomotive on the Liverpool and Manchester in 1829.

The remaining railways of Great Britain, in existence before these years of transition, were oddly scattered about the country. There were a few—very few and very short—colliery lines on the Cumberland coalfield. A line was projected, but never built, from the tiny scrap of coal measures, which a geological accident has preserved in the heart of Anglesey, across the Holyhead high road to the sea at Redwharf Bay[1]. Very interesting, though not very important, was the line which started from the Brecon and Abergavenny Canal, near Brecon, for Hay on the Herefordshire border. It was known as the Hay Railway: it was twenty-four miles long: it was not a mineral but a general line: it was built remarkably early in an out-of-the-way district: and it ran through the first railway tunnel in Great Britain. Another interesting general line, in an area which was no doubt influenced by the mineral lines of South Wales, Monmouth and the Forest of Dean, was the Gloucester and Cheltenham. It was built between 1810 and 1816 "with the twofold object of relieving the roads between Gloucester and Cheltenham from the carriage of heavy articles, and for bringing coal to the highly celebrated and improving town of Cheltenham."[2] As a coal carrier and reducer of coal prices it proved most efficient. Shortly after its opening, plans were started for providing a neighbouring district—that of Moreton-in-the-Marsh and Stow-on-the-Wold, on the other side of the Cotswolds—with the fuel which it very badly required. The result, after some years of financial struggle, was the sixteen-mile-long Stratford-on-Avon Railway from Stratford, where canal navigation ended, to Moreton.

In all the southern and south-western counties the only early lines of any importance were the Plymouth and Dartmoor, which was wriggling its way 1400 ft. uphill from the head of Plymouth Sound "to communicate with the Prison of War on the Forest of Dartmoor," between 1819 and 1821, and the Wandsworth and Croydon, otherwise known as the Surrey Iron Railway, the starting of whose works in 1801 had first acquainted Londoners with the new form of transport. This much-described line, which with its double track and double horseway measured

---

[1] [In previous editions it was stated that this line was built: the mistake is pointed out in Dodd, *The Industrial Revolution in North Wales*, p. 111.]
[2] Priestley, *op. cit.* p. 297.

24 ft. in width, deserves the notoriety that its nearness to London would in any event have ensured. It was both a public way and a carrier of general merchandise, and the Act sanctioning its construction was the first of the long line of railway Acts. Surrey was not a canal country in 1801, though in the next decade the Croydon Canal was struggling into an unprofitable existence; so the fuel question was prominent in the minds of the railway promoters. Coal and London manure were expected to be the chief down loads; and the up loads "lime, chalk, flint, fullers' earth and agricultural produce."[1] Business on the line was not confined to the contemplated staples, but the list is of interest.

The comparative ease with which railways could be constructed, as feeders for canals and rivers, over ground too difficult for remunerative hydraulic enterprise and the first experiments with locomotive engines had suggested to a few far-seeing individuals, before 1820, that the canal age would be short. In the opening years of the century, William James, an early railway engineer, was dreaming of a "general railroad company" with a capital of £1,000,000; and later, as the locomotive experiments proceeded, he argued with George Stephenson that speeds of twenty or thirty miles an hour might be attained, at a time when George was thinking only of eight or ten[2]. In 1821 appeared Thomas Gray's *Observations on a General Iron Railway or Land Steam Conveyance; to supersede the Necessity of Horses in all Public Vehicles; showing its vast Superiority in every respect, over all the present Pitiful Methods of Conveyance by Turnpike Roads, Canals, and Coasting-Traders. Containing every Species of Information relative to Railroads and Loco-motive Engines*. The *Observations* ran through five editions in as many years; and Gray, a single-minded enthusiast, poured out variations on his theme in articles, memoranda, and petitions to mayors and ministers. "Begin where you would, on whatever subject—the weather, the news, the political movements of the day—it would not be many minutes before, with Thomas Gray, you would be enveloped with steam, listening to a harangue on a general iron railway."[3]

But, so long as the locomotive remained imperfect and to the general public unknown, railways were popularly regarded

[1] Priestley, *op. cit.* p. 610.
[2] Jackman, *op. cit.* II. 509.
[3] Wm. Howitt, quoted in Francis, J., *A History of the English Railway* (1851), I. 85

at best as a subordinate part of "one great, compound, and connected system of Inland Navigation." The phrase comes from the 1819 edition of Rees' *Cyclopædia*, in which, significantly enough, railways are discussed under the heading "Canals." Popular opinion, at this time, coincided with fact. The railways of 1820–5 remained substantially what railways had been for a century and a half on Tyneside—a means of moving bulky goods over short distances at moderate speeds to and from tide or navigable water. Occasionally they formed links in a through route, and the idea of utilising them further in this way was familiar in technical circles; but, apart from the very imperfect locomotive, the technique of the permanent way, as it existed up to and even after 1820, gave some support to popular opinion and very little to the ambitious claims of men like Thomas Gray of the *idée fixe*.

Bridging, tunnelling in moderation, and embanking were thoroughly understood. The wooden and cast-iron rails of the eighteenth and early nineteenth centuries were the weak point. Narrow and thin bars of wrought iron—an inch and a quarter by nearly six-eighths of an inch—had been laid on top of the wooden rails at Alloa in 1785[1]. Twenty years later wrought-iron bars, an inch and a half square, "joined together by a half-lap joint with one pin,"[2] were tried at Walbottle Colliery near Newcastle. A few years later again, about 1810, the experiment was repeated at Lord Carlisle's Tindale Fell Colliery, near Brampton. As the rolling of wrought-iron bars was still a young industry, the lateness of these experiments is not surprising. Nor were they much followed up before 1830. The bars wore well; but if narrow they damaged the waggon wheels; to make them broad was too costly. So they failed to displace the various types of cast-iron rail. It was easy to cast rails which provided a broad running surface for the wheels. A rail whose section approached rather nearly to that flattened dumb-bell section, which was to become typical for British wrought-iron or steel rails, was the final product of the experiments with cast-iron edge rails; yet for heavy weights and high speeds the brittle cast metal could never be satisfactory[3].

About Newcastle the edge rail of cast-iron predominated. Waggons with flanged iron wheels had long been known there[4].

---

[1] Tomlinson, *op. cit.* p. 13.   [2] Wood, *op. cit.* p. 12.
[3] *Ibid.* ch. 2, with plates of the rails.
[4] Tomlinson, *op. cit.* p. 13–14, says since 1789.

So the essentials for speed and security were all ready. But in South Wales, where progress in railway construction had been more rapid since 1800 than in the North, and almost every-where else, the flanged plate rail was in vogue. In its most improved form this appliance without a future was composed of a horizontal running surface, with a vertical flange on the inner side to keep the waggon wheels in position and a second, downward, flange on the outer side which added to the strength of the whole—ingenious and cumbrous. It would take any waggon of the right width whilst edge rails needed the specialised flanged wheels.

In reporting on a projected railway near Edinburgh in 1818 Robert Stevenson—Stevenson of the Bell Rock lighthouse, the grandfather of Robert Louis—drew attention to the merits of the wrought-iron rails at Tindale Fell Colliery[1]. He sent a copy of his report to George Stephenson at Killingworth and Stephenson handed it on to Michael Longridge of Bedlington ironworks. A waggon way from a neighbouring colliery was needed at the time; and on this it was decided to experiment. John Birkinshaw, foreman at Bedlington, suggested, and in December, 1820, took out a patent for, a method of rolling the wrought bars into something like the shape of the improved cast-iron edge rail. These were the rails whose durability so impressed a deputation from the projectors of the Liverpool and Manchester Railway, who came to look at them in 1824, that eventually the rails of that line, and so of all other lines, were modelled on them. Their merit was still in dispute in 1825–30. Cast iron had its advocates. The cumbrous flanged plate rails were being manufactured both in cast and in wrought iron. But with the locomotive age the Bedlington type, im-proved, drove out all others[2].

When the Gloucester and Cheltenham Railway was being promoted in 1808–9 its advocates did not merely wish to ease the coal market at Cheltenham, but also to "relieve the roads" between the two towns, "from the carriage of heavy articles."[3] Their desire links the project with those continuous

[1] Dupin, *op. cit.* I. 215. Tomlinson, *op. cit.* p. 15. See also *D.N.B.*
[2] *Remarks on the comparative merits of cast metal and malleable iron railways,* etc., containing a letter from Michael Longridge, Newcastle, 1832. Wood, *op. cit.* p. 27, 41.
[3] Priestley, *op. cit.* p. 297.

efforts of legislators and administrators—very often the same persons in their varied capacities of Justice, Member of Parliament and Turnpike Trustee—to save their roads from being worn out by the wheels, or to turn wheels into rollers for the benefit of the roads. These efforts fill the longest chapter in the administrative history of the roads in the eighteenth century. Even in 1825 the chapter was not closed. By an Act of 1822, amended in 1823, it was prescribed that, as from January 1, 1826, all wheels for use on turnpike roads should be so made that, when the tire was over six inches wide its tread should not deviate more than half an inch from the exact horizontal, or, when it was less than six inches wide, more than a quarter of an inch. Further, no nail on the tire was to project more than a quarter of an inch[1]. It was not until 1835 that this wheelwright legislation, with its associated rules limiting the loads to be carried by vehicles of various types, was abandoned[2]. In the 'twenties Telford and McAdam, then at the height of their power, believed that roads should be adjusted to traffic and that they knew how to make them fit to bear the worst of it; but the parliamentary tradition in the other sense moved forward for a time by its own weight.

When the Act of 1823 came into force it could fairly be assumed, thanks to the work of the McAdams and the Telfords, that most turnpikes were no longer in need of such protective solicitude. Most, but not all. Dupin had noted with some astonishment before 1820 that "the great high roads which run into London, and which from their beauty are the admiration of foreigners, are formed of the most defective materials, and on this account are, perhaps, the worst roads in all England."[3] The worst main roads, he meant. To the bad material, a clayey gravel with small water-worn flint pebbles, was added a grotesquely exaggerated camber so that "carriages are obliged to drive along a dangerous slope, unless they are able to keep quite in the middle of the road."[4] It is this dangerous slope up to "the crown or arching centre of the road" upon which the action turns in De Quincey's *Vision of Sudden Death* when, "two or three summers after Waterloo," the English mail coach, with De Quincey (who had taken laudanum) as an out-

---

[1] Jackman, *op. cit.* I. 229.
[2] Webb, S. and B., *The Story of the King's Highway* (1913), p. 122 and *passim.* Jackman, *op. cit.* I. 232 and *passim.*
[3] *Op. cit.* I. 182.   [4] *Ibid.* I. 174.

side, nearly ran down a little "cany carriage."[1] Dupin's condemnation of the metropolitan roads was fully borne out in the evidence given before a parliamentary committee, in 1819, by the Postmaster General's superintendent of mail coaches and by responsible coach proprietors. Eight horses could do in the provinces work which required ten near London, and the working life of the eight was six years against three or four for the ten. Sometimes the mails lost twenty minutes in the deep loose gravel of a bad bit of road only a few score yards in length[2].

The House of Commons, provoked by Sir Henry Parnell and Davies Gilbert, was inquiring continuously into highways and turnpikes in 1819, 1820 and 1821[3]; but proposals for dealing with the metropolitan turnpike trusts—numerous, inefficient, extravagant and occasionally corrupt—were blocked until an Act of 1826 put 172 miles of roads and streets, formerly controlled by fourteen of the Middlesex trusts, under a body of competent and distinguished commissioners. Parnell and Telford worked together and, inspired by them, the Commission improved the main Middlesex roads between 1827 and 1831. Similar good work was being done, though on a smaller scale, by the consolidated Surrey and Sussex (Brighton Road), the Middlesex and Essex, and the New Cross turnpike trusts, on other sides of London. Consolidated trusts of the same type were at work in the later 'twenties about Bristol—McAdam's original English headquarters—Bath, Worcester, Hereford and Exeter. In the North the Manchester and Buxton, and in the far North the Alston trust in Cumberland, which controlled 130 miles of formidable Pennine gradients, were the most prominent examples of this class. But these ten big trusts and the Middlesex Commissioners managed only about 6 per cent. of the English roads.

Elsewhere...the thousand and odd little Trusts remained unconsolidated, each administering its ten or twenty miles of road...by its miscellaneous fifty or a hundred Trustees; gradually executing, it is true, the most elementary improvements, but for the most part squandering their tolls in extravagant administrative expenses, and piling up their debts until actual insolvency beset them...[4].

[1] The episode in *The English Mail Coach* is not, however, near London.

[2] Webb, *op. cit.* p. 190, based on *Select Comm. on the Better Construction...of Turnpike Roads and Highways,* 1819 (VI. 339).

[3] Webb, *op. cit.* p. 177 *sqq.* These sources have been so fully worked over by Lord Passfield and Mrs Webb and by Mr Jackman that, in this summary, detailed references are generally omitted.   [4] Webb, *op. cit.* p. 180.

Foreign visitors wrote with purple ink about the English roads partly because, with all their defects, they really were the finest in Europe, and partly because the visitor did not often desert the better turnpikes. It is to be remembered that out of about 125,000 miles of road in England in 1820 not 21,000 miles, and out of about 128,000 in 1838 only 22,000, was turnpike at all[1]. Less than a third of the Middlesex roads and only 10 per cent. of the Essex roads had been turnpiked by 1815. Now there is much clay in Essex; and off the clays it is, as men of Essex say, " 'illy and 'oley." The rest were left to the parish, the amateur unpaid parish surveyor of highways, the statute labour—never called in England the *corvée*—which had been grudgingly given by rural parishioners ever since it was started by the Act of Philip and Mary, and above all, in the twenty years between Waterloo and the Poor Law Amendment Act, to the pauper road-mender. There had been an element of relief-work in a good deal of the road enterprise since the peace. "In the winter of 1817, when the dearness of provisions reduced numbers of unemployed labourers to the lowest degree of misery, many great works...were undertaken...."[2] But though parish roads may have benefited from the laggard work of paupers, putting in time at filling ruts with dirt, the word enterprise is not here applicable. If the subordinates of the lesser trusts were still incompetent, and they certainly were, who shall measure the incompetence of lesser parish management? Parliamentary reports seldom refer to it. They were concerned with the main routes. Until all those roads which a French government would have graded as national were completely coachable, the rest must wait, picking up—as they certainly did, but at their own pace—the crumbs of sound method which fell from Telford's or McAdam's table.

National roads properly so called did not exist in England. The most national was the Holyhead road, and of that the most national part was in Wales. For about a generation before 1825 the Postmaster General had taken an active interest in the main roads and had got regular reports on them from his "riding inspectors"; but he could only exhort or persuade turnpike trusts and indict grossly negligent counties and parishes[3].

---

[1] Jackman, *op. cit.* 1. 234-5. Webb, *op. cit.* p. 193.
[2] Dupin, *op. cit.* 1. 160.
[3] For a study of the good old English method of road and bridge maintenance by indictment see Webb, *op. cit.* p. 99 *sqq.*

Union with Ireland had brought the Holyhead road into the political foreground: Sir Henry Parnell represented Queen's County at Westminster, and his experienced vigour had driven the Holyhead road through parliament, twenty-nine turnpike trusts, Bettws-y-Coed and Nant Ffrancon[1]. In England, the Holyhead Road Commissioners of 1815, armed with Telford's survey, with sums of money voted by parliament from time to time, and with the right to levy a sur-toll of 50 per cent. on all improved sections of the road, worked through the twenty-three existing trusts, each of which controlled on the average eight and a half miles of road. But the six Welsh trusts were amalgamated, and the eighty-five miles of Welsh road became a really national highway under Telford and his subordinates.

The Holyhead Commission had been modelled on the earlier Commission for the Highland Roads of 1803; since it was for Scotland that a semi-national system of road management had first been worked out. The military roads of General Wade and his successors had the engineering defects of their day (*circa* 1732–52); they were unsuited to the age of the English mail coach; and they had not been carried north of the present line of the Caledonian Canal. Under the Act of 1803 half the cost of any new undertaking might be borne by the state, provided local property owners would supply the other half. From 1804, however, the counties secured the right to contribute from county rates, so that the greater part of the money came from publicly controlled funds. Telford had established his reputation as engineer for the Highland Commissioners, for whom he had built or planned over nine hundred miles of road and twelve hundred bridges of all sorts, long before his Menai Bridge was opened[2]. In 1816 he had been called in to direct the expenditure of £50,000 which parliament had entrusted to the Commissioners for the remaking of an essential highland road outside the Highlands, that from Glasgow to Carlisle. In 1815 the road was ruinous. "The trustees seemed to be helpless...; a local subscription was tried and failed, the district... being very poor"; and a coach and horses had fallen through the bridge over Evan Water: hence this national action[3].

In Scotland the turnpike age only began after 1750[4]; but in

---

1 See his *Treatise on Roads*, 1833, for his grasp of the question.
2 Smiles, *op. cit.* III. 381–3.
3 *Ibid.* II. 428. Webb, *op. cit.* p. 181.
4 Sinclair, *General Report of the...State...of Scotland* (1814), III. 337.

the richer and more densely populated parts of the country the major trusts had done their work very creditably by 1825–30. A single engineer, Charles Abercrombie, a gentleman by birth, who took to civil engineering as a profession, had "lined out above 10,000 miles of road in Scotland" even before 1814[1]. Isolated dales in the South had been linked up with the Lothians, Berwickshire, and the English Northern Counties; and certain "very awkward machines" which "not a great many years since," as Sir John Sinclair wrote in 1814[2], had been the principal, almost the sole, Scottish vehicles had been driven into the far North-West and the Islands. They were the sledge and the "tumbler," a cart with solid wooden wheels fixed to an axle which rotated between wooden pins.

Apart from the Holyhead road, the highlands of Wales had been less fortunate than those of Scotland. There were no commissioners of Welsh roads. The industrial South had its fair share of road enterprise under turnpikes, and bridge-building activity had been general there in the eighteenth century. But, so late as 1813, the Welsh equivalent of the Scottish sledges and tumblers, the old "sliding-car" with one end on the ground and the other on two low wheels, was still "universal in some upland parts."[3] It was not a road vehicle. Anglesey had been so impossible before Telford went there that London coachmen, imported to run the mails, struck because the work was too dangerous[4].

On the eastern side of England the Great North Road and its principal feeders carried traffic forward, under innumerable trusts and with considerable expedition, to deliver it to the Scots. The Postmaster General, however, was not content with the facilities. His Office gladly availed itself of petitions from the North, and put pressure on the Treasury to sanction a new survey of the whole line from London to Morpeth[5]. The Scottish heritors, among others, had petitioned against the "ill-made, narrow crooked and dangerous" road "carried to the tops of the loftiest mountains"[6] between the Border and Boroughbridge. They themselves had made a good road from

[1] Sinclair, *op. cit.* III. 338. Webb, *op. cit.* p. 165.
[2] *Op. cit.* I. 233.
[3] Davies, *North Wales*, p. 121.
[4] Smiles, *op. cit.* II. 431.
[5] Webb, *op. cit.* p. 178.
[6] *S. C. on the State of the Northern Roads*, 1830 (x. 221), App. of Petitions.

Edinburgh to the Border. Telford began the survey in 1824 and made his plans for a completely new road of which "a hundred miles, south of York, were laid out in a perfectly straight line."[1] The scheme was embodied in a Northern Road Bill in 1830. It had plenty of predestined enemies, trustees of trusts to be interfered with, mayors and parliamentary representatives of towns on one or other side of Telford's hundred-mile straight from York to Peterborough, with all the critics of departmental extravagance—for its precursor, the Holyhead scheme, had cost first and last, including some harbour works, three-quarters of a million. Why should the people of the West and South pay for a road to Edinburgh? It was "a Scotch job to enable Scotchmen to mend their own roads with English money." The time from London to Edinburgh was already only 43½ hours. Why reduce it[2]?

The bill was thrown out in committee. And then the railways came and it was all forgotten; and the North Road still runs through Doncaster, Bawtry, East Retford and Tuxford.

---

[1] Smiles, *op. cit.* II. 433.   [2] Hansard, XXIV. 1335–45.

CHAPTER IV

AGRARIAN ORGANISATION

How the land of Britain was owned and held early in the nineteenth century is not known with statistical accuracy. Some important features in the landscape are rather clearer for Wales than for England, and for Scotland very much clearer; but there are obscure patches in all three. That by far the greater part of the island was owned by a comparatively small group of noblemen, gentlemen of family, and gentlemen in the making, is patent. It is tolerably certain that in the seventeenth and in the early part of the eighteenth century English land had been passing from the hands of the smaller owners—little squires and labouring proprietors—into those of the controlling class[1], which itself was continuously replenished with rich men out of trade. This transference of land continued in the later eighteenth and early nineteenth centuries; but there was not any important change in the balance of owner-ship between, say, 1785 and 1815; and it is far from certain that there was an important change between 1815 and 1830.

Again, it is clear that between 1750 and 1825 the unit of cultivation throughout Great Britain, the average farm in the agricultural sense of the word, was increasing in size, by the throwing together of ancient small holdings and the creation of new large holdings from heath down and fen[2]. But there are no trustworthy figures by which the movement can be measured; and, as is always the case in matters of this kind, there is a risk of misleading generalisation based on the areas where the movement was marked, and so was talked about, to the exclusion of those whose stagnation and lack of history may not have meant happiness but would have modified statistics, had there been any.

The problem of the transference of ownership has been complicated by the varying uses of the word yeoman, both by contemporaries and by historians. In the sixteenth and seven-teenth centuries the word had been used widely and loosely, and it was still so used in the late eighteenth century, though

[1] Johnson, A. H., *The Disappearance of the Small Landowner* (1909), ch. 7.
[2] See Levy, *Large and Small Holdings* (1911), *passim*, and all agrarian histories.

not by everyone. "My father was a yeoman but had no land of his own"—from the *locus classicus* in Latimer's sermon—would have been a contradiction in terms to Arthur Young, who, when he used the word, which was not often, meant "owner pure and simple."[1] Among Young's elder contemporaries some wide use still prevailed. To Blackstone a yeoman was a man with a county vote, and the county voters included lessees for lives: Adam Smith thought that in England "the yeomanry" became "respectable to their landlords" because "a great part of them" held leases for lives and so had votes[2]. That tenants without votes were also yeomen in his eyes is evident. He talks of the Scottish "yeomanry," and Scotland had no voting leaseholders and hardly any cultivating freeholders. Blackstone's use, which grouped among the yeomen all who had "lifehold properties" from which they could get a living—as opposed to leases for years—was a natural one, and was common enough.

But precisely in the years now under review, when Blackstone and Smith were long dead and Young had just died in extreme old age[3], the narrowest use of the word came more and more into fashion, until, in the evidence given before a Select Committee on Agriculture in 1833, experts reporting on the state of the "yeomanry" often took pains to make it clear that they did sometimes include with the freeholders owners of "lifehold properties,"[4] evidently feeling a doubt, which would not have troubled Blackstone and still less Adam Smith, as to whether such people were right yeomen or not. The narrowing use of the term is apt to mislead[5]; yet the agrarian history of the eighteenth and early nineteenth centuries does record a decline, though a decline neither continuous nor complete, of the yeomanry, in all senses of the word except Adam Smith's.

There was no general decline of the freeholding yeomen during the war years nor any strictly demonstrable decline of the copyholders and other "lifehold proprietors." But, though

---

[1] Rogers, J. D., *s.v.* "Yeomen," *Dict. of Political Economy* (1st ed. 1899): much the most useful account of the history of the term.

[2] *Wealth of Nations* (ed. Cannan), I. 367–8. Blackstone, *Commentaries* (ed. 1914), II. 714.

[3] In 1820, aged 81.   [4] Below, p. 103 *sqq.*

[5] It has misled, *e.g.* Mr and Mrs Hammond, *The Village Labourer*, 1760–1832 (1911 and 1920), p. 28–9, who assume that when Adam Smith talked of yeomen he meant freeholders.

precise evidence is lacking, some, perhaps a considerable, decline in the latter group may be assumed. Tenures for lives were becoming old-fashioned, and when they ran out or forfeited they might not be renewed[1]. The copyhold for lives was probably the commonest type; and although the tenant often had the customary right to "insert a life," the fact that this meant a bargain and the payment of a fine gave an opening to the landlord. The copyhold of inheritance, fairly common in the Midlands and South-East, like the "customary freehold" of the North and of Wales, could not run out, but might be bought out or exchanged for a leasehold[2]. Lifehold properties of different sorts were common[3] in the intermixed midland open-fields which at this time were being so rapidly enclosed; and although life interests in land, being real property, could not be swept away by an enclosure Act, the promoters of an enclosure would naturally see to it that as many as possible of these interests should have run out, or have been bought out or exchanged, before the enclosure was undertaken. Loose uses of the word yeoman by contemporaries have, however, tended to confuse the quite certain reduction in the number of holdings, which usually coincided with enclosure, with a reduction in the number of tenants for lives, or even of freeholders. "Upon all enclosures of open-fields," it was reported of south-east Warwickshire in 1794, "the farms have generally been made much larger; from these causes the hardy yeomanry ...have been driven into...manufacturing towns, whose flourishing trade has sometimes found them profitable employment."[4] No enclosure-promoter could make the farms of farmer-owners larger against their will, nor could he drive out holders of leases for lives by a mere order. Some of both classes may have sold out and migrated at the time of enclosure, but more probably the reporter was using the cant phrase "hardy yeomanry" when he meant simply small cultivators[5]. Perhaps

[1] E.g. Strickland, *A General View of the Agriculture of the East Riding* (1812), p. 33: copyhold, once very common, is disappearing.

[2] See in general *Williams on Real Property* (ed. 1920), p. 501 sqq. Holdsworth, W. S., *History of English Law*, VII. (1925), 298 sqq. To what extent forfeiture, arising from the tenant's failure to fulfil the terms of his copy, was an active force at that time I do not know.

[3] But not by any means universal—e.g. yearly or three-yearly tenancies the rule in Bedfordshire open parishes (*V.C.H. Bedford*, II. 132): common fields often let on short lease in Buckinghamshire (*V.C.H. Buckingham*, II. 83).

[4] Quoted in Prothero (Lord Ernle), *English Farming Past and Present* (1912), p. 296–7.   [5] Lord Ernle notes this.

he had read Adam Smith. The people in question may all have been ordinary yearly tenants or holders of leases for years, not for lives. How much they suffered, and whether the increased agrarian unit was a good thing or not, are matters not at present under discussion. That freeholders who had lived by their holdings sometimes vanished at the time of an enclosure is true enough. A small holding might not be of much use without its ancient common rights, and there might be inadequate compensation for the loss of them. When land was re-allotted allottees had to fence. The expense was heavy for a small man; he might decide to sell and use the proceeds either to stock a rented farm or to go into trade, or he might fall into debt. The proceeds of sale are sometimes said to have gone at the ale-house, and possibly the prices of some cheaply-bought life interests of copyholders, or of some tiny scraps of freehold by which the owner could never have lived, went there—a very great evil[1]; but hard-fistedness and ambition are vices more yeoman-like than rash spending. The patrimonies drunk away can hardly have been many. Truer to type is what Marshall wrote of some Norfolk yeomen in 1790—how, "seeing many who were recently their inferiors raised by an excessive profit which had recently been made by farming," they "sold their comparatively small patrimonies in order that they might— agreeably with the fashion or frenzy of the day—become great farmers."[2]

It is quite clear that the high prices of the war period provoked small owners sometimes to sell out and set up as great farmers, sometimes to buy more land from the encumbered members or the expiring families of their own class—there are always such—or from broken-up large estates when these, for similar reasons, came on to the market. Marshall wrote of what he called a *Terramania* among the yeomen, with the usual excessive prices, in the East Riding of Yorkshire and in Leicestershire about 1790[3]. The Kentish yeomen were said to be increasing and paying higher prices for land than anyone else in 1794[4]. Of Essex, Young wrote in 1807, "there never was a greater proportion of small and moderate-sized farms, the property of mere farmers, than at present. Such has been the flourishing state of agriculture...that scarcely an estate is sold, if divided into lots of forty or fifty to two or three hundred

---

[1] See below, p. 115.   [2] Quoted in Johnson, *op. cit.* p. 142.
[3] Prothero, *op. cit.* p. 292.   [4] *General View of...Kent*, p. 26.

a year, but is purchased by farmers."[1] The same thing was not happening, however, over the border in Hertfordshire.

The reports to the Board of Agriculture—from various dates between 1793 and 1815—suggest, in general terms and with no statistics, an increase rather than a decrease of small owner-cultivators or of owner-tilled land—it is not always clear which—in the North Riding, Norfolk, Essex, Kent, Hampshire, Central Somerset, Northern Wilts, Gloucester and Shropshire. There was a definite decline in Lancashire, but not for an agrarian reason—"the great wealth, which has in many instances been so rapidly acquired by some of their neighbours...has offered sufficient temptation to venture their property in trade."[2] In Cheshire the same causes were at work, though in neither case are we told what class of people had bought. In Westmorland, for other reasons, the statesmen—mainly customary freeholders—were "daily decreasing."[3] In the East Riding some owning cultivators had recently been bought out when the report was issued in 1812; but the class had never been numerous there[4]. In Hereford small states of from £400 to £1000 a year, occupied by their owners, were said to have declined[5]: these owners may have been descendants of yeomen but would not, it may be suspected, have claimed the title.

It is noticeable that all the districts from which an increase of "yeoman" holdings is reported are districts little affected by the recent enclosures of open-fields, except North Wiltshire. But that the maintenance and even the increase of small property was not, in the opinion of the reporters, incompatible with recent enclosure the Wiltshire case itself shows. The Report, it is of 1794, states both that there had been a good deal of enclosure and that "the property has been divided and sub-divided and gone into the hands of the many."[6] The Huntingdon Report, of 1793, explains that though in the old enclosed parts of the county large owners predominated, in the newly enclosed and open parts "property is pretty much diffused."[7]

[1] *General View of...Essex*, p. 39–40.

[2] Quoted in Prothero, *op. cit.* p. 295, where the counties mentioned above are also enumerated.

[3] *A General View of...Westmorland*, p. 302.

[4] Strickland, *A General View of...the East Riding*, p. 31.

[5] *V.C.H. Hereford*, i. 410.

[6] Quoted in Prothero, *op. cit.* p. 295.

[7] Maxwell, *A General View of...Huntingdon*, p. 7. Prothero, *op. cit.* (1912), p. 292 *sqq.*, quotes all the passages which suggest increase of owner-cultivation

Peace, as is known, made "one general malcontent" out of the "country patriots, born to hunt and vote and raise the price of corn," because "war was rent." To the farmer-owner war was profit, good living, good portions for his children, and a good gig. Eighteen years after Waterloo, and after the price-falls and fluctuations of the 'twenties, a Committee of the Commons reported of his class that "in the counties where Yeomen heretofore abounded...a great change of Property has recently taken place. The high prices of the last war led to Speculation in the purchase improvement and inclosure of Land....Prices have fallen, the debt still remains...most pernicious to this body of men."[1] The statement about the change of property is rather stronger than the evidence given before the Committee warranted. This evidence is, county by county, as follows. No decline, as distinguished from temporary distress, was reported among the Shropshire yeomen of Clun Forest[2]. In Wiltshire they had decreased "most materially" within the last fifteen years, but there were still "a great many."[3] There were "many" in Worcester, but "many" more had got tired of farming and had let their estates: others had sold[4]. In Norfolk were "a great many": very few had failed: "they are more economical than they used to be and generally they farm better."[5] In the North Riding the freeholders had been "regularly lessening for ten years"; yet in the witness's parish of 6000 acres "we are all freeholders, except a few tenants of little pieces, that some of the freeholders let off."[6] The decline in the Malton and Pickering country "did not begin directly

during the wars. Professor Gonner's *Common Land and Enclosure* (1910, p. 369–71) had repeated the view that, during the period covered by the Reports, there was a "widespread disappearance of the small farmer, and especially of the small owner": the complaint, he wrote, "seems to proceed indifferently from all quarters," but his references contain no further evidence about small *owners*. They are either references to consolidation of farms, or to apparently irrelevant passages, or to passages which seem to tell against his conclusion. *Essex*, p. 64, *e.g.*, is an argument against small farms, not a statement of fact: elsewhere in *Essex* comes Young's statement quoted above. Gonner refers to *Kent*, p. 26, where, he says, the reporter "doubts decrease in small farmers": what the Report says, p. 26, is "the number of yeomanry...is annually on the increase" (1794). Johnson, *The Disappearance of the Small Landowner*, Lect. VII, also quotes the main passages from the Reports. His conclusion is against decline in owners during the wars.

[1] *S. C. on Agriculture*, 1833 (V), p. x.

[2] Q. 421.   [3] Q. 1262.
[4] Q. 1691 *sqq.*   [5] Q. 2199.
[6] Q. 2439, 2531.

after the war, but within a few years after the war."[1] In the
West Riding about Doncaster the small yeomen, but they only,
"were nearly all gone."[2] In South Lancashire there were still
"a good many": they were sinking, though not fast, but were
more encumbered than formerly[3]. In Cheshire not many
remained. Here, as in many other counties, they were said to
have been too ambitious and lived too high during the war:
some had bought land at forty years' purchase and had suffered
for it[4].

In Kent there was no great change, though some yeomen
had sold out. The witness (a vague one) said of the average
yeoman that he "lived nearly as a workman."[5] Somerset still
had many yeomen; a few only had gone. It had also many
"lifehold properties," generally small[6]. "A great many have
fallen in," said a land-agent witness, "and in many instances
we could not recover the dilapidations, nor the heriots."[7]
Landlords were generally letting the leases for lives run out.
Another Somerset witness spoke of many yeomen in his area:
he said that only the more careless were selling, and he noted
that other small men sometimes bought[8]. A witness with
knowledge of Kent, Sussex and Essex spoke of "a great many"
yeomen and could not testify to decline[9]. Another, speaking
for Sussex and Hampshire, supposed there were still nearly as
many as in 1815, but "greatly reduced": before reduction
"many did live expensively."[10] A Derbyshire man said his
district had "perhaps as few as in any county"; but he did not
say they had declined[11]. About Loughborough there were
many, but the witness was certain that the gross number had
diminished[12]. Lastly, in Cumberland and Westmorland, the
statesmen were "constantly diminishing," the main cause being
the misguided burdening of their land with portions for big
families, which with fallen prices it could not carry. The buyers
were men who had made fortunes in trade or as large farmers[13].

---

[1] Q. 2534.   [2] Q. 3105.   [3] Q. 3601.
[4] Q. 5814–6.   [5] Q. 6046.   [6] Q. 4862–5.
[7] Q. 470–2.   [8] Q. 9196 *sqq*.   [9] Q. 7375.
[10] Q. 9923–4, 9035.
[11] Q. 12523. The Derbyshire *Report* of 1794 (p. 14) had noted the difficulty
of the smaller owner, "provincially statesman" to "preserve his estate...and...
improve his fortune on rational principles": often he "sat down in bewilder-
ment."
[12] Q. 8571.
[13] Q. 6697 *sqq*.

In view of this evidence and of the fact that seventy-seven years later more than 12 per cent. of cultivated English land was worked by its legal owners, a figure below 15–20 per cent. could hardly be suggested for 1825–30[1]. The cultivating owners of 1825–30, like those of 1910, were no doubt sometimes considerable landlords with farms in hand, or parsons farming their glebe. Others might be grouped in popular speech as large farmers; for an arrangement quite common in the early twentieth century, by which a man owns a little land, rents a good deal more, and is classed as a farmer, was not unknown to the ambitious yeoman who rented, or to the ambitious farmer who bought, a hundred years earlier[2]. Not every yeoman who made money in war time and wanted more land either bought all he wanted or sold all his patrimony to stock a rented farm. Some, it is true, bought steadily and prospered up into small squires, ceasing to cultivate and discarding the yeoman's name[3]. Some became agents, surveyors, attorneys, and let their patrimonies. Some went into industry and sold them. Some were ruined and went to the wall. Some remained and their descendants tilled their land through the two generations during which it was the fashion to say that such folk were extinct. Meanwhile the mistaken impression that there had been a cataclysmic downfall was strengthened by the too-common popular assumption that the word yeoman had always meant freeholder[4].

In Wales more primitive agrarian conditions were partially concealed by an identical legal terminology; but just because

[1] Whether 33 per cent. had ever been so worked may be doubted; but the problem has no precise solution. In 1910, 3,000,000 out of 24,500,000 acres in England were occupied by their owners (*Agricultural Statistics*, 1910, Cd. 5585, p. 61). [For yeomen surviving in 1832 see Chambers, J. D., *Nottinghamshire in the Eighteenth Century* (1932), p. 206.]

[2] *E.g.* Vancouver, *A General View of...Hampshire* (1810), p. 83. Many farmers "in addition to the land they rent are occupiers of their own estates."

[3] Noted and claimed as an original observation by Hasbach, *A History of the English Agricultural Labourer*, p. 107–8: a matter of common knowledge to students of family history.

[4] Steffen, G. F., *Studien zur Gesch. der Eng. Lohnarbeiter* (1901), I. 494, reacting against the cataclysmic view, suggested that the fall of the yeoman freeholder, if not actually an historical legend, was at least a not very important episode. Levy, *Large and small holdings* (1911), p. 27 *sqq.*, maintained against Hasbach and others that the yeomanry "disappeared in the course of the period 1760–1815." But by yeomanry he quite arbitrarily meant *small* freeholders. The 1833 evidence, which he did not use, shows that even these—who certainly had declined most—were far from extinct. [The conclusions in the text are confirmed by Davies, E., "The Small Landowner, 1780–1832, in the Light of the Land Tax Assessments." *Ec. H.R.* I. 87 *sqq.* (1927).]

the conditions were more primitive there are fewer problems of transformation. The bulk of the land was owned by the nobility or by "resident gentlemen of moderate means" as the Report of 1813 on North Wales put it[1]. There were no "petty lairds or tacksmen" (middlemen): the estates were managed directly by these resident gentlemen or by the agents of the nobility. Copyhold was very rare in the North, rather commoner in the South, in parts of which—particularly in the Vale of Glamorgan—agrarian and manorial conditions had at one time approximated to the English type[2]. A customary freehold, in which land was held for an anciently fixed quit-rent, was common both in North and South, and these customary free-holders were the equivalent of the English yeomen owners[3]. The accounts of 1813–14 have nothing to say of their increase or decrease, nor was there enough movement in the next fifteen years to arouse public solicitude. Both North and South Wales had so much waste mountain side, were still so largely pastoral in their interests, and had so very little open-field of anything like the English midland type that the problem of enclosure had been, and remained, a problem in hill-pasture. There was a "rage for enclosing waste lands"[4] during the wars, but it had little to do with questions of ownership. Holdings, it is true, had been a good deal thrown together, in the North, during the eighteenth century, but not—it would seem—so as to produce any acute social problem. Abundance of small holdings survived[5].

Taken as a whole, Wales was farmed by tenants in 1815. In the past their landlords had not done much for them. Great praise is given to a landlord in Brecon, who took his farms in hand in turn, remodelled their buildings, and made their lands fit for proper tillage[6]. The practice of undertaking capital improvements and charging the interest on the rent, as adopted by Lord Penrhyn, is described as a novelty: "several other proprietors have since adopted the same plan."[7] Year to year tenancies predominated in the North. In the South leases were rather more common. In both, the small holding was the rule.

---

[1] Davies, *North Wales*, p. 76.
[2] Davies, *South Wales*, I. 120. Rees, W., "The Black Death in Wales," *T. R. Hist. Soc.* 1920, p. 116–17.
[3] Rhys, J. and Brynmor-Jones, D., *The Welsh People* (1900), p. 404, 425.
[4] Davies, *North Wales*, p. 86.   [5] *Ibid.*
[6] Davies, *South Wales*, I. 128   [7] Davies, *North Wales*, p. 102.

Acreage estimates are not given for the North, except the statement that such a thing as an arable farm of 600 acres was exceedingly rare; but of the South we are told that most of the farms were from 30 to 100 acres, though there were also plenty even so large as 300–500 acres, and there were a few, a very few, greater still[1]. The tenants who became rich and famous were not, however, these few large arable farmers, but great graziers like Mr Williams of Pant-y-Siri in Cardigan— he was dead in 1814—who had managed to monopolise all the feeding on the high land between Tregaron and Builth. He was credited with 20,000 sheep, 500 wild horses, and "a vast number of wild cattle."[2] They called him the Job of the West. An inquiry into commons, thirty years later, showed that it was rather on these high—and generally unregulated—commons than in any transactions with arable land that men's fortunes rose and fell, as the "fighting shepherds" cleared, or failed to clear, ground for their masters' flocks[3]. Rise or fall in the fortunes of classes at this time was hardly perceptible.

Rights in and over land were more clearly ascertainable in Scotland than in either Wales or England. "In no country in Europe are the rights of proprietors so well defined, and so carefully protected,"[4] Sir John Sinclair wrote in 1814. "There is not a cot house and a kail yard that is not held by deeds as formal"—he felt bound to add "and nearly as expensive"— "as the titles to a valuable estate," wrote one of his collaborators[5]. Scotland, wrote the eighth Duke of Argyll, referring to the late eighteenth and early nineteenth centuries, had few "commonties" where "an indefinite number of persons had various and indefinite rights of use, founded only on customs," such as were then to be found in Wales and England[6]. Under the Scottish Acts of 1695 any proprietor having interest in a common could compel the other interested parties to divide; and during the next hundred and twenty years this had been almost universally done—though division of the proprietary rights had not necessarily carried with it physical enclosure[7]. The land,

---

[1] Davies, *North Wales*, p. 92. *South Wales*, I. 162. In 1851, of every 1000 Welsh farms, 719 were under 100 acres. *Census of 1851* (1854), *Population Tables*, II. clxxv.   [2] Davies, *South Wales*, II. 245.

[3] *S. C. on Commons Inclosure* (1844, V), Q. 1240, 1720.

[4] *General Report of the Agricultural State...of Scotland*, I. 112.

[5] Appendix 4, vol. IV. 221.

[6] Argyll, *Scotland as it was and as it is* (1887), II. 224–5.

[7] Sinclair, *op. cit.* IV. 230. The Acts excluded the Burghs in which freeholders,

legally speaking, was in very few hands. The number would be increased somewhat if "feuars"—holders of land in perpetuity under a "superior," subject to a fixed feu-duty and certain traditional "casualties"—were grouped with proprietors, as in practice rural feuars generally were. Most urban feuars were of a very different class; but the rural feuar, generally speaking, went with the lairds. The ultimate proprietors under the Crown varied in status from the Highland Dukes, with their whole counties, to a handful of petty lairds in the Lowlands, whose grandfathers had not lived so well as a Suffolk yeoman. But, even in the South, legal ownership was normally in great blocks. About sixty persons owned the county of Peebles and forty-eight others owned thirteen-sixteenths of Roxburgh[1]. Approximately one-third of the Kingdom of Scotland was strictly entailed[2].

Once there had existed in the South a certain amount of intermixed ownership in the run-rig arable fields. The Acts of 1695 had provided for redistribution in such cases and, "by a liberal interpretation of the act," redistribution was "extended in practice to pieces of land of a larger size, not in separate ridges, amounting perhaps to four Scots acres or five English, and lying intermixed."[3] At first not much used, these legal facilities had been eagerly adopted by improving landlords in the two generations from 1760 to 1825: by the latter date run-rig ownership may be said to have followed the commons. Run-rig agriculture was not dead; but where it survived—mainly in the Highlands—it survived among cultivators who were not the proprietors of their fields. So it could be got rid of by a landlord's administrative act without recourse to the English weapon of a private bill in Parliament.

Immediately beneath the landlord in the Lowlands now came, as a rule, the type of man fitly described in the Report on Peebles of 1814 as a "professional farmer"[4]—the man who had made

---

were numerous; so common wastes and even common fields survived in them. Cunningham, W., in *Sc. Hist. Rev.* XIII (1915–6), 185. Legally, enclosure under the two Acts of 1695, "took the form of a private lawsuit" among the heritors. Romanes, J. H., *An Enclosure Proceeding in Melrose*, 1742 in *Sc. Hist. Rev.* XIII. 101 *sqq.* [Cp. Hamilton, H., *The Industrial Revolution in Scotland* (1932), p. 41.]

[1] Findlater, *Peebles*, p. 29. Douglas, *Roxburgh and Selkirk*, p. 17. [For the history of feuing see Grant, I. F., *Social and Ec. Development of Scotland before 1603*, ch. V (1930).]   [2] Sinclair, *op. cit.* I. 105.

[3] *Ibid.* I. 265. Also Skene, *Celtic Scotland* (1876 *sqq.*), III. 372.

[4] *Peebles*, p. 31.

farming a reasoned art, not the old time peasant for whom it was an inherited habit. Everywhere these professional farmers had leases—twelve, nineteen and twenty-one years being favourite terms. There were no leases for lives. The farmers in occupation at the end of the wars rarely belonged to a later generation than the second of the men who had given the Eastern Lowlands the lead in British agriculture. Throughout the Lowlands improving landlords had picked their men, given them long leases, and, in some cases, the benefit of their own experience[1]. They had swept away most of the feudal survivals, some of which had been universal so late as 1750–60—the lord's privileged dovecot, the arriages or ploughings, bounages or reapings, and carriages or carting works of various sorts performed by the tenant, together with the rents in kind and the steelbow, or metayer, tenure; but strong remnants of thirlage, compulsory grinding at the lord's mill, survived to vex the nineteenth century, even in the South. In Aberdeenshire it was in full swing in 1794, and the complaints of the miller's "wanton insolence" recall the refrain of some anti-miller ballad of an earlier age. In Forfar, at the same date, the arriages, bounages and carriages were not extinct though "growing fast into disuse."[2]

When the reforming movement in Scottish tenures and agriculture began, at dates varying with the district, but all falling into the half century 1725–1775, in the Highlands and Isles a class of gentlemen-middlemen, the tacksmen, came almost everywhere between the great lords and the cultivators[3]. The tacksman farmed some land himself, his subtenants helping, just as the villani and cotarii helped to till the domain of a Domesday Knight who held under Gilbert of Ghent or Bishop Odo. The lands of the Lords of the Isles, in 1730–40, were all let in this way to Campbell and Maclean tacksmen, with beneath them tenants-at-will subject to all the uncertain personal services and exactions of the old Celtic feudalism[4].

---

[1] Sinclair, op. cit. I. 174, also his Analysis of the Statistical Account of Scotland (1825), I. 234 sqq.

[2] Anderson, Aberdeen, p. 47. Roger, Forfar, p 21. Findlater, Peebles, p. 89. For the services and steelbow see Fullarton, Ayr, p. 10, and Argyll, op. cit. I. 105; II. 44. For thirlage in particular, Sinclair, General Account, IV. 254.

[3] We have now a documented account of late tacksman-economy in Strathspey, in Miss Grant's Everyday Life on an old Highland Farm (1924), based on the papers of William Macintosh of Balnespick († 1784).

[4] Argyll, op. cit. II. 10 sqq.

Land was usually held by these subtenants in small groups, and its arable was cut up in run-rig—township farms, as such were called; an arrangement at that time also quite familiar in the Lowlands, for example in Ayrshire[1]. From about the years 1750–60, the Highland landlords set themselves to reform or to break down the tacksman system[2]. From 1755 onwards the new Argyll leases to the tacksmen forbade them to sublet save on precise terms—the subtenant's services were to be fixed, and redeemable at 1*d.* a day's labour, and he was not to be called away from his own land at seed-time or harvest[3]. But tacksmen were still numerous, and run-rig agriculture among their subtenants not extinct, in Argyll, Inverness, and the counties north of them in 1814[4]. Where the tacksmen had gone, often many of the subtenants had gone too, and in place of both were sheep and farmers from the south country with short leases. Rents were rising, for the landlord was "revaluing his estate on a basis of sheep."[5] The number of imported farmers and of sheep increased greatly in the next ten years, estates being cleared of their cottars, certainly unprosperous and often wretchedly poor folk, to make room for them. Legally this was easy, as the ordinary cottar was a tenant-at-will and the most favoured had at best a short lease.

Although it is impossible to estimate statistically the growth in size of the average holding in any part of Britain during the reign of King George III, there is no question that, at its close, the British conception of a small farm would have seemed unusual to a rural economist bred in a peasant land. In nineteenth- and twentieth-century Germany it was customary to call a peasant holding of under 12½ acres small; one between 12½ and 50 acres middling; one from 50 to 250 acres big. For purposes of classification in the England of 1825–30 farms under 100 acres might be called small; from 100 to 300 middling;

---

[1] Argyll, *op. cit.* II. 194. Fullarton, *Ayr* (1793), p. 9, referring to "forty years ago." Grant, I. F., "The Social Effects of...enclosure...in Aberdeenshire," *E.J.* (*Ec. Hist.*), Jan. 1926.   [2] Sinclair's *Analysis*, I. 296–7.
[3] Argyll, *op. cit.* II. 47.   [4] Sinclair's *Report*, I. 181 *sqq.*
[5] Adam, M. I., in *Sc. Hist. Rev.* XVII. 79, and above, p. 62–4. Some landlords refused to adopt the sheep system, but that did not make the cottars any more prosperous. Consolidation of holdings did—but that also meant emigration. As Miss Adam rightly argues, *any* improvement meant fewer people. See also her "Eighteenth-Century Highland Landlords and the Poverty Problem," *Sc. Hist. Rev.* XIX. 1 *sqq.*, 161 *sqq.*

from 300 to 500 large; and over 500 "extensive." Rough
estimates of the dominant type of farm, on this classification,
and occasional exact details as to size, are available for most
English and Scottish counties[1]. Welsh information is less precise, but the general situation in Wales is clear: it was a land
of really small farms, of which probably the majority were
cultivated without regular hired labour.

South-Eastern England was rich in small holdings. In Kent
there were many from 10 to 14 acres and few above 200;
though there was a handful of 500–700 acre holdings. In Sussex,
Weald farms averaged about 100 acres; but Downs farms,
comprising much sheep-walk, were gigantic, 1000 acres and
upwards. Surrey farms were of all sizes, but mostly small,
running from 40 or 50 to 300 acres. Middlesex was in much the
same condition. In the East Anglian counties holdings were
bigger, but there was no normal type. Essex contained some
of the largest farms in the Kingdom; but no county had "a
greater proportion of small and moderate sized farms occupied
by their owners."[2] "From 100 to 150 acres might be about
the average."[3] Suffolk holdings were mostly large, a very great
number being those of the substantial Suffolk yeomen. Norfolk, and with it Cambridge, covered the whole range, from
really small ancient fen holdings to great new farms on drained
land or on Coke's improved sands. In Hertford farms were
small, some very small—North Hertford was late enclosed—
with farmers reported "worse off than day labourers."[4] For
Buckingham what purports to be an exact average figure is
available: it is 179 acres. For Bedford there is an estimated
average of 150, and for Northampton one of 130–200. Leicester
had many 80–100 acre holdings; but 100–200 was more normal.
In Nottingham and Derby the really small farm predominated;
and in Oxford, with its few large estates and many "church
tenures," the small, and reputedly ignorant, farmer held his
own better than in some counties.

The southern and south-western counties, except Cornwall, are more vaguely described. Hampshire holdings varied,

---

[1] Loudon, J. C., *An Encyclopædia of Agriculture*, 2nd ed. 1831, p. 1125 *sqq.*
Loudon's summary is based on the county reports, Marshall's review of them,
and some later sources: it is reasonably accurate for the 'twenties. It agrees
rather closely with the more exact returns of 1851. See below, p. 451 *sqq.*

[2] Loudon, *op. cit.* p. 1225.

[3] *S. C. on Agriculture*, 1833, Q. 1546.

[4] Loudon, *op. cit.* p. 1137.

but as a whole were rather small. Wiltshire enclosed farms were medium to large, "customary tenements" small. Dorset had some very large farms. Somerset and Devon had nearly everything except very large farms, and Cornwall, "very much divided, subdivided, and vexatiously intermixed,"[1] was a county of small holdings averaging some £40 a year value.

In Gloucester the small holding was rare. All up the Welsh Marches and in Warwick and Worcester it was very common; but from these counties recent consolidation of holdings was definitely reported—from Stafford, Hereford, Warwick. For Warwickshire the average was put at 150 acres. The nearer the Welsh border the smaller were the holdings, great numbers in Shropshire being of 20 acres and under. Cheshire had many holdings under 10 acres and the county average was supposed to be 70: there was not much arable. Lancashire was also a county of very small farms. So was the West Riding: "for one of 400 acres there were a dozen under 50": "an occupier of 100 acres was styled a great farmer." The North Riding was much the same; and even on the rolling ground of the East Riding the really large farm was the exception.

Lincoln was more varied even than Norfolk. It comprised the Isle of Axholm, where "almost everyone is proprietor and farmer of 1–40 acres as in France"[2], a significant touch; the ridged wolds, newly enclosed, with great farms from 300 to 1500 acres; the coast "marsh" with many very small holdings, often yeoman property; and the belt just east of Lincoln where conditions were more normal. Last, the far North—Durham with a few great farms, but most of 50–150 acres; Cumberland and Westmorland nearly all cut up into tiny "parcels" worth £15–£30 a year; and Northumberland, very progressive, with farms larger the farther north you went up the coastal strip, but with very many small ones towards the hills.

The south-eastern arable district of Scotland[3]—Berwick, Roxburgh, and the Lothians—was a land of large farms. In East Lothian the average arable farm was 200–300 acres and the largest 500–600; though farms largely composed of hill sheep-walk might be three times that size. For the pastoral counties of the South—Peebles, Selkirk, Dumfries, Kirkcudbright and Wigton—not a quarter of whose surface was cultivated, acreage estimates would not be in any way comparable with those for

---

[1] Loudon, *op. cit.* p. 1172.   [2] *Ibid.* p. 1155.
[3] Based on Loudon, Sinclair, and the county reports.

arable or enclosed grazing farms of the ordinary English type. Of the South-Western lowlands—Ayr, Renfrew, Lanark, and Dumbarton—a half was cultivated in farms which were relatively small, but much larger than the little run-rig farms of 1760 had been. The North-Eastern lowlands, the coast lands from Kincardine round to Nairn, had fully mastered "the turnip husbandry and artificial grasses,"[1] which had brought with them some large farms; but the small farmer held his own. Farms in Aberdeenshire in 1794 had been tiny—smaller, it was supposed, than in the seventeenth century[2]—and there is no record of change in the next thirty years; though no doubt some change occurred with the progress of agriculture, for the tiny farms were reckoned an economic evil. Conditions in the central counties of Fife, Kinross and Clackmannan, Forfar, Stirling and Perth were exceedingly varied; but none of the counties would have been called a large-farm area. The Highlands and the Isles had their distinct agrarian systems to which some reference has already been made. Most of the tacksmen's subtenants, or the cottars holding from the supreme lord, were what are called in Germany dwarf-peasants, people who can rarely hope to live, never to live in any comfort, by their holdings alone.

There are figures in the census of 1831 which illustrate, with some precision, the extent to which really small farming had survived in Britain[3]. They are entirely destructive of the view that, as the result of agrarian change and class legislation, an army of labourers toiled for a relatively small farming class. Of 961,000 families engaged in agriculture, 144,600 were those of occupiers—owners or farmers—who hired labour; 130,500 were those of occupiers who hired no labour; and 686,000 were labouring families. That is to say, to each occupying household there were exactly two and a half labouring households; and to each occupying household which hired labour there were not quite five labouring households. If Scotland were omitted the figures for labouring households would be rather higher, perhaps as much as two and three-quarters and five and a half. Small as they may seem in either case, they will not surprise anyone familiar with contemporary British statistics who knows with how small a hired staff a farm of fair acreage might be

---

[1] Sinclair, *General Report* (1814), 1. 30.   [2] Anderson, *Aberdeen*, p. 49.
[3] See *Cambs. Hist. Journ.* (1923), 1. 92, for further details and references.

worked, even in the days when there was no agricultural machinery. In Arthur Young's *Northern Tour* (1770) a table of seventy-five farms, with an average acreage of 163, gives an average employment figure of one hired person—man, boy or milkmaid—per forty acres[1].

It is interesting to place beside these figures of 1831 Gregory King's often-quoted guesses at the numbers of the various grades of English society towards the end of the seventeenth century. Guesses they are and they must be treated as such; but they deserve quotation again. In England and Wales—not Great Britain—King supposed that there were 330,000 families of cultivating owners and farmers. There were 364,000 families of "labouring people and out-servants," exclusive of artisans and handicraftsmen, and 400,000 of "cottagers and paupers": total 764,000. He expressed the curious opinion that all these less fortunate families consumed more than they produced. Clearly they seemed to him "proletarian." If a quarter of them are assumed to be unskilled urban workers, a generous allowance, the proportion between rural occupying families and rural "proletarian" families is almost exactly 1 to $1\frac{3}{4}$ as compared with a probable maximum of 1 to $2\frac{3}{4}$ a hundred and forty years later[2].

Though the dependent class had not, it would appear, grown so disproportionately in that critical period as is sometimes implied, no comfortable statistics should be allowed to obscure either the hardships, injustices, and undeserved humiliations which the years from 1795 to 1825 had brought upon some of these labouring families, or the resulting changes in their relation to the social organisation of British agriculture. The guillotine, as the French statistician said, did not appreciably affect the tables of mortality. There is no doubt that the enclosures and consolidations of holdings, particularly during the war enclosure fever of 1790–1810, had driven into the labouring class many families of small holders, including those of some small ruined owners[3]. For these the humiliations of the black

---

[1] IV. 236 *sqq.*

[2] See *Cambs. Hist. Journ.* as above. The figures may also be looked at in this way: of the 275,000 "occupying" households of 1831, about 225,000 would be in England and Wales: King guessed at 330,000 such households for England and Wales: if he guessed right their number fell by just over 30 per cent. in 140 years: meanwhile the cultivated area increased.

[3] A generally accepted view. See Eden, *The State of the Poor* (1797), II. 591, and the discussions in Hasbach, *A History of the English Agricultural Labourer*, p. 107 *sqq.* Gonner, *Common Land and Inclosure*, p. 378. Above, p. 102, n. 7.

years must have been especially bitter. In considering ruined owners a distinction must be drawn, as has been already suggested, between the yeoman proper—in all its vicissitudes the term was never applied to a man who could not live by his holding—and the man who held an ancient copyhold cottage or some scrap of copyhold or freehold land in the open-fields, but lived primarily by wage labour. It has been argued that enclosure as such was not very likely to injure the former type, though it might turn him from yeoman into farmer or tradesman. The evidence goes to show also that owners of what were called common-right cottages, that is, cottages whose ownership carried with it a legal claim to the use of the commons, were compensated with an allotment of land when common was enclosed, as were scrap-owners in the fields when fields were enclosed[1]. But the allotment in lieu of common rights might be too small to be of use for grazing purposes, and the burden of fencing it disproportionate. There was a real danger that the few pounds tendered by the great man's agent at the right time would be accepted and go at the ale-house or, more probably and more defensibly, to meet the rising prices of war time. No statistical picture of these strippings of cottagers of such bits of property can be even outlined. Their extent must not be exaggerated. There is no reason to suppose that the average cottager in an area affected by enclosure had either a common-right cottage or land in the fields of his own[2].

More widespread, in England, was the grievance of the labouring family which had made some use of common and open-field stubble grazing, by sufferance and custom but illegally. At no stage in history, in arable districts with fairly dense population, had common rights been universal[3]. In the Middle Ages they were normally proportionate to the holdings in the fields. By the eighteenth century the proportion was generally deranged; in some cases all connection between

[1] Gonner, *op. cit.* p. 362.

[2] Davenant (*Works*, ed. 1771, II. 203), writing in 1688 of the 554,631 one-hearth cottages of 1685, says "but some of these having land about them, in all our calculations, we have computed the cottagers but at 500,000 families. But of these a large number may get their own livelihood and are no charge to the parish": to him a typical cottager was obviously landless and possibly a claimant on the rates.

[3] The fact that all the population at Epsom and at Barton (Cambs.) had Lammas rights was a matter for special comment in 1844. *S. C. on Enclosure*, 1844, Q. 5041, 5138. It had acted as "a formidable bar to enclosure."

common rights and holdings had been lost, for the whole system was in decay[1]. But almost everywhere, though with infinite local variations, the settled labouring people who had no holdings got access to the common, if only for turning out a few "stubble geese" or gathering two sticks. Opponents of medieval agriculture in the eighteenth century had taken no exception to this in moderation; though they were almost universally of opinion that an excess of commons, or unlimited access to them, was both demoralising to the settled population and attractive of undesirable immigrants. Harsh as the view seems, at least when applied to the settled population, there is much evidence in its favour[2]. Customary users of common had no legal claim to compensation in the event of enclosure; but the equitable claim of the settled users was recognised by almost all disinterested contemporary opinion. Unhappily, the commissioners, appointed *ad hoc* for each enclosure, pursued no uniform policy and generally neglected the equitable claim. "Taking a large number of awards throughout the country," wrote the most cautious and judicial modern student of the movement, "the recognition of ultra legal claims seems to be exceptional."[3] This applies to the whole period of enclosure by private Act in the eighteenth and nineteenth centuries.

Yet recognition was perfectly easy and—as the Reports to the Board of Agriculture show—was carried out in a few of the awards. The provision of allotments for labourers was also undertaken independently of awards by a few public-spirited landlords[4]. Norfolk has a rather good record of isolated equitable awards[5]. At Salthouse and Kelling a limited common was retained for the use of the small householders, the larger commoners being excluded. At Sayham allotments, which seem to have been adequate, replaced the old custom of common. In several parishes fuel rights were safeguarded. But in others, customs which gave the cottager the chance of keeping a cow—such valuable customs, it may be noted, were rare— were exchanged for half an acre on which no cow can live. An instance of half-compensation comes from Tuddenham in Suffolk[6]. The poor kept only asses and geese on the commons

---

[1] Gonner, *op. cit.* p. 80 n.
[2] Gonner, *op. cit.* p. 361.   [3] Gonner, *op. cit.* p. 365.
[4] Hammond, J. L. and B., *The Village Labourer*, 1760–1832, p. 157 *sqq.*, give instances.
[5] Gonner, *op. cit.* p. 363 n.
[6] Young, *Suffolk* (ed. 1804), p. 44.

and got firing from them. They were given a hundred acres of upland, and thirty of lowland for firing: they said it was enough: but there is no record of what they said about the asses and geese: possibly they still ran a few on the 130 acres. A striking case of what was possible comes from Sutton Cheney in Leicestershire. "For all those who had cows before," said the man who carried out the enclosure, "I left a sufficient quantity of land to maintain a cow."[1] There were thirteen cow-keepers and he left forty-four acres. This he laid out in four pasture fields and a common hay meadow with merestones, in which grazing was common after hay harvest. The arrangement might easily have been reproduced wherever the cottager's cow was found.

In Scotland, both the legal situation and the procedure were perfectly clear and hard. One sentence from Sir John Sinclair summarises both. "Even from the division of commons in Scotland, there is no injury to be dreaded by the labouring class, as their cottages give no right to keep cows on these wastes; and where they have a right of fuel that is always guarded in a...division."[2] Rights are precise: rights are the sole criterion, and they are respected.

The General Act of 1801 (41 Geo. III, c. 109), by which the methods of enclosing were standardised for England, referred to the possibility of grouping little allotments, for "proprietors and persons interested in...commons and waste lands," within one ring fence to save cost (clause 13); but whether "interest" might be held to cover extra-legal claims it was not the business of that Act to determine. In any case, little was done. This was in the year of Arthur Young's often-quoted saying[3]—"by nineteen Enclosure Acts out of twenty, the poor are injured, in some grossly injured.... The poor in these parishes may say *Parliament may be tender of property; all I know is I had a cow, and an Act of Parliament has taken it from me.*" "These" parishes were not the nineteen out of twenty. Cows were not so common as that[4]. But even if the cow were only an ass or three geese, the argument holds. Eighteen years later parliament was giving power to the Poor Law authorities to provide

[1] *S. C. on Poor Law*, 1818 (v), Q. 203.
[2] *General Report*, I. 278.
[3] *E.g.* Prothero, *op. cit.* p. 305.
[4] "Often" or "a great many" cases of cow-keeping cottagers are the most accurate statements which survive. See Hammond, J. L. and B., *op. cit.* p. 100–1.

allotments, and under this Act[1] something, some little thing, was done by the state during the 'twenties; though more was done by private persons. Public charity began to give to the labourer—viewed as potential pauper—what public justice should never have permitted him as a freeman to lose. In thinking of these things, if historical perspective is not to be distorted, the areas most affected by enclosure during the generation and a half before 1825, and those in which the labourer had rights or customs to lose, must constantly be borne in mind. There were many considerable areas, and innumerable single parishes, in which there had been no recent change, or no change worth mentioning[2].

Dependence on earnings, in money or kind, was made more complete, in many parts of the country, by a shortage of cottage garden ground. This, together with the difficulty in procuring milk or butter during the years of peak-prices from 1795 to 1820—a difficulty due in part to the decline of cow-keeping among cottagers—helps to explain the fearful monotony of diet in much of Southern England registered by Eden in 1797 and little altered during the next thirty years—"the unvarying meal of dry bread and cheese from week's end to week's end"; beer when they could pay for it; when not, "the deleterious produce of China" afforded "their most usual and general beverage." "If rich enough," they added roast meat, or bacon, once a week[3]. The fuel famine had checked frequent roastings in Eden's time. He contrasted with this monotonous dietary those of the North, Scotland, Wales and, he might have added, with some variants in detail, the counties of the Welsh Marches and the South-West—"porritch" eaten with milk butter or treacle; oatmeal crowdie; barley milk; pease kail; oat-cake; barley-bread; various cheap and savoury soups; and potatoes, which were much used and very good in the North. A potato propaganda was carried on during the next twenty years. Colquhoun, a potato enthusiast, reported in 1815 that south of Trent the consumption was still inconsiderable[4]. Late in the previous

---

[1] The Select Vestry Act (59 Geo. III, c. 12), § 12, 13.   [2] Below, p. 126.

[3] *The State of the Poor*, I. 496. But a Sussex witness in 1821 (*S. C. on Agriculture*, 1821, p. 54) said "very few" labourers did not get some meat every day, and a Scottish witness who had moved into Kent was surprised to find the labourers eating wheaten bread, drinking beer, and having "butchers' meat almost every day." *S. C. on Agriculture*, 1833, Q. 3295. For tea, see below, pp. 245–6.

[4] Colquhoun, *Resources of the British Empire*, p. 11. [Critics have noted local uses of potatoes earlier than any here quoted; but the generalisation stands.]

century it had taken Coke of Norfolk five years' experiment
with the potato to extract from his tenants the admission that
perhaps "'t wouldn't poison tha pigs."[1] But now it was making
progress, and by the late 'twenties potato eating for part of the
year was becoming general[2]. Also, in some places, the canals
and turnpikes had cheapened fuel. Yet the gain of the new
food to the labourer would not be great unless he had ground
on which to grow it.

Labourers as a class were short of land about their cottages,
but the majority, probably the great majority, in England in
1825–30 had either a garden, often it is true very small, or means
of getting a patch of potato ground[3]. There had been some loss
of garden opportunities in the previous forty or fifty years. It
is not safe to assume that all cottages in the eighteenth century had a fair patch of ground attached[4]; so the absence of
gardens, when found in the nineteenth, does not necessarily
prove a recent deprivation. But a certain amount of recent
deprivation is demonstrable. When farms were thrown together, the deserted houses might be cut up into labourers'
tenements and their gardens absorbed by the engrossing
farmer[5]. Then the owner might pull down the old cottages,
for, as a Surrey witness said in 1824, "the farmers have been
very anxious to get the gardens to throw into their fields."[6] If
the cottages were in the farmers' hands, the same witness
asserted, "they always prohibit...a pig and claim the produce
of the apple trees and of the vine which usually covers the
house." Whether this was an innovation or not is not stated:
probably it was. Of another of the home counties, Hertfordshire, the general statement is made that good vegetable gardens
were uncommon in 1818[7]: how far this was a new state of things
we are again not told. In Thanet Cobbett saw cottages with
not enough ground for a pig to lie down upon, as he put it[8].

[1] Stirling, A. M. W., *Coke of Norfolk* (1908), I. 281.
[2] *E.g.* in Bedfordshire, *S. C. on Labourers' Wages*, 1824 (VI. 401), p. 54: in
Hereford, *S. C. on Agriculture*, 1833, Q. 85.
[3] Hammond, J. L. and B., *op. cit.* p. 241, say, without qualification, when
summarising the events of the period 1760–1832, "they [the English labourers]
had lost their gardens." The evidence given is one extract from a Kentish
newspaper: p. 175, n. 1.
[4] Above, p. 115, n. 2.
[5] Cases in Hasbach, *op. cit.* p. 129 n.
[6] *S. C. on Labourers' Wages*: evidence of Hy. Drummond, J.P.
[7] *Lords' Comm. on Poor Laws* (1818, v), Q. 121.
[8] *Rural Rides*, I. 322.

Yet this same Cobbett, when delivering his soul against the Scots[1], boasts of the "neatly kept and productive little gardens round the labourers' houses" "of Kent, Sussex, Surrey and Hampshire, and, indeed in almost every part of England," which "distinguish it from all the rest of the world." Boys, the reporter to the Board of Agriculture in 1796, said that Kentish labourers often had large gardens and in many cases kept cows[2]. Marshall's review of the situation for the whole Eastern Department of England (1811) suggests that, in his opinion, it was about an even chance whether a cottage had or had not "a small garden."[3] On the line from Ipswich to Bury St Edmunds Cobbett found the cottage gardens, in March 1830, all "dug up and prepared for cropping." But of the Fens he complained that "where every inch of land was valuable, not one inch was the labourer permitted to enjoy."[4] In the South-West, from Dorset to Cornwall, gardens were the rule[5]; in Somerset they were at least common, and most labourers were said to keep a cider barrel and a pig[6]. In the Stroud valley Cobbett saw "a pig in almost every cottage stye."[7] In Hereford in 1830 "all careful men had a good fat pig"; so they had on the Gloucester-Worcester boundaries[8]. About Ludlow half-acre gardens were said to be general[9]. It should be added, however, that Marshall, in his General Report on the Western Department of 1810, had expressed the opinion that "a greater proportion of labourers fed a pig formerly than at present."[10]

Cottage gardens were general in Northumberland[11], though not on the factory farms, and at least in the better-to-do districts of Yorkshire[12]. In the North Riding, however, they were said to have been rare in 1800[13]. They were general, especially on the estates of large proprietors, in Derbyshire and Stafford-

---

[1] *Rural Rides*, I. 107: "Shut your mouths, you Scotch Economists; cease bawling, Mr Brougham...."
[2] Quoted in Hasbach, p. 147.
[3] *Ibid.* p. 130 n.   [4] II. 298, 314.
[5] *Lords' Comm. on Poor Laws*, 1818, Q. 129.
[6] *S. C. on Agriculture*, 1833, Q. 4774.
[7] II. 142: a manufacturing district, however.
[8] *S. C. on Agriculture*, 1833, Q. 8365, 10,522.
[9] *S. C. on Commons' Enclosure* (1844, v), Q. 2480: these gardens are not likely to have been created since 1830.
[10] Hasbach, p. 129 n.
[11] *J. R. Ag. Soc.* II. 185, quoting evidence from 1831.
[12] Evidence in Hasbach, p. 237.
[13] Tuke, *North Riding*, p. 41.

shire. Accounts from Nottingham suggest that the situation
there had been bad before 1830, and that only a few reforming
proprietors had adopted the "cottage-land" policy[1]. In
general, Cobbett's assertion "the more purely a corn country,
the more miserable the labourers"[2]—he had cottage land particularly in view—is borne out by nearly all other trustworthy
evidence. The worst accounts come from corn districts, and as
a rule from districts recently and scientifically enclosed, where
no scrap of land was "wasted."

The potato patch, coming rapidly into fashion in the South
during the years 1820–33, was often separate from the garden:
it might be an addition to it or, more likely, a substitute for it.
Generally it was in the fields and sometimes the farmer charged
an exorbitant rent for it: Cobbett found some outrageous, but
also some quite reasonable, rentals when riding through Wiltshire and Gloucestershire in 1826. "This fashion is certainly
a growing one," he notes with approval[3]. It was well known in
Somerset so early as 1818[4]. In Surrey it seems to have come
in only about 1830[5]. By 1833, at any rate, "a patch of land"
was common in Cambridge, even commoner in Norfolk and
Suffolk, though the pig—Cobbett's touchstone of labouring
comfort—was rare[6]. In Bedfordshire the potato patch had
begun "by the side of the road" before 1818, at the expense
of the King, one must suppose, not of the farmer: by 1824 the
potato was a general item in the Bedfordshire dietary, so presumably the patches were general also[7]. About Lewes potato
land became common early in the century[8]. These wide-
scattered illustrations show the ultimate success of the potato
propaganda.

The strain of high prices on a labouring class which had
become more than ever dependent on earnings was eased where
the ancient habit still survived of the unmarried labourer living
in with the farmer. In the North and North-West it was found

---

[1] *S. C. on Agriculture*, 1833, Q. 11,187; 12,258; 12,077.
[2] I. 321.
[3] II. 137, also 115. Mr and Mrs Hammond refer only once, incidentally, to
potato-ground (*op. cit.* p. 160) and only to quote the exorbitant rentals.
[4] *Lords' Comm. on Poor Laws*, as above, Q. 111.
[5] *S. C. on Agriculture*, Q. 10,249.
[6] *Ibid.* Q. 2134–5.
[7] *Lords' Comm. on Poor Laws*, 1818, Q. 76. *S.C. on Labourers' Wages*, 1824,
p. 54.
[8] *S. C. on Agriculture* (1821, IX), p. 53.

almost everywhere. "Men farming £400–600 a year would dine with their servants," in Cumberland. In the North Riding it was a regular practice. In Shropshire "house servants" were the rule[1]. But in the Midlands and the South-East it was decadent. There was still plenty of boarding in to be found in Kent in 1821, though not nearly so much as formerly[2]; and it may generally be assumed that old practices which survived in Kent survived, less or more, in most other counties. But the large farm, as it had developed during the wars, with its half-gentleman farmer, was unfavourable to the practice. The position of these big farmers of the South and East was summed up in the evidence given, in 1821, by one of them who came from Norfolk. He dated the decline from 1801, "when the high price of corn was." (You cease to feed your men when it is hardest for them to feed themselves.) After that it was discontinued owing to the flourishing state of agriculture during the wars: "people did not like the trouble of it: I believe that is the truth."[3]

Another advantage of some few at least of the North-country labourers was that they were allowed by their employer the feed of a cow. This allowance seems to have been general among the Northumbrian "hinds" and fairly common in parts of Yorkshire. And from Lincolnshire it was reported that "there was a practice in the marsh lands...between Louth and Grimsby...to give a carter so much and the keep of a cow."[4] The privilege was reserved for selected men, and existed only in selected areas.

The North-country labourer had the further advantage that his economic relations with his employer and the state had not been so generally deranged by the poor law administration as had those of his fellows in the South. But in innumerable rural areas, North as well as South, some poor law allowance in aid of wages had become part of the economic—or uneconomic—organisation of agriculture since 1795. With the allowance system was widely associated, south of Trent, the bread-scale—the guarantee by the parish of a weekly income

---

[1] *S. C. on Agriculture*, 1833, Q. 6647, 2499, 581.

[2] *S. C. on Agriculture*, 1821, p. 71.

[3] *Ibid.* p. 39. See below, p. 453; where it is shown that the decline in living-in has been exaggerated.

[4] *J. R. Ag. Soc.* II. 185, referring to 1831, for Northumberland: *S. C. on Agriculture*, 1833, Q. 74,961, for Lincolnshire: *Report on Women and Children in Agriculture* (1843, XII), p. 294, for Yorkshire.

to the labouring family varying with the price of bread and the family's size, a crude cost of living and standard of need index[1]. By the 'twenties, the system, born in a year of famine prices and matured during a succession of bad harvests and a national struggle for existence, was generally admitted to be vicious; attempts had been made locally to wipe it out; and careful inquiries into its extent and working had been undertaken. A questionnaire was circulated to poor law authorities by a parliamentary committee in 1824, of which the first three questions were:

(1) Are wages ever paid partly from the rates?
(2) Are allowances for children ever paid from the rates?
(3) Is such an allowance ever paid for the first child?

The very complex situation revealed was as follows[2].

An unqualified "No" to the first question, or an explanation that such relief was given only in cases of disablement or other exceptional need or that it was only given very rarely, came from every poor law area[3] in Northumberland, Cumberland and Durham; from 16 out of 17 areas in Lancashire; from 11 out of 12 in Cheshire; from 7 out of 8 in Stafford; from all in Derbyshire, Shropshire, Monmouth and Hereford; from nearly all in Worcester; from 12 out of 14 in Gloucester; from all in Somerset; from about half in Devon; and from nearly all in Cornwall. The West Riding said "No," without qualification; the East said "Yes," almost without qualification; and, surprisingly enough, the North Riding areas generally said "Yes," though often with qualification. In Lincoln 5 areas said "No"; 2 said "Yes." Wales gave an almost unvarying "No," except a few areas in Radnor, Glamorgan and Pembroke.

Most of these northern and western districts which answered "No" to Question (1) explained, in reply to Question (2), that sickness, misfortune, or large families were held to justify some help from the rates. The third question was rarely answered with precision, often not at all, from this group of counties,

---

[1] The formal bread-scale was not so general, even in the South, as is sometimes suggested; but the allowances made had food prices in view, e.g. no bread-scale in Bucks. before 1817, but prices were considered; none in Herts. or Beds. *Lords' Comm. on Poor Laws*, 1818, p. 94.

[2] From returns made to the *S. C. on Labourers' Wages* (1824, VI. 401) printed in 1825, XIX. 363. Historians have rather neglected these returns: neither Nicholls' *History of the Poor Law* nor Hammond's *Village Labourer*, for example, makes any use of them.

[3] The areas were generally hundreds or wapentakes and important towns.

which suggests that the exact proportioning of rate aid to numbers, generally connected with the Speenhamland policy, was not understood.

In Kent 7 areas out of 15 said "No" to Question (1); and in several of the remaining 8 it was explained that "some few parishes only" used the allowance system. Out of 10 Sussex areas, 4 said "No"; 4 said "Yes" with a qualification; 2 only "Yes" unqualified. Of 4 Surrey areas, 3 replied "No": of 17 Hampshire areas, 7 replied "No," 5 said the practice was rare, only 4 said "Yes" without reserve. In Dorset alone, of the counties south of the Thames, was the practice almost universal, though the Committee of 1824 got the impression that things were bad in Sussex[1]. But Dorset, Surrey, Sussex and most of Hampshire and Kent denied that extra relief was given with the first child. The Isle of Wight, however, sent in the significant note "no labourers are considered capable of maintaining three." North of the Thames the Middlesex and Hertford areas mostly replied "No" to the first question.

In Essex, 3 districts out of 10 said "No" to Question (1) and 6 others so modified their "Yes" as to make it clear that the county was not all given over to the system. Although more than half the Suffolk areas replied "No," the county, like Sussex, was unfavourably reported on by the committee. Norfolk was given over to allowances: 14 areas out of 17 said "Yes" and another would have said so a year earlier. The giving of extra relief for the first child was generally denied in East Anglia.

Counties with a record similar or inferior to that of Norfolk or Dorset were Bedford, Cambridge, Huntingdon, Northampton and Nottingham. Very little better were Berkshire, Buckingham, Leicester, Oxford and Wiltshire. The coincidence of the area in which wages were most systematically augmented from the rates with the area of maximum recent enclosure is striking[2].

Clearly all that was meant as a rule by the answer "No" to Question (1) was that the healthy unmarried man in regular work, or the married man with a small family, was not eligible for an allowance. The commissioners of 1834 found that North-country overseers might pride themselves on their freedom from "the abuses of the South," while giving allowances to

[1] *Report*, p. 5.   [2] See plate facing p. 20.

fathers of large families as a matter of course[1]. The 1824 returns leave room for, and even suggest, this policy. On the other hand, the 1834 commissioners drew no clear distinction between allowances to men in full work and allowances in respect of partial unemployment, condemning both with equal severity. Bread-scales ignored the question of cause entirely —a man was entitled to money enough to get x of bread, a man and wife $x + y$, and so on. Whether the money shortage which brought him to the overseer was due to two days' work lost or to a low standard full-time wage was immaterial. Consequently the system, though in some ways more scientific than the rough doles to men partly unemployed or to fathers of big families which often took its place, was more directly calculated than they to keep down the local standard wage. Perhaps some recognition of this, leading to a desire to make poor relief "deterrent," accounts for the fact that the bread-scales had often become less generous since the wars. Some scales of the period 1815–30 which have been examined show a serious fall in the minimum bread ration, the x and the y, as compared with the original scale issued by the Justices of Berkshire from the Pelican Inn at Speenhamland[2].

That the thoroughgoing adoption of the Speenhamland policy coupled with the working of poor law settlement tended to keep down the standard weekly money wage of agricultural labour there can be little doubt. For the dates 1794–5 and 1823–5[3] reasonably complete and trustworthy figures exist for most of England and—in less detail—for Wales. During the intervening war and post-war years, for which figures are much less complete, there had been considerable fluctuations. There was a rise, of varying amount according to the district, down to about 1812. A marked fall can be traced in some places, and inferred for most, between 1814 and 1821. Initiated by the great break in wheat prices of 1814, and encouraged by a

---

[1] *Report from H.M. Commissioners for inquiring into…the Poor Laws*, 1834 (octavo ed.), p. 26.

[2] Hammond, J. L. and B., *op. cit.* p. 184–5: Webb, S. and B., *The Old Poor Law* (1927), p. 183. An earlier case is in *V.C.H. Gloucester*, II. 169. The low rates of the 'twenties do not necessarily mean an unheard-of decline in the standard of life, as Mr and Mrs Hammond infer. (There was in fact a rise in the 'twenties: below, p. 127–8.) The Cambridge scale of 1821 was to be augmented "in all cases of sickness or…distress," also for "good behaviour" (*Report of 1834*, p. 21). It was disciplinary, brutally so it may well be.

[3] Also for 1832–3. For the statistical evidence see Bowley, A. L., *S. J.* 1898–9, and *Wages in the United Kingdom* (1900), p. 25 *sqq.*

redundant labour supply after the wars, the fall was completed by the more decisive price break of 1820–1 which may be taken as closing the age of war disturbances. Instances of the fall are the winter wage in the Isle of Ely which had dropped from something between 12s. and 15s. in 1813 to 9s. and 10s. in the 'twenties, or the winter wage in the Lothians, fallen still further, from 15s. and 18s. to "about 10s."[1] Farmers claimed, and price figures support the claim[2], that their men were at least as well off in 1821 as they had been in 1814—which however was not very well.

In agriculture the weekly money wage never tells the whole story, and what it fails to tell may grow more important as the stream of time is mounted. Extra earnings in hay and corn harvest there have always been; for these a quite satisfactory estimate for the age now under discussion can be constructed. If the pig and the cottage garden brought in less to the average British labourer in 1824 than in 1794—and it is on the whole likely that they did, though the matter is very uncertain—that must be considered. But very possibly the potato patch would, again on the average, balance the loss. Certainly, lost access to commons in those thirty years had worsened the lot of many men in many places, though it is doubtful whether, averaged over Britain, the loss in well-being due to the enclosures of commons would amount to very much. It has been exaggerated in popular retrospect; for it had little significance in many parts of England; still less in Wales; and in Scotland, for the pure labourer, none at all. The wage problem is complicated further by allowances in kind; by the difficulty of dealing with the food wage of the man living in and the change in the numbers of such men; and by the survival locally of other methods of remuneration in which the money wage tells nothing like the whole story. Extreme cases come from Wales and Scotland in the early nineteenth century, but approximations to them could be found in many parts of England, such as the payment in cow-feed of the Lincolnshire carter.

In South-West Wales, just before Waterloo, whole families worked for a farmer "at a fixed low rate per day without victuals."[3] But they might have hovels, gardens, and cow-feed at beneficial rates, potato strips, and bread corn at low fixed

---

[1] S. C. on Agriculture, 1821, p. 131, 323. [The Lothians of course were not a "Speenhamland" area, but the fall was found everywhere.]
[2] Below, p. 128.   [3] Davies, South Wales, II. 283–6.

prices all the year round. A very few years earlier the harvest
wage had taken the form of a "love reaping." The farmer
notified his day: all his dependents came: others came to pay
him with a day's work for a previous loan by him of a horse
for a day; and some came just for a share in the harvest meals,
for, as they said in the Middle Ages, those were wet boondays.

In spite of such curious survivals, estimates have been made
of the average earnings of English and Welsh agricultural
labourers for the two periods 1794–5 and 1823–5[1] into which
no risk of really serious error enters. To the abundant weekly
wage statistics for these dates a reasonably accurate estimate of
harvest and other miscellaneous earnings, and of the money
value of allowances in kind, can be added. For Scotland fewer
certain figures are available, and the situation in the 'twenties
is more conjectural. Sir John Sinclair was sure, in 1814, that
down to that date, Scottish wages had risen faster than the cost
of living[2]. Calculations based on the figures collected in the
Statistical Accounts of Scotland, which he inspired, show a rise
between 1794 and 1810 in the ratio of 35 to 55, so bearing him
out[3]. The wage fall in the Lothians, between 1814 and 1821, if
the rather vague figures quoted above can be relied on, coincided
very closely with the fall in the cost of living during those same
years. If this is at all typical, the Scottish labourer had at least
not lost ground.

A cost-of-living index, adjusted to the consumption habits
of the English labourer of this period, has recently been constructed[4]. Taking 1790 as base (100), a year in which the price
of wheat averaged 54s. 9d. a quarter and other prices were in
proportion, the Index for 1794 is 110 and for 1795, the blackest
year—as it then seemed—the year of Speenhamland, 130. The
highest point reached during the wars and bad harvests of the
next twenty years was 187, in 1813. For 1814 the Index falls
to 176 and for 1815 to 150. By 1824 it is at 113 and its average
for the whole decade 1821–31, thanks to cheap corn, is 111.
That is to say, leaving on one side such things as loss of access
to commons, leaving on the other side the new potato element
in the labourers' dietary[5], concentrating on earnings, and as-

[1] Also for 1832–3: the estimates are Professor Bowley's.

[2] *General Report*, III. 262.

[3] *S.J.* 1899.

[4] Silberling, N. J., *British Prices and Business Cycles*, 1779–1850 (*Supplement
to the Review of Economic Statistics*, Harvard, Mass., 1923), p. 234–5.

[5] Prof. Silberling could not take account of potatoes.

suming that employment on the land was not perceptibly more irregular in the 'twenties than it had been in the 'nineties—a fairly reasonable assumption—then the man whose earnings had not dropped below what his father was making in the year before Speenhamland, could buy with them just about as much as his father had bought, unless he was spending more on beer or on rent or on both. After 1830, when the beer duty was abolished, his beer certainly came cheaper than his father's beer: before that it was probably a trifle dearer. But the duty on small beer was always very low and the malt duty, after

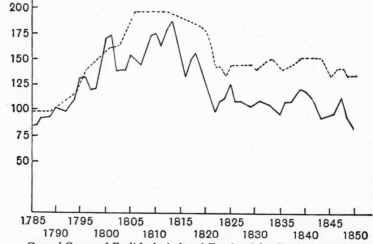

--------- *General Course of English Agricultural Earnings* (after Bowley). N.B. Information as to earnings is fairly ample for the periods 1780–94 and 1823 *sqq.*: the curve for the intervening period is less certain.

———— *Working-class cost of living Index* (after Silberling). For tables and notes, see Appendix.

1822, was only 1s. 2½d. a bushel above its pre-war level. Strong beer, taxed at 9s. a barrel in the 'twenties, was already paying 8s. in 1793[1]. There was no standard beer and there are no price statistics of any value; but no appreciable extra expenditure on this head was essential. For cottage rents also precise information is lacking; but the general movement between Arthur Young's day and 1850 was upward[2]. It is probable that, on the average, some extra earnings to cover this item would be required—perhaps 3d., certainly not more than 6d., a week.

[1] Buxton, S., *Finance and Politics* (1888), ii. 277–8.
[2] Caird, J., *English Agriculture in 1850 and 1851*, p. 474.

Now that rather vague figure the average English (with Welsh) labourer had improved his gross earnings—reckoned by adding an estimated percentage for harvest and other miscellaneous receipts to the recorded wages—by about £5 a year, say 1s. 11d. a week, between 1794 and 1824. But this average gain, enough to cover any possible rise in rents and in beer, with a small margin, was mainly due to the much more marked gain in counties north of Trent, where industry was offering alternative careers and the poor law was not so worked as to keep wages down. Miscellaneous earnings, the calculation assumes, moved with the wage, and in a number of counties the wage was definitely lower in 1824 than it had been in 1794. All these are counties of very well-developed Speenhamland systems. The fall in wages, expressed as a ratio, in the chief and best authenticated instances is as follows[1]:

	1794	1824		1794	1824
Sussex	86	81	Dorset	? 75–80	69
Huntingdon	62	58	Wiltshire	? 80–84	75
Suffolk	75	69	Hereford	? 70–73	64
Leicester	74	63			

Most other counties of Southern, Eastern, Central and South-Western England show either a very slight fall, a very slight rise, or a rise less than the national average. The chief well-authenticated exceptions are Middlesex, where the rise was much more than the national average, and Kent, where it about coincided with it. The explanation is obvious—London.

The West Midlands show a rise greater than the national average in Staffordshire and Warwickshire. Lincolnshire shows no appreciable movement. Northward from Derbyshire lies the area all of which, with the doubtful exception of Northumberland and the certain exception of the North Riding of Yorkshire, shows a rise greater than the national average.

Like those of the English North, Scottish wages had risen greatly in the thirty years, but their exact level during the 'twenties is, as has been seen, more uncertain. The rough estimate of "about 10s." put forward for the Lothians in the early 'twenties[2] would leave them in the same group—monetarily—as Lincolnshire, Cheshire, and the North Riding of Yorkshire. Between Scottish wages and the Scottish poor law there was no connection.

[1] Bowley, *S.J.* 1898, p. 702 *sqq.*
[2] Above, p. 126.

Whether the standard of comfort possible to the average English labouring family in the 'twenties, without any help from the overseers, was really higher than that possible thirty years earlier would depend, not only on the agricultural earnings of the head of the family, but on the total earnings of them all. Here enters the exceedingly difficult question of industrial by-employments, and in particular of spinning. The problem is not that of the earnings of the more or less professional woman spinner of the eighteenth century—there were plenty of these— but of the possible addition to family earnings by the work of the mother and, as they grew, of the girls in their spare time. The average pay for a day's spinning in 1787–8, based on returns from eighteen counties and from most of the textile trades, was as nearly as possible 6d. The figures were published by Young in his *Annals of Agriculture*[1]. How many full days' spinning could the mother of a young family in a cottage put in, before any of them could help her? When she could drive some of them to spin—this she did early—we hear of the augmenting of family incomes, in the regular manufacturing districts, by one or two shillings a week[2]. Widespread as the hand spinning of wool and flax for market still were in 1787–8, it can hardly be supposed that they were practised in every family in every county—or anything like it. For one thing, distaff spinning was going out and a wheel was not to be had for nothing. There must have been gaps in the business organisation for putting out the raw materials. When allowance is made further for the woman's constant pregnancies and confinements, her sickness, her household duties and so on, it would be most surprising if the average addition to family income, over a period of years, came to so much as 6d. a week.

The cutting off of even such a sum, just when the great rise in the cost of living took place (1795–1813), would be a disaster, and the condition of widows and others who had lived by spinning must have been deplorable; but with the fall in the cost of living after the wars came in other industrial by-employments[3], though it can hardly be supposed that these had effectively replaced spinning by 1824–30. Yet over the whole period 1794–1824 the loss to rural family earnings through the

---

[1] [From Pinchbeck, I., *Women Workers and the Industrial Revolution* (1930), p. 142.]

[2] Heaton, H., *The Yorkshire Woollen and Worsted Industries* (1920), p. 336.

[3] Below, p. 183. Agricultural by-employment (harvests etc.) had not changed much.

industrial revolution—still speaking in averages—cannot have been absolutely great; though even a loss of so little as 3d. a week, 13s. a year, to a family whose head made his £25 to £30 a year would be no light thing.

The conclusion of a difficult problem, which contains a number of doubtfully known quantities, is that whereas on the average the potential standard of comfort of an English (with Welsh) rural labouring family in 1824 was probably a trifle better than it had been in 1794, assuming equal regularity of work, there were important areas in which it was definitely worse, others in which it was probably worse, and many in which the change either way was imperceptible. In the bad areas the rates were drawn upon for the deficit[1].

The working of the poor law had not only tended to keep wages down and to perpetuate local inequalities by immobilising some of the population. After the wars the burden of rates, in certain areas and on certain shoulders, became intolerable. There is no need to treat as representative those extreme cases, often quoted in contemporary controversy, in which the rates equalled or exceeded the annual value of the land; but it is certain that everywhere the burden hung heavy about the neck of the small holder or proprietor. A rate of 10s. on the acre, such as that quoted from Great Shelford, Cambridgeshire, in 1834[2], might well be enough to push a small man with no financial reserves over the edge of bankruptcy, in one of the bad post-war years. So the system helped to depress the "yeomanry." It worked even more disastrously on the cot-tager-proprietor and the "scrap-holder." The fact that he, a labourer, had to pay rates to enable other labourers to be employed at an uneconomic wage was only part of the evil. In the thoroughly pauperised areas, farmers did not care to employ such men, because no one with property was eligible for parish relief and the standard wage was so low that, without relief of some sort, it was insufficient for a married man. How numerous such cases were is not known. The principle was tragically illustrated by one put in evidence in 1824[3]. A respectable land-owning cottager, known to be a good worker, could get no work for the reason given. His property excluded

---

[1] For the cost of Poor Relief in the various areas see below, p. 364.
[2] *Poor Law Report*, p. 54–5.
[3] *S. C. on Labourers' Wages*, p. 43.

him from the "poors' books." "We must therefore wait until we are ruined," said he. An enclosure was not needed to force this man's cottage or scrap of land on to the market; the law for the relief of the poor did that for him. So the system promoted that transfer of property from the small man to the greater which, exaggerated though it has been, was beyond doubt a feature of the age between the Speenhamland meeting and the Reform Bill.

In 1825 there was still some open-field and run-rig in Britain to be enclosed and much fen, wold, fell, moor and common to be improved and cultivated before the face of the land became wholly modern. But true open-field agriculture, with its routine compulsory on all holders in the village fields, was by this time rare. It had long been breaking down, quite apart from enclosure. "Whoever apprehends," wrote Thomas Stone in his report on Lincolnshire of 1794, "that the occupiers of a common field are necessarily tied down to any precise mode of management, by the custom of any parish, are grossly mistaken."[1] They were supposed to fallow by rule—though sometimes the rule was broken—but for the rest they did as they pleased. In the famous open-fields of Axholm, which still survive, cropping was entirely individualistic in 1794: fallow was extinct. Stone, who knew many counties, thought that the old three-course rotation of fallow, wheat and barley, oats and beans—in itself a slight improvement on the early medieval routine—was more strictly followed in the South Cambridgeshire open-fields than anywhere else[2]. He might have added Huntingdon. There were still in his day, and in Lincolnshire, two-course parishes where half the land lay idle each year; but there were no strict rules regulating the cropped half[3]. Generally speaking, districts which in the remote past had used a two-course rotation had improved it into a four-course, by a simple division of each field, before—often long before—the final act of enclosure[4]. During the thirty years which followed Stone's Lincolnshire report, most of the backward open-field belt in Cambridge and Huntingdon was enclosed, and the last continuous stretch of open three-field agriculture was broken up[5].

---

[1] P. 35.   [2] P. 53.
[3] Eden, *State of the Poor*, II. 394 (Louth).
[4] Gray, *English Field Systems*, esp. ch. IV.   [5] Above, p. 21.

The scattered open-field parishes which remained seem usually to have kept the fallowing rules, if no others, tolerably intact. So late as 1844 the cultivation of midland common fields was described as "universally two crops and a fallow."[1] The three-course rotation often survived the fields. Occasionally landlords had inserted it in covenants for the letting of newly enclosed ground. Or it might be that farmers, discouraged by what seemed to them the impossibly low prices of the 'twenties, fell back from inertia on the old system—or a worse. They got some support from a change in expert opinion. The eighteenth-century assailants of open-field agriculture, led by Arthur Young, in their anxiety to get rid of wasteful bare fallows, had attacked all fallowing so viciously as to produce a reaction. There was an anti-fallowing mania at its height about 1800, so men were saying twenty-five years later: it had "now spent its force."[2] So early as 1814 Sinclair was quoting with approval the dictum—"a complete over-years naked fallow forms, on all clay soils, the indispensable basis of all good husbandry."[3] Experts did not say that you must fallow one year in three on heavy clay; but that was the obvious thing for a discouraged clay-soil farmer to do. The much advertised "turnip husbandry" and the four-course rotations—turnips, wheat or barley, clover and rye-grass, oats; or some variant—might be all very well in Norfolk; but things were different in Bedfordshire. Even the two-course rotation survived 1830: a witness before the Select Committee on Agriculture of 1833 described, but did not locate, an estate which was tilled "partly crop and fallow and partly in the four-course shift."[4] Probably it was a light soil and the "crop and fallow" section the lightest and thinnest on the estate.

Between 1826 and 1832 farmers on clay soils were unusually gloomy. The inquiries made in 1833 help to explain their gloom and to illustrate the level of technique attained in the late 'twenties. Gloom had not first settled down in 1826. Ever since the break in prices of 1820–1 it had lain almost continuously over farmers and landowners. During twenty-one years up to October 1820, the average price of wheat in Norfolk had been 84s. 8d. a quarter: in June 1821 it was 53s. 5d.[5] During

---

[1] *S. C. on Commons' Inclosure*, Q. 3358.
[2] Loudon's *Encyclopædia of Agriculture*, p. 801.
[3] *General Report*, 1. 418.　　　　　　　　　　　　　　　[4] Q. 1514.
[5] *S. C. on Agriculture*, 1821, p. 26.

and since the wars corn-growing had been greatly extended in Ireland. While fighting continued, the military demand and the partial feeding of Spain and Portugal from the British Isles had drawn off surplus stocks, and helped to keep prices up[1]. Bad harvests between 1815 and 1818 had done the same. Then came excellent Irish harvests in 1819 and 1820, followed by the price break. In 1822 wheat touched 40s. and, though it was never so low again until 1835, the age of war and post-war prices was definitely over. In 1826 there was a bad drought; 1828 and 1829 were wet and ungenial; yet wheat prices never came within 9s. even of the old average. From 1830 to 1835 harvests were above normal, but the low grain prices which resulted were not likely to diminish the farmers' laments.

The weather conditions just before 1830 had not been favourable to the clays; and the clays were, generally speaking, both late enclosed and, largely, in consequence of this, very ill drained. Under-drainage had, of course, never been practised in the open-fields: they were thrown up into ridge-and-furrow and the water got away as best it could down the furrow, or stood there to ruin the crops in wet years. In a few enclosed counties, on the other hand, under-drainage was old established. Wedge-shaped drains, filled at the bottom with loose stones or brushwood, and covered over with earth were a regular "Essex practice" at the beginning of the eighteenth century. Many such drains were cut parallel in each field dealt with. The practice had spread to two or three adjacent counties; but it was quite unknown in most districts in 1830. Moreover, such drains were not very durable and, being shallow, were supposed to be not well suited for the drainage of arable land unless laid, as they sometimes were, in the furrows, between the great ridges where the plough seldom went[2].

Considerable progress had been made between 1760 and 1820 in the art of dealing with extreme cases of water-logged soil. The pioneer was Joseph Elkington, a farmer of Stretton-upon-Dunsmore, in Warwickshire. He had great skill in tracing underground springs, ascertaining the point at which the water was forced to the surface by coming up against some impervious stratum, deciding where best to cut it off, and how to lead the drains. His methods involved deep trenches—four and five feet—and much expenditure. The Scots, with their abundance

---

[1] S. C. on Agriculture, 1821, p. 207.
[2] Prothero, op. cit. p. 192–3, and below, p. 458.

of "spring bogs," were greatly interested in his methods and those of his imitators, as Sir John Sinclair's elaborate account of them in 1814 shows[1]. They had already met with considerable success before that date. But they were neither of universal application nor universally appreciated; and it was not until James Smith, of Deanston, in Perthshire, between 1823 and 1833, had shown how shallow drainage could be utilised for arable land that the movement became, so to speak, fashionable[2].

Fen drainage, on the other hand, had just entered on its final phase—that of efficient steam pumping[3]. Among the generally gloomy accounts of 1833, the evidence that the Cambridgeshire fens had never been so full of improvement stands out conspicuous. Norfolk, with its turnip and barley soils, also remained cheerful. It was "in as good a state now as ever I knew it," said a witness, while Suffolk and the shire of Cambridge, which also had a fair amount of light soil, were not much worse[4].

The highly farmed Lothians were holding their own fairly, except where, as in East Lothian, there had been too much concentration on wheat and neglect of stock, or on the inferior soils "where cultivation had been carried too far during the high prices of the war."[5] On these soils farmers were reverting to a system which recalled that of the old Scottish outfield agriculture. They let the land lie for several years in grass—but in sown not in natural grass, as under the old system—after a rotation of corn, turnips, and barley. In spite of such expedients emphasis was laid on the fact that many *prudent* farmers had been ruined[6]. Beyond the Forth, in the lowlands of Clackmannan and Fife from Alloa right round to the Tay, farmers had been helped greatly, ever since the price break of 1821, by the development of potato growing and export for the London market and by an intelligent use of new fertilisers—bone manure and rape dust. Farther north again, the new practice of sending fat beasts, sheep, and pigs to London by sea—by steamer that is—had been the chief alleviating circumstance[7].

The north-western side of England had not suffered, because wheat was seldom the staple crop and because the new towns, low as was the purchasing capacity of their people,

---

[1] *General Report*, II. 464 *sqq*. Elkington began his work in, or about, 1764.
[2] Below, p. 458.　　　　　　　　　　　　[3] Below, p. 445.
[4] *S. C. on Agriculture*, 1833, Q. 2101 (the Fens), 2033 (Norfolk), 2034 *sqq*. (Suffolk and Cambs.).
[5] Q. 2582. See also Q. 11,395.
[6] Q. 11,406, 11,525.　　　　　　　　　　[7] Q. 2859.

supplied fast-growing markets. In Cumberland some recently enclosed commons had slipped back across Ricardo's margin; but the man who spoke for the county in 1833 boasted that whereas it imported corn down to 1807 it had since become an exporter[1]. In the fells, away down to the Ribble, farmers were doing well with stock[2]. South Lancashire, a great potato-growing county, complained that it had grown potatoes until they no longer paid[3]; but such complaints are common form. It complained also of competition from Ireland. The new and regular steamboat connection had led to "immense importations of Irish produce," including no doubt potatoes, but above all, butter. "A very efficient man" was "much engaged" in this Manchester-Irish butter business[4]. Cheshire also had been hurt by Ireland, but it admitted to a fairly uniform, if slow, progress, interrupted only on the clays[5]. Much of it was under grass, and it shared with South Lancashire the urban milk trade, into which the Irish had not been able to cut. South Lancashire, when pressed, admitted that butter farms were rare and milk farms common[6].

Shropshire was most enthusiastically reported on[7]. Its agriculture, greatly improved in the last twenty years, had shown no falling off since 1821. No land had gone out of cultivation. Sheep-rot had hit the Clun Forest yeomen, but they remained upstanding. Rational crop rotations were more and more replacing the vicious old practice of repeated white cropping. Across the Welsh border Montgomery, Denbigh and Flint went with Shropshire and Cheshire. The more remote Welsh counties and districts—Carnarvon, Merioneth, Cardigan— were seldom referred to in the inquiries from 1821 to 1833. They were self-sufficient; barley bread, leek broth, cheese, pork, potatoes, cabbage and herrings were their food[8]; and the vicissitudes of wheat farming did not affect their slow emergence from very primitive agrarian conditions. Barley bread, it may be added, was a staple food throughout the North-West, in Cumberland, for instance, and in Cheshire, as well as in Wales. It had only recently gone out of use in Cornwall[9]. With it, in the North-West, often went oat-cake and the ancient *muncorn bread* of mixed wheat and rye[10].

---

[1] Q. 6588 *sqq.*   [2] Q. 3641.   [3] Q. 3750.
[4] Q. 3569 *sqq.*   [5] Q. 5779 *sqq.*   [6] Q. 3745.
[7] Q. 356 *sqq.*   [8] Q. 175.   [9] Q. 3431.
[10] Q. 6647, 5805–6. Also Loudon, *op. cit.* p. 825.

From Hereford, Worcester and Gloucester come the standard complaints of retrogression since the fall in corn prices, showing that we are back in an area where wheat growing for market predominated[1]. Retrogression was most marked on "common land which had not been enclosed many years, and thin clay soils"—marginal lands. It had just paid to drag these commons under cultivation during the wars: they had remained common until then because of their very barrenness: with wheat at 40s. to 60s., instead of 80s. and upwards, they were tumbling down again to grass and thorns.

Tumbling down to grass was not peculiar to ex-commons. One of the most experienced land agents and surveyors who gave evidence in 1833—an elderly and rather pessimistic Scotsman[2]—said that he had met with it in many counties and oftenest on old enclosed land "run out by cropping," that is, by neglect of proper rotation and fertilising. His evidence is a reminder that unscientific agriculture in the eighteenth and early nineteenth centuries had not been confined to unenclosed country. There were technical abuses in the old enclosed areas comparable with those familiar abuses of the open-fields which Arthur Young and his generation had denounced. Young had been so accustomed to associate enclosure with progress that he had been shocked when in France, much of which was old enclosed, to find that the association was not universally true[3]. His surprise is curious, because the association was not true in Wales nor yet in many another old enclosed district or patch of Britain. Witness the repeated white crops of Shropshire and Lancashire —"oats, oats, oats...for years together"[4]—the everlasting barley of Wales with intervals of grass[5], or the never varied oats of the old Scottish infield, which had given point to Sinclair's appeal for an occasional fallow. The facts are in no way surprising. The improved rotations of the eighteenth century had been purely empirical and had generally been introduced on newly enclosed land by pressure from above. No one really knew why corn and green crops should rotate. Some men of science supposed that vegetation was nourished by water only, and Jethro Tull, the best agriculturist of the age, had imagined

---

[1] Q. 1634 *sqq.*, 8292 *sqq.*   [2] Adam Murray, Q. 125 *sqq.*
[3] *Tour in France* (ed. 1794), I. 398.
[4] Holt, *Lancashire* (1794), p. 26.
[5] Davies describes a "democratic rotation" in South Wales as three or four successive corn crops and then as many years grass as you have had corn. I. 306.

that if the land were meticulously tilled according to his prescriptions it would carry the same crop for ever. Nor was he
entirely wrong, but his method was not fitted for the average
cultivator, least of all for the small farmer in old enclosed
country, bound by no village rules, who did what his father
had done before him. It was very possible that his father's
tradition would be inferior to that ancient tradition which had
crystallised into the improved triple rotation, as practised time
out of mind in the Cambridgeshire open-fields.

On newly enclosed land also, release from village routine
—which, as has been seen, had often preceded enclosure—
might be either used or abused. Greedy shortsighted farmers
under negligent landlords could very easily "run their land out
by cropping." Very few had yet tried, or even heard of, the
new fertilisers. Farmyard muck itself was not properly appreciated. Since 1821 little drainage had been done anywhere
except by the very best landlords, such as the Duke of Bedford[1].
The result of a combination of these circumstances is well seen
in a report on the arable districts of South Wales—which, for
the most part, were fairly old enclosed but contained some recent
enclosures. There had been no progress, it was said, since the
wars: yields were declining: weeds were flourishing: life leases
and sub-letting were common and, as a natural result of this
lack of control, "few farmers followed any regular rotation."[2]

Similar, though less comprehensive, accounts of decadence
came from heavy land all over the country. The farmers' losses
of profits and the landlords' losses of rents since 1821 had
checked drainage and the use of artificial manures, even where
the value of both was well understood; and poor rates had
seldom been heavier. Farmers with capital were seeking the
lighter and drier soils, where they could keep stock more easily
than on the undrained or imperfectly drained clays[3]. It was
said that even open drainage was neglected: the ditches were
not so well scoured as they used to be[4]. Where clays were
heaviest and most uninterrupted—as in southern Essex, the
Weald of Kent and Sussex, and many parts of the East Midlands—there complaints were loudest and stagnation or retrogression, after the furious activity of the last enclosure age,
most widespread. Stagnation meant a rather longer life for the

---

[1] *S. C. on Agriculture*, 1833, Q. 215.
[2] *Ibid*. Adam Murray, Q. 125 *sqq.*
[3] Q. 1046.   [4] Q. 1077 *sqq.*

surviving scraps of common, thinly scattered over a country which, for the moment, was satiated with enclosure.

In August 1830 began rick-burnings, demonstrations and risings among the Kentish labourers, which spread first to Surrey and Sussex, later so far to the west as Dorset and Gloucester and northward to Norfolk and Northampton[1]. "Captain Swing" was out and his threatening letters were issued in many counties where there was no open demonstration and no arson. The men's grievances were many and almost all legitimate—grievances against the poor law, the game laws, tithe, enclosures, wage rates, machinery; with a background of unemployment and dear bread, during the wet ungenial years 1828-9, against which had flared up the Paris Revolution of July. A promise of 2s. a day certain, wet or dry, often sent them away content. But they did not often omit to break the threshing machines. No explanation of their action is needed beyond one quotation from the letter of a Kentish landowner —"an industrious man who has a barn [in which he could thresh in winter] never requires poor relief; he can earn from 15s. to 20s. per week."[2] The threshing machine was the newly arrived forerunner of the machine age in agriculture. There is no wonder that it went the way of other machines which take bread out of honest men's mouths. A mob of machine breakers had been the recognised eighteenth-century counter to untimely invention.

Down to 1800 the threshing machine, which after many failures had been made a success by Andrew Meikle, the millwright of Dunbar, between 1780 and 1790, had been little known south of the Mersey. Dear labour had brought it into Lancashire before 1794[3]. There were two experimental machines reported from North Wales in 1798: by 1813 they were "too common to be enumerated" there[4]. But they spread slowly into the corn counties of the Midlands and the South-East, where the risings of 1830 were most serious and where the parochial concentrations of population under the old poor law made machinery most deadly to the labourers. In 1824 it was reported from Huntingdon that the use of threshing machines was going back, the alleged reason being the burden of poor

---

[1] See the moving account in Mr and Mrs Hammond's *Village Labourer*, ch. XI
[2] *Ibid.* p. 245.
[3] Holt, *Lancashire*, p. 45: it was hand- or water-driven.
[4] Davies, *North Wales*, p. 122.

rates[1]. During the next few years the portable, horse-worked, type was said to be "very common in Suffolk": sometimes, so it is said, a labourer saved up and bought one—they were not very elaborate—and moved about with it quite in the modern way, the farmer supplying hand or horse power to work it[2]. But such fortunate and undertaking labourers must have been rare. The use of threshing machinery in 1825–30 was "common in every part of Scotland" and "every year spreading. . .in England and Ireland"; but the flail, not extinct anywhere, was if anything commoner in the South of England than the threshing machine had become in arable Scotland[3]. In other words, the risings of 1830 occurred just when the battle of machine *versus* arms was well joined. They succeeded not only in smashing much machinery but in delaying its march. Some magistrates advised farmers not to replace the broken threshers. Some farmers no doubt were discouraged. Twelve years later an agricultural reformer spoke of the "miserable machines"— he meant miserable in design—which even then were only "creeping into use in the South of England."[4]

The only other important labour-saving machine which had in any sense established itself before 1830 was the horse hay-tedder, for tossing hay, invented by Salmon of Woburn about the year 1800. By 1825–30 it was "coming into very general use," especially "in the neighbourhood of London where meadow hay is so extensively made."[5] Apparently no exception was taken to its introduction, although perhaps it was sometimes included, and smashed, with other machinery by Captain Swing. The reaper was still in the future: it is "yet a desideratum" Loudon wrote in 1831[6]. For some time experiments had been going on. Henry Ogle, a Northumbrian schoolmaster, invented a reaper *which worked* in 1822; but no farmer could be found who would go to the expense of trying it. In 1828–9 experiments were made in Forfar, Perth and Fife with a heavy machine, invented by Bell, which was pushed by horses har-

---

[1] *S. C. on Labourers' Wages*, 1824, p. 31.

[2] Loudon, *op. cit.* (1831), p. 439. And see below, p. 461–2. In the Meikle type of machine the corn was pushed by hand under beating arms worked by simple machinery.

[3] *Ibid.* p. 435, 519.

[4] Greg, R. H., *Scotch Farming in the Lothians* (1842), p. 6. Poulett Scrope, G., *A second letter to the Magistrates of the South of England* (1831), p. 6. And see below, p. 461.

[5] Loudon, *op. cit.* p. 421.   [6] *Ibid.* p. 421.

nessed behind: Gladstone's bean-reaper, which was little more than a knife attached to a sort of plough frame, had "been used in several parts of Scotland with complete success"; but this was all mere experiment, and not very hopeful experiment[1].

Most other agricultural novelties were rather improved implements than machines and few, if any, displaced labour directly. The horse-drill, for sowing corn and other seed, required a good deal of attention and implied a high style of farming and a carefully prepared seed-bed. Horse-hoeing of root crops and beans, which implied drilling or some equivalent process of sowing in rows[2], had been coming in very slowly since Tull's day, and, like drilling, it was intended rather to increase the crop than to diminish the labour bill. Neither method was by any means general in the 'twenties, and Cobbett was always grumbling that "men were not to be convinced of the advantage of the row culture for turnips"[3]; they preferred to sow turnip seed as well as corn broadcast. Cultivators and grubbers, introduced to lessen the number of ploughings on fallow, led to economy in horse power rather than in man power[4]. The improvements in ploughs, harrows, waggons and other essential implements, which had been going on for three-quarters of a century and more, had just culminated in the all-iron plough and the all-iron harrow[5]. Shares, coulters, and harrow-tynes had long been made of metal; though far down the nineteenth century the wooden-tyned harrow, and all kinds of compromises of metal and wood in the plough, held their own in certain districts or for particular purposes. Before 1830 the all-iron plough had been tried rather widely in the Lowlands and a little in the North of England. There was even a "somewhat noted maker" of iron ploughs at Alnwick[6].

That was the country in which Cobbett first met, and, as his style of type indicated, grasped the significance of, "thrashing machines...turned by STEAM ENGINES."[7] Men, donkeys, horses, occasionally water or wind, turned the threshing machines south of the Tyne; but with Northumberland began the factory farm whose engine could be harnessed to a chaff

---

[1] Loudon, *op. cit.* p. 427.
[2] It might be only dibbling in by hand.
[3] *Rural Rides*, I. 274.
[4] For these in the 'twenties see *i.a.* Loudon, *op. cit.* p. 528.
[5] Lardner's *Cabinet Cyclopædia*, "Manufactures in Metal" (1831), I. 156.
[6] *Ibid.* I. 156.
[7] *Tour in Scotland*, p. 85; and above. p. 30.

or turnip cutter as easily as to a threshing machine. The type
was significant but it was not destined to extend much in
Great Britain. Even a hundred years after Cobbett the farms
using their own power—steam or another—in this way were
still few. The actual line of development was discerned at the
time, though not quite accurately, by one of those Scottish
agricultural experts of whom Cobbett could never speak without
explosion. After describing the enterprising Suffolk labourers
who moved about with their threshing machines, John Loudon
added, in 1831, "reaping machines and steam ploughing
machines will probably in a few years be owned and let out
for hire in a similar manner."[1] Twelve years later he had to
admit that even an efficient reaper had not yet arrived; but he
had the good sense not to delete his forecast[2].

[1] *Op. cit.* p. 439.
[2] *Supplement* to his *Encyclopædia* (1843), p. 1319.

CHAPTER V

INDUSTRIAL ORGANISATION

BECAUSE no single British industry had passed through a complete technical revolution before 1830, the country abounded in ancient types of industrial organisation and in transitional types of every variety. Even in cotton spinning the early wooden machinery with metal fittings was in common use; the "self-acting" mule, built of metal, was but newly invented and only used in the more progressive mills[1]. There were still plenty of wooden spinning jennies, turned by hand, in the Lancashire mills in 1824, though the drawing process, preparatory to spinning, was always done by power[2]. But nine years later "those that are now jenny-spinners are getting, I think, into the decline of life," so quickly was the industry moving[3]. Weaving by the new method was just entering on the stage of rapid development, after twenty years of experiment and hostility. The first Manchester steam-loom factory had been set up in 1806. Guest's estimate for 1818 was that fourteen such factories existed in Manchester, Salford, Middleton, Hyde, Stayley Bridge and elsewhere: he thought they contained about 2000 looms. Writing in 1823 he reckoned that "at present not less than 10,000" power looms were at work in Great Britain. They made chiefly common print cloth and shirtings, but were rapidly conquering new lines of work. He supposed that there were 360,000 cotton weavers in the country, but probably his guess was high[4]. An estimate made in 1830 put the figures for England and Scotland at 55,000–60,000 power looms and 240,000 hand looms[5]. Baines, writing in 1835, did not anticipate the rapid disappearance of the older instrument, and his anticipation proved right[6].

The wool industries, because of their antiquity, their long

[1] "In all manufacturing establishments....the machinery...is, in the greatest part, of wood." Sinclair, *Analysis of the Statistical Account of Scotland* (1825), II. 200. A progressive Glasgow firm is bringing in the "self-actor" in 1833. *S. C. on Manufactures, Commerce and Shipping* (1833, VI), Q. 5398. The firm of Fairbairn and Lillie (see below, p. 154) is substituting "slender rods of wrought iron" for "ponderous masses of timber and cast iron" between 1820 and 1830. Fairbairn in Smiles' *Industrial Biography*, p. 325.

[2] *S. C. on Artisans and Machinery* (1824, V), p. 413: Stockport.

[3] *S. C. of 1833*, Q. 10,684: also Stockport.

[4] Guest, R., *A compendious history of the cotton manufacture*...1823, p. 46–8.

[5] *S. C. on Manufacturers' Employment*, 1830 (X. 221), p. 3.

[6] *History of the Cotton Manufacture*, p. 237.

regulation by the state—which cotton had entirely escaped—their wide distribution, and the extreme diversity of their products, had as yet been very incompletely transformed. Even the flying-shuttle was not in "very general use" in the West Riding until round about 1800. Carpet weavers still threw the shuttle across the loom by hand in the old ancient way, down to 1840 and later[1]. The worsted, that is to say, the combed wool, yarn was now almost entirely mill spun on the frame, though even the distaff was not quite extinct in England in 1820; but the essential preliminary process of combing was a handicraft in spite of various experiments in machine combing[2]. There was an analogous gap in the process of woollen spinning. Here the preliminary business of carding had been among the first to be taken over by power in the chief manufacturing areas, carding "engines"—cylinders set with wire teeth and revolving against one another to open out the wool—being often installed in the old water-driven fulling mills. But, in between carding and spinning there came, in 1835, when Ure published his *Philosophy of Manufacture*, what he called a "handicraft operation," that of "slubbing" or preparing the rough rope of wool, which was to be spun on the mule, on a wooden, hand-worked, machine called a "billy." "The slubbers," Ure writes, "though inmates of factories, are not, properly speaking, factory workers, being independent of the moving power." He noted that a patent had just been announced in December 1834, by which a second carding engine could prepare and deliver, by the process now known as condensing, the loose rope for the mule. The general adoption of this critical invention only took place in the second half of the century[3].

In a backward district such as Gloucestershire, even the mule only began to come into use about 1828, the hand-worked "billy" leading to the spinning "jenny," also worked by hand; though carding and some other processes were done by power[4]

[1] *Hand Loom Weavers. Assistant Commissioners' Reports*, III. (1840), 586 n. Nine-tenths of the worsted weavers are said to have used the flying-shuttle in 1803.

[2] For the distaff Rees' *Cyclopædia*, 1819, *s.v.* "Worsted": for combing, Burnley, J., *Hist. of Wool and Woolcombing* (1889), p. 144.

[3] Ure, p. 8. For the origin of the billy, originally used to prepare rovings of carded cotton for the mule, see Daniels, G. W., *The Early English Cotton Industry* (1920), p. 123.

[4] *Hand Loom Weavers. Assistant Commissioners' Reports*, v. 370. Hammond, Mr and Mrs, *The Skilled Labourer* (1919), p. 148, speak of water power being applied to "the jennies and the other machinery" *circa* 1800. This is very

Of the weaving of wool and other textiles, it need only be said here that power was first tried experimentally, with the usual result—a riot, for the relatively light fabrics of the worsted industry in the early 'twenties, and that power weaving remained experimental down to 1830. For the heavier woollen broad-cloths, pilot-cloths, uniform-cloths, blankets and the like, the power-loom had not yet been tried. Nor had it, as may be supposed, in carpet-weaving, and only tentatively in the roughest linen-weaving and for some kinds of silks. A Committee reporting in 1830 discussed, as a speculative question, what might happen "should it ever be found practicable to make use of it extensively in the fabric of woollens or silks."[1] Next year Lardner expressed himself as "very doubtful whether" its use was "susceptible of much extension in any save the commonest branches of the silk manufacture."[2]

For flax-spinning, machinery had been invented in 1787 by John Kendrew, an optician, and Thomas Porthouse (or Porteus), a clock-maker, both of Darlington. Much improved a few years later for John Marshall of Leeds, it had made that town the centre of British flax-spinning and of the making of the necessary machinery. From Leeds, where steam was used from the first, machinery spread to Aberdeen, Dundee, and other Scottish linen towns. But down to about 1820 machinery was only used for the spinning of flax properly so-called, not for the shorter by-product, tow, for which the early machines were unsuited. Nor did the mills spin nearly enough flax yarn to meet all demands. There was still plenty of spinsters' yarn on the markets of Great Britain, and not much else on those of Ireland[3]. In

doubtful for jennies. Professor Daniels of Manchester informs me that he has found no case of power being applied to the jenny for cotton. [There are "no authenticated cases" in the American wool industry. Cole, A. H., *The American Wool Manufacture* (1926), I. 112.] The machinery referred to in the Report of the *S. C. on Clothiers' Petitions* (1803, v) was not spinning machinery, as Mr and Mrs Hammond seem to assume, but "gig-mills" for finishing. There were spinning mills in the West at that time, no doubt with power-driven carding engines and hand-worked billies and jennies.

[1] *S. C. on Manufacturers' Employment*, p. 3.
[2] Lardner, *Silk Manufacture* (1831), p. 275. See below, p. 196.
[3] Machine spinning in Ireland began about 1805–10; but only very coarse yarns were produced. There was considerable progress after 1820, but steam was not used till 1829. Gill, C., *The rise of the Irish Linen Industry* (1925), p. 266, 318. Gill (p. 265) makes Porthouse a cloth manufacturer, following Horner, J., *The Linen Trade of Europe*, who made him a cloth-maker. But he was certainly a watch- and clock-maker. Longstaffe, W. H. D., *Hist. and Antiquities of Darlington*, p. 313, 319. [It seems that he is called a clothmaker in his patent specification. Marshall, T. H., *E.H.R.* 1927, p. 626.]

Scotland there were yarn dealers all over the country-side and on a market day, in the High Street of Dundee, the spinster did a good trade with the manufacturer direct[1].

The flax industry had a parallel to the worsted combers in the hecklers who prepared the flax for spinning. Heckling machinery was started at Leeds during the wars, but not until "many years later" in Scotland, and even then for some time it "made little progress." Consequently the hecklers, controlling the bottle neck, "in some measure controlled the trade, dictating the rate of wages, number of apprentices, etc., and enforcing their demands, however unjust, by strikes," as a master wrote in his reminiscences long after[2].

Silk, not needing to be spun in the proper sense of the word, has a curious and important technical history. Silk-throwing, the twisting together of the fibres so that they may stand the drag of the loom, was the earliest textile process to be performed on a large scale by power—in medieval Italy. In England the process was introduced by Thomas Lombe at his famous water-driven silk mill on a river island at Derby, the precursor of Arkwright's cotton mill in the same county. Between 1719, when Lombe's mill was built, and Arkwright's day, similar mills, large and small, had sprung up in many parts of the country to serve the carefully nursed and protected British silk industry of the eighteenth century. The largest were at Stockport, where, in 1769, "six engines the buildings of which are of prodigious bulk," employing "near 2000 people,"[3] threw silk for the Spitalfields weavers. Engines and work people supplied "the whole framework of the factory system" when power-spinning of cotton began. The manorial water-rights and the silk mills were taken over by a cotton manufacturer named Marsland in 1783[4]. But water- or steam-driven throwing mills flourished not far away, at Macclesfield Congleton and subsequently Manchester, where the first steam throwing mill was opened by Vernon Royle in 1819–20[5]. In spite of a growing concentration in the South Lancashire and Cheshire area, the

---

[1] Warden, A. J., *The linen trade ancient and modern* (1864), p. 690–4, 596. For Ireland, Gill, C., *op. cit.* p. 318.

[2] Warden, *op. cit.* p. 598.

[3] From the 1769 ed. of Defoe's *Tour*, quoted by Unwin, G., in *Eng. Hist. Rev.* April 1922, p. 213.

[4] Unwin, as above, and more fully in his *Samuel Oldknow and the Arkwrights* (1924), ch. II.

[5] *S. C. on the Silk Trade* (1831–2, XIX), Q. 3022 *sqq.*—Royle's evidence.

industry remained curiously scattered—over more than twenty counties and "about fifty towns."[1] The steam mill was the victorious novelty.

Machinery had already gripped a number of the final textile processes. The grip was not always a new thing. For centuries, in the "fulling stocks," the big water-driven wooden hammers had thudded down on the wet cloth, beating and thickening it; though in eighteenth-century London the motive power was a horse[2]. Shearing the nap of the cloth mechanically instead of with monstrous scissors, had prevailed against the bitter opposition of the shearmen, and was in general use[3]. So was the printing of calico by rollers, an invention comparatively recent but quickly adopted because the rollers were easily driven even by ordinary "milling" machinery[4]. Metal rolling by water power was an old story and the mere mechanism was similar[5]. It was easy also to use power, instead of the "horses or men," which no doubt had sufficed John Gilpin's good friend, to drive the heavy "calendars or mangles"[6] used to glaze cloth, silk, linen and calico. Pressing and packing by hydraulic power followed rather rapidly on Bramah's invention of the hydraulic press in 1795; for they had penetrated to Dundee by the 'twenties[7]. The revolution in dyeing, by chemistry not by the machine, was as yet far in the future; but Berthollet's chemical knowledge had begun to revolutionise bleaching and help make a new industry. The old Scottish adjunct to the power of sun and rain for bleaching had been sour milk. This had been to some extent replaced, after 1764, by very dilute sulphuric acid. Twenty-one years later came Berthollet's suggested use of chlorine-water, which he had expounded to James Watt in 1786. Next year de Saussure—it is a string of great names—showed it to Professor Copeland of Aberdeen, whose business friends tried it at once[8]. By the early years of the nineteenth century, the commercial preparation of chlorine had been much improved by Charles

---

[1] *Ibid.* Q. 11,368.

[2] Campbell, *The London Tradesman*, p. 261.

[3] The early shearing frames did not, however, employ revolving knives, for which the first patent was taken out in 1815: Crump, W. B., *The Leeds Woollen Industry, 1780–1820* (1931), p. 44.

[4] They were the foundation of the Peel fortunes: see *i.a. V.C.H. Lancashire,* II. 397.　　　　　　　　[5] Boulton used it at Soho; but it was much older.

[6] *The London Tradesman*, p. 262.

[7] Warden, *op. cit.* p. 615.　　　　　　　　[8] Warden, *op. cit.* p. 720.

Tennant of Glasgow. His works at St Rollox were started about the year 1800[1]. By 1830 they covered ten acres of ground[2]. The main products were sulphuric acid, chloride of lime, soda and soap. Lancashire was rather later than Glasgow in producing chemicals on a large scale. The first important works for the manufacture of soda by the Leblanc process were started by Muspratt at Liverpool in 1823—the year in which Huskisson cut the excise duty on salt, the raw material, from 15s. to 2s. a bushel. Six years later, salt being now quite free of duty, after "bitter opposition from agricultural interests," Muspratt and a partner started manufacturing in the pleasant little country town which had grown up during the eighteenth century about St Helen's chapel, in the parish of Prescot[3]. Meanwhile Leblanc's process had taken root on the north-east coast in the old seaside salt industry. Experiments with it had been made so early as 1806 by William Losh who had worked under Lavoisier, backed by the Earl of Dundonald; but the serious start was made by the Cooksons at Gateshead and Losh at Walker during the 'twenties, in connection with the repeal of the excise duty[4].

The primary metallurgical industries had nearly completed the first of their revolutions by 1825–30; although Neilson's application of a hot-air blast to the furnaces, which trebled the ratio between iron produced and fuel consumed in Scotland, came only in 1828–9[5]. So recently as 1788 there had been still twenty-six of the old charcoal furnaces in Great Britain, producing about a fifth of the British pig iron. The total output was 68,000 tons[6]. Then came steam for the blast, followed by a long-sustained munitions demand after 1793. This was of the utmost importance for "during the eighteenth century iron foundery became almost identified with the casting of cannon," as Dionysius Lardner wrote in 1831[7]. By 1806, 162 coke and

[1] *D.N.B.* [In the 1st edn. a phrase from Sinclair, *General Report*, v. 313, was quoted as referring to Tennant's works. Actually it referred to another firm. Marshall, T. H., *E.H.R.* 1927, p. 625.]   [2] Above, p. 51.

[3] *V.C.H. Lancashire*, II. 399 *sqq.* Brockbank, J., *History of St Helen's*. Gossage, W., *History of the Alkali Manufacture*. The excise was repealed in 1825.

[4] *V.C.H. Durham*, II. 301. [For Losh see Lowthian Bell, *The Tyne and Engineering*, *Trans. Inst. Mech. Eng.* 1881, p. 445. He went back to Paris in 1813–4 and started work at Walker soon after.]

[5] Scrivenor, *History of the Iron Trade* (1854), p. 259 *sqq.*, and *D.N.B.*

[6] Scrivenor, *op. cit.* p. 87–8.

[7] *Cabinet Cyclopædia*, "Manufactures in Metal," I. 55–6. An overstatement, of course: see Ashton, *Iron and Steel in the Industrial Revolution* (1924), ch. VI

11 charcoal furnaces in blast were turning out nearly 260,000 tons—the proportion of charcoal iron being now almost negligible—and new uses were being found for cast iron daily[1]. By 1830, between 250 and 300 furnaces in blast had an output of from 650,000 to 700,000 tons, more than two-fifths of which came from South Wales and about a third from Staffordshire[2]. "Happily," said Lardner, "the business of cannon casting on the large scale appears to be at an end"; but by this time the new civil uses of iron, especially for gas and water mains, pillars, railings, cables and bridging material, kept up the stimulus. London even made experiments with iron paving—near Blackfriars Bridge and Leicester Square[3]. There was still a small amount of charcoal pig made, for tin-plates and sheets, in Furness, Worcestershire, the Forest of Dean and South Wales, but none in the Sussex Weald after 1828[4].

Meanwhile, methods of producing wrought iron quickly and economically had been perfected and widely adopted. The puddling furnace, in which the pig was melted and stirred to get rid of its impurities, and the application of grooved rollers to draw the iron rods were patented by Henry Cort of Gosport in 1783. Puddling and rolling, while the puddled iron was yet soft, were to replace the slow and laborious refining of pig iron under the hammer, and to provide abundance of tough metal for rails, plates, chains and the like, without which the new metallic age could not have entered in. Cort's process, itself not entirely original, was no great success until the Homfrays of Penydaren improved it by adopting, among other things, a coke refining furnace which preceded the puddling furnace proper, in which originally raw coal was used. For a time the process was so much confined to Wales that it was commonly known as "the Welsh method." It was well established in Staffordshire and other English iron districts by the 'twenties; but the first puddlers were only brought into Scotland about 1830. When Lardner wrote, both furnaces were coke-fired: in the second the lumps, now nearly free of carbon, were heated for half an hour, then puddled; and as they "came into nature,"

---

[1] Scrivenor, *op. cit.* p. 99: the charcoal iron was not 3 per cent. of the total.
[2] See the estimates in Scrivenor, *op. cit.* p. 136. Galloway, R. L., *Annals of Coal Mining*, First Series (1898), p. 477. Porter, G. R., *Progress of the Nation* (ed. 1851), p. 268, 475.
[3] Dupin, *Commercial Power of Great Britain*, I. 154.
[4] Galloway, *op. cit.* p. 477.

that is, began to show the mysterious ropy, almost muscular, structure of the wrought iron, they were taken out, hammered and rolled; again heated; and finished under "a ponderous hammer moved by water power." Water-power was no longer indispensable, for steam had been applied to the hammers since 1782, but it was still widely used[1].

Steel also was available in greater quantity, though its uses had hitherto not extended much beyond the weapons, cutting implements, "toys," and fittings of various kinds for which it had been used in the eighteenth century. Fine steel had originally been an imported article, coming in bundles of small bars, called gads. It began to be made in England about the close of the Tudor period. Early in the eighteenth century "blister-steel" was being made in Sheffield—bars of very pure iron, mostly Swedish, being bedded in charcoal and fired for twelve days or so, until they had absorbed some of the carbon. The name comes from their appearance at the finish. But in this process absorption is irregular. To produce perfectly uniform steel Benjamin Huntsman, a Sheffield Quaker, had worked out, about 1740, a method of mixing broken blister, scrap steel, and other ingredients in small clay crucibles and casting from them ingots of known quality. Another method of securing tolerable uniformity is to break the blistered bars and heat and hammer bundles of them into an ingot in which the irregularities are, so to speak, averaged out. This is "shear-steel," so called from its use for the best shears, or "German steel" as it was called in the eighteenth century, from its first home near Solingen. It was made by Ambrose Crowley of Newcastle from about 1730, but Sheffield was still importing from Germany until 1770–80. When the great wars were over the import had been reversed; and by 1830 Lardner was lamenting our export of high-grade raw material, when we should have been exporting it made up into high-grade tools. Forges for making "shear" had been set up at Sheffield in 1785, and these, together with

---

[1] For Cort see Ashton, *op. cit.* ch. IV. See also the parliamentary report on the applications of Cort's family for public assistance. *Reports, Committees*, 1812, II. 85, and Lardner, *Manufactures in Metal*, I. 83–4. For Scotland, Bremner, D., *The Industries of Scotland* (1869), p. 50. Puddling reached Sweden and France about 1820; Belgium, 1821; Rhenish Prussia, 1830; Silesia, 1835. Swank, J. M., *Hist. of Iron in all Ages* (1892), p. 88. [In the 1st edn. a reference at this point to Nasmyth's steam hammer, invented some years later, gave the wrong impression that all hammers were still water-driven when Lardner wrote. Marshall, T. H., *E.H.R.* 1927, p. 626.]

the cast steel works of which Sheffield had now had two generations' experience, furnished the surplus[1].

Whilst the textile and metallurgical industries were being partially transformed, engineering, as the nineteenth century came to understand the term, was being made possible. The material was assured in abundance by 1815 or earlier. Inventive skill came from sources of all kinds. How Brindley, the millwright on 3s. 6d. a day, and Telford the stonemason, on less, helped to create the profession of the civil engineer is matter of common knowledge. To Campbell, about 1750, a millwright was an ordinary craftsman, who needed less money to set up in business than a plumber: "the wages given to Journeymen is no more than that of a common carpenter."[2] But Campbell also knew of "Engineers"—mechanical engineers, in modern language—whom he classed with small capitalists, such as coach-makers, optical instrument makers, and anchor smiths.

The Engineer makes Engines for raising of Water by Fire, either for supplying Reservoirs or draining Mines....The Engineer requires a very mechanically turned Head....He employs Smiths of various sorts, Founders for his Brass-work, Plumbers for his Lead-work, and a Class of Shoe-makers for making his Leather Pipes. He requires a large stock [at least £500, is said elsewhere] to set up with, and a considerable Acquaintance among the Gentry....He ought to have a solid, not a flighty Head, otherwise his Business will tempt him to many useless and expensive Projects. The Workmen...earn from Fifteen to Twenty Shillings a week; and the Fore-man of a Shop, who understands finishing of the common Engines, may earn much more[3].

It is easy to picture the little shops of these makers of "fire engines," which are certainly "the shops" writ small. There is no suggestion, however, that the engineers themselves employed power. But some people who would not have been so described did. Matthew Boulton had several water-driven rolling-mills and lathes before 1770[4]. But power played a small part at Soho, the making of machines by machines a smaller. There was in existence at that time a most imperfect, hand or horse-

---

[1] Ashton, op. cit. p. 54–9. Lloyd, G. I. H., The Cutlery Trades (1913), p. 73 sqq.
[2] The London Tradesman, Appendix, p. 323.   [3] Ibid. p. 248.
[4] Smiles, S., Lives of Boulton and Watt (1865), p. 179. [In the 1st edn. it was stated on the authority of W. C. Aitken, Birmingham and the Midland Hardware District (1866), p. 262, that both a man named Twigg and Boulton used "fire-engines" for such purposes in 1760–70. If Boulton had done this however Smiles could hardly have missed it, and the technical difficulties involved suggest a mistake in the tradition about Twigg.]

driven "engine," for boring cannon. It was much improved by John Wilkinson, the great Midland ironmaster, under patents of 1774 and 1795, to Watt's no small advantage, for Wilkinson made his cylinders[1]. Yet long after 1830 the "boring bar" at Woolwich was still driven by a "four-horse mill"[2]; although all commercial engineers had by that time abandoned the live horse power.

The early wooden textile machinery was made by the men who used it; or directly to their order by mechanics of many kinds—loom-makers, clock-makers, cabinet-makers, instrument-makers, and men with the mechanical hobby; the "engineers" of that day being primarily pump-makers. Having learnt to make machines, the makers often set up as spinners, so that from both sides there was intermixture. McConnel and Kennedy of Manchester combined the two businesses in the early years of the firm[3]. Henry Houldsworth, who, after six years at Manchester, went to Glasgow in 1799, still called himself a cotton-spinner and machine-maker in 1824. "A great many manufacturers make their own machinery?" the chairman of the parliamentary committee of that year said to one expert witness: "they do," was the reply[4]. Some of the largest firms long continued to do so—the Strutts at Belper, for example[5]. But by 1820–30 the professional purveyor of machines made with the help of other machines, the true mechanical engineer of the modern world, was just coming into existence—in Lancashire and London where the demand was at its maximum.

The committee of 1841 on the laws affecting the export of machinery decided, after hearing some very competent witnesses, that a change in the use of the word "tools" had occurred since 1820, with the coming of the machine tool. Tools, the report reminded parliament, were not what parliament might suppose: it went on to explain what they now were[6]. The first stage in their evolution, not by any means clear at

---

[1] The account in Scrivenor, *op. cit.* p. 92, is much supplemented by Ashton, *op. cit.* p. 63, 103 n., and ch. III. *passim.* Ashton (p. 101–3) stresses the importance of such firms as Wilkinson's in the evolution of engineering.

[2] From an (unpublished) London thesis by Mr H. T. King (1923), p. 15.

[3] Daniels, G. W., *The early English Cotton Industry*, p. 124 n., 128.

[4] *S. C. on Artisans and Machinery*, p. 347.

[5] Ure, *Philosophy of Manufactures* (1835), p. 21. The practice was not extinct in the twentieth century when, *e.g.*, at least one great wool-combing firm made its own machinery.

[6] *S. C. on the Laws affecting the export of Machinery* (1841, VII), p. vii. Quoted also in Knowles, L. C. A., *Industrial and Commercial Revolutions* (1st ed. 1921), p. 75 n.

all points, had taken place roughly between 1800 and 1825. Bramah, the universal inventor (1748–1814), who began life as a cabinet-maker, is perhaps the starting point; though long before his day clock-makers had employed screw-cutting lathes, a "wheel-cutting engine" and a "fusee-engine," used for a very delicate bit of metal working. To make the locks which he invented—his list of inventions includes also the hydraulic press, the publican's pull-over bar-room tap, and the water-closet—Bramah devised a series of machine tools. Under him, from 1789 to 1796, worked Henry Maudslay and, between them, they evolved a heavy screw-cutting lathe, a slide-rest for holding the metal-cutting tool, and other machines or appliances of less general interest[1]. Very important progress in wood-working machinery was made at the royal dockyards after 1797, under the guidance of General Sir Samuel Bentham, Jeremy Bentham's brother, whose patents were described by an expert more than eighty years later as "truly remarkable examples of inventive genius": in them "the principles of many of the most important machines at present in use...[are] set forth in the clearest and tersest manner."[2] With Bentham were asso-ciated, as inventor, Isambard Brunel the elder, and, as maker of the machines, Maudslay. They set up, in 1808, the series of machines with the aid of which ten men did the work of a hundred and ten in blockmaking[3]. Their "mortising engine" became the parent of the engineers' metal slotting and paring machine, in the hands of Richard Roberts.

Roberts (1789–1864), a black country shoemaker's son, was in early life a pattern-maker to John Wilkinson, later a working mechanic under Maudslay. He settled at Manchester in 1816 and he was one of those who gave permanent form to the metal-plane, a machine whose origin is obscure. "We can only learn that somewhere about 1821, a machine of this kind was made by several engineers."[4] About the time of his arrival in

---

[1] The best account of these origins is still that of Prof. Willis in 1851 *Exhibition Lectures*, I. 307 *sqq*. Willis points out that a better slide-rest than Maudslay's is figured in the *Encyclopédie* of 1772. See also Smiles, *Industrial Biography*, *passim*, and esp. App. III, "The Invention of the slide-rest."

[2] Bale, M. P., *Woodworking Machinery* (1880), p. 2. And see also Willis, *op. cit.* p. 309.　　　[3] Fernie, J., in *Proc. Inst. Civ. Eng.* (1863), XXII. 604.

[4] Willis, *op. cit.* p. 314. Smiles, *Industrial Biography*, p. 178 and *passim*, knew of six claimants for the invention—Roberts, Murray of Leeds, Fox of Derby, Spring of Aberdeen, Clement and George Rennie of London. Wm. Fairbairn regarded Maudslay, Murray, Clement and Fox as the "great pioneers of machine-tool making," with Roberts as leader of the second generation. Smiles, *op. cit.* p. 299.

Manchester "the whole of the machinery was executed by hand. There were neither planing, slotting nor shaping machines ...[only] very imperfect lathes and a few drills." So William Fairbairn (1789–1874) said, many years later[1], of the Manchester of 1814, when he arrived there, coming from Tyneside, where he had started life as a colliery engine apprentice, *via* jobs in London and Dublin. In the next twenty years Fairbairn had built up the firm which, as Andrew Ure explained with reverent awe in 1835[2], would turn you out an equipped mill for any price, trade, site or motive power; but in this matter of tools he always gave the chief credit to Maudslay and Roberts. Fairbairn's brother Peter (1799–1861), of Leeds, was applying the new engineering knowledge to flax machinery; but during the 'twenties he was not in a large way of business[3].

Very few of the engineers were. They sprang from the most various quarters. There was no direct line of descent from the pump-making engineers of two generations earlier. They had to get control of capital and build up businesses. Maudslay, who did a miscellaneous trade—flour-milling machinery, saw-milling machinery, minting machinery, turning in the 'twenties to the making of marine engines—moved to Westminster Bridge Road in 1810[4] and built up a large business there. Just how large it had become by the 'twenties is uncertain; but it was the leading London firm. In 1824–5 Maudslay's old master, Bramah, employed about a hundred men; Alexander Galloway some seventy-five in 1824 and perhaps a hundred and fifteen in 1825. Bryan Donkin, John Martineau, and one or two other London engineers were also considerable employers, but most of the two or three hundred "master engineers" and master millwrights, who were said to exist in London in 1824, were certainly small folk[5], superior master craftsmen such as Campbell described: they cannot have used much power. Their kind of business was indicated before the 1813 committee on apprenticeship by a journeyman smith who said he was "called

---

[1] Before the British Association, Manchester, 1861.

[2] In the *Philosophy of Manufactures*.

[3] By 1841, however, he was employing 550 men. *S. C. on Export of Machinery*, 1841, p. 208.

[4] Smiles, *Industrial Biography*, p. 223. Maudslay died in 1831.

[5] Galloway's evidence, *S. C. on Artisans and Machinery*, 1824, p. 19–26. *S. C. on the Export of Tools and Machinery*, 1825 (v. 115), p. 41. Bramah, *op. cit.* 1824, p. 37. Donkin, Martineau, P. Taylor and J. Haigh were the other London witnesses.

a machinist and engineer": that the business was a new one: that millwrights had set up in it and employed smiths: and that they made steam-engines, lathes, and so on[1]. The largest employment figure quoted in 1824–5 was from the North— T. C. Herves of Manchester, whose firm, "extensively employed in erecting mills and fitting them with machinery," found work for 140 to 150 men[2]. From the evidence of those years can be got also fairly clear notions of the engineering personnel of the 'twenties and its recruitment. Galloway employed "workers in wood whom we call pattern makers"; iron and brass founders; smiths; firemen; hammermen; vice-men; filers; brass, iron and wood turners. Herves had collected his leading men from cabinet-makers and clock-makers; but he was now taking apprentices. John Martineau said that he could easily expand his business by taking on more men from depressed handicrafts, if only they would come: he instanced watch-makers and instrument-makers[3].

In 1824 Manchester's lead was recognised, except by the Londoners; but the chief Glasgow witness, Houldsworth, claimed that his adopted town was now "not more than three or four years behind Manchester," though it still got "specimens of improved machinery" thence[4]. One of Manchester's greatest assets, he noted, was the subdivision not of labour but of trades. The cotton manufacture there was so great that such things as roller-making and spindle-making were separate and distinct industries, whereas elsewhere the machine-maker was forced to turn out these articles himself—an interesting line in the history of subsidiary industries.

The relatively small scale of most machine-using industries other than cotton is sufficient to account for the smallness of the young engineering firms. The steam-engine itself, the prime mover, was still small and, outside a limited group of leading industries, comparatively little used: the group includes mining, where the use of steam for winding as well as for pumping became general from about 1790–1800[5]; blast-furnace work;

---

[1] S. C. on Petitions...respecting the Apprentice Laws, 1812–3 (VII. 941), p. 20.
[2] S. C. on Artisans and Machinery, p. 340, 27.
[3] Export of Tools and Machinery, p. 21.
[4] S. C. on Artisans and Machinery, p. 379. The London witnesses, especially Maudslay and Galloway, claimed that the London craftsman was decidedly the best in England and was sober. Bramah had no drinkers among his hundred men and Donkin's men "were a very respectable class of persons." Ibid. p. 37.
[5] Galloway, Annals of Coal Mining (First Series), p. 355.

cotton and, to a less extent, the other textiles; lastly, after 1820, coastal and river navigation. There are no comprehensive statistics for the country; but those which fortunately exist for Glasgow, at once a representative port and a representative manufacturing town of the newest type, are complete. In 1831, Glasgow and its suburbs contained upwards of 200,000 people and 328 steam-engines. Of these more than sixty were on steamboats. The largest steamboat was of 387 tons and it had two engines, each of 110 horse-power. The remaining engines were nearly all in the hundred and seven power-driven cotton mills, many of which contained several[1]. The average engine, land or marine, was of 25·6 horse-power, and the total horse-power of the city and the Clyde would have driven one modern cruiser.

Outside the industries already discussed the applications of novel machinery and of steam power were only tentative. In large flour-mills and breweries steam had been adopted. Printing by steam was spreading from *The Times* to other journals. Less than half a dozen steam pumping engines had been set up in the great fen before 1830. Throughout the primary metal industries, steam was replacing water for driving rollers and other simple mechanisms. In 1822 Richard Hawthorn of Gateshead began to use it to drive his lathes[2], and no doubt other engineers of the 'twenties did the same. But in the hardware and light metal trades the scale of business was usually much too small to allow of the use of power, so that what machines there were fall rather into the category of implements, like hand-presses or hand-looms. "Our Birmingham machines," a witness said in 1824, "are rarely, if ever, mentioned in the scientific works of the day. The Birmingham machine is ephemeral...it has its existence only during the fashion of a certain article, and it is contained within the precincts of a single manufactory or a town."[3] .It was, he added, invariably light and portable. Whatever types of machine he had in mind, they were probably for the most part of the implement class, though the description need not exclude power, and may well cover the beginnings of a system which became common in Birmingham during the next twenty years —a system in which a small man hired a room with power

---

[1] *Census of* 1831 (1833), p. 1000.
[2] *The Industrial Resources of the Tyne, Wear and Tees* (1864), p. 253.
[3] *S. C. on Artisans and Machinery*, p. 332.

"laid on" from a central engine, and attached his light machines to the shafting[1].

When the new power and the new machines, with their almost unlimited transforming capacity, were let loose on Britain, towards the end of the eighteenth century, they struck a society in which—although the old powers of water and wind were very extensively used, implements of many kinds were long familiar, and capitalism with or without machinery and power was well established—the most primitive forms of industrial organisation still survived, not merely as fossils or as curiosities. The Highlands were not representative; but it is worth recalling that the Highlander at the very end of the eighteenth century still "made his own shoes of his own tanning.... Every man there is Jack of all Trades."[2] The women extracted dyes from herbs trees and shrubs of their own growing. The spinning-wheel was just coming in; teams of women, who sang as they worked, did the fulling by hand. The cloth "will take another song," they would say[3]. But even the Highland women did not "in general now work at the loom as they formerly did," the loom of 1797 being less suited for women than the primitive "beart" which had been in general use a generation or so earlier[4]. In the Lowlands and Northern England this direct production by the household for its own use did not go so far, but it was still important in the 'nineties of the eighteenth century. North of the Trent

almost every article of dress worn by farmers, manufacturers and labourers is manufactured at home, shoes and hats excepted; that is, the linen thread is spun from the lint, and the yarn from the wool, and sent to the weavers and dyers: so that almost every family has its web of linen cloth annually and often one of woollen also.... Sometimes black and white wool are mixed, and the cloth which is made from them receives no dye. Altho' broad cloth...begins now to be worn by opulent farmers...within these twenty years a coat bought at a shop was considered a mark of arrogance and pride, if the buyer were not possessed of an independent fortune.

[1] Porter, *Progress of the Nation* (ed. 1851), p. 249. Of 289 engines built by Boulton and Watt down to 1800, 104 were for textiles, 58 for mines, 31 for canals and waterworks (pumping), 30 for metallurgy, 23 for brewing and distilling. Lord, J., *Capital and Steam Power* (1923), p. 175.

[2] Eden, *State of the Poor* (1797), I. 558–9.

[3] Grant, Miss K. W., "Peasant life in Argyllshire in the End of the Eighteenth Century," *Sc. Hist. Rev.* XVI (1918–19), p. 147.

[4] Eden, *op. cit.* p. 554–5.

Of "the Midland and Southern counties," however, it could already be said that "the labourer, in general, purchases a very considerable proportion, if not the whole of his cloaths, from the shopkeeper."[1] Eden had country-folk, including country manufacturers, in mind; and primarily small farmers, yeomen, and such. He allowed that some labourers were too poor to buy raw material, but omitted to explain how they got clothing; and parts of his account are obviously inapplicable to towns-men. But real townsmen were still a small minority in the North in 1797. The classes of whom he wrote retained some at least of these habits thirty years later, in spite of the growth of pride and broad-cloth. An observant child of the 'twenties remembered how the Dodson family, which had such particular ways of doing everything that "no daughter of that house could be indifferent to the privilege of having been born a Dodson, rather than a Gibson or a Watson," extended those particular ways beyond "making the cowslip wine, curing the hams, and keeping the bottled gooseberries"—things in which even a twentieth-century Dodson might show character—to "bleaching the linen." No doubt particularity did not stop at bleaching. The Dodsons, it will be recalled, lived near, if not on, the Trent[2].

The North and Scotland, it need hardly be said, clung to the habit of domestic baking: they cling to it still. Coal was within reach almost everywhere; and where it was not the population was generally thin enough, as in the Highlands, for the local supplies of peat or wood to suffice. Whereas in Berkshire, in 1831, there was a grown baker, usually no doubt a baker's wife and perhaps a baker's boy, to every 295 of the population, in Cumberland the ratio was one to 2200[3]. The new canals and the horse-power railways had already done something to remedy the fuel shortage, which had been a main cause of the abandonment of domestic baking and even, among cottagers, of the domestic fire in many Midland and Southern shires; but the habit once dead never revived. It persisted, however, in the more heavily wooded South-West and, sporadically, wherever firewood was easily available. So did brewing and cider-making. Domestic brewing was still very common in the

---

[1] Eden, op. cit. p. 554–5.

[2] The Mill on the Floss, bk. 1, ch. vi. Mary Ann Evans was born in 1819.

[3] Calculated from the occupation returns of the census: there is probably no serious risk of error in the enumeration of the bakers.

North Midlands and the North, among the more substantial country-folk. Quite recently it had been practised in much humbler homes, and in semi-urban surroundings. In the Dudley iron district the normal cottage in 1833 had a kitchen, two bedrooms, and what was called a brewhouse—but the brewhouse was sinking towards the mere Victorian scullery. It seems that no Dudley iron-worker still brewed; but there was memory of brewing[1].

When the Highland women abandoned the "beart" they had handed over weaving to a representative of that grade which, in the logical classification of methods of industrial organisation, comes next above household production proper, in which producer and consumer are one—to the household weaver as he was called in medieval England, the "customer weaver" of early nineteenth-century descriptions, who worked up the consumer's prepared material to the consumer's order. Throughout Scotland and parts of Wales in 1825–30 this was the normal arrangement in rural districts; it was still to be found in Northern England, though mainly for linen weaving alone, and it was not yet quite extinct south of the Trent. It has been said that "in the Midlands at the end of the eighteenth century 'in every parish there was a weaver; and he was never called by his own name, but *the weaver*.'"[2] The reminiscences here quoted come from Nottinghamshire and it is doubtful whether, even at the date referred to, any such general survival could be demonstrated for the southern Midlands; though certainly customer weavers were known there. Nottingham and Lincoln, as it happens, were the most southerly counties in which a fair number of them survived forty years later (1835–40) "These domestic artisans were at one time numerous in the counties of Lincoln and Nottingham. Their number is now much reduced."[3] That, too, is the country of their nineteenth-century representative in literature, Silas Marner.

They were reported from every Scottish shire by the careful schoolmaster officials of the 1831 Census, mixed up in the industrial counties, and in some others, with market weavers —outworkers for urban employers—but completely unadulterated in the far North. In the county of Inverness, for instance, there was a customer weaver for every 279 of the population.

[1] *S. C. on Agriculture* (1833), Q. 9802. Above p. 32.
[2] Webb, S. and B., *The Parish and the County*, p. 47 n.
[3] *Hand Loom Weavers. Assistant Commissioners' Reports*, II. 352.

At the other end of the country, in Berwickshire, if the figures could be trusted, there would seem to have been one for every 100; but as, besides the customer weavers, there were reported weavers "distinctly said to be employed by the Master Manufacturers of Edinburgh and Glasgow," probably some not so reported were also so employed. Behind the bald figures and brief notes of the Census can be seen going forward in Scotland a process which in England had begun certainly in the thirteenth century, and perhaps earlier, the transformation of these household weavers into piece-workers not for the consumer, herself a producer of yarn, but for the organiser of production in a town. Customer weavers in Scotland, during the decade 1820–30, still handled both linen and woollen yarns; but the transformation of the wool industry was tending to restrict that side of their work in the South. There, as in England, the customer weaver put up his last fight on a field of sheets and table-linen. Many years had gone by, if the Annals of the parish of Dalmailing in Ayrshire may be trusted[1], since, under the second wife of the Rev. Mr Balwhidder, "there was such a buying of wool to make blankets, with a booming of the meikle wheel to spin the same, and such birring of the little wheel for sheets and napery, that the manse was for many days like an organ kist." After her death, in 1796, the "weariful booming wheel" that span the wool was silent: doubtless no later minister's wife set it going again; but little wheels for napery birred on.

In Wales there were numbers of weavers working up homespun woollen yarn in every county in 1831. But in many cases weaving for the customer's use was not their sole, or main, business; for throughout North Wales there was a well-organised production of flannels for market, which in the county of Montgomery—at Newtown and Llanidloes in particular—was passing into the factory stage[2]. Even farmhouse-produced flannel went to market and it was hard to differentiate a weaver from a farm hand. "The farmers make their pieces in their own houses from their own wool," a Montgomeryshire witness explained seven years later[3], "and they bring them to Newtown market....Agricultural labourers about Llanbryn-

[1] John Galt's *Annals of the Parish* is not officially an economic history of Scotland during the industrial revolution; but a better has yet to be written.
[2] The flannels of Newtown were made "chiefly in factories" in 1832. *S. C. on Factories Bill* (1831–2, xv), Q. 6476.
[3] *Hand Loom Weavers*, v. 555.

mair are hired by the year; they can all weave or spin; the farmers employ them at out-door work in the summer, and at the loom or jenny in the winter." It will be noted that the jenny had beaten the wheel. But the true customer weaver was common even in 1838 in South Wales, and the account given of him then[1] had been applicable to more individuals and over a wider area ten or fifteen years earlier. "Thirty or forty years ago" [say 1800–1810] the "isolated parish weaver" "occupied a very prominent station in the country, ranking in point of number and importance with the blacksmith and the miller; there being generally one or more in every parish, with fulling-mills in proportion." "In the retired parts of the country this description of person might still be found [in 1838], in the proportion of perhaps one in every two or three parishes, or even more." The handspun and parish-woven cloth was reckoned three times as durable as "shop-cloth." The looms were heavy and "mostly very old, as new looms would scarcely answer the cost of making. Many of them are perhaps some centuries old." Even in South Wales, it should be added, tiny "woollen factories" with a staff of from five to ten, equipped with carding-sets, hand or water driven, hand-worked jennies and hand-looms, were thinly scattered over the country by 1838. It was their gradual appearance which had so much lowered the status of the parish weaver during the previous generation.

For the North of England, it is difficult to disentangle the surviving customer weavers from the market weavers; obviously so in Lancashire, Cheshire, the West Riding and Cumberland— which had an important textile centre at Carlisle—and Westmorland, which was dominated from Kendal. Of Northumberland the 1831 Census states that: "the woollen-yarn and linen-thread, still spun in the villages, employs about 300 weavers, scattered thro'out the County."[2] The North Riding was full of scattered linen weavers, but they were within reach of the market influences of Knaresborough and Leeds, and some were certainly market weavers congregated in the smaller towns. The customer weavers of Lincolnshire are referred to in the Census notes, as they are in the Hand Loom Weavers Report seven or eight years later, where the reference shows that they had mainly been working at linen. It can serve as their epitaph.

Their number is now much reduced, there being far less domestic manufacture [of yarn]. The cheapness of cotton goods is considered the

---

[1] *Hand Loom Weavers*, V, 571.　　　　[2] 1833, XXXVI. 474.

principal cause. Some...employ themselves partly in agriculture....In a commercial point of view these men are totally insignificant, and can excite no interest but as a remnant of a body once very numerous in the generations now gone past[1].

From the scanty and incomplete figures available it may be estimated that, for the whole of Great Britain, they numbered not less than 5000 and not more than 10,000 in 1831[2].

The customer weavers were the only important group of craftsmen who still worked up for the consumer material, often raised on the consumer's land, which had already gone through one process of manufacture in the consumer's home. But direct work for the consumer, on material supplied by him, was of course exceedingly common, as it still is, though now over a narrower field. Repair work on clothes, houses, furniture, vehicles and implements would normally be done by the working craftsman or craftsman-shopkeeper, at any rate outside London and the largest towns, where the capitalist shopkeeper came as a screen between the consumer and the craftsman-shopkeeper—tailor, carpenter, wheelwright or cabinet-maker. "Shop-cloth" and shop calico might be bought to replace home-spun in the country; but they would go to the working tailor or dress maker of the local market-town, when not made up at home. For much work of construction too, as distinct from repairs, the working smith, saddler and wheelwright, the mason, bricklayer, carpenter and house-painter, had direct relations with the consumer—constantly outside London and the largest towns, and not infrequently inside them.

The building trades had gone through no revolution in technique before 1825[3]; but it is evident that a partial change in organisation, begun long before in London, had accompanied the rapid urbanisation of the half-century since 1775. Right through the nineteenth century, in the full flood of capitalism, there was no industry in which the handicraftsman more frequently rose to be a small jobbing employer and perhaps, eventually, a builder on a large scale; and that process was not new in 1800. The term builder, for the entrepreneur, seems to have come into general use between 1750 and 1800. Campbell

---

[1] *Hand Loom Weavers*, II. 352.

[2] The figures are based on the Census, taking the totals for counties—such as Inverness or Cardigan—where there is no reason to suppose that any of the weavers were manufacturers' outworkers, and an estimate elsewhere.

[3] Above, p. 71–2.

used it incidentally in 1747, and Postlethwayt in 1751, but it does not appear in Campbell's table of trades among bakers, bankers, brewers and butchers, or as a heading in Postlethwayt's Dictionary. Architects Campbell knows, though he "scarce knows of any in England who have had an education regularly design'd for the Profession." "Bricklayers, Carpenters, etc.," he adds, "all commence Architects, especially in and about London, where there go but few rules to the building of a City House."[1] Bricklaying he counts "a very profitable business; especially if they confine themselves to work for others, and do not launch out into Building-Projects of their own, which frequently ruin them: It is no new thing in London, for those Master-Builders to build themselves out of their own Houses, and fix themselves in Jail with their own Materials."[2] He ranks master bricklayers with such small handicraft-tradesmen as bakers plumbers and glaziers. Two generations later, Colquhoun, in the year of Waterloo, placed "respectable Builders" in the fourth of his seven plutocratically arranged groups of British society, with the "Ship Owners, Merchants and Manufacturers of the second class, Warehousemen and respectable Shopkeepers."[3]

For the purposes of the 1831 Census, "builder" was a recognised class, in which 871 people were returned for London. But in the agricultural shires the class was often nearly empty—7 in Berkshire, 9 in Bedfordshire, 12 in Buckingham and only 147 in the whole of Wales. Without staking too much on the accuracy of these returns, and not forgetting that a Berkshire bricklayer or a Welsh mason might be a small "builder," it is noticeable that the distribution of "builders" agrees reasonably well with that of the urban population. The market towns in agricultural districts contained few people to whom the name was commonly applied, it would seem; and as the name was by this time in general use, it may be assumed

---

[1] *The London Tradesman*, p. 157.   [2] *Ibid.* p. 107.

[3] *Resources of the British Empire*, p. 107. Postgate, R. W., *The Builder's History* (1923), p. 9, post-dates the emergence of builder and contractor. He refers to a "significant" statement in Postlethwayt's *Universal Dictionary* "that some master bricklayers were beginning to live handsomely," which he dates 1774. The *Dictionary* says that "most" (not "some") masters live handsomely and that "some" "attain good estates"; the latter, being those who "employ many hands," are "commonly called master builders," and project, draw, plan and estimate for buildings. The passage occurs in the first edition, 1751: the edition of 1774 is the fourth.

that the thing also was generally absent. A landlord about to build would make arrangements direct with master bricklayers, carpenters, plasterers and painters in the old way, and they would come to work with their lads and mates. If he lived in Wales or rural Scotland, he might have to dispense with specialist plumbers and glaziers. All Scotland only reported 672 in the two groups combined and Wales 243, as against 11,000 in England. The craft and mystery of the plumber had been but a feeble growth in Scotland. Sir John Sinclair admitted in 1814 that "the number of plumbers was not very considerable," but he added hopefully that it was "daily increasing."[1] If he was right, and the parish schoolmaster of 1831 right too, the daily increase must have stopped somewhere between 1814 and 1830.

By the latter date the "respectable builders" of London were already specialised into definite groups. There was a small group, contractors as we should say, who did little but erect public buildings[2]. A second, larger, group devoted themselves to the building of shops and business premises. Third, perhaps not all respectable, came the descendants of Campbell's reckless bricklayers, those who took risks with private houses, "speculative builders" as they were already called. They were no new type. Bethnal Green had its "Carter's Rents" and "Richardson's Rents," mean dwellings in courts and yards, in Queen Anne's day[3]. Their methods have remained the same until our own time—the land rented in hope, materials secured on credit, a mortgage raised on the half-built house before it is sold or leased, and a high risk of bankruptcy. They had been particularly hard hit in the years of commercial collapse, 1816 and 1826[4]. The class was not confined to London. It grew naturally everywhere, and as quickly as its own often questionable houses. It had put up "more than half" the new houses in Liverpool[5]. Much and deservedly criticised as the jerry-builder has been, no one has even suggested how the ever-swelling British urban population could have been housed

[1] General Report, v. 289.

[2] S. C. on Manufactures, Commerce and Shipping, 1833, Q. 1659 sqq. Evidence of Thos. Burton. For provincial contractors see below, p. 595.

[3] George, London Life in the Eighteenth Century, p. 342. It is not, however, certain that Carter and Richardson had been "builders": they may have been only house-landlords.

[4] S. C. on Manufactures, etc., Q. 1677.

[5] Ibid. Q. 4822. Sheffield, Q. 2887.

without him. That the towns were not planned, and often neither paved nor drained, was not the jerry-builder's fault; nor could he supply first-rate sanitation when the water-closet and the iron water main were barely invented, and a cheap method of making earthenware drain pipes was unknown. His houses —sad as they were—compared favourably with the samples of human dwellings among which he had been brought up, whether his first brick had been laid in town or country[1].

The jerry-builder was normally a small man, self-promoted from the ranks of handicraftsmen, often destined to revert to the ranks. All the London building trades were full of small masters, who worked both "on their own" and more or less under the larger builders. Take, for example, the painters. In the later 'thirties there were about 1000 master painters in London[2]. There were supposed to be 3000 to 4000 regularly employed journeymen, and another 6000 to 8000 employed for about seven months in the year, of whom some no doubt would be seasonal immigrants[3]. The ratio of masters to regularly employed men is remarkably low. What was the working staff of a prominent London builder not quite of the first rank, at the time of the Reform Bill, may be learnt from the evidence of Thomas Burton, already quoted[4]. He employed, on an average, 170 men in the busy season. The highest number he had ever had on his books in sixteen years was 235. He paid his Irish bricklayers' labourers 17s. and 18s.: there were many out of work. His skilled journeymen he said averaged 5s. a day, plus overtime, making 30s. to 40s. a week when busy; but whether they were busy for more than the six or seven months, which Campbell supposed to be the working year of an eighteenth-century London bricklayer, he did not say[5].

The building trade, taken as a whole, covered the whole range of industrial organisation; for at the bottom, insignificant it is true, were the old-fashioned Scottish peasant, who ran up his own turf or sod hovel, and the English carpenter, who did

---

[1] Above, p. 27 sqq. Cp. Knowles, L. C. A., op. cit. p. 105.

[2] The evidence comes, curiously enough, from the *Hand Loom Weavers Report*, II. 279.

[3] The Census of 1831 reported just over 5000 painters in London: if correct, the figure suggests the masters and regular journeymen.

[4] Burton specialised in commercial building, warehouses, shops, etc. *S. C. on Manufactures*, 1833, Q. 1660.

[5] For a general discussion of the course of industrial wages see below, p. 548 sqq.

estate repairs and building from timber grown and felled on the
estate, so filling the same rôle as the customer weaver. At the
top was the respectable, capitalistic, contractor for Regent
Street or Waterloo Bridge with his mixed teams of Cockney
craftsmen and spalpeen labourers, part directed by mastercrafts-
man sub-contractors, for paintwork it might be or for paving.

Among the building workers, the smaller master painter or
plumber of London, and the master mason or carpenter in the
country, corresponded most nearly to the ideal handicraftsman
of the systematisers—the man who, controlling his own place
of work and trade, owning his own tools, buying his own
material, and working alone or with a prentice and a mate,
sells his goods or services to the consumer through no middleman or entrepreneur. How important was this type in the
industrial life of the country as a whole? It is not an easy
question, but an answer must be attempted. And it may be well
to begin with the most difficult problem—that of London.
Here for centuries the shopkeeper had been differentiated from
the craftsman in a large number of trades. But, even in highly
developed trades, there might be little selling masters and crafts-
man-shopkeepers who conformed more or less well to the
definition. Take, for example, the true London trade in which
capitalism was probably oldest—that of the goldsmith and
jeweller. By the nineteenth century not only were shopkeeper and craftsman normally separate, but there was a regular
intermediate grade. "There is a middle sort of people,"
said a working goldsmith in 1813, "who come in between
us and the shopkeepers...warehouse men...they purchase
the goods of the manufacturer [he is using the term in its
old sense] and by giving a long credit, they have acquired
the whole trade almost of the shopkeeper, except one or
two of the principals...."[1] Yet beside these working goldsmiths, themselves masters not wage earners, and the independent "chamber masters" in the—much subdivided—watch-
making trade, who made parts of watches and offered them for
sale, there were certainly plenty of the still surviving type of
small working watchmaker-jewellers, who, if they did not make
all the things they sold, at least knew how they were made and
could repair them, and had no master over them[2].

[1] S. C. on Petitions respecting the Apprentice Laws, p. 11.
[2] For watchmaking see George, London Life in the Eighteenth Century,
p. 173 sqq.

Boots and shoes are a parallel case. For a century at least the large London shops had not only not been run by London craftsmen but had not always even employed them. They had dealt in boots made far afield—mostly at Northampton and Stafford and in Yorkshire. "The Country Shoe-Makers supply most of the Sale-Shops in Town," Campbell wrote in 1747[1]. "Have not the bespoke masters [of London] become customers to you?" an M.P. asked William Collier of Stafford in 1813: "No, not in a greater degree than they used, they were always customers...for half the shoes they sell here as bespoke...are the manufactures of Stafford and Northampton."[2] And yet at the bottom of the scale in the London boot and shoe trades were small working masters who took apprentices, but worked mainly for the shops, and independent if unprosperous shoe-maker-cobblers, of the type predominant in the country. How far they were mere repairers; how far, that is to say, their working-class customers wore country or second-hand boots is not certainly known. The accounts of the Stafford, Northampton, Kettering and Wellingborough trades from 1813 to 1824 suggest that a good many heavy country boots may have been worn in town; and the "translator," who patched up old boots bought from rag-men, had been a familiar eighteenth-century figure. But, like the little watchmaker-jewellers, the cobblers and translators were independent masters of quite a medieval sort, with medieval standards of cleanliness and living too[3].

In short, however capitalistic it might be at the top, every London trade which relied on London labour had some handicraft masters at the bottom. The permanent characteristics and small-scale operations of London industry, as yet almost untouched by machinery—that industry of "fitting and finishing all the commodities requisite for the consumption and vast commerce of the metropolis," noted in the Census Report of 1831—helped to keep them in existence. There was, and there had been since the thirteenth century at least, a perpetual tendency for the successful master to become primarily a shopkeeper, dealer, employer. No doubt the London-trained handworker, more often—much more often—than not, was a lifelong wage earner or outworker by the piece; but he had fair oppor-

---

[1] *The London Tradesman*, p. 219.
[2] *S. C. on the Petitions relating to the Duty on Leather* (1812–13, IV), p. 55.
[3] See for the London shoemakers the excellent account in George, *op. cit.* p. 173 *sqq.*, 233. For the numbers of shoemakers in 1830, above, p. 73.

tunities in a large group of minor industries, and some opportunities in almost all, of becoming his own master, whatever that was worth: its value varied. But the unskilled masses of builders' labourers, dockers, cadgers, hangers-on and underlings of all sorts had not such opportunities.

There is a reflection of the state of affairs, as it was about 1830, in the condition of the London Companies. The greater, mercantile, Companies had long since acquired their modern character. Even in Tudor times there was a minority of drapers in the Drapers' Company: in the eighteenth century its connection with cloth-dealing was purely nominal[1]. But among the lesser companies, in the 'thirties, "in more than a score of cases half or two-thirds of the company followed the trade, and it was still usual for those who entered the trade to take up their freedom in the company."[2] The companies in question were by no means all connected with handicrafts in the strict sense of the word; but the list represents adequately those old-established London trades to which a semi-medieval organisation was still not inappropriate, though it cannot be assumed that, even in these, the rise from journeyman to master was a normal episode in a working life. It seems that, in the Bakers' Company, the "great majority of whose members were or had been practical bakers," journeymen liked to join not because they expected to rise to the rank of master, but because "the freedom was considered as conferring a certain degree of respectability."[3] It is clear, too, from other evidence that the journeyman baker of the early nineteenth century was usually a lifelong wage earner[4]. Read with these reservations, a list of a dozen of what may be called the effective companies in 1830 is instructive: Apothecaries, Barbers, Brewers, Butchers, Cooks, Curriers, Cutlers, Innholders, Masons, Plumbers, Saddlers, Stationers.

Outside London and the specifically manufacturing areas, the true handicraftsman, or the very small entrepreneur hardly distinguishable from him, was common everywhere though probably dominant nowhere south of the Highland line. Every

---

[1] Johnson, A. H., *The History of...the Drapers of London* (1914 *sqq.*), II. 163, etc.

[2] Unwin, G., *The Gilds and Companies of London* (1908), p. 344, based on the inquiries connected with the Municipal Reform Act of 1835.

[3] *Ibid.*

[4] See, for instance, the petition of 7000 journeymen bakers of London in the *S. C. on the Observance of the Sabbath* (1831, VII), p. 5.

illustration given in earlier chapters of the survival of technically unchanged industries and small-scale industrial operations
points in his direction, though it may not demonstrate his
existence[1]. First came the old country crafts, which had continued almost unchanged since the Middle Ages—blacksmith,
baker (in the South), wheelwright, saddler, shoemaker, with
the bricklayers, carpenters and masons. There were probably
at least 25,000 strictly rural adult blacksmiths in Great Britain[2];
and there cannot be any doubt that very many of the non-rural
blacksmiths were handicraftsmen, for the word was and is
specialised to that meaning. A handful of smiths working in
the young engineering industry or as repairers in the textile
mills are no doubt included; but of the total of 58,000 adult
blacksmiths in the 1831 census, it would be surprising if less
than, say, 45,000 should properly have been classed as handicraftsmen. Allow 5000 to 10,000 lads under twenty, and the
figure is between two and three times that of all the Northumberland and Durham colliers, young and old. The number
of the shoemakers and cobblers was almost unbelievably great.
For Great Britain the figure is 133,000 adults. This includes
the shopkeepers and their hands, also the outworkers for Midland manufacturers like William Collier[3]. But as the total
figure for London, where shopkeepers and their hands were
most numerous, is only 16,502; as some considerable proportion
of these were themselves independent, if rather low grade,
workers; as the London type of "sale shop" for shoes was rare
in other towns; and as the aggregate excess of shoemakers, in
those counties where the outwork industry was localised, above
the normal proportion of shoemakers to population in purely
rural counties, certainly did not exceed 10,000[4]—it is reasonably
safe to conclude that more than 100,000 out of the 130,000 were
not higher in the industrial scale than the craftsman-shopkeeper. That the 17,300 Scottish shoemakers, with very few
exceptions, were of this, or of a lower, grade is suggested by
an entry in Sinclair's account of 1814. After describing the
typical solitary rural cobbler, he says—"in the larger towns
regular manufactories are established, where the business is

---

[1] Above, p. 67 *sqq.*　　　　　　[2] Above, p. 66.
[3] Above, p. 167, and below, p. 181.
[4] Calculated from the counties, such as Stafford, where the capitalistic outwork industry is known to have been strong, with a conjectural allowance for
a certain amount of capitalistic outwork elsewhere.

conducted by a master employing journeymen and apprentices."[1]
The bigger craftsman-shoemakers, Scottish or English, would
have a lad or two working with them; possibly some "black
thumbed maids" like that "cobbler's girl in Milk Street" loved
by the Knight of the Burning Pestle; all told, a very great army.

In industry after industry, among those as yet little touched
by the new powers, wherever it is possible to come to close
quarters, the very small working entrepreneur is found holding
his own easily. Take tanning. It is not usual to suppose that
in early nineteenth-century Prussia any industrial process was
organised in larger units than in Britain; yet a leather-dealer
from Longacre, who had been apprenticed in Edinburgh, "saw
the largest tan yard he ever saw in his life" near Berlin in the
year 1813[2]. Bermondsey was at that time the greatest English
tanning and currying centre, and he must have known it. But
his evidence no longer surprises when placed beside that given
in the same place, an hour or two earlier, by a certain F. Moore
of Bridgnorth. "You carry on business very extensively do
not you?...There may be three or four tanners who do more
business than I do in the county." This very extensive tanner
had just said that he employed seven men, a woman, and a
stout apprentice. What can the small tanneries of the Welsh
marches have been like?

With another ancient industry, that of brewing, it is possible
to come to quite close quarters. In London were the "eleven
great breweries," among the largest business units in the country;
but also many small ones[3]. Household brewing was common
enough in rural districts. But there is a fourth type of producer
to be considered, what might be called the handicraft brewer,
the licensed victualler who made his own beer. Of these there
were only seventeen in the London area, so complete was the
power of the "eleven" with their tied houses; but in Great
Britain there were 23,572[4]. They were rare in Surrey, Kent and
Hampshire; but fairly numerous already in Hertfordshire,
Essex and Oxfordshire. We are getting to the boundaries of

---

[1] *General Report*, v. 297.

[2] *S. C. on...the duty on Leather*, 1813, p. 46.

[3] Above, p. 68. In 1836 the group of big London breweries, now twelve
in number, used 526,000 out of 754,000 quarters of malt consumed in London.
Barnard, A., *The Noted Breweries of Great Britain and Ireland* (1889), p. xiii.

[4] Based on the Excise Returns of 1830. 1830, XXII. 167 *sqq.*, 217 *sqq.* The
situation was altered further in favour of the handicraft brewer by the Beer Act
of 1830. Below, p. 560.

London influence: the "eleven," it is on record, had tied houses in the country. At the other end of England, the brewing victualler was rare in Northumberland, Cumberland and Durham, perhaps because home-brewing was so general or perhaps because there was a "boot-legging" trade in whiskey along the drovers' roads[1]. But in many parts of the country the great brewer was rare, the small brewer not very common, and the brewing victualler almost universal. In the Sheffield excise "collection"—*i.e.* town and district—there were 9 brewers, 15 retail brewers and 1071 victuallers, of whom 930 brewed. The ratios between class and class were not very different in the "collections" of Leeds, Halifax, Lancaster, Northwich, Derby, Coventry, Lichfield, Hereford and throughout the South-Western counties and Wales. The brewing victuallers were less numerous (700 out of 1113) in the Manchester "collection": they were almost absent from that of Liverpool (40 out of 1257). Is this due to big breweries or to tide-water rum drinking? Probably to a combination of the two. Liverpool had extensive breweries in the 'thirties[2]. The Hull figures are similar. In East Anglia the brewing victualler was fairly common (227 out of 674) in Suffolk and in the Cambridge "collection" (160 out of 998); but both he and the "retail brewer" were very rare in the Norwich "collection," where the figures are—brewers, 51; retail brewers, 3; victuallers, 1070; brewing victuallers, 37. Norwich, like London, was an old home of capitalism, and capitalism had extended to beer. The solid brewers of those parts were good men of business. From the other side of England comes the least capitalistic of all the "collections," that of Stourbridge—brewers, 1; retail brewers, 40; victuallers, 773; brewing victuallers, 753. For the whole of Great Britain the proportion of victuallers who brewed was almost exactly one in three.

Distilling, in England, was a concentrated and localised industry. Most of the great gin distilleries, like the great breweries, were in London[3]. Scotland, which, in the early 'thirties, produced twice as much spirits as England, could

---

[1] There were many prosecutions for illicit trade in Scottish spirits in Northumberland and Durham. Excise Returns, 1830, XXII. 217 *sqq.*

[2] See, *e.g.*, the account of Liverpool trades in Draker, *Roadbook of the Grand Junction Railway*, p. 71.

[3] In 1783 the London distillers claimed to produce "upwards of eleven-twelfths of the whole distillery of England." George, *op. cit.* p. 40.

also show some big concerns. James Haig and Son of Sunbury, and John Stein of Clackmannan, each had an output of over 250,000 gallons in 1831, and half a dozen other firms, all south of the Highland line, had outputs of over 100,000 gallons. But the average output of the 239 Scottish distilleries known to the excise officials in 1831–3, including Haig's and the rest, was only about 120 gallons per distillery per working day. The officials looked narrowly: they reported on one concern which could not squeeze out two gallons a day, and on many whose average daily output was only from 10 to 15 gallons; but possibly some stills in the glens and islands escaped them[1]. These lesser distilleries of the North were not all-the-year-round businesses. They were adjuncts to the farms of the tacksmen and the greater farmers. Distillation started after harvest and stopped when the spring ploughing began. Those familiar with the history of the industry conjecture that a production of a thousand gallons a year represented about a quarter of one man's yearly labour in a distillery of moderate size; and that therefore the average Scottish distillery, if such a thing can be conceived as a reality, was approximately a ten-man unit. John Stein and James Haig may each have employed all the time of from fifty to seventy men, the winter distilleries of the North half of the time of four or five[2].

As the greater industries, revolutionised or not, are approached the problem of the handicraftsmen becomes more complex. There is no difficulty in proving the continued existence of the very small producer, as opposed to the factory hand, in many of the great industries. But as these industries usually work for distant markets he can rarely sell to an ultimate consumer. He has acquired relations with some factor or merchant which may vary from ordinary free sale—the producer trying now one merchant now another, as best suits him—to complete dependence, the producer being a mere outworker for the merchant. Again, the small master may be the handicraftsman of the diagrams, working alone or with journeyman and prentice, or he may be a tiny employer, even with outworkers of his own. The problems are well illustrated in the Sheffield trades. Sheffield and its district were full of small men working

---

[1] *Seventh Report of Commissioners of Excise Inquiry*, part II, App. XIX.
[2] I am indebted for these facts and estimates to Sir Alexander Walker of John Walker and Sons, Kilmarnock.

—to outward appearance—on their own account[1]. Some were called masters, some journeymen. There were scythe and sickle makers, whose life was still in part agricultural, just outside the town. All told, its much subdivided trades employed about 8500 people in 1824—table-knife forgers, hafters, grinders; spring-knife blade forgers, spring forgers, scale forgers, hafters, grinders; for scissors five trades; for files four; and so on. In 1822 an Association, whose history is not relevant here, "for the protection of the Spring Knife, Table Knife, Scissor, Pressers, Fork and File Trades, and such other trades as may be hereafter admitted"—that is, potentially, for all the Sheffield trades—decided "that no person belonging to any of the Associated Trades shall have more than two apprentices at the same time except under certain regulations to be hereinafter stated," and "that no person shall commence manufacturing in any of the Associated Trades, who has not served a legal apprenticeship...and who has [? not] an Establishment, *i.e.*, a Shop and Tools, etc." All this reads like an extract from the rules of a fifteenth-century gild. But a later rule says, not very grammatically, "that all journeymen...shall provide a work book for each Master by whom he is employed, and shall see that his work is regularly entered in such books," showing that the journeyman might be an outworker on piecework for more than one master, an arrangement against which every medieval gild had legislated. Yet, even so, the journeyman had his own tools, some kind of domestic workshop, forge, or grindery. He could, and on occasion did, produce goods on his own account[2].

In the eighteenth century, merchants in Hull, who imported the fine Swedish or Russian iron, also financed the export trade in cutlery by giving long credits to the small Sheffield masters. They were succeeded by Sheffield factors, who performed the same function, and sometimes became the actual owners of numerous workshops, besides making advances and supplying tools to the small men. Great havoc was wrought among these merchant-manufacturers by the Napoleonic wars and the trade depression of 1816–17. As they got into difficulties, and unemployment grew, the small men, whether technically masters or not, tried their own hands in desperation.

---

[1] Lardner, D., *Cabinet Cyclopædia*, "Manufactures in Metal" (1833), II. 12–3. Lloyd, G. I. H., *The Cutlery Trades* (1913), p. 445 and *passim*.
[2] The rules are in Lloyd, p. 472–3. See also p. 191–2.

"The cheapness of the raw materials," it was said in 1820, "enables every man who can raise money or credit enough to purchase as much of them as he can manufacture in a week to set up master for himself.... Among the discharged journeymen therefore, the number of these 'little masters,' as they are called, has been amazingly multiplied...whereby goods to an incalculable bulk, but often very inferior workmanship, have been made and pushed off through new and strange channels on the meanest terms, for money, for stuff, for anything, for nothing."[1]

For the moment the trade was falling back on handicraft. But the power of capital and commercial knowledge was soon felt again; and in 1833 a witness, describing this episode of the "little masters," stated that now they might be "considered in fact the journeymen of the merchants."[2] Moreover, in 1823, the first cutlery factory, in the proper sense of the word, had been started by Messrs Greaves: in it all processes from steel-making to the hafting of the knife were performed[3]. Nevertheless the nature of the trades kept open avenues to prosperity for the capable workman: there was no sharp line of cleavage between men and "little masters": and the upward transition was constantly made. With fortune the master might rub out his "little," and rise, as Lardner in 1833 admitted that many had risen, to "property and respectability."[4]

The relation of handicraftsman or small entrepreneur and factor at Sheffield was reproduced, with modifications, in many of the Black Country trades. Late in the seventeenth century the locks made by the smiths of Wolverhampton and Willenhall were bought and put on the market by travelling dealers. Early in the eighteenth century these men started store-rooms at Wolverhampton or Birmingham to which the smiths took their locks, and other hardware, in wallets. This system continued far into the nineteenth century and in the 'twenties was still of considerable importance[5]. The smiths were handicraftsmen or small masters, and some form of apprenticeship was general—as indeed it was throughout the Black Country[6]. Similarly, in the bit and saddlers' ironmongery trades of Walsall and Bloxwich, the goods turned out by the small masters were

[1] Quoted in Lloyd, p. 194.
[2] S. C. on Manufactures, etc., Q. 11,604.
[3] Lloyd, p. 182.
[4] Op. cit. II. 13.
[5] Birmingham and the Midland Hardware District (1864), p. 85 sqq.: and below, 1825, p. 221.
[6] Report on Children in Manufactures (1843, XIV), p. 26.

handled and marketed by home merchants or factors. The horrible little workshops stowed away at the backs of houses, in incredible filth and squalor, of men "scarcely one of whom is sufficiently important to have his name over his door"— the special reference is to the Wolverhampton area—were described for all time by the Commissioners on Child Labour of 1843[1]. The much less repulsive Birmingham workshop of that date, in all the endless divisions and subdivisions of the Birmingham trades, accommodated from half a dozen to twenty or thirty workers[2]. "The industry of this town," wrote a Frenchman whose observations were made in the late 'thirties, "like French agriculture, has got into a state of parcellation. You meet...hardly any big establishments."[3] His impression was that "whilst capitals tend to concentrate in Great Britain, they divide more and more in Birmingham." Tiniest, and lowest in the scale, were the nail-making workshops of Dudley, Sedgley and Cradley Heath, in some of which the French traveller saw half-naked girls turning out a thousand nails a day. These were so-called "domestic" shops, some of them attached to small farmhouses; but here there was always a master—in fact, as an English observer had reported in 1817, generally at least two; for the masters were specialists and, whilst the father made one sort of nail for one of them, his wife and children generally made a different sort for another[4].

These "nailmasters," as they had long been called, were employers in a much more real sense than the factors of knives and locks, or the merchant ironmongers; and the nailer was in no sense an independent handicraftsman. There were supposed to be some 50,000 nailers in the Black Country about 1830[5]—men, women and children—and to them the masters gave out nail-rod to be returned as nails. It is a case of pure outwork. The small master in the Birmingham trades was normally in quite a different position. Whether he were making buttons or fire-irons or coffin-furniture, lamps or pins or gun-barrels or jewellery, he was independent; though he might be

---

[1] *Report on Children in Manufactures*, p. 27, 80.

[2] *Ibid.* p. 32. For Birmingham at the end of the eighteenth century see Hamilton, H., *The English Brass and Copper Industries* (1926), p. 272. There were a few big Birmingham firms, besides Boulton and Watt.

[3] Faucher, L., *Études sur l'Angleterre* (1845), II. 147.

[4] *Lords' Report on the Poor Laws* (1817), p. 207.

[5] See the excellent historical account by Ephraim Ball in *Birmingham and the Midland Hardware District*, p. 110 sqq.

working pretty regularly for a particular factor, who marketed his wares, or he might—a lower stage—have come more or less under the factor's financial control. The scale of operations was, in most cases, so small that passage upwards and downwards was easy. Unsuccessful small masters would revert to the ranks as journeymen, and successful ones might hope to employ by twenties and thirties instead of by half-dozens. There was not a single big man in the trades in 1833 who had not once been small. That prominent sort of employer who got to London as a parliamentary witness would speak proudly of his seventy or eighty workpeople, explaining how very exceptional he was, or sadly of the great days now gone by when he had actually employed a hundred and twenty[1].

In the metal-working trades, and certain others, instances of a very significant type of industrial organisation are found in the eighteenth and early nineteenth centuries, a type in which skilled men, "masters" or descendants of masters, work on the employer's premises but retain marks—varying with the circumstances—of an independence which, in some cases, had once been greater. At times the mercantile entrepreneur can be seen slowly turning masters into factory hands. Early in the eighteenth century Ambrose Crowley, "of London, ironmonger," organised his great hardware works at Winlaton in Durham. In their separate shops at the works, the masters—they were so called—of "Crowley's crew," who made nails, locks, chisels and all sorts of ironmongery—largely for export—got tools and material from the works "ironkeeper," employed their own hammermen and prentices, and were credited with the selling price of their goods less cost of material; in which, it must be assumed, would be included some overhead charges and profit for Crowley, now Sir Ambrose, "ironmonger." Parts of the work at Winlaton were conducted on true factory lines, but most was done as described. The business still existed in the first quarter of the nineteenth century; but the organisation for that date is less well known[2]. It would seem, but it is not quite certain, that Thomas Copestake, a jeweller of Uttoxeter, renowned throughout all the Midland counties, had

---

[1] See the evidence of J. Dixon, who employed the 70–80, and T. C. Salt, whose 120 men had sunk to 60, before the *S. C. on Manufactures of 1833*, Q. 4330 *sqq.* and 4540 *sqq.*

[2] *V.C.H. Durham*, II. 281 *sqq.* Ashton, *Iron and Steel and the Industrial Revolution*, p. 195–7.

a similar organisation about 1775. His workshops "where the lapidaries have their wheels" were "ranged round a square tree-shaded court...whilst above were the shops for the smiths and setters."[1]

In the nineteenth century, the former independence of the master in process of conversion into a factory worker was sometimes shown by his continuing to take apprentices personally. I "allow the men to have apprentices," said a Wolverhampton brass-founder in 1833, who had built up a fair-sized business in an area of very small ones[2]. How unnatural what was called a "factory apprentice," as distinguished from a personal apprentice, seemed to skilled men appears from the evidence given in 1817, at an inquiry into the watch-making trades of Clerkenwell and Coventry, in which latter place the system of factory apprentices had been introduced[3]. Among the shipwrights, who were very jealous of old customs, whose unions were in the thick of the fight in 1824–5 at the time of the repeal of the combination laws, and whose trade had always necessarily involved work by masters on an employer's premises, the men's self-assertion took the form of a claim to determine for themselves the composition of the gangs, or "companies," which took on jobs in the yards collectively at a bargained price. The price was for the ship per ton, or for a given job in repairing. The contracting group might consist of from five to twenty-five shipwrights. If they found they could not complete the job alone, they hired other wrights at a wage, dividing up among themselves the remaining proceeds of the bargained price[4]. These contracting groups also claimed to determine the limits of a job, *i.e.* whether or not it arose naturally out of one

[1] Meteyard, *Life of Wedgwood*, II. 398. The probability is that these lapidaries, etc. were semi-independent masters, because relations of at least semi-independence towards the trading jeweller continued among the handicraft masters right through the nineteenth century. The author has known a working master who had workrooms on a trading jeweller's premises, but worked for him as much or little as he chose.

[2] James Dixon, in the evidence quoted on p. 176.

[3] *Minutes of Evidence before the Comm. on Petitions of Watchmakers* (1817, VI. 287), p. 73. There were 102 sub-crafts in watch-making at Coventry to each of which a boy might be apprenticed—14 subdivisions of the movement makers, 5 of the motion makers, 4 of the case makers, and so on. The factories only did finishing, *i.e.* assembling the watches.

[4] The best account of the system is in the evidence of J. P. Grieve, an old Blackwall shipwright, before the *S. C. on Navigation Laws* (1847–8, xx), Q. 8003 *sqq.* In the out-ports such groups sometimes actually built ships without an employer: see *V.C.H. Durham*, II. 303.

entrusted to their company, and so was theirs by right. Such claims some of the larger shipbuilders were resisting successfully in the 'twenties. Lesser men accepted the custom, which was no new thing. "I had two companies that I regularly employed," said one; "I agree with one or two leaders...and don't force on them men they don't want." His explanation was simple: "when I was a working-man myself I objected to working with 'non-shipwrights.'"[1] The quarrel is familiar in Trade Union history. The men's claims were rooted deep in the traditions of an old and proud skilled trade, whose members —even if technically journeymen—objected to being treated as hands and to working with those who had been, until recently, "illegal men."

To allow a certain amount of independence and self-determination to the subordinate workers in a great concern may be merely an intelligent bit of organisation from above. Gang work, piece contracts by the gang, and control by the gang of entry into it, are found in the revolutionised iron works of the early, and in the revolutionised steel works of the late, nineteenth century, where they can hardly be survivals, since the rolling gangs that served puddling furnaces and the gangs at the great steel furnaces had no eighteenth-century predecessors; but in the cases given the self-determination, which was sometimes grudged, shows no sign of having been created from above.

When a medieval gild forbade journeymen to take work home or to work for more than one master, the policy, there can be little doubt, was intended to prevent them from becoming mere outworkers, not so much in their own interests—journeymen did not make the rules—as because, once outwork is well established, the master with most character and commercial skill outstrips his fellows, drawing into his own service a disproportionate share of the available labour. The gilds believed in equality of opportunity for masters. In the long run the gilds failed; and outwork became the predominant—though never the sole—form of capitalistic industrial organisation in Britain. Probably it was still the predominant form in the reign of George IV; for though it was losing ground on one side to

---

[1] *S. C. on Combination Laws, particularly*...5 *Geo. IV, c.* 95, *Minutes of Evidence* (1825, IV. 565), p. 247: evidence of Th. Snook of Rotherhithe.

great works and factories, it was always gaining on the other at the expense of household production and handicraft. Capitalistic outwork may be said to be fully established only when the material belongs to the trading employer, and is returned to him after the process for which the outworker's skill is required has been completed—the wool given out to be spun, the yarn given out to be woven, the shirt given out for "seam and gusset and band," the nail-rod to be returned as nails, the limbs to be returned as dolls, the leather coming back as boots.

Among British outworkers the hand-loom weavers occupied the most prominent place. Hand-spinning for an employer, whether on the distaff or the wheel, was all but dead in England —a generation and a half, at most, of mill-spinning had killed it—and was already decadent in Scotland and Wales. Apart from perhaps 20,000 to 30,000 cotton power-looms, and a few experimental power-looms in linen and worsted and silk weaving, every loom in Britain was hand worked in the late 'twenties. No census of them was ever taken: but there cannot have been fewer than 500,000 and there may have been very many more. The vast majority of the weaving families were employers' outworkers. There were the 5,000 to 10,000 customer weavers[1]. There were also a certain number of journeymen weavers, who worked looms belonging to small masters on the master's premises, and of factory or shop weavers employed in the loom-shops of large manufacturers; but even in 1841 it could be stated that "neither the factory weavers nor the journeymen form large portions of the weaving population."[2] Normally, the weaver owned his loom or looms—so much fixed capital at least was his—but sometimes he hired it, or hired some of the "tackle" for it. The latter arrangement was common in figured weaving, particularly the weaving of figured silks[3]. Where the employer was loom-owner or tackle-owner his hold on the workman was strengthened; but it was already strong enough, by 1825–30, owing to the growing competition among weavers, especially in the plain cotton trade, as the Irish

---

[1] Above, p. 162.   [2] *Report on Hand Loom Weavers* (1841, X), p. 2.

[3] Looms were supplied before 1700 by the Royal Lustring Co. Scott, W. R., *Early History of Joint Stock Companies* (1911), III. 79. For muslin weaving, *circa* 1800, the employer usually supplied "reels and gear for each class of work." Unwin, *Samuel Oldknow and the Arkwrights*, p. 46. The expensive Jacquard tackle for figured silk weaving was also beyond the means of most weavers; but it was not as yet much used: only about 100 out of over 14,000 Spitalfields looms employed it in 1828. *V.C.H. Middlesex*, II. 137.

crowded into Lancashire and the West of Scotland and the power-loom began to tell. Not every hand-loom weaver was a mere employer's outworker. In the North some had a foot on the land; but this did not help the cotton weaver much as competition grew more bitter.

"There are two distinct classes of hand-loom weavers in Lancashire," Blomfield, Bishop of Chester, reported in 1827, "those who are living in large towns and those in the country places among the hills...*they* are at this moment by far the most distressed class of persons in Lancashire; for it has been their custom to take small tracts of land at high rents, which the husband and his sons cultivate, while the woman and her daughters have 2, 3 or 4 hand-looms...from the profits of which they...pay their rents;...at the same time that their loom-work fails them, their poor-rates are increased for the relief of other weavers who have no land."[1]

The same situation had arisen about Carlisle[2]. Yorkshire, too, had its small-farmer weavers; but their stake in the country was not yet a burden to them. It still helped to maintain them as independent handicraftsmen—the more so as theirs was a land of small master manufacturers, a class with which the land-holding weaver had close ties.

Textile workers other than weavers were, by this time, mostly to be found on the employer's premises—in factory or shop. In wool-combing, however, the situation was complex. The comber might be a pure domestic outworker, combing by the piece for a worsted-spinner or wool-stapler, that is to say, wool grader and merchant. But he might also be a journeyman engaged in the "comb-shop" of a small master, an arrangement common in combing though rare in weaving. Small master-combers had been a recognised industrial type in the eighteenth century—before the days of spinning machinery—and, until combing machinery became generally effective, they survived. Work done for them was outwork from the spinner's, but not from the master-comber's, point of view. The need for combing to be done on an employer's premises had been increased

---

[1] *S. C. on Emigration*, 1826–7. *Second Report*, Q. 2262. This confirms Prof. Daniels' view (*The Early English Cotton Industry*, p. 137) that exaggerated notions of the extent to which weavers held land, and of the benefit to them of holding it, have been based on Wm. Radcliffe's account of the township of Mellor. The land-holding weavers "among the hills" were not rated for the benefit of the innumerable landless town weavers but for that of landless weavers also "among the hills."

[2] *Ibid. Third Report*, Q. 2824 *sqq.*

because, right down to the end of the eighteenth century, a large body of itinerant unmarried combers followed the wool-clips, as Irishmen followed harvest, and combed for local staplers. This class was declining with the concentration of the worsted industry and the death of cottage spinning—for in the old days wool could be both combed and spun conveniently near its place of growth—but it was not yet extinct. Lastly, some of the worsted-spinning mills collected hand combers on the premises, factory workers detached from the power[1].

Those branches of the clothing industries which were organised on a capitalistic basis, either by manufacturers or large shopkeepers, relied almost exclusively on outwork. But the organisation was not simple: the man who took work from the retail shop—the reference is to London conditions—might himself employ in- or out-workers. "There are tailors called sweaters," James Mitchell reported incidentally to the Hand-loom Weavers' Commission in 1839[2]: the sweater employs women and boys, perhaps as many as twelve: "he takes home the clothes and on Saturday he draws the money." The more skilled outworking tailors worked with their wives: in London "about half the trade had wives able to earn" 9s. a week. "A third part of the clothes made in London are said to be done by women who set up workshops, and employ other women and girls": this class would cover the dressmakers working directly for consumers and the women doing outwork jobs of all kinds for the shops. No doubt Mitchell's account, based on observations made in 1837-8, would fit the conditions of ten years earlier. What he said of the skilled tailor would apply also to the outworking bespoke shoemaker of London and the great towns. The big boot-making houses of Stafford, Wellingborough, Kettering and Northampton, who took the army and navy contracts, manufactured in the bulk for export, and had for so long supplied the "Sale Shops" of London, also relied on outwork. Horton and Co., of Stafford, had employed "near a thousand" men, women and children during the wars. After the peace, the workers had to be "stinted to six or eight pairs a week," and it was said, in 1813, that only those with big families could make as much as twelve shillings[3]. There is

---

[1] See James, J., *History of the Worsted Manufacture in England* (1857), and Heaton, *The Yorkshire Woollen and Worsted Industries, s.v.* "Woolcombing."

[2] II. 281.

[3] *S. C. on...the Duty on Leather*, p. 52.

no mistaking the industrial organisation implied. The outworkers were not only in the town but "in the surrounding
villages and parishes."[1]

Knitting and hosiery in their various branches, were essentially outwork industries, the hosiery employer owning not
only the raw material but very often the knitting-frame also,
for which the knitter paid rent. The renting out of frames,
which was commoner than the renting out of looms, was so
profitable that small capitalists outside the trade put money
into frames as an investment. Witnesses complained in 1812
that this was done by "bakers, butchers, farmers' sons and
others"; and it was suggested that, to avoid extortion by these
outsiders, only "the hosier, the lace manufacturer, and the
work-man" should be allowed to own frames[2]. Here, as in
tailoring, sub-employment was well known: "a bag hosier is
a master-stockinger; he is one that gets his materials from a
hosier and he and his men work them up, and receive money
only for the working part."[3] The trade was an important one,
with its principal headquarters in Leicestershire, Nottinghamshire and Derbyshire; but in the period now under review it
was stagnant and depressed. Nor was it comparable in importance with even a single branch of weaving. The best available
estimates of the number of frames in existence, not in work,
give about 20,000 for 1782; 29,590—a curiously and suspici-
ously exact figure—for 1812 and only 33,000 for 1832[4]. They
were nearly all in England, framework-knitting in Scotland
being confined to a few places in Selkirk, Peebles and Dumfries, though there was plenty of hand-knitting for market all
over the country[5].

Every industry in which the craftsman could still do his work
at home had provided openings for the development of outwork—first in its incomplete form, in which the craftsman
found the material but worked regularly for the commercial
entrepreneur, then in its finished form, in which the material
was the master's. An enumeration of British skilled urban
trades in which outwork in some shape was known would be
little shorter than the index to a complete British Tradesman.

---

[1] *Lords' Comm. on the Poor Laws*, 1817 (1818, v), p. 101.
[2] *S. C. on Framework Knitters' Petitions* (1812, II), p. 17, 28.
[3] *Ibid.* p. 30.
[4] Muggeridge, R. M., *Report on the Condition of the Framework Knitters*
(1845, XV), p. 15.
[5] Sinclair, *General Report*, III. 295.

There are also the rural craftswomen and half-skilled women to be considered. Spinning machinery, together with knitting and lace-making "implements," had left women's hands idle and family earnings curtailed all over the country-side, in an age of hunger and high prices. Any tasks that could be given out to cottage-women found ready and cheap workers. Business man, philanthropic gentleman, and poor law reformer were all interested: of these, the profit-seeker was the most active, if least sympathetic, agent of employment. The ancient bone- and pillow-lace industry of Buckinghamshire, which had been so flourishing about 1800 that, as has been stated—or over-stated—"no women's labour for agricultural work could be obtained in the county," had recovered after years of post-war difficulties, but was soon to suffer from machine competition[1]. Straw-plaiting, already well established where Buckingham Hertford and Bedford adjoin, was spreading fast. Introduced into North Essex by the Marquis of Buckingham, late in the eighteenth century, it proved so useful that, by 1840, women, children and even old men were all busy in the Halstead, Braintree and Bocking districts[2]. The old Dorset trade in string, pack-thread, netting, cordage and ropes, with sailcloth and sacking—the urban headquarters were at Bridport and Beaminster—extended far away into the cottages[3]. Across the county, about Shaftesbury and Blandford, was a village shirt-button industry[4]. Glove-making, with its main urban headquarters in Woodstock Yeovil and Worcester, had its *attributa regio* of outworking villages in Oxfordshire Somerset and Worcestershire. The seventy directing and organising glove-masters of Worcester, early in the century, were credited with 6000 workpeople, of whom some were finishers and ware-house-workers on the premises, but most outworkers. By 1826 the employers had increased to a hundred and twenty and the workers, presumably, to 10,000 or more; but Huskisson's with-drawal of the prohibition of French gloves thinned the ranks terribly before 1830[5].

---

[1] *V.C.H. Bucks.* II. 106. [Hand-worked lace machines, i.e. "implements" were invented in the 18th century. Power was first applied to the bobbin-net machine in 1818–20 and there were 22 power factories in that trade by 1831. Felkin, W., *History of the Machine Wrought Hosiery and Lace Manufactures* (1867), p. 237 *sqq.*]

[2] *V.C.H. Essex,* II. 275. Also in Suffolk, *V.C.H. Suffolk,* II. 250.

[3] *V.C.H. Dorset,* II. 350. Lord Ernle (Prothero), *English Farming,* p. 312.

[4] *Census of* 1831, *s.v.* "Dorset."

[5] *V.C.H. Worcester,* II. 304, and authorities there quoted. *V.C.H. Somerset,* II. 329, 427. *V.C.H. Oxford,* II. 255 *sqq.*

The total contribution to the welfare of the country of the cottage outwork industries, of which these are only leading samples, it is impossible to estimate: it cannot have been very great. But it was noted that during the incendiary outbreaks of 1830 the Somerset glove-making centres remained tranquil— because the women and children could help support the men[1].

When factory legislation began, cotton-spinners constantly protested against the singling out of their industry for control and the censure which control implies. Their arguments were often sound; but the action of the reformers and of parliament is easily comprehensible. Long hours and overworked children were certainly not confined to cotton-spinning; but there was a wholesaleness, a monstrosity, about the great cotton mills which marked them down for public notice; although the less observant and less sensitive public of the eighteenth century had paid little attention to the perhaps greater evils of silk-throwing mills, some few of which were almost equally monstrous[2]. Small concerns there were of course in quantity, in the early days of cotton-spinning machinery, and in them some of the worst abuses. Dan Kenworthy told a committee in 1832 how when he was a lad they constantly worked "day and night the back end of the week and all Sunday." Who? said the committee. "Only my sister and her husband and me; sometimes another boy." "Do you mean...these were all the workpeople employed. Yes; belonging to that business."[3] But the size of the average steam spinning mill in the chief manufacturing centres, even in 1815–16, was something unprecedented in British industry. Forty-one Glasgow mills averaged 244 workpeople each. Three mills in the neighbouring country, all owned by one firm—Jas. Finlay and Co.—averaged over 500; and, at New Lanark, Dale and Owen employed over 1600. In England, the Strutts, at Belper and Millford, had 1494 workpeople. A list of forty-three important mills, in and about Manchester, gave an average employment figure of exactly 300: two firms out of the forty-three, McConnel and Kennedy, and George and Adam Murray, each employed more than 1000. In the year of the Reform Bill, a similar list of about

---

[1] V.C.H. Somerset, II. 427.
[2] For the size of the silk mills see Daniels, The Early English Cotton Industry, p. 99, and for their evils, George, London Life, p. 261.
[3] Report of Comm. on Factories Bill (1831–2, XV), Q. 2069–2077.

the same number of Manchester mills gives a figure of nearly 401[1].

When the spinner also controlled the organisation of weaving, an arrangement rare in 1816 but become common before 1830, the aggregate figures of mill workers and outworking weavers were, in extreme cases, gigantic. Monteith, Bogle and Co., of Glasgow, in 1816, had 4000 workers on their books—spinners, some power-loom weavers, 300 dyers in two distinct dye-works, and an army of outworking muslin weavers[2]. At the same date Horrocks, Miller and Co., of Preston, employed 700 spinners, in four separate mills, and a whole country-side of hand-loom weavers, nearly 7000 people all told[3].

These all are the great concerns. Average figures would be immensely reduced were it possible to include the mills of the type in which Dan Kenworthy worked down to 1814. But when, in the course of the next twenty years, the smallest type had been almost squeezed out and the combination of spinning and power-loom weaving had become rather more common, the average cotton mill visited by the newly appointed inspectors, in the early 'thirties, employed on the premises certainly under 200, but probably upwards of 150, people[4]. An industry had been created in which the normal business had something like the employment figure of the few, selected, big enterprises in most other capitalistic trades. The Wedgwoods' Etruria works, world-famous for nearly two generations, contained 387 work-people in 1816 and the second shipbuilder on the Thames employed about 230 in 1825[5]. So late as 1850 it was not claimed, even by an admiring statistician, that the average British coal mine employed more than about eighty "men, women and boys under ground and above."[6] Twenty years earlier, in view of the

---

[1] For 1815–16, S. C. on the State of the Children in the Manufactures of the United Kingdom, p. 230 sqq. (Glasgow), 16 and 20 (Finlay and Owen), 217 (Strutts), 374 (Manchester); for 1832, Tables of the Revenue, Population, etc., of the U.K. (Porter's Tables), II. 102.

[2] Report of 1816, p. 162. Monteith, Bogle and Co. were the Scottish pioneers of he steam-driven power-loom; though the first successful use of a (water-driven) power-loom is claimed for Buchanan, of Catrine, in 1801. Marwick, W. H., "The Cotton Industry and the Industrial Revolution in Scotland," Sc. Hist. Rev. XXI. 207.   [3] Ibid. p. 270.

[4] For a discussion of the difficulties of early factory statistics see E.J. (1915), p. 477.

[5] Etruria in the 1816 Report, p. 60; the second shipbuilder is G. F. Young (1825 Report on Combination Laws, p. 197). The first Thames firm, Wigram and Green, "when in full run" had about 600. Ibid. p. 220, and above, p. 69.

[6] S.J. XIII. 84.

great number of pits which were mere delvings on the outcrop
—especially in Yorkshire—the figure must have been very much
smaller; although on Tyneside and along the Wear pits were
great and deep, with large average outputs and large working
staffs. In 1800 the old Wallsend colliery had been reckoned
capable of turning out over 160,000 tons a year[1]. In 1830,
forty-one working collieries on Tyneside had an output somewhere between 2,250,000 and 3,000,000 tons a year and a
working force, above and below ground, of about 12,000—say
300 workers, of whom 200 were underground, turning out
60,000 to 70,000 tons at the average colliery[2]. The Wear figures
were even higher. But, for coal mining as a whole, such figures
were exceptional. There was, however, certainly one most
ancient industry of the first rank and possibly a second, whose
average figures were comparable with those of the parvenu
cotton. The first is tin and copper mining, which was at the
height of its strength and output in the thirty years from 1826
to 1856, together with certain sections of the copper and brass
industries that were based on it. Since the foundation of the
Companies of the Mines Royal and the Mineral and Battery
Works under Queen Elizabeth, there had always been a strain
of capitalism in these industries. The greatest eighteenth-
century brass works—at Warmley in Gloucestershire—employed
some 800 workpeople; a few of the largest copper-smelting
works counted their workpeople by scores; and the two associated Anglesey copper companies—controlled by Thomas
Williams—when at the summit of their power (1790–1815),
employed 1200 miners in the island, "had smelting works at
Amlwch, St Helens, and Swansea; had rolling mills and manufacturing works at Greenfield and Great Marlow; and besides,
owned their own ships."[3] But these were outstanding, not
representative, firms. The manufacturing end of the brass and
copper trades was in a crowd of little businesses[4]. In mining
the average unit was big. Almost exhaustive Cornish figures

---

[1] *Report on the State of the Coal Trade*, 1800, p. 547.

[2] The figures are those of John Buddle, the leading Tyneside "viewer" of
the time, before the Committees of 1830 on the *Coal Trade in the Port of London*
(VIII. p. 1, Commons' Committee, p. 405; Lords' Committee: Buddle gave
evidence before both).

[3] Hamilton, H., *The English Brass and Copper Industries to* 1800 (1926), p. 252
and *passim*; also *H. of C. Report on the Copper...Trade*, 1799 (*Reports not
inserted in the Journals*, X 653).

[4] Above, p. 71.

—for 1838—covering 160 mines, yield an average of nearly 170 workers per mine[1].

A comparison of Dolcoath or Wheal Kitty with New Lanark or Belper would be strictly valid only for the scale of operations. There was a strong leaven of independence among the Cornishmen. True, there were plenty of ordinary wage earners —"day men"—and their number was growing. But there were also the old aristocracy of the mines, men who took on jobs of work after a regular auction of the "pitches" held by the captain of the mine on "setting day." Small groups of "tutworkers" would agree to sink a shaft or drive a level at a price. A regular debit and credit account was kept between them and the mine authorities, and payments were often made on account. Groups of "tributers" would undertake to extract and prepare the ore for an agreed-on percentage of what it eventually fetched, also receiving advances on account, called "subsist."[2] These men are comparable rather with Ambrose Crowley's "masters," or the companies of the Thames shipwrights, than with the pure wage earners of the cotton mills. Still the mine was a business unit, with the main characteristics of a factory—it was owned by investing adventurers, and absolutely dependent on the central power which kept it free of water. Dolcoath, the deepest, was already 228 fathom deep in 1808[3].

The second industry whose scale of operations was possibly comparable with cotton is iron-working. There had been ironmasters with great businesses long before the first cotton mill was built. Just when the textile inventions were being made, some of these businesses were already gigantic. Antony Bacon, iron merchant from Whitehaven, who began the creation of Merthyr "Tudful" in 1765, eventually became an M.P. and "considering himself as moving in a superior orbit...transferred, in the year 1783...his lease and ironworks at Cyfarthfa to...Rd. Crawshay Esq., reserving to himself and assigns a clear annuity of £10,000."[4] Unless he outwitted Crawshay, which is unlikely, for Crawshay also made a fortune, Cyfarthfa

---

[1] They are in the first volume of the *S.J.* p. 78–9.

[2] Lewis, G. R., *The Stannaries* (1908), p. 202–6, and *V.C.H. Cornwall* (also Lewis), I. 568. Both "tut" and "tribute" were already giving way to ordinary wage work, especially "tribute."

[3] *V.C.H. Cornwall*, I. 565.

[4] Davies, *South Wales*, II. 458. See also Smiles, S., *Industrial Biography* (2nd ed. 1879), p. 130, and Ashton, *Iron and Steel and the Industrial Revolution*, p. 210, etc.

must have been a very useful property. It was only a part of
Bacon's "mineral kingdom."[1] He sold Penydaren to Homfray,
the man who perfected the puddling process; Dowlais to Lewis,
one of whose partners was John Guest of Broseley; and the
Plymouth works to Antony Hill. Bacon's ordnance contract,
which had served him well in the Seven Years' War, had already
been transferred to Carron—the works which Roebuck developed and in which James Watt was for a time interested.
By 1814, having made "carronades" during many years of war
and taken advantage of the power which Watt had harnessed,
the Carron works were claimed, by a Scotsman[2], as "the most,
extensive manufactory in Europe": they employed 2000 men.
The average Scottish iron-foundry, however, at that date
employed only about twenty[3].

In the same group as Carron were the greater English and
Welsh iron works of the years after Waterloo. Crawshay also
has been credited with a working staff of more than 2000 men
during the wars[4]; and Cyfarthfa remained active. There were
said to be ten iron works in the Black Country in 1812, each of
which had cost over £50,000 at the start[5]. A traveller credits
the Low Moor and Bowling company, near Bradford, with
1500 men, in the 'twenties, including the colliers[6]. In 1824
Samuel Walker and William Yates employed 700 men in their
works at Gospel Oak, Staffordshire, and perhaps 1300 "colliers
and ironstone getters."[7] But they only had use for seven steam-
engines of 350 horse-power all told. The main business of the
Walker family, the Rotherham works, was, like many of the
greater ironworks, what a modern economist calls an integrated
concern—mines of both sorts, furnaces, forges, plate mills and
a foundry—which made most things from tinning plates and
wrought-iron work to cannon and suspension bridges[8]. William
Mathews, of Corbyn's Hill, King's Swinford, in his works near

---

[1] Scrivenor, *History of the Iron Trade*, p. 122-3. Bacon had a lease of forty
square miles about Merthyr from Lord Talbot, Smiles, *op. cit.* p. 130.

[2] Sinclair, *op. cit.* v. 286.   [3] *Ibid.*

[4] By Scrivenor, *op. cit.* p. 123.

[5] Ashton, *op. cit.* p. 100: no authority quoted.

[6] Meidinger, *Reisen*, I. 309.

[7] *S. C. on Artisans and Machinery*, p. 116 *sqq.*: Walker's evidence. It is not
Samuel Walker the first.

[8] *S. C. on Manufactures*, 1833, Q. 9506 *sqq.*: Walker's evidence. The only
Samuel Walker in the *D.N.B.* is a divine whose sermons were published post-
humously: for the Walker family see Ashton, *op. cit. passim.*

Dudley employed 400 to 500 men in 1833; he made, among his newer "lines," structural cast-iron, gas and water-pipes, iron fencing and iron barges[1]. Antony Hill, Plymouth Works, Merthyr, specialised on malleable iron. With seven blast furnaces, and puddling furnaces to match, his near 1500 men could turn out 20,000 tons of bar iron in a year; and he had "an iron-ore work" in Cumberland[2]. By 1830 the four great establishments which had grown out of Antony Bacon's "mineral kingdom" were sending over 70,000 tons of iron yearly down the Glamorgan Canal, their sole outlet for heavy stuff[3]. But as in the mid 'twenties the whole population of the parish of Merthyr, which contained all the works, was round about 20,000; as a few smaller works existed there; as women and children are of little use in iron-making; and as the works would require some food-supplying and miscellaneous population—it seems most unlikely that Hill's employment figure of 1833 can have been representative even for these four giant concerns. A population of some 20,000, which would include about 5000 males over twenty, will hardly yield 6000 iron workers, miners, and ironstone getters.

No figures are available for an exact comparison of the average firm in the primary iron industries with the average cotton firm or Cornish mine. If there were only a few small iron works about Merthyr, there were many elsewhere in South Wales, Monmouthshire, and the Black Country—the districts which together contained more than three-quarters of the British blast furnaces in 1830[4]. The combination of smelting with puddling and the subsequent processes was not by any means universal. Yet it seems probable that the average ironmaster, the primary producer, would rank, as capitalist and entrepreneur, on equal terms with the cotton spinner; though, as the Scottish figures of 1814 show, there were very many small foundries all over the country for utilising the now abundant and fashionable cast iron.

An industry of the second or possibly third rank which was normally organised in comparatively large units—and indeed always had been—was glass-making. There were 116 "glass-

---

[1] S. C. on Manufactures, Q. 9600 sqq.: Mathews' evidence.
[2] Ibid. Q. 10,207 sqq. Above, p. 50.
[3] Scrivenor, op. cit. p. 123.
[4] Firms with more than one or two furnaces were the exceptions. See Scrivenor, op. cit. p. 135, and below, p. 429.

houses" in Great Britain in 1833; but very often one firm owned
more than one "house."[1] The leading firm in the country, that
of Isaac Cookson, had seven "houses" in South Shields and
two in Newcastle. Trustworthy employment figures are not
available[2], but a rough idea of the scale of operations can be
gained from the excise returns. Cookson's paid nearly £60,000
in excise that year. Had all their "houses" been engaged on
common bottle-glass, this would represent an output of over
8000 tons, as the excise was 7s. a hundredweight. Cookson's
were in fact very large makers of bottle-glass, but they also
made crown-glass for windows, on which the excise was
73s. 6d. a hundredweight, and plate-glass which paid 60s.
However their output was divided between the three sorts,
it must have been reckoned in thousands of tons. Second, as
a revenue producer, to Cookson's came William Chance, of
Stourbridge. His three "houses" made little besides window
glass crown and "sheet," which was taxed at the same rate
as crown. As his contribution to the excise was £54,000, his
output must have been upwards of 700 tons. Third came
Sir M. W. Ridley and Co., of Newcastle, with £40,000 also from
three "houses"—bottle-glass and crown-glass; fourth Cour-
thorpe and Co., of Bristol, with £39,000 from two "houses";
and fifth Charles Atwood, of Southwick and Gateshead, with
£38,000, also from two. The average English "house" paid
more than £6000 and the average English firm more than
£9000 in excise—a figure which represents over 1200 tons of
bottle-glass, perhaps 160 tons of flint-glass, or over 120 tons
of crown or sheet per firm. These were the staple articles in
1833. Very little plate-glass was made at this time—only about
700 tons in all England[3]. In Scotland the scale of operations
in the whole trade was smaller, and in Ireland much smaller.

Isolated great businesses, more or less of the factory type,

[1] *Thirteenth Report, Commission of Excise Inquiry*, 1835; on which this
paragraph is based.

[2] There is a guess in J. R. McCulloch's *Commercial Dictionary*.

[3] The British Plate Glass Co., of Ravenhead (St Helen's), had the monopoly
of the manufacture in the late eighteenth century, under an Act of 13 Geo. III,
c. 38. It imported French workmen. It failed commercially and was bought
up in 1798; but plate-glass was made only at Ravenhead until about 1815
("about twenty years ago," *Excise Report*, p. 40) when Cookson and Cuthbert
of Newcastle began to make it—reducing the price in the next twenty years,
"I believe full two-thirds" (R. L. Chance in *Excise Report*, p. 131). Ultimately
Ravenhead passed to the Pilkingtons, "wine and spirit merchants and rectifiers,"
who had begun to make crown-glass in 1827. *V.C.H. Lancashire*, II. 405.

with or without power, were to be found in numerous industries in which the normal business was still small, or still organised on outwork or handicraft lines. Such, for instance, were Greaves' new cutlery factory at Sheffield and the big London breweries. Robert Hulton, a Dublin coach-builder, employed 222 men in 1825[1]. These "sports" had been known in the eighteenth and even in the seventeenth and sixteenth centuries. Among the small masters of the Birmingham district, Boulton is credited with accommodation for 700 to 800 workpeople at Soho in 1770[2]. Copestake, the capitalist manufacturing jeweller of Uttoxeter, is said to have employed from one to two hundred men; and Josiah Wedgwood the first certainly employed several hundreds. Before the invention of modern textile machinery, Sir George Strickland had once found work for a hundred and fifty people in his woollen factory at Boynton[3]. "Crowley's crew" at Winlaton, early in the century, was a large one. Thomas Lombe's silk-throwing mill at Derby "contained in all its building half a quarter of a mile in length[4]." So factories of a sort might be traced back to the half-legendary Stumpe of Malmesbury and Jack of Newbury.

One industry had just come into being, when the Regent became the King, in which the scale of operations was always and necessarily large. This was the gas industry. The London Gaslight and Coke Company in 1822, from its three works in Horseferry Road, Brick Lane and Curtain Road, worked 126½ miles of mains and employed a capital of £580,000. The City of London Company had about 50 miles of main: the South London Company from 30 to 40, and the Imperial Company in the Hackney Road over 20 miles.[5] The Edinburgh Gas Works had nearly 20 miles of main in 1818; and the Manchester Gas Works were supplying 100,000 cubic feet of gas per day in the depth of winter in 1823[6]. The parliamentary committee which reported on the industry in that year assured the public that

---

[1] S. C. on Combination Laws, 1825, p. 8.
[2] Smiles, S., Lives of Boulton and Watt, p. 129.
[3] Young, Northern Tour, II. 7.
[4] Anderson, History of Commerce, III. 91.
[5] Sir Wm Congreve's Report in S. C. on Gas-Light Establishments (1823, V. 195).
[6] Ibid. p. 89, 48. The Manchester Works were "municipal"—created without legal authority by the Commissioners of Police, to the natural satisfaction of Webb, S. and B., English Local Government, IV, Statutory Authorities (1922), p. 262.

the danger of using gas was less than had been supposed; that coal-gas was not in itself explosive, and that they could not "close their report without expressing their satisfaction that the Public have obtained so great and so rapidly increasing a means of adding to the convenience and comfort of society... and they are of opinion, that as a means of police, much benefit would be derived from its general introduction to light the streets of this Metropolis."[1]

In partially revolutionised industries the large power-using unit was becoming common, but was not yet really representative. This is true of the textile industries, other than cotton. There were, of course, large businesses and large wool linen and silk mills. English flax and worsted spinning were following in the tracks of the cotton industry. Marshall's flax mills at Leeds were quite comparable with the larger Manchester factories—and more unhealthy than any of them. There were already some big worsted spinning mills in the Bradford district. But weaving, both woollen and worsted, was still normally done "out," though some employers had gathered all their workpeople under their own eye, like Wormald Gott and Wormalds of Leeds, in whose mill—rebuilt after a fire in 1799 —"the whole process of manufacture... from the first breaking of the wool to the finishing of the piece... was conducted on a very extensive scale."[2] It is easy to exaggerate, in imagination, the size of the mills; and there are no general figures from the 'twenties with which to check the imagination. But from the 'thirties there are. Andrew Ure calculated in 1835, from the returns of the first factory inspectors, that the average woollen or worsted mill contained 44·6 persons, mainly women and children. A rather later and more exact calculation, based on material collected in 1839, gives a corresponding figure of 58, and shows that the average employment figure in 342 Yorkshire worsted mills, the giant concerns of the wool industries, was just over 75[3]. That is after ten or fifteen years of rapid growth both of the industries and of their constituent units. Mills were being built very fast in the early 'thirties; "enough

[1] *Report*, p. 4.
[2] Baines, E., *Yorkshire Past and Present*, III. 158, quoting a guide-book of 1806. The arrangement was common in the actual town of Leeds in 1834 *S. C. on Hand Loom Weavers' Petition*, Q. 500. "Cloth is woven mostly in the weaver's own house? No, not in the town: in the neighbourhood it is."
[3] Ure, *Philosophy of Manufactures* and *Second Report of S. C. on Mills and Factories* (1840, x), App. II.

to astonish anybody," said a witness in 1833[1]. If figures existed
for 1825–30, thirty-five to forty employees for factories in the
wool industries taken *en bloc*, and fifty to sixty for worsted
spinning, might not be unreasonable. Factory *plus* outwork
figures for the larger firms would be much greater; for in many
cases, particularly in the woollen industry in its then stage of
development, a minority of the work was done on the premises.
In worsted a man might be a spinner and nothing else, but in
the larger woollen firms the control of production from start
to finish was in the same hands—whether the work was done
"in" or "out." A maker of army broadcloth from Wakefield
told the committee on the combination laws in 1825 that he
employed over four hundred people, including his weavers,
and a Huddersfield witness, speaking of one of the great men of
his district in the fancy woollen trade, said: "we consider them
considerable men when they have a hundred weavers, but he
has nearly three hundred."[2] Eight years later, John Brooke of
Huddersfield "supposed he employed" upwards of a thousand
in- and out-workers, and "one of the largest superfine manufactories in the whole of the West of England" claimed fifteen
hundred[3].

On the other side of the account, whether the average business or the average factory is being measured, must be set the
big battalions of the Yorkshire domestic clothiers. In the first
decade of the century it was reckoned that more than 3000 of
them came in to sell their pieces in the two chief cloth halls of
Leeds[4]; and there were other important selling halls in the
West Riding, besides another small one in Leeds itself. Their
numbers had decreased by 1820; but even twenty-five years
later Leon Faucher was greatly impressed by their sustained
strength: "c'est en Angleterre qu'il faut aller pour voir, tant
que l'humble édifice subsiste encore, cette exception toute
démocratique aux progrès absorbants de la grande industrie."[5]
The edifice still had considerable resisting power; for in 1858
the historian of Yorkshire explained that only about half those
engaged in the woollen industry worked in factories—outside
were a great majority of piece-working weavers and a minority
of the still independent domestic clothiers[6].

---

[1] *S. C. on Manufactures*, Q. 1104.   [2] P. 59, 131.
[3] *S. C. on Manufactures*, 1833, Q. 1859, 1320–2.   [4] Baines, *op. cit.* III. 158.
[5] *Op. cit.* II. 18. For the decrease before 1820, *S. C. on Laws Relating to
Stamping Woollen Cloth* (1821, VI), p. 49.   [6] Baines, *op. cit.* II. 625.

Before the machine and factory days, there had been no sharp cleavage between those clothiers whom the famous parliamentary report of 1806 on the Woollen Industry first officially labelled "domestic" and those who, in the words of Queen Elizabeth's statute, "put out cloth to making and sale."[1] The small capitalist, who bought wool and worked at home with his family and his hired men, if prosperous, could give out yarn to some neighbouring weaver; if very prosperous, he could concentrate on the buying, giving out, and selling and become an entrepreneur. Unless he was in a very small way indeed, he would always need to get some spinning done outside his own domestic establishment, so long as the mechanical rule, one spinner one thread, remained valid. He was seldom able to do for himself the final processes of cloth-working or finishing. This business was concentrated in the towns and was done by, or for, the merchant. It was largely from these cloth-working merchants that the first mill-owning "merchant manufacturers" had been recruited; though the prosperous "giving out" clothiers of Yorkshire and of the West of England —where the true domestic type was almost unknown—were also in a position to set up mills of their own, as machinery came into use[2].

The domestic men reacted to machinery in different ways. Fulling had always been done for them on commission, often at old manorial water-mills. Now they might get some other process, such as carding which was early taken over by machinery, done in the same way. Slubbing and spinning they could do successfully at home on the hand-driven billy and jenny—not very expensive implements. Sometimes, instead of selling their pieces unfinished to the merchant—the traditional arrangement—they got finishing also done on commission, and "merchanted" themselves. "I am a bit of a merchant": "occasionally I get some pieces finished" and sell them; "when I have stocks; when trade is slack"—was a kind of evidence not infrequently given[3].

But by far the most interesting and important product of the domestic clothiers' reaction to machinery was the co-

---

[1] *The Statute "of Artificers"* (5 Eliz. c. 4), § 20.

[2] Some of the best evidence bearing on the rise of the merchant manufacturers is that given by J. Waterhouse, of Halifax, before the 1821 *S. C. on Stamping Cloth*, p. 7 *sqq.*

[3] *E.g.* John Hearnshaw, in 1821, *S. C. on Stamping Cloth*, p. 73.

operative mill, the so-called company mill. At the start these were water-mills, often on the sites of the old fulling mills; and the first, and always the most important, of the new machines installed there was the carding engine with its great wire-toothed cylinders[1]. Between 1810 and 1830 steam was generally adopted; and by the latter date the company-mill system was widespread. A dozen years later it was "not the exception but the rule."[2] The course of operations in 1843 was as follows: the clothier bought his wool already sorted; it was "scribbled," carded, and in the 'forties always "slubbed," at the mill; spun and woven by the clothier "at his own home"; fulled at the mill; sold unfinished, "in the balk," as the phrase was, and is; dyed and finished by the merchant. In the early days the clothiers clubbed together quite informally. From ten to forty of them would put up some £50 each; would buy land, build on it, mortgage it, get the machinery on credit, and put in a manager. Even those who had no share might use the mill, paying ordinary commission rates. Some of the joint owners could not write. In the early days no banking account was kept. The Common Law did not recognise these informal and unchartered joint-stock enterprises; so there were abundant opportunities for malversation and fraud. By the 'twenties, more care was being taken and regular partnership deeds came into use. One of these, of 1825[3], provided that all shareholders must be clothiers living within a mile and a half of the mill; that the mill should have its banking account; that there should be a committee and trustees; and that all action should be taken in the trustees' names. Even so, the arrangements were still irregular at law. Being unchartered, the companies could not sue or be sued collectively, nor could one partner sue another on a joint debt—save possibly in Chancery, and that kind of suit the Yorkshiremen thought, very properly in the days of Jarndyce v. Jarndyce, was out of the question.

[1] Above, p. 144.

[2] S. C. on Joint Stock Companies (1844, VII), App. v, p. 348. The best account of the early company mills, based on the evidence of J. Baker, a sub-inspector of factories, and John Nussey, of Birstall, a clothier. There is a good account of one 1831 company mill, at Farsley, in the Hand Loom Weavers' Report, III. 549. The Birmingham Brass Company of 1826, successor to an eighteenth-century company of the same name, had something in common with the Woollen Company Mills. It was formed on a co-operative basis by small manufacturers, who undertook to buy from it 5 cwt. of brass for every £20 share held—there were 700 shares. It died in 1830. Hamilton, Brass and Copper Industries, p. 237.

[3] Given in the 1844 Report.

13-2

The company mills were included in the factory statistics of the 'thirties; but as each of them did part of the work of producing cloth for a score or two of small manufacturers, they fall into an entirely different class from the privately owned factories. Yet their very existence was witness to the resistless advance of machinery; and their life as adjuncts to independent, domestic, manufacturing businesses might have been set its term by a far-sighted mechanic before 1830. When the hand-worked jenny could no longer compete with the power-driven mule, in the production of even second-rate yarn, weaving alone would remain domestic; and the mere domestic weaver had long ceased to be an independent producer. The mill would become the headquarters of production rather than the home; and though the subdivision of mills among different firms was well known in the 'thirties, 'forties, and later—"there are often several firms in one building": "sometimes as many as a dozen"[1]—subdivision among a score or two of firms was never possible. In some way or other concentration had to be attained. But the time of inevitable concentration was not yet: in the 'twenties the company mills were still a-making.

The flax and silk mills of the early 'thirties were, on the average, considerably larger than the mills in the wool industries. Ure's calculation (1835) gave an average employment figure of 93·3 for linen and 128·3 for silk, against 44·6 for wool and 175·5 for cotton. Nearly half the flax mills at that time were Scottish. Many were very new, and the aggregate of persons employed in them—including Ireland—was under 33,000. In view of the immense amount of customer and market hand-loom weaving, and the very considerable amount of hand-spinning, which went on in the 'twenties, the factory hands of Great Britain in 1825—of whom there may have been some 20,000—cannot be treated as, in any way, representative workers in the industry. For silk the position was different, though some of the same considerations apply. There was a very rapid growth of large steam silk mills, particularly about Manchester, between 1820 and 1830. The first Manchester throwing-mill was finished for Vernon Royle in 1819–20. By 1832 there were a dozen "what might be called Manchester mills."[2] Between 1825 and 1832 successful experiments were being made there with the steam power-loom, for weaving the

---

[1] S. C. on Mills and Factories, 1840, Q. 8, 648.
[2] S. C. on the Silk Trade, 1832: Royle's evidence, Q. 3022 sqq.

cheaper silks and the mixed fabrics of silk and other fibres, such as the so-called Irish poplins and the notorious Victorian bombazines. These Manchester mills would increase the average employment figure. On the other hand, silk-throwing and the associated processes had long been mill businesses, so that the mill figures would cover the whole of that section of the trade. For the year 1824 it was reckoned that the average throwing mill employed 176 people[1]. Only weaving remains. Its organisation was exceedingly complex, but it was not yet a factory industry, though at times some looms were collected on factory premises[2]. Not infrequently, especially in the North —Manchester, Leek, Congleton, Macclesfield—a man who was primarily a silk-throwster might stand in the same relation to the silk weavers as did Horrockses, the Preston cotton spinners, to their thousands of rural cotton weavers. Ayton, of Macclesfield, for example, an employer of this class, had 600 to 700 names on his books in 1818—"not half...in the factory."[3] Vernon Royle also was throwster and manufacturer.

Among the weavers, both the handkerchief weavers who predominated at Macclesfield and the ribbon weavers of Coventry—but not among the broad-silk weavers of Spitalfields—there was a class of "undertakers" corresponding almost exactly to the *maîtres ouvriers* of the contemporary Lyons trade[4]. The undertaker got silk from a master, employed journey-hands and prentices, and "to repay him for the winding, warping, shop-room and looms, he has a third of the earnings." Down to 1813 the Macclesfield rule had been that no undertaker should have more than two prentices. Since the repeal of the Apprenticeship Law the whole system was undergoing change. Masters were cutting out the undertaker and making the journeyman find his own loom tackling and shop-room.

In the Coventry district the undertaker system, or some equivalent, had been essential, because before 1820 the work had been done chiefly for masters in London. But as the master also had an agent on the spot, who dealt with the under-

---

[1] *Ibid.* Q. 11,360: evidence of J. Brocklehurst of Macclesfield.
[2] See *e.g. S. C. on Petitions of the Ribbon Weavers* (1818, IX. 5), p. 66—a Coventry ribbon man with thirty looms in and seventy out: p. 76, a Macclesfield bandanna man with fifty in and about one hundred out.
[3] *Ibid.* p. 66.
[4] *Ibid.* p. 68, 90, etc. For Lyons, Levasseur, *Hist. des classes ouvrières*; Pariset, *Hist. de la fabrique Lyonnaise*; Godart, *L'ouvrier en soie de Lyon.*

takers, it was possible—there also—to cut out these sub-employers. Apparently this had not been much done down to 1818; but with the rapid spread of the "engine-loom," which wove many narrow ribbons at once, between 1818 and 1832, the undertaker system declined[1]. In 1818 there had been some 3000 engine-looms and some 5500 "single-hand" (*i.e.* single ribbon) looms in the district. By 1832 hardly any single-hand looms remained in the town itself, but there were 4500 engine-looms; there was no "undertaking" in the "engine" trade—"the master finding warps and giving out the article ready for manufacture"—but the undertaker still dominated the single-hand trade of the surrounding villages[2]. By this time there were a good many masters domiciled in Coventry. They and the London masters had cut out the undertaker by themselves supplying engine-looms to the journeymen, so riveting their hold on them.

In Spitalfields, masters dealt direct with the weavers and the businesses were of all sizes, though the average business was probably rather large. In 1832 there were said to be seventy-nine broad-silk manufacturers in Spitalfields. In 1838 there were 6751 broad-silk looms (and 2551 velvet looms) at work in the district. The dates are too far apart, the figures too uncertain, to justify a simple division sum, and it is not clear whether or not the 1832 reference includes velvet; but they point vaguely towards a rather large average firm in the 'thirties. Taken as a whole, the silk industry was highly capitalistic, as exotic industries are everywhere apt to be. Big men might be interested financially in both throwing and manufacturing, perhaps also in importing. But its intricate organisation included units of all types and sizes. Only in throwing was the factory, properly so called, dominant[3].

It has been customary to think of the manufacturing firms of early nineteenth-century England, whatever their form of

---

[1] The engine-loom was not a power-loom: it was a variant of the Dutch or swivel-loom long in use in the Manchester small-ware trade.

[2] *Comm. of* 1818, p. 7. *Comm. of* 1832, Q. 968, 999, 1001, 1193.

[3] Above, p. 146. *Comm. of* 1832, Q. 4805 *sqq.*, 8612, etc. *Hand Loom Weavers,* II. 227. *E.J.* Dec. 1916, "The Spitalfields Acts." The figure of 79 is doubtful: the same witness said there had been 167 firms in 1826 (Q. 8612). It perhaps refers only to the larger firms; for "almost every man who employs 2 or 3 looms will be called a master manufacturer." *Second Report on Foreign Trade (Silk and Wine)* (1821, VII. 421), p. 29.

organisation, as so many blind aspiring growths, struggling upwards—in the brute indifference of their jungle—towards the sun of property and respectability. The custom is in the main just; but there is much evidence of rational, if ruthless, co-operation among growths with common interests, and it seems probable that there was more co-operation than there is surviving evidence[1]. "We rarely hear," wrote Adam Smith, "of the combinations of masters....But whoever imagines, upon this account, that masters rarely combine, is as ignorant of the world as of the subject. Masters are always and everywhere in a sort of tacit, but constant and uniform combination, not to raise the wages of labour."[2] He had in mind only this one aspect of masters' combination, doubtless the most important. During the currency of the great Combination Laws (1799–1825) this "tacit combination" sometimes became vocal; though as a whole the industrial history of that dark quarter-century bears out another saying of Smith's: "we seldom...hear of this combination, because it is the usual, and one may say the natural state of things which nobody ever hears of." Or, as a witness put it in 1824, masters' combinations were "a matter of daily notoriety."[3] Yet wage control combinations, and some others, can easily be traced in the records; and the former at least may often be suspected where not clearly traceable.

From the eighteenth century had been inherited a tradition of organisation among the "interests." "The West India Interest," with its West India Committee of persons resident in London but connected with the sugar colonies, was a continuous and powerful political force[4]. Associated tobacco-merchants, skilled in the methods of propaganda, had ruined Walpole's excise scheme[5]. Associated industrialists of many sorts, led—on this occasion not to his credit—by Josiah Wedgwood the first, and organised as the General Chamber of the Manufacturers of Great Britain, had helped to wreck Pitt's equally rational proposals for Anglo-Irish free trade in

[1] This section was drafted before the publication of Ashton's *Iron and Steel*, on p. 184 of which some similar remarks occur, with valuable instances of eighteenth- and early nineteenth-century combinations of masters.

[2] *Wealth of Nations* (ed. Cannan), I. 68.

[3] *S. C. on Artisans and Machinery*, p. 12.

[4] Penson, L. M., "The London West India Interest in the Eighteenth Century." *E.H.R.* July 1921.

[5] Brisco, N. A., *The Economic Policy of Robert Walpole* (1907), p. 92 *sqq.*

1785[1]. About the same date the "Associated Smelters" of copper —in Bristol and South Wales—were designing a market-sharing agreement with the new great power in the copper world, Williams of Anglesey[2]. The wars and the industrial troubles which accompanied them had necessitated much joint action —representations and petitions about taxes, workmen's combinations, monetary matters, convoy and prize, the orders in council, property lost abroad, machine-breaking riots and corn laws. Government's growing anxiety over the condition of England question, with its parliamentary committees and commissions, during the Great Peace[3], held together, or drew together, the criticised interests—cotton men, silk men, salt men, shipping men, and the rest. Some interests adhered naturally without external pressure.

"Is there not a committee to fix prices?" said the chairman of a parliamentary committee on the Use of Rock Salt in the Fisheries to a Cheshire salt merchant and manufacturer in 1817[4]. Replied; "the trade is under the control of several committees, situate at different places; but it is certainly wrong to say that these committees are appointed for the purpose of regulating the price; it is considered...a laudable. association to promote the...trade and improve it." Asked whether price regulation was not one way of promoting the trade; answered, "It is." Another witness who believed himself to be the largest salt proprietor in the kingdom[5], explained that this was the "second or third" such association. "It had been called a combination; but he called it an association for the improvement of the trade." Pressed a little, he admitted that "it was thought highly prudential to make an addition to the price." This important and experienced man of affairs added in self-defence: "I should suppose there is scarcely any trade which has not meetings of committees of a similar description." There is hardly a trade, affirmed another witness, "the trade to the Baltic, the trade to the Brazils, or any other trade, in which the parties are not associated together." Such observations, even though biased and not decisive of fact, are informing. It will

---

[1] Murray, A. E., *Commercial Relations between England and Ireland* (1907), ch. XII. O'Brien, G., *The Economic History of Ireland in the 18th Century* (1918), ch. XXI. Ashton, *Iron and Steel*, p. 169–74. Witt Bowden in *American Hist. Rev.* XXV. [Who holds that Pitt's proposals were not rational but ill-drafted and dangerous.]

[2] Hamilton, *The British Brass and Copper Industries*, chs. VII, VIII; above, p. 186.   [3] The term is Harriet Martineau's.

[4] 1817, III. 123, p. 22.   [5] Thomas Marshall.

be noted that the cases cited are of dealers rather than of manufacturers. They recall another well-known saying of Adam
Smith: "people of the same trade seldom meet together, even
for merriment and diversion, but the conversation ends in a
conspiracy against the public, or in some contrivance to raise
prices."[1]

"The meetings of [London] brewers to fix and lower prices"
—a pretty euphemism—were "not disguised by them but declared to be necessary" in 1818[2]. The employers in the silk
industry, that same year, were reticent. Macclesfield had a
committee. Its object, said the Macclesfield men, was to prevent pilfering of silk[3]. (This was a recognised function of
masters' organisations in outwork industries: the Worsted
Committee for this purpose was statutory[4].) Pressed, the
Macclesfield men allowed that "their objects were various."
Pressed again on the matter of pilfering—"can it be possible
that they meet only for that purpose?"—they evaded the issue:
"we meet very often for that purpose; I am sorry to say too
often." Spitalfields was just as discreet. There was a masters'
society with subscriptions. Its main object also was to prevent
silk pilfering. About its other objects the witness fenced with
some skill and managed not to commit himself[5]. In the course
of the combination law controversy of 1825 a good deal of
masters' organisation came to light, to half-light, mainly in the
shipbuilding and shipping trades. The Thames shipbuilders,
or some of them, had recently formed a society to fight the
shipwrights' union[6]. Thirty-two builders had been written to
and eighteen had met. The particular organisation seems new,
but it may have had formal or informal predecessors. At Newcastle the shipowners had reorganised their society in 1820.
They asserted, with seeming sincerity, that it was not a fighting
organisation against the seamen: "never except upon one
occasion" had they discussed seamen's wages[7]. What its
functions were they did not explain, but intelligent speculation

---

[1] *Wealth of Nations*, I. 130.
[2] *Report of the Comm. to whom the Petition of several Inhabitants of London...
complaining of the high price and inferior quality of Beer, was referred* (1818, III.
295), p. 4.
[3] *S. C. on Petitions of Ribbon Weavers*, p. 79.
[4] See below, p. 342–3.
[5] *S. C. on Petitions of Ribbon Weavers*, p. 191.
[6] *S. C. on Combination Laws*, p. 404.
[7] *Ibid.* p. 166.

is not excluded. In the Black Country the nailmasters met regularly, from before 1800, with the main object of fixing wages, though they never had occasion to give evidence on the point at Westminster[1].

Newcastle was the headquarters of the most long-lived and notorious employers' combination of the early nineteenth century—the committee for the "limitation of the vend," *i.e.* output and sale, of coal raised on the Tyne and Wear[2]. Ever since 1771, with certain interruptions—periods of cut-throat competition, or what was called " a fighting trade "—this organisation had been in existence. Its strength was the natural monopoly of supplying sea-borne coal to London and almost the whole of Eastern, South-Eastern, and Southern England which the Tyne and Wear had enjoyed for centuries. The opening of the Stockton and Darlington railway, following on the construction of coal-carrying canals and their associated railways, had interfered somewhat with this monopoly; but it was not yet seriously threatened. During the 'twenties the system worked thus. Each colliery sent a representative to Newcastle and the representatives chose a committee. Every colliery was rated, given—that is—a certain proportion of the total output and sale of each class of coal, according to its reputed capacity. From month to month—in later years from fortnight to fortnight—the total amounts which might be "vended" were fixed by the central committee, with an eye to the state of the market, and of these amounts each concern might ship its appropriate quantity. The object was, of course, to maintain a level of prices which the associated owners regarded as remunerative. Once a year the proprietors of the best coals named the price at which they proposed to sell during the next twelve months. Inferior sorts had their prices adjusted to those of best coals, and it was the business of the committee to sanction the maximum "issue"—as the periodical declarations of the total amounts to be "vended" were called—which was compatible with the securing of these prices. Naturally there were recurrent disputes as to the "basis," the share of

[1] *Birmingham and the Midland Hardware District*, p. 110. Ashton, *op. cit.* p. 184, where several combinations (not quoted here) are referred to.

[2] Dealt with in Porter's *Progress of the Nation*. The main sources are the *Report on the State of the Coal Trade* of 1800, the *S. C. on the State of the Coal Trade in the Port of London*, 1830 (VIII. 1) and the evidence taken before the Lords' Committee on the same subject (VIII. 405). For the geography of the trade, see the plate facing p. 236 below.

the total output which each old colliery was to enjoy or new one
to secure. The outbreak of such a dispute meant the beginning
of a spell of "fighting trade," when the collieries, instead of
selling peaceably to merchants, would often "hire vessels and
send their own coals to market"[1] in their eagerness to secure
the maximum "vend" for themselves. But always they
came back to agreement, and marginal concerns—in modern
economic language—which a continuance of "fighting trade"
might have forced over the edge and into the gulf, were again
able to participate in the profits of keeping Londoners warm.

The workings of the "limitation of the vend" were very
fully inquired into by the parliamentary committees of 1800 and
of 1830. The committee of 1824–5 in effect ignored them.
That of 1830, having heard that coal from the Tees was
beginning to compete in London with that from the Tyne and
Wear, and that the inland coalfields were able to cut into the
old monopoly areas of the vend committee, when its prices
were fixed too high, advised parliament to trust to free and
open competition for the prevention of monopolistic abuses,
expressing the hope that other areas would never be induced to
send representatives to the Newcastle committee[2]. Combination laws being abolished, and parliament much occupied with
other things at that time, the advice was taken. This is not the
place to inquire how far the system was an unqualified abuse
or how far the standard argument of those concerned—that it
gave stability to trade—justified its existence.

For obvious reasons, concerted action, apart from the inevitable tacit combination against wage earners—of which the
trade union history of 1825–35 has much to tell—was less
likely in young trades, and in trades undergoing rapid transformation, than in those with a more or less unbroken tradition,
such as coal-owning ship-owning and overseas commerce.
Your gild, in a relatively static age, meeting in order to determine a "just price," might have been accused, by a medieval
Adam Smith, of conspiring against the public: he might have
been right. What is certain is that its members, all working
in much the same way, were very likely to meet regularly that
they might "promote the trade and improve it." But the man

---

[1] S. C. 1830, p. 7. To a modern economist these are the familiar problems
of a *Kontingentierung-Kartell*. [For similar kartell-policies in Scotland see
Hamilton, H., "Combn. in the West of Scotland Coal Trade," *E.J.* (*Ec. Hist.*),
Jan. 1930.]   [2] *Report*, p. 17–18.

with a mill full of mules and a long bank account was less likely
to concert action with the men who could only afford jennies
and were trying to make them more effective by taking shares
in a company mill; though the jenny men might, and in fact
did, pull together. If attention is concentrated too much on
the industries, or sections of industries, which were going
through rapid metamorphosis, there is some danger of exagger-
ating the savage industrial individualism of the age. Collective
foresight and selfishness, in masters or men, may be little
better than individual foresight and selfishness, but they are
different. They grow very rapidly in any group of fairly equal
units with certain common interests, whether the units are large
or small. The Yorkshire domestic clothiers were definitely
"class-conscious." The master cotton spinners were developing
class-consciousness, under the spurs of public criticism and a
political grievance, between 1816 and 1833. The midland coke-
using ironmasters, almost as soon as they became a definite
group, were holding regular quarterly meetings[1], and they contributed a strong sub-group to the General Chamber of Manufacturers of Great Britain, in the 'eighties of the eighteenth
century. In the 'nineties they co-operated with South Welsh
Yorkshire and Scottish masters to fight Pitt's suggested excise
on pig iron. They won; and when the proposal was revived in
1806 they won again. The midland meetings certainly fixed
prices and regulated conditions of sale. So did a South Welsh
meeting held, though not quite uninterruptedly, at Newport
between 1802 and 1824 and a Yorkshire meeting, held in various
places, between 1799 and 1828. South Wales did some output
regulation, on "vend" lines; but this policy is not heard of
either in the Midlands or in Yorkshire before 1830. It so
happened that in that year ironmasters' combinations were in
poor health. The Welsh meetings ceased in 1824. Depression
after the trade boom of 1825 led to disloyal competition and
under-selling in all areas. The minutes of the Yorkshire meeting
stop in 1828 with a confession of failure. Joint action for the
curtailment of output in the Midlands and South Wales was
proposed, but not accepted, in 1831. But the midland meetings
apparently went on and, by 1839—when the next depression
came—they were to adopt the limitation policy. Iron, in short,

---

[1] The meetings can be traced to 1777 and probably were not new in that
year. Ashton, *op. cit.* p. 164.

had little to learn about industrial combination when the railway age began[1].

The workers had not had much to learn about it when the century began. The trade club or trade union, while it is doubtless a product of the capitalistic organisation of industry, is in no sense a product of the industrial revolutions of the eighteenth and early nineteenth centuries[2]. Rather did these revolutions—and the political accident by which the first of them coincided with *the* Revolution—interrupt and set back the natural development of the clubs, which was moving on steadily during the eighteenth century, in spite of a whole series of anti-combination laws[3]. Even the great combination Acts of 1799–1800 did very little to check the development, though no doubt they made trade club activity rather more dangerous to its leaders than before. But it had never been quite safe; and the history of the French *compagnonnages*, workmen's societies which functioned for centuries although continuously illegal, is a warning against attaching too much importance to Acts whose life was short, whose administration was ineffective, and whose aim every working man and some employers desired to circumvent[4]. A single episode illuminates the realities of the situation. One of the strongest, most widespread, and it would seem most high-handed of the eighteenth century trade clubs was that of the journeymen wool-combers. It had been illegal since the reign of George II. In 1812—just midway in the life of the combination Acts—the Home Office was informed that the wool-combers' union meant to hold a congress at Coventry. The Law Officers of the Crown were asked to advise as to a prosecution. They replied: "These combinations are mischievous and dangerous, but it is very difficult to know how to deal with them." And so nothing was done, even though the combers were said to be mostly dissenters suspected of republicanism[5].

[1] Ashton, *op. cit.* ch. 7, "Combinations of Capitalists," for the whole question down to 1831. The MS. Minutes of the Yorkshire meeting are in the Sheffield Public Library. For output regulation in 1839, Scrivenor, *Hist. of the Iron Trade*, p. 290.

[2] It is hardly necessary to refer to Mr and Mrs Webb's *History of Trade Unionism*, which created that history. See the 1920 ed. p. 45–6.

[3] The series is given in Cannan's edition of the *Wealth of Nations*, I. 68 n.

[4] [Mrs M. D. George, "The Combination Laws reconsidered," *E.J.* (*Ec. Hist.*), 1927, proves that the Laws were even less effective than is here suggested.]

[5] This episode was brought to light by Mr and Mrs Hammond in 1919. *The*

The story of this very club illustrates excellently the significance of the first industrial revolution in trade union history. While hand-work ruled the worsted industry, the combers were in the position which a trade union organiser best likes; they were indispensable skilled men, the cost of whose process, even if high, did not form an important part in the total cost of the finished article. So, like the flax-hecklers of the early nineteenth century, whose process is first cousin to wool-combing, they "in some measure controlled the trade, dictating the rate of wages, number of apprentices, etc., and enforcing their demands, however unjust, by strikes."[1] Down to 1825–30 no combing machine had been a real success; but the beginnings of machinery helped in the rout of the Yorkshire combers after their great strike of 1825. For another twenty years the machine was to hang over them; it fell and crushed their union to powder in the late 'forties. Thereafter, for more than half a century, few trades were so ill-provided with trade union machinery as wool-combing.[2]

Somewhat similar, but much less disastrous, is the story of the millwrights. Here the partial discomfiture, not, however, the permanent defeat, of the old trade clubs was facilitated by the repeal of the apprenticeship law in 1814, though its prime cause was the series of technical convulsions which threw up modern mechanical engineering. At the end of the eighteenth and the beginning of the nineteenth century, the custom was to pay all qualified and apprenticed millwrights by time[3]. There was a standard time rate—whether arranged by regular collective bargains or not the evidence does not state; but the presumption is that it was. Round about 1813 this rate was

Skilled Labourer, p. 200–1. The statement of Postgate, R. W., The Builders' History (1923), that "any union that...was in any way active was dealt with under these Acts" (p. 15), hardly fits in with the fact recorded seven pages further on, that in 1810 the London building trades—bricklayers, plasterers and carpenters—were "sufficiently well organised to strike" and raise wages from 28s. to 30s. Of course many trade unionists were prosecuted and punished. Webb, op. cit. p. 78 sqq. [but mostly for conspiracy under the Common Law. George, op. cit.]   [1] Above, p. 146.

[2] For the position in 1907, Clapham, J. H., The Woollen and Worsted Industries (1907), p. 209–10.

[3] This account is based on Alex. Galloway's evidence before the S. C. on Artisans and Machinery, 1824, p. 27 sqq. For the closeness of the old millwright societies in London (there were three of them) see Wm. Fairbairn's account of his experiences in 1811 in Smiles, Industrial Biography, p. 309: for the skill of which the millwright was justly proud, p. 314 (Fairbairn again)—"he was generally well-educated and could draw out his own designs."

42s. a week. The millwrights, the old aristocrats of mechanical industry—there were specialist millwrights before the Norman Conquest—when employed in the young engineering shops, insisted on this wage whatever work they did, even to turning a grindstone. Nor would they let non-millwrights do a millwright's work. But repeal of the apprenticeship clauses of the Elizabethan labour law enabled employers, as one of them put it, to "overwhelm" "the excluding party with new men." Further, to circumvent the policy of the millwrights and meet the ever-changing needs of the new industry, some of the employers decided, so far as possible, " to pay every man according to his merit and to allow him to make his own agreement," phrasing which points to previous collective bargains or at least to very precise and binding trade custom. Alexander Galloway, in 1824, called this payment by results with individual bargaining "the engineers' economy," and another witness— from Birmingham[1]—said that it was gaining ground generally. It had been most destructive to combinations and to the old millwright's policy, Galloway pointed out; so "that that trade that used to scoff and spurn at the name of an engineer [an interesting touch], are obliged to take up the name of an engineer, and conduct their business by the engineer's economy."[2] That economy had been applied also to the carpenters and joiners who had been transformed into pattern-makers for the new industry. Their old time-rate was 30s. Galloway paid his men from something below, he did not say how much below, that figure up to 42s., according to the nature of the work.

But, in spite of the repeal of apprenticeship clauses and the existence of combination laws, the millwrights put up a stiff fight. Herves of Manchester[3] said that with him they "scarcely ever worked by the piece," and admitted that he had checked the number of prentice millwrights in his works when the men cried enough. Whether millwrights or not, the engineers evidently soon acquired the professional point of view. Let Herves speak again: "the men will not allow other workmen to come into the trade; machine-makers more particularly, in our manufactories are not allowed to come in, unless they have

---

[1] Wm. Brunton. *S. C. on Artisans and Machinery*, p. 323.

[2] Maudslay (p. 39) had explained that, at one time, "the millwrights would not work with an engineer." Martineau (p. 6) thought that paying men "according to their quality" rendered it "impossible that combination can take place with us."　　　　　　　　　　　　　　　[3] *Ibid.* p. 341 *sqq.*

worked for five years at [making] cotton mills, flax mills, or woollen mills." He had acquiesced, for he had known his men "turn out" about it. "You mean to say that the men have succeeded...? Yes." Engineering, under whatever name, was so patently a man's job—unlike cotton spinning—and a job which needed years of probation, whether called apprenticeship or something else, that after the partial collapse of the old millwrights' traditions, new traditions not dissimilar—with clubs or unions to mould them—began to grow almost at once.

How a strong club might retain its strength, when threatened by no sudden mechanical revolution, the history of the journeymen paper makers union shows. The organisation of the union was elaborate. There were five "Grand Divisions"—Maidstone, Carshalton, Wells, Leeds, Manchester—each with its prescribed area. According to the evidence of an ex-secretary, given before the committee of 1825, it did almost everything that a trade union has ever done; in the teeth of the combination laws it had given strike pay[1].

Nearly all the old unrevolutionised London skilled crafts had their clubs and combinations though they did not often, if ever, include the whole body of journeymen. Francis Place, the best of witnesses, described to the Committee on Artisans and Machinery[2] the "perfect and perpetual combination," with its "all but military" system, of the London journeyman tailors. He added, "it is less perfect in other trades but all... have some organisation"; and he went on to describe that of the carpenters and plumbers. He was of opinion that the combinations were "generally successful." The London hatters were specially well organised and they corresponded with hatters' clubs in nearly every other town, they said[3]. They had sick, burial and out-of-work benefit; they used the tramping ticket; they voted assistance to non-hatters on strike; and—in defiance of combination laws and as though 5 Eliz. c. 4 had never been modified—they were very firm about their rule that no master should take more than two prentices other than his sons. The carpenters and joiners of London had "five

---

[1] *S. C. on Combination Laws*, 1825, p. 26 *sqq.*, and App. XVIII, where the rules are printed. Paper-making machinery was coming slowly into use, 1803-30, and in the latter year as much paper was made by machine as by hand; but, with an expanding demand, there was no displacement of labour. See Spicer, A. D., *The Paper Trade* (1907), p. 62-4.

[2] P. 44 *sqq.*

[3] Evidence of J. Lang, p. 91 *sqq.*

distinct societies "[1] of a more rudimentary sort: regular benefits were paid only in cases of loss by fire, loss of tools, and burial, unemployment being met by voluntary contributions. The bootmakers had two societies, one for London and one for Westminster. If some evidence given anonymously by an employer fourteen years later can be trusted they, like the tailors, were "all but military" in their discipline—"They hold the meetings and fix their prices." "They do not come to your shop to work? No, that is against their rules. I dare not keep a man at my shop to work for me; they would all strike if I did."[2]

In Spitalfields the weavers certainly had some organisation in the eighteenth century; but by the end of the first quarter of the nineteenth it had declined. Theirs was a trade verging on decay. Years back there had been an agreed-on book of weaving piece-rates. Whether it was agreed on informally, or by an *ad hoc* meeting, or between masters and representatives of a weavers' club we do not know[3]. After the passing of the Spitalfields Act, in 1773, a master's committee met a men's committee to thresh out the wage rates, to which the Justices subsequently gave legal binding force. This implies fairly good organisation among the men. From about 1795, the masters showed increasing reluctance to work the Act and eventually, in 1823, a majority of them—but by no means all—fell in with the successful agitation for its repeal. During the various inquiries which preceded repeal the men were very coy about their organisation, as indeed were the masters about theirs[4]. In 1818 a master put in evidence against the men a set of rules "To be observed by a few Friends called the Good Intent," of which rules Art. 3 provided out-of-work pay for a man refused work "that demands his legal price." (There was still a legal price but it was not being observed.) For the men, John Baker explained that subscriptions were "entirely optional": that they never struck: that "there was no committee at all": that there were "a few men who receive the money who are called the Finance": that, in case of a dispute, they did appoint what "you may call a committee if you think fit": and that

---

[1] P. 176.

[2] *Hand Loom Weavers*, II. 281.

[3] Clapham, J. H., "The Spitalfields Acts," *E.J.* Dec. 1916. For the book of rates, not used by the author in that article, but existing in the Goldsmiths' Library, see George, *op. cit.* p. 182: it is dated 1769.

[4] Above, p. 201.

there was a Secretary to the Trade[1]. With the repeal of the Spitalfields Act the foundations of this not very secure organisation were undermined. The industry was spreading fast outside London. Spitalfields, with its ancient tradition, lost first its pre-eminence, then its prosperity, and the opportunities for organisation there dwindled year by year.

In the old Macclesfield silk-handkerchief weaving there had been a recognised scale of piece-rates, or book as the men called it, down to 1814[2]. It was dropped by the masters because trade was leaving them and going to Manchester, and they feared undercutting. There is no direct evidence that it had been arranged by anything which could be called a union. Macclesfield in 1817 was full of sick and burial clubs, but a weaver testified that they had nothing to do with wages: "I never knew any application to any society of this nature, in consequence of want of employment, or anything of that kind"[3]: and his evidence was not traversed. On the other hand, there had existed, from 1807 to 1815, a most elaborate agreement between the undertakers and the weavers, regulating apprenticeship on quite medieval lines[4]. It was signed on February 11, 1807, by twelve undertaking firms, and by representatives of the men, which implies at any rate an *ad hoc* negotiating committee and probably a club or clubs in the background. The abolition of compulsory apprenticeship cut the ground from under this agreement.

Probably in Macclesfield, and certainly elsewhere, trade union activities were prosecuted quietly, and without leaving any traces, by some of the friendly societies, just as in the Middle Ages a fraternity might do the work of a regular trade gild. Complete direct evidence is naturally lacking; though the committees on combinations of 1824–5 traced, recorded, and regretted instances of benefit societies with trade union functions[5]. "There is no subject," it was officially reported in 1838–9, "on which the working classes are less ready to give information than as to whether they belong to benefit societies"[6]; but it was known that nearly all weavers who could afford did belong. In the West Riding such societies "were almost universally resorted to"—"less so, however, in the form

[1] S. C. on Ribbonweavers' Petitions, p. 59, 195.
[2] Ibid. p. 63.   [3] Ibid. p. 103   [4] Ibid. p. 90.
[5] S. C. on Artisans and Machinery, p. 590.
[6] Hand Loom Weavers, II. 255.

of societies certified under the Act of Parliament, than in that of free gifts, secret orders, sick clubs and funeral briefs."[1]

A series of Acts for the encouragement of regular friendly societies (1793–1829) had coincided with the maximum discouragement of industrial combinations. A return made in the year of Waterloo gave a recognised membership of nearly a million[2], to which must be added that of the informal "secret orders, sick clubs and funeral briefs." "These clubs," the Select Committee of 1825 reported, "were, in many instances, composed of persons working at the same trade; the habits and opportunities of association...doubtless afforded facilities of combination for raising wages and other purposes, all of which were then unlawful." Trade union leaders could imitate what Francis Place did in his journeyman days, when he reorganised the breeches-makers' trade club, in 1794, "under the guise of a Tontine Sick Club" to avoid detection[3]. But some trades gave too narrow a margin of earnings for much club or union activity. The most populous trade in the country, that of the hand-loom, marked by the Revolution for death though it was to be an unconscionable time in dying, already gave a very narrow margin in most branches of cotton weaving. Year by year the two chief forms of trade union activity possible to a body of outworkers—standard scales of piece-rates and strikes to enforce them—became, the one less practicable as the fashions shifted quicker with the quickened pulse of economic life, the other too dangerous as the power-loom began to clang in its shed, reminding the cottage weaver that once his own loom stopped it might never start again. "What is the reason that the weavers could not unite as well as the spinners, and carpenters and joiners?" a Manchester cotton weaver was asked in 1834. "Their extreme poverty and likewise their jealousy...if they give a halfpenny out of their pockets they must work for it again, and they will not give any aid to other men."[4] In 1824–5 there were, however, many groups of weavers as yet unthreatened and fully capable of carrying on effective trade union organisation. Several such organisations came to light. It is significant that much the most complete, well-managed,

---

[1] *Ibid.* III. 539.
[2] *S. C. on the Laws respecting Friendly Societies* (1825, IV), p. 6. The figure is 925,429. See below, p. 297.
[3] Wallas, G., *Francis Place*, p. 19.
[4] *S. C. on Handloom Weavers' Petitions*, 1834, Q. 6659.

and masterful of them was that of the Yorkshire fancy woollen weavers, a trade which remained unthreatened for almost another fifty years. This union's primary object was the control of piece-rates, and it had excellent striking machinery[1]. But for the hand-loom weavers as a class, these eighteenth and early nineteenth-century trade club and trade union beginnings, nipped by the Revolution, were to have no healthy maturity.

Strong as were the clubs and combinations in the old skilled crafts of London they were stronger—and far more turbulent—in Dublin. The Irish capital comes into the British picture because there was correspondence and co-operation between its clubs and those of Britain. Every trade had its club, the chief constable of Dublin said in 1824[2]. The combination laws were "wholly inoperative." Club law against unlawful (*i.e.* non-apprenticed) men, against men who worked below union rates, and against men who gave witness in the courts about club methods, was enforced by the bludgeon. Some of these societies—the case quoted in 1824 was that of the cabinet-makers—bargained collectively and openly with the masters. A number of them had arrangements for "blanks"—tramping cards which gave the bearer a right to assistance from his fellow-unionists when travelling in search of work—with corresponding societies in England. The cases quoted were the ironmoulders, foundrymen, curriers, hatters and "thickset cutters," a possibly incomplete list which includes some English societies of which little else is known.

The societies whose activities were most fully inquired into in 1824–5 were those of the ship-sawyers and shipwrights, which is fortunate, since theirs were typical and most important unrevolutionised crafts in a trade where capitalism and work on the employer's premises had necessarily existed time out of mind[3]. Liverpool employers accused both groups of great tyranny and violence. The sawyers, they said, refused piece-work, insisted on their men being taken on in rotation, and limited the employment of apprentices—apprenticeship in these trades having remained untouched by the repealing Act of 1814. Evidence from working shipwrights showed that their policies

[1] *S. C. on Combination Laws*, 1825, p. 27. The Knaresborough linen-weavers also did rough collective bargaining. *S. C. on Artisans and Machinery*, 1824, p. 540.

[2] *Ibid.* p. 289 *sqq.*: see also p. 421 *sqq.* and p. 465 *sqq.*

[3] Above, p. 69, 177.

were much the same[1]. Their society, it appeared, was a joint
benefit society and trade union, as was that of the sawyers.
It gave sick pay, burial pay, and wife's burial pay; and it kept
a club doctor. It boycotted ships where a dispute was on,
obliged all men who had served their time in Liverpool to join
its ranks, refused to admit outsiders who had not served their
time somewhere, checked overstocking of the yards with
apprentices and limited the day's work. It made rules about
the number of men required for particular jobs; and it had
abolished piece-work, so its secretary said, because under a
piece-work system the old men suffered. On the Thames, the
London Shipwrights' Provident Society, a new organisation in
1825 and certainly less powerful than that on the Mersey, was
pursuing somewhat similar policies and had come into such
sharp conflict with the masters, over a demand for a collective
bargain and the question of control of the composition of the
gangs, that, finally, they—or some of them—had refused to
employ its members[2]. On the Tyne, members of the four
unions of the wrights were declining to work with any master
who would not promise to retain the seven-year apprenticeship[3].

The seamen of the 'twenties were untouched by the revolution;
for steam at sea was yet little better than a toy. Against some
of them also the charge was made of refusing to work with
non-unionists[4]. It was reported that they called these non-
union seamen "scab-men," an early, perhaps the earliest, use
of a familiar scrap of nineteenth-century trade union slang.
Untouched also were the coopers, to whose very typical, strong,
London union the select committee of 1825 paid special
attention[5]. They attempted to raise and regulate wages, to
limit the number of apprentices, and to control the working
hours: their weapons were the simultaneous strike, the refusal
to work with non-unionists, and what was called—and may
very well have been—the persecution of "scab-men." There
were strong and rather brutal combinations too in "every
branch" of the old-fashioned Sheffield trades; they had been
known there—though this the committee of the 'twenties did
not report—for nearly a century[6].

[1] S. C. on Artisans and Machinery, p. 183 sqq., 202 sqq.
[2] S. C. on Combination Laws, 1825, Report, p. 6; Minutes of Evidence
p. 180, 250, 350 and passim. Above, p. 177-8, for the gangs controversy.
[3] Ibid. Minutes, p. 170.   [4] Ibid. Report. p. 5.
[5] Ibid. p. 2 of the Report and p. 58 sqq. of the Minutes of Evidence.
[6] Lloyd, The Cutlery Trades, p. 239.

Combination was at its strongest in the skilled crafts, but it can very rarely be proved that particular societies were old. Nor is trade-club history in the eighteenth century clear enough, even in its outlines, to make it certain that organisation of some sort was continuous in trades where it is known to have existed —the tailors for instance, whose clubs are first heard of in the first quarter of the eighteenth century. The committees of 1824–5 realised that, in many trades, combination was no new thing, but historical inquiry was not their business. Many of the societies whose rules they secured were apparently of recent date, but some may have been revivals of older organisations. The committee of 1825 was evidently surprised, and much impressed, by the very regular system of government in all the societies into whose organisation it penetrated, with president, secretary, committee and printed regulations, "by which they are ostensibly governed."[1] This all suggests old traditions in what may already be called the trade union world.

The new or revolutionised trades also had their unions, which—as in the young engineering shops—might transfer the tradition bodily, apprenticeship and all, from the old world to the new. But the fluid organisation of the rising trades, their rapid growth, the constant influxes of new men, the ease with which employers could use the combination laws against these mixed masses, and the frequent changes in location and processes made combination difficult. The traditional policy as to training and apprenticeship for example, reasonable enough in an old stable industry, seemed—and generally would have been— a mere stupid conservatism if applied unmodified to an industry which was neither. In the typical, already almost mature, product of the new age, the spinning mill, hordes of women and children posed an additional, and a new, problem. In spite of this the male spinners, taking over the tradition, had made noteworthy beginnings of organisation long before 1824.

At Stockport, the men who worked the hand-driven jennies in the factories still possessed their "old laws signed in the year 1792."[2] As the jenny was only patented in 1770, and did not get into factories immediately, this implies very rapid organisation in a new industry. The society which made these

---

[1] S. C. on Combination Laws, 1825, Report, p. 6.
[2] S. C. on Artisans and Machinery, p. 409. And see Chapman, S. J., The Lancashire Cotton Industry (1904), p. 193. [A reviewer in the Manchester Guardian points out that this society goes back at least to 1785.]

laws had failed and been broken up. A new one—the Stockport Cotton Jenny Spinners Union Society—had just been formed in 1824: it was "at present in its infancy," said a member. Among the frame spinners there was no union, for they were all women and children with a few male overlookers. At Glasgow, combinations among the male jenny or mule spinners were unknown in the early days of the mills. They first came to the notice of employers, about 1805, as bodies which undertook wage negotiations. In 1810, as a master put it, they "tried to determine whom we should employ."[1] There was a fight: they were beaten, and they were forced to sign a document repudiating the claims to control. These claims, of course, were all variants of one—the demand for the exclusion of non-unionists. To the spinner and other workers in new trades the non-unionist, the scab, stood for the "illegal man" against whom the journeymen of the old crafts struggled—the unapprenticed man with whom, down to 1814, those who had served their time had a legal right to refuse to work; for as the law applicable to old trades then stood he had no right to work himself. After their defeat in 1810, the Glasgow spinners took to methods of secrecy, and occasionally of violence, until the repeal of the combination laws: some instances of assault and vitriol throwing among them and among the Ayrshire coal-miners, who also had begun to combine, were severely censured by the committee of 1825.

Most of the combinations in the cotton trade—usually local and short lived, as was to be expected in the circumstances—occupied themselves with wages only, or at least fought only on the wage issue. A great strike of spinners in the Manchester district, which coincided with the Glasgow troubles of 1810, aimed at driving up wages—and failed, although the General Union which ran it seems to have been well organised[2]. Again, in 1818, at a time of political and economic ferment in Manchester, a wage strike of some 2000 spinners threw at least 20,000 people out of work. This strike also failed—thanks in part to the application of the combination law—in spite of a little financial assistance from trade clubs elsewhere, including the London shoemakers and more than one society of those resolute unionists the hatters[3].

---

[1] Hy. Houldsworth. *S. C. on Artisans and Machinery*, p. 476 *sqq.*
[2] Hammond, *op. cit.* p. 93.
[3] *Ibid.* p. 97, and Hammond, *The Town Labourers*, p. 306 *sqq.*

Coal mining was a trade in which the technical revolution was long drawn out: there was no revolutionary decade, hardly even a revolutionary generation. There is no reason, therefore, to expect either a stimulus to, or a drag on, movements towards organisation to set in at any particular date. In old mining districts, where the workings were of some size, the common life of the pit provided a natural platform for common action. On the other hand, the colliers of the eighteenth century had been a race apart, often ignorant, brutal, and cut off from the life of the towns and the traditions of the crafts. As a missionary to a barbarous land, John Wesley had penetrated among the mines of Kingswood. The Forest of Dean was officially pagan. "The great area of the forest being extra parochial, though very populous," there were few churches except on the extreme outskirts. Nonconformists brought about a striking reform in the nineteenth century, and "immense numbers of chapels" were built between 1810 and 1840; but it is not surprising that the traditions of forest life were clannish and secret, or that concubinage had usually taken the place of marriage[1]. Only in 1775 had that well-known Act of parliament (15 Geo. III, c. 28) passed whose opening words were: "Whereas many colliers, coal-bearers and salters in Scotland are in a state of slavery or bondage, bound to the collieries and saltworks, where they work for life, and are sold with the mines"—be it enacted, in short, that these things cease. The Act was not a success, and effective emancipation only followed an amending Act of 1799 (39 Geo. III, c. 56). Emancipated, the Scottish miner came but slowly into the current of national economic life. For a long time he was strictly endogamous. Even when he lived in a town, said an intelligent observer of the nineteenth century, "he failed somehow to get absorbed into the great industrial body"; and nearly a century after the Act of 1775 the same observer could write—"still, there appears to be a want of sympathy between him and the mason, the carpenter, the tailor, the shoemaker, and other tradesmen, and they rarely associate."[2]

During the first quarter of the nineteenth century the swift growth in the demand for coking and steam coals, followed by the new demand for gas coal, brought workers to the pits, in many districts, who were not of the old mining stock and did

---

[1] *Report on Children in Manufactures*, 1843, p. 158–9.
[2] Bremner, D., *The Industries of Scotland* (1869), p. 20.

not readily amalgamate with it. By 1830 the Irish immigrants had begun to appear on the Western coalfields, from Ayrshire to Glamorgan and Somerset[1]; but they did not get into the old fields of Northumberland and Durham. Here, as might be expected, combination of a sort began early. The Northumberland and Durham practice, down to 1844, was for men to be hired by the year—or rather for eleven months and a half, as a year would have given every man a legal "settlement" in the place where he worked. In 1765 the masters had tried to introduce a rule that none of them should hire a pitman who had not "a certificate of leave" from his last master. The object was to stop a scramble for labour at a time of growing demand for coal—but the parallel which leaps to the historian's mind is that of a medieval villein who required leave to work outside the manor. For the north-country pitmen there was the nearer Scottish parallel. Whether they considered it or not, they all turned out, to the number of four thousand, did a very little damage, and won[2]. But there is no record of permanent organisation during the eighteenth century. By 1810, however, when there was trouble and a strike on the Tyne and Wear, again about questions connected with the "yearly bond," the men certainly had a "brotherhood." Delegates from the various pits held meetings; but as the masters called in the law and the military, many a delegate found himself in gaol or its equivalent, the Bishop of Durham's stables[3]. This time the owners won. With the repeal of the combination laws the union came into the open, so that on February 26, 1826, Lord Londonderry was writing apprehensively to the Home Office that it was "entirely established," and that "if the Coal-Owners did not resist...they must surrender at Discretion to any Laws the Union propose."[4] They did resist, under Londonderry's leadership, imported outside labour, beat the men and broke the union in 1832, after a terrible long strike at a most inopportune

---

[1] Bremner, op. cit. p. 20, and above, p. 61.

[2] Hammond, The Skilled Labourer, p. 12–14, and Welbourne, E., The Miners' Union of Northumberland and Durham (1923), p. 21. Mr and Mrs Hammond's narrative suggests very little damage, Mr Welbourne's a very great deal—"riot and destruction swept along the whole Tyne valley." [Mr Hammond informs me that the statement in The Skilled Labourer is literally true so far as the H.O. papers and the local newspapers tell the story. There was a remarkable absence of violence except at a single colliery.]

[3] Hammond, op. cit. p. 22. Welbourne, op. cit. p. 24.

[4] Hammond, op. cit. p. 29.

time for both sides—for the Tyne and Wear were just losing their monopoly of the London market[1].

The aims of a miners' union in an old industrial district—where, however, the collieries were much smaller than those of the Tyne and Wear—are well illustrated in the, undated, rules of the Coal Miners' Union of Sheffield and its Neighbourhood which came into the hands of the committee of 1825[2]. The Union was managed by a committee of two representatives from each pit. The object to which its funds were to be mainly devoted was the maintenance of an "equitable price for labour"—how is not explained. Any alterations in "the list of prices as the standard for work" were to bring it into action. Finally, a very significant clause stated that as "improper persons," coming into the pits, had done much harm to the Sheffield pitmen, no one was to be allowed underground who had not worked as a coal-getter from the age of sixteen. There is nothing of the friendly society about these rules; it is a purely industrial programme. Once again, a sentiment like the old craftsman's dislike of the improperly trained "illegal man"—who is assumed incompetent—is felt at the back of the desire to avoid working with non-unionists. Even if Sheffield colliers were cut off a little socially from Sheffield forgers and grinders, they breathed an atmosphere impregnate with craft pride, prejudice, and exclusiveness, and very unwholesome to strangers. Their rules do not specify the "improper persons" who had got into the pits—in Northumberland and Durham they were hungry lead-miners from the hills[3]—but it is conceivable that their life was not an easy one.

[1] Welbourne, *op. cit.* p. 39–43.
[2] *S. C. on Combination Laws*, 1825, Report, p. 51.
[3] Welbourne, *op. cit.* p. 34.

CHAPTER VI

THE ORGANISATION OF COMMERCE

"THE prejudices of some political writers against shop-keepers and tradesmen," Adam Smith had written[1], "are altogether without foundation. So far is it from being necessary, either to tax them, or to restrict their numbers, that they can never be multiplied so as to hurt the public, though they may so as to hurt one another." Certainly their very rapid multiplication during the eighteenth century had made the problem one of general interest, whether Smith's confident solution of it were right or wrong. The multiplication of overseas traders was criticised by no one. All might not agree with Campbell of the *London Tradesman* that "other Arts, Crafts and Mysteries live upon one another, and never add one Sixpence to the Aggregate Wealth of the Kingdom"; but almost all would have endorsed the lyrical peroration of his article on the Merchant—who "draws his honest gain from the distant Poles....The Poor he sets to work, Manufactures flourish, Poverty is banished and Public Credit increases."[2] Criticism, in Adam Smith's day, was directed rather towards the armies of middlemen and retailers who had sprung up to meet, it may be in some cases to exploit, the needs of a community which had become the metropolis of a commercial empire, whose gigantic capital city was only kept alive by a very complex and cumbrous machinery of supply, whose industries, already specialised and localised but mostly in the hands of small producers, were—for lack of quick communications and quick news—only held together by trading chains of many personal links. Wool staplers and merchants and "jobbers" and "broggers"; graziers and drovers and cattle jobbers, Smithfield salesmen, carcass butchers and cutting butchers; cheese factors, who bought among the farmers, and cheese-mongers in the towns, who retailed or sold again to pure retailers—such lists are only samples from a few leading trades in the mid eighteenth century[3].

The improvement in communications and the increased size

---

[1] *Wealth of Nations*, I. 341.   [2] P. 284.

[3] See Westerfield, R. B., "Middlemen in English Business" (*Trans. of the Connecticut Academy*, 1915), *passim*.

of manufacturing firms, between 1750 and 1825, had made possible the cutting out of some of these personal links; but the opportunities had been seized more often in connection with manufactures—just because it was here that firms had grown— than in the trades which handled food and fuel. Matthew Boulton could dispense altogether with the local factors, who collected the hardware of the working masters, and with the London ironmongers and the London merchants, who handled it when it went abroad. He had discussed the art of continental advertisement with Wedgwood before 1770, and had "advised the method afterwards put so fully into force by Mr Wedgwood, that of distributing printed sheets containing engraved examples of various articles, to which should be added price lists and other particulars."[1] So the continental buyer could write direct to Etruria or Soho, or to other large firms in other trades who imitated their businesslike methods. And although the wars had interfered for a very long time with the Continental circulation of "printed sheets containing engraved examples of various articles," so that something like a new start had to be made after 1815, these more direct methods left their mark on the internal trade of Britain. By 1825 that most characteristic figure of the previous century, the packman merchant, the Manchester Man, was nearly extinct. The custom had been for such men to buy in the manufacturing districts the cheaper textile, cutlery, and other goods that were in universal demand, and to move with their trains of horses or mules "from one Market Town to another; and then at some Inn" to "profer their Wares to sell to the Shopkeepers of the Place."[2]

In 1823, Guest noted the disappearance of the Manchester Men[3]. Selling by sample, he wrote,

has now become general not only in this [the fustian] but in every other business; and it may now be asserted that the whole of the internal wholesale trade of England is carried on by Commercial Travellers —they pervade every town, village and hamlet in the Kingdom, carrying their samples and patterns...they form more than one half of the immense number of persons who are constantly travelling through the country in all directions and are the principal support of our Inns, the neatness and comfort of which are so much celebrated throughout Europe.

[1] Meteyard, Eliza, *Life of Wedgwood* (1865), II. 76.
[2] Westerfield, *op. cit.* p. 313: the quotation is from the late seventeenth century.
[3] Guest, *A Compendious History of the Cotton Manufacture* (1823), p. 11.

In the textile trades, with which Guest was most familiar, these bagmen, selling to retailers by sample, were usually not principals, like the Manchester Men, but agents for mercantile firms domiciled in the manufacturing districts or in London. But in trades where the scale of production was smaller, the principal might travel himself, only not with a stock of goods. A Birmingham writer in 1825 speaks of "the now universal custom of home merchants, *factors*, as they are called, travelling the country with specimens, or with *pictorial representations.*" So the buyer—in this case an ironmonger or other shopkeeper outside the Birmingham area—was no longer bound to "apply to the individual fabricators."[1] The wandering factor came to his doors with his pictorial representations.

A humbler type of peripatetic trader had formerly done a great deal of business, especially in rural districts and in the North of England, the pedlar, who went not to shopkeepers —the shop had not been universal—but direct to the consumer, as did that "polygamic potter" Peter Bell[2], who

> Had heard the Atlantic surges roar
> On farthest Cornwall's rocky shore,
> And trod the cliffs of Dover
>
> .   .   .   .
>
> And he had lain beside his asses
> On lofty Cheviot Hills;...

The most familiar type of north-country pedlar had dealt not in pots but in clothing. He was known as "the Scotchman," and his work was not confined to "lofty Cheviot Hills" and rivers' brims where the yellow primrose grows. But even "the Scotchman" was ceasing to be a principal and becoming an agent in the nineteenth century[3]. "I should think one-half of the population get their clothing" "from Scotchmen who travel," a witness from Stockport, already a considerable manufacturing town, said in 1833[4]. "There are some families that will deal with three or four or five of these men." So far the account might apply to men like James McGuffog, who,

---

[1] *The Picture of Birmingham*, 1825, p. 17: and above, p. 174-5.

[2] Wordsworth's note on "potter" runs: "in the dialect of the North a hawker of earthenware is thus described." *Peter Bell* was written before 1800.

[3] For shopkeepers, pedlars, and "The Society of Travelling Scotchmen of Bridgnorth" in 1789, see Daniels, *The Early History of the Cotton Industry*, p. 65.

[4] *S. C. on Manufactures*, Q. 10,582

starting life as an independent pedlar with a basket, got first a pack and then a horse and then a horse and van until requested, somewhere about the year 1770, "by the nobility and principal families and farmers around Stamford to open an establishment there for the sale of the best and finest articles of female wear, for which, for some time in his travelling capacity, he had become celebrated."[1] No doubt there were still independent wandering McGuffogs in the 'twenties. But those who clothed Stockport were mostly paid travellers. "I know one firm of this description in Manchester," the evidence continues, "which employs five travellers." It was described as one of more than twenty big firms of this class which existed at that time in Manchester, and it was evidently not very big; so perhaps the principals of some of the lesser ones still travelled in person.

The commercial traveller, the powerful wholesale dealer, and the local shop, following after the packman-merchant, had between them all but killed everything but the trade in livestock, foodstuffs, and merry-making at the fairs; although they had not reduced the number of links in the chain between producer and consumer—rather the reverse. A hundred years earlier, when Defoe wrote his description of Sturbridge—the last of the great fairs—he had noted already the "prodigious trade," exceeding "by far the Goods actually brought to the Fair and delivered in kind," done by "Wholesale Men from London and all Parts of England, who transact their Business wholly in their Pocket-Books, and meeting their Chapmen... take Orders."[2] Forty years later a London firm might still be announcing its intention of selling "extremely cheap...a large and elegant Assortment of Rich, Fancy and Plain Silks,"[3] at its booth in Garlic Row; and in the 'eighties Henry Gunning, with other undergraduates, haunted the great booth in which Mr Green of Limehouse and his pretty daughter, "Miss Gherkin," sold pickles and grocery at the lowest London prices[4]. But by that time the transformation was far gone. In 1773 Mary Snow, a dealer in glass and china, was advertising her

---

[1] Robert Owen, *Autobiography* (1857): McGuffog was Owen's first master.
[2] The larger chapman was hardly distinguishable from the Manchester Man; the smaller was just a pedlar. Westerfield, *op. cit.* p. 315. Defoe's *Tour* (1724), I, 124.
[3] *Cambridge Chronicle*, Sept. 17, 1765.
[4] Gunning, H., *Reminiscences* (1854), I, 170: Gunning took his degree in 1788.

intention of selling at her shop opposite the Red Bull "on the same terms as at Stirbitch Fair *all the Year Round*."[1] Notices from shopkeepers who intend "not to keep the fair" multiply. They have come perhaps "from Town," like Thomas Dales in 1790, "with a very large assortment of goods...which he is determined to sell under Fair prices at the great shop on the Market Hill."[2] Outside dealers still come, but in falling numbers. Some of them also are declining to keep the Fair. In 1800, J. Smith and Sons, "Woollen Manufacturers from Yorks," return thanks to the Public for past favours and announce their intention of not keeping the Fair; but they will sell their Superfines and Seconds, Mill'd Drabs and Kerseymeres at the Wrestler's Inn in Petty Cury[3].

From that time onward the notices of the fair have an increasing flavour of foodstuffs. It is still a great cheese-mart in 1820, not only for Cottenhams but for Cheshires and Gloucesters too. Horses are freely bought and sold but—in 1820 at any rate—there are few "of a superior kind." Hops, a great article of trade in Defoe's time and long after, are in small supply and their sales very limited. Perhaps because of this general flatness of trade, it is noted that the booty of the pickpockets "was not of any considerable amount."[4] By 1828, "in wool," another staple of trade in the eighteenth century, "scarcely a single sale was effected."[5] Sturbridge Fair was left sleepy, if still noisy, by its sluggish brook.

All over the country, the distribution of materials for clothing was fast settling down on lines which changed very little throughout the century, fastest in London and the larger towns. Thomas James, at the time of the Reform Bill, was a wholesale linen draper, silk mercer, and woollen draper in Cheapside[6]. He was one of a class. He bought direct from the factory, but probably also from the small home-trade merchants in the manufacturing districts, who were indispensable so long as the very small manufacturer survived[7]. He said that he supplied shops in nearly every English town, in many Scottish towns, and in some Irish towns. He explained that a few very large

---

[1] *Cambridge Chronicle*, Sept. 25, 1773.   [2] *Ibid*. Oct. 2, 1790.

[3] *Ibid*. Sept. 19, 1800.

[4] *Cambs. Chron. and Huntingdonshire Gazette*, Sept. 29, 1820.

[5] *Bury and Norwich Post*, Sept. 29, 1828.

[6] *S. C. on Manufactures*, Q. 1349 *sqq*.

[7] They are described in all the older accounts of the trade in woollens, and kept their position long after 1820–30.

retailers bought partly from the factory direct, partly from men like himself. Periods of credit, on both sides, had been much reduced since the wars. He used to receive anything from six to twelve months' credit. Now, the most was three or four, and as a rule he paid cash at the month's end. Some of his retailer customers were equally prompt. They all paid quicker, and so held smaller stocks, than they used to do. The account might almost come from a city wholesale house of the twentieth century.

At the final stage of distribution, the "bazaar" for fancy goods and the department shop had just made their appearance, in London and a few other large towns. In London "a few large houses" (in another place they are said to be "eight or ten") "have grown up, where a person wanting the articles which a shopkeeper sells, can be accommodated with every article at once; and it is very much the fashion to go now to these great houses."[1] Glasgow was exceedingly proud of the retail warehouses of J. and W. Campbell in Candleriggs St. "Sixty-four persons attend the customers." "Every kind of soft goods" are sold. "Purchasers of a halfpenny lace or a pennyworth of thread are equally attended to as those who make large purchases." Although J. Morrison and Co., Leaf Son and Cole, and Wynn Ellis "of London, turn more money annually, there is no house in the King's dominions that serves so many customers as Messrs Campbells of Glasgow."[2]

Everywhere, down to the smallest country towns and some of the villages, the shop—specialised or general—was supplanting the pedlar, the itinerant tradesman of the fairs, and the ancient custom of making clothes at home. Even before 1800, labourers in the South of England and the Midlands purchased "a considerable proportion of their cloaths from the shopkeeper of the nearest town."[3] The proportion grew. North of Trent "Scotchmen" found anchorage in drapers' shops, and the cloud of commercial travellers helped the smallest village general shop to keep abreast of the times. In Stockport local shops were even beginning to undersell the new type of Scotchman from Manchester[4]. The town shop was tricking itself out with glass-fronts and gold-leaf. In old-

---

[1] S. C. on Manufactures, Q. 527, 529.
[2] One of the attractive Scottish footnotes to the Census of 1831, s.v. "Glasgow."
[3] Eden, quoted above, p. 157.
[4] S. C. on Manufactures, as above, p. 221.

fashioned places, such as Shrewsbury, the kind of establishment in which "the goods were exposed...on open baulks or shutters, which, swung on hinges, were turned back and secured at night," was still to be found in the early 'twenties[1]; but the spell of activity, speculation and "progress," about the year 1825, had often led to its replacement by something more fitted for one of the London shopping streets—streets "lighted by gas in the finest style so as really to resemble enchanted ways. All that one has read...of the size and wealth of Bagdad, Damascus, Ispahan and Samarkand here one finds realised. Asiatic splendour is here united with the simplicity of the Grecian, and the variety and charm of the Gothic, taste." "Here" is the Regent Street or Strand of George IV's later years as it appeared to the sincere if sentimental Meidinger[2]. Quick transport by road and canal—the ten-mile-an-hour coach, the bagman's gig, and Messrs Pickford's fly-boats—kept the shops in easy touch with London wholesalers, or with manufacturers and home-trade merchants in the industrial Midlands and North.

The trades in home-grown foodstuffs—and at least nineteen-twentieths of the essential foodstuffs of all sorts were home grown—had changed less than those in clothing materials, though they, too, had been affected by quickened communications. But the new speed had seldom modified, and even seldomer simplified, an existing commercial organisation: it had, as a rule, only extended its scope. In many towns there had been little change in that direct dealing of producer and consumer which is carried on about market stalls and market-women's umbrellas. In Norwich's splendid old market-place Meidinger admired the arrival, from the country round about, of "astounding abundance of foodstuffs of every kind, vegetables, butter, fruit, cattle."[3] The new industrial towns often lacked the inherited market accommodation of the older places; but the business had, until recently, not been very different. Manchester and Birmingham had held their markets in streets and lanes and churchyards and shambles. Birmingham had recently set aside the area of the old manor house for market purposes; but "a piazza, hall, or other place of shelter" was still "wanted for the transaction of business" in 1825[4]. A year

---

[1] "As recently as 1823": Meteyard, *Wedgwood*, I. 206 n.
[2] *Reisen*, I. 14.   [3] *Ibid.* I. 204.
[4] *The Picture of Birmingham* (1825).

earlier, in Manchester, the Commissioners of Police had opened
a covered market for butchers and greengrocers—not for meat
and vegetables—in the London Road. Another "handsome
covered market," in Brown Street, followed in 1827, and a fish-
market in 1828. But there was still plenty of street marketing
and "the number of carts with farm produce which came from
every side of the country...was truly astonishing."[1] It was
the very capable unreformed Corporation of Liverpool which
had set this fashion in market halls when it opened, in 1822,
a hall "far bigger and more imposing than the Halles at Paris"[2]
—eleven hundred feet by two hundred, with cast-iron pillars,
four separate pumps of fresh water and, for illumination, gas.

The account of the new Manchester meat and vegetable
market shows how the dealer was coming between producer
and consumer. (For meat, the dealer had always been needed
everywhere, but not for vegetables.) The chain of intermediaries
was stretching out towards the London length[3]. In London
that chain—astonishingly efficient, when the difficulty of feeding
the place without rapid transport facilities is considered—
worked in deplorable grooves. There was "talk of building big
market halls as in Liverpool"[4]; but only talk. "On Monday
the City was almost impassable from the cattle"[5] driven to
Smithfield—a Smithfield inadequate, most insanitary, full of
oaths and cruelty to animals. Billingsgate too was "cramped
and dirty."[6] Such were the places from which—through
various intermediaries—King George IV got his beef and
Mr Creevey his fish.

Even those food trades, in London and the greater towns,
which had remained longest direct, or nearly direct, were requiring more intermediaries. The trade in fresh dairy produce
had formerly been strictly localised, with little room for intermediaries[7]. The steamboat now brought fresh Irish butter

---

[1] Wheeler, J., *Manchester, its Political, Social and Commercial History* (1836),
p. 347.

[2] Meidinger, *op. cit.* I. 321. For the control of Manchester markets by the
Court Leet, Webb, S. and B., *Local Government*, II. 108. In vol. IV ("Statutory
Authorities," 1922) the enormous significance of the Commissioners of Police,
Improvements, etc., in municipal history is brought out. For the Liverpool
Corporation, see vol. III. 414–24.

[3] Above, p. 219.   [4] Meidinger, *op. cit.* I. 67.

[5] *S. C. on Smithfield Market and the Slaughtering of Cattle in the Metropolis,*
1828 (VIII. I), p. 4.

[6] Meidinger, *ut sup.*, who never said hard things of England if he could
help it.   [7] Westerfield, *op. cit.* p. 204.

regularly to Liverpool and fresh West Country butter to London. The result was to strengthen the position of the butter wholesaler and make him a more essential link in the chain from farm to consumer. He had established his position in the eighteenth century, or earlier, by handling the heavy imports of salted butter, which came to London from points so far distant as Northumberland and Carmarthen. In 1730 a single London wholesaler, Abraham Daking by name, was supposed to turn over 75,000 firkins of salt butter a year.

Quickened transport had begun to affect even the milk supplies of London, and in the same way. Until the nineteenth century all London milk had been drawn from a very narrow area. The metropolitan cowkeeper might himself distribute or, much more usually, he might sell to the small distributor with his "milk-walk"—the person who employed the smart milk-girls of the old prints in genteel quarters, and slavish parish 'prentice girls elsewhere[1]. There is no suggestion of any elaborate organisation or of any operations on a large scale[2]. Towards the end of the eighteenth century a new development set in—the creation of capitalistic dairies in the London suburbs. "The most eminent" of these, in 1825–30, were two at Islington and the metropolitan dairy in the Edgeware Road. One of those at Islington, Rhodes', was then over thirty years old. It averaged more than 400 cows: they were never untied and they were fed mainly on brewery refuse: the ventilation was excellent. Laycock's of Islington was larger still, and the metropolitan, originally created by this milk-king Rhodes, kept 320 stalled cows: in both the ventilation was bad. "From 1822 to 1829 a number of other dairies sprang up...but like other bubbles of those years, they have nearly all burst." The survivors held big contracts for the supply of milk to institutions, and also sold to the milk-dealers, a class whose importance was apparently on the increase[3]. Meanwhile the milk-radius was extending with the improvement of the metropolitan roads.

[1] George, *London Life in the Eighteenth Century*, p. 90, 232. Milk-selling is not a "trade" recognised by Campbell.

[2] "Lactaria, the Inventress of the Lactarium in St George's Fields," where she supplied milk, syllabubs, and "rural elegance," may have been in a fair way of business. Advertisement of 1773 quoted in George, *op. cit.* p. 349.

[3] Loudon, *Encyclopædia of Agriculture* (1831), p. 1028–9. Rd. Laycock was not merely a milk purveyor. He had "an establishment for the feeding and taking in of cattle," *en route* for Smithfield, where he could house 1500 beasts under cover. *S. C. on Smithfield Market*, 1828, p. 234.

Cows were still driven to suburban houses and milked before
their doors, as a guarantee of purity; and the milkmaid with
her "Milk-below!" and her two pails, "just like Switzerland,"[1]
still did the actual distribution. But there was more organisation behind her; and "already," that is before 1831, "country
dairies...from five to twenty miles from London" were sending up milk—no doubt to the dealers—in closed vessels by
"spring carts, which go at a rapid trot." What a change the
railways will make in all this, was Loudon's comment when
describing it[2].

Capitalistic dairying is found, at the other end of the kingdom, in Glasgow. "At Whitsunday 1810, Mr Harley," of that
city, "first began to turn his attention to the formation of a
Dairy, on a large scale." At that time, and indeed much later,
only "a few farmers" brought in fresh milk to Glasgow,
though barrelled buttermilk was regularly brought. Most of
the fresh milk came from cows stalled in the town. Of these
there were 586 in 1816. The "Harleian Dairy," a wonderful
and most sanitary structure, contained 195, and 64 "cow-
feeders" managed the rest[3]. Ten years later, the Harleian
was still running, with 200 head of cattle and an associated
bathing establishment; for Harley had aimed as much at the
health of the town as at his own gain[4].

Further opportunities for extension of the middleman's
sphere had been provided by the growth of the London potato
trade. As the potato came into general use, in the eighteenth
century, it was grown in the London market garden area. By
about 1760 this area, which originally was all in Middlesex and
Surrey, had spread some way into Essex.

> Potatoes now are Plaistow's pride,
> Whole markets are from thence supplied.

By 1796, there were more than 1600 acres under potatoes in
Barking, Ilford, Leyton, Wanstead and East and West Ham.
In 1811 there were 420 acres in West Ham alone[5]. But by
that time potatoes were coming in as a field crop, and the long-
range import to London had begun. Thomas Stone had noted
in 1794 that the smallholders of the Isle of Axholm were sending

[1] Meidinger, op. cit. I. 67.
[2] Op. cit. p. 1029.
[3] Cleland, J., Annals of Glasgow (1816), I. 370-2.
[4] Meidinger, op. cit. II. 95.
[5] V.C.H. Essex, II. 474-7.

potatoes all the way to London[1]. Thirty-five years later Cornwall had just taken up the growth of early varieties, and they were on sale in Covent Garden[2]. At the same time the recent introduction of steam communication between the Thames the Forth and the Tay had enabled the farmers of Forfar and Fife to find relief in a time of depression by growing potatoes in the fields for the London market[3]. These big consignments from long distances required a large-scale organisation among the Covent Garden wholesalers.

The greatest of the home foodstuff trade—that in grain— had not been much simplified since the practice of selling by sample, which was in full swing early in the eighteenth century[4], had facilitated large-scale buying by middlemen of various sorts for the London market. Simplification was hindered by the horrible complexity of weights and measures. Newcastle sold by the boll of 2 or of 6 bushels; Carlisle by the bag of 3; Norfolk by the coomb of 4; London by the quarter of 8; Hertford and Bedford by the load of 5; the West Riding by the load of 3; Furness by the load of $4\frac{1}{2}$. At St Ives, in Huntingdon, one of the chief of the fenland markets, wheat was sold by the load of 5 bushels, oats by the last of $10\frac{1}{2}$ quarters, and barley by the quarter of 8 bushels. When the bushel measure of capacity was translated into weight, uniformity was no greater. For the same class of grain, Shropshire translated at 75 lbs., Yorkshire at 60, Lancashire at 70, Birmingham at 62, and Wolverhampton at 72; while in Staffordshire the weight varied "nearly with the number of market towns, and in some of the markets two or three different weights are used." When dealer dealt with dealer, the difficulty was got over by stipulating that the transaction should be in bushels of so many pounds per bushel, the system which the Select Committee on the Sale of Corn of 1834 recommended for general adoption; but as between farmer and dealer such commercial rationalism was never admitted[5]. Presumably the dealer saw his profit in the irrational.

[1] *General View of the Agriculture of Lincoln*, p. 30. Dr Slater seems to suggest that potato-growing in Axholm only became important after 1850 (*The English Peasantry and the Enclosure of Common Fields*, 1907, p. 57); but Stone is quite explicit.

[2] Loudon, *op. cit.* p. 849.

[3] Above, p. 135.   [4] Westerfield, *op. cit.* p. 145.

[5] See the *Report* of the Committee (1834, VII) and the evidence, *passim*. The quotation is from Q. 7.

In spite of the development of selling by sample, bulk selling was by no means extinct. According to the place where he lived, or the grain which he was handling, the farmer might sell "to the Factor, the Merchant, the Hoyman, the Miller, the Mealman, or the Maltster"[1]; but the names were no longer always those of distinct trades, as they had once been. In 1800 farmers were still selling at Mark Lane from samples which they brought in their pockets[2]; but by 1830 this practice seems to have died out. The factor to whom a farmer might sell was the agent of some bigger man, merchant or miller, who had not himself the local knowledge to handle Carlisle bags and Staffordshire bushels. But some of the large farmers in counties near London were in a position to deal with another type of factor, the man who sold for them in Mark Lane. Joseph Stonard, corn factor, had explained to the House of Commons Committee of 1800 that he sold mainly East Anglian grain and that the majority of it was "growers' corn": he got a commission per quarter sold[3]. Many farmers resident near the coasts of Kent were in the same position as these East Anglian growers: they sent their grain to London fortnightly, in charge of the "Kentish hoymen," shipmasters who were also factors at the Corn Exchange, who sold for them on commission[4]. The course of events between 1800 and 1830—improvement in communications and some slight increase in the number of large farmers—had perhaps increased the number of growers who were in a position to deal thus directly with London. But the average farmer sold outright to a factor, a hoyman, a local merchant, or a local miller[5].

If Cobbett is to be trusted, the local merchant was more often than not a Quaker.

The Quakers carry on the far greater part of the work. They are, as to the products of the earth, what the Jews are, as to gold and silver.... One would think that their religion bound them under a curse, not to work. Some part of the people of all other sects work...but, here is a sect of buyers and sellers[6].

---

[1] S.C. on the Sale of Corn, 1834, p. xiii.
[2] Appendix to Reports on the Corn Trade, 1801. In Reports from Comm....
not inserted in the Journals, IX. 156.
[3] Ibid. p. 147 sqq.
[4] Ibid p. 151, and Westerfield, op. cit. p. 154.
[5] According to Charles Savile, Esq., M.P., in 1800, all farmers outside Kent, Essex and Suffolk sold outright, Reports on the Corn Trade, 1801, p. 146.
[6] Rural Rides, I. 209.

The history of a good many merchant and banking families in country towns bears out at least the first sentence of this incisive and truculent generalisation. Such families, it would appear, were either ousting the factors of the greater houses or themselves acting as factors for them: the greatest days of the collecting factors had been those when Britain still exported grain and they operated for export houses, as is shown by the evidence given in 1800. Wheat, it was explained, was mostly sold to millers, but "at times of exportation"—there had been no such time since 1792—it was taken by "shipping factors."[1] After the wars the shipping factor was out of business, and the millers—who had been strong men for many generations[2]—dominated the situation. They took the bulk of the English wheat direct from the farmer in 1830[3], often combining in their own person the functions of miller corn-merchant and flour-merchant. Evidence given in 1800 shows that the millers already employed factors to buy for them at a distance, just as the wheat exporters did before them, and that they sold grain through selling factors on the London Corn Exchange. A fair quantity of wheat passed through the hands of various middlemen before it was milled; but the "circulation among middlemen" was commoner on the more primitive Irish markets in 1830[4]. The opening of steam communication with Ireland in 1824 had given a "prodigious" stimulus to Irish milling: the Irish wheat, though still inferior, had improved greatly since the peace, and it was fit to be sent over as flour, now that the risk of damage *en route* by sea water was so much reduced[5].

The miller had assumed the functions of the wholesale "mealman" without, as yet, destroying him. A hundred years earlier this type of tradesman bought corn, had it ground, and sold meal to the shop-keeping mealman—especially in London. But even in Defoe's time the millers were cutting into the one trade and the bakers into the other, the baker selling fine flour

---

[1] *Report*, p. 146. For Imports and Exports see the valuable return of 1830 (XXII. 5) covering the period 1697–1814. For the great exporters of the eighteenth century, Westerfield, *op. cit.* p. 166.

[2] For the miller-merchant, regarded as an abuse in the seventeenth century, *ibid.* p. 168.

[3] Evidence of Wm. Jacob of the Corn Department of the Board of Trade before the *S. C. on Agriculture*, 1833, Q. 8.

[4] Jacob's evidence, as above.

[5] Evidence of Jos. Sandars, Liverpool merchant, *S. C. on Agriculture*, 1833, Q. 4101, 4132.

to consumers[1]. Witnesses "in the mealing trade" gave evidence in 1800[2], and it was explained before the committee of that year that the London corn factors generally started as "factors and mealmen." House of Commons committees in the early 'thirties could still describe the mealman as one of the regular purchasers from the farmers; but evidently the trade, as a distinct occupation, had much declined.

In the barley trade, the maltster was in much the same position as the miller in the wheat trade: there were malting houses almost everywhere, just as there were mills, and the trade as a rule required no intermediaries, though barley, like other grains, sometimes passed through a number of hands. Malt had not been made in any quantity in the near neighbourhood of London for a century or more[3], during which time the demand of the London breweries had grown outrageously; so there had been ample opportunity for the development of large-scale operations in the basins of the Thames and its tributaries, from which most of the London malt came. Other large urban brewing centres, such as Norwich, exercised a similar influence. In the districts where victuallers' brewing and domestic brewing predominated[4] malting operations must have been on a smaller scale. How far the primitive practice of domestic malting survived no available record indicates.

Oats and beans, the committee of 1800 had reported, were sold by the farmer to "what are called Jobbers or Dealers"; "tick beans" went to shipping factors for the West India plantations—part of the economics of slavery; white pease were sold to factors for the navy, a very great consumer at that time, and to "persons who make a trade of splitting them and furnish the corn chandlers with them for general consumption."[5] With the necessary modifications in the demand from the plantations and the navy, the account would have been true twenty-five years later. Whether the jobbers (of oats and beans) were ever the same men as another small, but most important, group of London jobbers reported on in 1800 is uncertain—probably not. The group in question were the pure market dealers, the ancestors of all nineteenth-century produce exchange operators.

[1] Defoe, quoted in Westerfield, *op. cit.* p. 171
[2] *E.g.* Wm. Rustin, *Report* of 1801, p. 153.
[3] Campbell, *The London Tradesman*, p. 268: "but little malt is made in London in proportion to the consumption."
[4] Above, p. 170–1. [5] *Reports on the Corn Trade*, p. 146.

They appear to have operated in all kinds of grain—though less in wheat than in other grains, because so much of the wheat missed Mark Lane—but under considerable legal difficulties.

"About twenty" of these jobbers had stands in the Corn Exchange, and "there might be forty persons on the market who practised jobbing to some degree."[1] They bought on credit to resell and to "take advantage of momentary changes of the market which," as their critics alleged, "they themselves could occasion." As the market opened at no fixed hour, they were said to get in "before the fair buyer." A few years earlier they had frequently made purchases without taking delivery, an illegal proceeding at eighteenth-century law, but "the late trial, King v. Rasby had made them more cautious" in this respect. They were not yet a perfectly distinct group, nor were their operations very extensive: one witness thought that no people made jobbing their chief business—but he was only an ex-member of the Exchange and it would appear that his evidence was somewhat out of date[2]. He alone had a good word to say for "jobbing": he thought—quite correctly—that it steadied prices in time of plenty: he also thought that it was dangerous in time of dearth. There is no precise record of its development during the next quarter of a century, but the whole course of commercial evolution and of City opinion during those years favoured operations of this class.

The great coal trade of London and the Thames basin, one of the most important distributive organisations in the country, was regulated and ossified by statute and ancient custom. Here there was as yet little chance of simplification. More than seventy Acts of parliament had dealt with the trade between 1688 and 1800. After the inquiry of 1800, an immensely detailed coal-trade code had been embodied in the Act of 1807 (47 Geo. III. Ses. 2, c. lxviii) which was still in force. It was based upon the customs of the old Tyne-Wear-Thames coastwise trade. In 1800 there had been much talk of the regulation of possible abuses in this trade through the competition of "inland" coal. But nothing had come of this. When sea-borne prices were very high a little coal came in by canal, but a slight price fall was enough to stop it. The "Paddington coal," as it was called—*i.e.* Midland coal brought in by way of the Grand Junction

---

[1] *Reports on the Corn Trade*, p. 154 and *passim*.
[2] This was Charles Savile.

and Regent's canals—was reckoned at 1484 tons in 1826[1]. It fell to 547 tons in 1828, when there was a "fighting trade" from the North. Now the total London coal trade at the time was about 2,000,000 tons a year[2]. Tees coal, unknown in London before 1826, was just becoming an important factor in the market: even coal "from the Firth"—of Forth—had appeared there; but both classes, being sea-borne, came under the old rules which bore on the coal trade of London Pool.

From the coalowner, who might be either an owner-exploiter like Lord Londonderry or a royalty-paying lessee—and was usually an informal company of such lessees—Newcastle coal had all, at one time, been taken by the "fitter" who loaded it on the keels, which he usually owned. The fitter was a factor who transferred coal to the shipowner for a commission: he did not himself fix the price, which was normally controlled by the associated coalowners in their vend[3]. Under an Act of Queen Anne (9 Anne, c. 28) the fitter had still to send to the coal office of the Lord Mayor of London a certificate of the cargo which he had transferred to the shipowner. Latterly, however, direct loading into colliers at the staiths, and so direct dealings between the coalowner and shipowner, had been on the increase—one of the few points in the trade at which an old class of intermediaries was being to some extent cut out. The shipowner was a principal not an agent. So long as the vend operated, there was no temptation for the coalowner to cut into his business or his trading profit; but in a year of fighting trade, such as 1828, the coalowner might hire ships —hoping to make a better freight bargain than his neighbours —and himself sell in London.

In London the normal buyer was a big coal-merchant, who usually dealt with a factor representing the shipowner, and bought cargoes or parts of cargoes. He got twenty-one chaldrons for every twenty that he paid for, by the custom "called ingrain." But he might not unload his purchase without elaborate supervision. Coal paid all sorts of duties. The fitter, or presumably in his absence the coalowner, had to certify that,

---

[1] This was after the removal of the duties on inland coal by Robinson in 1824. See Smart, *Annals,* II. 196. The figures are in the 1830 *Report on the Coal Trade,* p. 67: that and the 1800 *Report* (in *Reports from Committees...not inserted in the Journals,* X. 538) are the bases of the following paragraphs.

[2] See Porters, *Progress,* p. 581, for figures of the London trade.

[3] Above, p. 202.

before shipment, Newcastle "spoutage" and the special Tyne duty known as the "Richmond shilling"—an old payment used by Charles II to endow one of his families, and bought back from the Dukes of Richmond by the State in 1799—had been paid. In the Thames there were mayor's dues, market dues, and the heavy King's duty, besides factorage, stamps, insurance and what not. Unloading was therefore supervised, and cargoes checked against the fitter's certificate, by the statutory "water meters." There were fifteen of these, nominated by the City, and they had 158 deputies. The work of unloading was done by another group with statutory pay, the "coal whippers." As this pay, fixed in 1807, was above current rates for similar work, the employing whippers, in collusion with publicans, insisted on a minimum consumption of liquor, charging their men 2s. a day for gin and beer, whether drunk or not.

The barges, into which nearly all coal was shipped, usually belonged to the merchants. They were not regulated, but only freemen of the watermen's company might navigate them. Arrived at the merchants' wharf, the coal came under the eye of the statutory "land meters," who measured the cargoes and saw that the coal was put into the three-bushel sacks, in which alone it might be delivered. From start to finish the measures were those of capacity, and as broken coal occupies more space than unbroken, it was to everyone's interest to break it. Land meters were perhaps the most useless of all the official hierarchy. They gave not even a nominal protection to the poor, who bought coal in less than sackfuls. Their absence, owing to a legal accident, in parts of Kentish London and from many wharves on the Regent's Canal was noted with approval[1].

The greater merchants, who kept wharves, sold as a rule to "second merchants." Of these the most important group were known as "accounters"—men who kept their own barges, might send them to take coal direct from the collier in London Pool, and carried on an upriver trade. Then there were the "brass plate coal merchants," "principally...merchants' clerks, gentlemen's servants, and other dealers." These were supposed to handle five-sixths of London's domestic fuel. A third group bought coal from the wharf-owner to peddle it in small parcels to the poor. Large consumers, such as "manufacturers on the waterside," and a few of the greatest public

---

[1] [Most of this code was repealed in 1831, but laws for coal-whippers survived to 1856. George, M. D., "The London Coal-Heavers," *E.J.* (*Ec. Hist.*), 1927.]

and private establishments, might buy from the merchant
direct; but evidently this direct trade was only a small proportion of the whole. It was, however, growing with the growth
of the new gas companies, whose demand was to be an important
factor in the gradual transformation of the London coal trade
and the elimination of intermediaries between coalowner and
consumer.

There was no full inquiry into the coal trade outside London.
But with the aid of the London accounts, and of a map constructed in 1830[1], it is not difficult to form some picture of it.
Near the coalfields intermediaries were of course fewer, and on
the fields they might be cut out altogether. For the Thames
basin the "accounters" can be pictured supplying upriver
depots, and perhaps selling to merchants of the "brass plate"
type, so far as a point between Windsor and Reading. To
Reading there now came canal-borne coal from Somerset, and
to Oxford canal-borne coal from Warwick and Leicester. All
round the South coast would be distributing port merchants,
handling mainly North-East coast coals east of Plymouth and
Welsh coals west of that point. Along the East coast were
ports whose shipowners had long been interested in the Tyne-
Thames colliering business. Yarmouth men, for example, had
enjoyed a great share of it in Defoe's day[2]. They supplied the
local depots also. Coal was the chief import of Ipswich, Yarmouth and Lynn—to take only a handful of East coast towns
from a great group—during the 'twenties[3]. In each case the cargoes had to be transhipped for inland navigation, and the trans-
shipment, it may be inferred, would often be accompanied by
a change of ownership. A 28-ton barge could go from Yarmouth
to Norwich without locking, and one of about the same size
from Lynn to Cambridge through three locks only. At the
ultimate inland distributing centre, Northampton it might be
or Cambridge, would be "second merchants"—or even third
or fourth—who often handled coal, timber, and grain. Many
men of this class had become bankers and, as such, might be
shedding off some commodity trades to lesser people. Quakers
would not be strange among them, and dissenters in general
very familiar.

[1] On which the Plate facing this page is based.
[2] Defoe, *Tour*, I. 193.
[3] See *e.g.* the references in Meidinger, *op. cit.* I. 200, 205, 213.

The mere bulk of the coastwise coal trade was gigantic: it dwarfed the foreign trade. More than twice as much coal was shipped to Ireland as to all foreign and colonial ports, and towards 1830 the Thames took nearly three times as much as all Ireland[1]. Down to 1825 the coal exports proper had never reached 280,000 tons. Rapid growth began only in 1830, with an export of over 400,000 tons. Neither Britain nor the world had tonnage enough for the carriage of many bulk cargoes over great distances. Foreign trade had not yet completely lost its primitive characteristic—the exchange of precious things. The whole tonnage of shipping engaged in it under all flags entering British ports during the years 1825–30 averaged about 2,750,000. Meanwhile, in short voyage colliers, the Thames got its 2,000,000 tons of coal every year.

Among the regular British imports there was one true bulk trade and one only—the timber trade. For several centuries great spars for the navy, with dyewoods and curious woods from the tropics, had of necessity been imported; but only in the eighteenth century had the exhaustion of British forests and the housing demand made, first, London and then the whole country absolutely dependent on the overseas supply. They had drawn naturally on Scandinavia and the Baltic. Campbell's London timber merchant in the middle of the century was "furnished with Deal from Norway, either in Logs or Plank; with Oak and Wainscoat from Sweden; and some from the Counties in England; with Mahogany from Jamaica; with Wallnut-Tree from Spain."[2] At the close of the century, between 1788 and 1802, the country imported nearly 200,000 loads of fir timber from Northern Europe every year[3]. The quantity coming from the American colonies was at that time negligible, though the trade had been helped by bounty or preference for ninety years. But fear of a timber-famine, when Napoleon's continental system was extended to Northern Europe in 1809–10, turned the course of trade. The duties on European timber were pressed upward from 6s. 8d. a load in 1793 to 65s. a load in 1819, while colonial timber was either admitted free or very lightly taxed[4].

---

[1] Figures in Porter, *Progress*, p. 279, 581.
[2] *The London Tradesman*, p. 167.   [3] Porter, *Progress*, p. 375.
[4] *First Report on Foreign Trade*, 1821 (VI), p. 3–11 and *passim*. Smart (*Economic Annals*, II), ch. 2. Tooke, T., *History of Prices*, II. 417.

The sharpest rise in the European rate, from 27s. 4d. to 54s. 8d., occurred in 1811, at the height of the struggle with Napoleon. The upshot was that whereas, down to 1809–10, the timber used in Britain had been mainly from the Baltic, in 1821 Baltic timber was used only "in the more valuable description of buildings."

In that year duties were revised—10s. a load was placed on colonial timber and the foreign rate was reduced to 55s., rates which remained unchanged for nearly twenty years. It was reckoned at the time that, allowing for the average difference of freight, this left to the Canadian timber the very substantial preference of 30s. a load[1]. Further, it was argued that the American colonies had a natural monopoly of big spar timber and a natural advantage in the supply both of very large trunks of free-working fir wood and of all the cheapest stuff; that consequently their trade was in no danger. The argument proved correct and the preference, in most seasons, ample. In 1821 the colonial imports were about three times the foreign in bulk; and the available figures suggest that this advantage for the colonial imports trade was fully maintained[2]. The total imports, judged by the standards of the day, had become very great indeed. In 1831, 546,000 loads of timber "eight inches square and upwards" were imported. For such timber the load of 50 cubic feet may be taken as a ton. The spars, deals, battens, staves, boards and so forth were not all entered either by weight or by cubic content. They would raise the tonnage to something between 600,000 and 700,000. Thirteen years later, when the first exhaustive estimate of imported timber was attempted, the figure stood at 1,318,000 loads—perhaps 1,250,000 tons— of which 922,000 loads were colonial. During the 'twenties a very large part, perhaps so much as a third, of the tonnage entering British and Irish harbours from overseas carried timber, and timber was the chief article of trade at most secondary ports. So numerous were the timber-ships, that critics of the policy which had created the colonial trade argued that Britain in fact gave a bounty to maintain the "superfluous shipping" of British America, much of it very inferior[3]. Any old ship was reckoned good enough to carry this unsinkable freight: C3's at Lloyds might come in "awash with sodden deals."

---

[1] *Report* of 1821, p. 9.
[2] Porter, *op. cit.* p. 579: there is a misprint under the year 1831.
[3] *Report* of 1821, p. 6.

Owing to the nature and modifications of the corn laws, the import trade in corn was erratic and intermittent, though sometimes large. Some trade there always was, because corn could always be warehoused for re-export, but it was often very small—about 13,000 tons all told in 1823, for example[1]. Merchants watched Danzig prices, the barometer prices of the day, in relation to official, ascertained, British prices with constant and strained anxiety. When the situation seemed hopeful, they began to fill up the bonded warehouses on the chance of finding ultimately an outlet to the home market. But, from 1820 to 1825, good harvests and the old corn law kept the true import trade insignificant. In 1821 only two quarters of wheat were imported for home consumption—save from Ireland—and in 1822 not even that. The import of foreign wheat for consumption continued negligible until 1825, although in 1824 something like 150,000 tons of grain and flour of all sorts arrived in British ports. With 1825 fears of shortage led to *ad hoc* easings of the law—the release of warehoused corn by order in council and special Act of parliament[2]. There followed the sliding-scale Act of 1828 (9 Geo. IV. c. 60), the corn law of the 'thirties and early 'forties. These changes in policy were accompanied and followed by a series of inferior or bad harvests. As a result the imports of foreign wheat and wheaten flour averaged some 130,000 tons a year, in the years 1825–8, and nearly 400,000 tons in 1829–31. The maximum quantity of grain and flour of all kinds entered for home consumption in any one year was the approximately 700,000 tons of 1827, a year in which the figure was swelled by unusually heavy admissions of oats. But, from 1832, this emergency trade melted away until 1837. For the four years 1833–6 very little wheat was imported and the total average imports of grain and flour of every kind were about one-tenth of those in the peak year 1827[3].

Ores or metals filled little of the inward tonnage. Less foreign iron was being used than for very many years past, owing to the recent development of the home industry. Swedish bars for the Sheffield trade were essential[4]; but a great many scissors and files can be made from a ton of blister-steel. At

---

[1] Figures in Tooke, *op. cit.* III. 293.
[2] Canning's Warehoused Corn Act of 1827 (7 & 8 Geo. IV. c. 57) brought in after the failure of a more ambitious scheme. In 1825 Huskisson admitted Canadian corn at 5s. See Smart, *Annals*, II. 274, 422; Tooke, *op. cit.* II. 134.
[3] Tooke, *op. cit.* III. 239.   [4] Above, p. 150.

the opening of the century about 40,000 tons was the annual import of iron. This may be compared with 11,000 tons in 1820, 10,000 tons in 1823, 15,000 in 1825, and 14,000 in 1828. It is true that the munitions demand had ceased, but the new demands for edge tools probably outweighed the loss of that for swords and bayonets. British iron was now good enough for many purposes for which, twenty or thirty years earlier, imported iron had been ordinarily employed. "Was that iron used for steel or for all purposes?" Joseph Hume asked Sir John Guest in 1840, referring to the imports of the late eighteenth century. "It was used for all purposes," the expert replied[1]. "The use of our own iron has superseded in a prodigious degree all other iron," an engineer told a parliamentary committee in 1824[2]. About 1800 the home make was to the import as four to one, or rather less: in 1828, it was as fifty to one; and in that year the exports of British raw iron—mainly wrought bars, not cast pigs—was 65,000 tons against an import of 14,000[3].

Copper ores were much shipped coastwise but were only just beginning to be imported—from South America, as a result of the innumerable mining ventures there of the years 1824–5[4]. The main supplies of the smelting centres, of which Swansea was chief, came from Devon, Cornwall, the dwindling yields of the great Parys and Mona mines in Anglesey, and the Isle of Man. It was said, in the early 'thirties, that the Great Hafod copper works at Swansea employed 150 coasters to feed them with ore[5]. From 1815 to 1825, Britain exported every year considerably more copper than she used at home; and for many years after that date it was still quite common for exports to exceed home consumption. In 1832 the export of British unwrought and sheet copper was nearly 8000 tons and that of

[1] Guest's evidence before the *Comm. on Import Duties* of 1840, Q. 381 *sqq.*
[2] Alex. Galloway. *S. C. on Artisans and Machinery*, p. 22.
[3] Figures in Porter, *op. cit.* p. 248, 575.
[4] See the *Return on Copper Imported and Exported*, 1833, XXXIII. 229. In 1832 just over 100 tons of copper (more than two-thirds of it old copper for re-manufacture) and 3500 tons of copper ore were imported. Over half the imports came from Colombia, and nearly all the balance from Mexico, Cuba and Peru: these were all new trades. Hamilton, *The English Brass and Copper Industries*, p. 210, says that "comparatively large quantities of unmanufactured copper and ore" had been imported down to 1797; but the average for the eight years 1790–7 was under 850 tons, and this includes Irish ore, *Ibid.* Ap. IX.
[5] Lardner, *Cabinet Cyclopædia*, "Manufactures in Metal" (1834), III. 149. For the eighteenth century see the 1799 *Report on Copper Mines and the Copper Trade* and Allen, G. C., in *E.J.* March 1923.

copper smelted in Britain from foreign ores 700 tons; but the latter figure grew rapidly during the 'thirties[1]. Tin was in much the same position as copper. The British Isles were still the Tin Isles of Europe, although two centuries earlier Siamese tin had begun to come West, and for a century the great deposits of Banca and Billiton in the Malay Islands had been worked[2]. But the Cornish industry had never been more active than under King George IV. The British output, which during the earlier years of the century had averaged not much over 2500 tons a year, touched 4100 tons in 1817 and 5500 in 1827, the average for the decade 1821–30 being 4400 tons[3]. Nearly half this make of tin was exported, although a few hundred tons of the East Indian tin were retained for special purposes and an entrepôt trade in it was beginning to arise in London[4]. Lead also was a British export, as it had been since Romans first cast lead pigs in the Mendips. The export was declining somewhat before the competition of the new, or revived, Spanish industry in the Sierra Morena: it fell from nearly 20,000 tons in 1821 to 8000–9000 tons in 1831. The Spanish lead as yet rarely came to England—only 554 tons were recorded in 1832—but it competed with the British in other markets[5].

So far, therefore, as a bulk trade in common or "half-precious" metals existed, it was a bulk trade outwards; but a very small mercantile fleet could carry it all.

A new inward bulk trade in what might be called a "half-precious" commodity—one of those things which the Customs House officials of the 'twenties measured, not in tons or loads, but in pounds—was in course of creation to feed Lancashire's iron wheels. Forty years earlier all the cotton used in the country—about 8000 tons a year—had not employed much shipping. But by 1800–1 space for 25,000 tons had to be found; after the wars for twice as much; and from 1825–30 for an average of more than 100,000 tons[6]. Cotton from the Levant

[1] The 1833 *Return*, also Porter's *Progress*, p. 578.
[2] Lewis, *The Stannaries*, p. 54 n.
[3] *Ibid.* p. 258.
[4] Lardner, *op. cit.* III. 21. The entrepôt trade grew fast in the 'thirties. In 1839 the true import was 900 tons and the re-export 1100. *Comm. on Import Duties* of 1840, p. 262.
[5] Lardner, *op. cit.* III. 58. The exports rose again, to nearly 14,000 tons, in 1832. *A. and P.* 1833, XXXIII. 441.
[6] Figures in Tooke, *op. cit.* II. 391 *sqq.* See also Chapman, *The Lancashire Cotton Industry*, p. 143.

the West Indies and Guiana, which had met nearly all needs down to 1794, had fallen into the background, as the export of American slave-grown and mechanically-ginned cotton mounted in the new century. But America did not really dominate the British market until after the wars. There were heavy imports from Surat and Bengal and Brazil between 1816 and 1820, besides the remnant of the West Indian trade which Georgia and the Carolinas were strangling. In 1822 Egyptian cotton, to the growth of which Mahomet Ali and his French technical advisers had turned the fellaheen, first came on the market; and in 1825 Egypt sent, but for the one year only, a considerable quantity. Yet by 1826–30 the American domination was established; for the United States were supplying three-quarters of all the cotton consumed in the United Kingdom[1].

Until the sudden rise of the factory system at the close of the eighteenth century, the imports both of raw flax and hemp, mainly from the Baltic, had been considerably bulkier than those of cotton[2]. Petersburg prices were the standard quotation for both commodities on the London market. The hemp trade —for obvious reasons—had been at its height during the wars. Ten years after the peace, the imports had settled down to a normal level of some 25,000–30,000 tons a year, from which there was not much variation. For many years not a great deal of hemp had been grown in the British Isles, so that the fluctuations in consumption are pretty accurately reflected by those in the imports. The flax imports—not from Russia only —were growing fast after 1820, the growth in this case having a double cause, an increased manufacture, due to the application of machinery, and a dwindling production of the raw material in Britain. During the boom-year 1825, the import nearly reached 53,000 tons and, although it was not again so high until 1833, it fell only twice below 45,000 tons in the interval.

No such figures were approached in the wool trade; for it was only very recently that the United Kingdom had become, to any marked degree, dependent on outside sources of supply. In the eighteenth century the government, following an old-established policy, had been more concerned to stop the smuggling of surplus British wool abroad than either to hinder

[1] Ure, *The Cotton Manufacture*, I. 144. Chapman, *op. cit.* p. 143. Ellis, *The Cotton Trade of Great Britain*, p. 86.
[2] Tooke, *op. cit.* II. 391.

or to encourage imports. It had not been very successful[1], and as soon as the prohibition of export was removed, in 1825, a regular export trade grew up, or came to light, about 125 tons of British wool being returned as shipped abroad in 1827[2]. The relatively small quantity of fine wool, mainly from Spain, required during the eighteenth century by the manufacturers of the West of England—it was not used at all in Yorkshire[3]— had been admitted duty free. By 1789 this import had grown to over 1000 tons and in 1800 it touched 4000[4]. Political conditions during the Peninsular War strengthened the trade connection with Spain and Portugal, and the quality of the Spanish wool was fairly maintained; so down to 1812 very little came from any other source. But when Europe fell open, in 1814–15, English merchants and manufacturers began to realise the excellence of the fine wool now grown in Silesia and Saxony, where the recently introduced merino sheep were "nursed up as you would nurse a race horse in England."[5] There was now a duty on foreign wool, which for a few years (1820–25) was so high as 6d. on the pound; but the fine wool was very valuable and came in over it, to the amount of 10,000 tons in 1824 —two-thirds being German. Next year the duty fell to 1d. a pound and the imports were nearly doubled; but 1825 was abnormal and during the next four years the average import of wool of all sorts went back nearly to the 1824 level.

Among the returns prepared for the Lords' Committee on the Wool Trade, in 1828, was one giving the quantities imported from all countries since 1800. Under the year 1806 appears the entry "New Holland," 245 lbs. In 1814 "New Holland" is credited with over 10 tons; in 1826 with nearly 500 tons, but in 1827 with less than 250. This was the result of the enterprise of John Macarthur of Camden, formerly captain in the New South Wales Corps sent out to garrison the convict station of Port Jackson. One sanguine witness, in 1828, thought the Australian prospects so good that "within fifteen years...or

[1] See the 1786 Report on Sheep and Wool Smuggling. Reports from Committees ...not inserted in the Journals, XI. 302 (English wool was freely used at Arras, Elbeuf, Louviers, Amiens, etc.), and, for an earlier period, Lipson, E., History of the English Woollen and Worsted Industries (1921), p. 88–91.

[2] Lords' Report on British Wool Trade, 1828, p. 350. As soon as export became legal shipments to the Channel Isles decreased. Ibid.

[3] So Benj. Gott, before the Lords' Committee, p. 285.

[4] The figures in the Lords' Report (p. 330) and those given in Tooke, op. cit. II. 391 do not quite agree.   [5] Henry Hughes, merchant, in 1828 Report, p. 40.

twenty years, this country will be independent of Spain and
Germany for these [fine] wools."[1] Benjamin Gott, the great
Leeds manufacturer, did not think the Australian clips would
"rival the Saxon," since they were but "a drop in the bucket."[2]
But, as John Macarthur the younger had written home in July
1825, "the Yorkshire men have always talked against the wool,
but have still bought"[3]; so conceivably Gott did not speak his
whole mind. The time was coming when those Yorkshire men
who wanted the best wool would buy very little else[4].

If the economic importance of an article of commerce is to
be measured by the multiplication of value into bulk—a form
of measurement for which there is something to be said—
then the most important inward cargoes during the reign of
George IV were the cargoes of sugar. They had been so regarded
for a very long time by statesmen[5], and the "West India
interest" which watched over them had been a force in politics
for nearly a century. "Strange that a manufacture which
charms infancy and soothes old age should so frequently occasion political disaster."[6] Not perhaps so strange, when the size
and wealth of the watching "interest" is appreciated.[7] The
normal import of sugar in 1821–30 was 220,000 tons a year.
The amount varied comparatively little from year to year,
though there was a general upward tendency. The value, untaxed, ranged with the seasons and the qualities from a rare
minimum of £11 to a rare maximum of £58 a ton. A representative price for a common quality ("East India, Brown, in
Bond") would be about £20[8]. Not all the 220.000 tons were
consumed or refined in Britain. The entrepôt business was
one of the most prized branches of the sugar trade. It had
developed greatly during the wars, and statesmen were anxious
to retain it by means of an efficient system of bonded warehouses. In this they had been fairly successful. From the

---

[1] 1828 *Report*, p. 48 (Hughes).   [2] *Ibid.* p. 287.

[3] Onslow, S. M., *Some Early Records of the Macarthurs of Camden* (Sydney,
1914), p. 416. Macarthur moved to Camden in 1805.

[4] In 1830, 730 tons of Spanish, 11,000 tons of German, and 880 tons of
Australian wool were imported. The home clip is unknown: perhaps it was
60,000 tons. Twenty years later Australian imports were 17,000 tons and
German 4000 tons. See Baines, T., *Yorkshire Past and Present* (1858), ii. 639.

[5] See Beer, G. L., *The Old Colonial System*, and Sombart, *Luxus und Kapitalismus*, for the story of statesmen and sugar.

[6] Disraeli, *Lord George Bentinck* (ed. 1906), p. 209.

[7] Penson, "The West India Interest," *E.H.R.* July 1921.

[8] Tooke, *op. cit.* ii. 391, 412–14.

import of 220,000 tons, 40,000 tons was about a normal re-export. As Ireland took less than one-seventh of the remainder, in spite of her great population, the British consumption in the early 'twenties may be put at 150,000–160,000 tons, or not much less than 20 lbs. per head per annum; and this in spite of a taxation which kept the retail price of the cheapest sugar at between 6d. and 9d. a pound[1].

Much less important, commercially fiscally and socially, were coffee and tea. The gross import of coffee varied from 17,000 to 23,000 tons a year, but a large part of this was re-exported —in some years very much more than half. This entrepôt business, concentrated in London, helped the British trade balance and nourished "the Wen," but was not otherwise very significant. More important than the business itself was the decline in it which took place between 1821 and 1831, as the result of a reduction of the duty on West Indian coffee from 1s. to 6d. a lb. in 1825. At that time only the preferentially treated West Indian coffee, mainly from Jamaica, passed into consumption; indeed there was not demand enough to carry it all off at the price. The balance, with all other sorts of coffee —which were so heavily taxed in the interests of the West Indies that they were not consumed at all—was re-exported. The change in the duty, which apparently more than doubled the average home consumption—these were the early days of the popular, as opposed to the genteel, coffee-house—gradually brought all the West Indian coffee into consumption. But even then (in 1831) the whole British demand was still under 10,000 tons, or a little over 1¼ lbs. per annum per head of the population. The British working man was a poor coffee drinker; though Mr Pamphitoris' coffee-house in Sherard Street, Haymarket, was already well patronised by "all classes from hackney coachmen and porters, to the most respectable."[2]

Nor was the wage earner in a position to become a heavy tea drinker, in spite of all that social inquirers had been writing for thirty years and more about his fondness for the "deleterious produce of China."[3] Tea was still held tightly in the grip of the East India Company. Every pound of it went

---

[1] S. C. on Import Duties, 1840, Q. 200, 154, and Porter, op. cit. p. 541.
[2] S. C. on Import Duties, 1840, Q. 201. His evidence and that of other coffee-house keepers fills a curious page in social history. For the commercial side see Porter's evidence and his Progress, p. 372, 549.
[3] Eden's phrase, above, p. 118.

through the Company's London warehouses. How far the monopoly actually drove up prices and restricted consumption it is impossible to say. Prices certainly were very high and consumption as certainly small—rather over 13,000 tons (in 1831) for Great Britain and Ireland. Consumption per head in Great Britain may have been so low as 1¼ lbs. and cannot well have been higher than 1½ lbs. The average price of all tea free of duty in the decade 1821–31 was 2s. 7d. The cheapest teas would no doubt go for 2s. or less. If they did, they paid 96 per cent. *ad valorem*; if not, 100 per cent. With various middle profits they can seldom have been retailed so low as 5s. a pound: the average retail price must have been above 6s.[1] How much "deleterious" tea at 6s. a pound might a labourer with a wife and three children, on 18s. to 16s. a week in town or 12s. to 9s. in the country, buy weekly? His household's exact share of the national consumption would be a little under 2 oz., perhaps eight pennyworth. The countryman can hardly have afforded that. If he did it cannot have done the five much harm.

Tobacco, like tea and coffee, was one of the commodities whose import and consumption had been checked by tremendous war and post-war taxation. The British consumption varied between five and seven thousand tons. Since the loss of the American colonies there had been no strong interest to fight for tolerable taxation, and it was an obvious luxury. The consumption in Great Britain, if the figures are to be trusted, fell appreciably between 1811 and 1821, while that in Ireland fell disastrously. By 1831 the British consumption was just about what it had been in 1811. Ireland was consuming some two-thirds of what she had consumed in 1811. In neither case, of course, was the consumption per head nearly so great as it had been. Nor is this surprising. The British duty in 1811 was 2s. 2d. and a fraction per pound. From 1820 to 1826 it was 4s.; in 1826, 3s.; from 1827 to 1831, 2s. 9d. During that time the price of Virginia tobacco in bond was seldom above 8d. a pound and was occasionally as low as 2½d. or even 2d.[2]

Wine was a stagnant and a relatively unimportant trade, though the imports of wine were of some significance to ship-owners. Statisticians supposed that the consumption per head

[1] Porter, *op. cit.* p. 552. *Customs Tariff of the U.K.* (c. 8706 of 1897), p. 204.
[2] Porter, *op. cit.* p. 566. *Customs Tariff of the U.K.*, p. 197. Tooke, *op. cit.* II 418. Rive, A., "The Consumption of Tobacco since 1600," *E.J.* (*Ec. Hist.*), Jan. 1926.

in the United Kingdom was not much more than a quarter of what it had been a century earlier. However that may be, the figures, such as they are, show a larger import, larger absolutely not merely per head, in 1801 than in 1821 or in 1831[1]. The decline was most marked in Ireland—sinking deeper into poverty and spirits—but was perceptible in Great Britain. Wine had long ceased to be a drink of the people, and the curves of its consumption record little of interest except changes in the dinner-table habits of the well-to-do. The United Kingdom put away in 1821–31 some 6,000,000 gallons a year of all the wines, or, say, the full cargoes of sixty 400-ton ships.

If the wine imports were relatively small, those of spirits were enormous. More rum came into the United Kingdom from the West Indies in 1831 than wine from all sources— 7,800,000 gallons as against 7,100,000 gallons. (More was not retained because the re-exports of rum were heavy.) This is recorded rum: there remains that which was smuggled, of which there is no estimate. There is, however, an estimate of what might be called the officially smuggled French brandy. It averaged 600,000 gallons a year during the five years 1827–31. For those years the French Customs recorded an average of 2,200,000 gallons exported to England, the English Customs an average of 1,600,000 gallons received from France. According to the British Board of Trade "the French government acted with a very doubtful kind of morality in these matters, and assisted its subjects very much in smuggling"[2]; but it can hardly be supposed that all, or nearly all, the smuggled brandy was entered at the French Customs before shipment. The real annual smuggling may have been 1,000,000 gallons or more.

The savage fluctuations of the grain trade and the efficient smuggling system make it hard to speak precisely of normal imports; but certainly timber, grain and flour, sugar, cotton, flax, hemp, coffee, wine, tea, iron, wool and tobacco—in that order, if graded by bulk, with spirits inserted perhaps between flax and hemp—were the leading imports of the years 1825–30. They accounted for something like three-quarters of the whole import trade, in bulk and probably also in value. The remainder was infinitely varied, including all the light valuable goods which escaped, as well as those which failed to escape, the notice of the Customs House. Among raw materials silk, and

---

[1] Figures in Porter, *op. cit.* p. 560. *Customs Tariff of the U.K.* p. 150–1.
[2] Porter, before the Committee of 1840, Q. 187, and his *Progress*, p. 560, 803.

among manufactured goods manufactures of silk, were perhaps the most important. After Robinson's reduction of the duty on the former in 1824 there is no evidence that much was smuggled, so that the 1500–2000 tons of very valuable "raw, waste and thrown silk," which is the normal figure in the late 'twenties, is probably correct; but the habit of smuggling French silk fabrics, like that of smuggling French lace and brandies and gloves, was so general, easy, and well organised that the replacement of the prohibition by a reasonable duty, in the same year, had by no means brought all French silks under the view of the Customs. Here again French returns help the student of smuggling statistics. More than half the silk goods entered in France as exported to England did not appear in the English returns as imported from France[1].

Even including the silks, smuggled or taxed, foreign manufactures formed a very small part of the imports. Mirrors and miscellaneous glassware from France and Germany came in fair quantities over the tariff: they were too fragile for the smugglers. Some woollen goods of various kinds came in both ways, the French fancy fabrics being often smuggled with the silks. Some gloves, more often than not smuggled, with straw-plait from Leghorn and linen from Germany France and Belgium complete the list of those manufactured goods which came at all commonly; though small quantities of every class of fine merchandise were imported from time to time for the use of the world of fashion. Most of the miscellaneous imports were foodstuffs and raw materials—such as turpentine and tallow and seeds, currants oils and brimstone, oranges rice and spices, dyewoods and indigo and hides[2].

Britain paid for her imports almost exclusively with the products of her manufacturing industry, and with re-exported "colonial wares." A growing, but relatively inconsiderable, quantity of coal, a fair amount of tin copper and lead, a little wool, a few thousand tons of pig iron and a few hundred tons of unwrought steel, a few slates from Lord Penrhyn's quarries, and some cargoes of china clay from the moors of St Austell is an almost exhaustive list of the raw materials exported. In 1827, and again in 1830, all these raw materials, together with all "goods upon which but little labour had been bestowed"— of which the most important was bar iron—as opposed to

[1] *Report* of 1840, Q. 188, and Porter's *Progress*, p. 223.
[2] Based on retrospective facts and figures from the 1840 *Report*, Q. 9, p. 208

"finished manufactures and goods into the value of which much labour had entered," represented only between 17 and 18 per cent. of the total declared value of British exports[1]. The total exports in 1827 were valued at £37,200,000 and in 1830 at £38,300,000. Of this latter figure just over one-half (£19,300,000) and of the former just under one-half (£17,500,000) was the value of the cotton manufactures exported—to such an extraordinary degree had the foreign trade of the country already become dependent on the great new industry. In both cases the figure includes yarn and twist as well as piece goods; and this export of half-finished goods, though not yet very large, was growing; for continental countries—first France, then Russia, then Prussia—were barring out the finished goods, partially or completely.

The fabrics of wool, which fifty years earlier had been the staple export of the country, were left very far behind; though the Customs authorities still enumerated them with a detailed traditional affection which they had not yet acquired for the cottons—cloths so many pieces, napped coatings so many, kerseymeres, baizes, stuffs, flannels and the rest, each so many pieces or yards. The average annual export of wool fabrics in the late 'twenties was worth almost exactly £5,000,000. There was as yet no perceptible export of woollen or worsted yarn. Linen yarn, on the other hand, from the new spinning mills at Leeds and elsewhere, was just beginning to leave the country in quantities of which the Customs could take account. The first recorded export to France was 55 lbs. in 1829[2]. By 1836 the figure would be 4,000,000 lbs. worth £277,000. But up to 1830 yarn had no serious weight in the total of from £2,000,000 to £2,500,000's worth of linen goods annually exported. Of this total about a quarter was of Irish origin, though in the last years during which separate records of the Irish trade were kept—the records ceased in 1833—the Irish share fell[3].

Cotton, wool, linen and silk manufactures together accounted for about £26,500,000 out of the £38,300,000 at which British exports were valued in 1830. If the value of the exported raw materials and "goods upon which but little labour had been bestowed" (£6,900,000) be deducted from the total, a relatively

---

[1] 1840 *Report*, p. 206: Porter's memorandum for the Committee.

[2] *Ibid.* p. 186.

[3] Porter, *op. cit.* p. 225. The average annual export in 1820–3 (in million yards) was—British, 31·4; Irish, 15·1. In 1830–3 it was—British, 48·7; Irish, 11·9.

inconsiderable figure remains for all finished manufactures other than textiles. Hardware and cutlery took the first place on this residuary list with £1,400,000; manufactures of brass and copper the second, with £867,000. After that no heading in the statistics showed so much as £250,000, and one only is of considerable interest—"machinery and mill work." The declared value under this head for 1830 was £208,000. But no one believed it. Permission to export any valuable kinds of machinery was only a few years old, and there were still legal and administrative restrictions on the trade. But then, as one engineer told the committee of 1824, evasion by misdescription was very easy, because no customs officer could identify a scientifically dismounted machine. Another engineer felt bound to say, with gratitude, of the customs people that "it was only in cases where it was impossible to shut their eyes, that they had ever ventured to keep them open."[1]

The distribution of the £38,200,000's worth of exports in 1830 was on this wise[2]. The United States, the largest single customer, took £6,100,000's worth, much of it in cotton goods. Prussia, the German States, Holland and Belgium together took £6,700,000; France, Spain, Portugal, Italy and the Balkan coasts £7,200,000; Russia and the Scandinavian States £1,700,000. All Asia was content with £4,100,000; all Africa with £744,000; Australia with £300,000. The British North American Colonies took £1,900,000, but the British West Indies £2,800,000, and South America with Mexico £5,200,000. The single island of Mauritius took £161,000 and the foreign West Indies over £900,000. The small balance went to Man and the Channel Isles. As might have been expected, the analysis brings out the predominant purchasing power of the raw cotton countries, the sugar countries, the favoured timber countries, and those South American States which had acquired purchasing power by borrowing on the London market. It was not "natural" for Scandinavia and Russia to be such poor customers; the British Parliament had willed it. Asia, it should be noted, took part payment for her exports in gold and silver, as she always had since she drained the Roman Empire of its treasure; and the precious metals are not included in these figures.

---

[1] *S. C. on Artisans and Machinery*, p. 9, 20: the quotation is from Alex. Galloway's evidence.

[2] *S. C. on Import Duties*, p. 206: the distribution in 1827 was almost exactly the same as in 1830.

With one important and one relatively unimportant exception, all British trade was handled by private mercantile houses.
The important exception was the trade of the East India Company, which, however, was now a very different thing from the
East India trade; the relatively unimportant exception that of
the Hudson's Bay Company. Under the Act of 1813 (53 Geo.
III, c. 155), which extended the East India charter for a further
—and, as it proved, a final—twenty years, the private trade had
been given a wide place. The rather meaningless complexities
of the system as it existed in the 'twenties help to explain
why it ended in 1833[1]. They also illustrate admirably that
tangle of antiquated trade regulations at which the political
economists were hewing. The thing, as Cobbett would have
said, was thus[2]. Private traders might ship any goods legally
exportable, in legal ships—that is, British-built ships with
crews three-quarters British, as prescribed by the Navigation
Acts—to any "East Indian" port and bring back the produce of
such port, if legally importable. An "East Indian" port was
any port east of the Cape of Good Hope and west of the Straits
of Magellan. But if the trader wished to invade "the Company's peculiar limits," i.e. all that coast which lies between
the mouth of the Indus and the straits of Malacca, he must pay
for the Company's licence. He had a right to this licence if
his ship were bound for Bombay, Madras, Calcutta or Prince
of Wales Island[3]. For other ports the Directors might refuse
a licence, but appeal lay to the India Board. Within what were
called "the Board's limits," an area containing Ceylon Java
and the Malay Islands generally, the India Board was the
licenser: it always issued the licence, and without fee. Trade
within the "Charter limits"—the Cape to Magellan's Straits—
was confined by the Act of 1813 to ships of 350 tons and upwards. Small craft, the Company had argued, were more apt
for smuggling and large ones more likely to maintain British
prestige. However, under 59 Geo. III, c. 122, small ships were
allowed to go to New South Wales. Not until 1821 had it
become legal[4] (under 1 & 2 Geo. IV, c. 65) for "His Majesty's
subjects to carry on Trade...between any ports within the
limits of the East India Company's Charter (except...China)

---

[1] Below, p. 486 *sqq.*
[2] Based on the *Third Report on Foreign Trade*, 1821 (VI).
[3] Or Penang, off the Malay coast.
[4] As recommended in the *Second Report on Foreign Trade* of 1821.

and any...Ports beyond the limits...belonging to any State ...in amity with His Majesty."

The clause excepting China touches the root of the trade problem of the 'twenties. Since 1814, while the general trade with India had grown, John Company's Indian trade had declined[1]. He clung the more tenaciously therefore to his monopoly of the China trade, his sole intact monopoly and the principal source of the dividends on East India stock. Even the China monopoly was intact only against the English shipowner, not against English goods. By a very odd anomaly, United States ships were, by treaty, in a position to load in British ports and clear for Canton. The Company's super-cargoes there had reported, in 1820, that 3000–4000 pieces of English broadcloth had come under the American flag direct from England; and some British goods even got into China overland through Russia and Kiachta. The Committee on Foreign Trade of 1821 could not quite bring itself to attack this anomaly, though it discussed the possibility—an awkward one—of opening the Canton trade to private enterprise yet retaining the Company's monopoly of tea. But its final conclusion was that the monopoly of the whole China trade must be left until the charter of 1813 should expire. It was property, state-guaranteed property, not to be lightly touched. The argument was unassailable; so tea remained dear, and broadcloth and "shalloons" for the China market were shipped either by the Company, or as part of the "Privilege Trade" of its captains and officers, or in American bottoms, or not at all.

"The Hudson's Bay territory," Porter the Board of Trade statistician wrote in the 'forties, "is so little known that its area cannot be given....The only purpose to which it is applied is that of hunting-grounds for the Hudson's Bay Company, through whose instrumentality the markets of the world are yearly supplied with the most valuable furs."[2] An account of it, he thought, might be well enough for a geographer but was no work for him, a student of "The Progress of the Nation, in its various Social and Economical Relations." Twenty years earlier similar people were still more indifferent. True, the Company was doing a good business with its furs at that time. The market value of its capital of £200,000 was well over

---

[1] *Third Report*, p. 3, and below, p. 486.
[2] Porter, *op. cit.* p. 797.

£400,000[1]; but neither the import of furs, nor the export of the trade goods which were bartered for them, was a really important part of the overseas commerce of the United Kingdom; and the future of that vast ill-known tract, "extending between 49° [the present boundary between the Dominion of Canada and the United States, west of the Lake of the Woods] and 70° North latitude, and from Cape Charles in Labrador... to the Rocky Mountains and the mouth of the Mackenzie river,"[2] was veiled from the owners of those two thousand hundred-pound shares in whose hands, by grant of King Charles the Second, lay the monopoly rights over it.

A few other ancient trading companies kept up, or had recently abandoned, a shadowy existence. The Company of the Merchant Adventurers of England, known in its later days as the Hamburg Company, had never recovered from the confiscation of its house in the Gröningerstrasse, and of all British merchandise found in Hamburg, by Marshall Mortier in 1806[3]. But the Muscovy, or Russia Company, the oldest of them all, was still claiming some power of levying dues on trade nearly sixty years later: a Presbyterian merchant disputed its right to vote the proceeds towards the erection of an Anglican organ in Moscow[4]. The Merchants of the Staple of England were too completely mummified to interest themselves in their chief ancient business, that of exporting wool, when that business once more became legal after being illegal for a century and three-quarters; but it would appear that they still dined[5]. The South Sea Company had enjoyed in name its exclusive trading rights down to 1807, when a tax was levied on certain goods imported from what had been "South Sea Company limits," to raise a guarantee fund to indemnify the shareholders for this hypothetical loss[6]. In 1821 the Levant Company, or Turkey Merchants, had surrendered their charter "as an offering to the enlarged and liberal spirit of commerce, which

[1] English, H., *A Complete View of...Joint Stock Companies* (1827), p. 41.

[2] Porter, *op. cit.* p. 797.

[3] It had enjoyed a little *imperium in imperio* at Hamburg, which was only formally abandoned in 1833, after long negotiations. Hitzigrath, *Die Kompanie der Merchants Adventurers und die englischen Kirchengemeinde in Hamburg* (1904), and Baasch, *Geschichte Hamburgs*, 1814–1918 (1924), p. 25.

[4] See the *Correspondence respecting dues levied by the Russia Company, with particulars relating to the Company's Income and Expenditure*, 1864. A. & P. LVIII. 56 3.

[5] There were some traces of the "home staples," *e.g.* at Southampton. Gross, C., *The Gild Merchant*, I. 145 *sqq.*

[6] *Dict. of Political Economy*, *s.v.* "South Sea Company."

now distinguished England"; and in the following years the
State was engaged in taking over those establishments which
the Merchants had kept up for the supervision of trade, such
as the Consulate at Smyrna, with its Consul, Vice-Consul,
"Cancelier," Chaplain, Surgeon, Dragomans, Students and
Janissaries[1]. But these companies were all phantoms and, in
fact, only the Muscovy Company, in its early days, and the
South Sea Company had ever traded, or proposed to trade, in
their corporate capacities. The rest had merely regulated the
private trading of their members and contended for their
monopolies against outsiders and interlopers. The British commercial world of the 'twenties took no sort of interest in any
of them.

A delicate, experimental, and easily abused credit mechanism
had been constructed—without design—and was being modified
from year to year—without supervision, save that of the unseen
hand of self-interest—to forward the overseas trade of the
private firms. Where a market was in the hands of a strong
company, well capitalised, the problem of "financing" trade
was simple; but the only such markets were those of China and
of America beyond 49° North. Some markets were financially
well equipped. The United States and the European Continent had their banks and bankers and financial houses, their
merchants who had left—more or less completely—the trade
in goods for the trade in bills, their brokers, and bourses and
correspondents for English firms; though the upheavals of
1789-1815 had so damaged some of this delicate machinery
that it was probably no more efficient, and possibly not so
efficient, as it had been in the days of the Fuggers of Augsburg[2].
But in many of the markets with which Britain traded there
was no banking system at all, and in some there were no regular
importing merchants with whom a British merchant or manufacturer could get into touch[3]. Financing was the business of
the British merchant and of those on whose help he relied for
accommodation. Among export merchants there had been—

[1] Dr H. W. V. Temperley has shown me copies of some curious correspondence about these transfers, from which the quotations are, with his permission,
made.
[2] See Tawney, R. H., *Introduction* (1925) to Wilson's *Discourse on Usury*, for
the sixteenth-century money market and financing of trade.
[3] See evidence of G. Larpent before the 1833 *Comm. on Commerce and Industry*, Q. 2148 *sqq.*

especially since the commercial crises of 1816 and 1825—some abandonment of the old system of "adventuring," in which the exporter bought goods out and out, loaded them on his own or his hired ship, and took the whole risk of finding an outlet for them. Instead of buying out and out, the merchant might reduce his risks by making only a percentage advance on goods consigned for sale to him, or to his overseas agent, by the manufacturer hungry for markets. This system is said to have become specially prevalent, about 1830, in the Glasgow and district cotton trade with India, and to have put dangerous temptations in the way of the smaller manufacturers[1]. It was not a marked feature of the Manchester trade. The strongest and best-known manufacturers of all—Boulton and Watt, Dale and Owen, the Wedgwoods, or the Gotts—had gone further and taken the risks of merchanting themselves, the more readily no doubt because very often such firms, particularly in the new textile trades, were mercantile in origin. Dale was a merchant before he put money into spinning mills and so was Gott, who, with others like him, was denounced by the "pure" manufacturers of Yorkshire as a dangerous hybrid, a man with a foot in both worlds, in short a "merchant manufacturer."

But, taking the trade of the country as a whole and the average manufacturer who was still—in most industries—in a very small way of business, the system of advances on goods produced may not unfairly be described as normal. It was so described in 1823[2], and such arrangements never die quickly. It became especially important when trade was slack[3]. The small manufacturer—for instance, in the hardware trade—went on producing as long as he could and got percentage advances on his goods from the local factor who sold for him. Beyond the local factor there might be a London factor, doing the same

---

[1] *S. C. on Handloom Weavers' Petitions*, 1834, Q. 100.

[2] In the Report of the *S. C. on the Law of Agents and Factors*, 1823 (IV. 265). This Report led to the Act of 1824 (4 Geo. IV, c. 18) which, *i.a.*, gave consignees a lien on goods to the amount of their advances, to which they had not previously been entitled at law. The occasion of the Committee was an old rule of law, long neglected but recently revived in the courts, which subjected a factor to liability who exceeded the authority derived from his principal, and was held to affect the title of a person dealing with the factor, *bona fide*, where such authority had been exceeded. This extension to a third party was based on the mysterious case, Paterson *v.* Tash, 1742, said to be nowhere properly reported. In illustrating the way in which the old rule was "inconsistent with present business" the Committee gave a full account of business methods.

[3] *Report* of 1823, p. 12–13.

thing for the local man, and relying for financial support, in his turn, on some strong mercantile house which took the goods for sale abroad. The whole chain was waiting on the ultimate sale for the adjustment of differences between the percentage advances and the bargain price. Bigger and stronger manufacturers preferred making to order, and as the business unit grew making to order grew with it. In 1835 Andrew Ure went so far as to write that "*formerly* there were large quantities of merchandise manufactured and kept on hand to wait the chance of a market; that is not the case now; the manufacturers take orders and these orders seem to occupy them fully."[1] But Ure was thinking in terms of the big manufacturing concern, the cotton mill especially; and the "seem" of his last clause shows that he was not quite sure of his ground even there. No doubt, however, the tendency was in the direction which he indicated, the overtrading of 1824–5 having scared into prudence some manufacturers of the class who looked ahead and could afford to curtail or suspend production when orders were scarce.

Important as the advance against goods was in the export trade, that had never been its main sphere of importance. The food and raw material shipments from countries on a lower level of economic development than Britain were what needed most financing.

"By far the greater part of our commerce," the Committee of 1823 reported[2], "is aided by advances at some period...and in many instances there is, first, an advance by the foreign shipper or consignor to the foreign proprietor [the farmer or planter is meant], then an advance by the consignee [in Britain] to the consignor...and subsequently an advance by some capitalist to the factor [the British consignee, who was not the legal owner of the goods] in consequence of the difficulty of finding a ready and advantageous sale."

The system was especially prevalent in the entrepôt trade. "Merchants and planters in all parts of the world" consigned their coffee or sugar or corn to London, "and drew [bills] in anticipation of the value immediately."[3] Much of the produce so consigned was unsaleable in this country—Cuban sugar or Brazilian coffee, the duties on which were so high that they had no chance against consignments from Jamaica, or corn consigned for warehousing when the price prevented its release for the British market. It was the consignee's business to dispose of

---

[1] *Philosophy of Manufactures*, p. 430.
[2] *Report*, p. 7.   [3] *Ibid.* p. 11.

consignments judiciously, as opportunity offered, either in this or in some other market. Stocks of corn, consigned in this way to London, formed a standing reserve which could be drawn upon as soon as the corn law permitted, or before, when government determined on a relaxation of the law by Order in Council, as in 1825–6[1].

A very slow realisation of consignments, in other words very long credit given by the London consignee—produce broker or merchant—was specially characteristic of the East India trade. The consignee "frequently kept the goods for months and even years"[2] before the final sale. "Most of our India houses, being very opulent," made advances on consignments freely, although they might "have no means of knowing to whom they belonged," because they dealt with a consignor who might not be the ultimate owner. The risks were considerable, and many carelessly managed houses of reputed opulence increased them by the recklessness of their advances. They gave advances on merchandise which existed, and on merchandise which was going to exist, and on sugar or indigo estates which might be expected to produce merchandise. Grave abuses are not demonstrable for the 'twenties but, when the commercial crisis of 1847 shook down many of the leading East India firms, abuses running back for many years came to light which illustrated the dangers inherent in the system.

"In the Mauritius trade, and other trades of that kind," a witness explained "the brokers have been in the habit...not only of advancing upon goods after their arrival, to meet the bills drawn against those goods, which is perfectly legitimate, and upon bills of lading which, to a certain extent might also be done [the normal system, as described in the 'twenties]; but, beyond that, they have done what is perfectly illegitimate; they have advanced upon the produce before it was shipped, and in some cases before it was manufactured."..."I had bought bills in Calcutta...the proceeds of the bills went down to the Mauritius to help in the growth of sugar; those bills came to England and about half of these were protested; for when the shipments of sugar came forward, instead of being held to pay those bills, it had been mortgaged...to pay previous engagements before it was shipped, in fact almost before it was boiled":

a pretty state of things[3].

That the risks in this system of advances against goods from

---

[1] Above, p. 239.   [2] *Report*, p. 15.
[3] Evans, D. M., *The Commercial Crisis of* 1847–8, p. 81, quoting the parliamentary inquiry into the crisis.

uncontrolled sources was recognised during the 'twenties is shown in the contrast drawn by the reporters of 1823 between the East and the West India trade. There was less risk in the latter, they pointed out, because most of the plantations were mortgaged to British merchants. Something was known about them in London, Bristol or Liverpool, and the consignee who made the advances was in a position to ascertain definitely whether he was dealing with the legal owner of the goods, the man who could mortgage them "to pay previous engagements," or with a consignor who, in the eye of the law, was like himself merely an "agent or factor." Yet, the reporters added, much coffee and other produce came from non-mortgaged estates, both in the West Indies and in South America, in the usual way, and the usual rather blind advances were made against it.

The risks run were, in a great degree, the necessary risks of new trading with countries recently opened up. They were least in the West Indies because the trade was old, trading conditions relatively stable, and information as to "the standing of parties" relatively accessible. They were greatest in those parts of South America where the Spanish trade monopoly had vanished only yesterday with the rebellions which created the new Republics. The East Indian trade also, as a trade for the independent merchant, was comparatively young and not yet fully open: new branches of it were always growing up. After all, in every trade—import or export—the risks incidental to the system of advances against consignments, when that system was managed with reasonable prudence, were less than those of the adventuring system. The two systems, of course, worked side by side. Very often the same man acted both as merchant proper and as factor or agent[1]. Some goods he bought outright, imported, and held till he could sell them; on others, consigned to him for sale, he made advances by accepting bills up to two-thirds or three-quarters of their probable market value before he had sold them. In his turn he might get advances, if he needed them, from bankers and other capitalists, on the security both of his own goods and of those consigned to him for sale.

The system of advances against consignments was by no means confined to the tropical and sub-tropical trades, though in these it was most essential if trade was to go on at all. Italian silk, for example, was sold by London brokers on account of

[1] *Report*, p. 4.

foreign consignors. Silk dealers and manufacturers in Britain were given such long credit—there was always long credit, handed back down the chain of supply, when the ultimate consumer was a person of fashion—that the seller often stood out of cash for six or twelve months. Meanwhile, he had made advances on account against bills drawn by the Italian consignor, who himself had made advances to the ultimate owners, up-country peasant silk-worm rearers very probably[1]. So also with the Spanish and German wool and the American cotton, though the delays were less outrageous, and the ultimate owners more likely to be persons of substance—Saxon or Silesian squires and planters in the Carolinas[2]. The importers of cotton —the business was now concentrated at Liverpool—almost always combined the functions of merchant and of factor for the American shippers. Behind the importers stood the brokers, the class of men who—since the close of the wars or thereabouts —had bought on commission most of the cotton used by the big spinning firms of Liverpool's hinterland. The Manchester cotton dealer and his fellows in the other manufacturing towns, who had performed important functions down to 1815, were being squeezed out. If far-sighted, they became brokers themselves. There were still over a hundred of them in Manchester at the peace, and only the railway gave the knock-out blow; but they were weakening steadily from 1815 to 1830. Knowledge of supply and demand was being concentrated in the broker class, founded in the eighteenth century by Drinkwaters Rathbones and Holts, and with it wealth and power. Some brokers bought; some sold; some both bought and sold. It was customary for the importer to get advances from them as the sale proceeded, although Liverpool terms of payment were promptness itself as compared with silk trade terms, or with the old Manchester cotton dealers' terms. They were ten days' credit and a three months' bill. Lancashire was speeding up the commercial machine[3].

The system of consignment and advances by the consignee ran all through the corn, seed, butter and provision trades, both foreign and domestic, being specially prominent and important in the Anglo-Irish trade[4]. It was said, no doubt

---

[1] *Report*, p. 6.   [2] *Ibid.* p. 7.
[3] *Ibid.* p. 14–15. Ellison, T., *The Cotton Trade*, p. 165 *sqq.* Daniels, G. W., "Early Records of a Manchester Cotton Spinning Firm," *E.J.* June 1915, p. 179–80.   [4] *Report*, p. 12.

truly, to be a great assistance to the less pecunious Irish producer. Here again the normal terms of credit were not so long as in some trades; but so anxious were consignors to touch good money that consignees—mainly London corn and produce brokers—were regularly drawn upon before they were in a position to reimburse themselves by sales. They were fulfilling the proper risk-bearing functions of the capitalist like their fellow-brokers of sugar and coffee.

Such firms were leading members of that final group of capitalists upon whose goodwill the consignment and advance system rested, a group described by the reporters of 1823 as being composed of "Bankers, Corn-Factors, and Brokers." It was they who were "accustomed to make advances to the merchants."[1] The corn-factors were selected for citation because the financing of the corn imports was of outstanding national importance. Their fellows, the produce and bill brokers, "distinguished by the Goods they mostly deal in," were "a very considerable Body of Men and of vast Credit" in Campbell's day, when they were still—so far as his information went—precisely what their name implied and no more. "Their Business is to transact Business for the Merchant; buy up Goods for him; procure him Bills of Exchange, for which he has [? they have] a premium call'd Brokerage."[2] Pure brokerage of this sort still went on extensively in 1830, but in the meanwhile—greatly helped by the system of consignment for sale—there had arisen from among the brokers many of the strongest British commercial firms, true capitalists who lived more by the judicious use of their accumulated wealth and personal credit than by their brokerage fees. In much the same way, a successful bill broker no longer merely procured for the merchant such bills of exchange as he might need; he was becoming, thanks to his capital, what the mid-nineteenth century bill broker essentially was—a bill merchant, who operated extensively in bills, home or foreign, on his own account. Thomas Richardson, of Richardson Overend and Co., the biggest "bill-broker and money agent" in London, turned over "about twenty millions annually, sometimes more," in 1820–3[3]. Besides the brokers there were true merchants who, having done

---

[1] *Report*, p. 10.   [2] *The London Tradesman* (1747–57), p. 296.
[3] *Report*, p. 79; they were largely produce brokers' bills, on the security of the goods. [Cp. King, W. T. C., *History of the London Discount Market* (1936), p. 25–6.]

well in business, did less and less "adventuring," and used their knowledge of men and markets to finance the adventures of others[1].

Just as in the home trade bankers might still be merchants, so in the foreign trade broker, merchant, and banker were not completely distinct types. Produce brokers were often engaged in mercantile operations, when adventuring on their own account, and in banking operations when giving accommodation to clients. From among the bill brokers Samuel Gurney, a partner in Richardson and Overend, soon to become Overend and Gurney, described himself to a parliamentary committee in 1833 as a "bill broker and banker"[2]: the public were to call him "the bankers' banker." Nor would a capitalist produce broker, whose special product happened to be raised both within and without the British Isles, confine his brokerage or his accommodation to either home or foreign transactions, any more than a bill broker would confine himself to paper arising in connection with overseas trade, at a time when the bill was a very prominent feature of the home trade. Slow communications gave the produce trade between London and remote counties something of a foreign character. The gigantic Irish produce trade was essentially foreign, in that it was carried on between countries geographically distinct, of widely divergent economic type, which, down to 1825, were in a position to raise duties from the trade passing between them. Nor did the banker pure and simple, if domiciled in a city with foreign trade connections, confine his advances to merchants of any one class[3]. But already a small group of firms were specialising in one particular method of financing foreign trade. They lent their names to importers and accepted bills drawn against consignments from abroad, so rendering the bills much more marketable and, by their knowledge of the parties concerned, facilitating and safeguarding the whole course of trade. A representative of the class gave evidence with Gurney in 1833[4]. Timothy Wiggin, such was his uncompromising name, had formerly been a Manchester export merchant. Asked to define his present occupation, he said he was a foreign banker. Asked

---

[1] Such people had existed in England since the sixteenth century. Tawney, *op. cit.* p. 66.

[2] *S. C. on Commerce and Industry.*

[3] For banking in general, see below, ch. VII.

[4] *S. C. on Commerce and Industry*, Q. 1930 *sqq.*

to explain his work, he said it was to "accept bills drawn abroad" and receive "bills remitted from various parts of the world to meet payment of them." This is the fully developed and specialised accepting house, or merchant-banker, described many years later by Walter Bagehot as one of the constituent elements of Lombard Street. Wiggin was a newcomer not unwilling to describe his work. There were certainly older, stronger, and more reticent houses engaged in it[1].

[1] The function was old; the specialisation in it comparatively new. Its evolution will not be clear until, and if, the records of various old City firms and families are thrown open. For some discussion of the point, see Powell. E. T., *The Evolution of the London Money Market* (1915), p. 332. [There is valuable new material by Cole, A. H., in the Harvard *Journal of Economic and Business History*, vol. I. p. 384 *sqq.* 1929.]

CHAPTER VII

MONEY, BANKING, INSURANCE AND SPECIAL COMMERCIAL ORGANISATIONS

UNDER King George IV the structure of British currency settled down heavily on the appointed bases from which it was not moved for nearly a century. "Peel's Act" of 1819 (59 Geo. III, c. 49) had ordered the Bank of England to exchange notes for bullion, as from May 1, 1821, at the rate of £3. 17s. 10½d., the mint price of gold per ounce. As from May 1, 1823, it was bound to cash all its notes on demand in the new gold coin of the realm, the sovereigns and half-sovereigns for the minting of which provision had been made in connection with the Act of 1816 (56 Geo. III, c. 68) when statesmen thought that the resumption of cash payments was near. Actually, it began to cash the small notes, those under £5, in gold on demand, on May 10, 1821[1]. Peel's Act had also swept away all ancient laws restricting the trade in precious metals; even British money might be dealt in—though not melted—freely. In fact it was melted, in Birmingham, "as regularly and almost as publicly as so much iron or copper"[2]; and the traffic in it had been "carried on before, although forbidden." An associated Act (59 Geo. III, c. 76) forbade the Bank for all time to make advances to government without parliamentary authority, but allowed it to buy exchequer bills, or advance money on them, provided the amount of such transactions was laid before parliament annually.

So, six years after the peace and twenty-four years after the Bank had first been permitted to refuse to cash its notes, the war-time emergency monetary system came to an end and gold monometallism was finally established.

As a gold-standard country the United Kingdom stood alone. England also stood alone in the possession of a banking system whose central, national, joint-stock bank had a monopoly of

---

[1] [Under the permissive Act 1 & 2 Geo. IV. c. 26 which also affected the bullion provisions of Peel's Act. See Wm. Ward's evidence before the 1832 Committee...on the Bank Charter (1831–2, VI. Q. 1944) and Acworth, A. W., Financial Reconstruction in England 1815–22 (1925).]

[2] Attwood, T., Observations on Currency...to Arthur Young, Esq. (1818), p. 121.

joint-stock banking, a monopoly of the banking business of the state, the care of the ultimate reserves of all other metropolitan banks, the only serious gold reserve in the country, and no statutory obligations except those of paying gold for notes on demand, of not issuing in the future notes smaller than £5, and of not lending to government without leave from parliament. It reared its head among some sixty London private banks[1], mostly of great strength and reputation, and nearly eight hundred[2] private country banks of most varied quality, all of which were as uncontrolled by the state—except in one single matter—as were the corn-merchants' offices, the chandlers', tea-dealers', or mercers' shops from which so many of them had sprung. The controlled matter was the denomination of their notes. Parliament had forbidden them in 1775 to issue notes for less than 20s., and in 1777 for less than £5. Later, the 20s. notes were restored; but in 1804 the notes were subjected to a stamp duty, and since 1808 the issuer had been obliged to pay for an issuing licence. The state at least knew what he was doing. The legislation of 1819 had contemplated that the issue of small denominations would again be forbidden; and the Bank of England had been instructed to find the gold to enable these small notes to be withdrawn. The gold was ready; but in 1822 parliament changed its mind. The country gentlemen were scared at the crack in the corn markets and anxious to slow down deflation; so the banks were authorised to go on with their £1 notes until 1833[3]. Rather later, parliament changed its mind again, and by an Act passed early in 1826 (7 Geo. IV, c. 6) no more English notes under £5 were to be stamped for duty, and none of those already stamped were to be re-issued after April 5, 1829. But what reserves, or what manner of reserves, a bank should keep against its notes and other liabilities parliament never debated.

None of the London bankers had issued notes of their own for fifty years or so[4]. They had found that Bank of England notes and cheques—the use of which for large payments was well established in eighteenth-century London—served all

---

[1] There were sixty-two in 1832: see G. Carr Glyn's evidence before the Committee of that year.

[2] In 1821, 781: Gilbart, *Practical Treatise on Banking* (1827), p. 95.

[3] See the Director's *Memorandum* for the Committee of 1832, p. 69*: and for the break in prices, above, p. 133-4.

[4] Carr Glyn's evidence, as above.

their needs. They lent money by opening credits on which
customers might draw instead of by handing to them promises
to pay cash on demand[1]. Country bankers, with few exceptions,
were essentially note issuers: the cheque was little used among
them. Their paper had provided a much-needed currency after
1797, especially in the industrial North, where, for lack of cash,
manufacturers had sometimes been driven to paying accounts
for a few shillings by accepting bills, and to paying hand-loom
weavers' wages in I.O.U.'s which were discounted by publican
"bankers."[2] Curiously enough the one important district outside the London area in which the Bank of England note was
really current, when cash payments were resumed, was South
Lancashire[3]. Small Bank of England notes were even used
there for wage payment. For this purpose they were helped
out with coin, local notes, I.O.U.'s and "truck." "A considerable amount of paper of the nature of tradesmen's drafts for
small amounts were likewise always floating about"[4]; and the
trade bills of well-known firms passed from hand to hand, by
endorsement, almost like notes, though this practice was less
common in 1821 than it had been ten years earlier.

Bank of England notes were not everywhere acceptable.
"No person in the more Northern counties will take a Bank
of England note if he can help it."[5] But every country banker
was likely to have some. In London he kept a correspondent
from among the city bankers, whose main business was to turn
country bills on London into cash for him as required. Now
that gold was again to be had, the country banker might naturally count on getting it by cashing bills or bank notes through
his correspondent. He had very often learnt his business under

---

[1] But Gilbert's very elementary explanation of the advantages of the cheque
system, in the *Practical Treatise* (sect. II, "The Utility of Banking"), suggests
much ignorance among the non-commercial public.

[2] Grindon, L. H., *Manchester Banks and Bankers* (1877), p. 33.

[3] Joplin, T., *On the General Principles and Present Practice of Banking in
England and Scotland* (Newcastle-on-Tyne, 1822: reprinted in *The Pamphleteer*,
1824, XXIV. 529—the edition here quoted), p. 545. See below, p. 269.

[4] Grindon, as above. Jones Loyd, who should have known, said that about
1825 the circulation in Manchester was nine parts bills and one part gold and
Bank of England notes (Gilbart, *Practical Treatise*, p. 35 n.). But the secretary
of the Country Bankers' Committee said in 1832, "there is a great mistake...
respecting the circulation of bills and of notes in Lancs....I know one Banker
...at Blackburn and at Manchester, that had a circulation of £1 notes exceeding
£140,000 in 1825." *Comm. of 1832*, Q. 5327.

[5] Joplin, as above.

the paper *régime* which had endured for over twenty years, and the keeping of a gold reserve was not one of his habits[1]. So now, as Huskisson said in 1826, the Bank, in time of trouble, had "seven or eight hundred drains [of gold]...at once opened through her."[2]

There were no strong traditions to guide country bankers. Each used the money that came into his hands just as he thought best. There was no standardisation of investments. Each district had its own peculiarities and needs. There was neither co-operation nor imitation. London, for example, allowed no interest on deposits but charged no commission for managing current accounts. In the country, commission was always charged and interest was sometimes given, but generally only on deposits left for a definite time, not on current balances; and such deposits were rare. As Gilbart put it in 1827, "a London banker takes care of his customers' money, but a country banker has chiefly to advance money to his customers."[3]

Some of the lesser country bankers were not well educated or wise and not all were honest. Their failures were astonishingly frequent, even apart from times of special crisis. There was never a year from 1815 to 1830 in which at least three banks did not break, and the total of bankers' bankruptcies for the fifteen years was 206. Usually failure was due to one of two causes, speculation with their resources or the giving of too much accommodation to a single firm, big enough to drag them down if it collapsed. Few had large resources with which to speculate. A wise bank of the lesser sort confined its business to the narrow round of "lending out that capital which it raises by the circulation of its notes, and the comparatively small sums deposited with it, mostly without interest...and to buying and selling bills on London." The loans would be "primarily confined to the discounting [with its own notes] of such short dated bills...as through its London agents can be turned at any time into cash."[4] This safe standard of wisdom, it would seem, not very many bankers were able to maintain.

In Scotland the position when cash payments were resumed was totally different. The number of banks was small—in 1826

---

[1] See *i.a.* the evidence of Vincent Stuckey, the West Country banker, in 1832: "certainly" he relied on the Bank for gold at a pinch. Q. 1145.

[2] Feb. 10, 1826. Hansard (N. S.), XIV. 237.

[3] *Practical Treatise*, p. 7.

[4] Joplin, *op. cit.* p. 536–7.

only 36, of which four were Edinburgh private banks which did not issue[1]. Few private banks now did important business, and hardly any issued. At the head of the banking system stood three old chartered joint-stock banks "presumed to be limited in virtue of the character of their incorporation"[2]—the Bank of Scotland, the Royal Bank of Scotland and the British Linen Company. Not chartered until 1831 but already very powerful was the new Commercial Bank founded in 1810. Even before 1700, the Bank of Scotland had experimented with branches in Glasgow, Aberdeen, Dundee and Montrose; but its successful development of branch banking dated only from 1774[3]. It had sixteen branches in 1826. A few years after 1774 the Royal Bank had followed its lead by starting a single insignificant branch in Glasgow; but in the early nineteenth century the Linen Company and the Commercial Bank were spreading their branches in all likely quarters. The Linen Company had twenty-seven and the Commercial thirty-one in 1826[4]. There was no branch banking at all in England. With its spread in Scotland, the Scottish banks had taken powers to increase their capital: in 1821 the Bank of Scotland and the Royal each had a capital of £1,500,000, the Linen Company of £500,000, and the Commercial of £450,000 paid up on a nominal capital of £3,000,000[5]. Apart from the Bank of England, the capitalisation—nominal or actual—of no single English bank was known to the public.

Below the central chartered Scottish banks came a series of local joint-stock banks, many of great strength, which were fast absorbing the remaining private firms. A typical first-grade house of this class was the Banking Company of Aberdeen founded in 1767. (The first bank of any kind in Manchester, it may be noted, was not opened until 1771[6].) Its original capital was £75,000, £30,000 paid up. Forbidden by its own rules to do any non-banking business, it had been continuously safe and successful. In 1821 a share in it, on which £150 had been paid, was worth £1400: in 1836 the price was £3000.

---

[1] S. C. on Promissory Notes in Scotland and Ireland, 1826 (III. 257). Report, p. 5, and Gilbart, Practical Treatise, p. 59.

[2] Kerr, A. W., History of Banking in Scotland (1902), p. 7. The British Linen Company was not officially a bank, but was so in fact.

[3] Kerr, op. cit. p. 28, 115.   [4] Report of 1826, p. 5.

[5] Kerr, op. cit. p. 161, 152.

[6] Grindon, op. cit. p. 4. [For banking functions performed by manufacturers, see Wadsworth, A. P. and Mann, J. de L., The Cotton Trade and Industrial Lancashire, 1600–1780 (1931), p. 92–3.]

There were 446 shareholding partners in 1826[1]. Such an institution was not a body corporate; for corporate privileges were procurable only from the Crown, and this Aberdeen Bank had just been made by Aberdonians. But as nothing in Scots law prevented the creation of joint-stock companies, their whole machinery was adopted, minus the corporate personality. This might involve some cumbrous procedure in legal transactions —the Commercial Bank in 1826 was, in the eye of the law, a firm with 521 partners—but otherwise the advantages of joint-stock enterprise, with unlimited liability of course, were fully secured.

Between the smaller banks of this class and private banks proper there was no very clear line. Most joint-stock banks, both large and small, had taken a local semi-public designation —the Paisley Banking Company, the Merchant Banking Company of Stirling, the Falkirk Banking Company, and so on. They had their transferable capital of definite amount divided into shares. But the fewness of their shareholders might assimilate them to the ordinary English bank with its handful of partners: "they were nothing more than banking firms, consisting of a few individuals, although taking a local designation."[2] The Paisley Bank in 1826 had six partners; the Stirling Bank seven; the Falkirk Bank five. The easy transferability of their shares gave them a dash of the public character, but in all else they were private. Lastly came the private banks proper, a rapidly declining group. By 1820 "it was only in Edinburgh that private banking, pure and simple, was still in active operation"[3]; and in Edinburgh unsuitably intimate relations had existed between the private houses and the public chartered banks, which had become somewhat lethargic. Competition from the new Commercial Bank, between 1810 and 1821, had provoked the chartered banks to a fresh activity and cut deep into the remaining business of the private firms. Every important Scottish bank, of whatever class, issued notes and the cheque system was not much developed.

Publicity, the branch system, the concentration of head offices in Edinburgh, and the smallness of "business" Scotland, had

---

[1] *Report* of 1826, p. 5.

[2] In 1826 there were 3 banks each with over 400 partners; 3 more with over 100; 6 with from 20 to 100; and 17 with under 20. *Report*, p. 5. The quotation is from Kerr, *op. cit.* p. 123.

[3] Kerr, *op. cit.* p. 160.

led to a great uniformity of banking practice. The large paid-up capitals and long lives of the chief firms had produced a natural confidence in them. Deposit was a general habit. The small depositor—with £10 and upwards to offer—was encouraged, whereas in England he was generally frowned out. Interest on the balances even of current accounts was almost universal. "A great many" people lived entirely on deposit interest, so a Scottish witness told a committee of the House in 1826[1]. At that time the same witness estimated the deposits in all the Scottish banks at "considerably over twenty millions." Notes of the various banks, especially the one-pound notes, were the general currency, and Scottish bankers boasted that "nine-tenths of the labouring classes...if they had their choice, would prefer a one-pound note to a sovereign."[2] No one feared that any of them would suddenly lose their value, as English country bank notes had so often done. Trust in the banks was increased, and with it the wealth of Scotland, by the famous system of "cash credits" under which sober and industrious men, starting with "a mere trifle, which trifle they have been known to make by their own industry," could secure advances up to a certain fixed amount, provided they could find "persons of, perhaps, a little more fortune, who, to encourage them," were ready to "become sureties for their...accounts." There were many instances of "young men...from low situations...servants...farm-servants even...that...have raised themselves by becoming farmers of considerable extent, or manufacturers in a way highly creditable to themselves and beneficial to their country."[3]

Cash payments had hardly been resumed when a group of Englishmen began to preach the merits of the Scottish system and to advocate its adoption south of the Tweed. In February 1822 appeared at Newcastle Thomas Joplin's pamphlet *On the General Principles and Present Practice of Banking in England and Scotland*, with a scheme for a Newcastle and district joint-stock bank. It was widely circulated and discussed at meetings of business men in Manchester, Liver-

---

[1] *S. C. on Promissory Notes in Scotland and Ireland*, 1826, p. 165.

[2] Robert Bell, a Scottish banker, to Gilbart: printed in the later editions of Gilbart (when his two books became *Gilbart on Banking*), *e.g.* ed. 1873, p. 500.

[3] *S. C. on Promissory Notes*, etc., p. 272. Evidence of a Scottish banker.

pool and elsewhere. Two years later a new edition, with a
sketch of the movement in the interval, was published at
London in the *Pamphleteer*. Joplin noted how, in the twenty
years preceding 1818 there had been 230 bankruptcies of English country banks, "an average of failures...in all probability
far exceeding that of any regular business"; how "sometimes,
as if epidemically, the banks of a whole district will fail together,
as was the case a year or two ago in the South of Ireland," and
a little earlier in Durham; and how not one Scottish joint-stock
bank had failed in over forty years. The Scots, he said, considered the credit of their principal banks "equal to that of the
Bank of England itself." Moreover, these banks performed
thoroughly what he held to be the essential function of a banker
in a way in which the English country banks, at any rate, most
certainly did not. The function was to act as a "capital merchant," a free, regular, and recognised buyer and seller of
capital. "Now, what a merchant is in other commodities, the
Scottish bankers are in the money market. They borrow of
those who have money to lend, and lend to those who want to
borrow, acquire a knowledge of both, and charge...one per
cent." As a foil to this, he sketched the narrow round of business and the limited group of not too confident depositors of
the average English country bank. Joplin was not a severe
critic of the Bank of England, but his scheme for strong provincial joint-stock banks implied the termination of the Bank's
monopoly of joint-stock note issuing business; though he was
the first to argue, in 1823[1], that the Charter of the Bank did
not, in fact, "prevent public banks for the deposit of capital
from being established," but gave only a monopoly of note
issue. He feared that a revision of the Charter might not be
practicable until the next renewal in 1833; but as "the exclusive right of banking, as a joint-stock company," was "of
no advantage...to the Bank, except in London and Lancashire";
and as the note circulation profits in Lancashire were "probably
the result of chance," he hoped that some arrangement which
would give full liberty to his Newcastle bank might be arrived
at earlier. To this end he set on foot an agitation and sought
interviews with the right people, including Ricardo. "I always
enjoy an attack upon the Bank," Ricardo had written to

---

[1] In his *Supplementary Observations to the third edition of an Essay on Banking*,
p. 84.

Malthus in 1815, "and if I had sufficient courage I would be a party to it."[1] He was now—in 1822, from his place in parliament—denouncing the Bank directors as ignoramuses in currency.

Early in 1822 government was, in fact, very ready to listen to any plan for strengthening the country banks, and—incidentally—increasing the currency; and Lord Liverpool was always deferential to Ricardian opinion[2]. Whether the action of government, which began in March or April, was due—as Joplin claimed—to his February pamphlet may be doubted. There was a negotiation with the Bank for an extension of its Charter to 1843, in exchange for an immediate alteration which would permit the establishment of joint-stock banks outside of a sixty-five-mile radius about London. Opposition from the country bankers and others led to the abandonment of the scheme, after it had been announced in parliament; and government contented itself with the expedient of extending the life of the country £1 notes, without taking any steps to strengthen the issuing firms or to allow stronger ones to compete with them[3].

Meanwhile, Ricardo was thinking of a plan for concentrating the whole note issue of the country, after 1833, in the hands of a body of five commissioners, who were to take over that side of the Bank of England's, and of every other bank's, business under the title of The National Bank[4]. He proposed "to prevent all intercourse between those Commissioners and Ministers, by forbidding every species of money transactions between them." By an arrangement which might have been singularly hard to work, £1 notes were to be procurable in the country but not in London. The scheme, however, was only an outline. Ricardo put it on paper during the summer of 1823; but on September 11 of that year "this enlightened, amiable and truly virtuous Senator" died, after a most painful illness[5]. His plan was published as it stood next year; and Thomas Joplin said that "if Mr Ricardo had understood the

---

[1] Quoted in Prof. Foxwell's *Introduction* to Andreades' *History of the Bank of England* (1909), p. xx.

[2] For Liverpool's share in the economic policy of the 'twenties see Halévy, E., *Hist. du Peuple Anglais* (1923), II. 197 and *passim*.

[3] Above, p. 264. Joplin in the *Pamphleteer*, p. 563–5. Castlereagh's speech of April 29, 1822. Hansard, VII. 160–2. Halévy, *op. cit.* II. 107 n. Smart, *Economic Annals*, II. 78 n.

[4] *Plan for the Establishment of a National Bank. Works*, p. 499.

[5] *Observer*, September 15, 1823.

theory of our country bank circulation, he would never have proposed" to set up "government agents" rather than joint-stock companies[1].

Trade activity in 1823–4 preceded the first great nineteenth-century eruption of such companies, that of 1824–5, during which, out of 624 schemes thrown up, 143 never got to the point of stating how much capital they wanted; 236 made that statement and issued prospectuses, but never issued shares; 118 had the satisfaction of seeing a market in their shares opened, but were subsequently abandoned; and 127 were still in existence in 1827, with an aggregate paid-up capital of £15,200,000 whose current value was £9,300,000[2]. Among the survivors were the Manchester and Liverpool Railroad, the General Steam Navigation Company, forty-four mining companies and, inevitably, no English Banks. But four new Scottish joint-stock banks were started, of which three were permanently successful[3]—the Aberdeen Town and County, subscribed capital £150,000, held by 470 partners; the Arbroath Banking Company, capital £100,000; and the National Bank of Scotland, a combination of three companies projected in 1824, with a nominal capital of £5,000,000 of which £500,000 was issued. Conformably to Scottish practice, the National at once began to organise branches: by 1833 it had twenty-four in operation.

When the crash came, at the end of 1825, Scotland did not escape; but her fully developed joint-stock banks, her new joint-stock banks, and all Edinburgh and Glasgow banks did. The Caithness Banking Company of Wick failed, but was absorbed by the Commercial. The Stirling Banking Company, with only eight partners, failed but paid in full. Only the Fife Banking Company, which stopped payment on December 15, 1825, but staggered on until 1829, finally collapsed with gigantic loss to its shareholders. There were calls on private fortunes of £5500 *per share*, to make good the unlimited liabilities. England had been harder hit. At the end of November, Sir William Elford's bank, one of the strong houses of the West, with headquarters at Plymouth, went down. It was followed at once by the reputedly strong Yorkshire firm of Wentworth

---

[1] *The Pamphleteer*, p. 573.
[2] English, H., *A Complete View of the Joint-Stock Companies formed during* ...1824 *and* 1825 (1827), p. 28.
[3] Even the fourth lived for ten years. Kerr, *op. cit.* p. 191.

and Co.[1] By December 3 Pole, Thornton and Co., a first-rate London firm, were staggering. They were agents for many country banks and for several in Scotland; so it was very important that they should be kept erect. Hurriedly the Directors of the Bank of England put £300,000 at their disposal. It was not enough and Poles stopped. Then Williams, Burgess and Co., an equally prominent house, went down; and there were others. For the two years 1825–6 there were no less than eighty commissions of bankruptcy issued against country bankers; though a considerable number of the broken firms were able to pay 20s. in the £ and resume business[2].

All current criticism of English banking law and practice seemed justified. Lord Liverpool, who spoke with knowledge and authority on currency questions, had long disliked both. He and Peel hastened to turn the criticism into law. In a speech of February 13, 1826[3], Peel gave even exaggerated praise to the rival Scottish system. But he did not praise it all—not the £1 note, this particular type of promise to pay having been fastened on by critics as specially dangerous. Peel and Huskisson thought that it tended to drive, or keep, the sovereign out of circulation, which the £5 note could not do. Moreover, the weaker the bank the more, so it was argued, did it rely on the issue of notes of low denomination. As a means of forcing the new sovereigns into use, and so creating that metallic reserve in the pockets of the public which was to become characteristic of British currency during the next eighty-eight years, the proposed abolition of the small notes was well timed; though this particular form of the argument for gold was not current in 1826. It was also much easier, in the conditions and with the knowledge then available, to abolish the small notes than to improve from Whitehall the methods and organisation of the seven or eight hundred banks which issued them. Scotland showed that there was no necessary connection between £1 notes and unsound banking; though it was open to an Englishman to point out that the permanent soundness of

[1] Macleod, *The History and Practice of Banking* (4th ed. 1883), II. 115 *sqq.* Wm Beckett, the Leeds banker, told the Committee of 1832 that Wentworth's was miserably managed.

[2] The figures are in Gilbart's *History and Principles* (1834), p. 95. Andreades, *op. cit.* p. 252, says there were thirty-six country failures: on p. 254 Peel is quoted as saying seventy-six: Macleod, *op. cit.* II. 116, says sixty-three: Powell, *The Evolution of the Money Market*, p. 330, says seventy-nine.

[3] Hansard (N.S.), XIV. 286. In this speech he referred to the 76 failures.

Scottish banking, in what was now a gold monometallic country with free trade in gold, depended on the existence of an adequate gold reserve somewhere. There had, in fact, been a " very large" gold demand from Scotland in 1825[1]. Scotland now, on hearing that government proposed to follow up its projected legislation against the small English note with similar legislation for the rest of the United Kingdom, rose solid against the encroaching and treacherous Southron, Sir Walter blowing the pibroch dressed as Malachi Malagrowther. The Southron withdrew behind a screen of inquiry committees from both Houses[2], and abandoned the position; the abandonment, if it was really due—as statesmen asserted—to the evidence of witnesses that Scotland knew how to manage £1 notes with safety, being itself an admission that there was no harm in those notes, apart from the alleged folly and undoubted financial weakness of some of those who issued them.

By the Act which dealt with the paper money—7 Geo. IV, c. 6—no more notes below £5 were to be stamped for circulation. Those already stamped were not to be issued or re-issued after April 5, 1829. The Bank of England, together with the country banks, was accused of over-issue during the early months of the trade boom. It had, in fact, after increasing its note issues against gold in 1824, increased them again without adding to its gold early in 1825[3]. It was now ordered to make returns to the Treasury of the weekly circulation of its notes under £5, and these returns were to be published in the Gazette. As no such obligation was imposed on the Scottish banks, whose issue was to go on indefinitely but not to cross the Tweed, a possible inference was that the Bank was less trustworthy than they. The contrast in treatment was the more marked because small Bank of England notes did not circulate everywhere in England, whereas those of the greater Scottish banks had circulated almost everywhere in Scotland, and to some extent in the Northern counties of England: "being Scotch...it would be in their very nature to travel South."[4]

However, the government did desire a wider circulation for

---

[1] So Carr Glyn said in 1832. *Report on Bank...Charter*, Q. 3074. A good Scottish witness had said in 1826 (*Report*, p. 50) that the demand was small. The fact seems to have been that most of the home banking demands for gold were relatively small. What people wanted was trustworthy money. Vincent Stuckey, for instance, took little gold, but £100,000 in notes, into the West. *Report on Bank...Charter*, Q. 1193.   [2] Those quoted above.
[3] Evidence of G. W. Norman, a Director, in 1832. Q. 2557. He thought the 1825 issue was a mistake.   [4] A saying credited to Lord Eldon.

the Bank's notes: hence, no doubt, this public watch over them. In the Act which dealt with banking organisation (7 Geo. IV, c. 46), it went out of its way to establish the right of the Bank to open branches. Probably such action would have been legal at any time; but government wished to remove all doubt. The clause was practically an instruction. Lord Liverpool had long wanted to sprinkle the provinces with notes from safe and partially controlled sources. He was "extremely keen upon having branch Banks of England," Huskisson once said[1]. Hitherto "the Bank had always declined it"[2]; now it was almost eager to start branches. "For the better regulating of copartnerships of certain bankers in England,"[3] the body of the Act authorised banks with an indefinite number of partners to operate outside a sixty-five mile radius from London, as contemplated in 1822, provided that they had no place of business in London and that all "partners" were liable without limit for all the debts of the business. This provided a more rigid discipline for banks than had been applied—at least potentially —to other companies by an Act of the previous year, when parliament was feeling kindly towards joint-stock enterprise. For under 6 Geo. IV, c. 91, which abolished all restrictions on joint-stock trading, the Crown had been authorised, in any future grants of charters to companies—which, as corporations, were persons—to provide that members should be "individually liable, in their persons and property, for the debts...of the corporation, to such extent and subject to such regulations and restrictions as His Majesty...may deem fit and proper." This left room for a liability limited by charter, while retaining complete individual liability in all unchartered associations such as the Scottish banks. It was evidently the intention of the Act of 1826 either to limit the discretion of the Crown under that of 1825 or to suggest to the Crown that banks should never be given charters.

Besides establishing the metropolitan banking radius, the Act of 1826 empowered joint-stock banks to sue and be sued in the name of their public officers. This was a real convenience, as those Scottish banks which had some hundreds of "partners" appreciated when they went to law.

---

[1] In conversation with Vincent Stuckey, the West Country banker. *S. C. on Banks of Issue*, 1841 (v), Q. 602: Stuckey's evidence.

[2] Evidence of J. Horsley Palmer, the Governor, in 1832. Q. 466.

[3] The official title of the Act.

Utilising at once its new statutory right, the Bank of England opened branches, before the end of the year 1826, in Gloucester, Swansea and Manchester. Within the next few years it opened also at Birmingham, Bristol, Exeter, Hull, Leeds, Liverpool, Leicester, Newcastle and Norwich[1]. Rather later came Plymouth, which replaced Exeter, and Portsmouth. These branches were by no means mere note issuers. They discounted bills at Threadneedle Street rates, which were often lower than country rates. They took "drawing accounts" without charging any commission, whereas most country bankers charged. *Per contra*, they gave no interest either on long deposits—six months or more—as many country bankers did, or on the balances of current accounts, as in Scotland; and they allowed no overdrafts. They issued letters of credit for the transfer of money on easy terms. They were opened not, as might have been expected from the circumstances of their origin, in districts where banking was specially weak and sound money desirable, but in districts with banks generally efficient and plenty of business for the Branch Bank to tap. It is probable—almost certain—that their competition drove down local discount and deposit rates; but their rigidity of policy was against them. In the Midlands and the North particularly, the business community liked to be able to overdraw. In the early days of the branches, country bankers were desperately annoyed by their refusal to accept from depositors any "country notes" unless the issuers had opened an account with them and kept a covering balance in it. The Bank of England Branch, it appeared, was to be both a privileged competitor and a semi-official censor of notes. This was not agreeable to the many strong and well-managed country banks which had always met their obligations and carried on a conservative, if not rigid, business in discount and advances on varied security. "Jones, Loyd's" Bank, of King Street, Manchester, and 43 Lothbury, London, was only in the second business generation from old Mr John Jones' tea-shop at 104 Market-stead Lane. Yet the partners in this great firm, one of whom had already sent his son, Samuel Jones Loyd, to Eton and Trinity, might well resent a policy which suggested that they were inferior to some Scottish commercial banking company, and had indeed hardly got beyond the irresponsible tea-shop banker stage. And what "Jones,

---

[1] There were eleven branches in 1833. Gilbart, *History and Principles*, p. 114.

Loyd's," who were not note issuers, might resent at Manchester, Gurneys at Norwich, or Attwoods at Birmingham, who were note issuers, might resent still more[1].

Twice, in 1827 and in 1828, the country banks memorialised the government against the Bank of England Branches[2]. Their establishment, they said, had "the evident tendency to subvert the general banking system that had long existed throughout the country." It could "be distinctly proved that the prosperity of trade, the support of agriculture, the increase of general improvement, and the productiveness of the national revenue" were "intimately connected with the existing system of banking." They "would not complain of rival establishments founded upon equal terms; but they did complain of being required to compete with a great company, possessing a monopoly and exclusive privileges." They feared lest "this great corporation" should become "masters of the circulation of the country... and thus be armed with a tremendous power and influence, dangerous to the stability of property and the independence of the country." This was in 1827: ministers replied that their observations "should receive the most deliberate and serious attention." What attention was given did not satisfy the country bankers. Their memorial of 1828 ended with an expression of deep regret

that your lordships [of the Treasury] do not feel justified in adopting measures for the withdrawal of the branch banks, and they hope that your lordships will be pleased, as far as lies in your lordships' power, to prevent any interference with the business of your memorialists; and that your lordships will be pleased to institute an inquiry into the system of country banking, and take into your lordships' consideration the claims of the country bankers to be regarded as parties in the intended application for the renewal of the bank charter, and that no special privilege or monopoly be granted or continued to the governor and company of the Bank of England.

Ministers promised not to neglect the interests of the country bankers in "any negotiation between the government and the Bank of England for the renewal of the bank charter," and their successors did in fact hold a full inquiry into the banking system

---

[1] The best accounts of the early relations of Bank of England Branches and country banks are in the evidence given in 1832 by William Beckett (Q. 1380 *sqq.*), C. S. Forster of Walsall (Q. 1497 *sqq.*) and Jones Loyd (Q. 3360 *sqq.*). For the history of Jones Loyd's, see Grindon, *op. cit.* 38 *sqq.*, 92.

[2] Printed in Gilbart's *History* under the respective years.

ot the country before the charter was renewed in 1833. But the Branches remained, except those which the Bank itself in its own interest decided to close, and from them the Bank-of-England-note-habit spread fast. By 1833 some leading bankers were becoming reconciled. William Beckett of Leeds thought that "upon the whole" the branch there "was desirable and ...added to the safety of banking." It had not cut much into his main business, and it was useful as a recipient or purveyor of gold. Speaking for the West country, Vincent Stuckey, and for South Wales, J. B. Wilkins of Brecon and Merthyr, agreed[1].

During the first years after the Act of 1826 Bank of England Branches grew about as fast in "the country" as joint-stock banks. Private bankers were naturally hostile, and the public was suspicious of the joint-stock concerns. Yorkshire was the first industrial district to move, well capitalised banks being started in Huddersfield and Bradford during 1827[2]. A small one was also opened that year in Lancaster and a more substantial one in Norwich. Not until November 1828 was a scheme for a Manchester joint-stock bank put forward. The scheme was "Scotch"—a central house with branches in the manufacturing towns round about. But Thomas Potter, afterwards first mayor of Manchester, one of the promoters, led an opposition to this Scottish system. He said that "a man is successful in business only when he can watch with his own eye everything that is going on, and that the same principle would apply in banking."[3] This poor argument prevailed for a time and the Bank of Manchester started business in March 1829, as a unitary bank with £300,000 capital paid up. Yet before the end of the year, a branch was opened in Stockport —apparently to meet the competition of a projected rival, the Manchester and Liverpool District Bank, which opened at Stockport in December 1829, and at Manchester in May of the following year. Its notes said that it had a capital of £5,000,000; but it "was nearly eighteen months without a board of directors" and "no account of its proceedings had ever

---

[1] Beckett, Q. 1447 (also 1370, 1435): Stuckey, Q. 1135: Wilkins, Q. 1668.

[2] A list of banks, with dates and authorised capital, was put in evidence by the Directors of the Manchester Joint-Stock Bank in 1832. *Report*, p. 323. It gives fourteen creations to the end of 1830 and one in 1831. Macleod's statement (II. 383), "not more than four or five being formed in as many years" [after the Act], is therefore wrong and Powell's estimate (*op. cit.* p. 310) of ten to the end of 1830 is too low.

[3] Grindon, *op. cit.* p. 241.

been published" down to 1832[1]. As its name and its policy indicated, the District meant to develop branches; and so the Manchester—which regarded the District as a very shady enterprise—is found later opening at Bolton and, curiously enough, at Newtown in Montgomeryshire[2]. Thus branch banking began in the home of the new industrialism. But it was a bare beginning. The same year (1829) a start was made in Halifax, Birmingham, Cumberland and Leicester, in each place on a small scale. Meanwhile a very interesting—and at the time unique—development had occurred in the South-West. Vincent Stuckey, in 1826, was head of a Langport bank, sixty years old. He was also a partner in four or five other banks. He early took advantage of the Act to unite them all, make his partners shareholders, and open branches, of which there were fourteen in 1832. The joint-stock men from Manchester thought his bank was not the genuine thing: it "took the name of a Joint Stock Bank," they said. But Vincent Stuckey was well content; he had found the arrangement "of the utmost convenience in all branches of his business."[3]

Liverpool acquired a strong bank in 1830; and in the same year two smaller concerns, the York City and County and the Whitehaven Bank were opened. By the end of 1833 the total of joint-stock banks had grown to thirty-two[4]. Two only had any considerable number of branches—Stuckey's and that ambitious concern, the Manchester and Liverpool District, which had sixteen.

London bankers had not been party to the movement of protest against the new activities of the Bank of England, which did not affect them. As a body they were strong, well organised and content with the arrangement by which the Bank issued for all London, kept their balances, discounted for them if necessary[5], and let them have notes or gold as required. They were in almost hourly intercourse with it and were satisfied with the assistance which it gave[6]. What internal reserves of

[1] Memorandum of the Directors of the Manchester Bank for the Committee of 1832.

[2] Grindon, *op. cit.* p. 241.

[3] The Manchester Memorandum and Q. 1008.

[4] *The London P. O. Directory*, 1834, quoted in Gilbart's *History*, of that year, p. 108.

[5] They had discounted with it a great deal during the wars and down to 1825: from 1825 the practice died out. Powell, *op. cit.* p. 331 n.

[6] Carr Glyn's evidence in 1832 (Q. 2829 *sqq.*) is the basis of this account.

notes or gold they ordinarily kept is not known. But they were certainly large holders of notes. Probably a very considerable part of the £15,200,000 of notes circulating in London in March 1832 was in their hands. That more gold was kept by them for any length of time than was needed for till-money is unlikely. We keep only "a small portion" of our reserves in gold, Carr Glyn said in 1832[1], and probably Glyn and Co. were not exceptional. In short, the Bank was the custodian of the British gold reserve; and it was not in a position to draw the new sovereigns and half-sovereigns out of the pockets of the public, now that cash payments were restored. Indeed, in difficult times, gold stuck to the pockets and went to them from the banks.

No law had placed the care of the nation's gold in the Bank of England's hands, and the Directors had been slow to recognise their liabilities in face of a situation which they had not created. In the late 'twenties and early 'thirties they aimed vaguely at the policy of keeping two-thirds of their total liabilities covered by securities—mainly government stock, exchequer bills, and a dwindling amount of commercial paper[2] —and one-third covered by bullion, when the exchanges were normal. They got near the mark in 1827 and 1828, but generally were far below it. When asked in 1832 whether they really maintained this one in three proportion, about which several Directors had spoken, the man who had been Deputy-Governor in 1825 said that "the thing was not to be brought to that precision."[3] In their bullion, it should be noted, they counted silver as well as gold; and occasionally so much as a fifth of the metallic reserve was in silver. Their declared policy was to aim at this rather arbitrarily determined and rarely attained metallic reserve and, after that, to remain passive; "the circulation of the country, so far as the same may depend upon the Bank, being subsequently regulated by the action of the foreign exchanges," as the Governor put it in 1832[4]. He meant that if gold was wanted overseas, when the exchanges were against us, it would be got by the public presenting Bank of England

---

[1] Q. 2870.

[2] From 1827 to 1832 the commercial paper was sometimes under £1,000,000: from 1805 to 1816 it had varied from £11,000,000 to £20,000,000. See the tables in Gilbart's *History*, p. 173.   [3] J. B. Richards, Q. 5029.

[4] Horsley Palmer, Q. 72. Rather too much has been made of Horsley Palmer's support of the one-third bullion policy, *e.g.* by Macleod, *op. cit.* II. 131; Juglar, C., *Des crises commerciales* (1889), p. 343; and Andreades, *op. cit.* p. 257.

notes to be cashed, and so reducing the circulation. "The plan has been, under ordinary circumstances, to let the Public act upon the Bank, rather than the Bank upon the Public."[1] Or, as Nathan Rothschild, one of the public, put it, "you bring in your bank notes, they give you the gold"[2]—and no questions asked. As a great handler of gold, he found the arrangement excellent. The Bank never sent gold abroad itself; but it sometimes sent silver, "for the purpose of operating upon the Paris exchange direct."[3] Nor did it try to manipulate the exchanges by way of its discount rate. Its own rate was kept well above the market rate because, although it had been a great discounter of commercial bills during the wars, its Directors now thought that it ought not to compete much with the banks for this class of business[4]. The rate was at 5 per cent. in 1826, and dropped through $4\frac{1}{2}$ per cent. in 1827 to 4 per cent. in 1828. There it remained. Above 5 per cent. it could not go because of the usury laws[5].

Domestic drains of gold from the Bank were only probable at times of special political or commercial anxiety. It is true that these were rather frequent between 1820 and 1832. Foreign drains were also exceptional. "In general the exchange is always in our favour," said Rothschild; "I experience it in my own business."[6] Heavy gold demands might possibly arise in connection with loans, public or private, to foreign powers; but, as the country grew richer, they generally did not. "For the last four or five years," it is still Nathan Rothschild speaking, "I have found when a new loan is made, most capitalists only changed one property against another, and very little property is wanted from this country." Monies held, or profits made, abroad were invested there apparently. But when there was even a risk of war, Rothschild explained, foreign princes would have gold and would pay outrageously for it; then nothing on earth could keep it in the Bank. He knew. The only other serious cause of a drain, he said, was one of those heavy and sudden imports of grain which the corn-law mechanism encouraged. Being intermittent, the corn trade was lopsided: there was not an adequate normal flow of British manufactures to countries whose corn we did not regularly buy.

The situation had been clearly illustrated in 1817–19, when

---

[1] G. W. Norman, Q. 2392.
[2] Q. 4848.
[3] Horsley Palmer, Q. 215.
[4] Horsley Palmer, Q. 171, 477.
[5] See below, p. 346 *sqq.*
[6] Q. 4804, 4876.

an attempt had just been made to get gold again into circulation. That attempt coincided with the flotation in London of important loans to continental nations, some parts of which went out in gold. In Russia—where the facts are precisely known—the loan operations coincided with unusually heavy exports to Great Britain of corn and other produce. It might have been possible to balance the loan by exports of manufactures, but it proved impossible to balance both the loan and the abnormal imports. Hence "the payments for a large proportion" of the loan "were made by exports of bullion thither," and the Russian exchange was against us[1]. So were other exchanges in 1818, particularly the French[2]. A very large part of the £7,000,000 of gold coin issued in 1817–18, with a part of which the Bank had begun to redeem notes in cash, was drained out of the country and the effective resumption of cash payments thereby postponed.

In 1825 home and foreign drains coincided. The foreign exchanges had begun to turn against England in November 1824. By August the bullion at the Bank was down to £3,600,000. By that time the Paris exchange was restored, but the Bank had to face the troubles of the autumn with depleted stocks. Happily for it, France had a bimetallic system, under which silver could easily buy gold. A quantity of silver was shipped abroad and gold came in return—very largely in English sovereigns, probably some of those lost in 1817–18. No doubt the gold, or some of it, came from the Bank of France—Horsley Palmer thought so[3]—but it was not a transaction between bank and bank. G. W. Norman, who was a Director at the time, "never heard it stated that a great portion of the gold that came over was brought from the Bank of France...never heard anything specific on the subject."[4] But naturally the Bank of France was cognisant of the situation. Had it shown ill-will—and its

[1] Tooke, *op. cit.* II. 95. Tooke was a Russia merchant.

[2] Tables in Tooke, *op. cit.* II. 385. France was borrowing to pay the war indemnity. Juglar, *Des crises commerciales*, p. 327.

[3] Q. 800, which is also the authority for the statement that it came in sovereigns.

[4] Q. 2727. See also Wm Ward's evidence, Q. 1882 *sqq.* It was hardly, therefore, as Mr Powell says (*Evolution of the Money Market*, p. 329), the adoption of the "expedient, destined...to become classic" of "the seeking of assistance to the extent of £2,000,000 from the Bank of France." There was over £1,000,000 less silver in the Bank of England in February 1826 than there had been in February 1825; but the figure of £2,000,000 lacks contemporary authority.

bullion transactions never had the automatic character which Rothschild so much appreciated in those of Threadneedle Street—the Bank of England might conceivably have stopped payment; for although its coin and bullion together did not get below £1,027,000, coin was short and bullion not legal tender. People in England, in a position to know, heard "that it was actually proposed to the Government of France to take measures for stopping the Bank of England."[1] If the proposal was really made, goodwill or good policy prevailed, and the gold was shipped.

Economy in the use of gold and cash in the city of London had been encouraged, and the city bankers had been held together for over fifty years, by the organised clearing system. A few of the most notable houses in London, like Coutts', "the principal part of whose business"—as Sir Coutts Trotter put it—"was not with mercantile men,"[2] were outside the system, together with some minor or newer city houses and the bankers of outer London; but the list of the thirty-two "clearing bankers," as it was in 1827, includes nearly all the great names of London banking history, names which might well be put beside Disraeli's list of "the men of metal and large-acred squires" who threw out Sir Robert Peel. There are among them Barclays and Bosanquets and Curries; Dorriens, Frys, Glyns and Grotes; Hanbury and Hankey and Hoare; Jones, Lubbock and Masterman; Smith and Spooner, Whitmore and Williams. "But the list is too long; or good names remain behind."[3]

The clearing-house stood among their premises, "in Lombard Street, adjoining the banking-house of Messrs Smith, Payne and Smith, whose property it was."[4] The house had long superseded the clearing meetings of clerks on the kerbstone. Each bank had its drawer into which clerks from every other bank, coming twice a day, dropped bills and cheques payable by the owner of the drawer. Debits and credits were totted up and checked by two salaried inspectors, and balances due were paid over. "No gold, silver, or copper is taken to the clearing house; the differences under £5 that may be left between the

---

[1] Horsley Palmer had "heard such a report." Q. 466.
[2] *Report of* 1832, Q. 3186.
[3] *Lord George Bentinck*, p. 195.
[4] Gilbart, *Practical Treatise*, p. 16.

clerks...are carried to account on the following day." There is mention also of the clerks leaving the house "to fetch the money they have to pay" but there is no mention—in this 1827 description—of payment by cheque on the Bank of England, the mid nineteenth-century practice. It would appear, from the reference to a £5 unit, that payment was still made in Bank of England notes. But as £5 was also, at this time, the lowest figure for which the Bank allowed its customers to draw a cheque[1], it is just possible that the clerks went to fetch cheques signed by their principals. In either case, the system was simplicity itself. It was worked by firms of a class whose names did not often appear on lists of bankrupt bankers.

When the first bank was started at Manchester in 1771 the following announcement appeared in the *Manchester Mercury*:

Notice is hereby given that the Manchester Bank, together with an Office of Insurance from Fire, will be open'd on Monday, the 2nd of December next, under the Firm and Direction of Byrom, Sedgwick, Allen, and Place. N.B.—Agents for the Fire Office in this and the neighbouring counties will be speedily appointed; and Persons insured in other Offices may remove into this free of all expenses[2].

The history of this enterprising attempt to divert fire insurance business from "other Offices" is not here in question. The point of interest is that Manchester, which had managed to do its business without any local bank, was already quite familiar with one at least of the main branches of insurance, and with the insurance agent, and that Manchester men patronised various unspecified offices. Five years later Adam Smith remarked that "taking the whole kingdom at an average, nineteen houses in twenty, or rather, perhaps, ninety-nine in a hundred, are not insured from fire"[3]—a rather misleading remark with a specious suggestion of accuracy. Yet it is possible that, literally, even his second estimate was correct. In "the Kingdom at an average" there were enough uninsured and uninsurable Irish cabins, Welsh and Scottish cots, and tumbledown English cottages to justify it. But if he meant to imply that only one-hundredth, or one-twentieth, of the value of house property in the Kingdom was insured, it is more than likely that, on either assumption,

---

[1] *Report of* 1832, Q. 329 (Horsley Palmer). Down to 1825 the minimum had been £10.
[2] Grindon, *op. cit.* p. 4.
[3] *Wealth of Nations*, I. 110.

he was wrong. For England he was almost certainly wrong. Twenty-nine years after the *Wealth of Nations* appeared, the insurances effected in English offices were for a sum of about £240,000,000; in Scottish offices for about £20,000,000; and in Irish for about £10,000,000. The interval was one of development, it is true, but all the strongest companies of 1805, except one, existed in 1776 in full activity. It would be very surprising if they were not insuring English houses to the amount of perhaps £50,000,000 in 1776; and it is not thinkable that English house property was worth £500,000,000, still less £5,000,000,000 at that time[1].

The old London companies, chartered and unchartered, joint-stock and mutual, which did nearly all the business in the eighteenth century, dated from the South Sea Bubble and before. The Hand-in-Hand, a mutual society, went back to 1696; the Sun, the first to do business outside London, had grown in 1709–10 out of Charles Povey's Company of London Insurances of 1706. The Union and the Westminster were not much younger. Two chartered companies were floated during the Bubble, both intended for the business of marine insurance, both forced, at a time when they "scarce subsisted but in the complaints the proprietors made of being cheated by the directors," to do fire-business for a living, both destined to continue doing fire business for two centuries. They were the Royal Exchange and the London Assurance[2]. After that no new fire insurance office was actually started in London or out of it for nearly fifty years, though one at least was projected[3]. There is a story that a ruinous fire at Blandford, in Dorset, in the year 1738, stimulated insurance in the provinces[4]. If this is true, it must have been the London offices which did the

---

[1] A great deal, it is not known how much, of the property insured in 1805 was merchandise. The assumptions in the argument are: that, taking £240,000,000 for 1805, a sum not below, and perhaps well above, £100,000 seems reasonable for 1776 and that of this sum a half seems reasonable for houses. For 1805 see Walford, C., *The Insurance Cyclopædia* (5 vols., unfinished, 1871–8), III. 420–1, 484. Walford's incredibly painstaking and comprehensive work, to which the following pages are heavily indebted, although not perfect, has not been used by historians as it deserves. It is not in the bibliography of Cunningham's *Growth of English Industry and Commerce*.

[2] Scott, W. R., *The Constitution and Finance of English, Scottish and Irish Joint-Stock Companies to 1720* (1911–12), II. 373 *sqq.*, 408, 481.

[3] Relton, F. B., *Fire Insurance Companies...during the Seventeenth and Eighteenth Centuries* (1893), p. 203.

[4] Walford, *op. cit.* III. 481.

work. Apparently these offices were doing work about Manchester thirty years later; for the only country offices existing
in 1771, so far as is known, were the Bath Fire Office of 1767
and the Bristol Fire Office of 1769. Possibly the Bristol had
an agent in Manchester so early as 1771, for in 1787 it had
"agents in all the towns of the North and West," and it was
underselling the London offices; but it seems more likely that
the "other offices" of 1771 were those of the metropolis[1].

Some twelve or fifteen English companies were set on foot
in various parts of the country between 1770 and 1800, of which
a few—notably an office started in 1797 which developed into
the Norwich Union—retained their importance in the nineteenth century. More important, historically, than any of them,
was the first addition to the London companies since 1720—
the New or Phoenix of 1782. It was started among the "sugar
interest" and was the first British office to open out business
overseas—in the West Indies, naturally. In 1786 it had an
agency in Hamburg which, no doubt, closed twenty years later
with the French occupation. The Phoenix thereupon sought
compensation in the United States. It had opened at New
York in 1805 and, from there, it extended its business to a
number of other American towns[2].

Meanwhile, in England, during the wars, fire insurance was
being organised rather quickly under county patronage and
designation—the Wiltshire the Worcester and the Shropshire
offices existed before 1800. They were followed by the Essex
and Suffolk; the Kent; the Hants Sussex and Dorset and the
County of 1807, this last a society which was intended to render
weak local organisations superfluous by working from London
through a series of county committees. The scheme was a
success; and while many county societies maintained a rather
feeble existence, the County became one of the strong concerns
of the early nineteenth century[3]. From the same period (1800–
10) date other important London societies, such as the Globe
the Imperial and the Atlas, and a number of country societies.
The years from 1810 to 1824 saw a few new creations, hardly
any of which were durable, except the Guardian, founded in
1821 among the London private bankers; but the upheavals
of 1824–6 threw up many more societies than they destroyed,

---

[1] Relton, *op. cit.* p. 208.
[2] Walford, *op. cit.* III. 485. Relton, *op. cit.* p. 218.
[3] Walford, *op. cit.* III. 490. Relton, *op. cit.* p. 214, 238.

among others the Alliance (1824), which was backed by Alexander Baring, Samuel Gurney, Nathan Rothschild and Moses Montefiore—a powerful group. The story is that Rothschild started it to provide a good post as actuary for his cousin, Benjamin Gompertz, the mathematician. However that may be, Gompertz served the society with distinction for twenty-four years[1].

In the year 1832 fire insurance in England and Wales was in the hands of thirty-nine companies, fifteen in London and twenty-four in the country; but the fifteen did seven-elevenths, and the twenty-four only four-elevenths, of the business[2]. It was a business involving insurances for some £500,000,000. Nearly half of it was done by the five greatest London companies, the Sun, the Phoenix, the Protector, the Royal Exchange and the County—two dating from the early, and one from the. late, eighteenth century, one from the early nineteenth and one (the Protector) a product of 1824. The Sun alone did almost one-sixth of all the business: in 1805 it had done one-third. A single country company held its own with the five great ones from London, the Norwich Union, which came only just below the Phoenix. The second country office—the West of England, founded in 1807—would have taken a place only with the seventh London office.

In Scotland the development of native fire insurance, unlike that of banking, had been late and slow. Possibly the nature of Scottish buildings had something to do with this. Stone towns and farmhouses do not burn easily and crofters' cabins are not insured. Edinburgh had had its mutual Friendly Insurance Society since about 1720[3], but there was only one other in Scotland in 1800. In 1805 there were five, with an aggregate business hardly one-twelfth of that of the Sun at the same date. Not all the five endured. In 1816 the chronicler of Glasgow records, "altho' there is now no Fire Insurance Office belonging to the town, there are no less than twenty-two branches of the London and Provincial Offices established in it."[4] Rapid development only began with the formation of the Scottish

---

[1] Walford, *op. cit. s.v.* "Alliance"; for the marine side of the Alliance see below, p. 291.

[2] *An Account of all Sums paid...for Duty on Insurance from Fire...1832* (1833, XXXIII. 423). Walford, *op. cit.* III. 422, uses a list of 1830 which gives some information not in this return: in that year there were thirty country societies.

[3] Walford, *op. cit. s.v.* Scott, *op. cit.* III. 374.

[4] Cleland, J., *Annals of Glasgow,* I. 406.

Union Society in 1824. Even so, all the business done by eleven Scottish companies in 1836, the first year for which such figures are available, was less than that done by the Norwich Union alone six years earlier[1].

The organisation of the fire offices varied greatly. Some few were companies limited by charters of incorporation. Most were joint-stock companies without charter, or extended private partnerships, not easily distinguished from joint-stock companies. The Sun had originally twenty-four shareholders; but in 1720 each share was cut into a hundred parts and these were put on the market. Eight years later the number was doubled, and from 1728 to 1892 the Sun Fire Office had 4800 shares[2]. The Phoenix was a private partnership whose shares had no fixed value and whose directors could refuse any new shareholders. The Union (of 1714), originally a mutual insurance society, reorganised itself as a joint-stock company in 1805 with 1500 £200 shares, £20 being paid up on each[3]. The County, two years later, constituted itself with 4000 £100 shares, £10 paid up. This system of reserved liability was very common: it provided an emergency fund for the companies. None of the companies started during the period 1800–24 was incorporate. To surmount the legal difficulties arising from their character of gigantic private partnerships, a number of them, between 1810 and 1815, secured Acts of Parliament enabling them to sue or be sued in the name of their secretary. The County, for example, took this precaution in 1813 (54 Geo. III, c. 11). This series of Acts forms an interesting link in the evolution of the modern joint-stock company[4].

As a form of regular business, marine insurance—in Britain and, still more, elsewhere—was far older than the insurance either of houses or of lives: there is no great difference in essentials between an insurance policy of 1555 or 1613—the dates of two of the earliest surviving British policies—1800 or 1900[5]. The first Act of Parliament to regulate the business

---

[1] Walford, *op. cit.* III. 423.   [2] Scott, *op. cit.* III. 387–8.   [3] *Ibid.* III. 379.

[4] The principle was adopted for banks in 1826; above, p. 275. The repeal of the Bubble Act (6 Geo. I, c. 18) in 1825 (by 6 Geo. IV, c. 91) left joint-stock companies to the Common Law, which was not adapted to them but was not hostile. Holdsworth, *History of English Law*, VIII. 221.

[5] Gow, W., *Marine Insurance, a Handbook* (3rd ed. 1903), p. 27. The 1555 policy is printed in Marsden, R. G., *Select Pleas in the Court of Admiralty* (Selden Society), II. 49, and reprinted in Gow, *op. cit.* p. 323.

(43 Eliz. c. 12) notes how "it cometh to pass, upon the loss or perishing of any ship there followeth not the undoing of any man, but the loss lighteth rather easily upon many than heavy upon few"—an obvious reference to that underwriting of fractional risks by groups of individuals which has been practised ever since. A hundred years later underwriting had become an important function of the mercantile group which haunted Edward Lloyd's coffee-house in Lombard Street. Then came the two Bubble Companies, which—taking their cue from the Bank of England—asked for, and got, a monopoly of the business of marine insurance by joint stock[1]. But the strength of the business remained with Lloyd's and private underwriters, who, fifty years after the Bubble (1769–74), as a means of excluding undesirables, organised themselves into the club which perpetuates the Restoration coffee-house keeper's name. The prime mover was that remarkable man John Julius Angerstein, a Petersburg Hanoverian who started life in 1749, at the age of fourteen, as clerk to a London Muscovy merchant, and died in 1823 after collecting the pictures which form the core of the National Gallery. With him was associated Martin Kuyck Van Mierop. (The City of the late eighteenth century attracted, and adopted, commercial ability from all sides.) From eighty to a hundred was the early membership of the club[2].

At this time there was no general habit of marine insurance. Here Adam Smith did not risk one of his specious arithmetical generalisations. He contented himself with the two safe propositions, first, that "the proportion of ships insured to those not insured" was much greater than of houses and, second, that nevertheless "many sail...at all seasons, and even in time of war, without any insurance."[3] The war impending as he wrote, and the far greater wars which opened within a few years of his death, established the habit; and "thus," as the Victorian chronicler of Lloyd's put it, "the war which made England great also ended in the greatness of Lloyd's."[4] Its committee was in constant touch with the Admiralty on matters of convoy; its news service was better than that of Whitehall; its member-

[1] Martin, F., *The History of Lloyd's and of Marine Insurance* (1876), p. 101. [Superseded by Wright, C. and Fayle, C. E., *A History of Lloyd's* (1928).]

[2] *Ibid.* p. 119 *sqq.*, and, for Angerstein, the *D.N.B.* According to J. Bennett, the secretary of Lloyd's in 1810, the membership was seventy-nine in 1771. *S. C. on Marine Insurance* (1810: reprinted 1824), 1824 (VII. 303), p. 107.

[3] *Wealth of Nations*, I. 110.

[4] Martin, *op. cit.* p. 162.

ship had grown, by 1810, to between fourteen and fifteen hundred, of whom from four to five hundred "took their seats every day"[1]; its members, good plain business men, insured all that wanted insurance, including neutral ships against capture by British men-o'-war. This could readily be done, "at a very high premium," Angerstein said. He had done it frequently, though it was not "expressed upon the policy." However, it was "not so much done now as it was."[2] The underwriters can hardly be blamed for doing it, for the law of the matter was of recent growth. Only by a decision of Lord Kenyon in 1794 had the insurance even of enemy property been finally declared "repugnant to public policy and consequently void"[3]; and the complications and shifting alliances of the great wars, during which a ship might be a neutral one year, an enemy another and an ally a third, must have encouraged the underwriters to take business where it offered until the law was made clear at all points. Their sole risk in accepting business "repugnant to public policy" was that they might not have to pay in case of loss. Such business was declared void, not treasonable; but in the Great Peace it had lost its interest.

The Report of 1810 had stated that there was no reason for continuing the monopoly of joint-stock marine insurance enjoyed by the Royal Exchange and the London companies. They had not done 4 per cent. of a business affecting property worth £162,539,000 in the previous year. Yet, in their interest, even partnerships among the underwriters were illegal; so that "in case of death" of an underwriter there was "no surviving partner to settle with."[4] In London, with its huge business and many strong underwriters, the inconveniences, though serious, were perhaps tolerable. But there was very real hardship in what were still called the outports. So there was illegality there, and in London too for that matter. The monopoly was infringed by informal underwriting associations, of which some twenty were said to exist. Two were in London, one of them a mutual insurance scheme among the owners of eighty-three government transports; the rest were mostly among collier-owners at Newcastle, Shields, Sunderland and Blythe.

---

[1] Bennett's evidence, as above, p. 107.

[2] Angerstein's evidence, p. 64.

[3] Brandon v. Nesbitt. See Walford, op. cit. s.v. "Enemies, Insurance of." [Wright and Fayle, op. cit. p. 80–1, 180.]   [4] Report, p. 7.

The merchants who had promoted the inquiry desired full liberty of association in insurance. They were not satisfied with Lloyd's, whose chief members were accused of absenting themselves in September, October and November to avoid the winter risks[1].

But Lloyd's, whose spokesman in parliament was Joseph Marryat—father of a greater Marryat—managed to get the proposals of the Committee rejected; and, with the great decline in marine risks after the peace, interest in the question died down for nearly ten years. Then Nathan Rothschild and his strong associates in the Alliance Insurance Company took it up, for they wished to extend their operations to marine insurance[2]. In parliament, Fowell Buxton secured for them the reprinting of the Report of 1810 and moved for the repeal of 6 Geo. I, c. 18, which gave the Royal Exchange and the London their monopoly. He got anticipated support from J. D. Hume Huskisson and Robinson; his Bill went through; and before the end of the year the Alliance Marine Insurance Company, with a paid-up capital of £250,000, was floated[3]. It was one of only thirteen, out of the many hundreds of companies projected or floated in 1824-5, whose shares were worth more than had been paid on them, at the beginning of 1827[4]. It did a fair business, but a business not seriously injurious to Lloyd's. The Alliance was followed, in 1825, by the less skilfully managed Indemnity, which had the misfortune to bank with Pole and Co. But it survived. In the outports, companies first appeared in 1826, on the north-east coast where the associations had been reported in 1810. Only one of these survived. The General Marine of London (1830) and the Liverpool Marine (1831) were more durable, but not at first very important.

Thus, at the close of the decade, marine insurance by companies, some of which were strong enough to carry very heavy risks, was recognised and growing; but Lloyd's, the individual underwriter, and the minutely subdivided risk had lost little of their importance.

Life insurance, like fire insurance, was no business for individuals or small partnerships, though sometimes they had

---

[1] *Report*, p. 15. [Fayle and Wright, *op. cit.* do not discuss this charge.]
[2] Martin, *op. cit.* pp. 231–52 and 290. [Fayle and Wright, *op. cit.* p. 307 *sqq.*]
[3] The parliamentary story is told in Smart, *Economic Annals*, II. 237–9.
[4] English, H., *A Complete View of the Joint-Stock Companies* etc. p. 6.

tried it. There had survived from the days of its doubtful beginnings a single incorporate organisation—the Amicable Society
for a Perpetual Assurance Office of 1706[1]. The Amicable was
a mutual society with a maximum membership, prescribed by
charter, of two thousand. "It is perhaps no small tribute to
the ability of the early management that it was able to keep the
undertaking in existence, when so little was known of the principles upon which this class of business should be conducted."[2]
The undertaking had still thirty-six years of separate existence
before it in 1830. Possibly the Royal Exchange and the London
Assurance should stand beside it as early incorporated life
offices; for both took powers to add life insurance, with fire
insurance, to their primary function. But in fact neither depended much upon this class of business in early days—the
Royal Exchange taking less than £11,000 in life premiums in
the forty years from 1721 to 1761[3].

The modern era in life insurance begins, as is generally
agreed, not with these but with the first directors' meeting of
the fully constituted Equitable at the White Lion in Cornhill
in September 1762. Seven assurances were effected that day[4].
In its youth the Equitable, like its predecessors, lacked the
actuarial knowledge without which all life insurance hitherto
had been but gambling, even if the judicious and conservative
gambling of the Amicable. But in 1774 William Morgan,
nephew of the great Dr Price, became its assistant actuary. He
did not retire from its service until 1830. His active life covered,
as his activities did much to determine, the development of
life insurance as a business based on a growing science[5]. As
an element in the economic life of the country, however, the
business was quite unimportant until his latest years. Adam
Smith had not thought it worth particular reference; and the
six London offices which, so late as 1800, were all that existed
had a limited if select patronage.

The events of the next few years suggest that, in life insurance
as in marine insurance, the necessities of war permanently
affected economic habits and organisation. Under the first

---

[1] Scott, *op. cit.* II. 390-2.

[2] *Ibid.* p. 391. See also Jack, A. F , *An Introduction to the History of Life
Assurance* (1912), pp. 234-6.

[3] Jack, *op. cit.* p. 236, following Walford.

[4] Walford, *op. cit. s.v.* "Equitable Society." Francis, J. F., *Annals, Anecdotes
and Legends...of Life Assurance* (1853), p. 108. Jack, *op. cit.* p. 233.

[5] *D.N.B.*

Income-tax Act, of 1799 (39 Geo. III, c. 13), that inquisitorial tax was not to be levied on life insurance premiums. This privilege was retained in the later income-tax Acts of the war period; though by that of 1806 (46 Geo. III, c. 65) it was confined to persons with incomes under £150. In that year nine companies were doing life insurance[1]. By the end of 1808 eight more had been started, some pure life companies, others combining life with fire business. The Albion, of 1805, insured in both kinds, but abandoned its fire business twenty-two years later[2]. Similarly, the Eagle, of 1807, did a mixed business until 1825, after that date concentrating on life insurance[3]. The Eagle and the Albion each had a paid-up capital of £100,000. Many of their contemporaries had less financial strength and far shorter lives. There was much reckless promotion, a little dishonesty, and a consequent heavy mortality in insurance companies of all sorts before 1825, indeed a heavier mortality before than immediately after the crisis. From the promoters of 1824-5 life insurance naturally received attention, though with the wars the fiscal stimulus to insure had ceased. That the demand for insurance facilities at that time was effective is shown by the relative success of this group of promotions. Six concerns were projected but never went to allotment. One only, the Aegis, was floated and abandoned with heavy loss to the shareholders. Some half-dozen new life offices, including the Clerical Medical and General, and a few mixed offices, survived[4].

Scotland had used the English companies for any life insurance which she required down to the time of Waterloo. In that year she began, as England had begun nearly a century earlier, with a mutual society—the Scottish Widows. By 1829 it had policies issued to the amount of over a quarter of a million. There were no further developments between 1815 and 1823, when the North British Fire Company began to do life work and the Edinburgh Life was started among the advocates and writers. By 1830 seven definitely Scottish societies were in operation[5].

Recovering from the fantasies of its early days, when the

---

[1] Francis, *op. cit.* p. 180.
[2] Walford, *op. cit. s.v.* "Albion."
[3] *Ibid. s.v.* "Eagle."
[4] Promotions, failures and survivals from English, *op. cit.*
[5] Francis, *op. cit.* pp. 317-23.

Safest and Most Advantageous Office, at the sign of the Carved Porter, insured marriages and servants, and the Beehive Society, at the Golden Beehive, Strand, insured against marriage and births and also against non-marriage[1] (was this for maidens or for fortune hunters?), insurance, in the late eighteenth century, had become essentially life insurance—a method of saving against one's own death[2]. It had reverted to something of its original variety by 1825–30. Though the regular offices dealt only in lives, they were ready to accept creditors' insurances of the lives of their debtors, the insurances effected in marriage settlements on the life of the wife in cases where —should she die—her property would pass from the husband, or other similar provisions against contingencies arising from death[3]. With all this, it is clear that the bulk of such contingencies remained unprovided for, even among those well able to make provision. More than twenty years later the first annalist of Life Assurance ended his preface thus—"The simple fact, that the payment of a small yearly sum will at once secure the family of the insured from want, even should he die the day after the first premium is paid, is sufficiently singular to the uninitiated; but it is more so, that very few avail themselves of an opportunity within the reach of all."[4]

"Within the reach of all"—well, of some. Although the Scottish bankers justly claimed that in their country means existed by which "young men...from low situations...servants...farm-servants even"[5] could get banking accounts, regular banking and the insurance of the great companies were not within the reach of wage earners and handicraftsmen, hardly within that of small cultivators or small traders. Recognising this, parliament—since first "the state of the poor" and the risk of revolution stirred it, in the seventeen-nineties—had encouraged their poor man's equivalents, the savings bank and the friendly society. The first was an excellent invention of well-to-do philanthropic people. George Rose, the parliamentary advocate of the savings bank in 1815–6, as he had been of the friendly society more than twenty years earlier, claimed

---

[1] Scott, *op. cit.* II. 392.

[2] The early marriage and apprenticeship insurances were akin to the modern educational and other endowment insurance, *i.e.* insurance against an anticipated expense. The system was being revived about 1800, but seems not to have been much used. Walford, *op. cit. s.v.* "Endowment Insurances," and evidence there quoted.

[3] Francis, *op. cit.* pp. 189–90.   [4] *Ibid.* p. viii.   [5] Above, p. 269.

the invention for the Society for Bettering the Conditions of the Poor, "of which he had long been a member."[1] Jeremy Bentham's literary executors argued that the notion came from the Frugality Banks which he had advocated in his papers on "Pauper Management" in the *Annals of Agriculture* for 1797–8[2]. Probably they were right; but whoever the inventor, the construction was recent. The second was an ancient, widespread, and natural growth, its roots running deep into "solemn and great fraternity" and gild and primitive funeral feast. Cambridge Thanes, of the eleventh-century Thanes' Gild, agreed to attend one another's funerals and help one another in time of trouble[3]. Newcastle shoemakers in 1719 subscribed 1s. every six weeks to a sick fund and 6d. each for the funeral of a brother[4]. Their society had 160 members in 1796. It was only one of innumerable humble eighteenth-century societies, most of which can have left no memorial.

"The lower part of mankind," Dr Price had written in the manner of 1771, "are objects of particular compassion, when rendered incapable by accident sickness or age, of earning their subsistence. This has given rise to many very useful societies among them, for granting relief to one another, out of little funds supplied by weekly contributions."[5] The method was so well recognised that, between 1758 and 1770, there had been on the statute book an unsuccessful Act (31 Geo. II, c. lxxvi) "for relief of coalheavers on the River Thames; and for enabling them to make a provision for such of themselves as shall be Sick, Lame, or past their labour, and for their Widows and Orphans"—in short a parliamentary friendly society[6]. In 1786 came John Acland's now famous project for a national friendly society which was to work, among other things, what would to-day be called a contributory scheme of old-age pensions[7]— a proposal which would have been merely ridiculous had not the friendly society and its methods been so widely known. When, therefore, the state, by Rose's Act of 1793 (33 Geo. III,

[1] Rose, Rt Hon. G., *Observations on Banks for Savings* (3rd ed. 1816), p. 3.
[2] *Works*, I. 73, and VIII. 358 *sqq.*
[3] Thorpe, B., *Diplomatarium Anglicum Aevi Saxonici* (1865), p. 605.
[4] Walford, *op. cit.* IV. 383, *s.v.* "Friendly Society."
[5] Quoted in Walford, *op. cit.* IV. 385.
[6] There was a similar Act for the Tyne keelmen (28 Geo. III, c. 59) which had a longer life. [For the coalheavers Act see George, M. D., "The London Coal-Heavers," *E.J. (Ec. Hist.)*, 1927, p. 233, 240.]
[7] Acland's pamphlet is entitled *A Plan for rendering the Poor independent on Public Contributions, founded on the Basis of the Friendly Societies, commonly called Clubs.*

c. 54), gave encouragement to societies "of good fellowship" "for raising by voluntary subscriptions...separate funds for the mutual relief and maintenance of the...members in sickness, old age and infirmity," enabling them to acquire many of the capacities of bodies corporate, to make rules which should be binding and hold funds of whose management the law would take cognisance, it was merely recognising and establishing an institution already known and used in almost every county and important town of Great Britain. About that time Hull had fifty-one societies, Sheffield fifty-two—all very reticent and suspicious of government—and Birmingham "innumerable" societies. Their relations to trade clubs is well illustrated from the figures of Kendal, where twenty societies existed. Two of these were for women, and seven of them were called trade clubs, because "they admit none into their Societies but persons of the same trade."[1] A few years later, with the great combination laws of 1799–1800, the confusion between friendly societies and trade clubs became complete[2]. The state blessed the seven Kendal clubs, if they still survived, with its right hand and cursed them with its left. Under Rose's Act, it blessed only rules which had been submitted to Quarter Sessions; but some things could easily be left out of the rules, and any body called a friendly society, even if it had not submitted its rules, sounded respectable until proved subversive. In 1795–6 nearly half the societies whose existence was reported to Sir Frederick Eden, when inquiring into *The State of the Poor*, had not submitted rules to Quarter Sessions; but the proportion declined later.

In his *Observations on Friendly Societies*, of 1801, Eden estimated that there were over 7000 clubs in England and Wales with a membership of 600,000–700,000. He had definite information of 5117 enrolled clubs, from a series of not quite complete private returns, and he added a third for the non-enrolled. "And if the average of each member's family be four persons...nearly a fourth of the population of England and Wales may be supposed to receive occasional relief from these useful establishments." In 1806, Patrick Colquhoun believed that there were some 800 enrolled and as many non-enrolled societies "in the metropolis and its vicinity." He reckoned that they had a membership of 80,000 "mechanics and labouring people."[3]

---

[1] Eden, *State of the Poor* (1797), where information, which Eden began to collect in 1795, is arranged under counties and towns.
[2] Above, pp. 210–11.   [3] *Police of the Metropolis*, p. 575.

A return made in 1815 puts the known membership for Great Britain at 925,000[1]. If correct, it suggests that the proportion of membership to total population was at least maintained in spite of war and high prices. There were also the unknown members of obscure and shy societies, very many. Good numerical estimates are lacking after this date, the statement of an Edinburgh reviewer, in 1820, that "above an eighth part of the population of the Empire" were enrolled not being quite in that class[2]. But there is nothing to suggest any slackening in the movement, and there is evidence of better organisation and sounder policies. Scotland, which had many societies before the passing of Rose's Act, was now covered with them. In the county of Aberdeen alone, two hundred had their rules approved by the justices between 1793 and 1824[3]. Many, there and elsewhere, were old handicraft trade clubs thrown open: "in almost every town we have the *Weavers' Society*; the *Wrights' Society*; the *Shoemakers' Society*, etc., although very few of them have any connection *now* with the trade from which they derive their name," a man with twenty years' experience of the movement wrote in 1821[4].

Both in Scotland and England there were constant discussions of friendly society policy, and a steady flow of pamphlets. Improved organisation is shown in the growth during this period of large, semi-federal, societies such as the Manchester Unity of Oddfellows. Originally, as their name suggests, societies of the best possible fellowship, the Oddfellows of Lancashire, by 1832, were fully organised, with an annual movable conference, district lodges, 31,000 members, and a future. They were claiming a past in the 'twenties: "the name of Odd Fellows was given to this order...by Titus Caesar, from the singularity of their notions,"[5] they said. Within ten years they were enrolling many more than 31,000 members annually. Sustained public interest in the societies is shown by the two select committees which discussed their affairs, in 1825 and 1827, and by the Act of 1829 (10 Geo. IV, c. 56) which consolidated the already considerable bulk of Friendly Society Law.

---

[1] See above, p. 211.   [2] January 1820, p. 158.
[3] *Report on Friendly or Benefit Societies of the Highland Society* (1824), p. 6.
[4] Burns, G., *An Inquiry into the Principles and Management of Friendly Societies in Scotland*, quoted in Walford, *op. cit.* IV. 409.
[5] An Oddfellows' document quoted in Walford, *op. cit.* IV. 400.

The typical society was still frankly convivial: it would meet perhaps at the Six Jolly Fellowship Porters. That, like graveside duties, was an old inheritance. Did not Anglo-Saxon gilds pay subscriptions in malt[1]? Does not the third of the earliest surviving set of Merchant Gild regulations in Europe begin *adveniente tempore potacionis*[2]? The Rev. Thos. Becher, Prebendary of Southwell, who must at least have drunk *Gentlemen! The King* and sherry at a funeral, calculated with a sigh in 1823 that, all told, there would be no less than 190,170 friendly society meetings a year, which, at 6*d.* per head per meeting, meant "that £347,039 a year was thus improvidently spent in ale-houses by the laborious classes."[3] Whether or not the expenditure of 6*d.* per head in ale was a moral defect, the societies had many defects of organisation. Their finance was often primitive, their actuarial knowledge negligible. Most of the pamphlets, and great parts of the legislation, of the period were intended to improve the one or the other. Some societies relieved only those members who were both sick and indigent. Down to 1819 at least, when the law stepped in to prevent it, some would insure members against the risk of fire, the risk of imprisonment for debt, or the risk of being drawn for the militia. Some were mere dividing societies whose yearly saving were directed only towards the Christmas goose[4]. They collapsed oftener than the banks, though never in such swathes as the joint-stock companies of 1825. Yet they cheered many humble lives and did solid work in social insurance, easing for their members the cares of sickness, lying-in, invalidity and old age, and for their heirs the expenses of seemly burial.

In the year before that in which friendly society law was consolidated, the savings bank acts had also been consolidated and amended (9 Geo. IV, c. 92). The first had been George Rose's Savings Bank Act of 1817 (57 Geo. III, c. 130). The first bank of the type which this law was meant to encourage was probably Miss Priscilla Wakefield's Charitable Bank at Tottenham, started in 1804[5]. Six trustees took the money and

---

[1] Rules of the Exeter Gild, *circa* 1040 A.D., Thorpe, *Diplom. Ang.* p. 612.

[2] Gild of St Omer. Fagniez, G., *Documents relatifs à l'histoire de l'industrie et du commerce* (1898), I. 105.

[3] *The constitution of Friendly Societies*, etc., p. 49. In his pamphlet on *The Friendly Society at Southwell* he contrasts his reformed type with "the old System of Mismanagement and Conviviality."

[4] Walford, *op. cit.* IV. 409–10.

[5] *Dict. Pol. Econ. s.v.* "Savings Banks": the *D.N.B.* says 1798.

allowed 5 per cent. on all deposits of over twenty shillings left with them for a year. The interest was too high and the trustees lost; so a later savings bank, that of Bath (1808) intended for domestic servants, reduced it by one per cent. After 1810 the cause made rapid progress among the charitable, Rose subsequently writing with special gratitude of the "talent, zeal and perseverance"[1] with which it had been taken up in Edinburgh. When first he put the case before parliament, in April 1816[2], there were nearly eighty such banks in the United Kingdom. The law which he fathered dealt only with England and Wales. There was a separate Act for Ireland but none for Scotland. It seems to have been thought that Scottish banking practice already gave facilities enough for the small depositor. The English Act forbade trustees ever to make profit from their position, and instructed them to remit all deposits, when their total exceeded £50, to the office for the reduction of the national debt. There a "fund for the banks of savings" was opened, which allowed interest at 3d. per cent. per day or £4. 11s. 3d. a year. As the rate of interest generally allowed to savings bank depositors was 4 per cent., this left a margin for expenses but nothing to tempt trustees to break the law.

Depositors were not permitted to pay in more than £100 in the first year or more than £50 in any subsequent year. A later Act, that of 1824, reduced the figures to £50 and £30, and prohibited the giving of interest on deposits above £200. Even so, these relatively high limits forbid any assumption that the very large funds which soon accumulated in the banks were built up mainly by direct deposits from the "laborious classes" proper. But a clause of Rose's Act had greatly facilitated indirect deposit by those classes; for it allowed enrolled friendly societies to become depositors in savings banks through their recognised officials. The permission was repeated in the friendly societies' Act of 1819 (59 Geo. III, c. 128), which also empowered the societies, like the banks, to take their funds direct to the office for the reduction of the national debt. How far they did so during the following decade was not officially disclosed. Five years after the Savings Bank Consolidating Act of 1828, under which the interest given by the national debt office was reduced from 3d. to 2½d. per cent. per day and that given to depositors to just under 3½ per cent., there were 408 trustee savings banks

---

[1] Op. cit. p. 4.
[2] Smart, Economic Annals, 1. 504.

in England and Wales with 425,000 depositors and £14,334,000 of deposits[1]. The relatively high average deposit, very nearly £34, suggests extensive patronage of the banks by small trades-men and others not entirely dependent on wages or the work of their hands for a living. But in any event, machinery had been created, during a most trying period in the social history of the nation, which brought opportunities for saving, with security and a modest interest, well within the reach of all who had any savable surplus.

The complete self-determination of the underwriters' club at Lloyd's was far more typical of the institutions auxiliary to British industry and commerce than was the, slight and belated, statutory regulation of note issue or the much more elaborate prescriptions for the control of savings banks and friendly societies. It was well within the tradition of the freeholder theory of society, as it has been called, which had exercised so much influence on thought and policy ever since the Glorious Revolution, that a greater measure of regulation, disciplinary or charitable, should be extended to the affairs of men with little or no property—persons below the freeholding level—than would have been counted tolerable for, or by, those property-owning persons—yeomen, gentlemen, merchants, and, as they rose to prosperity and respectability, manufacturers—for the defence of whose self-determination society had been conceived to exist. "Property," said the leading thinker of the early days of the French Revolution, "is the god of all legisla-tion."[2] The Abbé Sieyès was not much read in England, but he also was within the tradition: this doctrine of his had long been perfectly, if not always consciously, apprehended there: what we call the industrial revolution was its child not its parent. Had war-time emergencies not deranged the currency, and so forced the hand of government, it is unlikely that the statesmen of 1815–30 would have framed even the late and slight banking regulations of 1819 and 1826. They allowed a tangle of old rules to enmesh the East India trade, not for love of them, but out of solicitude for the property rights of share-holders. That the abolition of rotten boroughs was a blow at property was an argument which took some countering in 1832.

[1] Return of November 1833. *Dict. Pol. Econ.*
[2] Sieyès, E. J., *Vues sur les moyens d'exécution etc.* (1789), p. 72.

For fifty years and more self-determining commercial clubs, of which Lloyd's was a type, had been growing in numbers and strength, not without opposition and accusations of monopoly, but usually without governmental interference, so long as their members seemed to be persons of respectability. For a great part of the eighteenth century the respectability of the stock broker had been in question. Sir John Barnard's Act of 1733 (7 Geo. II, c. 8, "to prevent the infamous practice of stock-jobbing") had been aimed at some of his most characteristic activities, the time-bargains: "all wagers, puts and refusals, relating to the present or future price of stocks, or securities" were declared void, and attempts were made to prevent their reintroduction. Throughout the first three-quarters of the century, another struggle had continued intermittently between the stock-brokers and the authorities of the City. Were the brokers or were they not to be reckoned among that limited body of "exchange brokers" who, by ancient statutes defined and strengthened under William III and Anne, had to be licensed and badged by the Lord Mayor and Aldermen[1]? The brokers won. So late as the 1774 edition (the fourth) of Malachy Postlethwayt's *Dictionary of Commerce*, stock jobbers were still treated as sheer parasites, and twelve "Plain Reasons why stock-jobbing has been and still continues to be, detrimental to the commerce of the nation," together with the old laws against the jobbers, were its only contribution to the economics of the subject[2]. That Cobbett was with Postlethwayt fifty years later needs no reminder.

But all the while the stock jobbers were establishing themselves and there was no more legislation against them. Sir John Barnard's Act was never effectively operative; though it is said to have done some good, in the early days, by making dealers careful with whom they dealt[3]. Decisions in the courts whittled it away. In 1767 two test cases went in favour of the view that even government stock could be dealt in by brokers who had not the Lord Mayor's badge. Five years earlier, the principal and most substantial dealers in stocks, feeling after respectability, had adopted its symbol—a club, which met at Jonathan's Coffee House in Change Alley. Thence this "organ-

---

[1] Duguid, C., *The Story of the Stock Exchange* (1901), pp. 56–7.

[2] Postlethwayt died in 1767. The fourth edition was altered very little from the third (1766) and not very much from the first (1751).

[3] Duguid, *op. cit.* pp. 48–50.

ised nucleus of brokers"[1] moved, eleven years later, to their own Stock Exchange, as they called it, though it was still something of a coffee-house, at the corner of Threadneedle Street and Sweeting's Alley. After twenty-nine more years (1802), when the issues of nearly two decades of war and thirty years of canal building, *inter alia*, had greatly increased both their numbers and their respectability, they crossed the road, over five hundred strong not counting their clerks, to premises in Capel Court. The less respectable, with failures from the House, remained without, to haunt Change Alley and Sweeting's Alley, and to become the "little-go" or "alley" men of the early nineteenth century.

Surviving an attempt, in 1810, to start an opposition club, the House emerged from the wars to do the immense business of the "tax-eaters," its members to "skip backwards and forwards on the coaches" between Brighton and the city, enraging Cobbett. The funds were now everyone's investment, although "at the beginning of the late war," as Joseph Lowe wrote in 1822, they had been "comparatively little resorted to as a deposit for private property...in the provincial part of the kingdom."[2] In 1815 a French Government loan was dealt in for the first time on the London market; in fact, not merely dealt in but floated there. Loans for all the powers in Europe, and for many out of it, followed during the next ten years. In 1823 transactions in them began to be carried on in a separate building, the Foreign Stock Exchange, also in Capel Court; but this separate domicile was abolished after a short trial[3]. To canal companies were added dock and gas and insurance and waterworks and bridge companies and, in the boom of 1824-5, companies for every kind of thing, but principally for the exploitation of mines—from Wheal Turton to the Gold Coast and Peru.

When the map of Europe was about to be redrawn, towards the close of the wars, Castlereagh was discussing with Aberdeen the restoration of Holland, which for some years had been cut up into French Departments. "If in no other point of view

---

[1] Duguid, *op. cit.* p. 60.

[2] *The Present State of England, with a Comparison of the Prospects of England and France*, p. 309.

[3] Duguid, *op. cit.* p. 121. Down to the 'twenties all dealings in the British Funds took place in the Rotunda of the Bank of England. When Meidinger wrote, the Rotunda served "theilweise noch dazu." *Reisen*, I. 19.

than as the natural centre of the money transactions of Europe,"
he wrote in deplorable English, "all interested nations are
interested in its being again raised to its rank of a free and
independent state."[1] It had been so raised, and Belgium had
been added to it to increase its freedom and independence.
Again it became an important centre of money transactions;
but not the natural centre for Europe. That was now in
London, and of London the natural centre was the club in
Capel Court, with houses like Rothschilds and Barings grouped
about it and dependent on its mechanism for the implementing
of their designs. This club was constituted and governed not
by statute or ministerial *ordonnance*, as were the auxiliary commercial organisations of contemporary France, but by its own
votes and its own elected committee. When a fresh attempt was
made to abolish dealings in options, in 1821, the initiative came
not from any Sir John Barnard in parliament, still less from
the Chancellor of the Exchequer, but from the committee
itself. To this there was opposition from the democracy of
brokers—a democracy with a solid property qualification: a
secession from the club was threatened, and the committee,
feeling the sense of the House, withdrew[2].

The rather obscure early history of the London corn exchange
provides an illustration of a dealers' club which was never able
to centralise and control its own trade completely, partly because
of the inherent difficulty of the problem, partly—it would seem
—because of a lack of foresight and a narrow selfishness among
the directing group. Yet the survival of a tradition of legislative
control over dealings in grain seems to have interfered in no
way with its free development. "Until about forty years"
before the end of the eighteenth century the bulk of the London
trade in water-borne corn was carried on at Bear Quay, "on
account of its vicinity to the coasting vessels."[3] In the year
of George III's accession, or thereabouts, a group of corn
factors corn buyers and Kentish hoymen—leading dealers at
Bear Quay—bought a plot of land in Mark Lane and built an

---

[1] C. to A. November 5, 1813. *Cambridge History of British Foreign Policy*
(1922), I. 424 n.

[2] Duguid, *op. cit.* p. 122.

[3] *Reports from Comm. of the H. of C....not inserted in the Journals*, IX. 153
("Seven Reports on the Corn Trade," being evidence taken in 1801). Also
Westerfield, *Middlemen in English Business*, p. 153. And above, p. 229 *sqq.*, for
the general organisation of the corn trade.

exchange. It was a private venture, divided into eighty proprietors' shares and managed by a committee of the proprietors.
The number of "stands" was limited and their control soon
fell into very few hands. It was even said that holders of proprietors' shares could not always get stands. A powerful factor
from the directing group, giving evidence in 1801 [1], explained
that the proprietors had always given preference, in applications
for stands, to men who had served their time to the trade—
served that is as factors and mealmen—a principle which may
possibly have excluded some proprietors. Dealing on the
exchange was possible without the occupation of a stand; but
not enough grain was so dealt in to influence the market perceptibly. The position of a stand-holding factor was therefore
a very strong one, and naturally there were charges of rings and
price rigging. One witness, "in the mealing trade,"[2] grumbled
that London had no true—he meant open—corn market: the
Mark Lane exchange was both private property and much too
small.

But no suggestion of interference with this property was ever
discussed in parliament or out of it, so far as is known. Administrative machinery was so feeble that government had the
greatest difficulty in finding out what the prices of corn really
were, and so was in no position to control or influence prices
or price-making, except by tariffs, even had it wished to do so.
When, in 1820, petitions complaining of agricultural distress
poured in, the committee to which they were referred was
instructed to confine itself to an inquiry into the methods of
calculating average prices. It reported that "with the exception
of the returns taken at the Corn Exchange the greatest neglect
and inattention" had "universally prevailed"; that "a very
inconsiderable proportion of the quantity sold" was "ever
returned," and that, as a possible remedy, "the Board of Trade
should be furnished by law with greater means of general superintendence and direction [of the collection of statistics] than
they at present possess."[3] The fact that Mark Lane handled
only a part of the London trade, and more fodder grains than
wheat, sheltered it from criticism which might conceivably
have become acute, had its monopoly of business been at all

[1] Evidence of Jas. Stonor, p. 148.
[2] Wm. Rustin, p. 153.
[3] *S. C. on Petitions complaining of Agricultural Distress*, 1820 (II. 101),
pp. 5, 6, 9.

comparable with that of Capel Court. It continued to develop
in its own way, on the basis of private property[1].

The London Coal Exchange in Thames Street was, in history
and function, almost a perfect replica of the Corn Exchange in
Mark Lane; but—a vital difference—in 1807 it had been incorporated into the statutory regulative system which lay heavy
on the coal trade of the capital[2]. Freedom was the rule; but no
one sought uniformity. The London coal trade always had been
regulated, and regulation went on for a time by its own
momentum. Like the corn market, the coal market had been
removed from an open-air site—"Roomland," at the top of
Billingsgate Dock—to the new headquarters early in the reign
of George III[3]. The Exchange was a freehold property, divided
into sixty-fourths, held by coal factors, coal buyers, and the
owners of colliers. Trade was not confined to the proprietors
but was open to all subscribers of £3. 18s. 0d. a year or 6d. for
each market day; and—here the Exchange showed weakness,
if regarded as a club—subscribers need not be proposed by
existing members, nor made to face a ballot. Yet, as their number
in 1800–1 was not much over 150, and as it was obviously
advantageous for any prospective buyer to get access to the
"Subscription Room," where the "Public Letter" gave invaluable daily information as to the course of trade at Newcastle and most of the business was transacted, it would seem
that there must have been some more formidable impediment
than the 6d. fee. Non-subscribers did buy: "prices were never
refused to any applicant," a witness explained. The advantages
of the room must have been worth 6d. a time, and yet they
were not shared by everyone—that is clear—and not by anyone
who might be called a consumer.

The Act of 1807 had made of this private Coal Exchange a
national, or at least a municipal, institution. The Act applied
to London Westminster and parts of Middlesex, Surrey, Kent
and Essex—greater London in short. All coal arriving in
London Pool had to be sold at the Exchange, on one of its
regular 'change days—Monday, Wednesday and Friday, from
12.0 noon to 2.0 p.m. The contracts were to be entered in the

---

[1] [A second exchange was built in Mark Lane in 1828 where the main business
was in seeds. Dowling, S. W., *The Exchanges of London* (1929), p. 180. The
course of trade was the same in both.]   [2] Until 1831. Above, p. 235.
[3] *Report on the State of the Coal Trade*, 1800 (*Reports...not inserted in the
Journals*, x. 538 sqq.). And see Westerfield, *Middlemen in English Business*, p. 233.

factors' books and copies sent to the City Clerk of the market[1]. It was almost as if all transactions in stocks and shares had been driven into Capel Court by law, to the ruin of the "little-go" men—with this important difference, that the purchase of cargoes and part cargoes, the business which the law envisaged, was in the hands of a few strong firms, the "first buyers," whose members naturally frequented the Exchange. The 1807 arrangement appears to have encouraged the concentration of trade in the hands of this relatively small group. Once the coal was sold and delivered in London, with all dues paid, the law took no further notice of it. The first buyer sold freely to second buyers of all sorts—"accounters," "brass plate merchants," and pedlars of coals to the poor, the unorganised and less respectable "little-go" men of the London coal trade.

The eighteenth-century cloth-halls of Yorkshire had much in common with these London commercial exchanges and clubs, but being connected with staple localised industries they had a more definitely public character. They were usually built by subscription of the interested parties[2]—merchants, landowners and clothiers—and were managed by trustees, not by freeholding proprietors. But not one of them was in the proper sense municipal, or in the full sense public. When, for example, the third White Cloth Hall at Leeds was being planned, in 1774–5, merchants took the lead[3]. Contributions ranged from a guinea to £250. Among them was one of £100 from the Leeds Corporation. The Hall was a great place with no less than 1213 cloth-stalls; for it was meant to attract the democratic constituency of the domestic clothiers. Freeholding came in at this point; for "eventually it became possible to acquire the freehold of a stall by paying...£1. 10s. 0d. Such stalls were entirely the property of the clothier, who could sell them, let them...or bequeath them[4]." By 1806 they were worth from three to eight guineas according to situation. At that time the Hall had long been administered by seventeen trustees elected

---

[1] See the very elaborate Act (47 Geo. III, Ses. 2, c. lxviii) or the summary of its essentials in the *S. C. on the State of the Coal Trade in the Port of London*, 1830, p. 3–4. The Act covers 68 pages.

[2] But the first Halifax Hall was built in 1708 by Lord Irwin, that of Huddersfield in 1768 by Sir John Ramsden. Heaton, *The Yorkshire Woollen and Worsted Industries*, p. 379. Baines, *Yorkshire Past and Present*, II. 429. There were, of course, cloth halls much older than these eighteenth-century creations.

[3] Heaton, *op. cit.* p. 368   [4] *Ibid.* p. 369.

periodically from among the clothiers, on a territorial basis —two from Liversedge, two from Birstall and Gomersal, and so on. The older and even larger Coloured Cloth Hall of Leeds, built in 1756, with its 1770 stalls, not counting those in an upper storey added in 1810, was managed in much the same way—fifteen trustees to make by-laws, regulate business, collect dues, and maintain the fabric, and a mass of freeholding stall-owners[1]. Its big open courtyard—the building formed a hollow square—was the heart of the commercial and political life of the town far down the nineteenth century.

By 1820–30, however, the cloth-halls were past their zenith. The "Tammy Hall" of Wakefield had fallen into complete disuse before 1830[2]. Attendances at Leeds had so much declined, with the concentration of the industry and the development of new methods of marketing, that the trustees of the White Hall would probably have sold their site to the Corporation for a cattle market, in 1818, and moved their constituents to vacant stalls in the Coloured Hall, had not the trustees of the latter asked such outrageous prices for the accommodation[3]. But the declining importance of the halls had nothing to do with their private, self-determining, organisation; and the abortive negotiation with the town authorities is in itself an illustration of their thorough independence of government central or local.

Still more public in character than the cloth-halls, but yet —like them—spontaneous growths, free of all governmental control, were the few chambers of commerce which had come into existence between 1780 and 1820. The name was borrowed from the French, first by their old allies the Scots. Eighteenth-century Glasgow had its Merchants' House, or merchant guild its Trades House, or representative gathering of the fourteen incorporated trades, and above them its Town's Great Council[4]. But, with the rapid extension of commerce and manufactures on the Clyde, in the last quarter of the eighteenth century, these ancient unadaptable and privileged bodies no longer satisfied the more ambitious leaders of the economic life of Clydesdale. Inspired by Patrick Colquhoun, at that time Lord Provost, more famous later as a London magistrate and a statistician,

---

[1] Heaton, *op. cit.* p. 373.   [2] *Ibid.* p. 382.
[3] *Ibid.* p. 389.
[4] Lumsden, H. and Aitken, P. H., *History of the Hammermen of Glasgow* (1912), p. 106. Cleland, J., *Annals of Glasgow* (1816), I. 409.

they formed themselves into a Chamber of Commerce and Manufactures for Glasgow and its district in 1783[1]. To increase their weight and dignity they procured a charter of incorporation; but that did not give them governing authority; they had no powers but those of a club. Their charter spoke of "the protection and encouragement of trade"; the regulation of matters submitted to them affecting "any branch of trade or manufactures"; action for the redress of fiscal or legislative grievances; support for their members when dealing with the Trustees of Scottish Trade, the Convention of Royal Boroughs, or the Imperial Parliament; and lastly—the one absolutely precise object—the consideration of "all matters respecting the corn laws of this part of the United Kingdom." It is curious to meet so early, and at a time when the corn laws were not yet a theme of bitter controversy, the emergence of what was to become a characteristic function of the early chambers of commerce. That of Glasgow, like its much younger brother of Manchester forty years later, served mainly as a clearing-house for liberal ideas and a sounding-board for local opinion.

Edinburgh was not to be left behind. She, too, had institutions enough for the surveillance of her commerce, had they been entirely efficient. In particular she had the Company of Merchants of Edinburgh, a close body of many excellent philanthropic and other activities, which, even during the 'eighties of the eighteenth century, was engaged, like any medieval merchant gild, with the problem of "unfree traders," who set up shop temporarily in Edinburgh, yet did not pay the full town dues of freemen[2]. The Chamber of Commerce, which was started in 1785, meant to keep more open doors and scan wider horizons; but there seems to have been no sort of hostility between the two institutions. The Chamber made use of the Company's premises and the two bodies worked together to secure for Edinburgh its proper weight in the counsels of the kingdom. It is the Chamber which, in 1812, instigates the Company to petition parliament against the renewal of the East India Company's charter. It is the Company, *motu proprio* apparently, which declares for free trade in corn in 1813, 1814 and 1815[3]. When, in 1820, the merchants of London had pre-

---

[1] Cleland, *op. cit.* II. 377 sqq.

[2] Heron, A., *The rise and progress of the Company of Merchants...of Edinburgh* (1903), p. 136 and *passim*.

[3] Heron, *op. cit.* p. 158. The Chamber used the Company's premises all through the century. *Ibid.* p. 324.

sented their free trade petition to parliament, both Chamber and Company petitioned in the same sense, as did the Glasgow Chamber and the embryo Chamber of Manchester[1].

The foundation of the Chambers of Glasgow and Edinburgh was contemporary with the English movement which threw up the project for a General Chamber of Manufacturers of Great Britain and, ultimately, the earlier English Chambers of Commerce. The Birmingham Commercial Committee of 1783, which grew into the Birmingham Chamber, was partly inspired by those ironmasters who were realising in their own business the advantages of combination. Two years later came Pitt's propositions for a free trade with Ireland and the prompt refusal of the associated manufacturers, led by Josiah Wedgwood[2]. Manchester had its anti-free-trade committee—or Chamber, as Watt called it in writing to Wedgwood[3]—in those days; but apparently it died away, like the General Chamber of Manufacturers, when the emergency was over. Nine years later it revived, under the name of the Commercial Society, to watch over the affairs of Manchester traders with the continent, which had been upset by Great Britain's entry into the revolutionary wars[4]. There were similar societies in other towns, besides that of Birmingham. Delegates from the societies of Leeds, Halifax and Exeter meet delegates from those of Manchester and Birmingham, to discuss co-operation and matters of common interest, in 1797[5]. But the societies are not very vigorous. That of Manchester dies down in 1801, though never dissolved, leaving a balance of £157. 9s. 0d. with its bankers. That of Liverpool starts quietly in the same year. That of Birmingham makes some kind of a fresh start in 1803, and in 1813 takes on the full title of a Chamber of Commerce[6].

[1] Heron, op. cit. ch. IX. Levi, L., History of British Commerce (1872), p. 153. Smart, Economic Annals, I. 748, omits Edinburgh. The Company's free-trade zeal was not incompatible with a sturdy local patriotism: in 1816 it petitioned against a reduction of the export duty on small coals because Scottish coals were "flinty and large." Heron, op. cit. p. 158.

[2] Witt Bowden in Amer. Hist. Rev. xxv. 70. Ashton, Iron and Steel and the Industrial Revolution, p. 164 sqq. Wright, Chronicles of the Birmingham Chamber of Commerce, pp. 1–18. Above, p. 199, 204.

[3] Ashton, op. cit. p. 173, from the Boulton and Watt MSS.

[4] Helm, E., Chapters in the History of the Manchester Chamber of Commerce (1902), p. 1. Helm takes 1794 as the foundation year.

[5] Ibid. p. 48.

[6] Ibid. p. 60. Wright, op. cit. The Picture of Birmingham (1825), p. 17. For Liverpool, R.C. on Labour. A and P. 1892, xxxvi. Pt. 5, p. xxxii.

Manchester followed seven years later. The Chamber of 1820 came into existence, appropriately enough, in connection with the free-trade petitions of that year. It took over the balance, the archives, and many surviving members of the old Society[1]. Its free-trade faith was not yet quite secure. After the directors had collected evidence in 1824 for the Committee on Artisans and Machinery—apparently with a view to supporting free emigration and a free trade for engineers—the Chamber voted against the free export both of men and of tools, but decidedly in favour of the free import of corn. In 1825 its members "felt it their duty to declare their approbation" of Huskisson's fiscal policy. As the decade closes this, the most active Chamber of the 'twenties, is left petitioning against the revised corn law of 1828[2]. There was a recently established Chamber at Bristol, started in 1823 in deliberate opposition to the not very satisfactory Corporation and the exclusive Society of Merchant Venturers of that city[3]; but it had not yet grown into importance. As for the Birmingham Chamber, an anonymous local guide-book felt bound to write in 1825—"this society is still in existence, tho' not in a course of very active exertion."[4] The Chambers, in short, although characteristic British organisations, played only a subordinate part in the life of the country.

[1] Helm, *op. cit.* p. 1, 61.

[2] See the sketch of the political activities of the Chamber given by J. B. Smith, its President, before the 1840 *Committee on Import Duties*, Q. 2009–2014. Smith tried to argue that the 1825 vote only meant that Manchester thought Parliament ought to free corn before it freed artisans or tools.

[3] *Letters on the Trade and Port of Bristol* (1834), quoted in Webb, S. and B., *English Local Government*, III. 465.

[4] *The Picture of Birmingham*, p. 17

CHAPTER VIII

ECONOMIC ACTIVITIES OF THE STATE

MOST thinking people in Britain during the latter years of King George IV believed themselves to be ill-governed, and held that government showed special incompetence on the economic side. Not all would have agreed about the point at which incompetence was greatest; but one or other aspect of the national finance, or the corn law, would perhaps have secured most votes. Cobbett's numberless disciples had been told how war and public extravagance, pensions, sinecures and idle parsons, helped by the accursed paper money so recently abandoned and the funding system which ought to be abandoned, had made Britain a paradise of "stockjobbers" and "tax eaters." The middle and working class readers of Attwood, the Birmingham banker's son, were assured that the cardinal error in government had been precisely this abandonment of paper money—deflation, in short—and that the cure was the modification of Peel's Act and the provision of abundant currency to stimulate trade, not the squeezing of trade into the narrow box of the gold standard[1]. Educated Whigs, out of office these forty years and not at all certain that their country had done well to spend money fighting Napoleon —whom some of them idolised—relished Sydney Smith's picture of the dying Englishman, gathered to his fathers to be taxed no more, but leaving his executors to find money for the tax on his marble tombstone and the bill of the apothecary who had paid an extravagant Tory state "a license of £100 for the privilege of putting him to death."[2] Among the group now

---

[1] Cobbett was also an enemy of Peel's Act, not because he wanted more paper money, but because it paid to "tax eaters," in gold, debts contracted in paper. *Rural Rides*, I. 116, 276. Cole, G. D. H., *The Life of William Cobbett* (1924), p. 280. Typical passages from Attwood are: "let the circulation be kept on so ample a footing as shall create a greater demand for labour than labour can possibly supply"—"whilst bank notes were plentiful the country flourished although there were no guineas"—the country should maintain "the Bank Restriction Act...under the controul of a legislative commission" because "bank notes are more controulable...than gold, and...prices may be preserved more steadily, on a given ratio, by their use, than by that of gold" (price stabilisation *via* a managed currency, in the language of to-day). *Observations on Currency to Arthur Young, Esq.* (1818), pp. 39, 221, 253, 217.

[2] From the famous article in the *Edinburgh Review*, 1820.

known as the political economists, young J. R. McCulloch, in the year immediately following the war, had been so much scared at the burden of the debt that he had advocated a compulsory reduction of interest[1]—an advocacy of which later he did not care to be reminded—while his master Ricardo, with more courage, from 1819 until his death in 1823, upheld the policy of a capital levy[2]. To this no one paid much attention: it was one of Mr Ricardo's foibles. His friend Malthus was oppressed most by the swollen local expenditure on the poor —which had risen to its maximum, £7,870,000, in 1818— because, to him, poor rates tended to create a redundant population and so all economic ills. Both he and Ricardo were enemies of the existing corn law, though not of all corn laws, and both, together with the growing body of free traders among political economists, Benthamites, merchants and manufacturers, were bitter enemies of the tangled, irregular, tariff hedge of the early 'twenties. Ricardo did not live to see the first lopping of it during the middle years of the decade; his friends pressed for a second and a third.

Bentham himself, still taking his "ante-prandial circumgyrations" from Queen's Square Place and "codifying like any dragon," though nearing his eightieth year, was critical of most economic activities of the state. In his distrust of official persons, he had once even favoured the handing over of the Poor Law to a National Charity Company[3]; though in that Constitutional Code, on which he was always working, room was found for an Indigence Relief Minister[4]. His Trade Minister had few executive duties—beyond the prophetic one of collecting and circulating all kinds of information which might help to form the judgment, and the wealth, of dealers and manufacturers. Other limited, not less well chosen, and more or less economic functions were assigned to the Interior Communications Minister, the Health Minister, and that most interesting official whose duties overlapped his—the Preventive Service Minister, who was to take thought for the anticipation or mitigation of evils due to "collapsion [falls of things]; inundation; conflagration"; diseases peculiar to unhealthy dis-

---

[1] *An Essay on a Reduction of the Interest of the National Debt, proving that this is the only possible means,* etc., etc., 1816.
[2] See Cannan, E., *Ricardo in Parliament. E.J.* June and Sept. 1894.
[3] In 1797–9. "Tracts on the Poor Laws," *Works,* VIII. 358 *sqq.* Below, p. 314.
[4] The Code is in *Works,* IX: the ministries, p. 438 *sqq.*

tricts or trades; contagious diseases; dearth and famine. Under these various ministries an army of Registrars were to record not only births, deaths and marriages, but many other facts of political and social importance[1].

Besides the reasoning critics of government and those instinctive critics who, like the Luddites and some of the agricultural labourers of the South in 1830, struck out blindly at what hurt them most—magistrates or masters or machines—there were the isolated thinkers and small groups who had passed from a mere criticism of government to a criticism of society. The enclosure of the town moor, to their own profit, by the members of the Newcastle Corporation and a simple faith that, by natural law, not only commons but the earth should be the property of all, had made of Thomas Spence —that man "not more than five feet high...unpractical in the ways of the world to an extent hardly imaginable"[2]—a land nationaliser years before the French Revolution. He fell foul of Tom Paine's, to him, Laodicean proposal of 1795-6, that landowners should repay their debt to the community by a 10 per cent. death duty on landed estates, to be allocated to the endowment, on attaining their majority, and the pensioning, in old age, of all propertyless persons whatsoever. Later, he went to gaol for his faith and he died in 1814; but he left behind him a little band of fiery "Spencean philanthropists" and a contemptuous page in the later editions of Malthus, who argued that "the land for all" meant—in the long run and in accordance with the principle of population—not enough land for any[3].

William Godwin's frontal attack on the state and private property, and the counter-attacks on Godwin, were already battles of long ago. No edition of *Political Justice* appeared between 1798 and 1843. True, Godwin's "calculation" that "all the conveniences of...life might be produced if society would divide the labour equally among its members, by each individual being employed in labour two hours during the day," and the Godwinian, almost Spencean, proposition, "English reformers exclaim against sinecures—but the true

---

[1] The Registrar, at least for births, etc., came four years after his death by 6 and 7 Wm. IV, c. 86.

[2] Francis Place's description of him, quoted in Beer, M., *A History of British Socialism* (1920), I. 109.

[3] *Malthus on Population*, 6th ed. (1826), II. 45.

pension-list is the rent roll of the landed proprietors," had found places in the fifth note to *Queen Mab* in 1813. But Shelley had only a little following, who perhaps did not always read his notes, and Godwin—in the 'twenties—had become first the sponging pensioner of a landed proprietor, Shelley himself, then a borrower from every friend he had, to end— in the early 'thirties—as a sinecurist yeoman usher of the exchequer, by the favour of a Prime Minister[1]. Yet his sound had gone out beyond recall, and daring men at times challenged the rights of the state, the sacredness of property, or the need for a toilsome day, without knowing that they challenged in the name of a yeoman usher.

Robert Owen, in his fiftieth year when King George III died and already world-famous as a factory reformer and educator, had found, twelve months earlier, that even a committee which included Ricardo, Sir Robert Peel and the Duke of Kent could not interest the public, to the point of subscription, in an experimental Village of Union of twelve hundred persons on twelve hundred acres, housed and—when not engaged on the land—manufacturing with the aid of machinery in the great collegiate and communal ranges of buildings, laid out in rectangular courtyards, which the public called Owen's parallelograms[2]. Devised as a cure for unemployment and submitted, in an earlier form, to a parliamentary committee on the poor laws, the plan had become, for Owen and some few others, the hope of the world. Mankind was to sort itself into Villages of Union according to its affinities so that, in the programme put forward without a trace of satire or humour, community No. I might be composed of Arminian Methodists who were also ministerialists and community No. L of moderate reformers who happened to be Jews. The scheme, like all Owen's schemes, was not part of an attack on government, but part of a revelation of a new way of life. In 1820 two new chapters had been added to the revelation: the abandonment of the plough and the universal adoption of spade-husbandry were to make com-

---

[1] See his life in the *D.N.B.*, and Brown, F. K., *Life of Godwin* (1926).

[2] Podmōre, F., *Robert Owen, a Biography* (1906), 1. 218, 256. "Owen's Parallelograms" might perhaps be traced to Bentham. In his "Situation and Relief of the Poor," contributed to the *Annals of Agriculture*, 1797–8, Bentham advocated "Industry-houses upon a large scale...with each a portion of land (waste in preference) at least sufficient for the maintenance of its own population." *Works*, VIII. 369. [Prof. J. F. Rees has pointed out however that Owen reprinted John Bellers' *Proposals for raising a College of Industry of all useful trades and husbandry* (1695).]

munal agriculture as productive as Crompton's and Cart-
wright's machines had made the cotton industry; and communal
prosperity, rendering hoarding and money superfluous, was to
lead naturally to the adoption of the true standard of value—
human labour crystallised into units like foot-pounds or horse-
power[1]. Here Owen nearly joined hands with Attwood, becoming a common critic of government and Peel's Act. Like
any other currency fanatic, he suggested that his system—independently it would seem of communism—would "let prosperity
loose on the country."

But throughout the decade he and his disciples, in England
Scotland and America, by the press and by public debate,
through societies working towards the establishment of "villages of unity and mutual cooperation" and through actual
experiment with such villages, whether at New Harmony in
Indiana or at Orbiston in Lanark, were concerned not with the
criticism of government but with the founding of that better
way of life—the way of "the Communionists and Socialists"[2]
—which should render governments, as commonly understood,
superfluous. As a prophet Owen never spared false gods. He
might have been more successful as a social pioneer had he
been more willing to spare what he reckoned the falsity of all
religions. This he was too honest to do. That the political
institutions and the government of the 'twenties generally
escaped his formal condemnation was, however, no testimonial
to either. He was not much interested in them, because he
was less and less disposed to regard them as fundamental. They
were bad but not important. Religions were bad and also
important[3].

Historians have generally agreed that the country was, on
the whole, ill-governed under George IV. While giving credit
for this to Peel or Liverpool, for that to Wallace or Huskisson
or even Robinson, they point to the failure to deal firmly and
justly with taxation and the debt or to pursue a sustained and
well thought-out commercial policy; to the grudging repeal
of the combination laws; neglect of the claims of agricultural
labourers; blindness to the evils of unregulated town growth;

[1] Podmore, op. cit. 1. 267 sqq.

[2] The Co-operative Magazine, 1827, p. 509 n. [An early use of the word
Socialist. Prof. C. R. Fay has called my attention to an earlier, of 1824.]

[3] No attempt is here made to deal with all critics of government and society,
or to do more than illustrate what seem the principal lines of thought.

indifference to the rapidly spreading plague spots of the mines and the factories; tolerance of a poor-law administration both too severe and too lax; and the like. Each charge taken separately can be substantiated. But there is a limit—very soon reached—to the amount of workman-like creative legislation or administration of which any government is capable in a given time. There was no limit to the call on creative ability in a nation barely recovered from twenty-two years of war, shaken by ill-comprehended economic change, and bewildered by a growth in its own numbers without precedent in history. Judged as governments are perhaps entitled to be judged, not by what proved practicable in a later and more experienced day, nor by what reformers and poets dreamed and were not called upon to accomplish, but by the achievement of other governments in their own day, that of Britain in the late 'twenties of the nineteenth century makes a creditable showing. "I myself," Heinrich Meidinger wrote in 1827, "have travelled in the Low Countries, Switzerland, Germany, Austria, Prussia, Northern Italy and France, that is to say in the most civilised lands of Europe; but nowhere have I found countryman and townsman better off, the means of communication finer and more numerous, public spirit stronger, charitable institutions better ordered, and rational human freedom so dominant and secure as in England."[1]

Englishmen, with some knowledge of the conditions of life in town and country, and anticipating what the Poor Law Commissioners were to say seven years later about their leading charitable institution, may marvel at such praise—forgetting the miseries of other lands and how admirable might seem to some foreign eyes that gigantic and all-pervasive poor law system under which, however horrible its defects, people rarely starved[2]. In England, in the lean years after the wars, men suffered bitterly and Captain Swing was out; but they were not so ravaged by hunger and hunger typhus as were the rural hand-loom weavers of Silesia or the Rhenish peasantry. In Ireland, which had no poor law, men starved at regular intervals. George IV's London was amazingly insanitary, but not so

---

[1] *Reisen*, I. xxii.

[2] It did not seem admirable to all foreign eyes. Malthus (ed. 1826, II. 335) quoted with satisfaction the *Comité de Mendicité* of 1790 which had called it "la plaie politique de l'Angleterre la plus dévorante." Individuals *did* starve in England, expecially in the great cities, but there was no general "starvation."

insanitary as Charles X's Paris. The French death-rate in the 'twenties was nearly 50 per cent. higher than the English[1]. When cholera came in 1831–2, it, almost certainly, killed far more Frenchmen than Englishmen[2]. The diet of the British agricultural labourer—Meidinger's "countryman"—was often meagre enough; but nowhere did he live for six months every year "exclusively on potatoes and chestnuts," like some free peasants of the Department of the Tarn[3]. Nor did he go either barefoot or in sabots. Only in the Western Isles could any houses be found so bad as the older houses in Nogent-sur-Seine—"low, windowless,...buried in the ground...usually only of one room, lighted only through the half-door."[4] Though he called attention to the miserable diet of the lowest grade of Lancashire mill hands—"potatoes, oat-bread, buttermilk and at best a little bacon"[5]—Meidinger was certain that, when in regular work, Manchester wage earners lived better than people of a similar social grade in France or Germany.

That Britain may well have excelled her neighbours in the means of communication, in public spirit, and in "rational human freedom" needs no illustrative examples. Her other excellences were far from being all government-made, certainly they were not made by the particular governments which had been in office since Waterloo; but the over-governed continentals of the early nineteenth century rightly gave credit to governments which knew when to hold their hand, to *laisser faire—laisser passer*, and to governments which had been able to preserve a good inheritance reasonably intact.

Continentals agreed with the islanders that the islands carried a fearful burden of debt and a tax-system radically bad. It was seldom noted that one reason for the burden of debt was the politic and gentlemanlike refusal of Castlereagh and Wellington even to consider extracting from France war indemnities of any consequence. France, who had always made war at the expense of the conquered, found herself called upon to pay

---

[1] See, *i.a.*, Porter, *Progress*, pp. 18–19.

[2] Frenchmen 103,000 (Levasseur, *La Population Française*, II. 146). No general figure exists for this country. The deaths in and near London were returned at 5275 in fifteen months (Martineau, *History of England*, II. 73). Jephson, *The Sanitary Evolution of London*, p. 2, says 5000 deaths in a population of 1,500,000; this would mean some 50,000 in all on the certainly much exaggerated assumption that the rate was equally high throughout Great Britain.

[3] *La statistique agricole de* 1814 (1914), p. 534.

[4] *Ibid.* p. 89.   [5] *Reisen*, I. 302.

as indemnity, or compensation for damages, to all the allies a sum considerably less than that which the United Kingdom had paid out in loans and subsidies during the wars of the coalitions[1]. As these British payments, with a few exceptions, had been gifts not loans, there was little prospect of repayment lightening the British burden. Loans had been made to Austria, in 1796–7, but the Emperor was never in a position to pay even the interest on them. So, as Lord Liverpool explained twenty years later, "it became a maxim with every administration, after the experience of the Austrian loan, not to engage in any transaction of that kind."[2] The British public was much gratified when, as a result of some judicious diplomacy at Vienna in 1823, the Emperor at length offered to pay £2,500,000 "in satisfaction of the whole of the British claims upon his Imperial Majesty."[3] Brougham said that half-a-crown in the pound, which was about what this amounted to allowing for accrued interest, was not a very handsome composition for an Emperor, an ill-bred observation which annoyed Prince Metternich[4].

If there was no hope of further payments from abroad in relief of the debt, there was at least no important British overseas liability, such as the wars of the twentieth century created[5]. The total amount of the debt charges in 1827 was nearly £29,000,000—the capital of the funded debt was £780,000,000 —but, as Sir Henry Parnell put it in 1830, this was "in point of fact" but "a transfer of so much money from the pockets of one part of the public into the pockets of another part of it."[6] It need have occasioned no particular hardships had the "tax-eaters" and the tax-payers been, more or less, the same people. But they were not; and that gave Cobbett's nickname its cutting edge and led Parnell to conclude laboriously that whereas, with a well-arranged fiscal system, the principal injury which the taxes to pay the interest might occasion "would consist in the expense and vexation attending the collecting of them," as

---

[1] The total amount paid out from 1793 to 1816 was over £57,000,000 (Clapham, J. H., *E.J.*, "Loans and Subsidies in time of War," December 1917). France paid 700,000,000 francs as indemnity and 265,000,000 as compensation, or not much over £38,000,000 in all. See Webster, C. K., *The Foreign Policy of Castlereagh* (1925), pp. 82–85, 145.

[2] Hansard, xxxii, 1030 (March 1816). There were some other trifling loans (*E.J.* December 1917, as above).

[3] From the ratifying Act of Parliament, 3 Geo. IV, c. 9.

[4] Hansard (N.S.), x, 310, 358.

[5] The small windfall from Austria was used as income.

[6] *Financial Reform*, p. 274.

things were, "the debt was justly considered as a heavy burden on the industry of the country."

The charge of the debt accounted for just over one-half of the public expenditure of the United Kingdom, which in 1827 amounted to nearly £56,000,000[1]. The army and navy cost over £16,000,000 and the collection of the revenue nearly £4,000,000. The remaining £7,000,000, or rather less, covered the civil list, the civil services, bounties given to certain industries, and occasional expenditure under special Acts of Parliament. Taxes to meet this expenditure had to be drawn from a "general income," an annual flow of national wealth from all sources, which, for Great Britain, was currently estimated at something like £300,000,000[2]. No serious attempt had ever been made to estimate the "general income" of Ireland. In round figures, the people of Great Britain may be thought of as paying one-sixth of their total income in taxes, the tax-eaters among them receiving—on the average—one-twelfth of the national income back again from holdings in the funds.

There was singularly little arrangement of the tax-system according to individual ability to pay, though individuals might reduce their payments by abstaining from those semi-luxuries which yielded a very great part of the revenue. Sir Henry Parnell calculated that the principal taxes on luxuries were "paid by the wealthier classes...as these articles are not used by the labouring class but to a limited amount."[3] He had in mind a net revenue of over £27,000,000 derived from sugar (£4,500,000), tea (£3,250,000), coffee (£500,000), imported spirits (£3,000,000), English spirits (£2,250,000), Scotch and Irish spirits (£2,250,000), beer (£3,250,000), wine (£1,500,000), tobacco (£2,750,000), currants (£250,000) and other dried fruits, and from various luxurious imported manufactures[4]. The list of the articles which a well-informed and liberal-minded politician believed not to be "used by the labouring class but to a limited amount" is curious. His remark is half pure error—there was a heavy consumption of spirits, strong beer, and tobacco among wage earners—half a revelation of the mean living standard of that "labouring class" which could

---

[1] It is necessary, in all these figures, to include Ireland; but Ireland contributed a very small part of the revenue of the United Kingdom—between £3,000,000 and £4,000,000. Parnell, *op. cit.* p. 262.

[2] Parnell, *op. cit.* p. 16, and estimates there quoted.

[3] *Op. cit.* p. 43.

[4] The figures are those of 1828.

afford such a limited amount of sugar, tea, coffee and dried fruits.

The total net revenue from Customs and Excise in 1827 was upwards of £36,000,000[1]. The net revenue from all other forms of taxation was £13,000,000; and there was a non-tax revenue, from various sources, of over £2,000,000. Among the £13,000,000 were to be found those taxes which really were, in the main, paid by the wealthier classes—the land-tax, crystallized by Pitt and partially redeemed, but bringing in about £1,500,000; the "assessed taxes," on carriages, armorial bearings, men-servants, horses, dogs, guns and so forth, which although cut down in 1823 and in 1825 still brought in nearly £2,000,000; the window tax and house duty, yielding £2,250,000; and the probate and legacy duties[2]. The incidence of the remaining duties of importance was more varied and disputable. There were the different licence duties, including that paid by Sydney Smith's apothecary and those paid by auctioneers, solicitors and members of many other professions, including also the licences of drink retailers, hawkers, manufacturers and retailers of tobacco and snuff, pawnbrokers and makers of playing-cards. There were the various stamp duties, on bills, receipts, promissory notes, bank notes, mortgages and indeed almost all business instruments, a group which brought in upwards of £3,000,000. Stamp duties of another class included the hard-fought duty on newspapers and the duties described in the Act of 1812 as lying upon "all...pills, powders, lozenges, tinctures, etc., to be used or applied externally or internally...wherein the person making, preparing, altering, vending or exposing to sale the same, hath or claims to have any occult secret or art for the making or preparing the same."[3] Stamps and licences of all kinds yielded about £7,000,000.

Parnell selected for special attack the customs duties on non-luxurious agricultural produce and the raw materials of manufacture, and the excise duties on certain important domestic industries, a group of duties which yielded the difference between the £27,000,000, which he treated as justifiable taxation of luxury, and the net £36,700,000 yield of the Customs and Excise. The group included nearly £1,000,000 of duty paid on imported corn, for he was taking 1827, a year of heavy imports,

---

[1] The figures were much the same in 1828 and 1829.
[2] The term "assessed taxes" was sometimes used to cover land tax, house duty, etc.   [3] Buxton, *Finance and Politics*, II. 375 n.

as his basis[1]. It included also the small sums contributed by the import duties on other foodstuffs—such as 3*d*. a lb. on bacon, rather more than 2*d*. a lb. on butter, rather more than 1*d*. a lb. on cheese and rather less than 1*d*. a lb. on lard[2]. These relatively high duties kept imports down. Meat, other than bacon, might not be imported at all; nor might cattle, sheep or swine. The corn duty was therefore the only serious revenue-yielder in this sub-group; and it was intermittent. In the sub-group of raw materials things lay differently. "Cotton wool," although lightly taxed—6 per cent. *ad valorem* when foreign, and a nominal 4*d*. a cwt. when from British possessions—brought in over £300,000; raw and thrown silk—smartly taxed still, in spite of Huskisson's reforms—nearly £130,000; and wool—now admitted free from British possessions, and at not more than 1*d*. a lb. from foreign countries—over £105,000. The flax duty was nominal, only 1*d*. a cwt., and unproductive; but the hemp duty, much more irrational—for the United Kingdom produced a good deal of flax but very little hemp, and was in standing need of hemp for cordage—worked out at nearly 12 per cent., and produced over £100,000.

The timber duty was the great revenue-yielder among the import duties on raw materials. Its peculiar arrangement was a war-time legacy[3]. The country could not do without the Baltic fir logs, the Baltic deals, and the oak from Memel and Danzig, although British North American fir logs only paid 10*s*. a load as against the Baltic £2. 15*s*. 0*d*., and the most lightly taxed Baltic deals paid a duty more than nine times that on the corresponding American material. All told, the timber duties yielded about £1,500,000, of which over £1,300,000 came from fir logs, deals and battens. As a consequence, Great Britain, with her scanty forests, paid far more for her timber than any other country; for though the American timber was lightly taxed it had to bear the long slow Atlantic haul. Two further consequences were that, builders economised on their timber when running up cheap town houses—"to save timber they were apt to make the roof flat instead of sloping with a good pitch"[4]—and that, so it was argued, the North Sea and Channel fisheries suffered in competition with the bigger and cheaper fishing

---

[1] Above, p. 239.
[2] Butter was not supposed to be imported as a foodstuff: it had to be "spoiled" by putting a tarred stick into the barrel.   [3] Above, p. 237.
[4] J. D. Hume before the *S. C. on Import Duties*, 1840, Q. 1468.

boats of the French[1]. That the French boats at this time were bigger, better, and more numerous than the British, and that the British fisheries were none too flourishing, was admitted: how far timber made dear by duties—to which might be added cordage and provisions, both dear for the same reason—was an important cause is matter for debate; but cheaper timber would have helped.

Duties on raw iron were neither lucrative nor burdensome. The only foreign iron that Britain now wanted was the Swedish and Russian blister-bar, and the duty on this worked out at about 10 per cent. *ad valorem*, or rather more when the market sagged[2]. Its value was so much increased when Sheffield had done with it, that this duty was only a trifling handicap to its re-export as cutlery. Except for a few hundred tons of spelter —which paid £10 a ton!—other base or "half-precious" metals were hardly imported at all.

Scattered about the tariff were a number of quite irrational raw material taxes, which protected nobody and brought in no great revenue. Such were the duties of from 30 to 40 per cent. on common turpentine; those of 10s. a ton on rough brimstone and £6 a ton on brimstone if refined; and those on all kinds of gums. Last, most irrational, but most productive, was the imperial duty on coals shipped coastwise. At an English port such coals paid 4s. a ton: at a Welsh port 1s. 8d.: at an Irish port 1s. 7¼d.: at a Scottish port nothing[3]. Slates shipped coastwise were similarly taxed, and the two duties together brought in nearly £900,000, at the expense of innumerable consumers. The far heavier export duty on coal, which had developed from that retained a century earlier by Walpole when he got rid of most export duties, was helping to keep down what was to become one of Britain's chief export trades. It cannot lightly be dubbed irrational. At the back of it was the

---

[1] *S. C. on Import Duties*, 1840, Q. 2989. For other, and probably more important, causes of successful French competition in the fisheries see the *S. C. on British Channel Fisheries*, 1833 (XIV. 69). See also the *S. C. on Devon Fisheries* and the *S. C. on the Use of Rock Salt in the Fisheries*, both of 1817 (III. 117 and 123).

[2] It was 30s. a ton. It had been £6. 10s. 0d. a ton down to 1825. For the course of prices see Tooke, *History of Prices*, II. 406.

[3] These and all other duties, as they stood in 1827, are conveniently given in Parnell, *op. cit.* Ap. 1. Until 1824 there had been an additional duty, which worked out at 3s. 6d. a ton, on coals coming into London. See Porter, *op. cit.* p. 277-8. Smart, *Economic Annals*, II. 196. The Budgets of 1824-5 had, of course, greatly modified the tariff, but to call them "Free Trade Budgets," as Smart does, is excessive.

thought of conserving a unique national asset, whose export would help foreign competition[1].

The excise duties on manufactures which Parnell singled out for attack in 1830 were those on glass, paper, and printed goods. Had he written a year earlier he would no doubt have added leather. Vansittart had halved the leather duty in 1822, so bringing it back to what it had been before Queen Anne died, and Goulburn abolished the remainder—at a cost to the exchequer of over £340,000—in his budget of 1830[2]. The duty was characteristic of the decade and, like the other duties on home industries, of importance because of its effects on industrial technique and organisation. Closely associated with it until 1824 had been some rules of law—recently enacted— of a type sometimes supposed to have gone out of fashion long before the end of the eighteenth century. These were laid down by Acts of 1800 and 1801 "relating to the use of Horse Hides in making boots and shoes, and for better preventing the damaging of raw hides and skins in the flaying thereof."[3] They provided for the inspection of flaying, and the fining of bad flayers. Although inspection in London was said to have become "a mockery"[4] by 1824, in many places it was a reality. In Edinburgh, for example, the Acts only began to be enforced effectively during the 'twenties, and in some districts butchers had to send their hides considerable distances to be passed by the inspectors. Many experts in 1824 were in favour of retaining inspection on the ground that it maintained quality; but it could hardly survive in the competitive politico-economic atmosphere of Huskisson's day. However, so long as the leather-duties continued, some governmental control of manufacturing processes was inevitable. In the interests of the excise the trades of tanner and currier were not allowed to be combined—at any rate not on the same premises. "The excise," a witness had explained in 1813, "says we shall not...diminish the hide during...tanning, because there shall be the whole weight come to pay the duty. Now after it goes to the currier, the upper leather...has a great deal shaved off by the

---

[1] The argument was used by Torrens in 1826, quoted in Smart, *op. cit.* II. 379. The notion that the asset might be terminable was not yet current.

[2] Smart, *op. cit.* II. 80, 538.

[3] *Minutes of Evidence taken before the Comm. on the Bill to repeal two Acts of the 39th and 40th and 41st of his late Majesty relating to the use, etc.* 1824 (VII. 183).

[4] Parnell, *op. cit.* p. 111.

currier."[1] A tanner witness stated in 1824 that, but for this rule against combining the trades, the inspection Acts would have been superfluous. If a tanner's whole interest in the hide lay in the tanning of it, it did not greatly concern him that it came into his hands, and left them, somewhat damaged in the flaying: it would cost less and fetch less, but his charge for the tanning need not be touched. But were he also a currier, interested in the ultimate fineness and uniformity of the leather, he would be more likely to reject ill-flayed hides and so maintain the standard of flaying[2]. Thus the excise rules were an impediment to industrial integration and a force working for the maintenance of the small scale, almost medieval, organisation of tanning and its allied trades[3].

No such consequences can be ascribed to the excise on printed calicoes and muslins. The leading print-works were big and modern enough. The duty was very heavy—$3\frac{1}{2}d.$ a yard—but it was repaid as a drawback if the goods were exported; and so strong was the position of the cotton industry that more than two-thirds of the money collected was repaid in 1828[4]. Even so, there remained a net revenue of nearly £600,000, which means a home consumption of over 40,000,000 yards. The glass and paper duties, on the other hand, besides their obvious effect in adding to the home cost of essential articles of consumption—even second-class paper paid $1\frac{1}{2}d.$ a lb.—had, like the leather duties, a petrifying influence on the industries. Before the glass duties had been last raised, in 1812, the amount of British glass annually retained for home consumption was 413,000 cwt. In 1829 it was only 364,000. It had been 374,000 cwt. when the great wars began, more than a generation earlier[5]. In the interest of the revenue, every glass-works had at least two excise-men quartered on it. "We can do no single act in the conduct of our own business without having previously notified our intention to the officers placed over us,"[6] said one manufacturer in 1833. "We have to give notices all day long," said Lucas Chance. There was a licence on the glass house, a payment per pound for all glass melted in the

---

[1] S. C. on the Petitions relating to the duties on Leather, 1812–13 (VII. 593), p. 30. Evidence of Sam. Beddome of Bermondsey.

[2] Comm. of 1824, p. 25.

[3] Above, p. 170.

[4] Parnell, op. cit. p. 40.

[5] Lardner's Cabinet Cyclopædia, "Porcelain and Glass" (1832), p. 142.

[6] Quoted in Powell, H. J., Glass-making in England (1923), p. 153.

pots, and a further poundage on the excess weight of the finished glass over 50 per cent. of what had been in the pots. No wonder the excise men were always sounding the pots with iron "gauging rods."

But this was not the worst. The inside measurements of every pot had to be registered, and the annealing ovens had to be of a particular shape "with only one entrance," which could be locked. For the convenience of inspection each glass works had to turn out only one sort of glass.

Flint glass might not be made in a crown-glass factory, nor bottle-glass in a plate-glass factory. A common bottle-glass factory might not produce phials less in content than six ounces. A crown or German sheet-glass factory might not produce glass exceeding one-ninth inch in substance, and a plate-glass factory must not produce plates exceeding five-eighths inch or less than one-eighth inch in thickness[1].

There is no need to emphasize the effects of this system on organisation or invention. Incidentally, it produced illicit furnaces, dubious "little-goes" in dark corners, which made cheap articles out of re-melted broken glass. However, in spite of the harm done, more than a third of the British glass found markets overseas, and on this third the duty was returned as a drawback[2].

The main evil of the paper duty was its mere weight—3d. a pound on all printing and writing paper. The British make of the first-grade papers—rag papers—in 1831 was 45,000,000 lbs. The make of second-grade paper, taxed at 1½d., was only 15,000,000 lbs.[3] When the law which was operative in the late 'twenties (43 Geo. III, c. 69) had been passed there was no mistaking second-grade paper. It was defined as brown paper made "of old ropes or cordage only, without...extracting the pitch or tar,"[4] and it could be identified by its smell. But by 1830 much cheaper materials were available, and there were processes for getting rid of the smell. So papers could be made out of second-grade materials which competed with the first-grade papers. For the public this was no hardship, but it led to some confusion and friction in the trade, as the line dividing the grades, which once had been clear, became

---

[1] Powell, *op. cit.* p. 155.

[2] *Ibid.* p. 41.

[3] *Fourteenth Report of Commissioners of Excise Inquiry*, 1835, p. 74. The Irish make was 1,300,000 first-grade and 500,000 second-grade.

[4] *Ibid.* p. 10.

blurred[1]. Since the excise duty was not mixed up with the processes, like that on glass, but fell on the ultimate product, there is no reason to think that it hindered the natural development of the industry, save in so far as it discouraged improvement by setting a rigid limit to demand.

Most of the customs duties on manufactures did not yield revenue and were not intended to yield revenue. They were frankly, if now in most cases needlessly, protective. The changes in the tariff of 1824–5, generally credited to Huskisson, had not altered the system in any essential. Instead of being prohibited, French silks paid 30 per cent. *ad valorem*; but, in spite of prophesyings to the contrary, that proved enough to keep most of them out. "The whole amount imported since 1825," Parnell wrote with perfect truth in 1830, "forms scarcely a few days' consumption."[2] A consolidation of all duties on cotton manufactures at a uniform 10 per cent. *ad valorem* had not affected the imports perceptibly. A few special "lines" had come when duties were high: no more came when the duties fell to 10 per cent. A reduction of the woollen duties from 50 per cent. and upwards to 15 per cent. worked in much the same way; some more woollens came, but not enough to matter. So it was with glass and china and gloves and linen and lace and the rest. The final *omnibus* clause of the budget of 1825, which fixed the duty on all manufactures not specially dealt with at 20 per cent., shows the essential conservatism of the reforms. In view of Britain's industrial leadership, a general 20 per cent. was more than enough to close her ports to most foreign manufactures. "Little or no change," said Parnell, "was really made by the alteration of the protecting duties and prohibitions in 1825." "If free trade...is the right policy, the work of introducing it still remains to be done."[3]

Although the protective system, as applied both to manufactures and agriculture, remained substantially untouched, the bounties on export, for long closely associated with it, were almost all either dead or under sentence of death. The most important of them, the corn bounty—first tried experimentally under Charles II and erected into a permanent system at the Revolution—had been inoperative for over thirty years. That

---

[1] In consequence the duties were equalised, at $1\frac{1}{2}d.$ the lb., in 1836.
[2] *Financial Reform*, p. 73.
[3] *Ibid.* p. 72, 74.

for the encouragement of the whale fishery, almost equally old
—it dated from 1732, and had last been regulated by 55 Geo. III,
c. 32, in the year of Waterloo[1]—had been allowed to expire in
1824. Its work, it was believed, was done. Bounties on exported
silks—they were seldom paid—had been allowed to lapse in
the same year[2]. Linen bounties had also been condemned.
Originally it had been proposed to abolish those on the coarser
fabrics out of hand, and to allow those on the finer to die by
10 per cent. gradations. But Joseph Hume, the free-trade
Radical, whose constituents in Aberdeenshire, with other
Eastern Scots, made much coarse stuff, had urged equality of
treatment for the two sorts. Irish interests also had to be considered; and the making of linen—whether coarse or fine—
was held to be a civilising influence in Ireland. In the end
extinction by degrees was accepted for both sorts[3]. Over
£200,000 was still being paid in linen bounties in 1827; but by
an Act of the following year the death of the system was fixed
for January 5, 1832[4]. Bounties for the encouragement of
herring-fishing and herring-curing were also fading away
between 1824 and 1830. Those on curing went first. The
special grants to the Scottish and Irish fisheries—amounting
to nearly £100,000 a year—were condemned to extinction by
7 Geo. IV, c. 39, under Canning. "They are to cease," wrote
Parnell, "on the 5th of April, 1830." But as "the putting of
an end to them had, of late years, been so often enacted by
law, and so often postponed"[5] he did not feel confident that
they would really die. In fact they died.

Apart from the rather considerable linen bounties, the
revenues of Britain remained burdened, at the close of the
decade, with only one bounty, the exact amount of which was
then in dispute—the bounty on sugar re-exported. Sugar
being taxed on entry was entitled to a drawback on re-export.
In view of the method of calculating the duties it had been
maintained, in 1824, that this drawback worked as a bounty,
even when the sugar was shipped out unrefined. It was admitted, in 1824 and later, that the method of calculating the
drawback on refined exports involved a heavy bounty, "said

[1] Smart, *op. cit.* II. 194. For a modern defence of the whale bounty see
Markham, Sir Clements R., *The Lands of Silence* (1921), p. 189. Between 1732
and 1787 the number of whalers grew from something under 10 to 185.
[2] Smart, *op. cit.* II. 199 n.   [3] *Ibid.* II. 195, 213, summarises the debates.
[4] Parnell, *op. cit.* p. 130.   [5] *Ibid.* p. 132.

by some persons, of good authority, to be as high as 6s. or 7s.
a cwt."[1] Parnell, to be on the safe side, assumed that this "gift
of so much public money...to the exporting merchants, for
the benefit of the West India planters and the foreign consumers" might be reckoned at 5s. a cwt. or something over
£100,000 for the year 1828.

Bounties, in short, survived only as a very subordinate part
of the general system of preferential treatment for produce
raised within the Empire. The Irish linen bounty was defended
more on political than on economic grounds. Britain was held
to have no further need of bounties, even by those who had
no objection to them in principle. To the parliamentary political
economists there was the objection of principle that some tax
burdensome to producers or consumers had to be maintained
in order that bounties might be paid; and this applied to
bounties of every kind. The economists also objected to most,
if not all, of the preferential tariffs because of the resulting
burden on the productive power or consumptive capacity of
the mother-country. Parnell calculated that the East India
Company's monopoly of tea, which was of the nature of a
much exaggerated imperial preference, made the price of tea,
"exclusive of duty, double what it was at New York and
Hamburgh" and imposed "a tax of at least £2,000,000 a year
in the form of increased price"; that the preferential sugar
duties, by keeping out cheap foreign and East Indian sugar, were
"a tax on the public" of—at least—£1,500,000 a year; and that
"the monopoly of the timber trade enjoyed by the shipowners
and Canada merchants" cost more than £1,000,000 a year[2].

These, with coffee, hides and textile raw materials, were the
outstanding instances of preference; but the principle was
recognised on almost every page of the tariff. Argol and Ashes,
Boxwood, Cedarwood, Ebony, Mahogany and Cochineal; the
skins of Bear, Beaver, Cat, Fox, Martin, Mink, Otter and
Raccoon; Gum Arabic and Camels' Hair; Isinglass and Sperm
Oil and Tallow; Turmeric, Bees' Wax, Rosin and Castor Nuts;
with Soap, Pig Iron and Iron Bars—on these and some other
things, did they care to send them, colonies and overseas possessions received substantial preferences[3]. They, in their turn,
were required to give preferential treatment to the produce and

---

[1] Parnell, *op. cit.* p. 139; and see Smart, *op. cit.* II. 217, 265.
[2] *Financial Reform*, p. 5.
[3] They are tabulated, as they stood in 1827, in Parnell, *op. cit.* p. 313.

manufactures of the United Kingdom, with the result that the mother-country "still practically enjoyed all the advantages of the old monopoly with respect to supplying the colonies with her productions."[1] It was the heavy taxation of the alternative foreign article, rather than the preference *per se*, which drew the fire of the economists.

But something had to be taxed if the service of the debt and the really very moderate expenditure on other national services were to be covered without borrowing—unless parliament would accept again the "inquisitorial" Property Tax, swept away, against the wishes of the then Chancellor of the Exchequer, to the accompaniment of "a loud cheering...which continued for several minutes," by a majority of 238 to 201 on March 18, 1816[2]. All competent students of finance, ten years later, knew that its re-imposition in some shape was essential for any reform of the fiscal system. Lord Liverpool had opposed, and continued to regret, its abolition. "If it was in our power to do our duty," he wrote to Canning in 1824, "we should increase our direct taxes by at least £2,000,000,"[3] and cut four or five millions off customs and excise. The principle was actually accepted by the cabinet in 1827; but Goderich's ministry fell before it could be applied[4]. Writing in September of that year from Frankfort, Meidinger, obviously reflecting ordinary opinions collected during his travels of 1824-5-6, declared that a well-ordered Property Tax alone would enable the British Government to get rid of the excessive import duties[5].

"In selecting a new tax," Parnell was able to write three years later, "there seems to be but one opinion with respect to what that tax ought to be. Persons who hold the most opposite doctrines on the subject of our financial, commercial and agricultural difficulties, in suggesting remedies, have made an Income Tax a part of them."[6]

He suggested, without going into detail, a rate of $1\frac{1}{2}$ or 2 per cent. which, he thought, "would probably yield three millions." That same year, in debate, Huskisson, Poulett Thomson and

[1] Parnell, *op. cit.* p. 239.   [2] Smart, *op. cit.* I. 468.
[3] Quoted in Halévy, E., *Hist. du peuple anglais au* 19me *siècle*, II (1923), 183.
[4] Herries, C. J., *Life*, II. 1, 132.   [5] *Reisen*, p. xvii.
[6] *Financial Reform*, p. 267. Lullin de Chateauvieux, J. F., advocated it in his *Lettres de Saint-James*, p. 66, in 1822. The statement of Seligman, E. R. A., *The Income Tax* (1911), p. 117, that "it was not until about a decade later (than 1820) that any real interest was manifested in the subject" is based on too bibliographical a view of the matter.

Lord Althorp all accepted the principle, the last in his plain way declaring that to reduce taxes on commodities and to "impose a property tax to meet the deficiency thus occasioned, would be a very good measure."[1] It was a good measure which he never introduced, although as Chancellor of the Exchequer for many years he was to have every opportunity.

The British tax-system at the close of the decade, though unaltered in principle and still radically defective, was much more orderly and rational in detail than it had been in 1820. So much at least government might have said in self-defence. A still greater measure of order, coupled this time with small but perceptible changes of principle, had been introduced into the closely associated systems of colonial and navigation policy. Ever since the loss of the American colonies, awkward adjustments, by order in council and treaty, had adapted a colonial and navigation system, one of whose cardinal assumptions had been that all the New World was somebody's colony, to the existing facts. Meanwhile, by capture and settlement, new territories with new requirements and products had come within the Empire. Latterly, the successful revolt of Spanish America had covered the New World with states which were nobody's colony. The old rule of the navigation law that all American produce[2] must come in British ships, a rule which had been eased to meet the case of the United States after 1783, was manifestly out of date forty years later. The rule which directed that certain enumerated articles of colonial produce —of which sugar, tobacco, and cotton were the chief—must be shipped to Britain only had become curiously partial in its application to an Empire whose centre of gravity had shifted from Virginia the Carolinas and the West Indies. The ancient English jealousy of the Dutch was almost dead, and special legislation against them would have been singularly out of place at a time when the Congress of Vienna had just arranged to strengthen their kingdom—in England's interest—by incorporating with it the Belgic provinces, and to fortify it against the French at England's expense[3].

---

[1] Hansard, XXIII. 908.

[2] The rule applied, with certain exceptions, to African and Asiatic produce also.

[3] We paid out rather more than £1,500,000 in 1818–20 for the strengthening of the barrier fortresses—including Ypres. *E.J.* December 1917, p. 500.

Wallace's Acts of 1822 (3 Geo. IV, c. 41, 42, 43, 44 and 45) had recognised these things; had cleared from the statute-book a vast number of obsolete laws; had given legislative sanction to certain facts accomplished in defiance of the navigation laws; and had eased one or two minor buckles of the navigation system[1]. Huskisson's navigation Act of 1825 (6 Geo. IV, c. 109—"an Act for the encouragement of British shipping and of navigation") had codified the law but had abandoned no more principles. There were no special clauses directed against the Dutch; but there was still, as in the Act of Charles II[2], a list of goods, the produce of Europe, which might not be imported into the United Kingdom, *to be used therein*, save in British ships, or in ships of the country of which the goods were the produce, *or in ships of the country from which the goods were imported*. The clauses in italics indicate easings of the buckles, but easings for British convenience. What once had been illegal goods might now be warehoused in Great Britain to be re-exported, for the benefit of her entrepôt trade, and the attempt —wearisome and difficult beyond belief—to determine whether the goods which a foreign ship brought from one of its own home ports were really the produce of that country was abandoned, for Europe. As for non-European produce, it might now come either in British ships or in ships of the country from which the goods were the produce *and* from which they were imported. This allowed for self-determining "countries" in the remoter continents, since these now existed and some of them had ocean-going ships. It really applied only to America: China tea was not likely to come in junks, nor ivory in Zanzibar dhows. But America was tied rather more tightly than Europe —by an *and* instead of an *or*. Whereas a Portuguese ship might now bring Spanish wine from Lisbon, a United States ship might not bring Cuban sugar from New York to be warehoused in London[3].

The old rule that non-European produce might not come from European ports even in British ships was retained. Its object was to give to the British ship the long instead of the short voyage. It did not however apply to the produce of

[1] Smart, *op. cit.* II. 104–6.
[2] Not the Navigation Act proper but the "Frauds on the Customs" Act, 13 and 14 Car. II, c. 11.
[3] The preference for the sugar colonies prevented Cuban sugar from coming to be consumed here.

Asia or Africa when shipped from the ports of Turkey in Europe.

Coasting traffic and the whole carrying trade between Britain and her colonies were reserved, as they always had been, for British ships. "All intercourse between the mother country and the colonies, whether direct or circuitous," Huskisson had said in introducing his measure, "and all intercourse of the colonies with each other, will be considered as a coasting trade to be reserved entirely and absolutely to ourselves."[1] The territories of the East India Company, it should be noted, were not a colony within the meaning of the Act. The directors might regulate trading there by the ships of friendly powers as they thought fit; and, by a special arrangement made in 1819, United States ships might even clear with cargoes from Great Britain for the Company's ports[2].

From the earliest days of navigation and plantation policy, the plantations had been free to export many kinds of produce wherever they pleased. This freedom was now generalised. The obsolete "enumeration" list was dropped; but the immense tariff preferences on sugar of all kinds were as effective as any compulsion in bringing the whole colonial output into British ports, to the great gain of the West Indies and Guiana. The same is true of the coffee of Jamaica which had never been "enumerated." Every colony had now free ports through which it might draw foreign produce, provided always that the foreign country concerned itself pursued a liberal colonial policy, and was prepared to reciprocate. But not one of the great colonial powers—Holland France and Spain—was willing to concede full reciprocity. Holland was not prepared for reciprocity of any sort. In practice the main effect of the new system was to ease access to the colonies for certain articles of United States produce—mainly foodstuffs and tobacco.

The law did not state, as some ancient laws had stated, that the colonies must buy such manufactures as they could not produce from Britain only. But the end was secured by another means, the preferential duties on British produce required of the colonies. In view of the burdens which the British Government placed upon the British consumer in the colonial interest, there was nothing inequitable in this; but it curtailed the freedom of the free ports. Huskisson's laws, Parnell wrote in 1830,

---

[1] Hansard, XII. 1097.
[2] See below, p. 487.

have had no kind of effect in making the trade of the colonies more free than it was before....These [discriminating] duties are so high, that England still practically enjoys all the advantages of the old monopoly with respect to supplying the colonies with her productions. The failure ...which was foretold in 1825, of the attempt to establish a free colonial trade, and at the same time give protection to British manufactures, has come to pass...[1].

The famous series of reciprocity treaties which Huskisson initiated had, strictly speaking, nothing to do with the navigation laws. Under the old system, even when "legal" goods had been brought by a foreign vessel—port wine in a Portuguese ship or German linen in a Hamburger—various differential charges had been made, remnants of the old alien customs on the goods, and higher port, light, and harbour charges on the ships. Drawbacks on re-export also were less when goods were sent in foreign bottoms. The intended result was to give a preference to the British ship even in those trades which the navigation laws left open to the foreigner. Such a system, as Huskisson said in 1823, was possible only so long as foreign countries acquiesced. The first recalcitrant had been the United States. Great Britain withdrew in 1815, and conceded equal port and customs treatment to United States ships. Portugal followed; then Holland; then Prussia began to threaten retaliation. Huskisson's reciprocity Acts (4 Geo. IV, c. 77, and 5 Geo. IV, c. 1) gave Government power to offer, by treaty or order in council, equal treatment for all goods brought in or taken out legally in foreign bottoms, provided the foreign country levied no discriminating duties on British ships or on goods brought in them. By 1830 Prussia, Denmark, Sweden, the Hanse towns, Mecklenburg, Hanover, the United States, France, Austria, and nearly all the new South American Republics had accepted the offer; though not all of them were admitted to perfect equality of treatment, because they were not prepared to concede it. The Dutch, for instance, who could never be brought to the treaty point, were granted equality of port charges by order in council of November 1824; but two years later, because their fault was "offering too little and asking too much," Canning clapped "on Dutch bottoms just 20 per cent."[2] For more than ten years the 20 per cent. stuck.

[1] *Financial Reform*, p. 238-9.
[2] See Temperley, H. W. V., *The Foreign Policy of Canning* (1925), p. 295-6. For the reciprocity treaties, Clapham, J. H., "The last years of the Navigation Acts," *E.H.R.* July and October 1910.

What exactly the treaties of full reciprocity did may be illustrated from one of them[1]—that of April 2, 1824, with Prussia. Charges on vessels of the two powers in one another's havens are to be equalised. Goods the produce of either, which may be legally moved at all, may be moved to and fro in the ships of either indifferently. No special duties shall be levied by either power on any goods merely because they come in the ships of the other, provided their import is otherwise legal. Bounties and drawbacks are not to be withheld by England on the ground that goods legally exportable or re-exportable are shipped in Prussian bottoms. Two years later (in May 1826) Prussia also secured the right to trade with the colonies, the right which Holland never got because she would not give it. Prussia could not buy it with an identical concession, for she had no colonies. So she bought it by guaranteeing "most favoured nation treatment" to British commerce and navigation. Her right to trade with the colonies did not exempt her goods from the colonial duties discriminating in favour of British produce: it merely guaranteed to them right of entry and the same treatment, when brought in her own ships, as they would receive if brought in British ships. Hence Parnell's complaint of the maintenance of the old British monopoly system. Wallace, Huskisson, and those who carried on their policy, aimed at strictly limited objectives[2].

Thinkers among the parliamentarians of the 'twenties were coming steadily under the influence of the economists. Lord Liverpool knew his "duty" in fiscal matters, but regretted his inability to perform it[3]. Herries the High Tory, "old, grey-headed, financial Herries,"[4] was with him. Parnell the Whig, who stood godfather—if not father—to the corn law of 1815, explained to the House in 1827 that he had changed his opinion on closer acquaintance with "the science connected with it."[5] "Since 1813, the subject of rent had been fully explained for

---

[1] They, and the various orders in council, are conveniently collected in Macgregor, J., Commercial Statistics, 4 vols., 1844.

[2] They would have been puzzled by the statement that "owing to Huskisson's enlightened policy the old Navigation Laws had been repealed upon the condition of reciprocity." The Political History of England, XI. (1906), 207.

[3] Above, p. 329.

[4] Benjamin Disraeli to Sarah Disraeli, May 15, 1832. Disraeli's Life, I. 205.

[5] The speech (Hansard, XVI. 1101) is quoted at length in Smart, op. cit. II. 414–5.

the first time.... Since 1813, too, Mr Ricardo published his new doctrines regarding wages and profits and upon the tendency of low profits to promote the transfer of capital from this country to foreign countries." He went on to summarise the Ricardian argument that dear corn meant—sooner or later—high wages; high wages, low profits; and low profits, a capital shortage. But not all parliamentarians were thinkers; even the economists were cautious; and to all questions connected, or believed to be connected, with national power there was general reluctance to apply a too strict economic argumentation. A solid ignorant gentlemanly vote stood between Liverpool and his duty. Even in the third edition of his *Principles* (1821) Ricardo, discussing tariffs, had not gone beyond recommending "a gradual recurrence to the sound principles of an universally free trade"[1]: for special reasons, he favoured a fixed duty of 10s. on corn to the day of his death[2]. So did Malthus[3]. Adam Smith's preference of defence to opulence was in everybody's mouth whenever the navigation laws came up for discussion. So late as 1840, James Deacon Hume, the free-trade official of the customs who helped Ricardo and Malthus to found the Political Economy Club and Huskisson to revise the tariff, explained to a parliamentary committee, in very cumbrous language, that there existed "the cases of national defence, the health of the country and free labour, involving matters of security and morality, which were taken out of the class of free trade, because they were by law interfered with, for purposes independent of trade."[4]

Certainly there was not much dogmatic objection to interference in the mind of the average legislator. Spasmodic abandonments of regulative legislation—from that of the apprenticeship law to that of the Spitalfields Act and the combination laws—had been due more to lack of constructive ideas for dealing with the various problems as they arose, and

[1] *Works* (ed. McCulloch, 1852), p. 191.
[2] *On Protection to Agriculture* (4th ed. 1822), "Conclusion." He thought 10s. "rather too high as a countervailing duty to the peculiar taxes...imposed on the corn grower," but "would rather err on the side of a liberal allowance than of a scanty one."
[3] See the note to Bk. II, ch. 12, of the sixth edition (1826) of the *Essay on Population*. Malthus thought "perfect freedom of trade...a vision which it is to be feared can never be realised." *Ibid.*
[4] *Comm. on Import Duties*, Q. 1411. His remarks about free labour refer to the special taxation of "slave-grown" sugar, those about health to the quarantine laws.

to lack of administrative machinery adequate to enforce even such regulative legislation as survived, than to reasoned preference for so-called economic freedom. The regulative laws abandoned were working badly and partially—that was true of them all—and no one was ready with an alternative, or prepared to face big administrative programmes. When speaking against the Spitalfields policy, which—in modern language—was state enforcement of a trade agreement in a localised industry[1], Ricardo, who "could not help expressing his astonishment" that the Acts were still on the statute-book, only just managed to carry the House with him in an argument that, if the Acts were really so beneficial as their defenders maintained, why then they should be applied, first, to the whole of the silk trade and, next, to all the trades of the country[2]. This was meant as a *reductio ad absurdum* and, whether it was so taken or not by his hearers, a *reductio ad absurdum* it was. Good or bad, the thing was unthinkable, when industrial Britain was so little organised, so local in its outlook, and in such a state of flux that trade agreements over areas much larger than Spitalfields could not have been arrived at, or, if arrived at, maintained, because their proper supervision was administratively impossible. Were the Lancashire justices to ride into Manchester, to grapple with all the intricacies of cotton piece-rates and, if they did, what would come of their award in Stalybridge which happens to be in Cheshire? The strongest argument against the Spitalfields system was that it did not even extend into Essex.

If any regulative measure seemed workable it might well pass almost unchallenged, especially if it appeared to promote good conduct and the virtues appropriate to their station among the "lower orders," or to safeguard the power of Britain. The legislation for Friendly Societies was an interference which would not have been tolerated by, let us say, the Universities or Brooks's or White's: it was regulative enough[3]. When the snap repeal of the combination laws brought its natural crop of strikes, parliament—as is well known—gave very serious attention to a scheme which was to withhold recognition from

[1] Above, p. 209.
[2] The majority was 68 to 60: June 9, 1823. See Clapham, J. H., "The Spitalfields Acts" in *E.J.* December 1916.
[3] Above, p. 297.

every Trade Union which could not get a Justice of the Peace to act as its treasurer[1]. Solicitude for the sea-power of Britain was clearly shown in the debates which preceded the passing of 4 Geo. IV, c. 25, *An Act for regulating the number of Apprentices to be taken on...Merchant Vessels.* It was one of Huskisson's Acts and, like much else of his, was only a modernising of an ancient mercantilist policy[2]. Ten years before, apprentice-ship on land had ceased to be statutory; but now apprentice-ship at sea, which had never been taken from the statute book, was not merely confirmed but strengthened and buttressed up with new regulations. Shipowners were to see to it that a proper ratio was maintained between tonnage and apprentices; the bigger the vessel the more indentured apprentices must she ship, so that there might be plenty of well-trained seamen. The bill did not escape Ricardo. "It would not be more unjust to enact a law that every surgeon should take a certain number of apprentices to encourage the progress of surgical science," he said. He pointed out also that it tended, or might tend, to keep down seaman's wages, by getting too much of the work done by apprentices. Huskisson was able to reply that ship-owners were quite satisfied with the measure. So, he believed, was every member of the House except Mr Ricardo. When it came to the third reading even the Ricardian opposition ceased[3]. The shipowners, for whom Huskisson had retained most of what they valued in the navigation code, were thus still saddled—not unwillingly, it is true—with a compensating liability to the state. The King's Navy, it must be recalled, was still to be manned in emergency by impressment from the mercantile marine; and ordinary naval opinion, for many years to come, could see no other way of manning it[4].

Those regulative laws which prescribed in detail how things should be made or measured or bought or sold, a group still fashionable in the middle of the eighteenth century, had almost all been allowed to lapse, but many of them very recently. So late as 1765 a most complicated law (5 Geo. III, c. 51), the last but one of an innumerable series[5], had been enacted

---

[1] Webb, S. and B., *History of Trade Unionism* (ed. 1920), p. 106 n.
[2] It replaced a number of Acts running back to 2 & 3 Anne, c. 6.
[3] Hansard, VIII, 551, 663, 1125 and Smart, *op. cit.* II. 168.
[4] Below, p. 501.
[5] Heaton, *The Yorkshire Woollen and Worsted Industries*, p. 414, calls it "about the last." The last was an amending Act, 6 Geo. III, c. 23.

for repealing several laws relating to the manufacture of woollen cloth in the county of York, and also as much of several other laws as prescribed particular standards of width and length to such woollen cloths, and for substituting other regulations of the cloth trade within the West Riding...for preventing frauds in certifying the contents of the cloth, and for preserving the credit of the said manufacture at foreign markets.

For the first time since Magna Carta had talked about *una latitudo pannorum tinctorum*, it was now legal throughout England to make cloth of any size and weight which the maker might select. But the Act provided a whole hierarchy of searchers inspectors and supervisors to certify the length and quality of the cloths, to see to it that they had not been overstretched on the tenters, and so to "preserve their credit at foreign markets." Every piece of cloth made in the West Riding of Yorkshire—the county economics characteristic of old England are noteworthy: Lancashire had no searchers—must still be sealed. For a time all was activity. "When the Act was first obtained," a witness said forty years later, "we saw them [*i.e.* the officials] once, twice, or sometimes three times a day examining our tenters."[1] But when this testimony was given control had become ineffective[2]. Cloths were sealed as being of certain lengths; but many merchants paid no attention to the seal, and often preferred unsealed cloth from other counties to the sealed cloth of the West Riding. Seeing that the fine cloth of the West of England was never sealed, this was not unnatural. No action, however, was taken by parliament in 1806, and the West Riding laws dragged on for another fifteen years, becoming more ineffective yearly.

Then, in 1821, a select committee inquired into them[3]. The fact that they were Yorkshire laws only was presumptive evidence for abolition. It was clear, as the committee pointed out, that they could not be essential to the "preserving of credit at foreign markets," for there was no cloth more prized abroad than that of the unregulated Cotswold valleys. One witness, a merchant-manufacturer from Halifax, said cheerfully that he broke the law daily[4]. Another big man from Halifax said that he had been liable to penalties of £100 a day for the

---

[1] *Reports*, 1806, III. 157, and Heaton, *op. cit.* p. 416.
[2] Not perhaps quite so ineffective as Prof. Heaton implies.
[3] *S. C. on Laws relating to Stamping Woollen Cloth*, 1821 (VI. 435)
[4] J. Waterhouse, *Report*, p. 8.

last twenty-five years—a fine, round, bragging statement of liability[1]. The Halifax witnesses were both in a large way of business and in close commercial touch with Lancashire—only some ten miles distant—which had no sealing laws. But the little men, especially those of the heavy woollen district, clung to the law; though their reasons for so doing were not very clearly expressed. Robert Clapham of Batley and all his friends had held a meeting and were unanimous. Their main argument was the utility of the stamp in connection with debt and bankruptcy claims. "The stamp is what I go by; and I have recovered by it more than once or twice,"[2] said James Oddy of Birstall. As a further argument for the stamp, he stated that "there was not one cloth maker out of three that could measure cloth." Being asked to expand the remark, he said that there were "not many honest enough." From Idle and Shipley and Leeds also came evidence of the affection of the domestic clothiers for the laws. They "think them a protection between them and the merchant." If they did, probably the laws were a protection in some cases, since in a matter of this sort the domestic men should have known what helped them. But the general evidence was that the merchants went by their own estimates and not at all by the seal. One Huddersfield merchant-manufacturer admitted, not however until he had been a little pressed, that in buying from domestic men he paid less than the contract price if the cloth, when measured, was found to be "below the seal,"[3] *i.e.* shorter than the seal suggested, but did not pay more if it was found to be above. It looks as though the seal cannot have been much of a protection.

The committee faithfully reported the domestic men's point of view. They commented on the inconvenience of the law for the merchant-manufacturer, and its neglect in the Halifax area. They explained that about Leeds it was still popular, even among some merchants; but they were at a loss to explain its popularity, seeing that the measurement which determined price was now everywhere made by the merchant. They concluded that the laws might safely be repealed. Repealed they were by 1 & 2 Geo. IV, c. 116, and so ended the century-long story of the regulation of the manufacture of woollen cloth by the state.

[1] W. H. Rawson, *Report*, p. 22.
[2] *Report*, p. 88.
[3] J. Wrigley, *Report*, p. 5.

In this case, according to most ancient precedent, the parliamentary machine had been set in motion by petition. Similarly, the repeal, in 1824, of the Acts "relating to the use of Horse Hides in making boots and shoes, and for the better preventing the damaging of raw hides...in the flaying thereof," followed —in 1827—by that of the leather duties with the regulation which they involved, were intended to meet grievances which had more than once been brought before parliament by way of petition. The very full inquiry made in 1813, for example, into the effect of the leather duties on the organisation and health of the industry was a reply to petitions; and there was petitioning about horse hides in 1824[1].

The repeal of the Yorkshire sealing and stamping Acts had prepared the parliamentary mind for repeal of similar Acts relating to Scottish linen. Some Scots had also been active with petitions. For just under a century—since 1727—the Scottish Board of Trustees for Manufactures and Fisheries had been engaged in spending some of the money due to Scotland from England under the Act of Union ("the equivalent") upon the development of the linen manufacture. It had offered prizes to housewives, set up spinning schools, brought Frenchmen from St Quentin to Edinburgh and given awards to inventors, when George II was King. It is still most active in the early nineteenth century. Its inspectors having confiscated some very bad linen in 1803, the Board orders pieces of it to be publicly burnt on the market day at Forfar, Kirriemuir, Glamis, Dundee and Brechin. Four years later its agents are seizing faulty linseed and punishing people for giving bad measure. In 1813 it is rewarding the inventor of a sail-cloth loom driven by water. All the time it has been giving premiums for flax-growing and, through its stampmasters, enforcing a law of George I which required the inspection and stamping of all Scottish linen. (There were no such rules for linen in England[2].)

In July 1820 a motion had been made in the old constitutional organisation of the burgesses of Scotland, the Convention of Royal Burghs, to the effect that "the inspection and stamping of linen by stampmasters was useless, was a tax on the manufacture, and ought to be abolished."[3] It appears that

[1] Above, p. 323.
[2] Warden, A. J., *The linen trade, ancient and modern* (1864), p. 5, 17, 18.
[3] See the narrative in the *Hand Loom Weavers' Commission*, III. 693.

the stampmasters themselves broke the law, like the merchant-manufacturers of Halifax, and that none of the principal linen fabrics manufactured in Scotland were of the legal widths. On hearing of this motion the Board of Trustees, on November 21, 1820—present the Lord Chief Baron, the Lord Chief Commissioner, the Hon. G. Abercrombie, Sir John Hay, Bart., and Gilbert Innes, Esq.—resolved, firstly, "That as this system has been acted upon in Scotland for nearly a century, and, in the judgment of all intelligent manufacturers and dealers in linen, with the greatest benefit to all concerned...nothing could be more impolitic and unwise than to attempt its overthrow," and ninthly, "That the experiment made some years ago by ...weavers in Dundee, to carry on the manufacture of the fabric called Bagging," without inspection and stamping, had led to a progressive and "notorious debasement and depreciation in the same." In spite of this and of the seven intervening resolutions of the Trustees someone, presumably from the Convention of Royal Burghs, brought the matter before Huskisson a year or two later. The Trustees heard that Huskisson was against them and fought hard, but made no impression on him[1]. He introduced a bill in 1823 for the abolition of all the laws regulating the Scottish manufacture, laws passed as he said parenthetically "at a time when the House was in the habit of interfering with the business of individuals."[2] He asserted that his bill would be received with satisfaction and gratitude by the people of Scotland; and in the House no one contradicted him. With little debate the bill became law (3 Geo. IV, c. 40) and the ground was cut from under the feet of the Trustees. This did not greatly matter, as they were themselves abolished that same year.

During the brief debate on Huskisson's bill, Parnell declared that the principle ought to be extended to Ireland, which had also its statutory Board of Trustees for the Linen Manufacture, dating from 1710, and a whole quiverful of linen laws and seal-masters—356 of the latter in Ulster alone. The Trustees were notoriously unbusinesslike: "their great inattention...to their money concerns"[3] had been very strongly criticised by the Commissioners of Account for Ireland in 1810. But as a whole

---

[1] So Warden, *op. cit.* p. 19.

[2] Quoted in Smart, *op. cit.* II. 164.

[3] *Hand Loom Weavers*, III. 689, in a well-documented historical survey of the Irish law upon which this paragraph is based.

Ireland was not articulate and did not petition: very possibly regulative laws suited her level of economic development. It is certain that, even towards 1840, "the great portion" of the Irish linen trade "still looked to legislative regulation as essential to the well-being and protection of their interests,"[1] just like Robert Clapham and James Oddy, twenty years earlier, in Yorkshire. However that may be; although twenty-two Irish linen laws were repealed in 1825 (by 6 Geo. IV, c. 122) and four more marked for repeal next year; and although in 1828 the Board of Trustees was abolished, yet its powers were transferred to the Lord Lieutenant; and in the first year of Queen Victoria an elaborate Linen Code for Ireland, with County Committees, Sealmasters to protect buyer and seller, Market Inspectors, special penalties for weavers who embezzled yarn, and so on, was re-enacted for five years (1 & 2 Vict. c. 52).

Embezzlement or misuse of raw material and half-manufactured articles like yarn, by the domestic outworker, had been one of the permanent employers' risks under the outwork system. There had been endless legislation against such things. By an odd anachronism, statutory machinery for dealing with them survived all other legislative regulation in the English worsted industry—and the machinery still survives. In the worsted industry of the West Riding, which, by the beginning of the fourth quarter of the eighteenth century, was definitely capitalistic, with a sharp cleavage between employer and employed, the law—of which there was plenty—had seemed to the masters entirely inadequate. The men were organised; "and in case a master tried to put the law into force...he could obtain no blacklegs and his own person and property were endangered."[2] So the masters counter-organised, raised funds, and hired inspectors to harass dishonest outworkers. Then they petitioned parliament and in 1777, by 17 Geo. III, c. 56, they secured legal sanction for that Worsted Committee of the counties of York, Lancaster and Cheshire which still exists. It will be noted that they had the good sense to take powers over an industrial area instead of over a single county in the old style. Other areas imitated them; and by the end of the decade there were Statutory Worsted Committees for Suffolk; for

---

[1] *Hand Loom Weavers*, III. p. 708.
[2] James, J., *History of the Worsted Manufacture in England*, p. 202-3. For the general history, Heaton, *The Yorkshire Woollen and Worsted Industries*, p. 418 *sqq.*

Norfolk and Norwich; and for a wide miscellaneous area comprising Lincoln, Leicester, Rutland, Northampton, Bedford, Hunts, the Isle of Ely and Cambridge. But these, except Norwich, were dying areas, whose committees had no permanent significance.

The Yorkshire Committee—its headquarters were at Halifax —had remarkable powers. If one of the employers' agents, who gave out wool to be spun, was found with wool in his possession of which he could not give a satisfactory account, he was assumed to have come by it illegally. To escape, he must prove himself innocent. If a workman did not return materials properly worked up in eight days, he might be punished as if he had actually embezzled them. Parliament even gave the masters something very near the right to levy taxes. Soap was a dutiable article; but there was a drawback on soap used in manufactures. The Committee's agents were authorised to claim $2d$. in every shilling of this drawback to finance the Committee's work. This potent and masterful organisation, whose members were elected for life and replaced by co-option, had as its first chairman John Hustler, the Quaker wool-stapler who planned the Leeds and Liverpool canal.

Though it carried out its policy with considerable success in the heart of the manufacturing area, in outlying districts it sometimes came up against county Justices yet more potent and not less masterful. In 1801 the Justices of Richmond refused a conviction to one of its inspectors on the ground that "the Act of Parliament was arbitrary and not fit to be put into execution."[1] Such a challenge to the sovereign parliament was possible under what Disraeli used to call "our territorial constitution." The Committee was however not merely an organisation for disciplining workpeople. It took action against masters who paid in truck; fought those who smuggled combing-wool out of England, or attempted to get export made legal; encouraged improvements and inventions; and spent its fines on infirmaries and Sunday schools. The decline of domestic spinning in the nineteenth century naturally restricted its functions; but in the 'twenties it was hard at work and, with the growing industrial use of soap, very well provided with funds. By order of 1821, it paid its members two guineas per meeting for attendance and two shillings per mile travelling allowance[2]. Of the

---

[1] Heaton, *op. cit.* p. 429.   [2] *Ibid.* p. 436.

Norwich Committee the history has not been written: probably it had some significance in the 'twenties, for the Norfolk industry lagged behind that of Yorkshire in the transition from outwork to factory conditions.

Older than the oldest regulation which had been laid upon the manufacture of cloth, so old indeed as to be dateless—a kind of economic common law—was the Assize of Bread, still alive in the provinces in 1830, though moribund[1]. Under it some local authority—it was far older than the Justices of the Peace —had originally regulated the weight of the loaf in relation to the price of grain, the price of the loaf being assumed to be fixed. The object was to determine the rate at which bakers should be remunerated for their service to society: if they had to give so much more for grain they might sell a proportionately smaller weight of bread at a given price. It was, in the nature of the case, a system which mainly interested townsmen in the early centuries. Country bakers had grown up in parts of southern England during the eighteenth century, but not before. In the North, they had not emerged in 1820; and by a transference of country habits to the growing northern towns, helped by the ease of getting fuel in most of them, domestic bread-making remained customary, if not universal, beyond the Trent. At Manchester, in 1815, half the population was said to prepare its own bread, though the baking was done for a fee at public ovens[2]; from Leeds, a letter to the parliamentary committee of 1821 explained that the Assize of Bread was not "set" there at all, because most people baked at home. So, as sale-bakers developed, they had been left free[3]. There was trouble over the Assize in 1813 at Stamford, where the old shifting loaf was still in use—"ours are the assize loaves, they vary in weight"[4]—and also at Derby. Farther north the Assize might sometimes be set, but it can never have been of real social importance.

For London, the old methods of the Assize had been out of date before Queen Anne died, because bakers bought not grain

---

[1] For the history of the Assize see Webb, S. and B., "The Assize of Bread," *E.J.* June 1904.

[2] Fay, C. R., "The miller and the baker," *Cambs. Hist. Jour.* I. 91.

[3] *S. C. on the regulations relative to the making and the sale of bread*, Appendix.

[4] *Comm. on the Bill to alter and amend 31 Geo. II, and 13 Geo. III, so far as they relate to the Assize of Bread outside...London.*

but flour[1]. Therefore, in her reign, the metropolitan Justices had been instructed to take into consideration the price of flour. Late in George II's reign (1758) the rule was laid down that a 280-lb. sack of flour was to yield 20 peck loaves. The Assize in London, by this time, was "set" by fixing a price for the peck loaf. Later, by Acts of 1797 and 1805, in a period of high prices when interest in the Assize revived everywhere, the discretionary power of the Justices was abolished—the latter Act allowing the London baker a fixed remuneration of 13s. for turning a sack of flour into the proper amount of bread. This scheme left him with no interest in the price of flour: whether he bought well or ill his margin was the same. It was severely criticised by a House of Commons committee in the year of Waterloo; and this criticism, backed by petitions from eight hundred master-bakers, led to the abolition of the London Assize by 55 Geo. III, c. 49. But London retained rules dealing with the weights of loaves, with adulteration, and with the duty of bakers to keep legal weights and measures. Only the statutory bakers margin was abolished[2]. Four years later (by 59 Geo. III, c. 36) similar though not identical rules were extended to all those extra-metropolitan places "beyond the weekly bills of mortality and ten miles of the Royal Exchange where no assize was set."[3]

This, then, was the complicated situation in the post-war period. London had no Assize, but had bread-rules. Many other places also had no Assize—either it had dropped out of use or it had never been applied because the places were new —but had rather different bread-rules. In others again the Assize continued to be "set" in one form or another. Where the Assize was not "set," the Justices had powers, in years of dearth, under an Act of 1773, to force bakers to prepare and sell only one kind of bread[4]—the standard wheaten bread, resembling that to which the country again became accustomed in 1916–18. In bad times the Justices were not at all slow to act. In 1813, the peak year for prices in the early nineteenth century, country bakers, in places where the Assize was still

---

[1] *Comm. on the Petitions of certain Country Bakers*, 1813, p. 1, and Fay, C. R., *op. cit.* 1. 86.

[2] Fay, *op. cit.* p. 87. Webb, S. and B., in *E.J.* June 1904, p. 216.

[3] The Committee of 1821 was appointed to inquire into the working of this Act.

[4] Webb in *E.J.* p. 213.

set, had wailed to parliament about the Justices' harshness, which shows at least that the Justices were not always engaged —as is sometimes suggested—in grinding the faces of the poor. At Bath and Bristol they allowed the baker a margin of only 10s. a sack of flour against 13s. in London. In Oxfordshire they still "set" from the wheat in the ancient way. In Worcester there had been no rise in the bakers' margin for thirty years. The Justices thought a rise was "against the poor people." In consequence, it was alleged, no baker could live by baking alone[1].

By 1821 years of dearth seemed a thing of the past[2], and interest in the Assize and all other bread regulations decayed. The select committee of 1821 appointed to report "on the existing regulations relative to the making and the sale of Bread" was definitely in favour of an experiment in complete free trade—"for one year at least"—subject to an anti-adulteration law and a law requiring every baker to weigh his bread on demand. For some unexplained reason, the law resulting from these recommendations (3 Geo. IV, c. 106) applied only to the ten-mile radius from London. But parliament had shown its hand. More important still, bread became relatively cheap in the 'twenties. Only the bad harvests of the war and post-war period had kept the Assize and its ancillary legislation alive. It may have been "set" now and again during the late 'twenties and early 'thirties. But it was no longer of interest anywhere. It never had been of interest in the new industrial centres of the North. Manchester had reported in 1821 that, when bread was sold there at all, it was sold by the pound against all the rules: she boasted of her perfect freedom from restraint. Leeds also, as has been seen, had no rules. But it was not until 1836 (by 6 & 7 Will. IV, c. 37) that an Act, almost a replica of the London Act of 1822, finally abolished the power and obligation of the Justices of the Peace to regulate bakers' profits or the price of bread.

The difficult war and post-war years which had kept the Assize of Bread alive had very nearly proved fatal—so little do any given set of circumstances necessarily favour or discourage regulation—to a less ancient, but still respectable, body of regulative laws, those which were meant to stop usury. Having

---

[1] From the *Comm. on Petitions of...Country Bakers.*
[2] Above, p. 133-4.

come through these years intact, the usury laws—much evaded and almost impotent—were to survive for a whole generation. The existing law was that of Queen Anne (12 Anne, st. 2, c. 16) which had reduced the maximum legal rate of interest from 6 to 5 per cent., higher rates being allowed only for loans on *bottomry*, in which the ship was the security, and *respondentia bonds*[1] in which the security was her cargo. Throughout the greater part of the eighteenth century, according to Adam Smith, the statutory rate had been "rather above than below the market rate."[2] Smith had nothing to say against the law. Though his approval of the 5 per cent. legal rate as "perhaps as proper as any" suggests a possible impropriety in all, he goes on to attack a legal rate so high as eight or ten on the ground that, if any such figure be adopted, "the greater part of the money which was to be lent, would be lent to prodigals and projectors."[3] To this Jeremy Bentham had retorted in 1787—in letters, eventually printed, as the *Defence of Usury*, in 1816—that prodigals were not very likely to get hold of the mass of British capital and that, as for projectors, they were the source of most good things: "Tubal Cain himself was as arrant a projector in his day, as ever Sir Thomas Lombe, or Bishop Blaise."[4]

Bentham had also explained some neat ways in which a prodigal might circumvent the law, adding:

should the effect of this page be to suggest an expedient, and that a safe and commodious one, for evading the laws against usury, to some, to whom such an expedient might not otherwise have occurred, it will not lie very heavy upon my conscience. The prayers of usurers, whatever efficacy they may have in lightening the burden, I hope I may lay some claim to. And I think you will not...wonder at my saying that in the efficacy of such prayers I have not a whit less confidence, than in that of the prayers of any other class of men[5].

Although projectors and prodigals and business men in difficulties circumvented the law during the eighteenth century, for most ordinary business transactions evasion was unnecessary, because the market rate was below 5 per cent. But towards the end of the Napoleonic wars, when twenty years of public borrowing had driven up the market rate, the

---

[1] For these bonds see *Dic. Pol. Econ. s.v. "respondentia."*
[2] *Wealth of Nations* (ed. Cannan), I. 91.
[3] *Ibid.* I. 338.
[4] *Works* (ed. Bowring), IV. 27.
[5] *Ibid.* IV. 13.

British Government itself, "in allowing discount for prompt payment of a loan,"[1] frequently offered more than the legal rate. By 1816 the usury laws had all but killed ordinary mortgage business. A mortgage, with its legal formalities, was precisely the kind of undertaking in connection with which evasion was most difficult. Landowners, hard hit by the sudden fall in corn prices during the years 1813–15, could find no mort-gagees and were forced to borrow, in roundabout ways, from the insurance companies at rates which worked out at ten per cent. and upwards[2]; for the usury laws, as Bentham pointed out, had never extended to "insurance in all its branches, to the purchase and sale of annuities and of *post-obits*."[3] In 1817, Sergeant Onslow supported by Sir Henry Parnell, had brought in a bill for the abolition of the laws. He made special play with the needs of Ireland: Ireland "with a fertile soil, a great population, and a favourable climate, was deficient only in capital," and stood to gain more than any other part of the kingdom by free trade in money[4].

Onslow's bill was not pressed: its proposer agreed that the subject required further consideration. This consideration was given by the select committee of the House which reported in 1818. The best of evidence was taken. Ricardo testified that, in his circle, the law was evaded "upon almost all occasions." On the Stock Exchange evasion was easy through the "differ-ence between the money price and the time-price of stock." You could borrow at more than 5 per cent., if you had stock, and could lend at more, if "the difference between the money-price and the time price afforded a higher rate." This was "the usual and constant practice," and was not affected by the fact that most "time" dealings were, strictly speaking, illegal[5]. Expert solicitors explained the recent difficulties of would-be mortgagors, and a representative of the Sun explained the methods of lending practised by the insurance companies. Nathan Rothschild said similar laws were evaded in every country he knew, and that there were none in Holland or "Hambro'"; though a Dutch witness pointed out that in fact his country had such laws, but that they did not apply

---

[1] Ricardo, before the *S. C. on the Usury Laws*, 1818 (vi), p. 5.
[2] See Brougham's speech, of March 1816, in Hansard, XXXII. 392.
[3] *Works*, IV. 14.
[4] The discussion is summarised in Smart, *op. cit.* I, 475.
[5] *Report*, p. 5–7.

to commercial transactions, and an Englishman resident at Hambro' observed that the Hanse Towns also had usury laws but that Jews evaded them, as Nathan Rothschild had correctly stated[1]. Only Samuel Gurney, moved—it may fairly be assumed—by moral and religious considerations, gave evidence quietly favourable to the usury laws[2].

The committee reported for repeal, giving as an additional reason that the market rate of interest—with the cessation of war borrowing—had now again got below the legal rate, and that so the moment was opportune. But this very fact apparently cooled the interest of a parliament of landowners, who could once more get their mortgages on reasonable terms and disliked moneylenders and that damning word usury. Onslow's abolishing bill—he was persistent—was lost in 1821 in 1824 and in 1825. In 1826 it was withdrawn at the request of government, although Peel admitted that the laws had again given trouble when market rates of interest had jerked up, during the panic of the previous year[3]. For the next ten years the market rate kept below 5 per cent. and interest in the whole question lapsed, except among a rationalist minority[4].

"There is one right," Malthus was telling his contemporaries, "which man has generally been thought to possess, which I am confident he neither does nor can possess—a right to subsistence when his labour will not fairly purchase it. Our laws indeed say that he has this right," therefore, unless the principle of population is to be left to rage unhindered, "we are bound in justice and honour" to change our laws, and "formally to disclaim the *right* of the poor to support. To this end, I should propose a regulation to be made, declaring that no child born from any marriage, taking place after the expiration of a year from the date of the law, and no illegitimate child born two years from the same date, should ever be entitled to parish assistance."[5] For the coming generation the poor law —the product of an age when queens ordered the affairs of their subjects from the greatest to the least, and the state

---

[1] *Report*, p. 17 (Rothschild), p. 42 (Warin, the Dutch witness), p. 51 (Thornton of Hamburg).

[2] *Ibid.* p. 24.

[3] Smart, *op. cit.* II. 396. For the rates see the diagram in Jevons, *Investigations in Currency and Finance.*

[4] But the Bank of England was relieved from the law in 1833. Below, p. 509.

[5] Quoted from the sixth edition of the *Essay* (1826), II. 319.

accepted liability for all[1]—was simply to cease. Malthus was not merely a critic of current administration—that all well-informed men were: he attributed "still more evil to the original ill-conception, than to the subsequent ill-execution."[2]

The semi-malthusian poor law commissioners of 1832–4 were to go with him half-way; but they lacked his academic courage. It had been suggested to them that poor relief should be made a national and not a parochial charge. That there were arguments in favour of this change they admitted. But they hesitated to give the fullest national recognition to the right whose existence Malthus had denied, and preferred to leave it as a half-right, a low-grade parochial right. The parishes, they seem to suggest, are not quite "the government." They were saving at once their semi-malthusian orthodoxy and the fundamentals of the existing system. The national suggestion, said they,

is objectionable in principle. To promise, on the part of the government, subsistence to all, to make the government the general insurer against misfortune, idleness, improvidence, and vice, is a plan perhaps better than the parochial system as at present administered; but still a proposal which nothing but the certainty that a parochial system is unsusceptible of real improvement, and that a national system is the only alternative against immediate ruin, the only plank in the shipwreck, could induce us to embrace[3].

Yet they were proposing to put the law more directly under "government," the central government, than it had been since the days of Lord Burghley and Archbishop Laud. They buttressed their refusal to consider the plan with financial arguments characteristic of their day. The prosperous island of Guernsey had a single poor-fund; but this required "a general income tax of not less than three per cent."[4] It was implied that a general income tax of nearly $7\frac{1}{4}d$. in the pound, for the relief of the poor, was unthinkable. Even if you were prepared to face such a burden, how were you to deal with fund-holders "domiciliated in Ireland and Scotland," if you began taxing personal property for the sake of the English and Welsh poor?

Possibly even Malthus, if called to sit on a commission whose business was to lay down principles for immediate action, might have hesitated to press his time limit for the whole

[1] These are not Malthus' reflections.
[2] *Essay*, II. 295 n.
[3] *Report*, p. 179.   [4] *Ibid*. p. 180.

poor law. No statesman of the 'twenties would have contemplated it as a working policy. "I have often heard Mr Canning say, that it was to the poor laws of this country that England owed her successful struggles with Europe and America; that they reconciled the people to their burthens, and had saved England from Revolution."[1] Right or wrong, Mr Canning was representative. A modern scholar who received his training not at Eton but at Ruskin College, Oxford, was inclined to agree with him[2]. Older than the Revolution settlement, older than Whig and Tory parties, older than High Church, Low Church and organised Dissent, the regulative disciplinary anti-individualistic Act of Elizabeth was not merely a part of the English constitution, but was assuredly that part of it of which ordinary Englishmen in their daily lives were most continuously conscious. Few beside Malthus dared, or desired, to speak of "the original ill-conception." The commissioners of 1832, with how much sincerity in each case it would be interesting to ascertain, but with undoubted political wisdom, paid homage to the established dignity of the Act, and that in capital letters, by arguing that their policies demonstrably carried out "THE SPIRIT AND INTENTION" of the Elizabethans[3]. "The outdoor relief of which we have recommended the abolition," they went on to argue—for, as is well known, they hoped to set a time-limit to outdoor relief, especially relief in aid of wages—

is in general partial relief, which...is at variance with the spirit of the 43d of Elizabeth, for the framers of that Act could scarcely have intended that the overseers should "take order for setting to work" those who have work...; nor could they by the words "all persons using *no* ordinary and daily trade of life to get their living by," have intended to describe persons "who *do* use an ordinary and daily trade of life."

It was fitting that an Act older than Coke on Littleton should be so scrutinised and glossed.

Two centuries of varying administrative policies had covered the country with an irregular network of institutions connected with the administration of the code which had grown about the 43rd of Elizabeth. The oldest of these were the Houses of Correction, orginally intended and still mainly used for a special

---

[1] Lord George Bentinck, quoted in Disraeli, *Bentinck*, p. 127.

[2] Ashby, A. W., *One Hundred Years of Poor Law Administration in a Warwickshire Village* (Oxford Studies in Social and Legal History), III. 1912, p. 103. "If England had not maintained such a system...from 1785 to 1800 it is more than likely that her constitution would have suffered from violent changes."

[3] *Report*, p. 262.

class of poor persons—vagrants, prostitutes, the half-criminal, and the misdemeanants under the poor laws. A return taken in 1776 showed that most counties had carried out the Elizabethan order to build or buy such "Bridewells," and still maintained them: in a few counties there were several[1]. Since 1776 there had been no further development of the system; and in the early nineteenth-century poor law controversies the House of Correction hardly appears[2]. Next in order of time were those urban workhouses which had been erected, by special Acts of parliament, to meet the needs of whole towns, and so avoid the waste of purely parochial administration where urban parishes were small[3]. Of these the oldest was the house of the Corporation of the Poor of the City of London, a body created by parliament in 1647. "London Workhouse in Bishopsgate St." had been founded in 1698 under an Act of 1662[4]. The houses at Bristol, Hull, Exeter, Crediton, Liverpool and Lynn also dated from William and Mary's reign; the rest, for the most part, from those of the first two Georges. Between 1750 and 1800 some twenty metropolitan parishes—some of them as populous as Crediton or Lynn—set up houses of the same type, often on older foundations[5]. But, even including these and a few late eighteenth-century statutory municipal houses like those of Oxford (1771), Southampton (1773), and Shrewsbury (1783), the whole group did not number much over forty by 1800. In addition, from a dozen to twenty towns, and a few big town parishes like Bermondsey St Mary Magdalene and Deptford St Paul, had similar institutions for which no special Act had ever been sought[6]. Most of the towns with town workhouses, statutory or not, were south of the Thames; but the lists include Derby Liverpool and Preston. The greatest of these municipal workhouses, in the late eighteenth century, was that of Norwich. Created in 1711, it served the whole city. During

---

[1] Reports from Committees...not inserted in the Journals, IX. Report of 1776 on Houses of Industry, etc., sect. IV. Vagrants and Houses of Correction: county returns.

[2] The term is not in the Index of the Report of 1834.

[3] They are set out, with their dates of foundation, in sect. I of the Report of 1776. See also Webb, S. and B., English Local Government, IV. (1922), 115–17, and ch. 2, passim.

[4] George, M. D., London Life in the Eighteenth Century, p. 218–19.

[5] Webb, p. 110 n.

[6] Tabulated in sect. II of the Report of 1776. The lists are not quite complete. Birmingham does not appear, but it had an eighteenth-century workhouse.

the early 'seventies, when the population of Norwich was something between 20,000 and 30,000, it contained in mid-winter on an average 1200 souls, of whom 600 were able-bodied, the rest children and impotent folk[1]. At that time none of the London parochial houses contained so many as three hundred able-bodied poor, though St James', Westminster, and St Mary, Whitechapel, each had upwards of two hundred.

The first extension to a rural area of the principle of the association of parishes for the establishment of workhouses had only come in 1756, when the gentry of the hundreds of Carlford and Colnies in Suffolk, led by Admiral Vernon, took power to amalgamate the administration of twenty-eight parishes and to build on Nacton Heath the Nacton House of Industry[2]. In the next thirty years thirteen hundreds, or grouped hundreds like Carlford and Colnies, in Norfolk and Suffolk did the same; "so that, by 1785, over the greater part of the area of these two large counties the administration of the Poor Law had...been vested in fourteen new bodies of Incorporated Guardians."[3] Their Houses of Industry were generally large and sometimes splendid. That of the hundreds of Loddon and Clavering, Norfolk, had "eighty-three apartments." That of Loes and Wilford, Suffolk, had a chapel, "a mansion," living and working rooms, pesthouse, brewhouse, washhouse and millhouse. Some had small farms attached[4]. Altogether, in externals, they might have been working models for "Owen's parallelograms."[5] They had started with the highest hopes of justifying their name and giving real industrial training.

A similar group of experiments was made rather later on the other side of the country, on the borders of Shropshire and Montgomeryshire[6]. The Shrewsbury House of Industry of 1783, started in a building erected as an offshoot of the London Foundling Hospital but abandoned owing to a change of policy at headquarters, was for a time very successful and much praised. It ran a corn mill a woollen manufactory and a farm. In the early 'nineties, five adjacent rural districts followed Shrewsbury's lead. consolidating their poor law administration and

[1] Figures from the *Report* of 1776.
[2] Webb, *op. cit.* p. 122.   [3] *Ibid.* p. 125.
[4] *Report* of 1776, p. 254, where several of the houses are described.
[5] There may be a direct connection. Bentham's "Industry-houses" (above, p. 314, n. 2) were avowedly an improvement on the East Anglian type.
[6] Webb, *op. cit.* p. 118 *sqq.*

building Houses of Industry. All this was after one of the best-known pieces of eighteenth-century poor law legislation, Gilbert's Act of 1782 (22 Geo. III, c. 83), had provided general, but optional, facilities for the union of parishes; though in fact the Shropshire Unions were created by special Acts and were not Gilbert Unions.

During the fifty years between this Act and the commission of 1832, but mainly during the war years 1795–1815, over nine hundred parishes grouped themselves into some sixty-seven "Gilbert incorporations." But as the total number of parishes, or distinct poor law units of administration in England and Wales, was nearer sixteen than fifteen thousand, the new arrangement was not of great national importance. Moreover, these Gilbert incorporations were localised. Ten of them were in Leicestershire, nine in Norfolk, eight in Yorkshire, seven in Kent, five in Sussex. The rest were very widely scattered, but there were never more than three in any single county. There were none in Hereford, Worcester, Gloucester, Wiltshire, Dorset, Somerset, Devon or Cornwall; none in Cambridge, Huntingdon, Bedford, Buckingham and Oxford; none in Northumberland or Durham. About a seventh of all the Gilbertised parishes were in Leicester, where the unions were "most capriciously put together" and much intermixed. There would be a nucleus of one or two dominating parishes who associated with themselves other parishes, contiguous or not was immaterial, which seemed to them useful allies. Consequently a Gilbert Union by no means implied a well-placed central workhouse, though sometimes it had one[1].

Without either special Act of parliament or the adoption of Gilbert's Act many parishes, up and down the country, possessed institutions usually called workhouses, and very many more possessed houses which had never made any pretence of being houses of industry, but were simply shelters for the impotent and destitute poor. Some idea of the geographical distribution of the workhouses, towards the end of the eighteenth century, can be gathered from a series of returns made in (1776–7) at the instigation of Thomas Gilbert, of Gilbert's Act,

---

[1] For Gilbert incorporations see Twistleton, E., *Report on Local Acts. Ninth Report of the Poor Law Commissioners*, 1843 (XXI). The figures are difficult: Twistleton knew no accurate list of incorporations. For the Leicestershire unions see Hall, R., in *Second Report of the Poor Law Commissioners*, 1836 (XXIX), part I, 396 *sqq.*

at that time Member of Parliament for Lichfield. The returns are no doubt defective, as eighteenth-century returns often are; but they are unique. Nor is there reason to suppose that, apart from the creation of the Gilbert and other unions after 1782, there was any important change in the distribution and character of the workhouses between 1777 and the reign of George IV. That there was some change in the use made of the houses will appear as the later evidence is examined.

The 1777 return was an appendix to returns, then first made by all parishes, of the money raised by rates and spent for the relief of the poor[1]. The local authorities were asked to report also on the number of "workhouses" and the number of persons each house would accommodate. Monmouth reported no workhouses, Rutland four, Westmorland nine, Hereford seventeen—of which ten small ones were in the city and one big one at Ross—the East Riding of Yorkshire eighteen, all tiny except one at Beverley. Between twenty and thirty were reported from Berkshire, Cornwall, Derbyshire, Dorset, Huntingdon, London and Westminster, Norfolk, Northumberland, Nottingham, Oxford, Warwick and Worcester. All Wales reported nineteen, of which eleven were in Pembrokeshire. At the other end of the scale come the one hundred and forty-two houses of Essex, nineteen of which could hold more than fifty persons[2]; the one hundred and thirty-two of Kent; the one hundred and seventeen of Sussex; the ninety-four of Suffolk, of which Ipswich alone had thirteen, one to each parish; the sixty-seven of Surrey; the sixty-one of Middlesex and the sixty of Hertfordshire. Another well-housed group of counties was in the South-West, Devon with ninety-five houses and Somerset with seventy-five. The houses of Devon were mostly in its numerous small ancient boroughs—Honiton, Bampton, Axminster, Barnstaple, after their kind; but a house to hold thirty people is reported from the deep country of Sampford Courtenay, nor is it an isolated case. In the industrial North, the West Riding had ninety-nine houses, seven in Leeds alone; Lancashire fifty-five, that of Liverpool, with a capacity of 600, being one of the largest in the country; and Durham forty-seven. The remaining counties with more than forty were Leicester, Hampshire, Lincoln and Northampton.

---

[1] *Reports...not inserted in the Journals*, IX. 297.
[2] Essex contained at that time 413 parishes. *V.C.H. Essex*, II. 330.

The distribution and character of the houses in a completely rural county, whose largest town had under 10,000 inhabitants, is well illustrated from Cambridgeshire. Cambridge itself had nine parochial houses[1]. The parish of Rampton, which in 1801 had a population of 162, was said to have six. This is either a row of cottages or a misprint; for even six cottages seems a high figure for the population. The rest were scattered, never more than one in each place, among the few small towns—Ely, March, Wisbech, Chatteris—and the big villages—Cottenham, Soham, Wicken, Thorney, Haddenham—of the county proper and the Isle of Ely.

In the third quarter of the eighteenth century workhouses had, as a rule, deserved the name. Serious attempts were still generally being made to set the poor on work, in the Elizabethan phrase. Apart from the work done in the East Anglian Hundred houses and the model Shrewsbury house, weaving and spinning are found in almost all the old municipal houses[2]. At Chester the inmates were set to "their respective trades." In Gloucester some at any rate made pins; and so on. But already the Bristol house, the provincial pioneer of the system, had become a poor house and infirmary exclusively—there were no able-bodied poor in it except the nurses and servants. The big Norwich house was, as has been seen, mixed in character; so was that of Liverpool. All, it may certainly be assumed, had at least a flavour of the poorhouse. It may, however, be taken for granted that, when any place reported a workhouse in 1776–7, those who made the report meant to imply something more than the mere poorhouse—a cottage or two with a few impotent folk or orphans—which was to be found in a vast number of parishes. The Rampton return, among others, makes it clear that the two types of institution might be confused. A cottage where infirm women and children were supposed to spin might be described as a workhouse. But the returns of 1776–7 are in general agreement with the fragmentary reports of the Assistant Commissioners of 1832–4 about workhouse geography[3]. At that time, for example, workhouses are said to be rare in Oxford, in Hereford, in Monmouth and in Wales

---

[1] Created under the Act of 1722. They were for the deserving poor. Town undesirables went to the House of Correction, the "Spinning House," which survived till 1901; county undesirables to the House adjoining the Castle Gaol. Stokes, *Cambs. Ant. Soc.* XI. 70–142; Gray, *The Town of Cambridge* (1925), p. 100; Hampson, E. M., *The Treatment of Poverty in Cambridgeshire* (1934), p. 71.

[2] Facts from the *Report on Houses of Industry of 1776*.

[3] *Report of the Poor Law Commissioners*, Ap. A, "Workhouses," 1834 (XXVIII).

—just as in 1777. On the other hand, the existence, at both dates, of many poorhouses where workhouses were rare is also illustrated from Hereford. "The majority of parishes in Shropshire and Hereford possess...either a workhouse or a poorhouse," says the reporter[1].

The wholesale adoption of outdoor relief, in all its forms, after 1795 stopped the creation of new workhouses and tended to change the character of the old. Gilbert's Act was, in more ways than one, responsible for this. Whether adopted or not by a given parish or group of parishes, its 29th section, which stated that only "such as are become indigent...and are unable to acquire a maintenance by their labour," together with orphans, should be sent to poorhouses, was a definite legislative discouragement of any provision of work for the able-bodied; while its notorious 32nd section which instructed the authorities to find work for anyone "able and willing," "suited to his or her strength and capacity in any parish or place near the place of his or her residence"; to maintain such persons, or cause them to be maintained, until the work was found, "and during the time of such work"; and to make up any deficiency between their earnings and the cost of their maintenance from the rates, gave legislative encouragement to a system of supplementing wages which already existed[2], and prepared the way for that Speenhamland emergency policy which became, over so great a part of England, the standing policy for a whole generation. The obligation to find work "near the place of his or her residence" discouraged the provision of a central workhouse or poorhouse in large Gilbert Unions, especially in the chaotic and mixed up unions of Leicestershire.

The existing workhouses, some of which had ceased to deserve the name before 1782, rapidly dropped into line after 1795. "In general merely poorhouses and infirmaries," says the Index to the *Report* of 1834, *s.v.* "Workhouses." Work of a more or less disciplinary sort continued in some of the well-managed houses. The great Liverpool house, extended in the nineteenth century and now the largest in the kingdom—it could house 1750 souls—fell into the hands of a first-rate

[1] *Report of the Poor Law Commissioners*, Ap. A, "Workhouses," 1834 (XXVIII), p. 659.

[2] Ashby showed in 1912, *op. cit.* p. 156, that the supplementing of wages from the rates did not start at Speenhamland. Marshall, D. C., *The English Poor in the Eighteenth Century* (1926), p. 104, shows that it was "at least a century old" in 1795.

governor about the year 1804, who was still in office in 1832–4[1]. He laid great stress on classification; he kept the sexes rigidly separate; he paid a surgeon a stipend of £300; and he saw to it that rough work, such as oakum-picking, was done by the able-bodied inmates. Ramsgate in 1832–3 had a house which was "very well managed under Gilbert's Act"[2]: real work was done there. Other well-managed houses had dropped all pretence of work and concentrated on assistance to the sick and indigent. That at Manchester, "professedly and in fact a poorhouse," was well but expensively conducted: it was not in the least deterrent as "admission was rather a matter of favour."[3] The old house at Bristol continued to be what it had been fifty years earlier, "rather an infirmary and hospital" than a workhouse, and "extremely well regulated."[4]

Many of the old municipal workhouses were in a shocking condition. It was to their address that all the complaints of the commissioners of 1832 were directed in their main report; though the wage problem which was the commissioners' chief preoccupation was essentially a rural one. There was the notorious House of Industry at Oxford, of which it was said "there is in fact no government." The sexes were mixed; no work was done; ingress and egress were almost free; in a spacious and uncontrolled garden the inmates took their ease at all hours, and so there was every reason to suspect "internal bastardy." There was the ancient house at Lynn—now "very bad": "no classification; no employment." At Chatham the house was in a "dreadful state." No work was done; the residents went freely out and in; fed on the finest wheaten bread and supplied with good ale brewed on the premises, they stood out for porter and gin—and got them. Inside the house, under the dining-hall, with a grating opening on the court, was the Chatham "cage," into which the human scourings of a dockyard town were dumped day and night—there to remain sometimes for two or three weeks in daily intercourse, through the bars, with the impotent, orphaned, and able-bodied poor[5].

The reformers' campaign, naturally and rightly, kept these things before the public and has kept them before history. It is therefore equally right that other well-managed houses should be recorded here—the "excellent" house at Lincoln and the

---

[1] *Report* of 1834, Ap. A, p. 914.   [2] *Ibid.* p. 218.
[3] *Ibid.* p. 922.   [4] *Ibid.* p. 512.
[5] Oxford, p. 988, Lynn, p. 596, Chatham, p. 220.

well-regulated houses of Brighton, Chichester, Canterbury, Carlisle, Ongar—like Ramsgate, a Gilbert house—and Poole, to take illustrations from various parts of the country[1]. Good and bad houses alike had long since abandoned any thought of productive, as opposed to disciplinary, work for the inmates. Coventry had a large house, built under a local act. It would hold three hundred or more. Started as a House of Industry, it had become a mere poorhouse round about 1800, as the town clerk reported in 1818[2].

No better than the old municipal workhouses were the incorporations of East Anglia and Shropshire. Their decline in efficiency was probably inevitable, in view of defects in their constitution and management which were apparent almost from the first; but the actual course of the decline was determined by the spread of outdoor relief. One of them, the Incorporated House of Industry of the Suffolk Hundreds of Loes and Wilford, was dissolved in 1824 for two significant reasons—outdoor relief of one sort or another came cheaper to the ratepayer than relief in the House; and residence in the House was said to be ruinous to morals[3]. It was also said to be very attractive in all these East Anglian Incorporations—to a certain class of rather disreputable poor person, it may be assumed; perhaps also to the impotent and aged, for the houses were roomy. One thing at least, a severe medical Assistant Poor Law Commissioner reported in 1836[4], the East Anglian Incorporations had in common—"a departure from the principles of management on which they were originally founded," that is to say, the principles of classification of the inmates and productive labour. "Outdoor relief was rapidly substituted for indoor maintenance [during the nineteenth century]; the House...became merely a house of reception for the aged and infirm or for the able-bodied upon emergencies."[5]   In Shropshire the Union Houses of Oswestry and Ellesmere, visited by an Assistant Commissioner in 1832, were found in the same case—no true work; no proper classification; "a lamentable falling off in their

---

[1] Lincoln in Ap. A, part II (XXIX), p. 132. The rest in part I. p. 531, 533, 217, 321, 225, 12. The list is not exhaustive.

[2] *S. C. on the Poor Laws*, 1818. *Second Report*, p. 185.

[3] Ap. A, part I, p. 373, and *Second Report of Poor Law Commissioners*, 1836, Ap. B, p. 154. Report of J. P. Kay, M.D., on the East Anglian Incorporation.

[4] Dr Kay.

[5] This statement applies to Loes and Wilford: the other Suffolk houses were "not much dissimilar": those of Norfolk a trifle better. So Dr Kay, p. 154.

practical working and effect."[1] Only the Incorporated Guardians of the Isle of Wight—modelled on the Suffolk Incorporations in 1770; very famous in their day; and possessed of an ample workhouse in Parkhurst Forest—escaped the general censure. Their administration was said to be fair. There was real work done in their house. But the separation of the sexes was not so thoroughly carried out as the visiting commissioner could have wished[2].

When Sir George Nicholls, who had knowledge if some bias, wrote that the "parish poorhouses, mis-called workhouses," before 1832, "were actually little better than receptacles for the vile, the dissolute, and depraved, together with some who were infirm or imbecile, and a few who were simply destitute and dependent—the whole living promiscuously together... without discipline or classification,"[3] he presumably had in the front of his mind those houses of small one-parish towns and big villages which he knew best. He had himself helped to make a bad parish house into a "good" one in the little market town of Southwell, during the 'twenties, and that no doubt affected his mental picture. (Residence in the Southwell house had been made "as disagreeable as was consistent with...health."[4]) He speaks of buildings "not often constructed for workhouses, but often hired or purchased for the occasion...generally of insufficient size, and always unsuitable in arrangement," whose "management was subject to negligence, partiality, and fraud." "Such parish houses," he concludes, "the author has seen." The Southwell house served not only the town, which in 1831 had a population of 3051, but also the surrounding district: "the district poorhouse at Southwell increases the Population," is the footnote in the census[5].

True village poorhouses interested the commissioners of 1832 very little, and it is not easy to get a satisfactory picture

---

[1] *Report* of 1834, Ap. A, p. 660.

[2] *Ibid.* p. 305. For their history Webb, *op. cit.* p. 138.

[3] *History of the English Poor Law* (ed. of 1898), II. 101.

[4] *S. C. on Agriculture*, 1833, Q. 11952. Evidence of a Notts. witness who was proud of the Southwell reforms, which had been imitated elsewhere in the county. Among other measures adopted at Southwell were "to prevent any from going out or seeing visitors: to prevent smoking: to disallow beer." *Report* of 1834, p. 231. Nicholls, who up to 1815 was at sea in the East India Company's service, became overseer of the poor at Southwell in 1821. There he worked under Prebendary J. T. Becher who took up the problem of the Southwell poor in 1818-19.

[5] *Census of* 1831, Summary vol. p. 205.

of their distribution[1]. Accounts of their recent creation, as a means of economy and de-pauperisation, illustrate their sporadic character, at an earlier date, and confirm general references to the same fact. Leckhamstead, Berkshire, for example, one of the commissioners' model parishes, "by the establishment, in the autumn of 1827, of a poorhouse for the maintenance of the aged and infirm, and for the employment of children...reduced the expenses of the parish about one-third."[2] Llangattock in Brecon did the same, making "a small poorhouse out of some houses adjoining one another."[3] Both poorhouse and workhouse had been exceptional in Wales, especially in rural districts[4]. In England it would seem that the small parish poorhouse, like the larger workhouse, had either deteriorated or gone out of use during the period of indiscriminate outdoor relief, in those districts where it had been common.

In Hereford and Shropshire, as has been seen, most parishes were said to have either a workhouse or a poorhouse. In Warwick, on the other hand, poorhouses were not common[5]. In Wiltshire apparently they were. Poulett Scrope, who was a Wiltshire justice, wrote in 1831 of "the parish workhouse" where labourers were "shut away from their wives"—which suggests severe discipline—as a normal institution[6]. Workhouses were declining in numbers in Hereford, because the poor could be kept more cheaply by other means. Whether this applied also to poorhouses is not stated. A piece of evidence from Somerset, and the constant confusion at this time of the terms workhouse and poorhouse, suggests that it did. "There are small workhouses in almost every parish," a Somerset Justice said in 1818, "but more *in terrorem* than being fitted or regulated as a workhouse."[7] A picture rises of the Justice saying "it may come to the workhouse, you know," when sanctioning the grant of relief to a doubtful character, and of the character remaining reasonably undismayed. Since allowances and other forms of out relief were emptying the big East Anglian institutions, the decadence of small village houses may be assumed with some confidence, even where it is not recorded. A few

[1] There is abundant room for such county studies as that of Mr Ashby.
[2] *Report*, p. 231.   [3] *Ibid.*
[4] They were "not common and generally disapproved." Ap. A, part II. p. 173.
[5] Ashby, *op. cit.* p. 120.
[6] *A letter to the Magistrates of the South of England*, p. 8.
[7] *S. C. on the Poor Laws*, p. 174.

cottages put at the disposal of old sick folk, and arrangements for boarding out or apprenticing a few children, met the case as the parish officials saw it. Those six "workhouses" of 1777 at Rampton, Cambs.—if they really existed—would probably not have been so returned in 1821. Perhaps the parish put poor old folk into them without charging rent, an ancient and very common form of relief all over the country. Perhaps that was what it had been doing in 1777. Indeed, in many parishes at all times, little more was necessary. Fortunately not every place in England and Wales kept a group of able-bodied unemployed or half-employed; though very many kept families which, as things had worked out, could not live on their earnings.

With workhouse and poorhouse accommodation stationary or declining, a population growing fast, Irish immigration spreading to rural districts, rural wages held down in many places by the way the poor law was worked, and the price of bread—which regulated much of the relief—abnormally high, the growing drain on the poor rates, during the first twenty years of the nineteenth century, for allowances in aid of wages and other forms of outdoor relief is comprehensible enough. In the towns there were the special drains set up by decaying trades—at Oldham a strict poor law authority could not refuse to give regular help to hand-loom weavers in 1832[1]—by the demobilised men in 1815–16, and by those thrown out of work by the severe commercial depressions in 1816 and 1825.

In many successive editions, from 1803 to 1826, Malthus reproduced the rather misleading footnote—"if the poor's rates continue increasing so rapidly as they have done on the average of the last ten years, how melancholy are our future prospects." In the ten years before his 1817 edition the growth had no doubt been considerable; but there was no obvious rise in the ten years before the edition of 1826. The figures can be so handled as to show a fall of £1,000,000[2]. The peak year had

---

[1] *Report* of 1834, Ap. A, part 1. p. 918.

[2] By comparing 1826 with 1817. The figures are:

1815	£5,400,000	1821	£7,000,000
1816	£5,700,000	1822	£6,400,000
1817	£6,900,000	1823	£5,800,000
1818	£7,900,000	1824	£5,700,000
1819	£7,500,000	1825	£5,800,000
1820	£7,300,000	1826	£5,900,000

There are no figures for 1804–10: the figure in 1803 was £4,300,000. These are the sums returned as actually spent "on the relief of the poor." The references

been 1818; and under any system of public assistance, other than the starvation system, relief would have been costly in 1818. Low food prices in the 'twenties helped to balance a growing population; so that at the end of the decade the burden, unnecessarily heavy no doubt, was yet much less crushing than anti-poor-law controversialists invariably assumed, and could not fairly be described as "an evil, in comparison of which the national debt, with all its magnitude of terror, is of little moment."[1]

In 1830–1 the sum actually expended for the relief of the poor in England and Wales was £6,800,000[2]. The debt charge that year, including redemption, was £31,000,000, and the total national dividend of England and Wales, if Parnell's estimate of £300,000,000 for Great Britain was nearly correct, must have been upwards of £250,000,000. South Britain paid its poor, including considerable sums which should have gone to them in wages, less than $2\frac{3}{4}$ per cent., and paid in poor rates not $3\frac{1}{3}$ per cent., of its income—a very tolerable charge, curiously near the 3 per cent. income tax which the prosperous island of Guernsey spent on its consolidated system of poor relief[3]. Reckoned by heads, the sum actually spent in poor relief works out at 9s. 9d. a year for each soul in England and Wales, a formidable figure in the hands of anti-poor-law statisticians. It can, however, be looked at in a way which makes it seem less terrible. Something like 2s. per head per week was about the least on which a family of four or five could subsist, at the absolute minimum standard of comfort, during the 'twenties[4]. On that scale, the 9s. 9d. would have kept the whole population for rather less than five weeks, or between 8 and 9 per cent. of the population, including an appropriate proportion of infants in arms, for the whole year. A Frenchman, consulted by the commissioners of 1832, said that this was a burden which England could easily bear, and must bear, "parce qu'il est une conséquence forcée des faits de son histoire et de son immense

in Malthus are—ed. 1803, p. 536; 1806, II. 394; 1817, III. 176; 1826, II. 335. Ed. 4, between 1806 and 1817, is not in the B.M.

[1] Malthus, ed. 1826, II. 335.
[2] The total sum raised by rates was £8,280,000.
[3] Above, p. 350.
[4] There were places in Eastern England where a man and wife with four children were refused poor relief when they had 10s. a week; but in manufacturing districts 12s. for such a family was often treated as a case of urgent need. Bishop Blomfield before the *Committee on Emigration*, 1826–7, Q. 2298.

prospérité."[1] The Commissioners disagreed with him but printed his Memorandum.

But the burden can be regarded quantitatively in a way which, while it cannot add to its gross weight, indicates the points at which it galled and helps to justify contemporary alarm. Probably a sum not less than £3,000,000 out of the £6,800,000 was spent on the agricultural labouring class[2], and that mainly in the South. Lancashire and the West Riding, with all their urban poverty and the daily growing problem of the hand-loom weavers, only spent £293,000 and £275,000 respectively on relief of the poor, during the year which ended in March 1831[3]. Northumberland and Durham, spared the poverty problems of the textile industries and, like Lancashire and the West Riding, blessed with a very fair level of rural wages, spent only £74,000 and £82,000. Norfolk spent £299,000 (but she had a decaying textile industry), Suffolk £271,000, and the almost townless Sussex £264,000. Kent managed to spend £346,000; but she had the Thames waterside population to handle, from Deptford to Sheerness. Surrey, partly metropolitan, spent £265,000, and Essex, with a waterside if hardly as yet a metropolitan problem of poverty, spent £273,000. Hampshire Wiltshire and Devon, all three rural big and populous, were also heavy spenders.

There were some 600,000 families of agricultural wage earners in England and Wales in 1831[4]. Assuming an average family of 4·5 persons, requiring 9s. a week to keep them on the minimum scale, the £5 per family which £3,000,000 allows for would suggest that the average family was dependent for more than one-fifth of its minimum needs on the state. Enough was spent to allow of just over eleven weeks' absolute dependence every year for all. But it has been seen how little was spent in the North; and £289,000 sufficed for the whole of Wales. The single county of Sussex spent nearly as much as Wales, and

---

[1] J. F. Lullin de Chateauvieux, author of the *Manuscrit de Sainte-Hélène* (1817) and *Lettres de Saint-James* (1822). A Swiss by birth and death († 1842) he was effectively a Frenchman. A Memorandum on the problems of poverty in France and England, *Report* of 1834 (XXXVIII), Ap. F, p. 33.

[2] The figure has been arrived at by assuming that nearly all the Middlesex, Lancashire and West Riding expenditure; 40 per cent. of that of Surrey, Kent, Essex, Norfolk and Leicester; and 33 per cent. in all other counties was urban or industrial.

[3] *Poor Rates. Abstract of Returns*, for the year ending March 25, 1831 1831–2 (XLIV), p. 449.

[4] Above, p. 113.

nearly twice as much per head as the average for the whole
country (19s. 4d. in place of 9s. 9d)[1]. Enough was paid out
there to keep all the Hobden and Iggulden families, and their
like, alive for many more than eleven weeks in the year[2].

Scotland, so the Select Committee on the Poor Laws of 1817
reported, had managed a law very like the English law so
differently that the Committee was bound to ascribe the difference to the greater enlightenment of the Scottish parochial
administrative authority, the heritors and kirk session, compared with the churchwardens and overseers of England and
Wales[3]. Their admiration was paid to the economy and the
rarity of relief for the able-bodied which marked Scottish
administration. They had before them a somewhat complacent
memorandum on that system supplied by a committee of the
General Assembly of the Kirk[4]. But it seems that they did not
fully apprehend some fundamental differences in the laws of
the two countries. Deeply embedded in the English law was
the right of the "valid" poor man to maintenance in exchange
for labour. Whether that labour might be done anywhere or
whether it should be done only in workhouses, properly
organised and disciplined, was a matter of current controversy;
but only the small group who, with Malthus, spoke of the
"original ill-conception" of the Statute of Elizabeth were ready
to challenge the right. In Scotland no such legal right had ever
existed. The Statute of 1579, c. 74, on which the system rested,
recognised only the right of those who, either from age or other
disability, "of necessitie mon live bee alms"—the impotent
poor of the Elizabethan classification[5]. Nor was assessment,
the levying of a poor rate, compulsory. The local authority
might resort to it if it so desired; but down to the middle of
the eighteenth century it had resorted to it very seldom. Col-

[1] The county averages per head are given in Porter's *Progress*, p. 96. The
year here taken is 1831: in 1811 Sussex had spent 32s.! Sussex was always
the highest. Next to it, in 1831, came Bucks (18s. 8d. per head), Suffolk
(18s. 3d.), Essex (17s. 2d.), Oxford (17s. 1d.), Bedford (16s. 11d.).

[2] For these families see Rudyard Kipling's Sussex stories, *passim*. Sussex,
Suffolk, and Essex had been little affected by enclosure; the others a great
deal. Above, p. 20.

[3] *S. C. on the Poor Law*, 1817 (VI. I), p. 21.   *Report* of 1817, Ap. A.

[5] See the Memorandum of 1817, also Nicholls, Sir G., *Hist. of the Scottish
Poor Law* (1856); Lamond, R. P., *The Scottish Poor Laws* (1892); Loch, C. S.,
"Poor Relief in Scotland...1791–1891," *S.J.* 1898; "Poor Law, Scottish," in
Dic. Pol. Econ. [*Memo. on...the Scots Poor Law Prior to 1845*, by Prof. Smart,
in *Royal Commission on Poor Law*, 1909 (XXXVIII).]

lections in church and the investment of charitable bequests had supplied all that the heritors and session deemed necessary, and personal charity had done the rest. So it still was in nearly all the "landward," and in a few of the urban, parishes of Scotland in 1820–30. A good many landward parishes had tried assessment, but most of them—so the Committee of the Kirk reported—had dropped it before 1817, because it led to a pauper influx. But it should be noted that, without any formal assessment, the heritors not infrequently made up the difference between what was gathered in church and what the poor needed by a private levy among themselves, proportional to their property in the parish[1].

The parochial authorities grouped those who "of necessitie mon live bee alms" into two classes, the enrolled poor, impotent persons whose names were entered on the rolls of the parish as permanent claimants on relief, and the occasional poor[2]. The second class, originally conceived of as persons suffering from temporary disablement, sickness, or other misfortune, and described in 1817 as the industrious poor, might have been swollen in the industrial areas by the inclusion of those out of work or short of work; but apparently this had been little done. Scottish rural society, with its many small cultivators and its long-hired labourers living in or housed on the farms[3], had offered few temptations to the abuses most frequent in England. In a well-managed Scottish town parish, the elders administered relief in person, knowing their districts and their poor, and strict to observe the law.

With full justice, no doubt, the Committee of the General Assembly explained that the tiny grants made by the heritors and session in many country districts were to be explained by the strong family and neighbourly feelings among the Scottish peasantry, which ensured a measure of private assistance for nearly all the very poor.

"In the great majority of our Scottish parishes," Thomas Chalmers, the militant advocate of the old parochial system, wrote in 1823, "all which the administrators of the public charity profess to do is to 'give

---

[1] The point is emphasised in the patriotic English *Defence of the English Poor-Laws...being the substance of a Letter addressed to Mr Canning in 1823. By a Select Vestryman of the Parish of Putney.* 1831.

[2] The statistics of enrolled poor at the time of the Scottish *Statistical Account* (1791–8) showed 18·16 per 1000 of the population. A return of 1818 gave 25·04 per 1000, but this may include occasional poor, though probably it does not. Loch, *op. cit.* p. 279–80.   [3] Above, p. 30.

in aid.' They do not hold themselves responsible for the entire subsistence of any of their paupers; they presume in the general, on other resources, without inquiring specifically either into the nature or the amount of them. It says much for the truth of our whole speculation [that the absence of a compulsory provision for the poor stimulates both charity and self-help] that in this presumption they are almost never disappointed; and that whether in the kindness of relatives, or the sympathy of neighbours, or the many indefinable shifts and capabilities of the pauper himself, there do cast up to him the items of a maintenance."[1]

What sort of a maintenance was cast up by the indefinable shifts and capabilities of the Cowgate and the Trongate wynds in the 'twenties, even when the poor fund was helped out by an assessment, is a matter for inquiry and reflection. It was mean enough in the 'thirties and 'forties. Possibly Scottish urban conditions worsened, certainly they widened, between 1823 and 1843; the personal tie between the Kirk Session and the poor grew weaker; but evidence laid before parliament in 1844 drew something like a cry of disgust from that very unemotional statistician, G. R. Porter.

It requires, indeed, no small degree of forbearance to limit all comment to an expression of astonishment that in any country calling itself Christian, and especially in one where so much stress is laid on the outward observances of religion, a degree of heartless neglect as regards the calls of humanity, such as is recorded by the Commissioners, could have been allowed to exist[2].

Not even the largest Scottish towns, when Chalmers was writing, had gone over entirely to the system of assessment and compulsory provision. Scotland was at the cross roads and that was why he fought. "In most of the border parishes of Scotland [by infection from England], as well as in many of its large towns...there is a fund raised by voluntary contribution at the Church doors; and, to help out the supposed deficiencies of this, there is, moreover, a fund raised by legal assessment."[3] The parish of St Cuthbert, which in 1821 contained over 50,000 out of the 138,000 people of greater Edinburgh, had resorted to assessment about the year 1770[4]: it also had a work house. So had Edinburgh City; but the City had struggled on without an assessment until well into the nineteenth century[5].

---

[1] *The Christian and Civic Economy of Large Towns*, II. (1823), p. 199. Vol. III came out in 1826.
[2] *Progress of the Nation*, p. 101. And below, p. 585 *sqq*.
[3] Chalmers, II. *op. cit.* 94.   [4] "Over fifty years." *Memorandum* of 1817.
[5] "Only of late"—*Memorandum* of 1817.

Chalmers' campaign, for the maintenance of the traditional Scottish parochial organisation and the virtues which rendered it possible and were, in their turn, encouraged by it, coincided so exactly with the well-deserved outburst of indignation against the abuses of the English system that it gained a great access of power. The Committee of the General Assembly had explained to parliament in 1817 that the adoption of assessment in a Scottish parish had almost always led to a steady rise in expenditure: the poor, it was believed, ceased to operate their "indefinable shifts and capabilities" so soon as they knew that they could dip into a bottomless impersonal bag of parish rates. Many reformers in England were so anxious to develop the capabilities of the English poor, and to keep down English rates, that they were ready—as the 1817 report shows—to load the Scottish system with uncritical admiration, and wish Chalmers God-speed. Yet the Committee of the Kirk had admitted that where dissenters were many, or where the seating accommodation of the churches was far below the population, church-door collections did not in fact suffice. In urban England at least, these were the normal conditions.

Both existed, and tended to increase, in Glasgow, where Chalmers ministered and fought from 1815 to 1823. The city proper had only nine or ten parish churches, and a few chapels of ease, for a population of 75,000, in 1821. Besides these, it had for the secession sects—Burghers, Anti-Burghers and Relief Kirk—seven; for Methodists, Independents and Baptists, seven; for Jews, two; for Unitarians, Glassites, Bereans, Universalists and Roman Catholics, each one[1]. When Chalmers was inducted to the Tron parish, in 1815, the City had a compulsory assessment, to which the church-door contributions were added. The central organisation was the general session, the ecclesiastical authority of the ancient undivided parish of Glasgow, and its instrument the town hospital—an infirmary-poorhouse built in 1733. In the 'twenties the hospital had about 500 in-patients, and about the same number of out-pensioners. What money, raised by assessment and collections, was not spent centrally was returned for disbursement by the elders in the parishes. Similar arrangements existed in most Scottish towns. In scarcely any, except one-parish towns, was "there a pure independent parochial administration."[2]

---

[1] The list comes from the foreigner Meidinger (*Reisen*, II. 99), so may not be exact in every detail.   [2] Chalmers, *op. cit.* II. 97.

Chalmers spoke severely of the waste, ostentation, bureaucratic methods, and pauperising influence of centralised management.

The humble doings of a Kirk Session will not so mislead the families from dependence on their own natural and proper capabilities, as when the whole pauperism of the place is gathered into one reservoir, and made to blaze on the public view, from the lofty apex of a great and conspicuous institution[1].

On taking over the newly made parish of St John's, in 1820, Chalmers caused it to be cut off from the town hospital and the general session, and organised as a self-governing unit for poor relief[2]. The Outer-Kirk parish followed and others turned his way: his volume of 1823 was a cry to them to persevere, and so enable Glasgow to get rid of compulsory provision for the poor and return to a true Christian economy. He supported his appeal by arguments drawn from two Glasgow parishes which were not parts of Glasgow City—the Barony of Glasgow and the Gorbals. The Barony, the most populous parish in Scotland, had first resorted to an assessment in 1810. Up to that time its expenditure "for a large and wholly manufacturing population"—in 1801, 27,000, in 1811, 37,000—"seldom exceeded £600 annually," "proving," to Chalmers, "that for the legal system of relief, there exists no natural and permanent necessity"[3]; suggesting, to the historian, that the Barony poor must have suffered bitterly at times. It was perhaps not so deplorable as Chalmers supposed that, "after 1810, the expenditure became about five times greater than before, in the short space of seven years." Even £3000 a year would not be an outrageous expenditure for a wholly manufacturing population of nearly 30,000 souls, in the black years 1816–17.

The population of the Gorbals grew swiftly, from 5000 to 22,000, between 1811 and 1821. Its people were engaged in manufactures and riverside labour. Yet it "retained the simple parochial economy that was bequeathed to us from our ancestors and"—so Chalmers thought—"flourished under it." "This parish has never admitted an assessment—and the whole of its sessional expenditure for the poor is defrayed from a revenue of about £400 annually." Happy Gorbals! That its families were "in every way as well-conditioned, and as exempt from the rigours of extreme wretchedness, as are those of the assessed

---

[1] The blazing reservoir on an apex sounds hardly Scottish.
[2] Chalmers, *op. cit.* II. 139.   [3] *Ibid.* p. 181.

city to which it is contiguous"[1] may prove that assessment was
wasteful and did not of necessity cure social ills; it hardly
proves that the poor of the Gorbals had from society their
deserts. Perhaps some of them were driven into the assessed city.

The total Scottish official expenditure on the relief of the
poor in 1830-1 is not on record, but it can be estimated with
considerable certainty at about 1s. 3d. per head of the population. For the years 1807-16 the total from collections, sessional
funds, and assessments averaged 1s. 3¾d. per head and for the
years 1835-7, 1s. 3¼d.[2] There is no reason to assume any great
change during the intervening years. There can be no sort of
doubt that the Scottish poor helped themselves and one another
much more, and more effectively, than the English. It was not
mere ecclesiastical conservatism which made Chalmers fight
for "the simple parochial economy that was bequeathed to us
from our ancestors," nor a mere desire to lower the rates which
made English reformers admire the Scottish system. On the
other hand, there cannot be much doubt that the Scottish poor
lived harder than the English.

The results of that section of the English poor law which
dealt with destitute children had been—from one point of view
—unfortunate almost from the first. It was the duty of the
parochial authorities to apprentice them so that they might earn
an honest living. This duty was generally carried out during
the seventeenth and eighteenth centuries in some fashion. But
even before Queen Elizabeth died, the courts had ruled that
apprenticeship was not essential in unskilled trades; you could
become a costermonger without serving seven years. "So an
husbandman, tankard-bearer, brickmaker, porter, miller, and
suchlike"[3] were held to be trainable without apprenticeship.
In the skilled crafts, the ordinary apprentice came from a home
socially on a level with that of his master, and paid a substantial
entry fee. For such vacancies pauper children were not wanted,
and such fees the overseers did not very often care to pay. It
was inevitable therefore that the pauper apprentice should either

---

[1] Chalmers, op. cit. II. 185-6. Chalmers notes (II. 188) that the Gorbals
elders all lived in their parish and were personally concerned in its administration, a record greatly to their credit.

[2] Loch, op. cit. p. 283.

[3] Bland Brown and Tawney, English Economic History Select Documents
(1914), p. 356.

be bound to hard and exacting trades—like those of the land and sea—which required juvenile labour but held out no great prospects, or should fall into an inferior position when accepted by a skilled master-craftsman—like John Gilpin's friend the calender—or by a shopkeeping person like John Gilpin himself. In the house of Gilpin or the calender, the boy or girl apprentice was apt to be rather an underling or drudge than a pupil in craftsmanship or salesmanship[1].

New large-scale industries had come as a godsend to the parish overseers, during the third quarter of the eighteenth century. The outworker by the piece, who had been the typical industrial figure of the mid-century, was unable to relieve them of all their reserves of child labour[2]. The merchant, or the employer of outworkers, wanted only a small picked staff. But as the modern employer evolved there was a change. The situation as it was developing in the new industrial world of the Midlands, just before the rise of the cotton mills, is perfectly illuminated by a single sentence from a letter written by Matthew Boulton, Watt's partner, in 1768. He took no apprentices, he said, except " Fatherless Children, Parish Apprentices, and Hospital Boys, which are put to the most slavish part of our Business."[3] His was not "a scheme of business that will admit of a mediocrity of fortune to be employed in it...a person bred in it must either be a working journeyman...or he must be possessed of a very large fortune."[4] On these grounds he had declined to take a friend's nephew as apprentice. Boulton's business was an exceptional one, but his attitude towards parish apprentices and hospital boys was not. They were taken as a form of cheap labour, to pick up the rougher journeyman's jobs where no great skill was wanted, or—when taken on the land—to serve a master seven years for their keep, like the Lincolnshire poacher, and then become labourers[5].

[1] Dunlop, J., English Apprenticeship and Child Labour (1912), ch. 16, "Apprenticeship as a device of Poor Relief." George, M. D., London Life in the Eighteenth Century, ch. 5, "Parish Children and Poor Apprentices."

[2] Though pauper children were apprenticed to hand-loom weavers (Hutchins and Harrison, History of Factory Legislation, p. 20), framework knitters, journeyman shoemakers, and so on (George, op. cit. p. 233, 237, etc.) and, in the country, to small handicraftsmen (Marshall, D. C., op. cit. p. 357 above, n. 2).

[3] Lord, J., Capital and Steam Power (1923), p. 58, quoting the Tew MSS. of the Boulton family.

[4] Lord, op. cit. p. 91.

[5] "The neighbouring farmers willingly accept them." Porter, R., Observations on the Poor Laws (1775).

That they should have been drafted in considerable numbers from urban areas, especially from the metropolitan area, into the early cotton mills was perfectly natural. There, as all the world knows, many were shamefully abused; but not all. One of the largest of the early mills, Smalleys at Holywell in Flintshire, with its hundred and ninety-eight sash windows "which nightly exhibit a most glorious illumination," had no less than three hundred apprentices in 1795[1]. Boys and girls had their separate houses, "which were whitewashed twice a year and fumigated three times a week with tobacco smoke." There was a surgeon and a Sunday school. Three children to a bed was the maximum; "the larger sizes" slept only two; "and those who work in the night are so far from succeeding each other in the same beds that they do not even sleep in the same rooms." Of another model employer, Samuel Oldknow of Mellor by Stockport, local tradition preserves a fragrant memory. In the apprentice house of the early nineteenth century they had "porridge and bacon for breakfast, meat every day for dinner, puddings or pies on alternate days." Tradition also stands to the declaration that "no one ever had owt to complain of at Mellor."[2] Oldknow seems to have got most of his children from Clerkenwell Parish, the Duke of York's Orphanage at Chelsea, and other metropolitan sources. He only worked them from 6.0 a.m. to 7.0 p.m. There were factories whose hours were 5.0 to 8.0.

It was not the Smalleys and Oldknows but the rank and file of average sensual parish-apprentice-employing factory owners, including, oddly enough, himself, whom Sir Robert Peel the elder intended to control by his Health and Morals of Apprentices Act, 1802 (42 Geo. III, c. 73)[3]. It is not the least of Britain's debts to the Elizabethan poor law that this rider to it, for Peel's Act was nothing else, got on to the statute book early in the century. These were children for whom the state had accepted liability. For five-and-twenty years and more the state had been interpreting such liabilities more humanely than had once been its habit. Peel had no difficulty with parliament.

[1] Unwin, *Samuel Oldknow and the Arkwrights*, p. 95–6, quoting Pennant, T., *A History of...Holywell*, 1796.

[2] Unwin, *op. cit.* p. 173–4. Another witness puts "wheaten bread" in place of bacon in the breakfast *menu*. [For another model employer see the *Life of Kitty Wilkinson* quoted in Knowles, L. C. A., *The Ind. and Comm. Revolutions of the Nineteenth Century*, 1st ed. p. 92 n.]

[3] The fullest account is in Hutchins and Harrison, *op. cit.* p. 16–18.

He was the specialist: it is doubtful whether there was a single other employer of parish apprentices in the House: his colleagues, as he said later, were quite convinced of the necessity for action, and the first amendment carried was to insert the words "and other" between "cotton" and "factories."[1] Ineffective as it proved, Peel's Act stood unmodified in the 'twenties, and provided a rough framework into which other —and equally ineffective—legislation had already been fitted, and much more was soon to be introduced. It furnished the categories—working hours, for the parish apprentice, to be not more than twelve a day; work by night, for the parish apprentice, gradually to cease; sanitation and health to be cared for by two whitewashings of the factory every year, adequate ventilation, a free suit of clothes for each parish apprentice once a year, separate night quarters for boys and girls and one bed for every two of them (even when not of "the larger sizes"); education, of parish apprentices, to include the three R's and attendance at church at least once a month[2]; inspection, to be carried out by two justices of whom one was to be a clergyman. The Act applied to all cotton and woollen factories in which "twenty or more persons" were employed, presumably on the chance of their containing apprentices; it provided that all mills and factories should be registered with the clerk of the peace, so that the Justices might be kept informed of their liabilities; and, as its whitewashing and ventilation clauses were not made dependent on the presence of apprentices, they became, nominally at least, of universal application. Moreover, there was no age limit for apprentices: they might, in the language of the later factory code, be either children, young persons, or adults.

The Justices did not altogether neglect their duty, but the task was beyond them. The problem too was changing. Even before Peel's Act, some few apprenticing authorities seem to have regarded apprenticeship to a cotton mill as undesirable: the authorities of the Foundling Hospital maintained (in 1807) that only incorrigible girls had ever been sent to such places[3]. After the Act, the worse type of mill-owner realised that it was

---

[1] *Journal of the H. of C.* LVII. 303.

[2] In Scotland, they were to be examined by the Minister and, before the age of 18, to "be carried to the Parish Church to receive...the Sacrament." This was an amendment. *Journal of the H. of C.* LVII. 534.

[3] Unwin, *op. cit.* p. 172.

to his advantage to employ "free" child labour. That the Act was regarded as a serious nuisance by many manufacturers, petitions for its repeal from Manchester, Bolton, Stockport, Glasgow, Leeds, Keighley, Nantwich, Ashton-under-Lyne and other places show[1]. Failing to secure repeal they "declined to take apprentices and employed the children of paupers without any limitation."[2] Over a mill full of "free" boys and girls the intruding Justices had no power. It is true that from 1802 to 1811 the poor law authorities "within the Bills of Mortality," *i.e.* of greater London, still sent into the cotton mills three-quarters of the children apprenticed outside that area[3]; but on the average of the ten years this meant only 436 boys and girls a year, a less number than Owen found at New Lanark when he went there in 1799[4]. There were also local supplies of pauper children to be drawn upon. But the evidence is clear that, by the 'twenties, the apprentice problem had fallen into the background[5]. Steam had brought the big cotton mills to town and there were children enough at their doors.

So, when the movement for factory legislation was resumed after the wars, with Robert Owen as its prophet and organiser, and Robert Peel the elder once more as its leading parliamentary advocate, the question of principle was certain to be raised, although the discussions ranged along every question of expediency and detail. Here was not a mere problem of the poor law, of those wretched little wards of society to whose status there had always clung more than a touch of servility, since their wardship was first recognised in Tudor times, when an Englishman could still be a bondsman at law. Had the state any obligation to "free" children? Were not their parents the divinely constituted judges of all matters touching their welfare? If the state had an obligation to children in grave danger or distress, were these—the children in certain textile factories —the chief, or the only, claimants on its protection? And so

---

[1] *Journal of the H. of C.* LVIII. 148, 160, 191.

[2] Peel in the House, February 10, 1818. Hansard, XXVII. 264, quoted at length in Smart, *op. cit.* I. 658.

[3] From the *Report of the H. of C. Comm.* of 1815 on parish apprentices, printed in Hansard, XXX. 533.

[4] About 500 "pauper children." Owen's evidence, *S. C. on the State of...Children...in the Manufactories,* 1816 (III. 235), p. 20.

[5] It is doubtful whether, at any time, pauper apprentices formed a very large proportion of the cotton-mill staff. The London figures quoted are instructive in this connection.

to the problems of detail and expediency; whether or not the factory children really were overworked; the penalising of AB; the preferential treatment of CD; the undeserved slur cast upon the reputation of this industry or that great city, and the discouragement of "enterprise" and foreign trade[1]. Peel himself declared for free labour. But he could not think that little children who had not a will of their own could be called free labourers: he was suggesting that sixteen should be the age at which they acquired a will and the burdens of freedom[2]. In one debate the younger Peel skilfully used the existing law to turn his opponents' flank. No one had challenged the protection of apprentices. Yet the master had an interest in keeping his apprentice healthy; he had no interest in a child hired by the day or the week and replaceable at a moment's notice from the overplus of the adjacent alleys. Here protection by the law was far more urgently called for[3]. So his father's unchallenged rider to the poor law supplied the needed *a fortiori* argument.

Lord Liverpool, in the Upper House, in 1818, did not rely on precedents or forensic arguments. In debate with James, Earl of Lauderdale, himself an economist almost of the first rank, who had invoked "the great principle of Political Economy, that labour ought to be left free," and thereby succeeded in holding up Peel's bill for a year, Liverpool said that as, in his opinion, it was a principle of the common law that children ought not to be overworked, he would like to see that principle recognised in so many words in the Act[4]. Although this argument was, in its turn, parried by Lord Eldon, who said that as the overworking of children was already indictable at common law there should be a general law for all trades or none at all[5], it expressed well enough that opinion of the average

---

[1] See the full summaries of the debates of 1815, 1816 and 1818 in Smart, *op. cit.* I. 442–3, 505–6, 658 *sqq.* It was in 1815 that Francis Horner quoted the agreement, mentioned before the committee, between a London parish and a Lancashire mill-owner that the mill-owner should take one idiot with every twenty sound children (Hansard, XXXI. 626). The case appears to be genuine, but it is hardly so representative as its quotation in every book on the subject since written might suggest.

[2] Speech of February 23, 1818. Hansard, XXXVII. 582.

[3] Speech of April 27, 1818. Hansard, XXXVIII. 354.

[4] Debate of May 7. Hansard, XXXVIII. 548, summarised in Smart, *op. cit.* I. 668–9.

[5] In February 1819. Hansard, XXXIX. 654. His argument is made more "Eldonian" than it really was in Smart, *op. cit.* I. 703.

member of parliament which prevails in divisions and becomes the voice of the state. Children were being overworked in a new and obvious way in new and unusually obvious institutions. The thing was not old enough to have become an interest, with almost a constitutional position, like the West India Interest and its slaves or the Shipping Interest and its navigation code. Hardly anyone in parliament was directly concerned in the profits of it, so that natural humanity was not blunted. The argument that legislation for one type of institution only, before the whole industrial field had been surveyed and mapped, was illogical and perhaps unfair might have appealed to a French Chamber, but was not likely to deter an assembly which regularly arrived at many of its most important economic decisions piecemeal, by private act.

As it emerged from parliament the Act of 1819 was much narrower than the draft prepared by Robert Owen on which Peel, and after Peel the Houses, had been working. It was in some ways narrower than the Health and Morals Act of 1802. Only cotton mills—the biggest, the most obvious, and reputed the worst of the factories[1]—were touched. Owen would have included all textile factories. Peel's date for the beginning of freedom to be overworked, the sixteenth birthday, was accepted: the limitation of the working day to twelve hours affected no one beyond that age. Ten years was the age originally suggested below which no child might go to a mill at all. Nine was the age finally agreed upon. Most important of all, perhaps, Owen's proposal to appoint salaried factory inspectors, to which Peel had attached considerable weight, when first he had asked leave to introduce a bill, in June 1815, dropped out[2]. In the end, therefore, 59 Geo. III, c. 66, an Act "to make further provision for the regulation of cotton mills and factories and for the better preservation of the health of young persons employed therein," proved a most ineffective instrument of preservation. In six years, only two convictions were obtained under it, and there was no doubt, during the middle 'twenties, that its various clauses were regularly broken or evaded. Nor were the three small amending or extending Acts of 1820, 1825

---

[1] The early flax mills were probably worse, the new worsted, and the long-established silk-throwing, mills at least as bad.

[2] See his speech in Hansard, xxxi. 624. It is sometimes suggested that the salaried inspector was a great nineteenth-century invention; but he was in the direct line of descent from the searchers and sealers of the eighteenth-century textile regulative Acts. Above, p. 337 *sqq.*

and 1831 (60 Geo. III, c. 4; 6 Geo. IV, c. 63 and 1 & 2 Will. IV, c. 39) of any general significance or efficacy[1].

Unimportant as the bill of 1825 was, the preparation and discussion of it were revealing and prophetic. Cam Hobhouse had it in hand. He spoke to Peel the younger. Peel referred him to Huskisson, Huskisson to George Philips of Manchester, for Manchester now had a voice in the Commons, though the working of the constitution made Philips sit for Wootton Bassett. Philips referred him to the Manchester Chamber of Commerce, that recently established sounding-board for the home voice of Manchester[2]. Hobhouse, who either did not consult the Chamber or paid no attention to its advice, was quite prepared to extend his proposal beyond cotton but thought, very wisely, that to tackle one large industry was enough for one man: there was no department at his back and no prejudice against piecemeal legislation on the benches about him. Also it was easier to get accurate information about cotton than about anything else. He was able to show that, even under his bill, cotton children would still work longer hours than adult carpenters, masons, bricklayers, blacksmiths or millwrights.

Philips' speeches showed both the strength and the weakness of the Manchester case. His experience of the existing laws, he said, led him to believe that this Act would not improve anyone's condition. He was probably right. He was convinced that it was better to work in a factory than outside, particularly if one were a weaver. Here he was probably at least half right. To the limitation of the hours of child labour he was not opposed: it was an excellent thing, if possible. But it was not possible without limiting the work of adults; and that—it was implied—was unthinkable. Having admitted so much, he concluded his speech on the second reading by arguing that wage and work contracts should never be interfered with, and that parliament would do well not to amend but to repeal all interfering laws. In committee he tried to discredit the bill by tracing its parentage, correctly, to the organised workpeople, the Grand Union of Operative Spinners, at a time when the House was very sensitive on this point of combination. Throughout, the standing—and, on the whole, just—grievance of the cotton men, that their trade was being singled out and pilloried

[1] Hutchins and Harrison, *op. cit.* p. 30–2. Smart, *op. cit.* II. 314.
[2] Cam Hobhouse's *Diary*, March 21, 1825, quoted in Smart, *op. cit.* II. 313 For the debates, Hansard (N.S.) XIII. 421–2, 643 *sqq.*, 1008 *sqq.*

more than it deserved, gave to his criticism that touch of indignation which makes opposition effective.

Huskisson and Peel did not go all the way with Philips, but
on this occasion they showed no zeal for the policy of control.
"As Parliament had thought it right to interfere with respect
to the cotton mills, certainly the more fully the provisions of
the former bill [that of 1819] were carried into operation the
better." Doubtless there were many things in every sort of
labour that one would wish otherwise; but if one so interfered
that the children got less employment or less pay—and the
masters said that this was the option—what then? That was
Huskisson. Peel asked the House "to pause before entering
too extensively into this field of legislation." He had supported
the approach of 1819, but like Huskisson he feared that, if
control were made too strict, children might be thrown on the
streets. Better the bread of affliction for the children than a
risk of no bread.

In his hesitations, his postulates, his limits; in his honesty
of purpose, his receptivity, his mastery of to-day's business
and his often blurred view of its relation with to-morrow's
needs, Peel might be taken as the embodiment of the British
state of the mid-nineteenth century. And that naturally enough
—since if the state, the economic state, from 1819 to 1850
was not precisely Peel, it was much more Peel than anyone else;
while after 1850 he kept his hand on it from the grave through
Gladstone whom he had formed. "Wanting imagination he
wanted prescience,"[1] Disraeli said of him after his death.
"There is a gentleman who never sees the end of a campaign,"
the Duke is believed to have said of him while alive, which
comes to much the same[2]. The state, in his or in other hands,
lacked prescience and did not see to the end of many of its
campaigns. "Things were in the saddle and rode mankind,"
and the state let them ride. Sometimes it seemed to be acting
on a reasoned policy of abstention; more often, perhaps, it was
not acting simply because it had no clear notion of what to do
for the best. Again and again it turned to some immediate
problem with thorough apprehension, but seldom to handle it
as one of a great chain of linked problems. Perhaps that should
not be expected of it, even by implication, since the state equipped
with prescience and sustained co-ordinating imagination has
not yet come down from the treasury of the ideas.

[1] *Lord George Bentinck*, p. 198.
[2] *Life of Disraeli*, II. 104, quoted without reference and perhaps legendary.

BOOK II

❧

THE EARLY
RAILWAY AGE

And along the iron veins that traverse the frame of our country, beat and flow the fiery pulses of its exertions, hotter and faster every hour. All vitality is concentrated through those throbbing arteries into the central cities; the country is passed over like a green sea by narrow bridges, and we are thrown back in continually closer crowds upon the city gates.

JOHN RUSKIN, *The Seven Lamps of Architecture*, 1849.

Pasha. The ships of the English swarm like flies; their printed calicoes cover the whole earth....All India is but an item in the Ledger-books of the Merchants, whose lumber-rooms are filled with ancient thrones!— whirr! whirr! all by wheels!—whiz! whiz! all by steam.

A. W. KINGLAKE, *Eothen*, 1845.

CHAPTER IX

THE RAILWAYS AND RAILWAY POLICY

THE locomotive engine did not win an easy victory; nor, in its early form, did it altogether deserve one. Towards the end of the year 1828, when the permanent way of the Manchester and Liverpool was far advanced, the traction problem was still unsolved. The promoters called in two outside experts, a Londoner and a midland engineer, to report. The report was hardly decisive. The consultants thought that the road might be run most economically with stationary engines and cables, if it was to be heavily worked at once. "But if any circumstances should induce the directors to proceed by degrees, and to proportion the power of conveyance to the demand, then we recommend locomotive engines on the line generally,"[1] with stationaries on two inclines. Stephenson pressed this alternative; for the outsiders had allowed that locomotives might have greater possibilities of improvement than stationaries. So came the Rainhill locomotive competition of October 1829, and Stephenson's triumph. Next year there appeared in a standard text-book of the day, *Galloway on the Steam Engine*, a gloomy account of locomotive prospects, evidently based on pre-Rainhill data. In their report for 1827, the directors of the Stockton and Darlington had pointed out how "as the result of the strict scrutiny into the subject...there appears to be a saving of nearly 30 per cent., in favour of haulage performed by the locomotive engine, when compared with its being done by horses." Not 30 per cent., wrote *Galloway*[2], and that on a line made to carry coals, where fuel costs will be negligible!

"These loco-motive engines have been long in use at Killingworth," he continued; but "notwithstanding the great exertions on the part of the inventor, Mr. Stephenson...there cannot be a better proof of the doubt entertained regarding their utility than the fact that it has been determined that no locomotive engine shall be used in the projected railway between Newcastle and Carlisle."

[1] See Smiles, *Lives of the Engineers*, III. 258 n. The source is *An Account of the Liverpool and Manchester Railway...by Hy. Booth, Esq., Treasurer* (1830).
[2] *Galloway on the Steam Engine*, 4th ed., 1830, p. 334. [Criticism of the early locomotive is challenged by Warren, J. G. H., *A Century of Locomotive Building* (1923).]

He had in mind the bill for that line which had received the royal assent on May 22, 1829. Clause 6 actually prohibited the use of locomotives. It also prohibited even stationary engines "within view of the Castle of Naworth or Corby Castle, or of the several mansion houses" of some half-dozen specified gentlemen. This was no doubt an enforced concession. Probably the promoters would have preferred freedom to use the locomotive, but there is no evidence that, at this time, they wished to use it[1]. Their line, when complete, would have a few heavy gradients, and for many years even Old George, as the early railway world knew him, would never lay out a heavy gradient for his locomotives. He told the people of Sheffield in 1836 that they could only get them into their town *via* Rotherham, and neither over nor through their hills[2].

In 1834, when part of the Carlisle line was nearing completion and the rails had to be ordered, the directors were still discussing horses. Horses would require four sidings to the mile on a single-line stretch between Prudhoe Haughs and Hexham: a locomotive could manage with a single siding, a saving of nearly £700 to the mile[3]. On their committee of management sat Nicholas Wood, whose *Practical Treatise on Railways* was now nearly ten years old, who had been an expert advocate of each forward step in railway development. In the end they decided to ask parliament to rescind the anti-locomotive clause of their original Act; and they felt so confident in the result that they immediately ordered an engine from Robert Stephenson and Co., an engine from R. and W. Hawthorn—both Newcastle firms—and an engine from Edward Bury of Liverpool. Parliament did what was required of it and on March 9, 1835, Stephenson's "Rapid" pulled the passenger coaches "Expedition," "Sociable" and "Prospect"; and Hawthorn's "Comet" the "Despatch," "Industry" and "Transit" from Blaydon to Hexham[4]. After that date little more is heard of horse-traction on the new public railways. The wrought-iron edge-rail was equally well established[5]. It was now being turned out not only at Bedlington, where it was first patented, but with great success in South Wales. The "Rapid" ran into Hexham on rails weighing 42 lbs. to the yard, made at Dowlais

---

[1] Tomlinson, *The North-Eastern Railway*, p. 198.
[2] Stretton, C. S., *The History of the Midland Railway* (1901), p. 88.
[3] Tomlinson, *op. cit.* p. 262.   [4] *Ibid.* p. 263.
[5] Above, p. 90–1.

and Ebbw Vale, where production costs were low enough to stand this long transit. Three years later, in June 1838, loco-motives were running on edge-rails to Carlisle, from the Eastern almost to the Western sea[1].

By that time the new model railroad had lived down all pro-fessional opposition: engineers were converted and converting, and their ranks were filling rapidly to serve it. But on the financial side there was still some doubt among experts, and it is, on the whole, rather surprising that money was so readily found for returns which—in the majority of cases—proved to be rather remote and seldom generous. There was so much wild projection; so much necessary uncertainty as to the execu-tion of particular projects; so much ignorance of engineering problems among the public; and so much systematic opposition from interested, and hardly less from disinterested, quarters, that the successful flotation of company after company from 1835 onwards is, at first sight, remarkable. Down to 1835 the amount of experience gained by the actual working of finished lines with locomotives was small. To the Stockton and Dar-lington and the Liverpool and Manchester had been added, in 1830, the little Canterbury and Whitstable "oyster" line, mainly worked, however, by stationary engines[2], and in 1832 (its Act was of 1830) the Leicester and Swannington coal line, the oldest section of the later Midland system[3]. In September 1834, the Leeds and Selby followed—a twenty-mile line with no very apparent objective. The London and Birmingham, the Grand Junction—from Newton-le-Willows, on the Liverpool and Manchester, to Birmingham—and the London and Green-wich had secured their Acts in 1833; the London and South-ampton had been sanctioned in 1834; the Great Western was fighting its way through parliament in 1834–5, and many other projects were before the public[4]. The decisions of investors were necessarily based mainly on hope, and there were many publicists who made it their business to damp hope down. *Railroad Impositions Detected; or facts and arguments to prove that the Manchester and Liverpool Railway has not paid One Per*

[1] Tomlinson, *op. cit.* p. 314–18.
[2] *The Railways of England* (1839), p. 97.
[3] Stretton, *op. cit.* ch. 1.
[4] A good summary of this period is given in *A few general observations on the principal railways...with the author's opinion upon them as investments.* London and Liverpool, 1838. See also Jackman, *Transportation in Modern England,* II. 563.

*Cent. Nett Profit; and that the Birmingham, Bristol, Southamp-
ton, Windsor, and other Railways are, and must for ever be, only
Bubble Speculations* is the title of one substantial, and far from
contemptible booklet, which went through two editions in 1834[1].

The early finance of the Liverpool and Manchester is in
fact rather puzzling. The company was limited by its Act to
a 10 per cent. dividend. It soon reached this figure, after
"gradually progressing in prosperity,"[2] and had paid away
altogether over £400,000 in dividends before the middle of
1837. But all the time it was getting powers to issue fresh
shares and borrow to a much greater amount: in 1837 it was
trying to secure a loan of £400,000 from the Exchequer Loan
Commissioners[3], offering as consideration a first charge upon
its revenues. Each statement as to probable costs at every stage
had been greatly exceeded, and the directors complained
"heavily in all their reports of the excessive amount of their
expenditure."[4] On the other hand, if, as some critics alleged,
part of the new stock really represented profits over and above
the 10 per cent., distributed to shareholders in this concealed
form, the company was doing much better than it allowed the
outside world to know[5]. Certainly it never had any difficulty
in paying the interest on its borrowed money. A sober and
well-informed apologist, in 1838, writing from Liverpool,
admitted extravagance but defended the line as a "grand
experiment." It was not "a fair test for other railways as to
the expense of working" because it was so short and its terminal
stations in proportion to its length so needlessly costly; because
it had been obliged to carry out locomotive and other experiments for the whole world; because, having found twelve-ton
engines necessary, it had to relay a line designed for six-ton
engines; and because it had more "objectionable" inclined
planes than any other line. The admission of the directors, "that
the expense of working this line from 1830 to 1836 had been
about three-fifths of the whole income," was "a very startling

---

[1] By R. Cort, son of the inventor of the puddling process. The rather contemptuous references to this pamphlet in Smiles, *op. cit.* III. 303, Jackman,
op. cit. II. 531 n., and Sekon, G. A., *A History of the Great Western Railway*
(1895), p. 5, depend too much on a knowledge of the event.

[2] *A few general observations...*, p. 49.

[3] Established by 57 Geo. III, c. 34 "for carrying on Public Works and
Fisheries" etc.

[4] Wheeler, J., *Manchester, its political...and commercial history* (1836), p. 302.

[5] Jackman, *op. cit.* II. 530-1.

fact"; but the apologist found comfort in observing that working expenses included new engines, waggons and stock[1].

Meanwhile the Stockton and Darlington, in spite of occasional financial embarrassments—once, in 1826, Edward Pease had to find ready money to pay the wages[2]—had declared quiet Quaker dividends, which had risen to 6 per cent. in 1831 and were back at 6 per cent., after a rise to 8 per cent., in 1834–5[3]. The Leicester and Swannington also, "contrary to general anticipation, proved a good sound investment."[4] The average profit shown in the books for the three years 1837–9 was over 6 per cent. and the shares at that time stood at a premium[5]; but down to 1835–6 the "general anticipation" was what the outside public had to go upon. The Leeds and Selby was never very prosperous. It squeezed out 2½ per cent. in its first half year (1834–5), 1½ per cent. in 1836, the same in 1837, and nothing in 1838[6]. During the first half of 1841, the average dividend on the share capital of seventeen companies in what was to become the territory of the North-Eastern Railway was only about 3½ per cent., although the average was helped by the 15 per cent. of the Stockton and Darlington and the 9 per cent. of the York and North Midland[7]. Right down to 1850 the gross receipts—not the dividends—on all existing railways never reached 8 per cent. on the capital expended[8]. It was fully open to anyone to argue, in 1834–5, that there was no good prospect of dividends except on a coal-line, and no certainty there. Those who held that horse-tramways on the public roads were preferable to the locomotive railway were not yet silenced[9]. And then there was the steam-carriage, whose advocates were active down to 1840. Following George Shillibeer, who had introduced the horse omnibus to London in 1829 and—in later life—developed the Victorian hearse, came the pioneers of the steam omnibus, Goldsworthy Gurney,

[1] *A few general observations...*, p. 49 *sqq.*
[2] Tomlinson, *op. cit.* p. 138.
[3] *Ibid.* p. 357.
[4] *A few general observations...*, p. 20.
[5] Stretton, *op. cit.* p. 30.
[6] *S. C. on...Communications by Railway*, 1839 (x), Q. 3874: evidence of B. Gott, the Chairman.
[7] Tomlinson, *op. cit.* p. 359.
[8] Lardner, D., *Railway Economy* (1850), p. 281. Lardner gave this crude figure because "the receipts alone are ascertainable with precision; the expenses and profits are left to conjecture" (p. 279).
[9] *E.g.* Fairbairn, H., *The Political Economy of Railroads*, 1836.

Sir Charles Dance, Colonel Maceroni. Thomas Telford and Bryan Donkin had borne public witness to its merits, after travelling in one on the Birmingham road so far as Stony Stratford, on November 1, 1833. They hoped great things of it, especially if part of the road "were to be prepared and kept in a state most suitable for travelling in locomotive steam carriages."[1] Next year there existed at least the provisional committee of a company for putting the Holyhead Road into such a state and running steam carriages on it. Very appropriately, Sir Henry Parnell was on the committee, and Telford was named as consulting engineer[2]. But the public did not bite.

Hitherto railway success, such as it was, had been due mainly to the resolution of small groups of local business men; to the enlistment of local patriotism; and to the conviction and driving power of a few engineers, interested less in dividends than in construction. Much of the resolution was Dissenting: a disproportionate amount of it was Quaker, and that not only on the Quaker Line. The Society of Friends was extraordinarily well represented on the early boards of management—at Stockton, Liverpool, Leicester, Birmingham; Peases, Backhouses, Croppers, Listers, Ellises, Sturges. Among the Northumbrian rumblings of George Stephenson, in the early railway anecdotes, is heard from time to time the still voice of these enterprising and judicious persons—"friend...why didst thou say that whatever Stephenson's engine could do thine own could do," addressed to a boastful but defeated engineer[3]. In some places the promoting groups were in touch with the local government authorities. The story of a railway committee of the Corporation of York deliberating throughout 1833–4 on plans for a railway system radiating from the northern capital appears to be fictitious; but George Hudson, the well-to-do linen-draper of College Street, who was the mainspring of the whole movement, was already a prominent local politician and became mayor in 1837[4]. Bristol, when once aroused from the "apathy" and "party spirit" of which local railway enthusiasts complained[5]—a measure of apathy and party spirit are not surprising within a few years of the Bristol riots—made the

---

[1] *Railroad Impositions detected...*, Ap. No. 6, gives the document.
[2] Its prospectus is given *Ibid*. Ap. No. 7.   [3] Stretton, *op. cit.* p. 30
[4] The story is in Grinling, C. H., *The Great Northern Railway* (1898), p. 2. But see Tomlinson, *op. cit.* p. 272. Hudson sat on the York Board of Health from 1832 and in the Corporation from 1835.
[5] Jackman, *op. cit.* II. 562.

Great Western scheme almost a municipal affair in 1839. The mayor called a meeting at which the very thorough inquiry into the project by a promoting committee was laid before the public; and the Corporation, the Dock Company, and the Society of Merchant Venturers were officially represented on the provisional board of directors. It should be added that local subscriptions came in slowly, and that the Great Western would never have been built without the money not only of London but of Birmingham, Manchester and Liverpool[1].

Liverpool business men were particularly active in investment beyond their immediate area, which suggests not only that they had imagination but that the Liverpool and Manchester did pay better than it told. Stephenson was able to raise money at Liverpool for the Leicester and Swannington even before the Liverpool and Manchester was open; and the group on whose money he drew, known in the early railway age as the Liverpool Party—Croppers, Rathbones, Horsfalls, Booths, Sandars—not only took an important share in creating the central link-lines of England between Mersey, Humber, Thames and Severn but, with Stephenson, had the long through-routes before their minds from the first[2]. Lancashire almost owned the London and Birmingham[3].

Between 1825 and the end of 1835 fifty-four railway Acts of all sorts had gone through parliament, the lines sanctioned varying from the Paisley and Renfrew, $3\frac{1}{4}$ miles long with a capital of £33,000, to the London and Birmingham with its $112\frac{1}{2}$ miles and its capital of £5,500,000[4]. The result of this legislation, down to September 1838, when the London and Birmingham was opened, had been the production of something like 500 miles of operating public locomotive railway, of which the London and Birmingham and its continuations up to Preston, the Grand Junction and the North Union, accounted for nearly one-half[5]. During the two years 1836–7, thirty-nine more railway bills for new lines in Great Britain received the royal assent, besides a number for Ireland. After that, there was a check: in the years 1838–9 only five bills became Acts. Not one was passed in 1840 and only one in 1841.

---

[1] Sekon, op. cit. p. 2. Jackman, op. cit. II. 562–3.
[2] See Stretton, op. cit. p. 7–9, 33, 36–7, 47.
[3] Tooke, History of Prices, II. 275 (1838), says it held seven-eights of the capital.
[4] List in S. C. ...on Communication by Railway, 1839, Ap. 29, p. 410.
[5] Cleveland-Stevens, E., English Railways: their Development and their Relation to the State (1915), p. 9.

The thing had been overdone during 1836–7. From 1831 to 1835–6 the cost of living had been falling and the price of Consols rising. In 1830, £153,000,000, and in 1834 another £10,600,000 of Government stock had been converted from 4 per cent. to 3½ per cent.[1] Blind capital, seeking its 5 per cent., a totally different thing from the clear-eyed capital of the Quaker business men from the Midlands and the North, had accumulated for the raiders. The projector and the self-certified engineer settled on the City.

The press supported the mania; the government sanctioned it; the people paid for it. Railways were at once a fashion and a frenzy. England was mapped out for iron roads. The profits and percentage of the Liverpool and Manchester were largely quoted. The prospects and power of the London and Birmingham were as freely prophesied[2].

Hope, and the Liverpool and Manchester precedent, were still the main justifications. But they served. The railways were propagated blindly and wastefully like living things. Multitudes of eggs never hatched out into Acts. There were five competing schemes for lines to Brighton and the shares of all, at one time, stood at a premium. There were three companies, or projected companies, for lines to Norwich. "In one parish of a metropolitan borough, sixteen schemes were afloat, and upwards of one thousand two hundred houses scheduled to be taken down."[3] But there emerged numbers of live companies which built real lines of which the Bristol and Exeter, the Birmingham and Gloucester, the South-Eastern, the Midland Counties, North Midland, York and North Midland, the Great North of England, Taff Vale, Eastern Counties, Manchester and Leeds, the Glasgow and Greenock, the Glasgow and Ayr, and the London and Brighton were perhaps the most important. (Among the rejected bills was Joseph Gibbs' bill for a Great Northern railway *via* Cambridge Sleaford and Lincoln to York.) With the companies emerged, as a contemporary noted, some changes in the language. "Men talk of 'getting up the steam,' of 'railway speed,' and reckon distances by hours and minutes."[4]

Coinciding, as it did, with an over-rapid development of

---

[1] See, *e.g.* the price curve in Jevons' *Investigations in Currency and Finance* or in Silberling's *British Prices and Business Cycles*, referred to above, p. 128. For conversion Buxton, S., *Finance and Politics* (1888), I. 127.

[2] Francis, *A History of the English Railway* (1851), I. 290.

[3] *Ibid.* I. 293.   [4] *Ibid.* I. 292.

provincial joint-stock banks whose business was unregulated, with rising food-prices, and with Anglo-American trade relations which both produced a drain of gold from England to America and made unsound business[1], this preparatory railway mania of 1836–7 left even the survivors, above all the half-built survivors which were the vast majority, in a difficult position. Banking facilities were curtailed. The Great Western, a generously and expensively planned line, at one time had its cheques dishonoured. Its continuator, the Bristol and Exeter, saw its shares offered in the market with a premium for the buyer[2]. The London and Southampton was selling new shares at 50 per cent. discount to raise money. Even London and Birmingham shares would fall below par; although in 1837 the chairmanship of the still unfinished line was taken over by George Carr Glyn, a circumspect representative of that old London banking community which, hitherto, had taken no active part in railway promotion or direction, though it had always been prepared to accept railway accounts. The pioneer lines came through with credit. The Liverpool and Manchester continued to pay, and the Stockton and Darlington raised its dividend to 14 per cent. in 1837, held it there in 1838, and raised it again in 1839[3].

The promotions of 1836–7 had added something over a thousand miles to the potential railways of Britain. For five years the land was bridged and cut and tunnelled without much new promotion. The Littleborough summit tunnel on the Manchester and Leeds, nearly a mile and three-quarters long, and Brunel's Box tunnel on the Great Western, 250 yards longer, were completed to the universal admiration; and the great Woodhead tunnel on the Manchester and Sheffield was in hand. In 1841 some people were thinking that the railway system was not very far from complete. Since July of that year it had been possible to travel from London to Newcastle in seventeen hours—by rail, *via* Birmingham, Derby and York, to Darlington, and forward by coach[4]. By rail from Euston *via* Preston to Fleetwood; by steamer from Fleetwood to Ardrossan; and by rail again to Glasgow, the journey could be done in twenty-four hours. "What more can any reasonable man

---

[1] Below, p. 511 *sqq.*   [2] Francis, *op. cit.* I. 299–300.
[3] Tomlinson, *op. cit.* p. 357.
[4] Grinling, *op. cit.* p. 8: or forward by rail (the new coast lines) over a much longer distance in about the same time. Tomlinson, *op. cit.* p. 430.

want?" asked even the *Railway Times*[1]. In June 1843 there were some 1900 miles of line open in Great Britain, and there was only a small amount of unfinished line in hand[2]. The first burst of construction was over.

But the engineers and the great promoters were not content. Gibbs' scheme for a northern trunk line along the easy gradients of the East Midlands had been whittled down into the Northern and Eastern Railway from London to Cambridge—which had not yet got there. The boom of 1836–7 had not thrown up a yard of approved railway for Bedford Huntingdon or Lincoln and very little for Nottingham. No route through Wales had been sanctioned and Scotland remained cut off; though special commissioners had reported to the Treasury in 1840–1 on the problems of railway communication with Scotland and Ireland. Their fourth report, which appeared in March 1841, declared for a Scottish connection by way of Carlisle and Lockerbie— provided there was reasonable prospect of the difficult bits of line from Lancaster to Carlisle and from Carlisle to Glasgow being undertaken "within some definite time." Should there be delay, they thought the West coast projectors should stand down and let in those of the East, "upon the supposition that at present one Line of Railway only can be formed from the South to Edinburgh and Glasgow."[3]

The group now dominant among the East coast projectors were strong men, and their activities, on committee and in parliament, bridge the gap between the completion of the main works promoted in 1836–7 and the fresh outburst of promotions in 1844. In 1841–2, with Robert Stephenson surveying and George Hudson working in committee or arranging—when necessary—to pay dividends out of capital[4], or to accept huge personal liabilities, to forward his plans, they were engaged in intricate controversy with the Stockton and Darlington interest and with the amazingly grasping Dean and Chapter of Durham to secure the creation of a direct Darlington and Newcastle Junction, which Stephenson described as "the last step remaining to establish the east coast route to Scotland."[5] They got their main Act in June 1842, and a route-rectifying Act in the

---

[1] Quoted in Grinling, *op. cit.* p. 6. Fleetwood had been created by Sir Hesketh Fleetwood in 1836.

[2] Wyndham Harding, in *S.J.* XI. 323 (1848), gives 1990, but later estimates reduced this figure: accuracy was hard to attain.

[3] *A. and P.* 1841, XIII. 213, p. 65–6. Report of Sir F. Smith and Prof. Barlow.

[4] Tomlinson, *op. cit.* p. 433.   [5] *Ibid.* p. 432, 434, 438–9.

April of 1843. For the Newcastle and Berwick a survey was ready. In the spring of 1844 Hudson opened the campaign which led to the Newcastle High Level and the Berwick Royal Border Bridges[1].

By that time capital and opportunity were lying ready, amply ready, to his hand: he and all the smaller, and all the sounder, railway strategists could plan on what scale they pleased. Since the excellent harvest of 1842 wheat prices had been reasonable. Peel was cutting duties on imported foodstuffs. The poorest consumer had a little more to spend and every kind of business profited. The market rate of discount had never stood so long under $2\frac{1}{2}$ per cent. as it did in 1843–4[2]. There was no difficulty in converting the outstanding £250,000,000 of $3\frac{1}{2}$ per cents. into $3\frac{1}{4}$ per cents. in 1844; because in that year the 3 per cents. touched par for the first time since before the Seven Years' War[3]. At the very beginning of 1845 the new $3\frac{1}{4}$ per cents. were already well above par[4]. It was no longer at all easy even for the greatest land-owners to oppose railway construction on personal grounds. Only the bravest men of letters denounced "the snorting steam and piston's stroke" and the general public did not listen. The Prime Minister was very well disposed towards railway enterprise: there was a railway party—of directors and the like—in the House, and Hudson himself arrived there in 1845. "He wielded an influence in England unparalleled and unprecedented....His alliance was sought by patricians; his children were the companions of peers."[5]

Up to the end of 1843, the length of public line sanctioned by parliament, including a trifling amount in Ireland, was reckoned subsequently at 2285 miles. Of this length 1952 miles were open. The Acts of 1844 added more than a third to the sanctioned mileage—805 miles; those of 1845 added 2700 miles; and those of 1846 added 4538 miles, by 219 separate Acts. Then the figure fell to 1354 in 1847 and to 330 in 1848. By the end of 1848 a round 5000 miles of line were working in the United Kingdom, of which less than 400 were in Ireland. That is the statistical skeleton of the Railway Mania[6].

---

[1] Tomlinson, *op. cit.* p. 454.
[2] Jevons' diagram in *Investigations*.
[3] Jevons, and Buxton, *op. cit.* I. 127.
[4] $104\frac{3}{4}$. *The Economist*, February 1, 1845.
[5] Francis, *op. cit.* II. 218–19.
[6] Lardner, *Railway Economy*, p. 54–5.

On the map it blocked out almost the whole railway system of modern Britain—the chief exceptions being the St Pancras and Marylebone lines into London, the Midland Peak Forest line into Manchester, the Midland Pennine connection with Carlisle, and a good deal of railway north of the Highland line. Of trunk lines its main creations were the Holyhead line, authorised in 1844, the various lines—Scottish and English— which finished both the East and the West Coast routes into Scotland, others which opened out more completely the South-Western counties of England, and the Great Northern from King's Cross to York, the longest line yet authorised in a single Act. This bill received the royal assent on the same day as the corn law repeal bill (June 26, 1846). The fight over it had been not less severe, much longer, and very much more expensive. They painted Edmund Denison, M.P., the father of the line, as the fashion was, holding the costly instrument firmly in his right hand[1].

Among the defeated in that struggle was George Hudson. When the contest opened in 1844, by agreements, common directorships and the mere power of his personality,

his influence extended seventy-six miles over the York and North Midland; fifty-one miles over the Hull and Selby and Leeds and Selby; over the North Midland, Midland Counties and another [the Birmingham and Derby Junction], one hundred and seventy-eight miles; over the Newcastle and Darlington, and the Great North of England, one hundred and eleven miles; while over the Sheffield and Rotherham, the York and Scarborough, the North British, Whitby and Pickering, it affected nearly six hundred more, making a total of 1016 miles, all of which were successful in developing traffic, and equally successful in paying good dividends[2].

In October 1845 he had accepted the chairmanship of the far from prosperous Eastern Railway, and had set plans in motion by which the Midland lines, feeling East, and the Eastern Counties, feeling West, should cut off the projected Great Northern at Doncaster and hand on the traffic, unspoiled by competition, to the Vale of York and the Great North of England.

---

[1] Grinling, *op. cit.* p. 56 and frontispiece. The fashion persisted—
   "He would hold a scroll of something,
   Hold it firmly in his left hand."
                        Lewis Carroll, *Hiawatha's Photographing* (1858).
[2] Francis, *op. cit.* II. 216. See Grinling, p. 47–8. Stretton, *op. cit.* p. 67.

Up to that time there had been a good deal of co-operation, voluntary and compulsory, between adjacent companies, but only one great legal amalgamation. The first parliamentary amalgamation, it is true, came so early as 1834 (Local Acts, 4 & 5 Wm. II, c. 25), but it only joined up two tiny companies near Wigan[1]. In 1835 the Grand Junction absorbed the five-mile-long Warrington and Newton, and in 1836 the Great North of England secured powers, by its Act of Incorporation, to buy a branch from the Stockton and Darlington. Then, in 1840, the Grand Junction again absorbed a neighbour, the Chester and Crewe, 23 miles long. Three years follow with no amalgamation Acts and only a couple of Acts authorising the purchase or lease of lines as between companies. In 1844–5 there were six amalgamation Acts and twenty-two Acts for purchases and leases, and in 1846 twenty amalgamation and nineteen purchase or lease Acts[2]. It was Hudson who started the real amalgamation movement, with the creation of the Midland in 1843–4.

The Birmingham and Derby Junction, which abutted on the London and Birmingham and the Grand Junction at Birmingham, and the Midland Counties which tapped the London and Birmingham at Rugby and also ran to Derby, had been wasting their strength in competition. The North Midland, which carried on their traffic into Yorkshire and on whose board Hudson sat, was interested in, though hardly injured by, their struggles. All three were beginning to fear the competition of a possible London and York (Great Northern) on through traffic for the North, and some an "invasion" by Brunel's broad gauge from the South-West. The "Liverpool party," more or less interested in all three and at first hostile to amalgamation, was—it is said —brought into line by these external dangers[3]. Terms were arranged in the winter of 1843–4: Liverpool names disappeared from the consolidated directorate: the Act received the royal assent in May 1844, and George Hudson took the chair, with John Ellis of Leicester as his deputy. What parts interest and ambition, the economic and the uneconomic motive, played in

[1] Cleveland-Stevens (who made a special study of amalgamation), *op. cit.* p. 18 *sqq.*

[2] Table in *ibid.* p. 25.

[3] It is perhaps necessary to remind non-Victorian readers that the Great Western, to which Brunel was engineer, had its distinctive broad-gauge. For the creation of the Midland see Stretton, *op. cit.* p. 67 *sqq.* Cleveland-Stevens, *op. cit.* p. 42 *sqq.* Grinling, *op. cit.* p. 15.

the affair will never be known. Within a year the Midland had taken over the Birmingham and Gloucester; within two, the Gloucester and Bristol. Its line of policy for the next two generations was already laid down—to strike outwards from the counties of its birth.

In 1845 the Grand Junction, an absorbent line, ably guided by the best railway diplomatist of the day, its general manager, Captain Mark Huish, took over no less a neighbour than the Liverpool and Manchester together with two smaller Lancashire companies. Some complex diplomacy followed. The Great Western was now really trying to drive the broad gauge into the industrial Midlands, and the "battle of the gauges" was joined over projected broad gauge lines to Rugby and Wolverhampton. The London and Birmingham, Carr Glyn's line, was negotiating for an alliance with the Manchester and Birmingham (which geographically was only a Manchester and Crewe). Into these discussions the Grand Junction intervened, with evidence by its secretary in favour of the broad gauge and a petition to parliament, signed by Huish, against the monopolistic schemes of Carr Glyn and his board (June 1845). The captain was manœuvring for position. Within five months the Grand Junction shareholders were summoned to approve of an amalgamation with Carr Glyn's board. The Manchester and Birmingham was also to join. On July 16, 1846 (9 & 10 Vict. c. 204) the London and North-Western Railway came into existence, with 379 miles of line; and Captain Huish was general manager under Carr Glyn[1].

That same year, whilst at least one bill for a new railway was passed on every parliamentary day, and the navigator in "white felt hat...velveteen...square tailed coat, scarlet plush waistcoat with little black spots, and...corduroy breeches,"[2] drinking "whisky by the tumbler and calling it white beer,"[3] was alarming and ripping up innumerable country-sides, the Manchester and Leeds was beginning the amalgamations which were to turn it, in 1847, into the Lancashire and Yorkshire; the Manchester, Sheffield and Lincolnshire began its fifty years' life under that name; amalgamations created the London, Brighton and South Coast; and by lease and purchase numerous minor lines and canals came under the control of the great

---

[1] Based on the excellent study of the amalgamation in Cleveland-Stevens, op. cit. p. 51 sqq.

[2] Smiles, op. cit. III. 321.   [3] Francis, op. cit. II. 70.

emerging companies. The next year saw an important amalgamation in East Anglia and the creation of the York, Newcastle and Berwick—the backbone of the future North-Eastern—out of 360 miles of line whose construction had been the work of eight separate undertakings. The railways of the country, still very far from complete, were settling down into a railway system[1].

As an important adjunct to that system the electric telegraph had just emerged from the experimental stage. The practicability of the telegraph, said one of the English pioneers in a lecture in 1838, "is no longer doubted, either by scientific men, or by the major part of the public." He prophesied that the telegraph would "one of these days, become an especial element in social intercourse." "Should the system ever be adopted generally throughout Europe, what a vast field does it open to us."[2] Cooke and Wheatstone had applied for their first patent the year before; and, the year after, the imaginative and experimental Great Western Company had laid wires in an iron tube from Paddington to West Drayton, to work one of their early instruments[3]. Experiments were also made in 1839–40 on the London and Birmingham and the Blackwall Railways; but these early instruments were expensive and the experiments on the London and Birmingham were dropped[4]. For some years little progress was made. Even the Great Western moved slowly: it did not lay wires through the Box tunnel until 1847[5]. Only in 1846–7 did the York and North Midland, the York and Newcastle and the Newcastle and Berwick, equip the East Coast main line to Scotland with the telegraph. They had trouble with their station-masters, against the name of one of whom it was entered in the minutes—even in 1852—that "he had not learnt to work the telegraph, or at all events paid no attention to it."[6] At the beginning of 1852 the Great Northern had no telegraphic organisation at all[7]. By 1846 the instruments had been greatly improved. Also it

---

[1] Cleveland-Stevens, *op. cit.* esp. p. 25–8.
[2] Edward Davy, quoted in Fahie, J. J., *A History of Electric Telegraphy to the year* 1837 (1884), p. 405, 408, 412.
[3] Sekon, *op. cit.* p. 58.
[4] See *Fifth Report on Railway Communications*, 1840 (XIII), Q. 349–50, and Sabine, R., *The Electric Telegraph* (1867), p. 38.
[5] Sekon, *op. cit.* p. 49.
[6] Tomlinson, *op. cit.* p. 532–3.   [7] Grinling, *op. cit.* p. 140.

had occurred to Cooke, in 1843, that the wire had better be suspended from posts, from which it now rang "shrilly, taut and lithe, within the wind a core of sound."

While, abroad, the new means of "social intercourse" was generally kept in the hands of government, in Britain the Electric Telegraph Company was formed in that critical year 1846 to exploit it. The Company bought up most of Wheatstone and Cooke's patents, together with those of Alexander Bain and other inventors, and pressed telegraphy on the railways and on the public[1]. During the first four years of its existence it had no rival, and it was able to charge high rates for ordinary messages[2]. By the middle of 1848, over 1800 miles of railway, "that is about half the railways open,"[3] had their telegraphic equipment. How essentially the telegraph was a railway adjunct in its early years is illustrated by the position in London so late as 1854. The Electric Telegraph Company, at that time, had seventeen metropolitan offices, including its head office in Lothbury. Of the seventeen, eight were at the great railway terminuses and three, as Dionysius Lardner wrote with some pride in 1855, were "open day and night."[4]

Some of the earliest railways were built expressly to break down a canal or "navigation" monopoly. This was notoriously the aim of the Liverpool and Manchester, along whose route the waterway companies maintained a strict and illiberal alliance. Stephenson raised money at Liverpool for the Leicester and Swannington because John Ellis told him that the rich men of Leicester were mostly "in canals" and were not likely to favour competition[5]. When the line was opened, the canal men are said to have looked dejected, which, seeing that the Erewash Canal—one of those likely to suffer—had paid 50–60 per cent. in the 'twenties, is not unlikely. Everywhere the canal interest was in natural opposition to railway projects; but down to about 1840 railway competition developed so slowly that the canals made no attempt to improve their own competitive capacity[6]. Although a few, specially open to railway attack, like the Ere-

[1] Levi, L., *History of British Commerce* (1872), p. 214–15.
[2] Lardner, D., *The Electric Telegraph popularised* (1855), p. 273.
[3] Harding in *S.J.* XI. 336 (August 1848).
[4] *Op. cit.* p. 273.
[5] Stretton, *op. cit.* p. 7.
[6] For their defects see above, p. 82 *sqq.*

wash and the Loughborough, had suffered heavily in pocket, some had improved their financial position between 1825 and 1840. Many had maintained it and many more, though reduced for reasons not necessarily connected with railways, were still excellent paying propositions. The Leeds and Liverpool, which paid 16 per cent. in 1825, was paying 20 per cent. in 1838-9. The figures of the Grand Junction for the same two years were 13 per cent. and 12 per cent.—the London and Birmingham Railway being just open in 1839. Corresponding figures for some other representative canals, from various parts of the country, were as follows[1]:

	Dividend	
Canal	1825	1838-9
Northern		
Trent and Mersey	75*	$32\frac{1}{2}$
Ellesmere and Chester	$2\frac{4}{5}$	$2\frac{4}{5}$
Barnsley	$8\frac{3}{4}$*	13
Huddersfield	Nil	$3\frac{3}{4}$
Midland		
Oxford	32*	30
Birmingham	70*	12
Coventry	44*	46
Worcester and Birmingham	2	$1\frac{3}{4}$
Stafford and Worcester	$28\frac{1}{2}$	$28\frac{1}{2}$
Warwick and Birmingham	11	30
Ashby-de-la-Zouch	Nil	$3\frac{1}{2}$
South-Western and Welsh		
Stroudwater	$15\frac{1}{3}$	24
Glamorgan	8	8
Monmouthshire	10	$4\frac{1}{2}$
Swansea	14	15
Southern		
Thames and Severn	$1\frac{1}{20}$	$1\frac{1}{2}$
Thames and Medway	Nil	Nil
Wiltshire and Berkshire	Nil	$1\frac{3}{4}$
Basingstoke	Nil	Nil
Kennet and Avon	$2\frac{1}{2}$	$3\frac{1}{8}$

* With a bonus.

As soon as a directly competitive railway was opened a canal had to cut its rates; but nothing is heard of rate cutting to forestall competition. Between Liverpool and Manchester the railway cut the old canal rate of 15s. a ton on light goods to 10s.

[1] Figures for 1838-9 from *The Railways of England*, 1839, p. 127 *sqq.*: for 1825 figures see above, p. 81.

The Irwell and Mersey Navigation and the Bridgewater Canal had to follow. The opening of railways from Manchester to Hull, in the 'forties, reduced the through water rate on manu-factures by nearly one-half. The Erewash Canal cut its coal rate from 1s. to 4d. a ton: the Grand Junction, for the long haul into London, cut its coal rate from 9s. 1d. to 2s. 0¼d. The Aire and Calder Navigation cut its general goods rate from 7s. to 2s. 3d. a ton to meet the Leeds and Selby; and so on[1]. But before 1840 such necessities had been rare.

Then, in six years, the whole weight of railway competition, actual and potential, exaggerated by the popular frenzy, fell upon the unprepared canals. They spent, in fruitless parliamentary opposition, money which could have been much better spent on their own equipment. Where their routes were naturally well fitted for water transport they continued to do plenty of carrying. In 1839, for instance, the tonnage of goods carried by water between Manchester and Liverpool was not quite twice that carried by railway: in 1845 and in 1848 it was a good deal more than twice[2]. From that time forward, the Bridge-water Canal, on the Lancashire side of the Pennines, like the Aire and Calder Navigation on the Yorkshire side, was always busy. But canals with many locks, or with difficulties of water supply on the watersheds, and all those canals which had never earned a margin of profit into which competition might cut, without cutting to the quick, felt themselves between the devil and the deep sea. Some were scared and surrendered to the railways at discretion; some were out-manœuvred; some black-mailed railway companies with threats of opposition; nearly all were ready to close with any good offer. And so, under Acts of 1845–7—mainly of 1846, again the critical year—canals with a mileage of 948 were bought or leased by the railways; and the consolidated Birmingham Canals became dependent on the London and North-Western Railway, by the Birmingham Railway and Birmingham Canal Arrangement Act of 1846[3]. There remained, however, some 2750 miles of independent canals and "navigations" in Great Britain[4].

[1] Mainly from Jackman, op. cit. II. 639 and Ap. 10. The Aire and Calder cut is from Six Reports from the S. C. on Railways, 1844 (XI), Q. 6176.
[2] Jackman, op. cit. II. 741.
[3] Cleveland-Stevens, op. cit. p. 91. [For canal blackmail of railways see S. C. on Rail. and Canal Bills, 1852–3 (XXXVIII), p. 11.]
[4] Calculated from returns in S. C. on Rail. Amalgamations, 1872 (XIII), p. xix.

The Birmingham Canals, prior to this, had taken powers to become a railway company; but, as things worked out, they came under one. The Trent and Mersey (Grand Trunk) Canal was more fortunate. It really made a railway. It had seen its superb dividends so cut into by the competition of the Grand Junction and the Midland that shares worth £1200, in the days of 75 per cent., had fallen to £450—a still respectable figure. But it retained vitality enough to turn itself, by a series of Acts in 1846–7, into the North Staffordshire Railway Company, in which capacity it managed a railway and a waterway parallel to the main line of the railway, with very fair success for over seventy years[1]. Perhaps it is worth recording that the chairman of the Trent and Mersey, at the time of its metamorphosis, was a Ricardo[2].

The worst placed canals had still a part to play in the transport business of the country, even when they were in danger of losing ultimately all but the slow bulky local traffic. In the early railway age their real competitive power was strengthened by the slow development of goods traffic—especially of cheap and bulky goods traffic—on many of the railways. Where the rail carried most goods, in the far North of England, there were no canals. That railways whose projectors had thought mainly of merchandise often found themselves occupied principally in the carriage of passengers is well known[3]. The miscalculation was not so universal as is sometimes suggested. Of sixty-six railways, whose returns were analysed in 1845, twenty-two derived a greater part of their gross revenue from merchandise than from passengers[4]. But the majority of the twenty-two were short coal lines. In Stephenson's country the lines were built for minerals and carried minerals. "The passenger traffic ...was considered very much in the light of a by-product. On the Stockton and Darlington...it was for eight years in the hands of certain coach-proprietors."[5] Even the Newcastle and

[1] Cd. 3719, p. 333. The transformation was not quite "unique," as Cleveland-Stevens says (p. 93 n.). By 1 & 2 Wm. IV, c. 60, the Manchester, Bolton and Bury Canal became the M. B. and B. Navigation and Railway Co. The intention was to make a railway of the canal: in fact both were worked. *S. C. on Railways*, 1839, Q. 4076 *sqq.* The Chard Canal Coy. got similar powers by 9 & 10 Vict. c. 215.

[2] J. L. Ricardo, M.P. for Stoke, 1841–62. The main Act is 9 & 10 Vict. c. 84. [In the 1st edn. it was stated that the management gave "satisfaction" to the district. Prof. J. F. Rees has shown that this is doubtful. *E.J.* June, 1927.]

[3] Lardner, *Railway Economy*, p. 277. Francis, *op. cit.* I. 203.

[4] Graham, W. A., *S.J.* VIII. 215 (September 1845).

[5] Tomlinson, *op. cit.* p. 364.

Carlisle, the longest and least "mineral" of the far Northern lines, drew a larger gross sum from merchandise than from passengers.

But immediately south of Teesdale, in the mid-'forties, the predominance of passenger traffic began[1]. The Great North of England drew more than 60 per cent. of its receipts from passengers, as did the Manchester and Leeds and the Manchester Bolton and Bury, in an infinitely more industrial area. These Manchester lines showed an extraordinarily rapid and heavy development of third-class passenger travel. On the Hull and Selby, however, passenger receipts only just exceeded merchandise receipts, and on the Liverpool and Manchester the merchandise figure was well over 40 per cent. It was on the metropolitan lines that the greatest, and most unexpected, predominance of the passenger showed itself. The London and Birmingham had anticipated a revenue of about £670,000, derived almost equally from passengers and merchandise. In its first year, it took more than £500,000 from the passengers and a bare £90,000 from the goods[2]. In 1844–5 it still drew more than three-quarters of its income from the passengers. The Great Western and the South-Western drew more than four-fifths from passengers, and the Eastern Counties 90 per cent.[3]

For all the railways of the kingdom, in 1845, passenger fares contributed 64 per cent. of the gross receipts. By 1848 the percentage was 57[4]. During the whole nineteenth century it never got so low as 40. Having learnt the value of this side of their business, the companies stimulated it, and the traveller responded to every stimulus. Even before 1850 he found "at those points of his route where the train stops for the purpose of refreshment, magnificent salons, luxuriously furnished, warmed and illuminated. [These a later age would call early Victorian waiting-rooms.] In these are established buffets," whose attendants "neither desire nor expect gratuities."[5] No wonder the traveller responded to a stimulus so wisely applied. He soon ceased to travel by canal, of which he had never been very fond. He used to like spanking bays: now he liked "getting the steam up" and "railway speed." The canals con-

---

[1] Graham's calculations, as above.
[2] Francis, *op. cit.* I. 203.   [3] Graham.
[4] Lardner, *op. cit.* p. 277.
[5] *Ibid.* p. 147.

tinued to carry merchandise and pay reduced dividends. "Strange to say," traffic in stone and coal on the Manchester, Bury and Bolton Canal was increasing in 1839, though there was a parallel railway all the way[1]. In 1840, Lucas Chance of Stourbridge still sent five-sixths of his glass to London by water[2]. But the canals attracted no new capital and, with few exceptions, carried out no improvements all through the nineteenth century.

When giving evidence in 1839 before a parliamentary committee on the turnpike trusts, the younger McAdam spoke of "the calamity of railways" which had fallen upon them[3]. That the railways were a calamity for many trusts there is no doubt. They were a calamity too for many of those who worked the traffic of the main highways, most of which were turnpiked. But, in discussing the effect of the railways on the roads, too much importance may easily be given to the trusts, because parliament took so much interest in them, and to the turnpiked highways, because they were the classic roads of England and the English Mail Coach—the Brighton, the Dover, the Portsmouth, the Bath, the Great North Road, the new Holyhead Road. So near London as in Essex, only 10 per cent. of the roads were turnpikes in 1815; and though in Middlesex the percentage was over 30, for the whole of England it was only 17, in 1838[4].

Like the canals, the turnpike trusts had fought the railways and lost. Unlike the canals, very few of them had been really prosperous, and many were loaded with the debt and bad administration of a century. McAdam did not regard the calamity of the railway as the prime cause of their distress. It had only, he said, "aggravated the evil," an evil which had its sources in debt, mismanagement, lack of co-operation, the competition of river and coasting steamers, and the recent loss to the roads of statute labour under the General Highway Act of 1835 (5 & 6 Wm. IV, c. 50). The trusts had nearly £9,000,000 of debt in 1836 and over £9,000,000 in 1839[5]. It

---

[1] S. C. on Communications by Railway, 1839, Q. 4274.

[2] Ibid. 1840, Q. 2865-6.

[3] S. C. on Railways and Turnpike Trusts, 1839 (IX. 369), Q. 427.

[4] Above, p. 94, and Webb, S. and B., The Story of the King's Highway, p. 225.

[5] S. C. on Turnpike Trusts, 1836 (XIX. 335), p. vi, and S. C. on Railways and Turnpikes, 1839, p. iii.

was "annually increasing, in consequence of the practice prevailing in several of the trusts of converting the unpaid interest into principal."[1] For some of them, the interest on debt was more than the gross income. McAdam said that he knew roads from which there were sixty years of interest due. Statute labour with pick and shovel by the labourer—other than the pauper—seems to have died out before 1835; but the farmers had often preferred sending their carts and teams for road work to paying a rate. The Act abolished both the obligation to labour and the compositions in lieu of it which had been arranged in some places. As the transfer of a stretch of road to a trust had not abolished the obligation to do statute labour on that stretch, the Act had deprived the trusts of an income, in money or work, which McAdam, in 1839, estimated at no less than £200,000 a year. On top of all this came the calamity of the 'thirties.

The blow was far deadlier for the trusts than for the canals, because it was precisely from that passenger and parcel traffic which the railways took over at once that the trusts had drawn most of their tolls. Farm carts used the roads free and low-grade bulky loads paid little or nothing. The effect of a railway on the tolls was instantaneous. Those levied at the Eccles bar on the Manchester and Liverpool road were farmed for £1700 in 1830. Next year they were offered at £800 and found no bidders. The Irlam bar, on the same route, which had fetched £1300, could not be let for £500[2]. The New Cross Trust lost £2500 the year after the Greenwich Railway was opened[3]. On the London and Birmingham road, £28,500 was taken in tolls by eight successive trusts during 1836. The takings in 1839, when the railway was open, were £15,800. The mortgage interest of the eight trusts was £16,500[4].

If a trust had the good fortune to cross a railway line, the situation was reversed. "In many cases the lateral roads have increased considerably in revenue,"[5] said McAdam; but illustrative figures are not available. Yet, as by far the greater number of trusts operated on trunk routes along all of which, sooner or later, railways were constructed, a final breakdown of turnpike finance was inevitable. Between 1837 and 1850 the receipts

[1] S. C. of 1839, p. iii.
[2] Jackman, op. cit. II. 617: from the Manchester Guardian.
[3] S. C. on Railways and Turnpikes, 1839, Q. 64.
[4] Ibid. App. I.   [5] Ibid. Q. 428.

of the trusts fell off by a third[1]. Before the Select Committee on Turnpike Trusts of 1839 appeared Lewis Levy, the greatest farmer of turnpike tolls in the country[2]. Once upon a time, he said, he had farmed £500,000 worth, which was about a third of all the tolls in the kingdom. "He had not come prepared" to tell the committee what his business now was; but it was a great deal less than that. He half confirmed a member's suggestion that perhaps it was £100,000. It would be very interesting to know in what direction Levy was diverting his activities, and how soon he had recognised that the turnpike ship was sinking.

Calamity to the turnpike trusts, it need hardly be said, was not calamity to the horse-drawn road traffic of the country. That, as all agreed and as the increase in the issue of licences for vehicles conclusively proved[3], grew steadily all through the early railway age. The railways were fed, in the jingle of the nursery, by "coach, carriage, wheelbarrow, cart." In London the ponderous two-horse hackney coach, that "remnant of past gentility...hanger-on of an old English family, wearing their arms and in days of yore escorted by men wearing their livery,"[4] was dying. The swift hackney "cab," in its various forms, was driving it out. In 1843, J. Aloysius Hansom patented his safety cab; but the Victorian hansom actually sprang from another patent taken out by another man two years later. Side by side with it, between 1836 and 1840, there developed the one-horse Victorian four-wheeler[5]. As for the steam-carriage, it passed almost out of memory: Goldsworthy Gurney turned to other inventions, for which he was knighted, and Colonel Maceroni died.

Carts and cabs increased, but coaches and posting-houses decayed. Journeys behind horses multiplied; but long journeys behind horses stopped. Immediately before Lewis Levy, in 1839, E. Sherman, of the Bull and Mouth Inn and posting establishment, gave evidence[6]. Fifteen coaches daily, he said, had ceased to run from the Bull and Mouth on the North Road since the London and Birmingham Railway was opened. "Mr Ormsby-Gore. Is the Tally-ho taken off? E. Sherman.

---

[1] Webb, op. cit. p. 216.   [2] Q. 204 sqq.
[3] Jackman, op. cit. II. 611.
[4] Dickens, Sketches by Boz, "Hackney Coach Stands."
[5] Morse, H. C., Omnibuses and Cabs (1902), p. 216, 224–5.
[6] Q. 132 sqq.

Yes, everything." The inflections of the two voices are perfectly audible. The tragedy was repeated on each trunk route as the sleepers and metals were laid along it. No coach started for Bristol after 1843 or for Plymouth after 1847. The "sleepy Leeds" had been run off the road the same year as the Bristol coaches. Railway development in the East Midlands was slow, and there was still a Bedford coach in 1848. But the exact dates are of little consequence. The effect in every case was instantaneous and inevitable.

The coaching interest argued that it suffered from overtaxation. Railways were taxed $\frac{1}{8}d$. per mile per passenger carried: coaches were taxed $\frac{1}{4}d$. per mile per seat licensed for passengers moved through a mile: coasting steamers were not taxed. This $\frac{1}{4}d$. per mile stage-coach duty was by no means all. There was a £5 licence per coach; a manservant's tax on coachman and guard; and the assessed tax on every horse. Then there were the turnpike tolls[1]. On the formal point of taxation the coaching interest was no doubt right. There was no way of justifying the inequality between the $\frac{1}{8}d$. and the $\frac{1}{4}d$.; and the inequality was made more patently unjust when the Treasury —for lack of experience and railway statistics, it would appear —allowed the companies to compound for this passenger tax on absurdly easy terms. But the coaching interest never referred to the subjection of railway property to poor rates, which had already begun[2]; nor did they mention, when lamenting over the tolls, the huge sums which the railways had paid for the right to make roads to run on, for the construction of those roads, and for keeping them in working order. The whole discussion was both necessarily inconclusive and, had a conclusion been possible, as necessarily idle. No tax remission or new tax which any government could have contemplated would have saved the coach run in direct competition with the railway. At best, it might have given the Tally-ho a spell of shabbygenteel life. It was better to go down with honour while the paint still shone and the wheelers were still glossy.

While railway building went forward slowly, that is to say down to the accession of Victoria, neither the making nor the staffing of the lines presented a labour problem of magnitude

[1] *S. C. on Railways and Turnpikes*, 1839, p. v, and Jackman, *op. cit.* II. 619 *sqq.*
[2] "The railways, by sharing the burden, have exercised a very beneficial influence on the rates." Caird, *English Agriculture in* 1850 *and* 1851, p. 125.

or serious novelty. Canal and road building and drainage
works had provided the traditions, and to some extent the
cadres, for a small army of contractors, still called "undertakers," and of more or less professional "navigators." Recruits were easily raised, most easily among the immigrant
Irish and the redundant population of rural districts. When
the Stockton and Darlington was building, the earthwork had
been "let in lots to small contractors and sets of workmen, who
formed temporary partnerships amongst themselves"[1]—methods which remained typical for the next quarter of a century.
As there was not much surplus rural population in Durham,
and as the Irish had not yet arrived there in force, some recruits
were raised among keelmen thrown out of work by a strike
in 1822.

The Manchester and Liverpool was built, as the directors
themselves once had occasion to explain, by men "the great
body of whom were either Irish or natives of the soil."[2] It has
been said, however, that some of the best, a minority of pro-
fessionals, "came from the fen districts of Lincoln and Cambridge, where they had been trained to execute works of
excavation and embankment."[3] No doubt such men would
become first-rate gangers for Stephenson when he was tackling
Chat Moss: "rough looking as they were, many of them were
as important in their own department as the contractor or the
engineer."[4] When it came to the laying of the permanent way
and, subsequently, to the working of the locomotives, experienced Northumberland and Durham men were given a certain
preference[5]. A few had been employed as overlookers from the
start. When construction was finished, in 1832, out of some
six hundred workmen, about sixty were the North-country men
of Stephenson's tail; the rest had been recruited locally by the
directors[6]. There was no difficulty in raising this small body
of permanent railwaymen; nor did the few new careers thus
created much affect the labour market of South Lancashire.

About eighteen employees of all sorts per mile of finished
line was, in this case, the direct effective demand of an

---

[1] Tomlinson, *op. cit.* p. 88.
[2] *Liverpool and Manchester Railway. Answer of the Directors to an Article in
the Edinburgh Review for* 1832 (Liverpool, 1832), p. 5.
[3] Smiles, *op. cit.* III. 321: no authority quoted.
[4] *Ibid.*
[5] *Answer of the Directors*, p. 7.
[6] *Ibid.*

operating railway for labour. If this proportion had been maintained, the five hundred or so miles of railway which were open towards the end of 1838 might have employed nine thousand men, and the four thousand five hundred miles open at the end of 1848, eighty-one thousand. But if the employment figures reported to parliament for June 30, 1849, are correct[1] —and there is no reason to doubt them—the high proportion of employees to mileage on the Liverpool and Manchester was not representative. Those figures show that all the companies of the kingdom, including a few in Ireland, with an open mileage of over five thousand, employed fifty-six thousand persons of all sorts, from secretaries and engineers to platelayers and labourers, or about eleven to the mile. But fifty-six thousand directly employed was already a large figure, comparable with the total employment of many old-established industries. The new careers opened out had now become important.

Meanwhile the huge, and quite distinct, demand for railway constructional labour had barely begun to slacken. The parliamentary committee which reported on the condition of the railway labourers in July 1846, estimated that "for several years to come...not much less than two hundred thousand men" would be employed continuously on the various works[2]. For the period of maximum constructional activity (1846-8) this estimate proved to be not very far out. A return made as for May 1, 1848, showed that 188,000 men were at work on lines not yet open to traffic, of whom 147,000 were classed as labourers, 6000 as miners or quarrymen, and 29,000 as artificers[3]. But rather more than a year later (June 30, 1849) the figure had fallen to 104,000, of whom something over 84,000 were the navigators and their foremen[4].

The term navigator had by this time a general and a special meaning. There were the gangs of experienced men who had professional skill and commanded a corresponding wage, the navvies proper, and there were the rough diggers of the rank and file. "As far as my experience goes," said a Scottish witness, "in Scotland we have not yet any of the class of people called navigators; they are generally mere labourers who come for the occasion, and probably do not return to that sort of

---

[1] Quoted in Porter, *Progress of the Nation*, ed. of 1851, p. 336.
[2] 1846, XIII. p. 13.
[3] Quoted in Lardner, *Railway Economy*, p. 58.
[4] Quoted in Porter, *op. cit.* p. 336.

work afterwards."[1] For the most part they were Highlanders or Irishmen. In the North of England "perhaps one-half of the navigators,"[2] in the wider sense, were Irish; but in the South, where rural population was denser and rural wages lower, most of the labour was local. The South Devon Railway, for example, was being built in 1846 principally by Dorset, Somerset, Wilts and Devon men who had worked their way down along the line of the Great Western. There were a few, but "very few," North-country men and the Irish are not mentioned[3]. Nor were there at that time any of the specially expert navvies on the works[4]. Such men wanted something like 5s. a day, and work was being done in South Devon at rates varying from 2s. 6d. to 4s. 3d., the maximum being paid to "miners" on tunnelling, which was really an expert's job[5]. The 5s. experts were only called in to do jobs of special difficulty, or when it was necessary to work against time: the "contractor generally knows where to put his hand on a body of these men."[6] Occasionally they formed a large proportion of the working staff. The five thousand Englishmen who made the Paris-Rouen railway were mostly "true navigators," for, as the contractor explained, "we had some long tunnels."[7] These were the men whose meat-eating and day's work so astonished the French. Their wages, even in England about double those of an average unskilled labourer, left a wide margin for steak, plush waistcoats, and whisky. What proportion they formed of the whole body of the railway makers it is impossible to ascertain; but the evidence suggests that, at least in 1844–8, that proportion was not high, since whole railways managed without them.

Already the great contractors were coming to the front. Thomas Brassey, who began life as the articled pupil of a land surveyor, was at work on the London and Southampton and subsequently on the Great Northern; but he was not as yet quite in the first rank. More conspicuous was Thomas Jackson, a "practical mechanic"[8] as he described himself, who had started on railway work in the early 'thirties. He had contracts in 1846 on three different lines, including the Chester and Holyhead, and he employed 3500 men. But the leading figure among

---

[1] *Comm. on Railway Labourers*, Q. 167.
[2] *Ibid.* Q. 1043.   [3] *Ibid.* Q. 184.   [4] *Ibid.* Q. 311.
[5] *Ibid.* Q. 185.   [6] *Ibid.* Q. 311.   [7] *Ibid.* Q. 328.
[8] See his evidence in 1846, Q. 1886 *sqq.*

the contractors of the 'forties was undoubtedly Samuel Morton Peto[1]. Nephew and apprentice to one of the great building contractors of the early nineteenth century, whose firm rebuilt the Houses of Parliament, Peto, when he threw over ordinary building for railway work, in 1834, at the age of 25, had both experience of large operations and a useful name. Twelve years later he was employing, directly and indirectly, about 9000 men: between 1847 and 1850 he was credited with 14,000[2]. Beneath and beside these great names were the innumerable small undertakers and navvies' groups, who did most of the straightforward work.

It was usual for the great contractors not to sublet the more critical undertakings. Jackson always did tunnelling with direct labour and Peto, in 1846, had 3700 men under his own hand on the rather awkward line through the heart of the fens and over the Bedford rivers, from Ely to Peterborough[3]. But sub-contract and sub-sub-contract were the rule. Peto, a model employer, had trained up his own sub-contracting gangers and required them to pay their men in cash weekly; but even Peto admitted that he had some difficulty in keeping the gangers to his system. In most cases the main contractor or the company, where it dealt with a number of small men, had neither the knowledge nor the desire to do anything of the kind. The second-grade contractor was usually, so Isambard Brunel said[4], a man with a capital of not more than £1000 or £1500, who sublet his brickwork to small master bricklayers, and his earth-work usually to excavator gangs. How these gangs worked was explained by John Sharp, a self-made contractor who, in twenty years, had made his way up from the pick and shovel. "There are in some works what are called butty-gangs; there they are all alike, and one receives the money and shares it among the others. In other places one man takes the work and employs men...and receives the benefit of it himself."[5] The best men, Sharp thought, preferred the butty-gang, where all were equal and where—as a navvy witness put it—wage quarrels could be settled "with an odd blow on the head and a quart of beer or two extra."[6]

---

[1] Brunel, *Comm. on Railway Labourers*, Q. 2047, said he was the largest contractor in the world. His own evidence is Q. 1230 *sqq.* And see Francis, *op. cit.* 1. 266 *sqq.*

[2] By Francis, in 1851.   [3] Q. 1976, 1230.
[4] His evidence is Q. 2047 *sqq.*   [5] Q. 2797.
[6] Thos. Eaton, Q. 2997.

Weekly payment in cash, on which Peto insisted, was one of the reforms in the organisation of railway labour which the select committee of 1846 wished to see generalised. It had already made considerable progress. It was coming in steadily in the West of England, John Sharp said: he himself paid fortnightly, making advances to the men between whiles if desired, but he would have no objection to the enforcement of the weekly payment in cash by law—a suggestion which the committee were considering. (He did not mention, but another witness did, that even fortnightly pay had only been secured recently on the South Devon line by means of a strike[1].) Thomas Jackson had imitated Peto, and weekly pay was well established on the Chester and Holyhead. But pay fortnightly, monthly, or sometimes at even longer intervals, was still quite common. The only witness to defend the system was Isambard Brunel. He was a great believer in the small contractor who undercut the big firms and kept prices down. "The prices at which railways are constructed compared with those at which large government works were constructed thirty years ago," he said, was "a strong instance" of the benefits of such competition: "in those days there was a monopoly by the large contractor."[2] He thought that the small man could not be expected to pay cash weekly without endangering the economy of the contract system.

Pay at long intervals was associated often, though by no means always, with the system of "tommy-shops" and advances to the men in the form of shop-tickets. The tommy-shop might belong to the contractor, or to the ganger, or to someone who paid one or other of these a commission for the right to run it[3]. Such a man was likely to make his profit by selling bad or dear goods. "They pay for the coarsest joints what I pay for the best," said a witness who had acted as a navvies' chaplain[4]. Sometimes the tommy-shopkeeper would supply cash against tickets—at a discount of a penny in the shilling. In itself, the system of shops on the works was no abuse. Peto said he could dispense with them even in the fens, where villages were wide apart and rather inaccessible, by notifying butchers and bakers in the market towns of the amount which he expected to disburse in wages on the coming Saturday: they soon sent out their carts[5]. But the man who made the Woodhead tunnel[6],

[1] Q. 196-7.   [2] Q. 2063.
[3] The *Report*, p. iv.   [4] Q. 212.   [5] Q. 1268.
[6] W. A. Purdon, engineer to the Manchester and Sheffield: Q. 1544 *sqq.*

ten miles over a Pennine hill road from the nearest town, argued conclusively that central organisation of supplies, what he called a "colonial system," was inevitable and might well be worked in the men's interests. Some witnesses testified to well-run shops; but the predominant opinion seems to have been summed up by a navvy of twenty-seven years' experience, who said that "tommies" meant "daily imposition" and "a great deal of inferior stuff."[1] The committee, having heard all the evidence, raised no objection to the employer acting as caterer; but they recommended the extension to railway work of the Truck Act of 1830–1 (1 & 2 Wm. IV, c. 37), so that the employer would have to pay in cash, and would only secure his men's custom for the shop if the shop deserved it. "The great objection to the truck system," they said, was "the door which it...opens to fraud on the weaker party to a contract." And as "the Legislative...already interferes widely with the free power of parties to contract," there should be no objection on principle to this extension[2]. With the abolition of truck was to be associated compulsory weekly payment, so as to avoid the riot and debauch of the monthly pay-day.

For the housing of navvies the committee had more revolutionary proposals to make. The facts were undisputed and, as usual, utterly diverse. At the Woodhead tunnel the company had built good stone cottages. Peto, when he was unable to get lodgings, built wooden barracks to hold about twenty-five men each, with hammocks and a steady man and wife in charge, to whom each occupant paid 1s. a week. At Bangor, Jackson had run up wooden cottages, which were mostly used by his married men; and so on. But even the best contractor could not stop the overcrowding of already crowded villages, which any large-scale lodging of navvies entailed, and the average contractor was content with the very roughest of shanties for his men—particularly his Irishmen. In Midlothian a Scot was lodged, an Irishman was hutted, a middleman hut-keeper—inevitable phenomenon where there was an Irishman to exploit—getting in between him and the contractor[3]. In Devon the huts were of mud and turf and the contractor got 3s. a week for one such "room": I "never saw anything to be compared to them," said the witness[4]. Isambard Brunel admitted that the Great Western accommodation, even in their new colony at Swindon, was still very defective; but he maintained

---

[1] Q. 3041–2.   [2] P. vi.   [3] Q. 8437.   [4] Q. 188.

that it was improving[1]. All the evidence in fact pointed towards improvement in the last few years; but the committee was rightly dissatisfied with the pace. Navvies should not be collected, they maintained, until adequate lodging was either known to exist or known to have been provided. The accommodation should be passed by inspectors under "the public Board which may be charged with the general supervision of railways." The proposal, they said, was doubtless novel; but then so was the problem. The lodging of these industrial armies in the field, like the lodging of Her Majesty's forces, should be the care of the state[2].

The conclusion suggests Edwin Chadwick, who was, in fact, one of the chief witnesses. His main interest, however, was in the question of employers' liability in relation to railway work, a matter in which he carried the committee, and nearly all the witnesses except Brunel, with him[3]. Taking as precedents the liability sections of the Code Napoleon, as extended in France to railways since 1840, and the recent British Factory Act (7 & 8 Vict. c. 15), which imposed on the employer the duty of fencing dangerous machinery and liability for accidents if it was left unfenced, the committee pressed for such "a considerable alteration of the present General Law of England" as would make the railway companies civilly responsible for all accidents to life and limb among their workpeople, the burden of proof that the sufferer was wilfully careless being thrown upon them, instead of the sufferer being called upon to prove that the company had been neglectful of its reasonable duty towards him. They wished at the same time to remove a grotesque anomaly of the law whereby a man, or corporation, was civilly responsible for the injury which another received by his, or its, wrongful act or neglect of duty, provided that injury was not unto death. As a preliminary, it was necessary that official statistics of accidents should be collected. Actually none existed. The committee were confident that the tables "if accurately made out would be both formidable and distressing."[4]

Incidentally the committee-men learned a great deal about navvy-life beyond their main subjects of inquiry. Peto had never heard of any trade unions among the navvies[5], and none

---

[1] Q. 2113.   [2] *Report*, p. vii.   [3] His evidence is Q. 2163 *sqq.*
[4] P. viii. The case of Priestley *v.* Fowler, 1837, the first in which "an action was brought against an employer for an injury caused by one of his servants to another" (Holdsworth, *Hist. Eng. Law*, VIII. 480), had turned lawyers' attention to problems of liability.   [5] Q. 1302.

of the evidence submitted suggested that he was wrong. But he noted that they nearly always organised sick clubs which they managed themselves. "They support their sick extremely well," another witness testified: "every man pays towards the sick...they make a little weekly payment."[1] There was a real solidarity among these rough fellows. When one of his men died after an accident, Peto paid the funeral expenses and made an allowance to the widow; but there is no reason to think that this was the average contractor's policy. Probably the sick club had a burial department. To the men's ignorance, especially of religion, there was a great deal of evidence from a few devoted clergy who had served as volunteer navvies' chaplains. The Catholic Irish were not less ignorant than the rest; but it was reported of them that they subscribed generously to the stipends of their priests.

"You speak of infidel opinions. Do you believe that many of them are Socialists?"[2] "Most of them in practice," replied the clerical witness to whom this question was addressed; "though they appear to have wives, very few...are married." A narrow interpretation of the word, but one which a particular aspect of Robert Owen's preaching—far removed from his practice—had made exceedingly common. That the infidel navvy, living in concubinage, was a hard drinker, a stout fighter, a lover of dogs and pigeons and other men's orchards and poultry yards, and a hardened "utterer of base coin"[3] witnesses were hardly needed to prove. All the world knew it. Yet his standard, it was said, had gone up markedly since about 1842. "We are eliminating the tramp type," Jackson explained[4]. There had been a time when the navvy was counted a barbarian outcast; when decent countrymen had preferred their 10s. or 12s. a week on the land to the fine wages of savagery and sin with him on the works of the London and Birmingham[5].

The recommendations in favour of strict state control of railway labour made by this committee of 1846, small things in a year of great railway developments, sprang from an outgrowth of parliamentary opinion important in its day, and much more important in retrospect, but on the whole barren. That

---

[1] Q. 307: the Chaplain mentioned above.
[2] Q. 2528.   [3] Q. 3095-7.   [4] Q. 2006.
[5] Evidence of R. Rawlinson, who had been four years on the London and Birmingham, Q. 889 sqq.

comparison of the navvies to the Queen's troops no doubt
seemed a most dangerous symptom to the political mind of
the main stock, which was ready to denounce almost any scheme
for railway regulation as "a very extraordinary interference
with property."[1] Parliament had begun by treating the railways as things of purely local interest, and had applied to them
the precedents of the turnpike trust and the canal. If they
could make out their case before a private bill committee, then
they were given, like the canals, that really great "interference
with property," the right to buy land compulsorily, subject,
however, always to elaborate safeguards—sworn and impartial
commissioners, or a jury to see that the to-be-expropriated
landlord was not imposed upon. He rarely was. The landed
interest, in the years before sale to a railway was recognised
as very sound business, was restless under this interference[2]
Specially offensive to it was the practice of enterprising railway
promoters of surveying land, without leave or licence, to see
whether it was suitable for their purpose. Innumerable stories
are told by the early railway historians of the dodges by which
the landowners were outwitted. Samuel Smiles, who would
certainly have been grieved had anyone sneaked into a cotton
mill on Sunday to count the bales with a view to their compulsory purchase, thought it an excellent jest that the Stephensons' chainmen, having been refused leave to survey the property of a certain clergyman, waited for a Sunday and "entered
his grounds on the one side the moment they saw him fairly
off them on the other," to perform his Sabbath duties[3]. Such
devices were not often necessary after 1837, and the companies,
forgetful of the great interference with property from which
they sprang, became very sensitive about proprietary rights.
The main limitations on their right to do what they would with
their own, contained in the decisive Liverpool and Manchester
Act, were first, the formal recognition that their road, like a
turnpike, was open to all users, with their horses or other
means of traction; second, the insertion of a skeleton schedule
of maximum ton-mile tolls for goods of different sorts, and for
conveyances with travellers or cattle, moved along the line by
such users, and a corresponding schedule of maximum rates

---

[1] Edward Baines, M.P.: see below, p. 415.

[2] See below, p. 415 n., for an instance of this restlessness—Lord Londonderry.

[3] *Lives of the Engineers*, III. 306.

which might be charged when the company did the work of transport itself; third, a limitation, never applied to any canal company, of the dividend to a maximum of 10 per cent.

This last limitation was inserted by Huskisson, when the bill was in committee, as a sop to its opponents. No subsequent bills contained it. The schedules of maximum tolls came to be nearly meaningless, because they had been fixed so high. The Liverpool and Manchester might charge up to $1\frac{1}{2}d$. per ton-mile, as a mere toll, on coals moved along its line by traction which it did not supply: in 1845 the average charge of twenty-two companies for actually hauling coals was only $1 \cdot 83d$. per ton-mile[1]. It was the same when maxima for passenger traffic began to appear in the bills: the Grand Junction the London and Birmingham and the Great Western might charge up to $2\frac{1}{2}d$. a mile for carrying people in open trucks[2]. The right of the public to use the roads like turnpikes soon broke down before the facts of locomotive traction. Carr Glyn said, in 1839, that his company had indeed received one or two applications to put strange locomotives on their line, but as these were from "unknown parties" they had been ignored. He added that if such locomotives had appeared he would "certainly not" have expected his signalmen and other officials to give them any help[3]; so that the chances of a successful run would have been poor. Thus, throughout the 'thirties and the early 'forties, the companies had a very free hand.

Their freedom was not uncriticised even in the 'thirties. During the little railway mania of 1836–7, Londonderry once said in the Lords that it would be an excellent thing if every railway bill contained a clause that after a certain period, when they had earned enough to have repaid capital and interest, "the railways should revert to the public."[4] He said this by way of comment on a proposal of Lord Wharncliffe's, referring to the absurd variety of schemes for a Brighton line, that the determination of the best route for a railway between any two points should be the business of the state. The aristocrat was the most probable *étatiste* in those days. When a little gentle

---

[1] Graham in *S.J.* VIII. 222 (September 1845). It is not stated whether the coal was always in private waggons: it generally was.

[2] Cohn, G., *Englische Eisenbahnpolitik* (1874), I. 45 *sqq.* deals exhaustively with the early bills.

[3] *S. C. on...Communicn. by Railway*, 1839 (x), Q. 110, 117.

[4] Hansard, 3rd Series, XXXI. 671.

railway regulation began, a few years later, Wellington voted for it warmly, said he had always wanted it, and regretted only its modesty[1].

There were a few *étatistes* in the Commons also. James Morrison, M.P. for Ipswich, who had made in drapery a fortune which he continuously augmented, was arguing, in 1836, that all canals and railways were of the nature of monopolies, and was illustrating their possible monopoly revenues from the dividends of the more successful canals[2]. Even if two served the same route, he added, some understanding between them was almost inevitable. With these and kindred arguments he supported his motion of May 17, that "in all bills for railways or other public works of that description, it be made a condition, that the dividends be limited to a certain rate, or that power be reserved to parliament of revising and fixing at the end of every twenty years the tolls chargeable."[3] His first alternative came in for well-deserved criticism: it would lead to improvidence, or evasion, or both. His second, though the bill in which he embodied it never got beyond a first reading, was obvious common sense. Why, he asked, should any body corporate be given "power to levy certain specified tolls and charges in all time to come"? No one ever answered him, but parliament went on throwing such powers about. Peel and O'Connell and Mark Philips of Manchester had all opposed his bill; and it was to it that Edward Baines, the Leeds Radical, had applied the phrase "a very extraordinary interference with property."

In 1839 parliament, which hitherto had limited its general railway legislation to certain standing orders regulating the submission of railway bills to parliamentary committees, set up a strong select committee to look into the whole question[4]. Many facts of interest came to light. After hearing Carr Glyn, the committee decisively condemned the notion of the free engine and the associated tolls principle, based on the false analogies of the turnpike and the canal. How was the free engine to get water when the company owned the stand-pipes? They

[1] Hansard, LV. 1251 (1840). Londonderry also wanted to abolish the compulsory land-purchase clause in railway Acts, and Wellington complained that railways were killing coaches.

[2] See *D.N.B.* Cleveland-Stevens, *op. cit.* p. 66 *sqq.* Cohn, *op. cit.* I. 60 *sqq.*

[3] Hansard, XXXIII. 977 *sqq.*

[4] The *S. C. on...Communicn. by Railway*, quoted above. On it sat, among others, Peel, Graham and Sir John Guest.

pointed out that in fact the Liverpool and Manchester, the Leeds and Selby, the Newcastle and Carlisle, and the Grand Junction were already the sole carriers on their respective systems[1]. The London and Birmingham supplied the rolling-stock and traction, but allowed Pickfords and their like to use them. On the Bolton and Leigh all the business was "let to a single carrier." Only on the Stockton and Darlington were there, besides the company using locomotive power, "other parties using horse power," as originally contemplated[2]. The committee made some animadversions on railway finance and the invariable excess of expenditure over estimates; criticised certain abuses of the companies' by-law-making powers and the incidence of the tax of $\frac{1}{8}d$. per mile per passenger; began a tentative discussion of "some controlling authority" for railways; and said that the whole matter required more time.

Reappointed in the next session, they talked of many things —taxation, tunnels, telegraphs, canals and carriers, level-crossings and accidents[3]. But what they recommended was the creation of a public body to examine railway works, to watch the execution of railway Acts, to supervise railways' by-laws, and to collect statistics. The things which they did not place within even the sphere of inquiry for this projected body —rates, dividends, monopoly revenues, amalgamations—are conspicuous. It is fair to add that the problems of amalgamation were present, in 1840, only to anticipatory minds like Morrison's. But the committee had recorded, in 1839, an elementary point in the economics of monopoly—that a curtailment of the facilities offered accompanied by a rise in the price charged may increase the net monopoly revenue: the Leeds and Selby had raised fares, reduced the number of travellers, and gained £1300. However, as that line remained a very lean monopolist, and as, at no time in the history of British railways did they, or any of them, secure monopoly revenues of even tolerable size, when reckoned in percentages, the indifference of this and other committees to the theory of monopoly is perhaps explicable.

[1] *Report*, p. viii. The Grand Junction allowed the London trade, brought to it by the London and Birmingham, to remain in carriers' hands, but itself arranged for the carriage of all consignments originating in Birmingham or north ot it.

[2] There was still plenty of horse traffic in the North-Eastern area in 1854. Tomlinson, *op. cit.* p. 527–8.

[3] *Reports (Five) from the S. C. on Railway Communications*, 1840 (XIII. 129).

The direct result of this Report was Lord Seymour's Act of 1840 (3 & 4 Vict. c. 97), the Act whose modesty Wellington regretted, with its amending Act, Gladstone's, of 1842 (5 & 6 Vict. c. 55). These Acts did little more than collect into the hands of three men[1], called the Railway Department of the Board of Trade, the existing rights of the state to be told how corporations were carrying on the work which it had entrusted to them, and to punish them for neglect or illegality. No railway intended for "the public conveyance of passengers" might be opened without notice given to the Board. The Board might send inspectors "at all reasonable times." It had to sanction by-laws, collect statistics of traffics and accidents, and move the Law Officers of the Crown to proceed against law-breaking companies. It might postpone the opening of lines with whose construction its inspectors were not satisfied, and might decide disputes between adjoining railways about the management of through traffic, on the application of either party to such a dispute. These Acts laid the foundation for a very effective control of railway construction, in the interests of the travelling public, but did little else. The work of the Railway Department of the Board, as Samuel Laing the Secretary explained in 1844, was "almost entirely limited to regulations with a view to the public safety."[2] The rather ambitious arbitration clause was never used and, as the Board was given no jurisdiction of its own, it must sue before the courts for the penalties to which companies that defied it were liable. This it never did, as its gentle monitions were not worth defiance[3].

When, in February 1844, Gladstone, recently promoted President of the Board for which Samuel Laing worked, rose in the House to propose a fresh railway inquiry by committee, problems of competition and amalgamation dominated his mind as, from another angle, they dominated those of the Hudsons, Huishes, Glyns and Denisons. Gladstone was himself a considerable railway shareholder with private access, by

---

[1] G. R. Porter, Sir F. Smith, R.E., and Samuel Laing.

[2] *Six Reports from the S. C. on Railways*, 1844 (XI), p. 2.

[3] Between the two Acts quoted came an abortive Bill of Labouchere's in 1841. That was the year in which a *S. C. appointed to consider whether it is desirable for the Public Safety to vest a Discretionary Power of issuing regulations for the Prevention of Accidents upon Railways in the Board of Trade* (1841, VIII) advised (p. v) that the Board should proceed "by way of suggestion rather than...positive regulation." For the legislation generally see Cohn, *op. cit.* I. 86 *sqq*.

way of his father and his father's Liverpool friends, to excellent sources of railway information—though, if he used them, his biographer has not told us. He approached the subject with far fewer reservations than did his chief, who made it clear in the opening discussions that he would not encourage interference with companies already at work and powers already granted—whereas the committee, certainly expressing the views of Gladstone, its chairman, while admitting that "positive enactments" in favour of existing railways must be respected, held that "nothing in the nature of what is called a vested interest...ought to be recognized by Parliament as attaching to"[1] them. It was Gladstone's hope, at first, that the state might bargain for increased control as the existing lines came forward in turn to ask for increased powers and territories.

The committee worked hard and quickly, issuing six reports between February and July, after hearing Glyn, Hudson, Laing, Huish, Captain Laws of the Manchester and Leeds, Saunders of the Great Western, Edward Cardwell at that time a young director of the South-Eastern, Rowland Hill who had recently become chairman of the Brighton line, Charles Vignoles the railway engineer, and a few others. Little was overlooked, though—under the chairman's guidance—the whole mass of matter was viewed in its relation to the central problem of control. Among many other things, the committee learned, especially from Laws and Hill[2], how systematically the companies felt for the maximum revenue by constant experimental shifting of rates and fares. Hudson, who hated competition—with his lines—made it clear that a concession by parliament to a competing line could never guarantee effective competition against a line suspected of monopolistic abuse. They would come to terms: "competition in railways must lead to compromise, it is as clear as possible."[3] Nearly all the most responsible witnesses, except Saunders and Hudson, were in favour of some increase in state control. Laws advocated nationalisation without delay and even Glyn said that, if a new start were being made, he would be for a state system: as things were, he fell back on Morrison's plan of a revision of charges by the state every twenty years[4].

---

[1] *Fifth Report*, p. 20. See also Hansard, LXXII. 232 *sqq.*; Cohn, *op. cit.* I. 102 *sqq.*; Cleveland-Stevens, *op. cit.* p. 102 *sqq.*; Morley's *Gladstone*, I. 268–9, a single inaccurate paragraph.

[2] Q. 6227, 6254–5, 6407.   [3] Q. 4204.   [4] Q. 5173 *sqq.* and 3254.

The young minister, apparently, was so keen on action before the army of railway projects, which were marching steadily through private bill committees without any reference to his department, should become a disciplined army of vested interests, that he brought in his bill on June 20, before the Sixth Report of his committee was issued and within a month of the appearance of the Fifth, which contained the evidence. In spite of his zeal, his more ambitious clauses were hamstrung in advance by Peel's pledge to the companies. These clauses authorised the Board, after a period of fifteen years from the charter of any railway, either to buy it up on certain prescribed terms; or to revise all its charges if it had made substantial profits (10 per cent. for three consecutive years), and, after revision, to keep a tight hold on its management, amounting almost to complete control. But no railway which had secured its charter before the session of 1844 was affected by these clauses—that is to say, upwards of 2000 miles of the most important lines in the country. In spite of this, the railway interest aided by Cobden, Bright and Macaulay fought the bill hard. Before the end of June a deputation headed by Hudson, Glyn and Saunders, and speaking in the name of £50,000,000 of railway capital, had begged Peel and Gladstone to hold the bill over. There was a not ill-founded feeling abroad that Gladstone was rushing parliament and the country. But Peel would not give way so feebly. No doubt he had sanctioned Gladstone's tactics without committing himself to the whole bill; and so far his honour was involved. Rebuffed, the deputation caused to be drawn up, published in the press, and despatched to shareholders and M.P.'s a strong memorandum against the bill. They argued that parliament's willingness to sanction competing lines disproved the statement, or implication, that railways were monopolies; that the lowness of average dividends proved that their charges were not extortionate; that nothing which British governments had ever done or left undone made it likely that they would prove good railway managers; that centralisation was un-English and that railway shares were property like any other[1].

What happened in the departments during the middle of July is not known. The bill got an easy second reading, but its drastic clauses were transformed by Gladstone himself for the

[1] *Railway Times*, July 6, 1844. The whole episode is fully dealt with in Cleveland-Stevens, *op. cit.* p. 105 *sqq.*, and Cohn, *op. cit.* I. 146 *sqq.*

third. Either he or Peel had recognised that the railway opposition was too strong for them[1]. Instead of fifteen years appeared twenty-one, in the clauses relating to rate revision and state purchase. All the clauses by which the Board of Trade was to secure a tight hold on a "revised" line were dropped; and neither a revision nor a purchase was to take place without a fresh Act of parliament. Whether the original bill was a good one from the point of view of an advocate of more effective state control, or from any point of view, is doubtful: there can be little doubt of the fatuity of these purchase and revision clauses of 7 & 8 Vict. c. 85.

Even the famous clause in the Act which created the Victorian parliamentary train—to run at least once each way on every week-day, except Good Friday and Christmas Day, and on Sundays too if the line ran Sunday trains at all; at a rate of at least twelve miles an hour, including halts; to stop at every station; to be composed of carriages with seats protected from the weather to the satisfaction of the Board of Trade; at a maximum charge of a penny a mile, children under three years of age free, children from three to twelve half price, and 56 lbs. of luggage free--even this clause applied only to new lines or lines seeking new powers. In exchange for it, the companies were freed from the passenger tax in respect of travellers by such trains. Only new lines were forbidden to issue interest-bearing debentures in excess of their authorised capital without parliamentary permission: old lines which had already done this were allowed to renew such debentures for another five years. There were also clauses dealing with postal traffic in a fashion very kindly to the companies—the Postmaster-General had to pay at excess luggage rates should his officials travel with heavy mail-bags: they were not entitled to travel by express, though the mails must move at 27 miles an hour—and a clause by which new railways were not to charge for soldiers on duty more than a penny a mile, third, for officers twopence, first. There was a clause authorising the erection of telegraph lines on land belonging to the railways, with suitable compensation, and giving the public access to all lines erected on railway land. The Board of Trade was once more instructed to move the Law Officers of the Crown, when necessary, to take proceedings

---

[1] See Cohn, *op. cit.* I. 165 *sqq.* Mr G. Kitson Clark of Trinity College, looking at the author's request, has failed to find any evidence bearing on these transactions in the Peel MSS.

against law-breaking railways; but if ever railway purchase should come up, the Treasury not the Board was to act for government.

At the close of the session the Act received the royal assent. It was called "an Act to attach certain conditions to the construction of future railways...and for other purposes in relation to railways." Gladstone was already restless in office, principally because of Peel's religious policy in Ireland. But he told Peel in July that "the connection of his family with the railway interest" made it very awkward for him to do that part of the Board of Trade business[1]. Early in 1845 he resigned. Gladstone was to have authority over commerce and finance very often during the next half-century: he never again attempted railway legislation on the grand scale.

Before leaving the Board he had strengthened its Railway Department to administer the new Act (August 1844)[2]. Another thing he had done which did not help the Department. By a standing order of 1837, projected railway companies were obliged to make a deposit of 10 per cent. of their capital as a pledge of *bona fides*, when their bill came before the Commons. He had pressed on the House[3] the reduction of this deposit by one-half, and had carried his proposal. He left his successor, Lord Dalhousie, and his four coadjutors, the Five Kings as they were called by their innumerable enemies in the railway world, to grapple with the full flood of projects in 1845. Their powers were not clearly defined. They had to examine railway bills to see that they were in order, that rules for public safety were complied with, that "provisions of magnitude which might be novel in principle" did not slip in unnoticed; and they had to recommend them, or not, to parliament, stating their reasons. But this departmental examination and a railway bill inquiry, with counsel, before a private bill committee might go on concurrently. Dalhousie wished to make the examination a real means of shelving undesirable or redundant schemes. But as his Department's function was only advisory, the exact weight to be assigned to its decisions was uncertain. The railway interest disliked the whole procedure and was able to point out errors in the Board's reports, which, seeing that it had to handle projects for some eight thousand miles of line within

---

[1] Parker, C. S., *Peel*, III. 161.   [2] Cleveland-Stevens, *op. cit.* p. 133.

[3] In his speech of Feb. 5 asking for a committee (above, p. 417). One of his reasons was that the Lords had a standing order requiring only 5 per cent. His argument is not fairly summarised in Cohn, *op. cit.* I. 103.

a year, is not surprising[1]. *Laissez-faire* journalists were intensely suspicious.

"Though parliamentary committees are in many respects obviously inconvenient and *most unsatisfactory* tribunals for hearing and deciding on the merits of a multiplicity of railway schemes," the *Economist* wrote on Feb. 15, 1845, "we have often expressed our opinion, that one of the most dangerous tendencies of our legislation of late, in imitation of the worst principles of other countries, has been to centralize power in the hands of government."

There must be some "open tribunal," and a parliamentary committee was better than none, much better, it was implied, than the Five Kings. So far the *Economist*. If the Kings reported early on a scheme which they reckoned of first-rate importance, and late on one which they believed to be frivolous, they were accused of partiality. Disappointed people "carried their...hostility into society and into Parliament" and great ladies "swept society from side to side" for recruits to their cause[2]. Partisans, and every one making haste to be rich by railways, from the Hudsons through the railway barristers to Jeames of Buckley Square—who "thirty thousand guineas won, in six short months, by genus rare"[3]—had hard words for those interfering Five Kings.

Either Peel was sceptical of the utility of the Board's reports from the first—as he well might be; for it really had neither the equipment nor the powers to exercise a fully informed and effective censorship of projects—or he was unwilling to incur the hostility of many members from all parties in their defence. He always said that they were not in any way binding on the House[4]. The *Economist* was able to record with satisfaction of a debate in which both he and Sir James Graham took part, during February 1845, that "the tone even of ministerial speeches tended to disclaim attaching weight to the decisions of the Board of Trade."[5] Many times private bill committees disregarded those decisions, notably in the case of the London

---

[1] Lee-Warner, Sir W., *Life of...Dalhousie* (1904), 1. 76 *sqq.* Dalhousie's speech in the Lords, July 10, 1845, Hansard, LXXXII. 388. Grinling (a typical railway enemy of the Five Kings), *The Great Northern Railway*, p. 31.

[2] *Dalhousie*, 1. 78.

[3] Thackeray, W. M., *Jeames of Buckley Square: a Heligy*. The hard words, in this case, are an inference.

[4] He said later that the reports were to supply information and that he had not had "the most distant intention of compromising the neutrality of the government." Hansard, LXXVII. 171.   [5] *Economist*, February 15.

and York (Great Northern) a scheme to which the Department was hostile[1]. Finally, after the Department had been thrown over in the House by Peel—on June 20—in the case of the Oxford and Wolverhampton[2], it was practically abolished. The Board of Trade had still railway work to do; but the formal reporting to parliament on railway projects ceased, and there were no more Five Kings. They had not been a success in spite of Dalhousie's strenuous and disinterested work.

That inquiry into railway problems should go on almost without interruption during the years 1844–6 was natural. Besides the six reports of 1844, the labour report of 1846, and various reports on the technical business of dealing with railway bills, on London terminal stations, and on the broad and narrow gauges, there was a Board of Trade report on amalgamations of 1845[3], and two thin reports from a select committee on the same subject in 1846, which recommended, within a year of the dissolution of Dalhousie's Railway Department, the constitution of "some Department of the Executive Government...charged with the supervision of railways and canals."[4] Before this committee had reported[5], Morrison, the protagonist of the policy of control, had moved for another and had carried his motion, after a little duel in the House with Hudson. The Railway King, abler and less scrupulous in fence, had pinked him more than once, although the umpires decided for Morrison. Morrison's committee was a strong one and its chairman knew his ground. He pointed out the fundamental error of treating a railway bill as a "private" measure: nothing could, and should, be more public. In France, Belgium, Prussia the state in one way or another reserved its ultimate rights over the railways. "In England alone are companies allowed the possession of lines in perpetuity subject to no available conditions": he wished to see all railway concessions made only for terms of years[6]. The committee, without going so far, recommended once more "that a Department of the Executive Government, so constituted as to obtain public confidence [this

---

[1] Cleveland-Stevens, *op. cit.* p. 140–1.

[2] Hansard, LXXI. 972 *sqq. Dalhousie*, I. 79. Peel said—"I shall exercise no influence to support the decision of the Board...and neither shall I exercise any influence in support of...the Committee"; but he voted for the committee.

[3] 1845, XXXIX. 153.   [4] 1846, XIII. 93, p. v.

[5] The Report is May 6, Morrison's motion March 19.

[6] From the so-called *Second Report* (1846, XIV.) which was really Morrison's draft report published by mistake.

was to the address of the Five Kings], be established for the superintendence of railway business."[1] Yet another committee, of the Lords, had already reported in the same sense[2].

Late in August, in a parliament exhausted emotionally by the corn law struggle, dazed with the roar of the railways and the chink of their promoters' pence, pulled one way by the fashionable economic philosophy, which had no respect for the principles of France or Prussia, and another by the need to "do something," there was carried, by that common consent of tired men which is of so little value, the Act for Constituting Commissioners of Railways (9 & 10 Vict. c. 105). A vague Act, as might have been expected, it prescribed some generous stipends but left powers indeterminate. The powers were never to be determined: the stipends and the Commission ceased within five years. Its establishment reflects a phase of the public mind at the close of the early railway age—nothing more.

[1] *First Report*, first resolution.
[2] 1846, XIII. 217.

CHAPTER X

IRON, COAL, STEAM AND ENGINEERING

At once effect and cause, railway development coincided with a development of metallurgy and mining quite without precedent. What had seemed both to Englishmen and foreigners the amazing output of iron in Great Britain, towards 1830, at the rate of over 2000 tons per working day (650,000–700,000 tons a year) was soon left behind. The figures are rather uncertain but the course of the production curve is

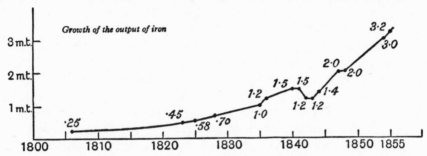

Growth of the output of iron

not. About 1835 it touched 1,000,000 tons; 1,500,000 was probably reached in 1840–1. A slide downwards followed and then came the rise to 2,000,000 tons in 1847–8. Within a few years (1853) a most competent observer was wondering whether the figure of 2,700,000 lately reached could possibly be maintained, "whether reckless make has not brought us to a position from which, unless mineral fields, at present unknown, come into operation...we must retrograde...and reduce the manufacture to somewhat more moderate limits."[1]

This doubting reflection was inspired by the principal event of the previous twenty years, the sudden and gigantic expansion of the Scottish iron industry, and by the belief, which was to prove correct, that Scottish output from Scottish ores would not be maintained. In 1830 there were only twenty-seven furnaces in Scotland. They turned out about 37,500 tons of pig. In 1838, forty-one furnaces in blast made 147,500 tons:

[1] Scrivenor, *History of the Iron Trade*, p. vi. Compare Scrivenor's figures with those in Porter's *Progress*, p. 268, 575, those given by Sir John Guest before the 1840 *Comm. on Import Duties*, Q. 381 *sqq.*, and the retrospect and criticism in *Royal Commission on Coal Supply*, 1871 (XVIII), 879–80.

in 1847, eighty-nine furnaces in blast made 540,000 tons—more than a quarter of the British output[1]. The Scottish industry had three principal foundations, geological, technical and commercial. Geologically, it relied on the limited stock of blackband ironstone, a ferrous ore "alternating with coaly matter,"[2] found in most of the coal measures, but particularly rich in iron about Airdrie and Monkland. It was sometimes called Mushet-stone, from David Mushet who discovered it in 1801 "in crossing the river Calder, in the parish of Old Monkland."[3] For many years he alone used it, at the Calder ironworks, mixing with it the more ordinary and poorer clay ironstone (Sphærosiderite) of the coal measures. After 1825 it was used unmixed, and in the 'thirties and 'forties it was mined fiercely. The technical foundation of the Scottish iron industry was Neilson's discovery of the hot-air blast in 1828-9. By 1831 it had been ascertained that the hard "splint" coal of Lanarkshire could be used in furnaces with the hot-blast without being first coked. This became the practice at most Scottish works. By 1833 a ton of iron could be made with one-third the amount of coal, and of limestone for flux, previously considered necessary. Soon Scottish pig iron began to alarm the ironmasters of England and Wales. By 1842 it was being denounced by the *Times* as the cause of unemployment and rioting in the Black Country. Fortunately for the English ironmasters, puddling was not really established in Scotland before 1836, and the Scottish iron did not puddle so well as to become a dangerous competitor with Staffordshire and Yorkshire bars or South Welsh rails[4]. Commercially, the Scottish industry of 1836-46 rested on the English and overseas markets and on the easy access to tide water which enabled it to supply them cheaply. (There was as yet no through railway communication with England.) In 1845 about one-half, and in 1846 not much less than three-quarters (377,000 out of 522,000 tons), of the Scottish make of iron was shipped down the Clyde[5].

Between 1830 and 1847, while the Scottish make was multiplied by nearly fifteen, that of South Wales grew by about 150 per cent., and that of Staffordshire, North and South, by

---

[1] *Royal Comm. on Coal Supply*, as above.
[2] Woodward, H. B., *Geology of England and Wales*, p. 189.
[3] Mushet, *Papers on Iron and Steel*, p. 127, quoted in Scrivenor, *op. cit.* p. 261.
[4] Scrivenor, *op. cit.* p. 260-4. Bremner, *The Industries of Scotland*, p. 50.
[5] Scrivenor, *op. cit.* p. 264.

not quite 100 per cent. Between them these three districts produced over 1,600,000 out of the 2,000,000 tons of the British make, in the latter year. Tyneside, Derbyshire, Shropshire and the West Riding—in that order—were the other important areas of production. The hot-blast had been introduced in many places "but not with the same extraordinary effect as in Scotland."[1] Owing to differences in the local coals, there was nothing like the same saving of fuel in Staffordshire and Glamorganshire. The fuel expenditure with the cold-blast seems to have been extraordinarily high in Scotland; and there was a strong opinion, or prejudice, among English and Welsh ironmasters that, especially when the primary object was wrought iron, the cold-blast made better stuff[2]. Meanwhile, they laboured to improve puddling; with the result that whereas Cort's original process used two tons of pig to make a ton of bars, and Homfray's improved process 30 to 35 cwt., by the 'forties the ton of bars could be made from 26 or 27 cwt. of pig[3]. Nasmyth's steam-hammer, invented in 1839 and patented in 1842, was just coming into use for "shingling" the masses that came from the puddling furnace, before they were rolled into bars. Apart from the huge home demand, a splendid export demand rewarded every effort after efficiency, as the non-British world moved into the railway age. France was laying down British rails on her new iron roads and the United States, where right down to 1844 there were "no facilities for the manufacture of heavy iron rails,"[4] was doing the same. In the 'twenties about a tenth of the British output of iron was exported in one form or another: by 1840–1 the exports were more than a fifth: in 1847–8 they were considerably more than a quarter of the immensely increased make[5].

The railway demand, direct and indirect, dominated the home market also. Fluctuations in the home consumption, so far as they can be ascertained, coincide closely enough with the flow and ebb of railway construction. Apart from new construction, railway demands were always growing. Almost every year the weight of rails and chairs increased. In 1830–2, 32 or 33 lbs. to the yard was a good weight for rails: in 1841 rails of

---

[1] Scrivenor, op. cit. p. 261.

[2] "Best Yorkshire" wrought iron was still being made with the cold-blast in the twentieth century.

[3] Scrivenor, op. cit. p. 252–3.   [4] Swank, J. M., Hist. of Iron, p. 432.

[5] Porter's Progress, p. 575.

73 lbs. were being rolled at Middlesbrough for the Stockton
and Darlington, and the weight of iron, in rails and chairs,
used for a mile of single track was 156 tons as against 53½ tons
in the early days[1]. On some such basis, the 2000 miles of new
line opened in the years 1847-8 must have used about 400,000
tons of iron for rails and chairs alone, allowing for sidings,
shunting yards and double tracks. If the iron required for
rolling-stock, bridge building, station building, fencing and all
the minor requirements, together with the demands of the
3000 miles of line already open on December 31, 1846, be added,
the railway companies' share of the not more than 3,000,000
tons retained for home use in Great Britain during these two
years can be roughly conceived.

Comprehensive figures by which the growth of the business
unit in the iron industries could be tested, either by output or
employment given or capital turned over in the year, do not
exist. Smelting might be a separate business or it might be
combined with other lines of work, and the combinations with
puddling, rolling, casting and various finishing processes varied
greatly; but the smelting figures alone, such as they are, suggest
the general trend. The blast furnace was growing in size,
efficiency and output. In progressive works, the cylindrical
form had been generally adopted by 1840, with a height of from
40 to 60 feet. "From 90 to 100 tons per week from a furnace
is now by no means unusual; in fact, throughout most of the
works of South Wales, the average make is seldom below 80
tons per week."[2] Not only was the furnace far more productive,
but the average firm had more, though not many more, furnaces,
if some Scottish figures may be taken as a guide. The twenty-
seven Scottish furnaces of 1830 had an average annual output
of about 1400 tons, or a weekly output of 28 tons each, if all
were in blast for fifty weeks in the year. In fact their output
capacity may have been anything from 28 to perhaps 40 tons,
but hardly more. They belonged to eight firms. The forty-one
furnaces of 1838, with an output which works out at over
70 tons a week even supposing that all were in blast for fifty
weeks in the year, belonged to only eleven firms. For the whole

[1] Tomlinson, *History of the North-Eastern Railway*, p. 405-6.
[2] Scrivenor, *op. cit.* p. 248-9. Scrivenor's first edition appeared in 1840.
The 1854 edition merely has a supplementary chapter; so that "now" down to
p. 279 means 1839-40.

of Great Britain, in 1847, Porter believed "upon what is considered good authority"[1] that 433 furnaces in blast (out of a total of 623 in existence) turned out nearly 2,000,000 tons of pig iron, which, on the assumption of fifty weeks' work—in this case perhaps not far from the mark—means over 90 tons per furnace per week. The eighty-nine Scottish furnaces in blast that year, on the same assumption, now averaged 120 tons a week. This difference might be anticipated, for Scotland had been setting the pace, so that England and South Wales had more of the old-fashioned installations. Therefore, the Scottish figures will not be quite representative. How many firms controlled the furnaces of 1847, in any of the three countries, is not precisely known; but evidently they had not grown in proportion to the number of furnaces in blast, still less in proportion to the growth in the output per furnace. However, they must have numbered at least 150, more probably between 175 and 200.

At no time hitherto had firms with more than four furnaces been common. In 1823 Dowlais, under John Guest, had eight, Cyfarthfa of the Crawshays eight, and Sirhowy six; but no Staffordshire firm had more than four and only three had so many. Low Moor and Bowling, the greatest in Yorkshire, had four and three respectively[2]. In 1839, Hill's Plymouth works at Merthyr, where the largest furnaces in Wales were to be found, had seven: an eighth was added in 1846[3]. By that time Cyfarthfa had risen to eleven and at Dowlais Sir John Guest, now the acknowledged leader of the British iron industry, had actually eighteen in blast—though by no means of the largest size: they averaged only 66 tons of pig a week each[4]. But no other firms in the country are known to have had ten furnaces. The business was exacting and fluctuating: competition between the different districts was fierce: the older ones were full of furnaces out of blast and of rather small, marginal, firms halting on the edge of extinction. In 1839 there were 122 South Welsh furnaces in blast, only five out of blast, and thirty-two building: there were fifty-four Scottish furnaces in blast, six out of blast and eighteen building: there were 120 South Staffordshire furnaces in blast, 106 out of blast, and none

[1] *Progress*, p. 269.
[2] Finch's tables quoted in *Comm. on Coal Supply*, 1871 (XVIII), p. 1142.
[3] Scrivenor, *op. cit.* p. 251.
[4] Wilkins, C., *History of Merthyr Tydfil*, p. 185, 207, 213.

building[1]. In the commercially gloomy year 1847, North Wales, a small dying area, had more furnaces out than in; of the furnaces in South Staffordshire 62 per cent. were out, whereas Scotland had only 31 per cent. out and South Wales 22 per cent.[2] The whole period was one in which conditions were not favourable to the expansion of the business unit except in Scotland and South Wales. Eighteen years later (in 1865) fifty-eight firms in South Staffordshire averaged not quite three furnaces each and barely two each in blast[3]. Such figures suggest that an average of four furnaces—in or out—per firm in Great Britain would be too high, and that three to three and a half would be nearer the mark for 1847. If three and a half were taken, it would give 177 separate firms in 1847, each with an average annual output of 11,300 tons. Two years earlier, at Dowlais, Sir John Guest could beat that average in ten weeks; but his firm was altogether exceptional.

The exact course of the increased consumption of coal, so closely connected at all points with that of iron, is much more difficult to determine, owing to greater uncertainty about the starting point, the obscurities of domestic consumption, and the fact that the definite finishing point falls a few years outside the early railway age[4]. When statistics were first collected officially, for 1854, it appeared that Great Britain was producing 64,500,000 tons of coal[5]. Only two years earlier an estimate of 34,000,000 tons had been put forward; though some estimators were by that time of opinion that the 50,000,000 line had been passed by, or before, 1850. During the 'forties, the estimates most current were certainly too low, as for instance McCulloch's 34,600,000 for 1845. De la Beche, the geologist, had supposed that a higher figure, namely 36,000,000 including the coal wasted at the pit mouth and subsequently, had been reached by 1839[6]; and the figure for 1854 suggests that this was perhaps not much too high. Possibly the curve of output steepened hard

---

[1] Mushet's estimates, the best of these early figures. *Comm. on Coal Supply*, p. 880.   [2] From Porter, *op. cit.* p. 269.

[3] *Birmingham and the Midland Hardware District*, 1865, p. 2–3.

[4] See the discussion and table of the various estimates in the *Comm. on Coal Supply*, 1871, p. 880 *sq.* Those for the eighteenth century are, of course, specially doubtful.

[5] *A. and P.* 1856, LV. 469 *sqq.*: the initial returns of the modern mineral statistics.

[6] But, bowing as it seems to the doubtful authority of McCulloch, De la Beche wrote in 1851: "the annual weight raised...is usually now estimated at 35,000,000 tons." 1851 *Exhibition Lectures*, I. 44.

between 1846–7 and 1852, as an almost finished railway system came into complete working and the growth in the number and size of industrial steam installations, which was very marked in the 'forties, produced its full effect. But it seems probable that the curve was fairly smooth throughout the forty years after Waterloo. Domestic consumption was presumably growing with, but faster than, a fast-growing population, as more and more people were brought within range of fuel at possible prices. The industrial steam-raising demand, the export demand, and, after 1830, the transport demand were also no

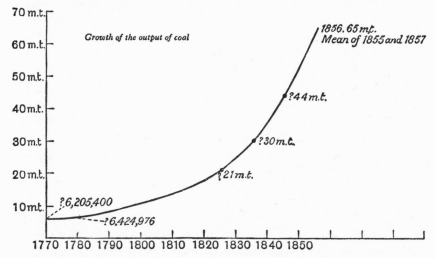

Growth of the output of coal

1856. 65 m.t.
Mean of 1855 and 1857

?44 m.t.

?30 m.t.

?21 m.t.

?6,205,400

?6,424,976

70 m.t.
60 m.t.
50 m.t.
40 m.t.
30 m.t
20 m.t.
10 m.t.

1770 1780 1790 1800 1810 1820 1830 1840 1850

doubt growing faster than the population and increasingly faster, but not, at least until the huge railway openings of the late 'forties, in jerks[1]. The smelting demand, one of the most important, was prevented from growing so fast as the output of pig by the spread of the economising hot-blast; but it was nevertheless growing fast enough, and carrying with it a secondary demand from the puddling furnaces, which became very important with the huge requirements of rolled railway metal in the 'forties. If an output of some 16,000,000 tons for Great Britain in 1816 be accepted as a starting point, some such progression as the following may be suggested as not unlikely: 1826, 21,000,000 tons; 1836, 30,000,000 tons; 1846, 44,000,000 tons; 1856, 65,000,000 tons.

When the British make of iron rose to 2,000,000 tons, as it

---

[1] There was an upward jerk in coal exports in 1844–5. Porter, *op. cit.* p. 279.

did in 1847, it was supposed[1] that the smelting alone consumed 8,000,000 tons of coal; for although the best hot-blast furnaces could do much better than four tons of fuel to one of iron, many cold-blast furnaces did much worse. The various subsequent meltings and heatings at puddling furnace, foundry, and forge were also expensive of fuel. So early as 1835, it was estimated that the Sheffield steel, cutlery, and allied industries, which were engaged in making steel from imported raw material, melting it, and forging it, and so fell outside the figures of British iron production, consumed over 300,000 tons of coal a year[2]. The figures suggest that at least a quarter of the coal raised in the later 'forties may have been used in metallurgy. How the rest was divided between domestic consumption, industrial steam raising, steam raising for transport, and such miscellaneous industrial uses as baking, glass-making, and pottery, cannot—in the entire absence of proper statistics of industrial steam raising in Britain throughout the nineteenth century—be even conjectured. The only figure ever suggested by a trustworthy contemporary was Lardner's 750,000 tons for the coal consumed by British locomotives during the year ending June 30, 1849[3].

Mining engineers, at the close of the first quarter of the nineteenth century, had longer traditions than any other engineering group. They had learnt to sink and work pits approaching 1000 feet in depth; though it was a common opinion, about 1830, that the 1200 foot line would prove the limit of profitable operation[4]. But in many districts shallow pits and open workings were common. Even in Northumberland, the getting of coal through sloping "drifts" from the surface still survived in the 'forties on the western edge of the field, at the outcrop of the coal measures, near Prudhoe. A few other northern mines, in Lancashire, Yorkshire, Cumberland and Scotland, retained similar "drifts," known by odd dialect names—bear-mouths, bout-gates, breast-eyes, futterils —either for getting the coal out or, when the coal was hoisted vertically, for letting the workpeople in[5]. There were open-

---

[1] By Porter, *op. cit.* p. 280.   [2] Quoted in Porter, *op. cit.* p. 250.

[3] *Railway Economy*, p. 83.

[4] Galloway, *Annals of Coal Mining*, I. 477. Galloway's excellent technical narrative is the main source for the following pages.

[5] Galloway, *op. cit.* I. 474; II. 348–9, based mainly on the facts brought out in the *Report on Children in Mines*. [Some "drifts" survived into the 20th century.]

workings, coal quarries, in Shropshire and Staffordshire, though
the best known of these, near Dudley, was regarded as something of a curiosity in the 'forties. South Wales was full of
mines worked by drifts, or levels, and contained also important
open-workings. The valleys of Glamorgan and Monmouth, deep
cut through the coal measures, make the open-working and the
level natural methods while the more accessible of the good
seams are still unexhausted. At the time of the inquiry into
child-labour in the mines (1841–2), it was reported that there
were probably more level-worked mines than vertical pits. Two
years later the Tredegar Iron Company was "working a fine
vein of housekeeper's coal, 15 feet thick, which is only 10 in.
from the surface. It has the appearance of an immense stone
quarry, and is within half a mile of the railway that leads to
Newport."[1]

If open-workings and working by levels were curiosities outside South Wales, most coalfields except that of the Tyne and
Wear had plenty of old-fashioned shallow pits. Among the
famous rough sketches, introduced for the first time into a
government publication in the report on child-labour in
collieries, is one to illustrate the hardships of children when
getting to and from their work. A boy and a girl face one
another, holding a rope and sitting astride of a pole or plank
which is fastened to the end of it. Close above them, probably
somewhat nearer in the sketch than in real life, is an old woman
turning the handle of the winch which is hoisting them to the
upper air. Such crude arrangements or slight improvements
on them, in which a horse or a very small steam engine replaced
the old woman, were commonest in Yorkshire, Derbyshire,
Staffordshire and, as might be expected, in the small outlying
fields like those of Dean Forest and Somerset, where the pits
were often "mere well holes measuring only four or five feet
across."[2]

But, outside Wales, most of the coal which really drove the
country came from the deeper and deepest pits. In 1854, the
Northumberland and Durham fields were yielding more than
a quarter of the English, and nearly a quarter of the British,
coal. In the 'forties their preponderance must have been
greater and in the 'thirties greater still. It was a district of
deep pits: in the early 'thirties Monkwearmouth had been

[1] *Mining Journal*, XIV. 309, quoted in Galloway, *op. cit.* I. 349.
[2] Galloway, *op. cit.* I. 475.

driven down to 1590 ft., though this immense depth was unique[1]. The opening up of Durham by railway had produced an astonishing and sustained activity in development, at immense cost. In 1829–30 witnesses from the North spoke with deep respect of sums ranging from £10,000 to £150,000 being spent on the creation of single collieries[2]. Ten or twelve years later such figures had been left far behind. Probably the most formidable enterprise of the period was the sinking of three shafts for the Murton Colliery, belonging to Colonel Bradyll and Partners (the South Hetton Coal Company) between 1838 and 1843[3]. The shafts pierced a bed of quicksand, ten or twelve yards thick, which nearly beat the sinkers. So destructive was the sand to the leather working bands and buckets used in pumping, that three tanyards, it is said, were needed to keep up the supply; but the tanyards of the 'thirties were small[4]. Sums variously estimated at £250,000, £300,000 and £400,000 were spent before the company struck the Hutton seam at 1483 ft. Other enterprises had spent more. In 1836–7, coincident with the first railway boom, two joint-stock companies, the Durham Coal Company and the Northern Coal Mining Company, each with a capital of £500,000, appeared on the Durham field. They did a great deal of boring and pit sinking and then failed. The shareholders of one lost nearly all their capital, those of the other, owing to unlimited liability, all and as much again. Other people divided up the bankrupt inheritance, and development fell back into the hands of the old type of private partnership, in which pits were owned, like ships, in halves, quarters, eighths, sixteenths, thirty-seconds, and sixty-fourths, "which I think is the smallest I know of," as John Buddle said in 1829[5].

Tyneside proper, especially the north bank, was less active than Durham during the 'thirties; and some famous old collieries, such as Wallsend, were in low water. But they were revived by improved methods of working, and by the world-wide demand, in the 'forties, for a steam coal to burn fiercely

[1] Galloway, op. cit. I. 471.
[2] Coal Trade...in...London, 1830, p. 45, 50.
[3] V.C.H. Durham, II. 329 sqq., following Galloway.
[4] Above, p. 170.
[5] Coal Trade...in...London, p. 270. For the two joint-stock enterprises V.C.H. Durham, as above, and Galloway, op. cit. II. 11 sqq. They were not such frank swindles as the contemporary Northampton Coal Mining Co. which sank 900 ft. and then struck coal which the men had put in. Ibid. II. 19.

with a clean ash—such as they could supply. Sinking of new pits was resumed, among which the North Elswick reached the Beaumont seam at 588 ft. in 1845[1].

Lancashire, which in the 'fifties raised more coal than either South Wales or Scotland, and probably came second to the great Northern field in the 'forties and 'thirties, was also relying mainly on its newer and deeper pits. Even in the early 'thirties, although barges still moved along the adit which Brindley had made into the Duke of Bridgewater's Worsley collieries, most of the Lancashire coal came from pits 100 ft. deep and upwards; and in the Ashton and Oldham districts depths of 700 and 900 ft. had been reached[2]. Great and decisive sinkings began in the later 'thirties. At Pendleton, between 1838 and 1840, a seven-foot seam was reached at 1392 ft. and an organisation set up which could send into Manchester 1000 tons of coal a day—an appreciable fraction of the total Lancashire output at that time. A year later, and rather farther to the west, a four-foot seam was struck at about the same depth. The Wigan field, which supplied Liverpool and even America, was mainly worked at easier depths, 1200 ft.—the supposed limit of profitable working in 1830—not being reached in any pit before 1849; but it had ceased to rely on really shallow workings[3].

The Yorkshire mining engineers were not forced to go nearly so deep anywhere; but its heaviest consuming areas and the export trade in Yorkshire coal, which grew up with the railways, could not be supplied from the outcrop mines. Sheffield, even in 1819, had drawn its coal from pits which averaged between 300 and 400 ft.[4] Similar depths, with a maximum of under 600, were reported from Barnsley by the Children's Employment Commissioners more than twenty years later. While they were drafting their report, the greatest Barnsley colliery of the 'forties, the Oaks, was being driven down to 848 ft. South Staffordshire, whose wonderful "thick coal" —"the ten yard seam" and other seams—had been quarried or won from numberless small and shallow pits crowded against one another, had discovered, about 1840, that a thick coal, though not so thick, could be got by driving down to nearly 1000 ft. through beds of red sandstone below which,

---

[1] Galloway, op. cit. II. 6, 9.
[2] Ibid. I. 473.
[3] Ibid. I. 473; II. 17.
[4] Ibid. I. 473, following Hunter, History of Hallamshire.

it had been supposed, no coal was to be had[1]. South Wales, having learnt and taught the world the unique steam raising qualities of certain of its coals, between 1828 and 1838, was sinking deep when necessary, though it was not yet often necessary, to get them. Scotland's deepest pit was one of the many Victoria Pits of the period, near Paisley, which got just below the 1000-foot level in or about 1840. In England, much the deepest—so far as is known—was the Apedale Pit, in North Staffordshire, near Newcastle-under-Lyme, which had been driven below 2100 ft. even in the 'thirties[2].

All this deep sinking, and outputs such as those from the Pendleton pits, would have been impossible but for the progress of mining engineering during the 'thirties, mainly in the hands of the Northumberland and Durham experts—and for some little borrowing from the Continent. For a long time, approximately down to 1840, the winding engines were of no great size, often as small as 20 or 30 h.p., and that at important collieries Monkwearmouth had an engine of 66 h.p., but it only lifted 36 cwt. at a time[3]. Some of the Scottish pits, as the public learnt after 1840, did without winding machinery—women carrying the coal incredible distances up ladders and on their backs. With the 'forties came engines of 100, 120, 150 and even 175 h.p. for the deep pits of Lancashire and the North.

From the little winding engines of the 'twenties and early 'thirties ran a hempen cable on which the coal was hoisted, hanging free, in great wicker-work corves made of hazel rods. The adult miner came up, also hanging free, with a leg through a rope-loop on the cable; and the spirited mining lad, freer still, gripped it with hand and knee. Coal-raising in metal carriages, hung under a cross-bar which ran in guides, had been tried even before 1800: the method was common in the shallow Yorkshire pits by 1830. But a method suitable for deep pits was only worked out by T. G. Hall at the South Hetton Colliery, Durham, and afterwards at the Glebe pit, Ryton-on-Tyne, in 1834–5—the two-decker metal cage, into which the coal was loaded in iron tubs and the miners packed with something approaching comfort and safety. It was fitted with shoes so that it could run smoothly on iron guide rods, as it does

---

[1] *Report on Midland Mining*, 1843 (XIII), p. iv, xxvi *sqq.* Woodward, *Geology of England and Wales*, p. 188. Galloway, *op. cit.* II. 18.

[2] Galloway, *op. cit.* II. 351.

[3] *Ibid.* II. 326–7: facts mainly from the *Children's Report*.

still. Its introduction coincided with the invention of the wire rope, first used effectively at Clausthal in the Harz Mountains in 1834, and first patented in England by Andrew Smith in the following year. Wire ropes were being fitted to the more powerful winding engines of progressive collieries between 1842 and 1847. In 1849 a weight of over four tons was raised at Monkwearmouth through 1716 ft. in sixty-five seconds[1].

Far back in the eighteenth century, and first in a few Derbyshire and Staffordshire pits, some small circulation of air in the colliery workings had been secured by hanging so-called coal-lamps—iron baskets with fire in them—at points where motion was most needed. Later, in the nineteenth century, more effective currents were set up by great furnaces placed either at the top of one of the shafts or, latterly, at the bottom of the "upcast" shaft. By the 'forties, this second method had become almost universal in the deeper pits of the Northern field; and much attention had been given to the proper direction of the air through the workings. Northumberland and Durham, where the mines were deep and "fiery," had been driven to study ventilation. Lancashire, except for some of the best managed deep collieries, was backward: "in the great majority of cases the ventilation appears to have continued in an inefficient and unsatisfactory state."[2] In most other districts it had not received much attention before 1845, either because pits were shallow, or because they were not fiery, or for less defensible reasons. Very little had been done in Yorkshire; but considerable progress was made there in the later 'forties. The Midland fields had not got much beyond the fire lamp. Atmospheric changes might easily reverse the currents, when nature was left to control them—air tending to come down the upcast shaft and up the downcast. Then, in colliers' language, "the pits were fighting each other," and until the contest was decided work must stop[3].

Furnace ventilation was a crude method, with patent drawbacks and dangers. The upcast shaft was not always a mere chimney: there might be traffic in it with the smoke: in consequence its heat could not be allowed to get above 80° or 90°. A descent was, for laymen, a rather terrifying experience. If

---

[1] Galloway, *op. cit.* I. 479 *sqq.*; II. 330 *sqq.* *Industrial Resources of the Tyne, Wear and Tees* (1864), p. 256–7.

[2] Galloway, *op. cit.* II. 264; see also I. 252, 284, 327, 520.

[3] *Ibid.* II. 265.

the furnace did not get enough fresh air it might precipitate
an explosion. If it got plenty it might fire adjacent coal beds.
If an explosion occurred, *motu proprio*, the furnace must be
put out: then ventilation stopped: then the ugly decisions,
when and how to re-light the furnace, must be made. There
was consequently much discussion and, especially after 1840,
a considerable amount of experiment with alternative methods
—the creation of air-currents by the discharge of high-pressure
steam and by various kinds of air-pumps, screws, and fans.
But the decisive steps towards better ventilation were only
taken in 1849[1]. Health and safety were waiting on the inventor
and the mechanical engineer.

Welsh, Tyneside and Wigan steam coal had found a growing
but a slowly growing, market among the steamers, as the steam-
boats or steamships were now vulgarly called. "The ships
employed in the butter and cheese trade are of a peculiar
description; they are steamers, or vessels propelled by steam,"
a witness told a parliamentary committee in 1847[2]. The committee cannot have been quite so ignorant as the stilted phrasing
suggests. Steamers had been well before the public eye for
over twenty years. There were 924 of them on the British register
that year, with a tonnage of 116,000, in a mercantile marine of
some 3,000,000 tons: there had been 531 of 51,000 tons in
1837, and ⌐32 of 23,000 tons in 1827[3]. It is a slow growth, less
than the carrying capacity of one good-sized modern tramp
per year from 1837 to 1847; and the average tonnage of the
steamer of 1847 ($125\frac{1}{2}$) is diminutive. The tonnage of sailing
ships built in the United Kingdom in 1847 alone was almost as
great as that of the whole British mercantile steam fleet. Actually
there was something "peculiar," if not in a steamer, at least in
the fact that a complete trade should have got into steamers'
holds, as the cheese and butter trades—primarily Irish, but
since a recent change in the tariff, in part French—apparently
had. In spite of some considerable achievements on the

---

[1] "By Mr W. P. Struvé and Mr Wm. Brunton, in the South Wales coalfield,
almost simultaneously in 1849." Galloway, *op. cit.* II. 296. But ten years later
an expert could argue that mechanical ventilation had not yet "supplied the
same quantity of air" as the furnaces, "in well laid out mines." Taylor, T. J.,
Trans. Inst. Mech. Eng. January 1859, "On the progressive application of
machinery to mining purposes."
[2] *S. C. on Navigation Laws*, 1847 (x), Q. 2324.
[3] Porter, *op. cit.* p. 317–18.

Atlantic and in the East, the steamer remained what it had been from the start—a river boat; a tug; a mail and packet-boat for the narrow seas. The building of some sixty to seventy sets of small marine engines a year, an output which fully met the demand down to 1847, was not a broad enough foundation for a separate industry, although a few firms gave special attention to the work[1].

Even slower than the growth of the steamer fleet was the progress of the iron ship. Cort and those who perfected the methods of rolling wrought iron for its plates and girders had made it a possibility. An iron barge or two was all that the eighteenth century had produced. More iron canal boats, for horse traction, followed early in the nineteenth. Then, in 1822, Aaron Manby built in sections at Tipton the iron steamer which he called by his own name. As he was an ironmaster both in Staffordshire and at Charenton—and a little later at Creusot—he had it put together in London and navigated down the Thames and up the Seine by the future Admiral Sir Charles Napier. This feat might have been expected to fire imagination in two countries; but it did not; although, two years later, it was said that Manby had "established iron steam-boats on almost every river in France."[2] A little steamer for the Shannon is heard of (1825) and iron boats for the Irish canals, built by John Laird at Birkenhead, but nothing more till 1830. In that year the Council of the Forth and Clyde canal, in prompt fear of railway competition after the Rainhill trials, called William Fairbairn from Manchester, where he was designing mills with iron framework, to tell them how to meet it. He advised iron steamboats; he built two or three—stern-wheelers—in Manchester, after experiments which Laird and his brother attended, and sailed them down the Irwell Navigation. The Lairds did better: they built the *Alburkah* in which Macgregor Laird sailed up the Niger in 1832[3].

The Lairds had tide-water. Fairbairn determined to go to

---

[1] *E.g.* Maudslay had done so in London (above, p. 154), and on the Clyde, Robert Napier: see *D.N.B.*

[2] *S. C. on Artisans and Machinery*, p. 8: evidence of J. Martineau.

[3] See Fairbairn's *Treatise on Iron Shipbuilding* (p. vii, "This embraces almost entirely my own personal experiences"); and his *Remarks on Canal Steam Navigation*, 1831. He built over 100 iron ships at Millwall between 1835 and 1850. Smiles, *Industrial Biography*, p. 329. See also Laird, M., and Oldfield, R. A. K., *Narrative of an Expedition into the interior of Africa in the steam-vessels Quorra and Alburkah*, 1837.

it, "in order not only to carry out what appeared to him an entirely new and important principle of construction, but to prove that his previous researches were entitled to consideration, both on the part of the Government and those connected with the commercial enterprise of the country"; so he opened up at Millwall in 1835 in the face, as he said and as can well be believed, of "opposition from every quarter," especially "from the great builders and shipwrights of the capital."[1] On the Clyde, Robert Napier, who had made his first marine engines in 1823, began building iron ships to put them in in 1839–40. In 1846 was founded the firm which became the Thames Iron-works and built the first ironclad in 1858; and in 1847–8 Patersons of Bristol built the *Great Britain* of iron, and of 1200 horse-power[2]. These are the greatest of the early names.

But in 1847 iron ships were so rare and so little understood that Lloyd's had made no regular rating arrangements for them. The practice of the surveyors reflects their distrust of an innovation and the still somewhat experimental character of the iron ship. Instead of rating it A 1 for a term of years, as a wooden ship was rated, they made it only a yearly tenant of that honourable class[3]. They could have given good reasons. True, the *Aaron Manby* had needed no repairs to her hull in twenty-five years[4]; but she was small and in France and did not go to sea. It is very doubtful if so many as 150 sea-going iron ships had yet been built, and of these a large part had not run for five years. The Admiralty had had less than two years' experience with the *Birkenhead*, its first large iron ship, which Lairds began in 1845. No iron ship was seen on the Tyne till 1840 and very few were built there before 1850[5]. The Peninsular and Oriental Company, whose success with the iron ship did perhaps more than anything to establish it, had certainly not had five years' experience in 1847. In June 1844 they had owned one iron steamer for eighteen months, and another was building, so B. G. Willcox, their managing director, told a select committee[6]. Willcox was a convert and something of

---

[1] *Iron Shipbuilding*, p. 4.
[2] *V.C.H. Essex*, II. 499. 1851 *Exhibition Lectures*, I. 563. For Napier, the *D.N.B.* and Cornewall-Jones, R. J., *The British Merchant Service* (1898), p. 120.
[3] *S. C. on Navigation Laws*, 1847, Q. 3383.
[4] According to Porter, *op. cit.* p. 575.
[5] *Industrial Resources of the Tyne, Wear and Tees* (1864), p. 241. [See generally Smith, Capt. E. C., *A Short History of Naval and Marine Engineering* (1938).]
[6] *S. C. on British Shipping*, 1844 (VIII), Q. 1124 *sqq.*

a prophet. He held that "eventually almost all steam vessels would be built of iron"—sailing-ships too, perhaps: he knew one that had run for six years and was as good as new, and she was 10 to 15 per cent. cheaper than a first-class oak ship.

Between 1844, when Willcox expressed these opinions, and 1848, both houses of parliament made extensive inquiries into the condition and prospects of the British mercantile marine, in connection with the projected repeal of the navigation laws. No iron shipbuilder or maker of marine engines was examined. Scattered about the thousands of pages of evidence are a few references to steam and iron, besides those already quoted. One London shipowner in 1844 thought that steam had accentuated the depression in shipping[1]: he hardly recognised a steamer as a ship. A Liverpool owner agreed that the regular movements of the steamers had, of course, injured the sailers, but urged that they had been "almost the making of Liverpool."[2] Captain James Stirling, R.N., the first Governor of Western Australia, a critic of the press-gang and an advocate of a more professional "standing navy," had "no doubt," in 1847, that the use of steam would spread on Her Majesty's ships[3]. Money Wigram, the great Thames builder, gave one very important piece of evidence incidentally in 1848. Referring to the innovation which Willcox, four years earlier, had called an "archimedean screw," which Wigram now called a propeller, he declared that there was a decided advantage in making "propeller ships" of iron, and that iron building was cheaper in Great Britain than elsewhere[4]. But the main discussions turned, and in the then state of marine engineering if not of iron shipbuilding were bound to turn, on the cost of live-oak, treenails, shipwrights' labour, and "twelve-year" teak ships; and on the competition of the reputedly very inferior "colonial builts," from the seaboard states of British North America, or of the deadly, efficient and marvellously well-built Yankee clippers, with their cotton sails, from lower points on the American coast.

In the early days of factory inspection (1834–5) figures which the inspectors knew to be defective, and which ought therefore

---

[1] *Comm. of* 1844: G. F. Young, Q. 194.   [2] H. C. Chapman, Q. 1564.
[3] *Comm. of* 1847, Q. 4686.
[4] *Lords' Comm. of* 1848, Q. 6182 *sqq.* The famous competition of screw *versus* paddle—Rattler *v.* Alecto—occurred in 1845.

to be increased from 10 to 20 per cent., suggested that the cotton industry—the steam industry *par excellence*—used 30,000 h.p. of steam and 10,000 h.p. of water. The steam power installations were almost all in the Lancashire, Cheshire and Glasgow areas where the industry was highly concentrated. Of the 30,000 (? 34,500) h.p. Lancashire and Cheshire had nearly 25,000 (? 28,750) and Scotland, that is to say, the Glasgow area, 3000 (? 3450)[1]. The figures were collected on the eve of a period of very rapid development; for by 1838 over 15,000 more horse-power of steam had been, or were being, added in Lancashire and Cheshire alone[2]. The commercial and social difficulties of the 'forties, following on a cotton crisis in 1837, slowed down the rate of development. In 1850, the next year for which comprehensive factory figures were published, there were 71,000 h.p. of steam, and 11,000 h.p. of water, available for the whole of Great Britain[3]. This store of power was divided among about 1800 cotton "factories," giving 45·5 h.p. per "factory."[4] The word factory, as used by the inspectors in the 'thirties, 'forties and 'fifties, meant neither firm nor mill—for one firm might have several mills (each entered as a factory) and one mill might contain a number, sometimes a considerable number, of power-renting firms (each also entered as a factory). But even when some allowance has been made for the few firms which owned several mills, the power average per firm in 1850 would certainly be low. The aggregate use of power is low also.

All the other textile factory industries of the country at that time used only 34,000 h.p. of steam and 13,000 h.p. of water. More than a third of the power used in the English and Welsh woollen mills was water-power (12,600 steam; 6800 water). In the infant woollen mill industry of Scotland, there was nearly twice as much water-power as steam-power (1653 water; 880 steam). The worsted factory industry, already completely con-

---

[1] From figures supplied by the Inspectors to Edward Baines for his *History of the Cotton Manufacture* (1835). See the discussion there, p. 384–94. They do not include printing or bleach works.

[2] *S.J.* i. 315 (September 1838).

[3] For comparison it may be noted that the cotton industry of the United Kingdom, including a small section in Ireland, used 1,239,212 h.p. of steam and water *plus* some comparatively small amount of electric power, in 1907. *Census of Production* (Cd. 6320), p. 340.

[4] Returns issued in 1857 (LVII. 338) for the years 1850 and 1856.

centrated in the West Riding of Yorkshire which contained
71,000 out of the total of 79,000 workpeople, was more modern
in equipment: it used 9900 h.p. of steam and only 1600 h.p.
of water. It had an average power equipment per "factory"
of over 23 (steam or water), whereas the woollen industry's
average worked out at 14·6[1]. Among the woollen factories of
the 'forties were a great number of those company mills, with
many owners, which were such a feature of Yorkshire industry;
so it cannot be assumed that the average British woollen
manufacturer could lay his hand on the power of much more
than ten horses. Now these textile industries, with cotton, were
the great power users of the second quarter of the nineteenth
century, in manufacturing industry proper[2].

Such scattered figures as are available of the rate at which
power was adopted in other industries emphasize this fact.
While over 15,000 h.p. were being installed in the cotton mills
of Lancashire and Cheshire, between 1835 and 1838, 2036 h.p.
were installed in all the other industries of these highly industrial counties[3]. Of this total 592 h.p. were at collieries and
351 h.p. were to be used to help machines to make each other.
A considerable but unspecified amount would be used in those
branches of the cotton industry not yet classed as factories, as
some Manchester figures show. The total steam-power of
Manchester and Salford in 1838 was 9924½ h.p. Cotton spinning and weaving used 6036: bleaching, printing, and so on,
1277: "machine making, foundries, etc.," 734[4].

A series of carefully compiled figures to illustrate the progress of steam-power in Birmingham, from the beginning down
to December 1838, is illuminating[5]. The first modern engine
is said to have been erected there in 1780. In 1803, to quote
a few selected years, 4 were installed; 10 in 1816; 13, averaging
12·5 h.p., in 1826; 21 in 1836; 12 in 1837 and 18 in 1838.
There had been little increase in the average size of new installations between 1826 and 1838, for these 51 engines of 1836–8
averaged 12·6 h.p. In 1838, when the population of Birmingham (with Aston and Edgbaston) was about 175,000, the town
contained 240 engines of 3595 h.p., of which 2155 h.p. were

---

[1] All figures from the returns of 1857.
[2] The increase in output capacity was, however, greater than the increase in
power employed; for textile machinery was speeded up greatly between 1830
and 1850. Forbes, H., *The Worsted Industry*, in 1851 *Exhibition Lectures*, II. 301.
[3] *S.J.* I. 315.   [4] *Ibid.* II. 280.   [5] *Ibid.* II. 440.

used in its staple metal manufactures and the rest in miscellaneous and unspecified industries. Birmingham was a town of small businesses which turned out goods that were mostly light; but in view of the size of engines at coal mines and in cotton mills in the 'thirties, and of those in the woollen industry so late as 1850, it cannot be assumed that these figures are unusually small for the power-using industries of the country as a whole.

The industries which had either not begun, or barely begun, to adopt the new power must not be overlooked. There is, an expert wrote in 1816, "no manufactory of any kind that I know of in which so little improvement has been made for the last thirty years as that of grinding corn"[1]: there were no very conspicuous improvements in the next thirty, and the chief of them were improvements in windmills[2]. Steam driving, so far as is known, spread very slowly after the Albion Mills in London—the first to try it—were burnt down in 1791. It was adopted in South Lancashire in 1801, at Warrington, and in 1817 at Liverpool[3], and no doubt elsewhere; but the industrial district of the West Riding was still fighting for emancipation from the soke rights of old royal and manorial watermills in the 'thirties and 'forties. Only under 2 & 3 Wm. IV, c. 105 were "the inhabitants of Ossett-cum-Gauthorpe" discharged "from the custom of grinding corn at certain watermills in the townships of Wakefield and Horbury." Leeds bought the soke rights of the old king's mills in 1838: Wakefield did the same in 1843. At Bradford soke rights in malt were enforced many years later[4]. In a large town the existence of such rights did not necessarily mean that there was no free milling, for the rights might be enforced languidly or only financially; but their late survival indicates the toughness of the old legal organisation, and suggests the toughness of the old economic organisation, of the milling business. Apart from the Irish wheat, which no doubt was much used at the steam mills in Liverpool, Britain lived mainly on her own grain from 1830 to 1846. What the country districts and small towns consumed was ground on the spot, as it always had been, by water or wind; and the

---

[1] Sutcliffe, *On Designing and Building Watermills*, quoted in Bennett and Elton, *History of Corn Milling* (1898–1904), II. 199.

[2] *Ibid.* II. 307.   [3] *Ibid.* III. 293–4.

[4] *Ibid.* III. 256 *sqq.* The Manchester Grammar School held the soke of the malt-mill on the river Irk down to 1884, when it sold its rights for £1000 a year to the Lancashire and Yorkshire Railway. III. 282.

great towns, though making some use of steam, arew a large part of their supplies already ground from the country[1].

In the wood-working trades little machinery and less power was anywhere in use; and that in spite of the brilliant inventions of Bentham, Brunel and Maudslay during the wars[2]. Their work was half-forgotten and no mechanical progress was made from 1810 to 1835. Even the circular saw, first used in England about 1790, and the planing machine only began to make real headway in the mid-'thirties—and then only in the larger urban works[3]. In the country, in innumerable sawpits, the taciturn sawyers—"top," the expert, and "bottom," the drudge whose "view went no further than the end of the pit"—plied their monotonous craft and were to ply it long. Their epitaph, lately written by one who knew and honours them, is an axiom rather than an insult: "in my experience they were drunken to a man."[4]

In agriculture, the factory-farms of the Scottish type, whose steam engines had so much impressed Cobbett, made very slow progress indeed: "few farms in this Kingdom at present have these appendages," a most competent witness wrote in 1843[5]. And although the Ransomes of Ipswich—one of the few firms in the country who had used steam in the making of agricultural implements before 1840—won a prize from the Royal Agricultural Society in 1842, for "the application of portable locomotive steam engines to threshing,"[6] it was still necessary, at the time of the Great Exhibition, for the reporter on agricultural steam engines in general to beg their makers "to attend more to the proportions of the various working parts, and less to external ornament'"[7]; while the official commentator on threshing machines took his illustrations from those driven by horses. There was, however, real progress in the application of steam to the drainage of "marishes and fenny grounds."[8] Joseph Glynn, one of the pioneers, had dealt with 90,000 acres in the eight or ten years preceding 1838. But, in fen drainage, very little power is needed for great areas, as the

---

[1] Above, p. 231.   [2] Above, p. 153.
[3] Bale, *Woodworking Machinery* (1880), p. 3. 10, 79. Willis, 1851 *Exhibition Lectures*, I. 312.
[4] Sturt, *The Wheelwright's Shop* (1923), p. 37.
[5] Ransome, J. A., *The Implements of Agriculture*, p. 166.
[6] *V.C.H. Suffolk*, II. 284.   [7] 1851 *Exhibition Lectures*, II. 29.
[8] As they are called in the first drainage Act, the Statute of Improvements of 1601.

engine need never rest. A 20 h.p. low-pressure beam engine, installed for the South Holland Commission in 1833, drained 6000 acres[1]. To replace the seventy-five windmills that gyrated about Littleport Fen, Glynn set up two steam engines, one of 30 and one of 80 h.p.; and for all his 90,000 acres he only used 620 h.p. of steam[2]. Though much had been accomplished by 1846–7, the work was by no means finished, windmills being still very numerous especially in the fens of the Witham valley, from Boston to Tattershall and towards Lincoln[3].

Every windmill or engine in the fens in 1850 drove a "scoop-wheel." A centrifugal pump was one of the sights of the Great Exhibition: its inventor was commissioned to make one for the drainage of Whittlesea Mere and so to open the last phase in the control of the fenland waters[4].

The mechanical engineers of the later 'forties were becoming, but had not yet become, equipped for the work which they were to perform in the second half of the century. In the 'twenties they had been getting hold of rough machine tools; but they lacked instruments of precision to guide their work, and there were as yet no standards of manufacture, though Maudslay had made a beginning with a standard screw. For measurement they had only the rule, callipers and straight edge. Every fitting was, as has been said, personal[5]. Round about 1830, Roberts of Manchester who had worked out the self-acting mule in 1825, to counter a spinners' strike, and had greatly improved it since, was faced with a brisk demand for duplicates. He made standard templets—apparently for the first time—to aid his workmen in reproducing the parts[6]. In 1833 Joseph Whitworth, toolmaker, aged thirty, a pupil of Maudslay, set up in Manchester in a small way of business and began, in the intervals of his everyday occupations, the work of perfecting measurement and introducing absolute precision into engineering by the utilisation of the plane surface and the

---

[1] Wheeler, *A History of the Fens of South Lincolnshire*, p. 119.

[2] Glynn's account in *Trans. Roy. Soc. of Arts*, LI (1838), 15.

[3] Wheeler, *op. cit.* p. 189–90.

[4] Wheeler; *V.C.H. Lincs.* II. 351; 1851 *Lectures*, I. 415. For the scoop-wheel, see above, p. 19.

[5] Several points in this paragraph are drawn from the unpublished dissertation of Mr King, referred to on p. 152 n. 2.

[6] Ure, *The Cotton Manufacture*, II. 197–8 and *Philosophy of Manufactures*, p. 368. [There had been experiments with the self-acting mule before Roberts.]

gauges that bear his name. The work of devising and constructing was long, that of securing adoption longer. Neither, least of all the second, was complete in 1846-7. As for thorough standardisation, essential, as Whitworth recognised, if perfect measurement and precision were to lead to the maximum of economy and efficiency in manufacture, that was far from complete two generations later.

"An eminent engineer," said the great Dr Whewell in 1851, "has proposed a system by which uniformity would be secured in the dimensions and fitting of machinery; and especially with regard to screws; fixing thus their exact diameter and pitch, as it is called—a process which would have the effect of making the construction, application, and repair of all work into which screws enter vastly more easy and expeditious than it now is."

And again, "Mr Whitworth would classify screws, and wheels, and axles as the millwrights have classified toothed wheels."[1] Whitworth's system was in fact something more than a proposal, but very much less than a habit.

Yet under the influence of the technique worked out by men like Roberts and Whitworth, imperfectly developed and adopted as it was, old machine-making firms which dated back to the days of machinery that was mainly built of wood had become specialists in the new metal machinery and its adjuncts. Such, in the cotton-machine industry, were Dobson and Barlow of Bolton and Asa Lees and Co. of Oldham, both firms dating back to the eighteenth century[2]. Galloways of Manchester started in 1790, and in their early days were largely occupied with wooden water-wheel gear. In the 'thirties and 'forties they were giving special attention to the boilers with which their name has ever since been connected. Meanwhile, young firms were rising from the struggle at the bottom, among the ranks of those of whom there is no—or only a statistical— memorial, to a position which has made posterity interested in their beginnings. In 1821 Henry Platt, a small maker of carding machinery, started business at Oldham. Nine years later he was joined by William and Collin Mather, whose father had also been a machine maker of the old school, and together they worked at the "wheels of iron." One of the great cotton-loom-making firms of the late nineteenth century, R. Hall and Sons, was started by Robert Hall at Bury in 1844. Hall—naturally— worked with his hands and three men worked with him[3].

---

[1] 1851 *Lectures*, I. 27. The proposal had first been made ten years earlier.
[2] *V.C.H. Lancashire*, II. 369.   [3] *Ibid.* II. 370.

Railways brought the locomotive firm, or turned older firms to locomotive building. There was the Vulcan foundry at Newton-le-Willows, in which the Stephensons were for a time interested, and the Newcastle firm which bore their name. The firm with which Roberts was connected, known in the 'thirties as Sharp Roberts and Co., also did locomotive building, among other things. So did the Hawthorns of Gateshead, whose business had been founded for work of a different kind in 1817[1]. In 1836 at Leeds, James Kitson founded a specialised locomotive business which grew rapidly in the next ten years. And there were others.

There had not been time, since engineering began to take its modern form, for many of them to grow great, and the total number of men and boys engaged in the engineering trades proper in 1846–7, which may have been 40,000–45,000 in all Britain, would not have provided a working force for many businesses comparable with the principal cotton mills. The Census Commissioners of 1851 secured employment figures from 677 English "engine and machine makers."[2] Of these 457 employed less than 10 men; 147 employed from 10 to 39; 39 from 40 to 99; 9 from 100 to 199; 8 from 200 to 299; 3 from 300 to 349; and 14 employed 350 men and upwards. At that time 113 cotton firms and 34 woollen or worsted firms were reported in this last category. There can be no doubt that a census taken four years earlier would have shown an appreciably smaller scale of organisation in engineering and not an appreciably smaller scale in the textiles. Engineering and engineering firms were growing with extreme rapidity precisely at this time, as the Census Commissioners noted. Joseph Whitworth, for example, had 172 names on his books in 1844: ten years later he had 636[3]. No doubt he had passed into the topmost category at the time of the census. So had the Kitson works at Leeds: there were 259 men at work on the last pay-day in 1845: in 1851 the figure was 431[4]. Of William Armstrong at Elswick this is more doubtful, yet is probable. He became managing director in 1847 with only about 200 men under him; but in

---

[1] *Industrial Resources of the Tyne, Wear and Tees*, p. 252.

[2] Population Tables II, *Ages…Occupations, etc.* (1852–3, LXXXVIII. parts I and II), p. cclxxvii. The results are imperfect, as 160 firms made no return; but it is safe to assume that most of these were small.

[3] *V.C.H. Lancashire*, II. 572.

[4] From the books of the firm, figures supplied by Mr E. Kitson Clark.

the next few years Elswick grew very fast[1]. It would not be at all surprising to find that in 1846–7 not more than half a dozen—possibly not so many—firms of "engineers and machine makers" were in the topmost category, while it would be most surprising were fewer than a hundred cotton firms in that category at the same date. For in cotton the great firm was well established, with a reasonably complete mechanical equipment, at a time when, as William Fairbairn said, "the whole of the machinery was executed by hand,"[2] and engineering proper, as opposed to machine making, did not exist. In 1846–7 the mechanical engineer was getting ready to turn the world upside down and to "mix me this zone with that."

[1] *Industrial Resources of the Tyne, Wear and Tees*, p. 252.
[2] Above, p. 154.

CHAPTER XI

AGRICULTURE

IT is not to be supposed that the slowly changing framework of British rural society could be much altered in little more than half a generation—in half of any generation; and during the early railway age it was hardly probable that even the rate of structural change normal to modern times, whatever that may be, would be kept up. It was, in a sense, a waiting time. War was long since over and gone; its aftermath had been reaped and was being enjoyed. The Reform Bill did not put the government of England, and no economic upheaval put the land of England, into fresh hands. Enclosure in the lowlands had pretty well done its work: what remained to do would scarcely show on the statisticians' gauges[1]. The railways themselves were beginning to affect function: they had not had time to tell on structure. Lastly, down to 1846, the agricultural policy of governments was uncommonly stable.

The census of 1831 had registered for the whole of Great Britain 275,000 families engaged in agriculture and occupying land which they cultivated with or without the assistance of hired labour[2]. The more exact and trustworthy returns of 1851 gave the, comparable, figure of 286,000 "farms"—agricultural units carrying families—excluding, in some Scottish counties, a large number of "crofters and other holders of small portions of land."[3] There may have been similar omissions in England and Wales, but as the crofter type hardly occurred in either they would be unimportant. Little change is shown here during the twenty years. Again, in 1831 it was said that 47·3 per cent. of the occupiers in Great Britain employed no hired labour. In 1851, 44·7 per cent. of the "farmers" either employed no hired men or omitted to state the number they employed[4]. The figures are surprisingly close. That those of 1851, and therefore

---

[1] Lord Ernle's statement (*English Farming*, p. 355) that "in 1837 the open-field system still prevailed extensively" is rather misleading. Properly speaking, it did not prevail anywhere: it survived in various places. See below, p. 454.

[2] Above, p. 113.

[3] *Census of* 1851, "Population Tables" (1854), II. 1025 and I. cclxxxii.

[4] Above, p. 113, and *Census of* 1851, as above.

presumably those of 1831 also, are not seriously vitiated by omissions is shown by an analysis of the very detailed statistics of the former year. There are some obvious omissions: 134 farmers, each of whom held over 600 acres, made no labour return; but of the 128,000 farmers all told who made no such return, over 102,000 were men with holdings under 50 acres, holdings of the type on which outside labour is not normally required. No doubt many thousand holders of farms from 50 to 75 acres, and some thousands farming more than 75 acres, did—as they declared—work without hired labour, at any rate without regular hired labour. The tables suggest that failures to make returns would not reduce the 128,000 much below, say, 120,000 or the 44·7 per cent. much below 42 per cent. Certainly this type of family-worked farm was declining during the early railway age; but decline must have been very slow.

Therefore it is to be expected that the exact statistics of the sizes of farms and of the varying ratios of employers to employed in different parts of the country, as brought out in the 1851 Census, should confirm rather than diverge from the much vaguer data of twenty or thirty years earlier[1]. "*Two-thirds* of the farms in Great Britain," the Commissioner of 1851 reported with emphasis, "are under 100 acres." The average farm, that unsubstantial entity, was of 102 acres[2]: for England and Wales it was of 111: for Scotland of 74. But in Wales and Yorkshire more than seven-tenths of the farms were under 100 acres and in Lancashire and Cheshire nearly nine-tenths; whereas in the south midland area—extra-metropolitan Middlesex, Hertford, Buckingham, Oxford, Northampton, Huntingdon, Bedford and Cambridge—appreciably less than half the farms were under 100 acres.

Of 1810 farms reported on in Buckinghamshire, 872 fell into the groups between 100 and 300 acres, and 229 into the groups above 300 acres, much the largest groups being those of 100–150 acres (322 farms) and 150–200 acres (229 farms), figures which confirm roughly the curiously precise estimate made many years earlier, that the average Buckinghamshire farm was of 179 acres[3]. Buckingham was generally representative of the whole south midland group except Cambridge, of whose

---

[1] As summarised above, p. 111 *sqq.*

[2] i. lxxix. The Census officials noted, as a curiosity, how near this was to the 120-acre hide of Domesday. The figures exclude mountain pasture attached to farms.　　　　[3] Above, p. 111.

3291 holdings 1919 were under 100 acres, and whose largest single group (346 farms) was that of holdings between 10 and 20 acres[1]. In Lancashire, still and always the county of maximum *morcellement*, out of 15,450 farms not 600 exceeded 150 acres and nearly 10,500 were under 40[2]. In Scotland there was "at once a great excess of *small* and *large* holdings. There are 360 farms in Scotland, and 771 farms in England, of 1000 acres and upwards. There are 142,358 farms in England, and 44,469 farms in Scotland, each of which is under 100 acres."[3]

The economic and territorial dominance of the large farm, already well established before 1830, was first fully revealed in 1851. Of 24,700,000 acres of farmed land reported on for England and Wales[4], covering "two-thirds of the English territory," considerably more than a third (8,821,000 acres) was laid out in farms of from 200 to 500 acres, and nearly another sixth (3,954,000 acres) in farms of 500 acres and upwards. The farms of 100–200 acres covered more than a quarter of the whole area (6,556,000); leaving to the 142,358 farmers of holdings under 100 acres considerably less than a quarter, or 5,345,000 acres. So far was the average farm of 111 acres from being representative. The same was true, *mutatis mutandis*, for Scotland. For neither country was it new. The movement towards the large farm, the complement of the movement away from the subsistence farm, was of necessity equally slow.

Rough occupation statistics collected for the Census of 1831 had shown that for every household holding and cultivating land in Great Britain there were 2½ households of agricultural labouring folk[5]. The 286,000 farms of 1851 could draw for their labour on 1,078,000 people of all ages and both sexes —71,000 were women—classed as outdoor agricultural labourers, and on 364,000 indoor farm servants, of whom 128,000 were women and girls and 236,000 men and lads—or exactly five wage-earning workers per farm[6]. No doubt many of those classed as outdoor agricultural labourers were not in work, or not in regular work, at the time of the Census; but for the

---

[1] From the tables in *Census of* 1851, I. 238–40.   [2] II. 658.
[3] I. lxxxi.   [4] I. lxxix–xi: again excluding mountain pasture.
[5] Above, p. 114.
[6] I. cxxiii. As, in the personal returns, 307,000 persons called themselves farmers or graziers, some of whom were retired from these callings, the 286,000 farms must be a fairly accurate figure.

moment that fact is immaterial. Close comparisons between data collected on such different principles are impossible; but so far as comparison is justified, the view that the structure of rural society had changed very little in the twenty years is fully borne out. Of the 1,442,000 wage earners and potential wage earners of all sorts, the 404,000 under twenty years of age would mostly come from rural wage-earning households. Many such households would supply two adult members to the national labour force. If the average contribution were the father and one full-working child, under or over twenty, which is not improbable, the old proportion of 2½ labouring households to every farm would be precisely maintained. The persistence of old conditions is further illustrated by the remarkable number of male indoor farm servants, mostly aged from fifteen to twenty-five, found precisely in those counties where the vaguer evidence of 1820–30 would lead one to expect them. There was still nearly one of these to every farm throughout the United Kingdom; and very many farms would not need one. Out of the 236,000 there were 160,000 in England, 31,000 in Wales and 45,000 in Scotland. In Surrey, Hampshire, Cornwall, Warwick and Stafford, in North and South Wales and in Scotland, their number very nearly equalled that of the farmers. It was slightly greater than that of the farmers in Kent, Hertford, Berkshire, Leicester, Lincoln, the North Riding and Cumberland. It was appreciably greater in Cheshire and Nottingham, and much greater in Devon, Shropshire and the East Riding. It was much less in counties with many small grass farms—Lancashire, Derbyshire, the West Riding; and also in Northumberland, Durham, Dorset, Somerset, Wiltshire, Worcester, Sussex, Oxford, Buckingham, Northampton, Huntingdon, Bedford, Cambridge, and all East Anglia[1]. The class includes the grooms and house boys of the big farmers; but its distribution shows that the majority were real farmworkers, often no doubt—as in Lincolnshire or Cumberland

[1] Examples from the various groups of counties:

County	Farms	Male indoor servants		County	Farms	Male indoor servants
a { Surrey	1,814	1,596	d { Devon	11,150	15,277
{ Warwick	3,580	3,289	{ E. Riding	4,263	7,451
b Kent	4,659	4,994	e Lancashire	15,986	8,720
Lincoln	10,189	10,878	f { Durham	3,715	2,725
Cheshire	6,380	7,279	{ Wiltshire	3,084	1,046
			{ Norfolk	6,473	2,355

to-day—horsemen or waggoners. Its decline has suffered exaggeration in popular historical retrospect, partly because it was most serious in East Anglia and those recently enclosed Midlands whose agrarian history too often serves as the agrarian history of England, partly because historians are not always well acquainted with contemporary England, where the class is far from extinct.

There were counties in which enclosure was very nearly finished by 1830: only 800 acres were dealt with subsequently by Act of Parliament in Middlesex and only 2200 acres in Kent[1]. There were none in which much enclosure of arable remained to do. Only a hundred and twenty-five special enclosure Acts and one general Act (6 & 7 Wm. IV, c. 115) got on to the Statute Book during the 'thirties[2]. So little known were the more perfect specimens of open-field husbandry by the 'forties than an experienced witness, before the Select Committee of 1844, expressed himself as "very much surprised indeed" to find whole parishes with hardly any several land in Yorkshire, Oxford, Berkshire and elsewhere[3]. Under the resultant Act (8 & 9 Vict. c. 118), 259 applications, affecting something over 160,000 acres, were made to the Commissioners during the three years 1845-8[4]. The small average area dealt with, about 600 acres, is noticeable; and yet the applications included a few big moorland propositions, such as the 3370 acres of Malham Moor above Airedale. Now and again some large part of an open-field village occurs among them—Milton Common Fields, 2090 acres, in Oxford; Wilburton Open Fields, 779 acres, and Isleham fields, 1359 acres, in Cambridge; Golding-ton, Bedford, 1092 acres; and so on—but the main business of the Commissioners was the handling of hill common, moor and down. By 1847 only about half-a-dozen open-field parishes were left in Cambridgeshire, where they had been so numerous twenty-five years earlier[5].

The gloom which hung over so much of rural England when the early railway age began deepened for five years, never lifted

---

[1] *Return of Inclosure Acts* (Cd. 399), 1914, p. 38, 22. [In the first edition it was wrongly stated that the last Middlesex Act was of 1825, after *V.C.H. Middlesex*, II. 109.]   [2] *S.J.* VI. 269.

[3] *S. C. on Commons Inclosure*, Q. 185. W. Blamire, Tithe Commissioner.

[4] *Third Report of Inclosure Commissioners*, 1848 (XXVI. 201).

[5] *J. R. Ag. Soc.* VII. 38. Jonas, S. "Report on Cambridge": and above, p. 20.

decisively, and when the age closed—with the corn laws repealed—was at its deepest. To the end of 1835 wheat prices slid along an almost smooth downward line—from a mean annual price of 62s. 4½d. in 1830 to one of 38s. 1½d. in 1835[1]. Wool, it is true, was moving the other way—South Down, which had averaged 1s. 1d. a lb. from 1821–30 averaged 1s. 4¾d. from 1831 to 1837, and the corresponding Lincoln averages were 9½d. and 1s. 2d.[2]—but neither butter nor beef moved to the producer's advantage, and the other grains generally followed wheat[3]. It is not surprising that the parliamentary Committee on Agriculture of 1833 was followed by another in 1835; or that the chairman of the second, Sir James Graham, a most capable working land-owner who had been a soldier in his youth, cheered himself with the thought that, if such prices were possible whilst population grew apace and nine farmers out of ten were farming worse than they need, there was a fair chance that the British Isles might remain self-sufficing.

From 1836 to the second week of January 1839, wheat prices climbed, with vicissitudes, to 81s. 6d.—while workmen in the towns became Chartists and Manchester started the Anti-Corn-Law League—to fall again, also with vicissitudes, to 45s. at the end of February 1845; so that "the Manchester confederates seemed to be least in favour with Parliament and the country on the very eve of their triumph."[4] In 1846, the year of repeal, 47s. 5d. and 56s. 3d. were the extreme limits of the fluctuations of weekly prices; but the Irish Famine year, 1847, saw 66s. 10d. in January, 102s. 5d. in May and 53s. in December. And so down again steadily to an average little above 40s. in 1850, and below 40s. in 1851, with no general compensating rise in wool or butter or beef[5].

Low or violently fluctuating prices for the staples of agriculture were not sufficient to stop movements already well under way, especially when those movements were such as the enterprise of scattered individuals could maintain; but they added much to the difficulties of initiation. Coke of

---

[1] Based on Tooke, T., *History of Prices*, II. 390.

[2] *S.J.* I. 56.

[3] For butter and beef are taken, as more or less representative, and for lack of anything better, the Irish wholesale prices in Tooke, *op. cit.* II. 408.

[4] Disraeli, *Lord George Bentinck* (ed. 1906), p. 6.

[5] Price figures from Tooke and Jevons' diagram in *Investigations in Currency and Finance*.

Norfolk worked on to his death, in his ninetieth year, in 1842, and he had imitators in most counties. The Southdown sheep which, with the marling of sandy soils to make them fit for wheat, were among his chief interests, spread steadily and so did the shorthorn cattle—the first of all the herd-books had been started, for shorthorns, in 1822[1]. Jonas Webb, of Babraham, in Cambridgeshire, was improving and spreading these two standard breeds during the 'thirties and 'forties. So far away from their places of origin as North Wiltshire, they drove out the horned Wiltshire sheep and the long-horned cattle almost completely, between 1815 and 1845[2]. Root and seed-crops were now known everywhere, if not everywhere used or intelligently cultivated. To the ordinary turnip, which would rarely keep beyond February, had been added the swede—first heard of in Britain just before 1800—and the mangel-wurzel, both more resistant to frost[3]. The very depth of depression turned the attention of active minds towards manuring. Bone dust had been widely tried, as a rule with good results, and by 1840 at least it may be said to have become generally known. It did wonders on the pastures of Cheshire between 1835 and 1844—and was described in the latter year as of "incalculable value" in Wiltshire[4]. Rape-dust had established itself locally in the Humber counties—Yorkshire, Lincoln and Nottingham— but was known only to the specialists elsewhere. There had been experiments with nitrate of soda: it had great successes and great failures: to some it seemed rather a mystery, to others "to have had its day" by 1845[5]. Lastly, but only in the 'forties, came guano and mineral superphosphate[6]. By 1842, Philip Pusey had come to the conclusion that guano was excellent for roots, "if properly applied"; and, four years later, when the import of guano had reached nearly 300,000 tons in one year, Lord George Bentinck was submitting to the House of Commons one of his "original and startling calculations"[7] about it. "'Multiply then,' exclaimed Bentinck with the earnest air of a crusader, 'six million six hundred and sixty-six thousand, six hundred and sixty by fifteen, and you have no less than

---

[1] Lord Ernle (Prothero), op. cit. p. 354. The next was in 1837.
[2] J. R. Ag. Soc. v. 179 (1845). [3] Ibid. III. 201.
[4] Ibid. v. 168; for Cheshire, v. 68. See also III. 210.
[5] Ibid. v. 168: the main source is Pusey's article in vol. III (1842).
[6] The first cargo of guano is credited to 1835 (Lord Ernle, op. cit. p. 366), but it took some years to "come": Pusey calls it "this last new manure" in 1842.
[7] Disraeli, op. cit. p. 67. The imports were, 1846, 283,000 tons; 1847, 89,000.

ninety-nine million nine hundred and ninety-nine thousand and nine hundred pounds of mutton as the fruits of one hundred thousand tons of guano.'" Though an excellent manure, it hardly worked so arithmetically as that.

John Lawes secured his patent for the manufacture of mineral superphosphate—from coprolites—in 1842 and started the manufacture at Deptford next year, the year in which his agricultural inquiries and research took permanent form in an experimental station at Rothamsted[1]. Superphosphate was being tried in the late 'forties and Rothamsted was exciting attention; but neither had yet really made itself felt. In fact, there was much misunderstanding and disappointment connected with the early days of agricultural chemistry. The foundation was laid, for England, with the publication of Liebig's *Organic Chemistry in its applications to Agriculture and Physiology*, in 1840[2]. Immense zeal was aroused, but the zeal was sometimes misdirected. Having learnt, for instance, that the chief chemical contribution of farmyard manure to plant growth was ammonia, some argued that it was therefore advisable to plough the manure in fresh so as to waste as little ammonia as possible[3]. Not all Liebig's own views were to stand criticism; so it was natural that his popularisers should err, and that the errors should confirm the great majority of unlearned farmers in their inherited knowledge or superstitions. Even fallible popularisation was a very slow process.

Knowledge of new fertilisers, whether applied wisely or imprudently, was therefore the monopoly of a few. James Caird, travelling through the country as an agricultural explorer, in 1850–1[4], wrote much about the new methods because he wished to instruct; but it is clear that what he called "antiquated farming" still dominated all but a few selected areas—such as northern Northumberland, central and northern Lincolnshire, or Coke's country in Norfolk. In "antiquated farming" it was usual to find even farmyard manure "treated as a troublesome nuisance,"[5] "the solid manure lying about the yards, and the liquid draining itself off to the watering-pond or the nearest open ditch."[6] In average districts intelligent and "antiquated" farming were constantly found side by side,

---

[1] *D.N.B.*   [2] Edited from Liebig's MS. by Lyon Playfair.
[3] Pusey in *J. R. Ag. Soc.* III. 208.
[4] *English Agriculture in 1850 and 1851.*   [5] P. 499.
[6] P. 6 (Buckinghamshire).

and in many intelligence was exceptional. "The successful practices of one farm, or one county, are unknown or unheeded in the next."[1]

Depression and the manager of a Scottish cotton mill were the proximate causes of the interest in the problem of drainage widely shown during the late 'thirties and 'forties. The method of ridding heavy soils of excessive moisture by means of a series of numerous parallel drains had long been known and practised in Essex, especially on the "marly" (*i.e.* not very heavy) clays of "The Roothings," south of Dunmow[2]. It was known, too, in Suffolk, Hertford and South Norfolk. Outside this area, and the fens, drainage had consisted mainly in the tapping of actual springs. Drains were few and deep. There was also, before 1830, some furrow drainage in the heavily ridged-up fields of the true clays—where ridges had almost everywhere survived the open-fields—an actual drain being laid in the furrow to help carry off the water. Some drains were filled with haulm, peat, ling or thorns—the old Essex way; some with stones, broken or on edge; some with tiles, flat or "sole" tiles for the bottom, bent "horseshoe" tiles above, to keep the water channel open.

Between 1823 and 1833 James Smith, manager of the Deanston factories in Perthshire, found that by laying drains from 16 to 21 ft. apart, $2\frac{1}{2}$ ft. deep, filled with stones, and by stirring the subsoil with a specially designed heavy plough, he could turn "a rush grown marsh into a garden."[3] In 1831 he published his *Remarks on Thorough Draining and Deep Ploughing* and in 1835 gave evidence before Sir James Graham's Agricultural Committee of that year. Thenceforward his method was in the mouth of all rural improvers; and when the Royal Agricultural Society was founded, in 1838, its *Journal* soon filled with discussions of Deanston methods. Graham pointed out, in the first number (1840), that "furrow draining and deep ploughing had been practised in England for half a century; yet the introduction of an analogous system into Scotland is regarded as almost a discovery."[4] It was true; but the English cry of "they manage these things better"—in France, Scotland, or Germany according to the thing or the age—has its uses;

---

[1] *English Agriculture in* 1850 *and* 1851, p. 499.

[2] Above, p. 134, and the valuable notes on early drainage in *J. R. Ag. Soc.* IV. 23 *sqq.*

[3] Lord Ernle, *op. cit.* p. 364.   [4] *J. R. Ag. Soc.* I. 29.

and in fact most of the rare English furrow drains had been unscientifically laid.

Two years later Philip Pusey, while announcing his "accidental discovery"[1] of the East Anglian anticipators of James Smith, maintained that nevertheless one-third of England would still be the better for Deanston or Essex "through" drainage. Cost was the chief obstacle, since those parts of England which most needed drainage often lacked the stones ubiquitous in Scotland, and the rough Essex methods were not everywhere trusted. In 1835, Beart of Godmanchester was using a tile-making machine which enabled him to sell at 22s. a thousand tiles which elsewhere fetched 40s. to 60s. These were the old "sole" and "covering" tiles[2]. Many years earlier[3], experiments had been made in Kent with hand-made clay pipes. Somewhere about 1840, a pipe made by a rough machine "seems to have originated in Essex": before 1842–3 it had "taken root" in Suffolk and Sussex and was being tried in parts of Kent[4]. The Royal Agricultural Society fostered it by prizes and experiment. By 1847 Josiah Parkes, the Society's consulting engineer, was able to report with proper gratification that the judges now had difficulty in selecting "the most meritorious pipe machine."[5] In less than three years, while Bentinck was working equations in guano and mutton and Peel was falling from office though not from power, the maximum daily output per machine grew from 1000 feet of pipe to 20,000. The thing could now be done; and in 1846 Peel was consulting Parkes at Drayton Manor. Prestige and publicity were secure; but not very much of Pusey's drain-needing third of England had got its thorough drainage when Peel died in 1850.

As "commissioner" for *The Times*, in 1850–1, Caird reported again and again on the deficiency. In the Vale of Aylesbury there was "great room for improvement by drainage, though the grass lands, especially those of prime quality, have generally been drained by wedge or wood drains."[6] In Wiltshire some landlords were supplying pipes but most tenants were putting them in badly. It was the same in Hampshire: "much of the country, where nothing but drainage is required to render the

---

[1] *J. R. Ag. Soc.* III. 169.
[2] *Ibid.* II. 93; III. 193.
[3] "Some thirty-five," *ibid.* IV. 372.
[4] Josiah Parkes in *J. R. Ag. Soc.* IV. 369.
[5] *Ibid.* VII. 249.
[6] In the Essex style (Caird, *op. cit.* p. 1–2).

soil abundantly fruitful, is...either imperfectly drained or not drained at all." Essex clung to its cheap and rather short-lived haulm-filled drains, "because in very few instances does the landlord contribute one farthing to the permanent improvement of his land." This was on the lighter clays: "in the heavy clay district tile drainage is not approved of. The land is...laid into narrow stetches, with water furrows to carry off the surface water." Suffolk drained its clay soils effectively but cheaply in the old style, without pipes. In Warwickshire there was too much of the defective furrow-draining of heavily ridged fields. Staffordshire was doing well, "the experience [of handling water] acquired in the mining operations of the district having proved very valuable"; but plenty still remained to do[1]. Much of Cheshire also had been well cared for, the fortunate landlords of the dairying districts being in a position to find the tiles. But there had been a deal of bad work by farmers. "He who could 'bury' the greatest number of tiles accounted himself and was generally accounted by his landlord the best tenant." Five years earlier it had been reported that the drainage of Cheshire as a whole was "lamentably defective."[2] Two-thirds of the Fylde district in Lancashire was "still undrained, and comparatively unimproved." There was activity in the Vale of York, where many landlords were "availing themselves of the drainage loan"[3]; and results were anticipated in a year or two, but "by far the greater portion of it" was still "undrained and badly farmed." "An immense extent of tile drainage had been made" in the rain-drenched fields of West Cumberland, but unhappily much of it had been "comparatively of little effect, from having been done too shallow." In Durham draining was still "greatly neglected." In Northumberland, where it was more attended to, "in many cases...drains are still being put in with the old expensive 3-inch horsehoe tiles and soles." And it was little less true in 1848-50 than it had been in 1842 that "a great portion...of the North-West of England and Wales" was "undrained grass land, almost in a state of nature, divided into very small fields by rambling, uncouth hedges."[4]

In contrast to this, the high farming on the coastal strip of the Lothians, in the Carse of Gowrie, and in Southern Perthshire

---

[1] The references, Wiltshire to Warwick, are p. 75, 89, 135, 152, 225, 230.

[2] Caird, *op. cit.* p. 256, and *J. R. Ag. Soc.* v. 77 (1845).

[3] Under Peel's "consolation" Act of 1846, 9 & 10 Vict. c. 101.

[4] Lancashire to Northumberland, p. 281, 326-7, 361, 335, 378: for 1842 Greg, *Scotch Farming in the Lothians*, p. 5.

—to name the leading Scottish districts—was, already in 1842, entirely based upon thorough drainage, on which the farmers had spent huge sums, more often than not without assistance from the landlords but relying on their 19- or 21-year leases. "There are no trees in the hedgerows, and few furrows, *the [drained] land being laid down flat*," the English admirer reported[1], his italics bearing witness to a common survival of the traditional ridge and furrow south of the Tweed. But not all Scotland was drained and farmed like the Lothians.

The Lothian farmers also, with the best farmers of Northumberland, retained the lead in the use of machinery secured before 1830. Nearly everyone now had his steam engine, usually a 6 h.p. high-pressure type, costing from £110 to £120. Threshing was its main business, for which it was harnessed to an £80 or £90 thresher of a type made at Corstorphine; but sometimes it was put to other uses. Even when worked only in harvest it paid: it is "a stud of horses which eat nothing except when at work," wrote one user[2]. The Scottish threshers were said to be "infinitely superior to the miserable machines creeping into use in the South of England,"[3] in 1842. There, the travelling steam-driven machine had just arrived, but still had to win its way. Portable machines, "frequently the property of individuals,"[4] had long been known in East Anglia, but they were hand- or horse-driven. In the first number of the *Journal of the Royal Agricultural Society* steam power had been suggested, and in the third number (1842) Pusey was able to announce that Ransomes of Bristol and other firms had put such machines on the market[5]. But right through the 'forties the progress of any kind of threshing, or indeed other, machinery was excessively slow. Pusey could write, in 1842, of whole districts "where the flail is exclusively used."[6] In the following year "neither modern machinery nor artificial manures" were to be found at Hanwell; a solitary winnowing machine, but no other modern device, existed in the parish of Northwood; and the first threshing machine had just reached Ealing. Its owner

---

[1] Greg, *op. cit.* p. 7. See also his *Scotch Farming in England*, p. 9.

[2] Greg, *Scotch Farming in the Lothians*, p. 6, 14–15. For machinery in Scotland and Northumberland generally see *S.J.* I. 401 (1838); *J. R. Ag. Soc.* II. 178 (1841).

[3] Greg, *op. cit.* p. 5.

[4] Ransome, J. A., *The Implements of Agriculture* (1843), p. 151: see above, p. 140.

[5] *J. R. Ag. Soc.* III. 215.   [6] *Ibid.*

was blamed for injuring the labourers, and that "at a farmers'
ordinary."[1] Seven years later, even the winnowing machine
was unknown in parts of Surrey, and Sussex farming was
incredibly primitive—six bullocks to an all-wooden plough,
"within a couple miles of Brighton," linking the days of Queen
Victoria to those of the Empress Matilda. In Oxfordshire
threshing machinery, of a sort, was used "on the large farms"
for wheat; but even on large farms barley was threshed by the
flail, partly to find work for labourers and partly "because the
machines in use cut the grain too short, and thus injure it for
the maltster." There were travelling threshing machines in
northern and western Wiltshire, but not the steam sort. They
were hand-driven: four men and a boy reckoned twenty-four
bushels of wheat a good day's work. Meanwhile, just across
the Dorset border, the steam engine of Mr Huxtable, the
farmer-parson, "threshes and winnows the corn, cuts the...
chaff, turns the stones for grinding the cattle food into meal,
and by a separate belt, when requisite, works a bone-crusher."
Such installations were rare south of the Tyne and had failed
to set a fashion. "The same day on which we saw the steam
engine of Mr Thomas of Lidlington in Bedfordshire, with
which he is enabled to thrash his wheat crop for 1d. a bushel,
we found other farmers paying four or five times as much for
the same operation, not so well done by hand."[2]

As for reaping, an effective machine was still to seek. There
is none "which gives promise of soon meeting general regard,"
a Scotsman wrote in 1840, and ten years later there was still
none[3]. Ransome and May of Ipswich employed more than
800 men, in 1850, and made "upwards of 300 distinct varieties
of the plough," besides scarifiers, harrows, threshing machines,
clod crushers and many other implements, but no reaper. Nor
did Garretts of Leiston, near Saxmundham, whose drills and
horse-hoes were the best known in England[4]. These implements at least were now well established. Pusey, who knew
best the relatively backward counties of Berkshire, Wiltshire,
Oxford and Hampshire, had been able to write in 1842 that
"the sower is now seldom seen"; though, in Suffolk, wheat, and

---

[1] *S.J.* VI. 120 *sqq.* Tremenheere, H., *State of Five Parishes in...Middlesex.*
[2] Caird, *op. cit.* p. 123, 127–8, 21, 78, 67, 499.
[3] Dudgeon, J., "Essay on Scottish Agricultural Implements," *J. R. Ag. Soc.*
I. 96.
[4] Caird, *op. cit.* p. 149.

in many places beans, were "dibbled in by hand."[1] Caird was still selecting for commendation, in 1850, places where the "corn is all drilled and horse-hoed"; but his occasional entry, "the corn is sown broadcast," records not average, but definitely backward, conditions[2].

Backward conditions of one kind or another were curiously common in the near neighbourhood of all the large towns where easy monopoly gains kept farmers apathetic. Small skill was required or exerted on the little meat milk and potato farms, undrained and unimproved, about the industrial towns of the North-West[3]. The land of the "weaver-farmers" in the West Riding was "believed to be the worst-managed in the district," since only when trade was dull did the weaver "become a more attentive farmer." It was farther from towns, "in the sheltered valleys of the mountain limestone," that Caird, passing through this land "not of farmers but of graziers," saw "everywhere evidenced a skilful and painstaking management of grass."[4] Durham, in spite of its growing industrial population, was badly farmed and low-rented; so were Surrey and Sussex. Northwood, Hanwell, and Ealing showed of what backwardness Middlesex was capable.

These Middlesex farmers, in 1843, were bitter against the new railways. At Northwood and Perivale "a fall in the price of livestock was imputed" to them, no doubt rightly; and the Northwood men, perhaps wrongly, ascribed a fall in the price of hay to the decline in the number of post-horses[5]. Years before, the Lancashire farmers had grumbled in just the same way at the steamers which brought fresh butter regularly from Ireland[6]. But the railways could not begin to tell everywhere until the late 'forties. Still, in 1842, "every autumn...cattle moved across England, from Devon, Hereford, parts of Yorkshire and Scotland," in the old leisurely drovers' fashion, "to the eastern coast, where they were fattened"; thence, when fat, they moved by road towards London[7]. By 1850, when the rail had got through to Norfolk, the 28 lbs., by which a bullock fell in

[1] *J. R. Ag. Soc.* III. 194.

[2] P. 375 and, *e.g.*, p. 409.

[3] Greg's *Scotch Farming*, originally letters to the *Manchester Guardian*, was meant to stir them up.

[4] P. 286–7, and above, p. 50.

[5] Perhaps wrongly, because post-horses declined but not horses: above, p. 403.

[6] Above, p. 136.

[7] Pusey in *J. R. Ag. Soc.* III. 205.

weight on the march from Castle Acre to London—"waste, entirely, lost to everybody"[1]—was being saved. Milk was coming in by rail from a distance of 30 miles about Liverpool and Manchester[2]; but the milk radius of Birmingham, with its 200,000 inhabitants, was only two or three miles and Caird was suggesting that the farmers of Northern Hampshire, within 30 or 40 miles of London, should make good their losses on corn by sending to metropolitan markets by rail milk, butter, and vegetables. Apparently they had never done so. Similarly, the South Hampshire farmers had allowed the French to supply Portsmouth with most of its potatoes[3].

"Antiquated farming" was not shown only in neglect of modern implements, drains, means of transport and fertilisers. Even surer signs were the primitive or wasteful crop rotations, to be found more or less everywhere, and the careless management of grass land in old enclosed Western and North-Western counties. "Water stagnates in the soil, the industry of the farmer is paralysed, the energy of the labourer deadened—nothing seems to thrive but the gigantic trees, whose roots in the smaller fields cover nearly their whole substratum like a network," is Caird's account of the ancient dairy farms of the Vale of Gloucester[4]. The "two crop and fallow" rotation of the old three-field system was still very common, especially on the Northern clays—in the East Riding, the Vale of York, "over all the strong undrained land" of Durham, and throughout Southern Northumberland. Fallow, wheat, oats was the standard Northern clay rotation. Fallow, wheat, beans was a variant, on the clays of Nottinghamshire. On Buckinghamshire and Oxfordshire clays "three crops and a fallow" was a recognised rotation, beans pease and clover being inserted between the two white crops. But as this was found only "on the better class of clay farms," in South Oxfordshire, the unimproved triple course may be assumed on the worse. Bare fallow, as a means of resting the ground after stupid and wasteful successions of crops, was general on heavy soils so far apart as those of South Lancashire and the Surrey and Sussex Weald[5].

Meanwhile, good farmers everywhere were varying their

[1] Caird, *op. cit.* p. 169.
[2] *Ibid.* p. 228.
[3] *Ibid.* p. 94–5. The reason of Birmingham's narrow milk-radius was that 1000 cows were stalled in the town.
[4] *Ibid.* p. 42.
[5] Caird, *op. cit.* p. 315, 326, 334, 371, 207, 9, 19, 267, 120, 127.

rotations empirically, without abandoning the essential discovery of the new agriculture. "The Norfolk or four-course
rotation is undoubtedly the one most generally approved, but
it is to its principle of alternate corn and cattle crops, rather
than to a strict adherence to its original detail, that this approval
is accorded."[1] Sometimes it drew out into a five or six-course
rotation, with varying crops in the various sequences. In the
wet West, good arable farmers found that they could safely take
two corn crops and then two green crops, instead of the strict
alternation. Near towns, where manure was abundant and the
demand for meat and vegetables keen, it paid the farmer to keep
only a third of his land in corn and two-thirds in green crops
—clover, turnips, potatoes for man and beast. West of Cobden's
famous line, "from Inverness to Southampton," beyond which
men were little interested in legislation about the import of
wheat because most of them grew so little, arable rotations
were subordinated to the needs of grazing and dairying, and to
the fodder crops which helped to meet those needs. East of
that line, which he drew rather differently, Caird calculated
that English rents were on the average 30 per cent. less than
west of it[2]. For Scotland no corresponding calculation exists,
but the situation must have been similar.

In an era of low prices and discouraged farmers, rapid improvement in social conditions on the land was not to be
expected. The early railway age felt also the biting social
cautery of the poor law amendment Act (4 & 5 Wm. IV, c. 96)
applied without anaesthetics. Systematic supplementing of
wages from the rates in agricultural parishes had been legally
discouraged, if not exactly prohibited, by 2 & 3 Wm. IV,
c. 96, and the bill of 1834, as originally drafted, had said that
on July 1, 1835, all outdoor relief to able-bodied men should
cease[3]. The clause, however, did not stand, and the statutory
Commissioners, "the three bashaws of Somerset House," were
able to enforce the policy only gradually and partially; but as
the years passed the labourer was everywhere forced to rely
more and more exclusively on his earnings. Parishes were
steadily grouped into unions, and the unions furnished with
"bastilles"—the biggest buildings except the places of the

---

[1] Caird's summary, p. 501.
[2] See his map reproduced on p. 467 below. [This map necessarily only gives a
rough picture of the facts, e.g. Oxford had much arable, Middlesex very much hay.]
[3] Nicholls, Sir G., *History of the Poor Law* (ed. 1898), II. 214–5, and II. 313 n.

nobility and gentry in many, if not most, rural districts. By
1846, the 643 poor-law units in England and Wales—unions
or single large urban parishes—had 707 workhouses, with an
average capacity of about 270 inmates; though, even in
1853, there were a number of "very imperfect" workhouses and twenty unions or parishes with no workhouse
at all[1].

It was fortunate for the villager, and for the Commissioners,
that bread was cheap for a couple of years after the Act of
1834. During 1838–41, the cost-of-living curve for the average
English agricultural labourer came a trifle nearer to the earnings
curve, and in 1847 perceptibly nearer, than it had been since
1825. Then, as prices fell after the famine, corn now entering
England freely, the curves drew apart farther than they had
been for over two generations. The cost-of-living index—taking
1790 as 100—which had touched its maximum at 187 in 1813,
and its maximum for the 'twenties at 128 in 1825, was at 99
in 1835, at 123 in 1839, at 116 in 1847, and at 83 in 1850.
Average earnings fell slightly between 1825 and 1845, but not
nearly enough to outweigh this gain to the labouring man from
free trade and agricultural "depression." Contemporaries
recognised it. "The change in the price of provisions," Caird
wrote, "has added greatly to the comfort of the labourer.
Within the last ten years [1840–50] the decrease in price of the
principal articles of his consumption is upwards of 30 per
cent."[2] But the marked improvement had come only since
1847. The average wage, here compared with prices, covered
a range of particular wages which had not changed in general
character since 1830, though the variations had been accentuated. Weekly wages, in the manufacturing North, Caird
calculated, were now 37 per cent. above those in the agricultural
South. "The line is distinctly drawn at the point where coal
ceases to be found."[3] In ten northern counties the average
wage was 11s. 6d.; but the average for the eastern, the arable,
side of the North was 6d. lower. In eighteen southern counties
the average was 8s. 5d. The extremes were 14s. in the West
Riding and 7s. in Gloucester, South Wiltshire and Suffolk.

[1] Nicholls, op. cit. II. 377, 427. [Webb, S. and B., English Poor Law History,
Part II (1929), chs. 1 and 2.]

[2] P. 518. This agrees very closely with Prof. Silberling's recent calculations:
his index figure for 1840 is 121: a 32 per cent. drop on this would give 82·3:
his actual figure for 1850 is 83. See above, p. 128–9.

[3] P. 512. See his map reproduced on p. 467.

South Scottish wages, for a slightly earlier date, yield an average of about 9s. 6d.[1]

Social habits engendered by the working of the old poor law died hard, as was inevitable, and the change from old to new

CAIRD'S MAP OF
ENGLAND IN 1850
*North of line . . . . , high
wage area*
*East of line ━━ main
arable area*

brought evils of its own. High among the inherited evils stood the distinction between "close" and "open" parish; the close where land was in few hands, or in a single hand, and where the number, and—it is fair to add—sometimes the quality, of the

---

[1] Bowley, *Wages in the United Kingdom*, p. 57. All the figures exclude harvest etc., earnings and are intended merely as illustrations of regional differences.

cottages had been severely controlled, originally, with a view to limiting parochial poor-rate liability; the open where, as Caird put it, "property being more divided there is not the same combination against poverty,"[1] but where there were often grasping speculating butcher and baker and beer-house keeper landlords, who had recently run up " the cheapest of all possible hovels."[2] There was no levelling out of rate-paying liability among the constituent parishes of the new unions; for under clauses 28 and 29 of the Act of 1834[3], when a union was formed, the Commissioners were to take three-year-average poor relief expenses, for the various parishes when separate, and assess the parishes to the common union fund on the basis of these averages. The original apportionments might be revised; but there was obviously nothing in the system to force, or even encourage, a lowly rated close parish to shoulder more than its pre-1834 share of the burden of the poor. And so it was

the commonest thing possible to find...labourers lodged at such a distance from their regular place of employment that they have to walk an hour out in the morning and an hour home in the evening—from forty to fifty miles a week....Nor is this the sole evil of the practice, for the labourers are crowded into villages where the exorbitant cottage rents frequently oblige them to herd together in a manner destructive to morality and injurious to health[4].

No statistical inquiry into the distribution of open and close parishes was ever made—it would not have been easy, for closeness was a matter of degree; but it is certain that no part of England was free of the contrast and its consequences.

From open villages were recruited those organised agricultural gangs of which parliament first heard in the early 'forties. West Norfolk and the Fens were their places of origin. Fen drainage, enclosure of sandy heath, the establishment of large farmsteads where no farms had previously stood, and the technical perfection of Norfolk agriculture had created demands for labour to meet which the resident population was unsuited or inadequate. Cottages or bothies might perhaps have been

[1] P. 516.

[2] *Seventh Report of the Medical Officer of the Privy Council*, 1864, II. 11 (1865, XXVI). For a full discussion of the open and close village, see Hasbach, *The English Agricultural Labourer*, p. 195 n., 268, 400–1.

[3] See the full analysis in Nicholls, *op. cit.* II. 275.

[4] Caird, *op. cit.* p. 516.

run up and "redundant" labour settled in from outside, as in
Scotland and Northumberland. But, partly because of the
working of the close parish system; partly because of the
seasonal or temporary character of much of the work to be
done—turnip-hoeing, the first weedings of newly drained fen,
or the first clearings of flints from land enclosed from rabbit-
warren; partly because Irish migratory labour was not plentiful
on the Cambridge-Norfolk border; partly, no doubt, owing to
the accident of individual enterprise in organising a system
which, when organised, proved convenient and cheap, the gang
system established itself[1]. Its beginnings went back to the
'twenties, and its birthplace seems to have been Castle Acre on
the Norfolk sands—a neglected open village, with eight farms
each of over 1000 acres, and many more of over 500 in the close
parishes round about[2]. When temporary or seasonal work
pressed, the farmer would apply to the Castle Acre gang-
master, whose mixed following of "both sexes and all ages"
would be marched out, bedded down somehow, and kept until
the work was done.

The system, which was always strictly localised and affected
only a tiny proportion of the workers of rural England, acquired
notoriety because of its patent abuses and its relation to the
poor law. Historians have been a little apt to treat as suspicious
and interested characters those contemporaries who argued
that the system was not essentially bad, but required regulation.
Yet the migratory harvester, hop-picker, sheep-shearer, fruit-
picker, or vineyard worker has been an essential factor in rural
life in very various lands and times. Migrants of some sort
were probably as essential in these gang areas—for the first
cleansings of the land at any rate—as were migratory navvies
for railway-making. But the savage exploitation of child labour
by many of the gang-masters, and the social neglect which had
allowed reservoirs of such labour to fill up in open parishes,
from which it was easily and cheaply drawn, gave the East
Anglian gangs their deserved ill-fame.

It must have been mainly in villages of a type intermediate
between the perfectly open and the effectively close, that Caird
registered the frequent survival down to 1850 of a habit created

---

[1] The best account is in Hasbach, *op. cit.* p. 198–9 *sqq.*

[2] *Women and Children in Agriculture*, 1843 (XII. 1), p. 220 *sqq.* A local witness
recalled the start of the system: he said it was due to high farming (p. 274).
[A rather earlier start is suggested in *Children in Agriculture*, 1867 (XVI), p. xxi.]

before 1834—"the rate-payers of a parish agreeing to divide amongst them the surplus labour, not according to their respective requirements, but according to the size of their farms."[1] He blamed the practice because it handicapped the farmer skilled "in economising one of the chief costs of production," and because since all labourers were paid alike, it furnished no motive to excel. A bare living was secure, as in the days of the bread-scales, and honourable ambition was discouraged. Except for survivals of this sort, the labourer of the 'forties had to rely on the wages which he and his family could earn in free and open competition, coupled with some prospect of outdoor relief—which reformers had failed to abolish—in time of sickness or abnormal misfortune, and a pretty certain prospect of the workhouse in old age. The allotments provided by the Bishop of London at Ealing, Tremenheere one of the Assistant Poor-Law Commissioners wrote in 1843, had acted admirably, especially for the aged—"in deferring the period of refuge to the union workhouse."[2]

In rural housing there had been, on the balance, but little change—slight improvement in some directions being offset, perhaps more than offset, by the natural course of decay throughout a series of years during which landlords felt poor[3], and by the upspringing of certain new abuses. Inquiries made in the 'forties, 'fifties and 'sixties make it possible to draw some of the lines of the picture with greater precision than was possible for the 'twenties, but do not alter its colour scheme. The blackest lines come from Edwin Chadwick's 1842 *Report on the Sanitary Condition of the Labouring Population*. Chadwick and his informants were looking for the causes of fever and so described in most detail the worst housing conditions; places in Dorset where the clay floors of cottages below the road-level became sodden in wet weather; places in Bedford where whole families slept in single rooms; places all over the country where cottage, dung heap, and pigsty were huddled together; or the one-room, "dry stone," hinds' cottages of Northumberland. But though these things were the worst, average conditions were not greatly better. A fresh evil had come of late in Dorset

---

[1] Caird, *op. cit.* p. 515.   [2] *S.J.* VI. 126.
[3] See *Women and Children in Agriculture*, 1843, p. 20, and the retrospect over "twenty or thirty years" in the *Seventh Report of the Medical Officer of the Privy Council*, 1864, p. 8.

and Somerset out of the reform of the poor law. The new union workhouses were throwing the old parish houses out of commission[1]. Attempts had been made to use these buildings for poor law purposes, but, as Sir George Nicholls himself records, "it rarely answered."[2] So they might be turned into barracks for the lowest class of labourers—the single door serving as the common entry for families who were given one room each. This particular account comes from Somerset[3]. Poor houses of any size were not numerous enough, in the country as a whole, to make the abuse typical; and there are cases on record of very fair accommodation being provided in them, when the transformation was properly done and the building not overcrowded[4].

Other exact lines for the picture of English rural housing about the year 1850 are supplied by inquiries made fourteen years later[5]. In 821 parishes chosen for examination, scattered all over England, 69,225 cottages had housed 305,567 people in 1851, or a cottage of some kind for every 4·41 souls. A close inquiry was made in 1864 into 5375 of these cottages. Overcrowding had increased a little since 1851; but the cottages were seldom new, and the figures of 1864 cannot mislead appreciably if accepted for 1850–1. Not 5 per cent. of the selected cottages had more than two bedrooms: just over 40 per cent. had only one. The single bedroom type averaged four people, two of them normally children, per bedroom; the two-bedroom type averaged just under 2·5 people per bedroom. So stated, the average amount of overcrowding does not appear excessive. But whereas, when the law came to deal with common lodging-houses[6], it accepted reluctantly a minimum of 240 cubic feet of air-space per person, in these selected cottages about 150–160 feet was the amount available. Sometimes there was no window, or only a bit of glass stuck in a hole in the wall, rarely a fireplace, often a wet or rotten floor, or a leaky roof, to these cramped bed-cabins.

Counties honourably mentioned in Chadwick's 1842 Report because of the activity of great landlords in building good cottages were Bedford, Norfolk, Suffolk, Lincoln and Stafford[7].

---

[1] For these see above, p. 354–5. [2] *Op. cit.* II. 296.
[3] Chadwick's *Report*, p. 10. [4] Dr Hunter's Report, as below.
[5] Dr Hunter's Report on Rural Housing in *Seventh Report of the Med. Officer*, 1864, Ap. VI.
[6] In the 'fifties. [7] P. 262 *sqq.*

The Duke's Bedfordshire houses all had "two rooms on the ground floor, and two or three sleeping apartments upstairs. They are fitted with kitchen range, and copper—and one fireplace upstairs—outbuildings for wood, ashes, and other conveniences—and an oven common to each block of cottages."[1] They cost the Duke, in 1850–1, from £90 to £100 each to build, hollow bricks being used. Outside the Duke's estates, unhappily, Bedfordshire and the adjacent parts of Cambridgeshire contained some of the worst open villages in England[2], although the Duke himself provided housing for all labourers who worked on his farms, and kept the houses in his own hands, so that farmers should not have too much power over their men.

The Bedford cottage standard was considered rather too high by most reforming contemporaries. A building of stone, where it was easily to be had, or of clay "in preference to brick or stud-work," because cheaper and warmer; thatched, because tiles or slates are intolerably hot and cold in an unceiled bedroom; a kitchen and "pantry" below; two bedrooms above; this was the practical ideal of the winner of the Royal Agricultural Society's Prize Essay on Cottages in 1843[3].

There can be no question that, even where cottages were deteriorating, allotments and potato-grounds were becoming commoner. The "fashion" was a growing one in 1826, as Cobbett noted[4]; although in the opinion of a parliamentary committee, seventeen years later, "it was not until 1830"— the year of the labourers' revolt—that the allotment system "was much resorted to."[5] The Bishop of London's Ealing allotments were laid out in 1832. The Poor Law Commissioners of 1832–4 blessed the movement, with reservations—they disapproved of large allotments—and were able to report considerable progress[6]: there was hardly a parish in Wilts or Dorset "in which the labourer has not the use of land"; North Welsh labourers frequently had land enough "to occupy their leisure time"; the movement was "beginning...to be very generally adopted" in Cambridgeshire; and so on. In 1843 further progress was reported in the South-West, especially in Devon; Somerset was more backward[7]. West Kent had its

[1] Caird, op. cit. p. 437–8.
[2] See, e.g., the account of Gamlingay in Seventh Report, p. 161.
[3] The Rev. Copinger Hill, J. R. Ag. Soc. IV. 356.   [4] Above, p. 121.
[5] S. C. on Allotments, 1843 (VII. 201), p. iii.
[6] Report, p. 181 sqq., and Appendices.
[7] Women and Children in Agriculture, p. 15.

allotment society. When started, in the mid-'thirties, farmers opposed it; now their hostility was said to have been overcome[1]. But seven years later "all" Oxfordshire farmers still complained of allotments "as injurious to the steady industry of the labourer and a heavy tax on themselves."[2] Although there were few parts of Kent Surrey and Sussex where the allotment could be said to be general, in 1843, there were fewer where it had not been tried[3]. Norfolk and Suffolk reported progress, and an established custom in some places. Allotments were said to be "nearly universal" in Lincolnshire; but it is not easy to accept without reserve broad generalisations, good or bad, about so wide and varied a county. "You find a fat pig in the house of every labouring man" is another sanguine Lincolnshire pronouncement[4]. Certainly the constant complaints of the sanitary reformers of the 'forties about pig-sty location and pig-sty management—from far-scattered counties—suggest that the pig, Cobbett's test of labouring felicity, was exceedingly common. It might not always help to feed its master. One Devonshire witness explained, in 1843, that its use was to pay the shoemaker's bill.

For much of central England there is not the same official evidence of allotment progress in the 'forties as for the South-West, South-East, and East; but some progress may be assumed. In Yorkshire, the allotment proper, that is to say the bit of land from a rood to an acre held by the labourer as rent-paying tenant, was almost unknown; but potato ground, allowed to the labourer by the farmers, was becoming common. There was one excellent reason for the scarcity of allotments—the frequency of good gardens and "cowgates" in the more prosperous parts of the county. In the Dales, there were no labourers except the farm servants, and in the East Riding even married men were fed in the farmhouses[5]. It was in late-enclosed corn districts, where gardens had been deficient in the 'twenties and the poor law most abused, that allotments had attracted reforming landlords and parsons. In Northumberland and the Scottish Lowlands they were little known; but that was because the permanent farm-hands, the hinds or "bondagers," all had

---

[1] *S. C. on Allotments*, Q. 1–29.

[2] Caird, *op. cit.* p. 29: this is Caird's only reference to allotments.

[3] *Women...in Agriculture*, p. 143.

[4] *Ibid.* p. 220, 261. [That this was sanguine is shown by the statement that in 1867 in N. Lincs. allotments were scarce. App. C, § 28, *Children...and Women in Ag.* 1867–8, XVII.]　　　　　[5] *Ibid.* p. 294–5.

cottages with gardens, were able to fatten two pigs, and might also have the equivalent of the Yorkshire cowgate[1].

The allotments committee of 1843 played with the notion of placing the provision of land for labourers under some department of state. As the law stood, by Acts of 1819 and 1831 (59 Geo. III, c. 12, and 2 Wm. IV, c. 42) the poor law authorities might provide them[2]; but little had ever been done under these laws and, since 1834, nothing. The committee explained that the poor law authority was unsuitable, but suggested no other. They hesitated to interfere with that "care of the neighbouring poor which properly devolves upon the proprietors of the soil." Allotments, they observed, were astonishing diminishers of crime; they fostered "thankfulness and respect"; they gave back to the people that access to the land which had so often been lost. The committee left the matter to the good feeling of "The House and...every landowner"—not entirely in vain[3].

When through any rural district one of the first railways began to be driven, the quartering of navvies in and about the villages increased congestion and brought with it other evils. Some venturesome men enlisted with them, so relieving the pressure on employment if not on accommodation. But, down to 1842 at any rate, the responsible authorities held that railway-making had done more harm than good to the agricultural population. The railways, said the Poor Law Commissioners in that year, "offer an almost imperceptible addition of employment to the resident labourers, which employment is of so demoralising a nature it would be better were it not offered at all; they bring heavy burdens on parishes by reason of the accidents which they occasion; they increase bastardy; and they double, if not treble, the amount of crime."[4] This was in days when the navvies, largely old hands and Irishmen, were

---

[1] For "bondage," see S.J. I. 319, 397; J. R. Ag. Soc. II. 183. [Some one from the cottage, hind or "bound woman," had to stand by to work at any time.]

[2] The Act of 1819 is the so-called Select Vestries Act; that of 1831 was concerned primarily with allotments: it referred specially to "allotments (under enclosure Acts) made for the benefit of the poor, chiefly with a view to fuel (for which see above, p. 116), which are now comparatively useless," and might be turned into cultivated allotments.

[3] Report, p. v–vi.

[4] Comm. Report of 1842 (Ap. B, p. 241), quoted in Report of Royal Comm. on the Poor Laws, 1909 (Cd. 4499), p. 231.

still regarded by decent country folk, as well as by the somewhat professionally minded Commissioners, with aversion[1].
Yet, a few years earlier, one of these Commissioners, in sanguine mood, had anticipated "at no distant date," from railway work alone, "the entire absorption of all the surplus labour
of the country."[2] The poor law statistics of the 'forties belied
his anticipation, partly because the poor law itself had bitten
deep into the rustic mind the fear of losing one's "settlement";
but by 1845 at the latest, railway work as navvy—better still
as platelayer or porter—was becoming a recognised career for
village lads. In thousands of new "Railway Inns" the chances
of life in towns where the railway ended, or even over the seas
to which the railway led, could be seriously threshed out.
Some few navvies made their way and came back to the land.
"'Railway men,' that is to say, men who have made a little
money by railway contracts," are found competing for the
small grazing farms of North Lancashire by 1850[3].

[1] Above, p. 412.
[2] In 1836: quoted, without source, in Cd. 4499, p. 306.
[3] Caird, *op. cit.* p. 281.

CHAPTER XII

OVERSEAS TRADE AND COMMERCIAL POLICY

A COMMON argument of free traders, during the early railway age, was that the fiscal policy of the country, and above all the corn law, which deliberately checked imports, checked also—by the inevitable working of economic law—the growth of the industries which manufactured for export. The argument, as a general proposition, is sound and it was used outside Britain, by the public men of agricultural states, to justify a policy of industrial protection: if Britain would not take their wares, why should they take hers? In 1836, an informal agent of the Board of Trade, who was inquiring about the prospects of a commercial treaty with the recently established Germanic Customs Union, was told that England must begin "with a reduction of her corn duties," which were far more unreasonable than the Zollverein taxes on manufactures. When the agent suggested alternatives, the Prussian stubbornly "took his stand upon corn."[1] Good as the argument was, an age less conscious of its industrial power, or a class less eager than the British manufacturers to make that power felt throughout the world, might well have been content with what trade expansion there had in fact been. For whereas the declared value of British and Irish produce and manufactures exported—nearly all, in fact, British—had averaged £35,600,000 a year for the five years between the opening of the Stockton and Darlington Railway and the opening of the Manchester and Liverpool, it averaged £50,000,000 a decade later (1835–40) and only £61,000,000 a decade later still (1845–50) after many of the restrictions on imports had been slashed through. The growth during the decade before the corn laws were repealed was greater than it seemed, for prices were falling[2].

[1] John Macgregor to the Board of Trade, July 9 and 14, 1836. *Letters of the Board.*

[2] The average price index number (Sauerbeck's) for these periods was, 1825–30, 95·4; 1835–40, 100·4; 1845–50, 82·6. But prices of British exports, mainly manufactures, were falling faster than this index number, in which corn prices play the dominant part, would suggest. Some indication of the fall can

Britain had been able to take goods enough from outside to allow of this very rapid expansion, although some appreciable part of her exports was not immediately paid for in goods, as it represented capital sent abroad for investment or shipping and other services rendered. Corn she had not been prepared to take at all freely, down to 1846, except from her colonies; she was reluctant to take European timber or "slave grown" sugar, or coffee raised outside the Empire, or fine French wines and manufactures, or German linen, or a number of other things. But she would not, in any case, have needed to take foreign corn regularly in heavy quantities before 1846; for when—the corn law in abeyance—she was facing poor harvests and a devastating famine in Ireland, during the four years 1846–9, the whole United Kingdom, Ireland included, only imported an annual average of under 900,000 tons of wheat and wheaten flour, and in 1848 managed with under 500,000 tons. She could get what timber she needed, at a price, from the colonies, with some contribution from Europe; though but for her tariff system she would probably have bought a greater aggregate and would certainly have bought more from the Baltic[1]. "Colonial wares" were in somewhat the same position as timber. She would take any amount into bonded store; but her preferential system, as worked during the 'forties, tended to keep down the quantities passing into home consumption. German linens—about which Prussian statesmen spoke to Macgregor in 1836—were fast ceasing to be "competition-capable," as the Germans would say, with British mill-made or part mill-made fabrics; and fine French wines and manufactures, which were always perfectly able to compete, would not have provided a very important element in the demand for British goods, even had they all been admitted on really easy terms, a policy which not the most hardened free traders contemplated.

Britain's reluctance to take most kinds of European, and many kinds of non-European, produce and manufactures, was offset by a greedy absorption of raw cotton and raw wool, to the entry of which there had been no serious obstacle since the

be drawn from a comparison of "official" and "declared" values of manufactures. The official values per unit—much out of date—did not vary. In 1830 the declared value of cotton goods exported was £19,500,000; the official value £41,000,000. In 1844 the declared value was £25,800,000; the official value £91,000,000. See Porter's *Progress*, p. 178, for the intervening years.

[1] See above, p. 237–8.

tariff adjustments of the 'twenties[1], and of timber which she could not do without, whatever the duties. The hundred thousand tons of cotton, imported in an average year of the late 'twenties, had very nearly doubled by the late 'thirties. The import touched in 1849—after great vicissitudes: in 1846-7 it was below the average of 1835-40—the tremendous figure of three hundred and forty-six thousand tons, of which, however, over one-eighth was re-exported[2]. Of values it is not easy to speak, owing to the varieties of grades and the annual fluctuations; but "middling uplands" was worth about 6d. a lb., or about £56 a ton, in the late 'twenties, about 7d. or £65 in the late 'thirties, and about 5d. or £47 in the late 'forties[3]. Allowing for the lower grades and the fluctuations, the average annual import of raw cotton in the late 'thirties cannot have been worth less than £10,000,000, or in 1849 less than £15,000,000.

The growth in the import of wool, though in no way comparable with that of cotton, was steady and considerable. From over 11,000 tons in the late 'twenties, it rose to over 22,000 tons in the late 'thirties and to over 33,000 tons in 1849. The imported wool was nearly all fine—Spanish, German or Australian—worth perhaps some 2s. 4d. a lb. on the average, towards 1840, and some 1s. 8d. in 1849, a year of low prices[4]. This would give a value of about £5,000,000 for the average imports of the late 'thirties, and of not quite £6,500,000 for those of 1849.

In the latter part of 1842 the Custom House adopted a new method for charging the duties on timber. "All kinds, whether square, or sawn and split"[5] were reckoned by their cubic content in loads—and so, for the first time, fairly accurate estimates of the bulk imported and of the value became possible. Fluctuations in the imports were precipitous, as might be expected in years when the railways were a-making and the timber duties were altered in almost every budget. In 1843 some 900,000 loads of colonial timber worth about £3 a load were brought in, and some 400,000 of foreign, worth about £4[6]—approxi-

---

[1] Down to 1845 the duty on foreign cotton was about $\frac{4}{5}d.$ a lb., that on British was merely nominal. Both were repealed in 1845. The maximum wool duty (on wool worth 1s. a lb. and upwards) was $1\frac{1}{20}d.$ It was repealed in 1844.

[2] The tables in Porter, *op. cit.* p. 178, and Ellison's *Cotton Trade*, Ap., do not quite agree.

[3] Prices from Tooke, *passim.*

[4] Tooke, *op. cit.* III. 434 (prices of fine Spanish wool, taken as fairly representative).

[5] Porter, *op. cit.* p. 579, and see above, p. 238.

[6] Prices from Tooke, *op cit.* III. 432.

mately £4,300,000 worth. The gross import touched 2,000,000 loads—from £7,000,000 to £8,000,000—in 1846, to fall again below 1,700,000 loads and perhaps £6,000,000 in 1849. The value of the annual timber imports for the years 1835–40 may be placed conjecturally at from £3,000,000 to £4,000,000.

That is to say, at a time when the export of United Kingdom produce, which required an annual equivalent in imports, was something well under £50,000,000, the expansion of population and manufacturing—themselves conditioned by the possibilities of export—were enabling the country to absorb some £20,000,000 worth of only three raw materials—timber, wool and cotton; the first all used at home; the second principally used at home; the third—and by far the most important—mainly destined for export as yarn or cotton cloth or cotton hosiery or lace. The average annual export of these things in 1835–40 was worth nearly £24,000,000 as compared with less than £6,000,000 for wool manufactures of every sort, and about £20,000,000 for everything else[1]. It is not surprising that Britain's foreign trade presented itself almost as a problem in cotton, or that Manchester claimed a great share in the determination of the commercial—and industrial and social—policy of the country.

It is on the whole unlikely that, whatever fiscal policy the United Kingdom had pursued between 1830 and 1848, a much better vent for her cotton and other textile goods would have been opened on the European continent than was in fact enjoyed. France was resolute in prohibition. Down to 1834 it was illegal to import textile yarns or fabrics of any kind. In 1834 prohibition of the very finest cotton yarns was replaced by a duty, because they were essential for the muslin industry of Tarare and had been smuggled systematically—from England or Switzerland—while prohibition was maintained. But that was the only relaxation[2]. Huskisson's replacement of the prohibition of French silks by duties did not affect French policy; nor did Peel's general reconstruction of the British tariff in the 'forties. Russia, with simple thoroughness, had prohibited the entry of all foreign manufactures in 1810. Her

---

[1] The highest figure for wool manufactures in the years 1830–49 was £8,200,000 in 1844; for cotton £26,700,000 in 1849.

[2] Houdoy, J., *La filature de coton dans le Nord de la France* (1903), p. 43. Reybaud, J., *Le coton* (1863), p. 133.

tariff of 1822, the foundation of her commercial policy down
to 1844, did not go quite so far; but it prohibited 301 articles
and placed very high duties on the rest[1]. All through the period
she took a considerable amount of cotton yarn but, even after
1844 when her tariff was eased a little, only trifling quantities
of finished goods. The tariff-ordinance of 1835 for the Austrian
lands—excluding Hungary—also prohibited 69 articles and laid
heavy duties on 1600. In connection, however, with an Anglo-
Austrian commercial treaty, signed June 18, 1838, duties—high
duties—replaced the prohibitions of cottons, woollens, linen,
earthenware, "fire engines" and some other manufactures[2].
But there were trade channels, reasonably open, into the heart
of Europe through Belgium, Holland, the Hanse Towns and
the hinterland of German states, all the way to the Austrian
and Russian frontiers.

The maintenance of these channels was a prime object of
British commercial diplomacy. This was why the Board of
Trade was so much interested in Zollverein politics. It was not
only for their own trade's sake that the Board and the Foreign
Office valued the German states: they furnished also excellent
smuggling bases. Leipzig was the base, and the Elbe the route,
for contraband traffic with Bohemia[3]; it was a very important
traffic up to 1838, when the disappearance of prohibition in the
Austrian dominions reduced it. From Leipzig also, Jewish
smugglers took English cotton goods in most satisfactory
quantities—when Macgregor was there in 1836—for transit
into Russian Poland[4]. Similarly, before the Zollverein came
into being on January 1, 1835, the imperial cities, and especially
Frankfort, had served as bases for contraband with less open
German territory. Henry Addington, our representative at
Frankfort just before 1830, had supported the free-trade—and
short-lived—*Mitteldeutscher Handelsverein* because it "would
afford immense facilities for carrying on the contraband trade
in the dominions of Prussia, Bavaria, Würtemberg and Darm-
stadt."[5]

---

[1] Schmoller, G., *Volkswirthschaftslehre*, II. (1904), 610.
[2] Macgregor, J., *Commercial Statistics* (1844), I. 20.
[3] Sir F. Lamb to Palmerston, November 2, 1836. *F.O. Austria*.
[4] Macgregor to the Board, April 29, 1836.
[5] Addington to Lord Dudley, May 27, 1828, *F.O. Germany*. For a German
view, Treitschke, *Deutsche Geschichte*, III. 637, 644. The Mitteldeutscher
Handelsverein comprised Saxony, Hanover, Hesse-Cassel, Brunswick, Weimar,
Bremen, Frankfort and a few others.

The Zollverein had no prohibitions and its tariffs were never unconscionable, but they had a tendency to move upwards, in the interests of German producers; and even when they did not move, they appeared increasingly burdensome upon the steadily cheapening products of British mechanical industry, because they were fixed rates, not *ad valorem*. Conceivably the abolition or thorough reorganisation of the corn law by the Whigs in the 'thirties, coupled perhaps with a reduction of British duties on linen, might have prevented the few increases in Zollverein duties, beyond the level of the older Prussian duties, which were made between 1835 and 1848; but it is most unlikely that the basic Prussian levels would have been reduced. Germany remained much the best European market for British textiles, but not a very expansive market; and she would probably have been both whatever the British commercial policy. More than half the cotton twist and yarn exported in 1839 (60,000,000 out of 106,000,000 lbs.) was shipped to Dutch or German ports[1]. Ten years later the quantity was almost the same, and it was a smaller proportion of the whole (65,000,000 out of 149,000,000)[2]. The exports of cotton piece-goods, plain dyed or printed, were also almost identical in 1839 and 1849. For the heavier and older fashioned woollen goods Germany was never a very good market: she had her own flocks and her own industries, in Saxony and elsewhere. But she had no organised worsted (combed wool) industry, for making the lighter fabrics for women's wear—"stuffs"—and so there was no demand in Germany for special taxation of these goods from Bradford. For them she remained England's best customer, taking in 1849—when probably her dealers were filling up stocks, after a spell of short food and revolution—about a quarter of all the British export.

The demand of markets in Europe, which no amount of tariff manipulation or reciprocity could have opened very much wider, was supplemented by the almost unlimited demand of unprotected markets in the tropics and sub-tropics. Manchester lived on "shirts for black men," and yellow men, and brown men, and for the Moslem world. While the German market remained stagnant, and the French market shut, the markets of the Turkish Empire and of the East were in brisk motion. Between 1839 and 1849—halfway through the early railway

[1] *A. and P.*, 1841 (XXIV). *Commercial Tables*, p. 123.
[2] *A. and P.* 1851 (LIV). *Commercial Tables*, p. 125.

age and about its close: both years of normal good trade, whose figures would fall on, or near, the ascending line of exports— the plain cotton goods shipped overseas more than doubled (380 to 795 million yards); those shipped to India and Ceylon and to the Turkish Empire more than trebled; those shipped to China and Hong-Kong (acquired for a trade base in the interval) grew from something not separately set out in the returns to nearly a tenth of the whole. The black men of the British West Indies and of the Brazils were also high on the list of customers, the Africans of Africa not nearly so high as yet.

The United States, from which nearly all the raw cotton came, with tobacco, and some corn and timber and miscellaneous wares, was naturally not a heavy buyer of plain cotton cloth —which she could very well make at home, apart from any question of duties. During most of the years under review she had a moderately severe protective system (the tariffs of 1832 and 1842[1]) with an interlude of freer trade. But the duties did not prevent her from being a good customer for British dyed and printed cottons, or from being by far the most important customer of the wool manufacturers. In 1839 she took more than a third of all the woollen cloth and of all the carpets exported, nearly a third of all the stuffs, nearly two-thirds of all the blankets and "blanketings," and nearly a half of a new kind of fabric, mixed wool and cotton, very suitable for warm climates, which Yorkshire had begun to produce[2]. In the next ten years the exports of these mixed fabrics grew from 2,400,000 to 42,115,000 yards, and still the United States bought nearly half. Her proportion of the old-style cloths—a declining commodity in all markets—and of the stuffs had fallen somewhat, that of the blankets and carpets had slightly increased. Tariffs in America were regulated by the relative political strengths of the purely agricultural South, exporting produce which Britain took eagerly, and the more industrial North, anxious especially for protection of its textile and miscellaneous manufactures. Corn the United States could ship, but not, as yet, in very great quantities; for the shipment of timber the British North American colonies were better placed. In the circumstances, it is almost inconceivable that

---

[1] See generally Taussig, *Tariff History of the U.S.A.*, and Dewey, *Financial History of the U.S.A.*, and references in these works.

[2] The so-called Orleans cloth. *A. and P.* 1841 (xxiv), p. 124.

changes in the British duties on food and raw materials would
have influenced Congress. To Britain's tariff on manufactures
the United States were entirely and properly indifferent: they
sent her none.

Of all the goods exported from the United Kingdom from
1830 to 1849, the United States took almost exactly one-sixth,
by value; the share rising sometimes to nearly one-fifth
(1847 and 1849) or even to nearly a quarter (1835 and 1836)[1].
She was a great buyer of the finer miscellaneous manufactures,
which she either did not produce at all or did not produce in
sufficient quantities. She was much the most important buyer
of that group of British exports which was growing more
rapidly than any other, even than cotton, especially in the
'forties—iron, in bars, bolts, rods, pigs and castings. From
73,000 tons in 1829 to 191,000 tons in 1839 and 554,000 tons
in 1849, the total shipments grew, with the vicissitudes inevitable
in a trade working largely to an intermittent constructional
demand, but without any real setback. In 1839 America took
an amount almost equal to the whole export of 1829 (68,000
tons), and in 1849 she took full three-fifths (329,000 tons) of
what seemed to contemporaries the immense shipments of
that year.

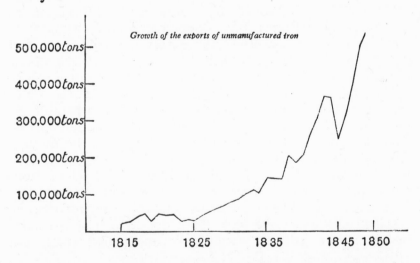

Growth of the exports of unmanufactured iron

America was also a great buyer of the rougher and heavier
manufactures of wrought iron, which the Customs authorities
classified with the unworked material, and not with either

[1] See the table of export distribution in Porter, *op. cit.* p. 360.

"hardware," "cutlery" or "machinery and millwork." Into this intermediate group fell nails, barrel hoops, anchors, chain cables and the like—but not anvils or awls or fire-irons or stirrups, which were "hardware." No doubt at many points the line of division was perfectly arbitrary. By 1849, the United States were taking very nearly a quarter of the 108,000 tons of these rougher iron wares, and a fair proportion of the finer goods grouped by the Customs as hardware and cutlery. This last group was, both in weight and value, a somewhat stagnant section of the export trade—presumably because it dealt in goods nearly all still made by hand, which every civilised and half-civilised country made, less or more, for itself. Its value had risen to over £1,600,000 in 1831: it only once rose above £2,250,000 (in 1836) before 1850. The weights corresponded very nearly with the prices; for there was no great cheapening of these goods between 1830 and 1850, as there had been between 1815 and 1830—when British iron had first become really abundant and the military and naval demand had almost ceased[1].

Side by side with the exports of iron, but not so fast, grew the export of coal—a commodity that no country which required it could well refuse to take, especially after the repeal of the general export duty in 1834. America did not require it, but France and Russia did[2]. Measured by the standards of the later nineteenth century, the export was trifling—it first passed 1,000,000 tons in the year of Queen Victoria's accession and was still under 3,000,000 tons in 1849. More than half of it went on the short North Sea, Baltic and Channel routes —France taking from about a quarter to about a fifth of the total, and Germany, in the later 'forties but not in the 'thirties, approximately as much as France, either direct or through Holland. The three countries together took, in 1839, 714,000 tons (out of a total of 1,428,000) and, in 1849, 1,198,000 tons out of 2,731,000. Denmark, having no coal of her own, was from the start a regular and, in proportion to her size, an excellent customer: she took about one-twelfth of the shipments. Russia and Italy were the remaining considerable, but

[1] See Porter, op. cit. p. 247.

[2] [But France taxed it, even differentially, to favour land borne Belgian coal.] In 1831 the tax on all sea-borne coal ceased. An export duty remained of 3s. 4d. a ton on coal in British ships, or in foreign ships under reciprocity treaties, and 6s. 8d. on coal in other ships. After 1834 there remained only a 4s. duty on coal in such ships.

less considerable, buyers, in the 'forties[1]. There were other buyers or consignees all round about the world, where places called "coaling stations" were beginning to grow up, to meet the needs of the "steamers, or vessels propelled by steam."[2]

If the Customs returns are to be trusted, the "machinery and mill-work" sent out of the United Kingdom was worth only £100,000 in 1831; less in 1832; nearly £500,000 in 1837; but still much less than £1,000,000 in the later 'forties. It is certain that, down to 1843 at least, the returns are not to be trusted; for here was working, and working most imperfectly, the last British export prohibition. The deliberations of two parliamentary committees in the 'twenties had shown up the defects of the system then existing[3], but had not led to its abolition. There were schedules of prohibited machines in the Customs Regulations Acts of 1825 and 1833, but the Board of Trade retained its old power of issuing licences for their export. In 1834 and 1835 it was still taking the duty seriously[4]—licences were refused for spinning-frames, and even for castings for the framework of looms and of cloth-raising machines; for cloth-shearing machines; for carding engines; for bobbin-net machines; for "a cutting and dividing engine for cutting the teeth on wheels"; and for "a set of cutters for slitting iron-rod for making nails." Yet paper-making machinery was allowed to go. So were copper-rolling machinery; "a machine for tearing in pieces woollen rags," *i.e.* the "devil" that makes the shoddy; packing presses; calico printing rollers and flax-breaking, but not flax-spinning, machinery. The *reductio ad absurdum* of these decisions was one which recommended a licence for the export of machines which would card and spin tow, "subject to all the penal consequences of the law," in case it should be found that they could be used for flax wool or silk.

In June 1841 a committee of the Commons reported on the matter[5]. They said that export licences were now given for

---

[1] See *A. and P.* 1841 (XXIV), p. 80, and *A. and P.* 1851 (LIV), p. 79, for 1839 and 1849. For the general growth Porter (who does not quite agree with the figures in the *A. and P.*), p. 279.

[2] See above, p. 438. Local coals were also being exploited for the purpose: the Burdwan mines in Bengal already had an output of 14,000 to 15,000 tons in 1830. *S. C. on East India Company's Affairs*, 1831 (v. vi), Q. 301.

[3] The *S. C. on Artisans and Machinery*, 1824, and the *S. C. on the Export of Tools and Machinery*, 1825 (v. 115).

[4] *Minutes of the Board*, 1834, 1835, *passim.*

[5] *S. C. to enquire into the operation of the...laws affecting the export of machinery.*

nearly everything except spinning and weaving machinery; that there was abundance of evasion and abundance of smuggling; and that as machine tools had been invented since the laws were made, "all these elaborate tools... are allowed free export," which suggests either that the Board of Trade's 1834 policy of not licensing an "engine for the cutting of teeth on wheels" had been dropped or, and more probably, that exporters of machine tools did not trouble to apply for licences, because the Customs officers "must go by schedule"[1]—and machine tools were certainly not scheduled. Very few people did apply for licences in 1841. The position was that a well-known machine —a loom or a frame—was likely to be stopped in the Customs, but an ingenious novelty was likely to go through without licence. There was in any case a heavy, and perfectly legal, export of models and drawings, much more harmful to British industry than any export of British-made machines could possibly be. As this tiresome and ineffective law was the sole surviving legal interference with the export trade, the committee recommended repeal. Repeal came in 1843 (6 & 7 Vict. c. 84).

Nine years earlier, in April 1834, and under an Act of the previous year (3 & 4 Wm. IV, c. 85), the Honourable East India Company had lost its last monopoly, that of the China market, and had ceased to be a trading body. How far the expansion in the Eastern trade, which took place between 1835 and 1848, is to be connected with the Act of 1833 is uncertain: a connexion there certainly was, but it may easily be overrated. For India itself, the decisive event had been the termination of monopoly trade there in 1814. Private firms had multiplied—mainly in Calcutta—and the export trade from Britain, other than that in Government stores, had passed completely into their hands before 1833. Their number was not yet very great. To the five or six old Calcutta houses, which did agency and banking business even before 1814, had been added twelve or fourteen new ones between 1814 and 1831[2]. But in 1828 the total number of Europeans resident in India, who were not serving the Company or the King, was—so far as the Company could ascertain—only 2016[3]. The number had been 1501 in 1815. Commercial freedom seems to have added about forty people

---

[1] *Report*, p. v.   [2] *S. C. on E. I. C.'s Affairs*, 1831 (VI), Q. 1.
[3] *Ibid.* Ap., p. 769. Of the 2016, 1595 were in Bengal.

a year to the tiny unofficial population, more than half of which was domiciled in Calcutta. But it was enough to handle all the British produce imported. Down to 1820–1 the Company had still taken a large share in this business. It sent out £576,000 worth of trade goods in that year. In 1826–7 it sent none[1]. But it went on exporting Indian produce to the last, though the commodities which it handled were always dwindling. By 1831 they were reduced to raw silk, some silk piece goods, saltpetre and indigo. (Sugar had been recently discontinued, and before that muslins.) On this trade the Company made a loss[2].

It was only kept up for financial reasons—remittances from India and exchange operations were more easily managed, so the Directors believed, when there was some considerable flow of their own goods which could be drawn against. (The amount in 1828 was about £1,500,000.) Critics pointed out that such a trade, not conducted "on the ordinary conditions of profit and loss"[3] but as a convenient by-product of the business of governing India, to facilitate transactions connected with the Company's territorial revenue, was very disturbing to the free traders who had to think of losses.

Why, a committee-man asked Wm. Simons, chief clerk of buying and warehouses in India House, in 1832, why, since you have ceased exporting British goods to India, do you still send them to China?[4] As a duty arising out of our monopoly, said the faithful servant: "I think I may affirm it was considered a moral obligation." There was a ritual for dealing with these goods. They were bought in no common way, but "by tender and contract," as for the state. They were inspected faithfully—and the rejects were sometimes bought by Americans and shipped to China all the same[5]. The Company shipped more than £600,000 worth in 1828—longells, camlets, Colchester baize, striped duroys, seraglio ratteens, templars, vigonia shags, and little else[6]; for the traditions of this trade were from the years when wool was king, and statesmen of the eighteenth century had liked the China market because it took

---

[1] *S. C. on E. I. C.'s Affairs*, 1832 (x), Ap., p. 767.
[2] *Ibid.* (VIII), p. 57–8, and *Papers relating to the E. Indies*, 1829 (XXIII), p. 115.
[3] *S. C. on E. I. C.'s Affairs*, 1832, Q. 1973.
[4] *Ibid.* Q. 887.
[5] *Ibid.* 1830 (v), Q. 4756: and see above, p. 332. [Also Morse, H. B., *The East India Coy. Trading to China* (1926), III, 363.]
[6] *Papers relating to the E. Indies*, 1829, p. 150, 159.

these things with the fantastic names. But it did not take nearly enough to pay for the tea, in 1828–32. To adjust the balance the Company—instead of sending bullion as formerly —sent, or encouraged its officers and private merchants to send, Indian cotton. Opium from India, "the trade in which was altogether contraband," was handled entirely by private merchants; but the Company was cognisant of its utility in helping cotton to balance the trade. The Americans, who practised a perfectly free trade in Canton, bought two-thirds of their tea and China produce with hard dollars[1].

The monopoly abolished, the China trade became more varied, as the Indian trade had become after 1814, when many British goods began to be shipped which India House had never considered[2]. Above all, the Manchester goods got a new outlet, as the Manchester men had hoped they would when giving evidence against the monopoly[3]. But the China trade grew slowly. Its growth was painfully and ingloriously bought. The Company, in its last trading years, had sent annually some £650,000 worth of baize and camlets and the rest: private trade sent only an average of £1,700,000 worth of all British goods, during the years 1845–9, and in the bad years of the opium war (1839–41) the Company's figure was barely exceeded[4]. War also checked the fall in tea prices at home, which had set in soon after 1834; but the fall was resumed in 1843, so that for 1845–9, the untaxed price was not much over half of what it had been twenty years earlier, and the consumption was twice as great[5].

During the discussion of 1831–2, there had been agreement that "the want of returns" was the great trouble of the Indian trade[6]—an odd reversal, due entirely to Manchester, of the classical seventeenth and eighteenth century difficulty of finding in England anything but bullion with which to pay for the precious things of the East. This "want of returns" had made the Company cling to the excellent "return" of China tea. India was still sending some muslins and other cotton fabrics —over 100,000 pieces in 1848—and considerable quantities of

[1] S. C. on E. I. C.'s Affairs, 1830, p. ix–x, and Q. 5647.
[2] Ibid. 1831, Q. 2753.
[3] E.g. John Kennedy. S. C. on E. I. C.'s Affairs, 1830, Q. 5016.
[4] For the Company's trade, Papers Relating to the East Indies, 1829, p. 111: a table for 1834–49 is in Porter, op. cit. p. 370.
[5] See above, p. 245–6, and for tea prices, Tooke, op. cit. II. 416; III. 433.
[6] S. C. on E. I. C.'s Affairs, 1831, Q. 1084.

silks, the maximum for the period being no less than 728,000 pieces in 1845; but these were the only manufactures. After the Company's withdrawal from trade, private enterprise worked up important new exports—linseed, wool, rum; and greatly increased some of the old—shellac, hemp, sugar, cotton. After 1835, when the preference given to West Indian over East Indian coffee in the home market ceased[1], attempts were made to develop coffee-growing in India. Nearly all failed; but in Ceylon success was rapid, so that the island was paying for her Manchester goods with coffee in the 'forties[2].

The opening of the railway age had coincided with a sharp rise in the outward flow, not only of goods but of men, from the United Kingdom. Since the repeal of the laws forbidding the emigration of skilled artisans, there had been no legal obstacle; and every year—with the growth of population and the improved means of transit, in Britain and in America—the incentives to move and the ease of motion increased. Imperfect figures for the whole of the United Kingdom suggest an emigration which rose for the first time, with a jerk, above a previous maximum of some 30,000 a year, towards 60,000 in 1830, to reach a —temporary—maximum of over 100,000 in 1832. The next peak is nearly 130,000 in 1842. The age closes with over 130,000 in 1846 and the tremendous average figure of well over 250,000 a year for the triennium 1847-9[3].

Throughout, and above all during that triennium of famine, this emigration was predominantly Irish. No regular and separate Irish returns were made before 1851; but one series of fairly trustworthy figures suggests that, down to 1845 when the Irish proportion suddenly increased[4], two-fifths British and three-fifths Irish was about the normal division. The series comes from British North America, which was reasonably representative of the emigrant-taking countries[5]. Between 1830 and 1843 the chief agent for emigrants at Quebec reported the arrival of 338,800 people from the United Kingdom. Of these, 92,500 were English or Welsh, 42,200 Scottish and 204,100

---

[1] See below, p. 497.

[2] Tables of these various trades in Porter, *op. cit.* p. 742-3.

[3] Johnson, *Emigration from the U.K. to North America*, p. 344-5. More-house, F., *Migration from the U.K. to North America*, 1840-50. (Manchester Ph.D. Dissertation.) [Carrothers, W. A., *Emigration from the British Isles* (1929).]

[4] From 1845 to 1849, both inclusive, the Irish proportion was four-fifths, 812,000 out of 1,028,500 in the aggregate.   [5] Given in Porter, *op. cit.* p. 129.

were Irish. These arrivals at Quebec formed about a third of the United Kingdom emigration for the thirteen years. Another 100,000 sailed for points in British North America other than Quebec, and 445,000 sailed for the United States. The departures for Australia and New Zealand, which only became numerous in 1838, numbered 112,000. Emigration was slack in 1844–5, as it often was in years of cheap corn, only 164,000 people leaving the whole of the United Kingdom in the two years. With the famine in 1846, and the Californian gold discoveries two years later, a new era in emigration began, whose history falls outside the early railway age.

On the assumption that two-fifths of the total emigration down to 1846, as officially recorded, was British—and if two-fifths is possibly low, one-half would certainly be high—the emigrants from Great Britain, from the end of 1830 to the end of 1845, averaged only about 31,000 a year, not an important subtraction from a population reputedly redundant, indeed a subtraction probably still less, as British emigration from 1815 to 1830 had certainly been less, than the yearly arrivals in Great Britain from Ireland. The official figures are too low, and for one economically important class of emigrants probably much too low; but that class was not so numerous as it was important, and even a generous allowance for error and under-statement could hardly raise the annual average up to 35,000.

The class in question is that of the skilled men who went to the continent, together with the commercial emigrants to India and elsewhere, most of whom no doubt came back and none of whom, presumably, went out in the first instance definitely as emigrants. But when allowance has been made for this, the official figures of emigration to "all other places" than North America, Australia and New Zealand seem quite inadequate. An entry of 1063 for 1820 probably reflects the organised movement of that year to South Africa, though it is too low[1]; but the 58 for 1831, the 202 for 1832 and the 227 for 1839 are almost meaningless. Even the annual average of nearly 2000 for the years 1840–7 can hardly be enough.

Before 1825 the skilled men who did so much to spread the industrial revolution on the continent took care not to be enumerated, and perhaps the habit of slipping away quietly persisted. While emigration was still illegal, Galloway told the Committee on Artisans and Machinery that 16,000 British

[1 The number was 3659. Johnson, *op. cit.* p. 228.]

artisans had arrived in France alone during the years 1822-3. Aaron Manby at Charenton, and Edwards at Chaillot, each employed, it was said, from 300 to 500 Englishmen. There were "immense numbers" of Englishmen near Calais in the lace trade; Englishmen at Dixon's machine works in Alsace; in other machine works at Rouen; in "almost every manufactory" of the modern type for woollens or cottons; and so on[1]. During the next fifteen years, with the progress of the new industry in Western Europe, it ceased to be necessary to take out trained men for puddling and moulding, as Aaron Manby had done. But the demand for foremen and directing personnel became wider. John Macgregor knew the continent well. "We find in France," he told the Import Duties Committee of 1840, "that the principal foremen at Rouen and in the cotton factories are from Lancashire; you find it in Belgium, in Holland, and in the neighbourhood of Liège." As far away as Vienna, "the directors and foremen" in the cotton mills were "chiefly Englishmen or Scotsmen, from the...manufactories of Glasgow and Manchester."[2] These were all picked men not ordinary redundants, and their loss was deplored.

"You find British capital," so Macgregor's argument continued, "going into Belgium, France and Germany to a very great amount; and this very British capital, employed there producing manufactures which meet us in the markets of the Mediterranean, the United States, Cuba, Porto Rico, South America and the East Indies." English capital and English labour, he added, had also gone into the New England manufactories[3]. When he spoke, this export of capital by private firms for private business purposes had been going on for a quarter of a century, but there is no means of guessing what its amount may have been. The loss of this capital and of the picked skilled men who went with it was—to free traders of the Macgregor type—a result of the restrictions placed on imports into the United Kingdom. Being unable to bring in goods to the value of those which her unique manufacturing capacity enabled her to send out, she left the value of the surplus

---

[1] *S. C. on Artisans and Machinery*, p. 8, 16, 101, 103, 108.

[2] Q. 1046. The passage is quoted in Hobson, C. K., *The Export of capital* (1914), p. 109. Macgregor was a good observer but not a man of judgment. "We had a very bad adviser in Macgregor, secretary to the board of trade"— "a loose-minded free trader"—Gladstone, in Morley's *Gladstone*, I. 250, 252.

[3] Q. 1047.

as fertilising capital in foreign countries, to be managed by her trained men who could not find equally profitable occupation at home. So the argument ran. The capital doubtless represented the surplus exports; but whether there would have been a smaller surplus, whether its owners would have refrained from seeking high rates of profit abroad, and whether the monopoly value of the trained men to half-industrialised countries would have been any less, had Britain pursued a different commercial policy, are open questions. The subsequent adoption of free trade neither reduced foreign investment nor checked skilled emigration; and the assumption which lay at the back of some British free-trading minds, in the 'twenties and 'thirties, that foreigners might be induced to grow food and raw materials "for ages,"[1] if only Britain would buy and use them freely, rested on questionable political assumptions, as an examination of French policy might have suggested.

Besides the money thus regularly invested in foreign businesses, there were the sums, individually perhaps not very great but in the aggregate considerable, taken by the half-million of British emigrants during the years 1830–45. Few, if any, of these were what might be called capitalists, but, apart from some of the poorest Highlanders, probably fewer were penniless. A Canadian estimate suggested that incoming settlers, in the single year 1834, brought with them £1,000,000[2]. Some 12,000 British and some 20,000 Irish went to Canada that year. The Irish probably took little; but it is very possible that the British averaged the £70 to £80 a head which the estimate would require. On some such basis, from £20,000,000 to £30,000,000 (£40 to £60 per head) of unrecorded capital, over and above that invested by the Manbys and Edwardses, may well have been taken overseas, and from the narrower British point of view lost, between 1830 and 1845. The only direct returns were successful emigrants' remittances to the old country; and the remittance habit was better developed among the poor Irish emigrants—to help their desperately poor relations at home—than among the richer British[3].

The recorded foreign investments—somewhat imperfectly recorded—were those made in state loans and joint-stock

---

[1] S. C. on Export of Tools and Machinery, 1825, p. 15.

[2] Porter, op. cit. p. 132. Also quoted in Hobson, op. cit., to which the following paragraphs are much indebted.

[3] See Johnson, op. cit. p. 353. Irish remittances were often to help relatives to emigrate; Morehouse, op. cit.

enterprises. It was reckoned in 1827, when the crash of 1825 was over, that £93,000,000 of English money with an "annual obligation" for interest of £6,000,000, was already invested in foreign government securities—French, Russian, American, German—and in American bank and canal shares[1]. The losses in Spain and Greece and the mythical republic of Poyais had been written off before this estimate was made, together with those in South American mines. In the 'thirties, new European borrowings were rare and South America was out of fashion, though its states floated a few more loans; but United States' borrowings more than filled the gap. The States, the canals, the banks—but mainly the States—borrowed freely, and London was the easiest place in which to borrow. Many banks broke and some States repudiated[2]; but it was after the chief bankruptcies and repudiations that Andrew Jackson estimated the European investments in United States stocks and shares at $200,000,000[3]; and instead of European he might almost have said British.

After that, American railroad bonds and continental railway shares began to attract the investing public. Some of the French and Belgian companies were half English, in capital, management, and design. On the Paris and Rouen—one of the lines for which Brassey was contractor—full half the work was done by English navvies; and long after the French had learnt to do without Englishmen for rough work they still hired some English plate-layers and other specialists[4]. By August 1845, regular quotations in financial newspapers included the stocks of most European and of many South American states; of thirteen of the United States, one of which—Pennsylvania—had six separate issues listed; of the United States Bank and the Bank of Louisiana; of half-a-dozen colonial joint-stock banks and of the bank of the Ionian Islands; of New Orleans and New York cities; the bonds of the Camden and Amboy and of the Philadelphia and Reading railroads, with the shares

---

[1] *Statistical Illustrations of the British Empire* (1827), quoted in Hobson, *op. cit.* p. 104.

[2] Michigan and Mississippi, with Florida, a Territory. [For the whole subject see L. H. Jenk's brilliant *Migrations of British Capital to 1875*, New York, 1927.]

[3] Hobson, *op. cit.* p. 111.

[4] Brassey, T., *Work and Wages* (1872), p. 79. "Upwards of 4000" workmen out of 10,000 were Englishmen, and they did more work than the French. This was in 1842 and the following years. On the later Dieppe line "Englishmen were still employed on the more difficult work"—plate-laying and tipping. *Ibid.* p. 82.

of eight French railways, one Belgian railway—the Sambre and Meuse—and the Dutch-Rhenish railway. Among the shares of the French lines, only two were fully paid up at that time, the Paris and Rouen and the Orleans. Both stood at over 100 per cent. premium[1].

By the beginning of 1847, the quotations of foreign and colonial railways had risen to thirty-four, though the effective export of capital for many of these had not yet begun. Fourteen of the railway shares quoted were French, three fully paid up, one 90 per cent. paid up, and two half paid up or more. Indian and Canadian lines now appear in embryo—such as the Great Indian Peninsula, 5s. paid up on a £50 share, or the Great Western of Canada—together with companies for Spain, Ceylon and Demerara, and the Jamaica South Midland Junction[2]. The calls on these various lines, amounting to nearly three millions for the first six months of 1847 alone[3], were helping to pave the way for the financial crisis in the autumn of that year.

This crisis and the revolutions, which ran through Western Europe like fire in the stubble during the early months of 1848, frightened the investor and checked the eastward flow of British capital. The *Economist* said in March 1848, "There is one circumstance which is particularly fortunate for this country. There probably never was a period, at least for many years past, when so little English money was invested in continental securities or credits; the events of the last eight months having led to the realising of the one and the contracting of the other."[4]   The months of actual revolution were not a time in which much realisation of foreign securities was possible. The *Economist* had itself noted a fortnight earlier that "Great Northern of France, Boulogne and Amiens, and all other French securities continue much depressed, and a market is not very readily found for them."[5] Frenchmen and Germans were sending money to London for safety but not—it may confidently be assumed—for investment in continental securities. The realisation to which reference was made had occurred

---

[1] The *Economist*, August, 9, 1845, quotes all but the last two, which occur elsewhere. The *Economist* only quoted the most marketable stocks and shares.

[2] *Economist*, January 2, 1847.

[3] *Ibid.* July 3, 1847, quoting the *Bankers' Magazine*. The actual figure given is £2,898,677.

[4] March 18, 1848. [Jenks, *op. cit.* p. 380 has shown that this statement, which was criticised in the first edition, is strictly correct. What follows is based on his account.]   [5] March 4, 1848.

principally during the summer of 1847 in connection with the abnormal food imports, the dear cotton, and the bullion drains of that troubled year[1]. Continental securities had been sold to redress the trade balance and make good the losses of the commercial crisis. It had been estimated in November that £6,000,000 worth had been disposed of. There had also been contraction of bankers' and merchants' credits to the continent. Investors having lost both money and nerve, hardly any fresh long-period continental investment was made either in private business or in public securities until Europe settled down again. In any case, the losses of 1846–7 had cut deep into the surpluses available for investment. Whether, when this brief pause in the outflow of capital took place—precisely at the end of the early railway age—the total sum invested overseas, excluding that "lost" with emigrants, was two, three or four times the reputed £93,000,000 of 1827, there is no good means of determining[2].

The main lines of the free trade programme for increasing the wealth of the kingdom by stimulating its overseas trade were laid down, in form convenient for digestion by politicians and the public, in Sir Henry Parnell's *On Financial Reform*, which appeared in the year the Liverpool and Manchester railway was opened[3]. Simplicity is the programme's badge. Taxes on imported raw materials, as an obvious abuse, are to go. Further, "as the progress of industry and the increase of capital are greatly promoted by everything that adds to the annual amount of imports, the right policy is to remove all obstruction in the way of importation, without the slightest reference to what course foreign governments may think proper to adopt."[4] The sentence applied primarily to manufactures. In appendices Parnell scheduled, first, the British manufactures not liable to injury from foreign competition, yet protected, and, second, those "erroneously supposed"[5] to be so liable and also protected. The first list comprised all the main articles of export, the second books, china, glass, gloves, leather goods, linen, paper, silks, refined sugar, watches, and a few more. As for the colonial trade, all restrictions on colonial economic freedom ought to go and, when they have gone, the

---

[1] Below, p. 529 *sqq.*

[2] [Bowley, A. L., *England's Foreign Trade*, Edn. of 1905, p. 75, estimated the British foreign investments of the early 'fifties at upwards of £400,000,000. Jenks, *op. cit.* p. 413, is "unable to account for" much more than £200,000,000.]

[3] See above, p. 318 *sqq.*   [4] P. 24.   [5] P. xxxvi.

colonies "will have no longer any claim to the monopoly of the British market."[1]

Parnell made compromise with what was to become orthodox free trade doctrine on only two points. "If protection must be given" to agricultural produce—he was thinking of a political necessity—let it be "a fixed duty of about £10 or £12 per cent.," which would yield a large revenue and so "would come in aid to the repealing of duties on raw materials and manufactures, and in this way make some amends for the injury it would still do to industry, in raising the price of food."[2] To export prohibitions and duties he was thoroughly hostile; but he was prepared to buy off the "prohibition to export" machinery—the limited and ineffective workings of which he, perhaps, did not fully apprehend—by "a moderate duty" on the export, which he expected would raise "a considerable revenue."[3]

Ten years later the Committee on Import Duties, of which Parnell was a member, used its opportunity, so far as its terms of reference permitted, to repeat the same programme loud and clear in the ear of parliament; for in the interval nothing of first-rate importance had been done. There were still duties —some, it is true, only trifling—on imported flax, silk, cotton, wool, iron, hides and other raw materials, much as Huskisson and Goderich had left them; though Althorp had cut the hemp duty from 4s. 8d. a cwt. to a nominal 1d.[4] The duties on manufactures, both those generally agreed to need no protection and those "erroneously supposed" to need it, were untouched. At the beginning, and again at the end, of their years of office the Whigs made a feint against the timber duties; but in the year of the report (1840) they raised them without touching the "colonial monopoly." Foreign hewn logs now paid 56s., colonial logs 10s. 6d. a load, and sawn or split wood rather more. Before it could be settled whether the feint of 1841 was to be followed by a blow, the Whigs were out of office. So, too, with sugar: there was a parting suggestion of drastic changes

---

[1] Parnell, *op. cit.* p. 246.

[2] P. 70-1.

[3] P. 42. There was not an absolute prohibition when he wrote: see above, p. 485-6.

[4] There are very convenient tables of the duties on the principal articles of merchandise and the changes in them, 1840-7, in Tooke, *op. cit.* III. 426 *sqq.* For Althorp, see Buxton, *op. cit.* I. 34.

from the Whigs, following an actual raising of the duties[1].
When they left office Empire-grown sugar paid 25s. 3d. a cwt.,
and foreign 63s. Empire coffee retained a preference of $9\frac{9}{20}d.$
a pound. (Tea paid 2s. $2\frac{1}{4}d.$, but as there was no Empire tea
there was no problem of preference.) But the Whigs had at
least got rid of intra-imperial preferences, doing away with
differential rates on sugar and coffee which had placed the
East Indian shipments at a disadvantage as against those from
the spoiled West Indies. They had also got rid of the general
export duty on coal, taxing the export only if made (as doubtless
it seldom was) in the ships of countries with which the United
Kingdom had not signed reciprocity treaties[2]. Corn duties
they left where they were, crying over their shoulders as they
were being pushed out of office that a reasonable fixed duty,
such as Ricardo had approved and Parnell just tolerated, was
the right thing[3]. They left export duties on wools and skins,
china clay and "cement stone"; and they left the machinery
export prohibitions.

Peel was not the man to apply simple formulae simply.
He was hammering out a policy—completing his education,
or appropriating other men's ideas, as Disraeli when kind, or
when unkind, put it. "Line upon line, line upon line...here
a little and there a little" was his way, his way both by temperament and by the necessity of a most difficult political
position. When he fell, in June 1846, the free trade programme
was in the ascendant, but there had been few clean cuts. Live
animals and most kinds of meat had been given free entry; but
butter—which had been prohibited down to 1842, unless
"spoilt" for food—cheese, hams, tongues and cured fish were
still taxed. Had there been no Irish famine, it may be conjectured that in the overhauling of the corn law, which he
contemplated in 1845, he would have aimed at a fixed duty on
corn, a very low fixed duty, but possibly somewhat higher than
the "registration" duty of 1s. a quarter, the figure at which
the downward sliding of duties, as provided for in the corn
bill of 1846, was to cease. This 1s. a quarter was the actual

---

[1] As part of the general 5 per cent. added to all import duties, except those
on corn, spirits and timber, in 1840: timber duties were raised specifically not
by the general percentage. Tooke, op. cit. III. 426. Buxton, op. cit. I. 325.

[2] Above, p. 484, n. 2.

[3] Lord John Russell had suggested a revised sliding scale in cabinet, in
February 1841. This was criticised, and the 8s. fiscal duty suggested instead.
Spencer Walpole, Lord John Russell (1891), I. 383-4.

duty levied from February 1, 1849, onwards, when the corn-law suspensions of the famine years were over[1].

It was under Peel that machinery export finally became free. He also abolished the small export duty on wool[2]. But he himself revived for a time (1842–5) a general export duty on coal; and he left at his fall that odd remnant of the duty, the tax on coal exported in ships of powers with which Great Britain had not signed reciprocity treaties[3]. He also left the export duty on china clay. In one matter he was almost logical. He swept away nearly all the duties on imported raw materials —those on every textile material, those on raw iron and steel, on hides and skins, on ashes, cochineal, indigo, logwood, tar and certain oils. But he left—among others—small duties on copper, lead, tin and tallow, and considerable duties on timber.

Timber duties, like the sugar duties, raised the imperial issue with which Peel had not Parnell's short way. So long as he thought it possible to retain corn duties of any size, he increased the colonial preference on corn[4]. He touched the timber duties more than once, finally arranging—in the budget of 1846—for a fall in two steps, to be taken in 1847 and 1848, to duties of 15s. a load on foreign and 1s. a load on colonial timber[5]. Sugar duties he, like every other statesman, found intractable and politically dangerous. Since they had been forced by the Act of 1834 to grow sugar without slaves, the West Indians could claim—over and above £20,000,000 compensation—that their sugar, "free grown" sugar, deserved very special consideration. "Free grown" was an excellent parliamentary catchword, which the Tories had used successfully against a Whig sugar duty proposal in 1841. Whether from conviction or from political necessity, Peel left the duties on "slave grown" sugar prohibitory, though he had brought those on "free labour foreign sugar"—Javan or Philippine—within about 1d. a lb. of the rates on British Empire sugars. He also left a preference of 2d. a lb. on Empire coffee and preferences on pepper and

---

[1] The "repeal" Act of June 1846 (9 & 10 Vict. c. 22), under which duties—though low ones—were levied even when corn was dear, was suspended in January 1847. It remained in suspense until March 1, 1848, when the duties provided for by it (4s. when the price was at or above 53s. and more when it was below) automatically came into force. Eleven months later the 1s. duty began.

[2] Above, p. 243.   [3] Buxton, op. cit. 1. 60 n. And above, p. 484, n. 2.
[4] By the Canada Corn Act of 1843 (6 & 7 Vict. c. 29) under which Canadian corn was admitted at 1s. a quarter.   [5] See Buxton, op. cit. 1. 344.

spices. Two months after his fall from office, Russell wiped out the line between free and slave grown sugar, and timed the expiry of the colonial preference for 1851. On this issue Lord George Bentinck fought him, in the interest of the West Indies, and won: the date of expiry was postponed and Empire sugar was guaranteed its preference of over 1*d.* a pound for six years[1].

Even Peel's treatment of manufactures would have seemed half-hearted to Parnell. He reduced all the duties, and he got rid of a number of duties, in Parnell's first category—the goods with which foreign competition was almost unthinkable—but he left 10 per cent., or 5 per cent. if the imported goods were Empire made, to every manufacture with which effective competition was at all likely; and by a special act of tenderness for an industry parts of which at any rate—in spite of Parnell— were certainly liable to injury from foreign competition, he left duties of 15 per cent. on manufactured silks[2].

It was not to be expected that reforms, all but one of which were conservative, would produce marked effects in a short time; though during the years of brisk trade, 1843–5, Peel was able to point to the satisfactory financial and commercial working of the earlier series (those of 1842–3) in defence of the more daring steps taken in 1845–6. Yet there were some prompt and striking results, nearly all in the food-stuffs trades. The imports of butter had leapt up to over 15,000 tons and those of cheese to over 18,000 tons by 1847—"and yet...the home producer has every year been receiving better prices," the *Economist* noted with triumph[3]. Live animals imported—nearly all cattle and sheep—increased from 5000 in 1842 to 216,000 in 1847; bacon from a few odd tons to 43,000; salt pork and salt beef, not so remarkably, yet very fast[4]. The increase might have been less, and prices for British producers less satisfactory, had Ireland, a natural supplier of all these things, not been ravaged by famine. She continued to send them over into Britain: at the height of the famine Irish butter in its thousands of tons was arriving on the London market[5]; but her exporting

[1] Disraeli, *Lord George Bentinck* (ed. 1906), p. 209, etc. Disraeli's *Life*, III. 92–3, 97. Buxton, *op. cit.* I. 96.

[2] The silk duties, since Huskisson, had been 30 per cent. The complete abolition of some 500 duties on articles of no importance had little effect on national welfare one way or the other.

[3] *Economist*, March 4, 1848: Trade Review of 1847.

[4] Figures from the *Economist's* annual Trade Reviews.

[5] See the reports on Provision Markets weekly in the *Economist*, 1847–8.

capacity cannot have been normal. Some of these provisions imported in 1846–7–8 therefore were of the nature of emergency supplies, like the extra five and a half million quarters of grain or flour brought into the United Kingdom in 1847[1].

The sources of the abnormal grain imports of 1847, when trade was completely open, are worth notice. They themselves, however, are not quite normal because there was food shortage throughout Western Europe. Maize for Irish relief—the maize which was ground into "Peel's brimstone"—was nearly all American. Of the 1,100,000 quarters of wheat which passed through the London market, about two-fifths of the whole British import, 370,000 quarters came from Russia, 253,000 from Prussia, 125,000 from the United States and 37,000 from the British Empire. Three-sevenths of the London barley was Danish, and more than three-sevenths of the oats were Russian. There was no Empire barley, and only 7000 tons of Empire oats. These London figures may be assumed to be fairly representative[2].

While Peel ruled, the imperial sugar monopoly remained unbroken: in 1845 240,000 tons of British sugar, and under 4000 tons of "free labour foreign" sugar, paid duty and were consumed. Russell set open the bonded warehouses, and in 1847 nearly a sixth of all the sugar consumed was foreign, mostly "slave labour"; yet the consumption of British sugar had not declined. The changes in timber duties did not, in the early years, much affect the rate of growth in consumption or the relative consumptions of British and foreign timber. In 1843 three-quarters of the whole consumption was British; in 1845 two-thirds; in 1847 five-ninths; in 1848 five-eighths[3]. The total consumption, like the total consumption of textile raw materials, was influenced more by the course of trade than by the course of tariffs. There was much less timber consumed in 1849 than in 1846; less wool, and much less cotton, in 1847 than in 1845; and so on. As for foreign manufactures—a considerable increase in the import of European silks can be traced, with some difficulty, through a change in the tariff classification; but it coincides with a decrease in the import of Indian

---

[1] "Extra" means beyond the level of 1846, which was itself 1,600,000 qrs. above 1845.

[2] They are given in the *Economist*, January 29, 1848, and are the London grain brokers' figures. A regular analysis of the sources of origin was not, at this time, given in the Annual Trade Returns.

[3] Figures in Porter, *op. cit.* p. 579.

silks[1]. There is some increase in gloves and an increase in tanned hides, both probably connected with the tariff—for the rest, nothing. The Customs officials of 1848 did not regard foreign cotton or wool or linen or iron or steel manufactures as "principal articles of merchandise," worth separate entry in the ordinary trade returns: no doubt the officials were right.

With the imperial sugar monopoly Peel left untouched the primarily imperial navigation code; but it may be assumed that he was dissatisfied with it. Yet it had been revised within a few months of the first announcement of potato disease in Ireland, when the last act "for the encouragement of British shipping and of navigation" (8 & 9 Vict. c. 88) went through parliament without discussion[2]. Partly because some of its sections were obsolete; partly because trade had for generations been adjusted to it; partly because it was so intricate and technical that only "a few official persons and a few inquirers in political economy"[3] understood it, the code had escaped the critical notice of eager and informed free-traders. It had not even been attacked by James Wilson in the *Economist*. It was vaguely known to restrain something, and so was suspect to the men of *laissez passer*, but it was allowed by them to be "rather of a political than of a commercial character."[4] Adam Smith's approving dictum about defence and opulence carried weight both with economists and with politicians. The Admiralty had been taught to believe that the law was really a mainstay of our defence[5].

No changes of importance had been made since Huskisson's time[6], though at a revision in the early 'thirties (3 & 4 Wm. IV, c. 34) the ancient list of goods, the produce of Europe, which might not be imported to the United Kingdom to *be used therein* (they might be warehoused here), except in British ships or ships of the country from which the goods came, had been enlarged by the addition of a dozen commodities, including wool, brimstone and oranges; which shows that

[1] For the tariff classification see *Economist*, March 4, 1848.

[2] Some points connected with navigation law, in the wider sense, are in 8 & 9 Vict. c. 86, 89, 93.

[3] Harle, W. L., *The total repeal of the navigation laws discussed, etc.* (Newcastle, 1848), p. 27.

[4] *Economist*, January 30, 1847.

[5] See the questions put by naval men in any of the Reports quoted below or Lord Hardwicke's speech in the Lords, February 25, 1848 Hansard, XCVI. 1313.

[6] Above, p. 331.

someone in the Board of Trade took the list seriously[1]. It still contained the main articles of European trade—timber, grain, hemp, flax, dried fruits, olive oil and wine. This was its undoing; for, although the rule worked well enough in ordinary times—the British mercantile marine being so strong—it had to be suspended during the famine. "While it does not prevent foreign ships from bringing food hither to be stored up and used in France and Holland whenever they choose," the *Economist* now wrote, "it did prevent, until it was suspended, that food being made available for our own people."[2] The law, of course, did not prevent foreign ships in general from bringing food for our own people; but it forbade a Dutchman to load for London in Danzig, or a Hamburger in Odessa, and in famine time even these prohibitions could not be maintained, though it is probable that their removal did not affect very many corn cargoes.

The famine having revealed some of the mysteries of the code to its predestined critics, they began to inquire into its other economic aspects and its political utility. They failed to find very many hard cases in the home trade. One was that of John Bright's friend, who bought cotton in Havre but might not bring it to England[3], because the old rule intended to preserve the long haul for British ships forbade the shipping of the produce of the remoter continents from European ports. James Wilson also had a friend, in great need of indigo, who bought it in Holland and brought it home *via* the United States, for the same reason[4]. Raw Javan sugar might not come in from Rotterdam; but refined sugar was a Dutch manufacture and might come in—a rule which seemed to make business for the Dutch refiner[5]. But, although there were other cases of the same sort, Wilson admitted from his place in parliament, when two years' inquiry and debate had beaten on the laws, that "the evils were more real than apparent. The mischief was more accidental than regular."[6] This was at once a testimony to the adjustment of trade to the law and a claim that such forced adjustment was not in trade's permanent interest —Rotterdam and Havre were good markets which should be made accessible.

[1] Six commodities were dropped from the list—salt, pitch, rosin, potashes, sugar and vinegar—it is not easy to say why.
[2] January 30, 1847.   [3] Hansard, LXXXIX, 1007 *sqq.*
[4] *Ibid.* CIII. 485.
[5] *A short review of the history of the navigation laws. By a barrister* (Sir Stafford Northcote), 1849, p. 60.   [6] Hansard, as above. March 9, 1849.

Within governing circles, some political difficulties arising from the law were very familiar. Various angles of it had in the past collided with the United States, who had stipulated for their removal. A straining of it, in connection with the arrangement of commercial treaties in the 'thirties, had troubled British relations with various European powers, particularly Holland and the Zollverein. First in a treaty concluded by John Macgregor with Austria in 1838, and afterwards in several other treaties, ports not on the territory of the other contracting party had been recognised by Great Britain as its "natural outlets" for all navigation law purposes. The procedure was illegal when first adopted and had to be regularised later[1]. The extreme case was the concession to Mecklenburg-Strelitz, which has no more sea coast than Bohemia, of the right to use Danzig, Königsberg, Antwerp and Rotterdam as its natural outlets. Whether it ever used any of them, except possibly Danzig, may be doubted; but the treaty and others of the same series, one of whose main objects was to keep free trade German states out of the Zollverein, were very irritating to Prussia, the more so as her own shipping laws were less restrictive than those of the United Kingdom.

Prussia, speaking for the Zollverein, began a diplomatic move against the laws in April 1846[2]. Bunsen indicated that the price of a renewal of an existing Anglo-Zollverein commercial treaty might be some maritime concession. He suggested that as England was about to abandon the corn law she might go on to abandon the navigation law. He assured her that "Prussia...never could think of disputing" her "preponderant power" on the seas, but would like greater freedom there. Two years later he was saying that the unequal treatment of Zollverein shipping was "deeply felt" as an "infraction of German honour," and that if the British navigation laws continued they would be imitated in Germany[3]. Meanwhile the question had come up awkwardly in Anglo-Dutch commercial diplomacy (in 1846) and much less awkwardly, but quite definitely, in Anglo-American diplomacy in the autumn of 1847[4].

[1] By 3 & 4 Vict. c. 95. See E.H.R. xxv. (1910), p. 687 sqq.
[2] Memorandum handed by Bunsen to Aberdeen. F.O. Prussia, vol. 268.
[3] To Palmerston, January 24, 1848. F.O. Prussia, vol. 292.
[4] The Dutch resented the working of our "natural outlets" policy, not extended to them. Relations with America were friendly, thanks to Bancroft, the American ambassador. See, i.a., Bancroft to Palmerston, November 3 and 17, 1847, in F.O. America. vol. 478. A fuller discussion is in E.H.R. xxv.

Colonial opinion was even more important than the opinions of foreign powers. Corn grown in the North American colonies had always enjoyed preferential treatment, and since 1843 had been admitted at the nominal fixed duty of 1s. a quarter. Peel's 1846 policy would destroy this preference and, at the same time, he was cutting into the preference on timber. It was natural for some people in the North American colonies to argue that imperial restrictions ought not to survive imperial preferences. If there were no navigation law, freights might fall with the admission of the highly efficient United States mercantile marine to the imperial carrying trade. From August 1846, resolutions and petitions from official and unofficial bodies in British North America flowed in steadily. Russell's sugar policy roused the West Indies also. The islands got most of their flour meat and lumber from the United States: the marketing of their sugar might be easier if they were allowed to load it for England in these United States bottoms; for there was sometimes a shortage of British tonnage in the Caribbean Sea[1].

As timber and sugar retained substantial preferences until after the repeal of the navigation law in 1849, the discussions turned mainly on corn, the more so because the sugar people wanted something, but by no means all of them, or always, repeal. Jamaica spoke with two voices, in 1847 and 1848, and Demerara was in favour of the law[2]. Favourable views also came at times from North American timber interests, who saw that repeal might lead to the termination of their preference, should the unprotected British shipbuilder insist on buying in the nearest market. The most significant of the long series of colonial documents is probably a petition of December 14, 1848, from the Montreal Board of Trade. The cessation of preference on corn, the majority of the Board agreed, would ruin the trade of the St Lawrence; therefore they demanded repeal of the navigation law and a 5s. British duty on foreign corn. A free trade minority repudiated the demand for preference but endorsed that for repeal[3].

---

[1] The resolutions and petitions from Canada and the West Indies are given in the Appendix to the *House of Lords' Reports on the Navigation Laws*, 1847–8 (xx), and in *Accounts and Papers*, 1849 (LI).

[2] See, *i.a.*, Stanley's speech in the Lords, May 8, 1849. Hansard, CV. 95–9.

[3] In *A. and P.* 1849 (LI). [Already in Aug. 1846 the Montreal Board had argued the case against the Navn. Laws arising out of Corn Law repeal, 1847–8 (xx), 935.]

Whether or not these various petitioners interpreted rightly the general and permanent interests of their respective colonies, their petitions carried weight in parliament. During the prolonged inquiries and discussions of 1847-9 Peel, who though out of office influenced them as much as any man, once arranged in order the considerations which determined him to favour a complete revision of the law. They were—colonial opinion: the offers and demands of foreign powers: the troublesome complexity of the reciprocity treaties: and the "mutilated and shattered state" of the law itself[1].

The offers to which he referred were primarily those of Prussia, prepared to guarantee complete freedom of navigation in return for complete freedom, and of the United States, made through Bancroft[2]. The States were ready to abolish all restrictions on navigation, by treaty, except the monopoly of the coasting trade. This was a serious exception. In the debates of 1848 and 1849[3] Gladstone argued, with great force, that American coasting trade was oceanic, in fact imperial; and that the British Empire ought to bargain for its opening to British ships, in return for the abandonment of the British imperial monopoly. America, he remarked, "was not a lover of free trade in the abstract." That was just what Britain now was, the repealers maintained[4]. Moreover, Gladstone's bargain policy would perpetuate the existing troublesome diversity of shipping rules—so much disliked by Peel—since not all bargains work out alike. After long parliamentary struggles, the repealers won, although the final margin was narrow in the Lords; and from June 26, 1849, the only remnants of a navigation code nearly two centuries old were the restriction of the British coasting trade to British ships with British crews, and the stipulation that every ship on the register must be manned by a crew at least three-quarters British.

That the law—on the eve of its repeal—was doing much to maintain shipping cannot be demonstrated. The "shipping interest" could never counter the free trade argument that already, in the most important trades and the most expanding

---

[1] June 9, 1848. Hansard, XCIX. 646.

[2] See Bancroft to Palmerston, November 3, 1847, and Bancroft's recapitulation of the offers to Labouchere, March 10, 1849. F.O. America, vol. 506.

[3] June 2, 1848, and March 12, 1849. Hansard, XCIX. 251 and CIII. 540. The quotation is from the second speech.

[4] Wilson's speech of March 9, 1849.

trades, they did very well without any protection, against the shipping of all the world. But the free traders, on their side, could not prevent the shipping interest from keeping open an uneasy ear to President Polk's proud message to Congress of 1847—should American shipping increase as it has increased of late, "the time is not distant when our... commercial marine will be larger than that of any other nation in the world."[1] Buried in a recent blue-book, and not quoted by either side, were a question put to B. G. Willcox, of the Peninsular and Oriental Company, and his reply—"And this country can beat the rest of the world so far as iron is concerned? Decidedly."[2]

[1] It was quoted by Hardwicke in the Lords, February 25, 1848.
[2] *S. C. on British Shipping*, 1844, Q. 1244. Above, p. 440–1.

CHAPTER XIII

BANKING, PRICES AND THE MONEY MARKET

WITH the return of an effective system of gold mono-metallism during the 'twenties, the United Kingdom had finally hitched its economic chariot to the *metallum solis*. It is not possible to establish easy and exact connections between gold supplies and prices in gold-using countries, especially when those countries are changing tariffs which vitally affect their price levels and modifying their banking practice, as the United Kingdom was between 1830 and 1849; but there is little doubt that the general falling trend of gold prices, between the decade 1820–30 and the gold discoveries of 1848–51, was evidence of a relative shortage in the world's supplies of gold, in relation to the world-demand for it in currency and in the arts. But the downward heave of the prices of primary foods and raw materials, which may be connected with, though not traced precisely or exclusively to, the gold position, was almost completely disguised for those who moved with it by the far steeper year to year waves and troughs. From an average index number of 103, for the decade 1820–9, there was a fall to an average of 88 for the decade 1840–9[1]. The tops of the waves never got above the starting level, though they touched it in 1839–40; but the last wave and trough are represented by the steep figures—1843, 83; 1847, 95; 1849, 74. Actual famine was needed in 1847 to bring the wave crest within 5 per cent. of the starting level.

If Thomas Attwood and the "Birmingham School" had had their way, a continuance of the Bank Restriction Act, "under the controul of a legislative commission," would have provided for the reversal of the downward heave and a smoothing out of the waves and troughs by a generous, but well "controuled," issue of paper[2]. Attwood's political and economic activities

---

[1] These are Sauerbeck's index numbers, in which the datum line (100) is the average of prices for the eleven years 1867–77. They are based on the price of thirty-one commodities down to 1846, and of forty-five from 1846. These are all primary food-stuffs and raw materials, the most "manufactured" article being common bar iron.

[2] See above, p. 311, n. 1.

were at their height in the days of the Reform Bill; but he tried
to harness Chartism to his currency theories; and he lived to
hear them treated with great contempt by Peel, in his speech
on the Bank Charter Act of 1844, and to read—and presumably
reject—a refutation of them by Mill in 1848[1]. In 1844 his
Birmingham followers were saying—"coin the ounce of gold
into £5 [instead of £3. 17s. 10½d.] and we shall then have relief
of our burdens, and encouragement to industry and trade."[2]
But, although they broke into a number of government inquiries[3], the Birmingham doctrines were as barren of results
as they were—in Peel's view—nonsensical. Attwood never had
a chance of showing how, in practice, "prices may be preserved
more steadily, on a given ratio" by the use of notes "than by
that of gold"; although his views might not appear so exclusively nonsensical to all students to-day as they did to Peel in
the 'forties.

The Directors of the Bank of England had now come round
completely to the doctrine of Ricardo and the Bullion Report
of 1810, as they understood them. They had no views of which
record has survived about the stability of prices; but they
desired the link between British currency and gold to be so
tight that no divergence between the purchasing powers of
the two should ever appear. They recognised that, broadly
speaking, adverse foreign exchanges and a foreign drain of
gold suggested a price level in this country rather too high—
as compared with the commercial world in general—and ought
to be met by a contraction of the paper circulating at home.
But their plan, as explained in 1832, was to keep a decent
metallic reserve and leave the rest to "the Public"—really to
the very small group of bullion dealers who were concerned
with foreign drains of gold, who would present notes to the
Bank to get the gold for export, and so perhaps reduce the total
circulation[4]. The process was not automatic, because there was
nothing but its own power of self-control to prevent the Bank
from increasing its note issue, and because there was some tendency for any gap in the circulation to be part filled by an increase

[1] Hansard, LXXIV. 726 (Peel's speech of May 6, 1844). Mill, J. S., *Principles
of Political Economy*, bk. III. ch. 13, sect. 4. Attwood died in 1856.
[2] From a pamphlet by "Gemini," quoted very contemptuously by Peel in
the House.
[3] For example, the 1832 *Comm. of Secrecy on the Bank...Charter* (1831–2, VI)
Q. 5567 *sqq.*
[4] Above, p. 280–1.

of " country " notes[1]. But by the late 'thirties, the leading country bankers at any rate had learnt how to read the signs of the times. Adverse foreign exchanges made them "prudent and cautious," as Vincent Stuckey put it. Wholesale provision prices, in their practical experience, did tend to fall after a foreign drain; and "in time" this told on their issues, by bringing down country prices and so reducing the amount of country bank notes required for a given volume of trade[2].

Whether the Bank's self-determined passive methods were adequate, and whether the complete liberty of issue still left to the country bankers was wise, were the central currency problems of the early railway age, with which statesmen and publicists occupied themselves sometimes to the point of currency-madness. There was less talk about drawing credits and cheques, the use of which was nevertheless spreading steadily, if in silence[3]. Nor was there enough intelligent comprehension among statesmen, and on the Board of Directors, of how the Bank might influence circulation and prices by a judicious handling of the rate of interest and discount, a method of wider range than any little changes in the supply of bank notes payable to bearer, because it acts on the general supply of purchasing power[4].

That greater liberty in connection with discount was desirable was recognised, though rather timidly, by the Act which renewed the Bank's Charter in 1833 (3 & 4 Wm. IV, c. 98). When discounting bills of a shorter currency than three months, the Bank might now disregard the usury laws, that is, go beyond 5 per cent. The Act also made Bank of England notes legal tender, which they had never been before[5], though they were to be legal tender only so long as the Bank cashed them on demand, and so were not legally tenderable for payments by the Bank itself: it provided for a repayment by the Treasury of a quarter of the £14,520,000 which the state owed the Bank, accompanied by a reduction of what the Bank received for managing the public debt: it recognised the formal right of

---

[1] S. C. on Banks of Issue, 1841 (v), Q. 96 sqq., 465 sqq.
[2] Ibid. Q. 502, 528.
[3] See below, p. 519.
[4] The method was explained admirably by Thomas Tooke in 1838, when criticising Bank policy. History of Prices, II. (1838), 296.
[5] That was why Lord King had been able, during the suspension of cash payments, to demand gold rents from his tenants and so force on currency inquiry. Smart, Economic Annals, I. 298.

"any body politic or corporate, or society, or company, or partnership, although consisting of more than six persons," to carry on in London all banking business except the issue of notes payable on demand, and the right of note-issuing country banks to have an agency in London, "for the sole purpose of paying such of their notes as might be presented there": and it obliged the Bank to send regularly to the Chancellor of the Exchequer statistics of its deposits, notes and bullion supplies. In return, its charter was renewed for eighteen years, with power to the state to suspend it after twelve.

The clause about banking in London was declaratory of an interpretation previously placed by the law officers of the crown upon the series of charters which had created and sustained the Bank's monopoly—that its monopoly of joint-stock banking extended only to issue. This interpretation the Bank had hotly contested, but the contest was now settled. The Bank accordingly did what it could, within the circuit of the law, to block the business of the first London joint-stock bank—the London and Westminster, opened in March 1834, with J. W. Gilbart as manager. Gilbart's bank had to fight not only the Bank of England but the London private bankers, the law, and a very suspicious public opinion. The general legal sanction of joint-stock banking, by the Act of 1826, applied only outside the sixty-five-mile radius from London, the formal declaration of 1833 notwithstanding. The London and Westminster was only a gigantic partnership at common law; and when it tried to get a private Act of parliament, allowing it to sue and be sued in the name of its Chairman[1], its enemies, with Lord Althorp's help, were strong enough to defeat the bill in the Lords. (Gilbart accordingly arranged to make all his contracts through trustees[2].) City capital was so hostile that the funds for the bank were mostly raised in the country. The clearing bankers refused the facilities of the Clearing House and the Bank of England would not let Gilbart open a drawing account[3].

---

[1] Such as insurance companies had often got (above, p. 288). The Act of 1826 had generalised this right for the joint-stock banks (above, p. 275).

[2] Gilbart, *The Principles and Practice of Banking* (ed. 1873), p. 466. An injunction was also secured in the Common Pleas restraining the London and Westminster from accepting short bills, on the ground that no partnership or corporation of more than six members could do this without infringing the Bank of England's privileges. "The only result was that the Bank paid the bills drawn upon it without acceptance."

[3] Gilbart's evidence in 1841: Q. 1307.

That public opinion was doubtful about joint-stock banking is not surprising. The Act of 1826 left the new institutions perfectly free in all matters of constitution, management, issue and account[1]. Gilbart was a great banker, and most of the joint-stock banks of the early railway age were to have long and honourable lives. But the original law gave too much latitude, changes made in it were not always judicious[2], and promotion was too quick for general safety. Liability was unlimited, but so might be the inexperience of the personnel. Consequently, for a generation and more, "ghosts of fraudulent joint-stock banks" haunted the Victorian mind.

At the close of 1833, there were thirty-two English joint-stock banks in full existence, the majority in the industrial areas. Promotion went on steadily in 1834–5, and with a rush during the boom of 1836. Very frequently existing private banks amalgamated with joint-stock concerns, or joint-stocked themselves, for safety or to be in the fashion; and the number of separate banking institutions was declining steadily. By the end of 1836, seventy-nine English joint-stock banks of issue were in existence, besides the non-issuing London and Westminster of 1834, the London Joint-Stock of 1836, and some eighteen country joint-stock banks which had never issued or had ceased to issue. The joint-stock note circulation at the end of 1836 was £4,258,000. Of the seventy-nine note-issuers no less than twenty-one, with issues of nearly £1,000,000 in the aggregate, were in Yorkshire, and much the largest single issue was the £231,000 of the Yorkshire District Bank[3]. There was at that time no joint-stock circulation at all in metropolitan England; none in the Eastern Midlands; none in Oxford or Berkshire or Hereford or Cheshire[4].

In March of 1837, the bank-note circulation for England and Wales was divided thus: the Bank of England, £18,200,000; the Private Banks, £7,200,000; the Joint-Stock Banks, £3,700,000. Four years later, at a time of bad trade just before Peel came into office, the figures were: Bank of England, £16,200,000; Private Banks, £6,200,000; Joint-Stock Banks, £3,700,000. There were also £2,900,000 of Scottish, and no

---

[1] Except that they might not issue £1 notes.

[2] For instance, Peel's Joint-Stock Banking Act, 7 & 8 Vict. c. 113, was found unsuitable and repealed in 1862.

[3] See the elaborate statistics given to the S. C. of 1841 by Gilbart: Q. 912–40.

[4] Gilbart's evidence: Q. 940.

less than £5,500,000 of Irish notes, including the issues of the chartered Scottish banks and of the Bank of Ireland[1].

By 1841 the number of English joint-stock banks had grown to 115—including three more in London. Private banks had fallen from the 781 of 1821, through 554 in 1826 and 436 in 1831, to 321[2]. Of the 321 private banks 287, and of the 115 joint-stock banks 91, were banks of issue—most of the non-issuing private banks being, of course, in London[3]. There was an important group of 25 country banks, mainly joint-stock, which employed Bank of England notes exclusively and had special arrangements with Threadneedle Street. Ten of them were in South Lancashire, where the Bank of England note had early got a footing, six in Birmingham and four in Newcastle[4]. In Scotland, the process of banking concentration went on more slowly because it had already gone so far: the 36 banks of 1821 had only fallen to 29 twenty years later. Many of the 29 were new creations like the Ayrshire Banking Co. of 1830, the Western Bank of Scotland of 1832 or the North of Scotland of 1836[5]. Ireland, like Scotland, was relying more and more on branch banking and had now not very many separate institutions. There had been fearful mortality among the old private banks in 1820, when "the circulation of a province, or nearly two, was swept off in a week."[6] After 1826, the Bank of Ireland had set up branches actively and the Provincial Bank of Ireland, projected in 1824–5 by Joplin and always directed from London, had been even more active. The last private bank outside Dublin, De la Cour's of Mallow, stopped payment in 1835 and even the Dublin private banks were dying out—only Ball and Co. were issuing in 1841. A batch of new Irish joint-stock banks had sprung up in 1834–6, but not all had endured[7].

Scottish banking in the 'thirties was strong and was not likely to trouble London much, even in difficult times. The Bank of Scotland, for example, kept a reserve of gold and Bank

---

[1] S. C. of 1841, Q. 937, and Ap. 13 a of the same report. In July 1844, the Private Banks had a circulation of £4,624,000 and the joint-stock of £3,340,000. Powell, E. T., *Evolution of the Money Market*, p. 413.

[2] Table in Powell, *op. cit.* p. 412; for 1821, above, p. 264.

[3] S. C. of 1841, Ap. 13 a.

[4] *Ibid.* Ap. 2. And see Grindon, *Manchester Banks and Bankers*, p. 254.

[5] S. C. of 1841, Ap. 13 a, and Kerr, *History of Banking in Scotland*, p. 215–16.

[6] S. C. on the State of the Poor in Ireland, 1830 (VII), Q. 1164.

[7] Gilbart, J. W., *A History of Banking in Ireland* (1836). Gilbart had worked there. Ap. 13 a, as above. For the banks of 1834–6, Tooke, *op. cit.* II. 286.

of England notes equal to a quarter of its own circulation, in 1841; but as it never paid much gold or many English notes across the counter, there was no great risk of the reserve being depleted[1]. Ireland was less stable, and the close linking of its banks with London increased the sensitiveness of the monetary position there.

That position had been very severely tested between 1836 and 1841. Early in 1837, the Bank's reserve of bullion had been down to £4,000,000 and late in 1839 to £2,500,000, when, as a private banker said two years later, the convertibility of Bank of England notes was "virtually at an end."[2] The Bank's liabilities were such that the ideal reserve, suggested by Directors in 1832, would have been over £10,000,000 of bullion in the 1837 pressure and £8,000,000 in that of 1839. Reserves, no doubt, exist to be used in time of pressure, but—on the second occasion at least—they were all but used up. The Bank made bad blunders. Some of the new joint-stock banks, especially those of Ireland, made worse. The public in 1835-6 was itching for higher returns on its savings—from railways or banks or Spanish bonds or the Safety Cabriolet Company[3]. But another projected company of 1836, the British and American Intercourse Company, capital £2,000,000, pointed to the immediate cause of the monetary trouble—the close and dominant commercial and financial relations which now existed between Great Britain and the United States. The States supplied the material for the ruling British industry; they were the greatest purchasers of British exports; they were absorbing British capital and playing with it as a young country, with a continent in reserve, is tempted to play with any tool or toy; and they were operating on the gold to which the economic life of Britain was hitched.

In January 1835, the national debt of the United States was paid off and arrangements were made for distributing the surplus federal revenue—no longer wanted for interest—among the States, where it got into banks which wanted to use it[4]. In 1836, after a long struggle, President Andrew Jackson beat the United States Bank. Its charter was allowed to lapse that

---

[1] *S. C. of* 1841, Q. 1791, and Ap. 23 *a.* For some failures of Scottish private banks, Kerr, *op. cit.* p. 213.

[2] *S. C. of* 1841, Q. 248: H. W. Hobhouse.

[3] Above, p. 388, and Poulett Thomson's speech of May 6, 1836, quoted in Tooke, *op. cit.* II. 276-7. See also Tooke, *op. cit.* II. 282-4, 386; III. 78.

[4] Dewey, *Financial History of the United States,* p. 219 *sqq.,* and references there.

year, and the government monies were spread about among
Jackson's "pet banks," instead of being concentrated as
hitherto in a central institution. The pet banks were in funds.
There were land booms and railway booms, and there were
nearly two hundred more banks in the United States in 1835–6
than there had been in 1834. Cotton prices were bounding up.
America imported far more merchandise than she exported,
between 1830 and 1837, and the foreigner in effect left the
proceeds of his surplus sales to earn American rates, preferably
in municipal and State bonds. "Our good fortune fired the
imagination of even the dull Europeans," as an American
biographer wrote later[1].

Since the late eighteenth century, the United States currency
had been—nominally—on a bimetallic basis. The ratio of silver
to gold was 15 to 1; but this was not high enough and no gold
worth mentioning had been minted. Now, by Act of June 28,
1834, it had been decided to lighten the gold eagle so as to make
the ratio very near 16 to 1, raising the mint par of exchange
between sterling and dollars from $4·44 to $4·87½[2]. Jackson's
government, which meant to have gold in circulation, required
the "pet banks" to pay a certain proportion of all demands
made on them in gold coin, and also arranged to draw gold
from Europe direct. The United States Bank was raising a
considerable loan in London, where money was cheap, in
1835–6, "to facilitate the settlements upon the expiration of
the charter."[3] There was also Dutch and other foreign borrowing in the easy London market. Unusual amounts of American
securities of all kinds were sent to Europe for sale (with the
ultimate object of securing gold); and upon these "credit had
been given by some of the principal houses in England, in
anticipation of the sums they were expected to realise."[4]

The unanswered charge against the Bank of England was
that it took no adequate measures to parry, or to minimise the
risks of, these foreseeable drains on the gold of Europe—
rather the reverse. It increased its securities and its issues,
and only raised its rate of discount to 5 per cent. in August

---

[1] Shepard, E. M., *Van Buren*, quoted in Dewey, *op. cit.* p. 226.
[2] Palmer, J. Horsley, *Causes and Consequences of the Pressure on the Money
Market, from October* 1, 1833, *to December* 27, 1836 (1837), studies the question
from the British side. It is used in Tooke, *op. cit.* II. 282 *sqq.*
[3] *Causes and Consequences, etc.*, p. 30. Also Tooke, *op. cit.* III. 73.
[4] *Ibid.* [A full analysis in Jenks, L. H., *The Migration of British Capital* (1927),
p. 92 *sqq.*]

1836. For no month in 1835 was appreciably more than a fifth of its assets in bullion, and the notes were throughout nearly three times the bullion[1].

In the course of 1836 the home situation was strained. It is not the case that the new English joint-stock banks inflated the actual note currency dangerously, as was thought at the time and has been sometimes suggested since[2]. Many of their issues replaced those of absorbed private banks, and in fact the total English country bank issue—private and joint-stock—though it averaged a million, or about 10 per cent., more in 1836 than in 1835, was declining from April to December of 1836[3]. Irish issues of all kinds increased a little, but only a little, between December 1835 and June 1836; and Scotland was steady. But some of the joint-stock banks—though not they alone—did bad business, discounted doubtful paper, and made advances on all sorts of questionable security. To increase their available resources, they re-discounted their holdings of bills freely in London—not in itself a banking vice, but danger-ous when the bills, or the uses to which the funds gained by their re-discount are put, have any taint[4]. Suddenly, in August, the Bank of England accompanied the belated raising of its discount rate by a positive refusal to discount any bill which already bore the signature of a joint-stock bank of issue. It was natural that, in joint-stock circles, this discrimination should be resented and treated as the act of a jealous rival, "to whom the extension and competition of the joint-stock bank system was most obnoxious."[5]

With the autumn failures began. An Irish joint-stock bank, the Agricultural and Commercial, went down in November. The other Irish banks, headed by the Bank of Ireland, antici-pating the failure and fearing a run, had already arranged for a heavy shipment of gold from London. In November, too, the Northern and Central Bank, of Manchester, which had

---

[1] See the criticism in Tooke, op. cit. II. 285 sqq., and his tables, Ibid. II. 386

[2] Tooke (II. 316) admits that he thought they were doing this in 1836, but found later that he was wrong. Powell, E. T., The Evolution of the Money Market (1915), repeats Tooke's original mistake.

[3] Powell, by quoting the issues of the joint-stock banks only, gives the im-pression that "the country banks" were increasing their issues in these months. The figures are in S. C. of 1841, Ap. 23 a.

[4] For a sober mid-nineteenth-century view on re-discount, see Rae, G., The Country Banker (ed. 1903), p. 223.

[5] Tooke, op. cit. II. 304. For the Bank's action see Macleod, Theory and Practice of Banking, II. 140.

thirty-nine branches in that area of American influence, was in difficulties. Threadneedle Street—so it is said[1]—was at first for letting it break but, fearing repercussion on its own depleted reserves, decided, on December 1, to go to its aid. In January 1837, the Bank was giving help in the London banking world, and in February it became involved in the affairs of the "three W's"—Wiggin, Wilde and Wilson—Liverpool houses which did merchant-banking business for the American trade and were reputed to have, between them, £5,500,000 of accepted bills outstanding[2]. After holding them up for a time, the Bank, on June 1, refused further assistance. Thereupon the three W's suspended payment. A few other firms followed. There was no general collapse, but the jerk was quite sufficient to pull up the car of trade and impose caution[3].

The special American gold drain was over; gold was coming back to London from Ireland; the normal position of Britain, the great exporter, as a country with favourable exchanges was reasserting itself, and the Bank's bullion reserve was rising. It rose steadily from May 1837 to January 1838, when it stood just below £9,000,000, or nearly the ideal third of the assets and almost exactly half the January note circulation. From March to May it was over £10,000,000. "The Bank," Thomas Tooke wrote that year, "having scrambled through its difficulties into a position of safety, may naturally claim merit from the event."[4]

Fortunately the spell of good harvests of the mid-'thirties had made corn-importing during these difficulties unnecessary. But the harvest of 1838 was reputed the worst since 1816 and that of 1839 was not much better. At the turn of the year 1838–9 wheat touched 80s., and it seldom got below 70s. during the next twelve months. The accumulated effects of these harvest failures, which involved an abnormal import of something like £10,000,000 worth of food grains, were felt mainly in 1839. During 1839 the financial world was reasonably cheerful. The Bank was much occupied with the liquidation of the securities which it had accepted from the tottering bankers

---

[1] By Macleod, *op. cit.* II. 151. The accounts in Macleod, Andreades' *History of the Bank of England* and Levi's *History of British Commerce* all derive, generally without acknowledgment, from Tooke, than whom there is no better authority; but this statement is not in Tooke.

[2] *Annual Register*, 1837, p. 183. Above, p. 261. [Jenks, *op. cit.* p. 86 *sqq.*]

[3] Tooke, *op. cit.* II. 306–8.

[4] II. 308.

and merchant-bankers in 1837. There were large sums owing from America, and the Bank began to concern itself with the internal affairs of the United States. Pressed by the commercial world, "through the medium of the newspapers and banking circulars,"[1] to do something for trade with its fine stores of bullion, it had reduced its rate from 5 to 4 per cent. in February 1838, and, with the object of reviving Anglo-American trade, had shipped something under £1,000,000 of the bullion to aid those American banks which had suspended cash payments. In the late autumn it was offering short loans at $3\frac{1}{2}$ per cent., when the market-rate had already got higher in anticipation of a difficult year in 1839[2]. The directors, as Tooke wrote bitterly, "had before, upon principle, disclaimed to act upon anticipation"[3]—the public was to "act upon the Bank,"[4] and the Bank still had over £9,000,000 of bullion in reserve on January 1, 1839. The public acted so quickly that in May the bullion was down to £5,000,000. The Bank then (May 16) shut the stable door with a bolt of 5 per cent., and sold £760,000 worth of government securities to improve its reserve.

Meanwhile, the American banks were helping the cotton-planters to hold up cotton prices against England. What cotton came over was paid for, at the high rates, by advances from the British consignees. The Lancashire spinners went on short time to force the dealers to put prices down, and the export of cotton manufactures, the mainstay of the export trade, became stagnant at a time when—owing to the food position—it was most desirable that it should increase[5]. At the same time American securities were flowing hard into Britain—especially State bonds and banking securities, including those of the United States Bank, which though it had lost its federal charter was continuing an adventurous career under a charter from the state of Pennsylvania. The continent also came into play. There, just as in Britain and in America, there had been a joint-stock and banking boom since 1836[6]. Prices had been driven up and treasure driven out. Some of it was in London. Late in 1838 the Bank of Belgium stopped payment and there

---

[1] Tooke, *op. cit.* III. (1840), 79.
[2] The market rate had been down to 3.
[3] III. 83. This section is based on Tooke, *op. cit.* III. 73–83.
[4] Above, p. 508.
[5] For the small takings of cotton in 1839 see a table in Porter, *op. cit.* p. 178.
[6] Juglar, C., *Des crises commerciales* (1889), p. 347.

was a run on Lafitte's bank in Paris. The treasure began to move back as continental prices shrank. Further, Russia was believed to be collecting treasure—silver, not gold; but then the Bank of England included silver in its bullion figures—with a view to the re-establishment of a silver, instead of a paper, rouble, finally ordered by ukase of July 1839[1]. So the drain on London spread and grew, and the second light harvest brought the inconvertibility of the Bank of England note almost within sight. Abroad, dealers in exchange had been anticipating inconvertibility since June.

When the Bank raised its rate and sold securities, in May, it also arranged for short bills to be drawn on Paris to the amount of £600,000. But as their maturity approached it was not ready for them. On June 20, to safeguard its resources, it put its rate up to $5\frac{1}{2}$, for the first time in history, advances at this rate to be made "on bills of exchange only."[2] This suggested that a client would not be able to get an advance even on an Exchequer bill; but it was not enough, and in July the directors —through Barings—"resorted to the discreditable expedient of applying for assistance to a set of Paris bankers who, after much hesitation, and much humiliating inquiry, consented to grant it."[3] The credit was for £2,000,000 and the Bank of France stood behind the Paris bankers. Another £900,000 credit was arranged in Hamburg[4]. On August 1 bank rate was raised to 6 per cent. After these "circumstances of almost national humiliation," as Tooke called them[5], things mended. The Bank's metallic reserve was at its lowest, £2,400,000, early in September. The food position kept it low all the autumn; it was not above £3,000,000 till January 1840; and it never got really high again until the good harvest of 1842 made the trade balance of the country definitely favourable. For nearly two and a half years the Bank rarely had more than one-fifth of its assets in bullion, and often not one-sixth[6]. But in those dark years of hunger, Chartism and unemployment, risky commercial experiments were unlikely, and there was no serious drain from without.

All the time discussion of banking reform went on. A strong

---

[1] Tooke, *op. cit.* III. 76—as a Russia merchant Tooke was well-informed.
[2] *Ibid.* p. 87.   [3] *Ibid.* p. 88–9.   [4] Macleod, *op. cit.* II. 145.
[5] *Ibid.* III. 90. [To the modern mind there is no humiliation in this skilful and successful international operation.]
[6] Tables in Tooke, *op. cit.* IV. (1848), 436–9.

committee sat in 1840 and 1841[1]. It included Peel, Joseph Hume, Grote, Abel Smith, Mathias Attwood—Thomas Attwood's brother—and Morrison the critic of the railways. It heard everyone worth hearing. Samuel Jones Loyd pointed out that the Bank's policy of keeping a fixed share of the assets in bullion, even if carried out, established no link between bullion and notes: "through the demands of the depositors" the bullion "may be wholly drained out without any contraction of the circulation."[2] (In fact, in March 1838, there had been a circulation of £18,600,000 backed by £10,000,000 of bullion; in October of 1839 there was a circulation of £17,600,000 and £2,500,000 of bullion.) Loyd was for tying the stocks of notes and bullion tight together, and had been expounding schemes to that end in various pamphlets[3]. Norman, of the Bank directorate, advocated a single bank of issue and "a... mechanism to displace the circulation of the country bankers."[4] Peel must have listened attentively to these two witnesses: he had always trusted gold and disliked unregulated paper money. H. W. Hobhouse of Bath defended the threatened private country bankers against the charge of careless handling of their notes, and argued that, if these notes were to go, the currency void "must be filled up by bills of exchange or checks or something else."[5] Vincent Stuckey spoke for the country joint-stock banks and explained how, so far from pouring out notes, they now encouraged even farmers to use cheques in order "to save the circulation": "that is a mode which has been introduced lately very much."[6] William Rodwell of Cobbolds, Ipswich, said the country bankers were all right even in times of pressure. "We have always had plenty of gold in the country; in 1839 particularly"[7]—true no doubt, but gold tucked away in the country helped no one. James Gilbart, as might have been expected, did not content himself with a defence of his own type of bank, which indeed was not much attacked, since the committee was obsessed with the problem

---

[1] *S. C. on Banks of Issue*, 1840 (IV); 1841 (V). There was also a *Committee on Joint-Stock Banks in* 1836; 1837 (XIV).

[2] 1840, Q. 2907.

[3] Including *Reflections suggested by a perusal of Mr J. Horsley Palmer' pamphlet on the causes and consequences of the pressure on the Money Market* (1837), *Remarks on the Management of the Circulation, etc.* (1840).

[4] So described in 1841, Q. 783. His evidence is in 1840, Q. 2002 *sqq.*

[5] 1841, Q. 173.   [6] 1841, Q. 456–7.

[7] 1841, Q. 781.

of note issue and the London and Westminster had no notes. From the high ground of his most extensive banking experience[1] he bombarded his enemy the Bank of England. He showed statistically how the country notes had their regular tide, lowest in August and highest in April, and how difficult it was to force their circulation up unduly[2]—for, as Hobhouse had explained, people came to the country banker with a bill or cheque and the banker said, "will you have it in coin, Bank of England notes, or country notes?": "that is the way our notes get into circulation."[3] But the Bank of England, Gilbart argued, could easily increase its circulation by buying gold and securities of all sorts with its own notes, a thing no country banker could do. And its notes did not return to it quickly as all other banks' notes did; for as it never allowed "interest for lodgements"[4] [deposits] no one was tempted to lodge. Although Gilbart was not in favour of Loyd's notion, the "currency principle" as it was beginning to be called[5], of making the note circulation fluctuate in exact correspondence with the amount of gold in the Bank of England—he criticised it while the Committee was sitting, in the *Westminster Review* for January 1841—nor yet of Norman's scheme for centralised issue, his evidence suggested the need for severe control of the Bank's issue policy. If the Bank were to be severely controlled, how hardly could the country banks of issue escape?

These, it is to be assumed, were the conclusions which Peel was drawing as he listened. The committee of which he was the leading member drew no real conclusions at all. It was "not in a position to make a final report," and its sole recommendation was that there should be issued "an account showing with greater accuracy, and at shorter intervals, the average amount of...notes which are in circulation in England and Wales, together with the average amount of bullion in the Bank of England"[6] and the Scottish and Irish circulations. Attention

---

[1] Clerk in a London firm who were agents for twelve country banks: manager of an Irish joint-stock bank of issue: general manager of the London and Westminster.

[2] *S.C. on Banks of Issue*, 1841, Q. 912.

[3] 1841, Q. 31. But of course, as Stuckey admitted (Q. 465), country bank loans tended to increase country bank circulation: only there was not much evidence that they had done so dangerously of late years. Above, p. 515.

[4] 1841, Q. 1361.

[5] Tooke (IV. 166) thought the term was first used in Norman's evidence of 1840, Q. 2018. See Gilbart's discussion of "currency principles" and "banking principles" in 1841, Q. 932–3.   [6] 1841, p. 3.

was not called to the way in which the currency void might be filled if country issues were curtailed or abolished; and, in spite of the evidence of Hobhouse and Stuckey, the word "check" did not occur in the index issued with the minutes of evidence and the two lean reports.

Within three years of the issue of the second of them, there having been no further public inquiry into banking questions, Peel—who had meanwhile balanced the budget and seen the country enter on a spell of active trade—decided to utilise that clause in the Act of 1833 which empowered Government to revise the Bank Charter in 1845, in order to put banking as it affected currency into order once for all. In May of 1844 he was expounding his monetary views[1], and parliament adopted them with perfect docility, the Commons by 185 to 30 and the Lords without a division. The Act (7 & 8 Vict. c. 32) was, as a great banker once said, less a Bank Act than a Bank Note Act[2]. It was made so by Peel quite deliberately. He was thinking of the convertibility of the bank note and of that alone. Whether he was thinking of it with perfect comprehension and clarity is doubtful. He had no more intention of regulating the business of banking, except where that business touched "the issue of money...a prerogative of Sovereignty," than of regulating the business of brewing. He had told his cabinet that, if he were "about to establish in a new state of society a new system of currency," he would find it hard to reject the conclusion—Ricardo's conclusion—that issue and its profits, like minting, should be a government monopoly: "a board would be constituted, independent of Government but responsible to Parliament, charged with the issue of paper, convertible into gold, to be a legal tender." Having rejected this line of action for reasons of practical convenience, the chief of which seems to have been "the risk of applying at once to three parts of a great Empire, in each of which there is a different system of currency, any unbending uniform rule"[3]—he had not forgotten the Scots £1 notes and Malachi Malagrowther—he decided to begin with England; to prohibit no bank from issuing which

---

[1] May 6 and May 20. Hansard, LXXIV. 720 *sqq*, 1330 *sqq*. From the economist's standpoint the speeches are not very good (see Tooke, *op. cit.* IV. 143, Macleod, *op. cit.* II. 151), but Peel was speaking to the Commons not to the economists. The praise lavished on them by Peel's political biographer, Parker, C. S., *Peel*, III. 139, is, however, misplaced.

[2] Lord Avebury, quoted in Buxton, *Finance and Politics*, II. 15.

[3] From his cabinet memorandum in Parker, *op. cit.* III. 134 *sqq*.

already issued; to stop forthwith, for all time and in all parts of the United Kingdom, the creation of new banks of issue; to limit the issues of all old ones in England to their existing dimensions; to provide facilities for their gradual transfer to the Bank of England, and to tie the Bank of England note firmly to gold. It was a characteristic balancing of vested interests and sovereign rights.

Hence the familiar clauses of the Bank Charter Act. Country banks, private or joint-stock, might never have more notes in circulation than their average for the twelve weeks preceding April 27, 1844. Their notes were not to be legal tender. If a bank broke, it forfeited its rights of issue. If two or more banks combined, they might combine their issues, but if the combined bank had more than six partners it might not issue at all—a clause meant to speed up the reduction of country issues at a time when combinations, and particularly combinations with a joint-stock, were frequent. Any bank ceasing to issue, for whatever reason, could never again put its own notes into circulation.

The obvious and avowed aim of these clauses was the gradual concentration of issue into Threadneedle Street. The process was to be slower than Peel probably anticipated: the country issues of England and Wales, which varied from about £8,000,000 to about £11,000,000 in the early 'forties, and were fixed at a maximum of £8,631,647 in 1844, were still between £1,000,000 and £2,000,000 fifty years, and were not quite extinct seventy years, later[1].

The Bank of England was cut—at law—into the distinct departments of issue and banking[2]. The issue department might create £14,000,000 of notes against securities (including the outstanding government debt to the Bank of some £11,000,000) and as many more as it liked against gold coin and gold or silver bullion[3], the silver bullion never to exceed one-fourth of the combined gold bullion and coin. By order in

---

[1] June 20, 1914, £84,831. The last bank with issuing rights—Fox, Fowler and Co.—was absorbed by Lloyds Bank in 1921.

[2] As advocated by Jones Loyd since 1837. Hence Disraeli on Peel. "There was always some person representing some theory...exercising an influence over his mind...Mr Horner or Sir Samuel Romilly...the Duke of Wellington, the King of the French, Mr Jones Loyd—some others—and finally Mr Cobden." *Lord George Bentinck*, p. 199–200.

[3] Silver because it was useful in case of a drain from bimetallic or silver-standard countries. Peel, May 20, Hansard, LXXIV. 1335.

Council, the issue against securities might be increased to any amount not exceeding two-thirds of the issues abandoned from time to time by other banks. Any member of the public might demand notes from the Bank in exchange for standard gold bullion at £3. 17s. 9d. an ounce. The Bank was to publish its accounts weekly in a prescribed form; it was exempted from the payment of stamp duty on its notes; its fixed payment to the Treasury in return for its privileges was increased and any profits on issue against securities, beyond the first £14,000,000, were to go to the public.

While the bill was before the house, the London bankers as a body, and at least one of their number—Mr Bosanquet—as an individual, begged Peel to make it more elastic for times of emergency[1]. Bosanquet pointed out how in crises bills of exchange and cheques—the "credit-currency"—cease to function, wholly or in part, and how, therefore, "a larger circulation than usual will be required at such periods, while in all probability an efflux of bullion is producing a diminution of the quantity," so that the Bank may not have the power to increase its issues while no other bank will have the right. No doubt, in the long run, he said, larger cash reserves would be kept by bankers to meet such emergencies, but he feared "very great difficulties...during the period of transition from the present lax to the future stringent system of currency." He suggested a five-years' permit to the Bank to make abnormal advances, at not less than 8 per cent., on the deposit of Exchequer Bills[2]. The high rate would render it certain that the permission would only be acted upon in the most critical times. Bosanquet's letter was acknowledged with thanks. To the bankers' memorandum in somewhat the same sense Peel stiffly replied that "her Majesty's servants do not consider it to be consistent with their duty to apply to Parliament for a discretionary authority to be vested in any public department...to sanction an increase of issues by the Bank upon securities, excepting under the circumstances provided for in the Bill."[3]

"If the same consequences are hereafter to follow," he wrote to the Governor of the Bank on June 4[4], "which did follow

---

[1] Bosanquet to Peel; Parker, *Peel*, III. 140-2.
[2] "Also that discretion should be given to the Bank either to issue their ordinary notes on such occasions, or notes receivable in payment for taxes, but not convertible into specie" (p. 141).
[3] III. 142.　　　　　　　　　　　[4] III. 139-40.

when both species of issue [Bank and country] were practically uncontrolled, the whole measure is a delusive one." He held that there was a difference in kind between "a promissory note payable to bearer on demand [*i.e.* a bank note] and other forms of paper credit, and between the effects which they respectively produce upon the prices of commodities and upon the exchanges."[1] Both in his memorandum for the cabinet and in his speeches he exaggerated the importance and the dangers of the English country issues; and he seems to have believed that the Bank, regulated as he proposed and relieved from the reputedly important price-inflating flood of the country notes, would be able and anxious to regulate the total supply of money as he defined it, *i.e.* notes and coin, in exact relation to the state of the exchanges. Jones Loyd had pilloried the old régime because under it the Bank's bullion might be "drained out without any contraction of the circulation"[2]; and Peel thought that provision—though not infallible provision—had been made against the recurrence of such a situation by the new Act. He supposed that, as bullion left the Bank, the money in circulation would decrease, pull prices down, and check the drain of gold: or if he did not suppose this his references to the exchanges had no meaning. Yet, as was shown within three years, the Bank, by holding a large reserve of its own notes which like buried treasure would not affect prices, and using them in times of difficulty, could pour out bullion while keeping up the effective circulation. Francis Baring declared in December 1847, that, during the discussions of 1844, "it never entered into the contemplation of anyone then considering the subject...that £7,000,000 in gold should run off, and yet that the notes in the hands of the public should rather increase than diminish," as happened between September 1846 and April 1847. "The question of the reserve was not sufficiently considered either by those who were favourable or those who were opposed to the bill," Baring said[3]. Peel spoke

---

[1] He did not say a difference in kind, but "a material difference" (speech of May 6); still his argument goes against the view that "had it [the legislature] recognised that the check currency...was likely to drive the bank note out of circulation for the ordinary purposes of commerce...it may be supposed that it would have dealt with its creation in an equally drastic manner." Withers, H., *The English Banking System, U.S. National Monetary Commission* (1910), p. 70.

[2] Above p. 519.

[3] Hansard, xcv. 615–16 (December 3, 1847). This criticism is substantially that of Macleod, *op. cit.* II. 160 *sqq.*, who quotes these passages from Baring's

later in the debate but left the reserve and Baring's statements undiscussed.

He had supposed in 1844 that he was "taking all the precautions which legislation can prudently take against the recurrence of a monetary crisis." But he had faced the possibility of recurrence.

"It may occur in spite of our precautions, and if it does, and *if it be necessary* to assume a grave responsibility for the purpose of meeting it, I daresay men will be found willing to assume such a responsibility. I would rather," he added, "trust to this than impair the efficiency and probable success of those measures by which one hopes to control evil tendencies in their beginning, and to diminish the risk that extraordinary measures may be necessary."[1]

This was his way of saying that he preferred a bracing law, which might have to be suspended, to a law which by providing ways out of difficulties would encourage bankers to slide into them.

A few years later, the highest officials of the Bank when asked "do you consider that the Act...relieved you entirely from any responsibility as regarded the circulation?" replied "Entirely."[2] The responsibility, they held, lay with the law and in view of the things that had been said about the law they can hardly be blamed. Further, they took the view, again with Peel's expressed approval, that as bankers they were to compete openly for business. The reluctance to concern themselves very actively with discounting, which had marked their policy since 1825, ceased. They set about "canvassing for discounts and fomenting transactions under the new principle that in the Banking Department they are to act on the same principle as private bankers," Samuel Gurney said[3]. As a bill-broker he was a prejudiced, but was never an inaccurate, witness.

In 1845 Peel legislated further for Scotland and Ireland. The clause of the Act of 1844 which stopped the creation of banks of issue had already frozen the Scottish banking world—the nineteen banks which were issuing in May 1844 getting a

speech. Baring was wrong in saying that opponents of the bill had not sufficiently considered the question of the banking reserve—Tooke, for one, had. Tooke, *op. cit.* IV. 309.

[1] To the Governors of the Bank, June 4, 1844. Parker's *Peel*, III. 140.

[2] *Secret Comm. on Commercial Distress*, 1847–8 (VIII), Q. 2652. Evidence of the Governor and Deputy-Governor of the Bank.

[3] *Lords' Comm. on Commercial Distress*, Q. 1098. For the earlier policy, above, p. 281.

monopoly of a country in which, since all first-rate banks issued, new non-issuing competitors would have a hard life[1]. There was not much left to do by 8 & 9 Vict. c. 38. Peel would not touch the £1 note. He allowed the issuing banks the £3,087,209 note circulation ascertained, as for England and Wales, in 1844, plus an extra issue up to the amount of the gold and silver held in their head offices; and he allowed amalgamating banks to retain their full rights of issue, whatever the number of their partners. So amalgamation could go on, though the creation of new banks could, or rather did, not. The note issue grew as the banks, in course of time, built up metallic reserves[2]; and Scotland continued to make a much greater use of bank-notes than England.

The Irish Act (8 & 9 Vict. c. 37) abolished a monopoly radius against joint-stock banks, hitherto enjoyed by the Bank of Ireland about Dublin, retained the £1 note, and regulated the general note currency as in Scotland. Neither in Ireland nor in Scotland were Bank of England notes to be legal tender. Against English provinces the Bank gained privilege; against the associated countries it gained nothing. Its weaker counterpart, the Bank of Ireland, lost privilege. In Scotland, a system of legal equality among banks was strengthened. Amalgamation of banks which valued their issues was discouraged in England but not in Scotland. Certainly Peel was not applying to "three parts of a great Empire...any unbending uniform rule."

The Scottish and Irish bills received the Royal assent on July 21. Within two months the first reports of potato failure in Ireland came over. In Britain the railway pack was in full cry. Prices of structural, and many other, goods were rising fast[3]. But there was as yet no awkward strain on the machinery of credit and currency. The market rate of discount, which had been for so long abnormally low in 1843–4, only got above 3 per cent. in 1845. Railways were fixing capital, wasting capital, and making much capital not wasted temporarily unproductive to its owners, and all this was very visible; but when completed, by increasing the pace of business, they were invisibly economising the circulating capital locked up in stocks of material,

[1] Kerr, *op. cit.* p. 237–42.

[2] But the increase came after 1848: the highest Scottish issue before was £3,900,000 in December 1846. In March 1841, the whole English issue was £26,300,000, the Scottish £2,900,000: in March 1901, the English was £29,600,000, the Scottish £7,400,000.

[3] *E.g.* bar iron, lead, tin, copper, timber. Tooke, *op. cit.* IV. 427 *sqq.*

fuel, and finished goods. Joseph Pease said subsequently that "there was no appearance of any want of floating capital"[1] in 1845–6. Wheat prices were reasonably low, though not so low as they had been between the harvests of 1843 and 1844, and the English cost of living index was still lower than it had been at any time between 1800 and the harvest of 1843[2]. Up to September 1845, at any rate, there was no reason to apprehend a foreign drain of gold to buy food, like that of 1838–9. At the end of June 1845, there were nearly £14,000,000 of gold and over £2,000,000 of silver in the Issue Department, and nearly £600,000 of coin in the Banking Department, of the Bank of England. Twelve months later, the first year of food trouble in Ireland had caused so little disturbance that the total of bullion and coin was not £1,000,000 lower[3].

There had, however, been a moment of financial anxiety during the winter of 1845–6. Parliament had decided that a 5 per cent. deposit on every railway scheme should be paid in bank notes, to the credit of the Accountant-General in Chancery[4]. The stock of notes outside the Bank's own reserve was about £20,000,000. Late in November, a calculation appeared in *The Times* intended to prove that £59,000,000 of notes would have to be deposited early in February, and that it could not be done. The figure gives some indication of the mass of capital nominally involved in the railway projects of 1845. Apparently its publication helped to kill off some of the feebler among them. In the end only between £11,000,000 and £12,000,000 was deposited. With a little ingenuity in arranging the hours and minutes of note payments in and out, the Bank could probably have handled a larger sum without stripping the country of currency, and in any case a full supply of Bank of England notes was not so essential to business as the public—its head full of currency debate—usually supposed; but the temporary locking up of so much capital in Chancery created an acute, if short, monetary stringency, the market rate of discount running up to 5 per cent. for the first time since 1841[5]. It had already fallen when, in April, Peel and Dalhousie pushed through parliament a bill to facilitate

---

[1] *S. C. of* 1847–8, Q. 4583.　　　　　[2] Above, p. 128.
[3] *Economist*, June 28, 1845, and June 27, 1846.
[4] Above, p. 421.
[5] For this episode see Evans, D. M., *The Commercial Crisis*, 1847–1848 (1848), p. 18–29. Evans was city correspondent of *The Times*.

the winding up of derelict railway schemes which had never secured parliamentary sanction—Lord Dalhousie's dissolution Act, as it was popularly called[1] (9 & 10 Vict. c. 28). The bill, which fell in the middle of the corn law debates, gave Disraeli an opening for a spoken essay on Peel in the style of his later saying—"wanting imagination, he wanted prescience."[2] Why let all this rubbish accumulate and then ask for special powers to remove it?

Although the Irish situation, in April 1846, was far easier than Peel had anticipated when he decided to touch the corn law, and although the price of wheat in England went on falling until the eve of harvest, it was apparent, from early spring, that trade was on a downward slope. Responsible business opinion—which however is not quite decisive, in the necessary absence of statistical evidence—argued that railway building had now gone so far that the appropriate balance between fixed and circulating capital was already seriously deranged. "An additional demand of about £40,000,000 per annum, which the new projects would require," one trade circular wrote, "must be fraught with the most ruinous consequences, for it is utterly impossible that...a diversion of such immense sums from the industrial pursuits of the country, should not deprive them of their very life-blood."[3] The February stringency had supported the argument. Prices certainly were falling and stocks accumulating. Apprehension, whether fully rational or partly irrational is immaterial, hobbled enterprise. All Eastern produce was down—tea, indigo, silk, cotton[4] Even iron was down. British bars had been at their highest in the second quarter of 1845. The drop was not great—about 10 per cent. below the maximum in the second quarter of 1846[5] —but any drop in the material for the iron roads themselves was remarkable.

At the end of that quarter Peel's corn bill passed the Lords. The Irish potatoes failed again, far worse than in 1845, and the British with them. Much of the wheat was good; but the British harvest worked out short, and the continental harvest shorter still. As the potato gap had to be filled, the effect was

---

[1] Evans, op. cit. p. 43.   [2] Lord George Bentinck, p. 198. Hansard, LXXXV. 951.

[3] Messrs Collman and Stolterfoht of Liverpool, quoted in Evans, op. cit. p. 37: but see Joseph Pease's opinion, p. 527, above.

[4] Tooke (IV. 68) argued that fears of dear corn prices "checked, for a time, the demand for articles of secondary necessity."

[5] It had been lower in the interval. Tooke, op. cit. IV. 428-9.

cumulative. In June the gazette price of wheat was steady about 52s. It fell to 45s. 1d. in August, after the new corn Act had opened the bonded warehouses on to the home market. This deferred the rise, so that the price never got appreciably above 60s. in 1846. But for the three months ending May 29, 1847, it averaged 80s. 6d. On May 29 it touched 102s. 5d. "A sale was made in the Uxbridge market at 124s."[1]; and for the six weeks ending June 26 the average was 94s. 10d. Then a better harvest, better potato prospects, and heavy imports of corn —for which the world had been ransacked—brought the price down plumb. On September 18 wheat was at 49s. 6d. The average for the six weeks before Christmas was 52s. 10d.[2] For the whole of 1848 the average was under 50s.

Such precipitous fluctuations were bound to do damage in the corn market. The gambling spirit of the railway mania had left the general trade of the country full of weak spots; and events developed so dangerously that older and more secret weaknesses were in time laid bare. A spectacular commercial collapse in the autumn of 1846, apparently quite unconnected with the general movement that was making for disaster, revealed one such weakness in advance and served as a sort of curtain-raiser for 1847. In October, Jeremiah Harman and Co., Russia merchants and agents for the Czar, failed for over half a million with assets of £100,000. The firm, it appeared, "had been utterly insolvent for nearly a quarter of a century."[3] This, coming at a time when the food outlook was darkening and gold was leaving the bank, made the City anxious; but the gold drain ceased in November; corn was not very short for the moment, as its price showed, and there was a temptation not to look too far ahead, a temptation to which the Bank of England—leaving circulation to the law—apparently yielded.

Yet, by January 1847, there was "an ascertained deficiency of the supply of cotton."[4] The food position evidently demanded caution. So did the railway position. Calls on railway shares were steadily fixing more and more of the country's free capital; and as many of these calls were from the foreign railways into which so much money had been put, they might easily occasion

---

[1] Tooke, op. cit. IV. 32.

[2] Economist, December 25, 1847.

[3] Evans, op. cit. p. 49, and the statement of affairs of December 1825, there quoted.

[4] Tooke, op. cit. IV. 72.

or accentuate a gold drain abroad, since for the moment they made Britain a debtor. In January 1847, the aggregate calls came to £6,150,000 of which £1,650,000 were foreign[1]. (This at a time when £5,000,000 was about the monthly value of the exports of the United Kingdom.) All that the Bank of England did was to put its discount rate[2] up to 3½ per cent., then 4 per cent. in the second half of the month; although gold had been flowing out since Christmas, and very fast in the first fortnight of January, when the rate was still at 3 per cent. The rate was kept at 4 per cent. until April, while treasure at the Bank fell from £13,900,000 on January 16 to £9,800,000 on April 10, the circulation both of Bank of England and of country notes being nearly the same late in March as it had been early in January[3].

Much of the gold had gone to France, where the Bank was in trouble by the end of 1846. As in England, railway finance and harvest failure were the causes. Between July 1 and January 1 reserves had fallen from 252,000,000 to 80,000,000 francs. Among its measures of self-defence were a raising of its discount rate to 5 per cent., for the first time in twenty-seven years, and the securing of a credit for £1,000,000 through the Barings —in effect from the Bank of England[4].

Disregarding this 5 per cent. danger signal, the Bank of England ran on at 4 per cent. through February and March, until for the week ending April 3 its treasure was down to £10,200,000 and its reserve of notes and coin in the Banking Department, which had been nearly £9,000,000 on January 2, stood at £4,400,000. Then, on April 8, it raised its rate to 5 per cent. and, as Jones Loyd put it later, paused and "declared it could do no more for the public, but must now take care of itself,"[5] by limiting severely the amount of accommodation which it would give even at 5 per cent. Its care for itself became closer in the following weeks, as both of its reserves continued to fail, the banking reserve being at its minimum on April 17 and the bullion reserve on April 24[6]. "In the third week of

---

[1] Evans, *op. cit.* p. 54.   [2] That is, its minimum rate on three months' bills.
[3] The Governor of the Bank subsequently admitted the error of delaying to raise the rate. *S. C. on Commercial Distress*, Q. 601, 605. See also Tooke, *op. cit.* IV. 445 *sqq.*
[4] Juglar, *op. cit.* p. 417. Tooke, *op. cit.* IV. 72–3. There were also gold withdrawals for the U.S.A.   [5] *S. C. on Commercial Distress*, Q. 5123.
[6] Banking reserve, April 17. £3,080,000; bullion reserve, April 24, £9,200,000.

April it was understood that only bills of the first class, due in May and June, were discountable at so low a rate as $5\frac{1}{2}$ per cent."[1] Meanwhile, and very naturally, the market rate for first class short bills was at 7 per cent. Longer bills, even of good quality, were paying up to 12 and 13 per cent.

But the desired effect was produced, though the brake came on with an unpleasant jar. Gold earmarked for America, "and even some that had actually been placed on board,"[2] was employed at these attractive rates in England. The drain ceased: during May the Bank lent and discounted freely at 5 per cent.: the bullion reserve crept up again to a maximum of £10,500,000 late in June; and the crisis passed without important bankruptcies.

But as rates for money dropped, in June and July, the American drain of bullion was renewed, for cotton was dear in 1847. Once more the Bank had to take special precautions. In spite of them it entered September—while wheat prices were tumbling down and maize prices had broken utterly— with less than £9,000,000 of treasure in both departments, and a reserve of notes in the Banking Department of under £4,200,000. Ever since August 6 there had been failures of corn firms, with commitments undertaken before the prices broke, "exceeding...anything which had ever before been experienced in Mark Lane."[3] Among them was the firm of W. R. Robinson, the Governor of the Bank of England[4]. By September 1 eight London corn firms, with total liabilities of over £1,500,000, five provincial corn firms—three of them in Liverpool—and five other mercantile firms of importance, most of which had had a finger in corn, were down. It is fair to them to state that the ransacking of the world for corn had been an act of national duty in 1847. The world had been too thoroughly searched. In September, East and West India houses began to go, and on the 20th Sanderson and Co., billbrokers, stopped payment. Among the East India houses was Reid, Irving and Co., whose senior director had been Governor of the Bank during the trouble of 1839[5]. Creditors' meetings

---

[1] Tooke, *op. cit.* IV. 73.
[2] Tooke, *op. cit.* IV. 74.
[3] Tooke, *op. cit.* IV. 316. See also Evans, *op. cit.* p. 67.
[4] But it paid 20s. in the £ subsequently. Evans, *op. cit.* p. 68.
[5] The affairs of many of these firms are summarised in Evans, Appendix, xliii.

and subsequent inquiry revealed, in a number of cases, internal conditions which showed that the storms of 1847 and the Act of 1844 were the occasion rather than the cause of fall. "They fail," Peel said in the House in December, "and then like this gentleman whose liabilities are to the extent of £50,000, and his assets £3000, they exclaim, 'This infernal Act of 1844, this detestable restrictive act of Peel's, is the cause of all our difficulties.'"[1]

In October came the turn of the banks, of Scotland, and of the North, while City failures—including those of bill-brokers, stock-brokers and colonial brokers—continued. The provincial and Scottish failures were almost entirely commercial, though the list included Liverpool soap-boilers, Manchester cotton spinners, Halifax worsted spinners and Glasgow calico-printers[2]. Seven private banking firms, ranging from Honiton to Manchester, went down, and four joint-stock banks. The banking collapse was especially marked at Newcastle, where the Newcastle Joint Stock Bank failed, and at Liverpool where the Royal Bank, "a concern...standing in the first rank among the banking institutions of the Kingdom"[3] stopped on Monday, October 18, although the Bank of England had advanced to it £300,000 on the security of bills of exchange. It had a paid-up capital of £800,000 and it had advanced £500,000 to a single commercial firm.

The Bank had terrified the commercial world by announcing, on October 1, that for the present it would make no advances upon public securities; but, while refusing many demands, it was giving all the support it could at the most threatened points, as the case of the Royal Bank of Liverpool shows. It even made heavy advances, quite against its custom, on the security of real property and on approved personal security[4]. But railway calls went on and, when there was delay in payment, companies borrowed "almost regardless of the rate of interest,"[5] in order to carry on their works. Runs on provincial banks had begun, and the public was hoarding notes and coin[6]. "Then came a fearful aggravation of the supposed danger": some Scottish banks asked for assistance—sound,

---

[1] Dec. 3, 1847. The firm in question was Bensusan and Co.
[2] Lists in Evans, *op. cit.* p. 91–2.   [3] Tooke, *op. cit.* IV. 317.
[4] Evans, *op. cit.* p. 75–6, 79.   [5] *Ibid.* p. 76.
[6] *S. C. on Commercial Distress*, Q. 2675 *sqq.*, evidence of the Governor and Deputy-Governor of the Bank of England.

model, Scottish banks with their relatively "enormous deposits." Runs on them would soon empty all reserves, and their securities "though solid, were not easily realised."[1] Money, in Peel's sense, was nearly exhausted: a little more hoarding, and there might be none.

The Bank return for October 23 showed only £1,547,000 of notes and £447,000 of coin left in the banking reserve. It is true that dividends had just been paid and that therefore some money might be expected back in a few days[2]. But Lord John Russell and Sir Charles Wood were advised that the time had come "to assume a grave responsibility," so wrote the classic letter of October 25 encouraging the Bank to "enlarge the amount of its discounts and advances," but only at a minimum rate of 8 per cent. They promised a bill of indemnity if this "should lead to any infringement of the existing law," that is, to an issue of notes against securities, for use by the Banking Department, beyond the £14,000,000 of Peel's Act.

The Bank Directors accepted the advice but passed a resolution at the same time stating that they were confident of their ability to carry on without infringing the law. In fact they never did infringe it. James Wilson of the *Economist* thought the letter did harm; that confidence was returning without it; and that it actually delayed the return. He also thought that the alarm and panic were unfounded, and that the Act of 1844 "must now be considered as a matter of history."[3] Although panic is not the less dangerous because Pan is a phantom, it is just possible that Wilson and the Directors were right, right at least in believing that the letter was not absolutely necessary to salvation—it is very hard to believe, against all kinds of evidence, that, in the then state of the public mind, it did harm[4]. But the Directors, when they passed their stout resolution, had the letter on the table, and Wilson had not to handle the situation himself.

Carr Glyn and Samuel Gurney, among others, saw the crisis from within. Glyn was confident that the letter "produced the same effect as if the Bank of England had made an issue, because

---

[1] Quotations from Sir Charles Wood's speech of Nov. 30. Hansard, xcv. 374 *sqq.*
[2] *Economist*, November 30, 1847, p. 1255.
[3] Leading article of November 30, 1847.
[4] *E.g.* Evans, *op. cit.* p. 86: it "immediately changed the entire aspect of business." *Lords' Comm. on Commercial Distress*, p. xii: all witnesses agreed that the letter did good.

it brought out the Hoards of Notes and they went into Circulation."[1] Gurney told the Lords' Committee how his firm had

required about £200,000 and had it at Nine per Cent. On the Monday... we had again a heavy Demand; and we applied to the Governor, and said that, to supply Lombard Street with what was wanted, we should require £200,000 more. It was a Case of Difficulty for the Bank under its reduced Reserve, and under the Limitation of the Act. The Governor postponed a Decision...to two o'clock. At one o'clock the Letter from the Government...was announced. The Effect was immediate. Those who had sent Notice for their Money in the Morning sent us Word that they did not want it—they had only ordered Payment by way of Precaution....From that day we had a market of comparative ease[2].

With the letter in hand, the Directors could allow the banking reserve to drop again: it was at £1,600,000 on October 30. After that it rose fast; the notes came back, and the bullion reserve rose also, for there was no foreign drain with corn so cheap. By the end of November, the banking reserve was at six millions, the issue reserve at ten. Financial clearing up after the crisis took many months, and it was not facilitated by the political troubles of 1848; but right through that year of revolution the purely banking and currency situation in Threadneedle Street was perfectly comfortable—with a banking reserve rarely under eight millions and an issue reserve rarely under twelve. Supporters of the Bank Act argued that it had done more good than harm because the convertibility of the note into gold had been maintained: Jones Loyd even argued that the Chancellor's letter was no departure from the principles of the Act[3]. Its enemies, especially Thomas Tooke the ablest of them, were sure that it had done more harm than good by its separation of the Bank into departments and by its rigidity[4]. Tooke said that with all that gold, far more than in 1838–9, the Bank could easily have handled the situation on the old system; and he was able to prove that mere fluctuations in the amount of notes had not the importance which the currency school and Peel—with their memories of inconvertible paper, and their dogma that notes were money in a very special sense —had always assigned to them. He could emphasise also the proved efficacy of his own chosen method of dealing with gold

---

[1] *Lords' Comm. on Commercial Distress*, Q. 1736.
[2] *Ibid.* Q. 1120.
[3] Before the Lords' Committee, Q. 1400 *sqq.*
[4] *E.g.* his evidence before the Commons' Committee, Q. 5309 and *passim.*

drains—the manipulation by the Bank of the rate of discount[1]. But, in spite of Tooke's arguments and evidence and of James Wilson's confident declaration that "the Act must now be considered as a matter of history," it was neither modified nor repealed. The railways began to pay. Bread was cheap. Great Britain had escaped financial and political revolution. She left people interested in such things to discuss "fiat money" with John Mill—though members of the Birmingham School were still wearying parliamentary committees with it in 1848[2]— and she went on with her business.

[1] Above, p. 509.

[2] Commons' Committee, evidence of T. C. Salt and P. H. Muntz, both of Birmingham, Q. 84 *sqq.*, 99 *sqq.* A section of the Commons' Committee of 1847–8 wished to condemn the Bank Act, but was out-voted.

CHAPTER XIV

LIFE AND LABOUR IN INDUSTRIAL BRITAIN

DURING the early railway age the people of Britain, swept along in their own machines, were "thrown back in continually closer crowds upon the city gates."[1] The age closed, as shown in the census of 1851, with half the population urban—a situation which had probably not existed before, in a great country, at any time in the world's history. It is true that most of what were to become the largest English towns, and Glasgow, had grown more rapidly between 1821 and 1831 than they were ever to grow again. These were mainly textile centres, some of which were rising from very small beginnings; but Sheffield and Birmingham were among the number. (Bradford had the highest percentage growth in that decade of any town in Britain, except George IV's Brighton.) Yet since population as a whole was growing fast, and since the railways worked powerfully on the middle-sized towns, the ports and the iron centres, during the late 'thirties and the 'forties, besides rendering an almost indefinite growth of London possible, the actual addition to the population of towns with 20,000 inhabitants and upwards in Great Britain, which had been 1,100,000 between 1821 and 1831 was 1,270,000 between 1831 and 1841, and no less than 1,800,000 between 1841 and 1851[2]. Ruskin's "continually closer crowds" was, by chance, statistically correct. And in many places neither city nor town, with populations less than 20,000, the crowds were getting closer, the air denser, the streams fouler.

The towns, in the mass, were mainly inhabited by immigrants, as London always had been. Out of 3,336,000 people, of 20 years of age and upwards, living in London and 61 other English and Welsh towns in 1851, only 1,337,000 had been born in the town of their residence. London itself was now more thickly set with its own children than the average town, so violent had been the movements provoked in the industrial

---

[1] Ruskin, J., *The Seven Lamps of Architecture* (1849), p. 359.
[2] Weber, A. F., *The Growth of Cities in the Nineteenth Century*, p. 40, 47–59. London, thanks to the railway, grew faster in 1841–51 than in 1821–31.

districts. Of 1,395,000 Londoners over twenty years of age in 1851 not much less than one-half (645,000) were London born. Leeds, Norwich and Sheffield were the important towns with the largest percentages of natives. In Leeds 55,000 out of 95,000 of the adults, and in Norwich and Sheffield almost exactly one-half, were native; but in Manchester-Salford, in Bradford and in Glasgow the proportion of natives was only just over a quarter, and in Liverpool considerably less than a quarter. The large town with the smallest proportion of native residents, but little over a fifth, was however Brighton[1].

"Hitherto," William Farr wrote when presenting these facts to Sir James Graham, "the population has migrated from the high or the comparatively healthy ground of the country to the cities and seaport towns, in which few families have lived for two generations. But it is evident that henceforward the great cities will not be like camps—or the fields on which the people of other places exercise their energies and industry—but the birth-places of a large part of the British race."[2] The conclusion was obvious. Let the towns be so arranged and controlled "that the worst of all birth-places—the crowded room, or the house of many families—will never be the birth-place of any considerable proportion of the British population."

It is possible that Farr, a sanitarian and a close ally of Edwin Chadwick, when he spoke of the towns as camps was echoing a terrible sentence from Chadwick's *Sanitary Condition of the Labouring Population* of 1842. "Such is the absence of civic economy in some of our towns that their condition in respect to cleanliness is almost as bad as that of an encamped horde, or an undisciplined soldiery."[3] "The prisons," Chadwick said elsewhere, "were formerly distinguished for their filth and their bad ventilation; but the descriptions given by Howard of the worst prisons he visited in England (which he states were among the worst he had seen in Europe) were exceeded in every wynd in Edinburgh and Glasgow, inspected by Dr Arnott and myself. ...More filth, worse physical suffering and moral disorder than Howard describes...are to be found amongst the cellar population of the working people of Liverpool, Manchester, or Leeds,

---

[1] Census of 1851 (1852–3, LXXXVIII), *Ages, Occupations...and Birth-place of the People*, I. clxxxiii *sqq.*

[2] *Ibid.* I. xlv. Farr did the heavy work of the Census and, although he signs second on the report, it is here assumed that he wrote it.

[3] P. 43.

and in large portions of the metropolis."[1] The prisons were now better than their surroundings: "At Edinburgh, there were instances of poor persons in a state of disease committed from motives of humanity to the prison, that they might be taken care of and cured."[2] That was the indictment, the true bill. There was danger that the improvement in the health of the country and of its towns which, hard as it is to believe, had undoubtedly taken place between the middle of the eighteenth century and the decade 1820–30, might be lost now that an uncontrolled, or improperly controlled, town had become the home not of a minority but of the representative citizen.

The Commissioners for Paving, Lighting, Sewerage, Police, Improvement—or whatever they were locally called: there were three hundred of them—together with the best of the unreformed municipalities had done work not to be despised before 1835[3]. Paving, to take a single instance which Chadwick himself quoted, had saved Portsmouth town from "intermittent fever" in 1769, and drainage had subdued the "aguish disposition" in the adjacent parish of Kilsea in 1793[4]. Paving had probably not been undertaken anywhere with a direct view to the public health, but it made towns healthier; and fortunately nearly every body of commissioners and every tolerable municipality had done some paving. But the task was too great for the machinery, even had there always been a good will which assuredly there was not; and neither help nor guidance had come from parliament, when Chadwick reported in 1842 or when, two years later, Friedrich Engels studied *The Condition of the Working Class in England*. The commissioners, or the municipalities which took over from them after 1835, had paved the main and some of the by streets; but who thought of paving all the tangled maze of the old town of Manchester? There, "wherever a nook or corner was free, a house has been run up; where a superfluous passage remained it has been built up."[5] Who could pave properly among the "three rows of houses, of which the lowest rise directly out of the river," one above another on the steep bank of the Irk? From the filthy stream below in dry weather, "bubbles of miasmatic gas constantly arise and give forth a stench unendurable even on the

---

[1] Chadwick, *op. cit.* p. 212. [2] *Ibid.* p. 214.
[3] Webb, S. and B., *English Local Government* (IV), *Statutory Authorities*, *passim*.
[4] Chadwick, *op. cit.* p. 37. [5] Engels, *op. cit.* (ed. 1888), p. 37.

bridge, forty or fifty feet above the surface of the stream"—that stream "checked every few paces by high weirs, behind which slime and refuse accumulate and rot in thick masses."[1]

The "new towns"—every place had one or more, whether so called or not—had come so fast. That of Manchester stretched "up a hill of clay." "Single rows of houses or groups of streets stand here and there, like little villages on the naked, not even grass-grown, clay soil...the lanes are neither paved nor supplied with sewers but harbour numerous colonies of swine penned in small sties or yards, or wandering unrestrained through the neighbourhood." It is the pig scavenger of the Middle Ages. Even in a better-looking section of the new town, "many streets are unpaved and without sewers"—"private" streets these, of one-brick-thick houses, timed to fall down before the short ground lease ran out and all reverted to the landowner[2].

What was true of Manchester was true, *mutatis mutandis*, of every other growing industrial town and of all the new fringes of London: mere paving was heavily in arrear.

Scavenging, another elementary civic duty, was, if anything, still more neglected owing to incompetence, apathy, and obstructive proprietary rights. Although, in the ordinary clearing of the main streets, great progress had been made in most towns during the thirty or forty years preceding 1830, that was only a part of the problem[3]. "Several nuisances exist," the Bradford Highway Surveyors reported simply to the Commissioners on the State of Large Towns in 1844. "One of these is in the most public part of the town and in the very centre of business, and consists of refuse, offal, etc., from the butchers' shops, necessaries, ash places and urinaries....This is private property and therefore the surveyors understand that they cannot cause the removal of these nuisances."[4] Mr Boffin's dust-heaps, so called by courtesy, were not "in the most public part" of London. But a dust contractor explained in 1842 that "the site of the New London University was a place in which the refuse was deposited [*i.e.* before 1827], so was the site of the new row of grand houses in Hyde Park Gardens. I think the site of Belgrave Square was another place of deposit."[5] From Greenock

[1] Engels, *op. cit.* p. 34.   [2] *Ibid.* p. 39.
[3] Webb, *op. cit.* p. 316 *sqq.* "A notable advance" had been made (p. 333).
[4] *Report*, p. 338.
[5] *Report on the Sanitary Condition*, etc., p. 381: also quoted in Webb, *op. cit.* p. 339 n.

in 1840 comes this story: "in one part of the street," Market Street, "a narrow back street," "there is a dunghill—yet it is too large to be called a dunghill. I do not mistake its size when I say it contains a hundred cubic yards of impure filth ...it is the stock-in-trade of a person who deals in dung; he retails it by cartful. To please his customers he always keeps a nucleus, as the older the filth is the higher is the price."[1] Even the progress made in street sweeping down to 1830 left main roads bad enough, lanes, courts, wynds and closes unspeakable. Manchester in 1842 cleaned its main streets once a week, its third grade streets once a month: "but this provision leaves untouched...the courts, alleys, and places where the poorest classes live and where the cleansing should be daily."[2] During the years of progress, town refuse had a value and people were glad to contract for the removal of "dust"; but by 1842 there was in London "no filth...that now, as a general rule, will pay the expense of collection and removal by cart, except the ashes from the houses and the soap lees from the soap-boilers; and some of the night soil from the east end of the town," where market gardens were handy[3]. So the young municipal authorities of the late 'thirties and 'forties were faced with a losing service and, having no sanitary standards and no obligation to government, were tempted not to press too hard, even where pressure was possible, on the dung-hill dealers and nuisance proprietors—in spite of the cholera warning of 1831–2[4].

Their failures with drainage and sewerage were rather more excusable. Streams and rivers had always been used to provide power and carry off refuse. While population was thin, they could perform both functions without too grave public inconvenience, especially where the current was swift or tidal. The new industry brought new foul effluents and demanded more and more weirs and mill-dams, as on the Irk at Manchester. The Irk came out of a district in which there was no regulative authority into a town which was dominated by industrial

[1] *Report on the Sanitary Condition*, p. 47. Mr and Mrs Webb (*op. cit.* p. 339 n.) think this "the climax of horrors." The Bradford case might claim equality: so of course could any medieval or early modern town. "Sanitation" was the new thing, not stenches.

[2] *Ibid.* p. 53: also quoted in part in Webb, *op. cit.* p. 344.

[3] John Darke, cleansing contractor. *Report on Sanitary Condition*, App II, p. 379.

[4] A nuisance might be abated, but could be repeated. Anyone could set up a slaughter-house anywhere. See Jephson, *The Sanitary Evolution of London*, p. 38.

interests and, in any case, had neither the knowledge nor the legal right to deal with that foul ditch. Flowing swift, "clear and cool," from the limestone hills of High Craven, "the river Aire, which in its natural state would have had a strong and regular current," had "been dammed up in several places for the purposes of mill power, and for the purposes of an important water communication [the Aire and Calder Navigation]. These dams thus act as a series of catch-pits for the sewage of a population of 120,000 persons.... The authorities having control over the town drainage, even if they had been so constituted as to have been competent to execute or maintain systematic works, would have no jurisdiction or control over the natural outfalls...."[1] Those of Leeds could not stop those of Bradford—in a side valley upstream—from discharging their main sewers "either into the brook or into the terminus or basin of a canal which runs into the lower part of the town." There were similar catchpit dams in Sheffield and Halifax, to name only places visited by the Commissioners of 1844, "and the effect of the miasma from the stagnant pools produced is most pestilential."[2]

The northern towns at least had a government which might be stirred up and given powers. London had about three hundred governments—"jostling, jarring, unscientific, cumbrous and costly"[3]—parishes, sets of paving trustees, and various commissions of sewers, some of considerable antiquity but all now working under private local acts. The commissioners for the City itself—really a statutory committee of the Corporation—seem to have done their work pretty well[4]. Those of Holborn and Finsbury had done theirs excellently: their surveyor in the 'thirties, John Roe, was a competent sanitary engineer[5]. Those of Westminster, nominally in charge of most of the drainage of the West End, were "bossed" by a strong, interested and corrupt chairman and a gang of property-owning "ward politicians." Those of the Surrey side were heavily in debt and completely inefficient. All along the low ground—Lambeth, Vauxhall, Southwark—in 1832 "the channels and ditches for carrying off the water remain in their

---

[1] *Report on the State of Large Towns*, p. 19.
[2] *Ibid.* p. 315, 319.
[3] Jephson, *op. cit.* p. 13; and see Webb, *op. cit.* esp. p. 80–100.
[4] For them Webb, S. and B., *The Manor and the Borough*, p. 640–1.
[5] See his evidence in *Report on Sanitary Condition*, App. I.

natural state, overflowing with filth and impuritys."[1] No improvement followed the cholera.

The Acts of parliament, from which these bodies derived their powers, generally, as Chadwick said, "either presume that no science, no skill, is requisite for the attainment of the objects, or presume both to be universal."[2] They, and what might be called the common-law of sewers behind them, ran back to times when a sewer was a thing for carrying off not solid refuse but land water. It was nominally illegal in London to link up "houses of office" with the sewers, though liquid matter from cesspools might pass into them; but as water-closets were gradually fitted, first into the best, and then into the better, London houses, between 1810 and 1840, the prohibition broke down. But the sewer might be higher than the cesspool that it drained, or it might run up hill. With cesspools the whole town was honeycombed, east to west. Among them, in poorer quarters, were the pumps, still much used because "company water" was not everywhere laid on. "If the soil through which the rain passes be composed of the refuse of centuries," wrote a medical officer of St Giles' in the 'fifties, "if it be riddled with cesspools and the remains of cesspools, with leaky gas-pipes and porous sewers, if it has been the depository of the dead for generation after generation...[it] cannot yield water of any degree of purity"[3]: agreed.

The technical difficulties presented by the problem of London sanitation, above all of London drainage, have always to be borne in mind when judging the sanitary failures of the day. Local government had not been much considered from that point of view. There was no articulate dissatisfaction with the system of the metropolitan Commissioners of Sewers until the late 'thirties[4]. In the 'forties Members of Parliament and would-be reformers were "bewildered by the technicalities and con-flicting opinions of the budding experts on the sizes and shapes of drains, the respective values of gully-holes, grates and traps, and the mysteries of hydraulics."[5] Sanitary science was as new and raw as its name. Chadwick was explaining in 1842—not as a neglected commonplace, but as a recent discovery—how

[1] *The Extraordinary Black Book*, quoted in Webb, *Statutory Authorities*, p. 101.
[2] *Report on Sanitary Condition*, p. 37. [3] Quoted in Jephson, *op. cit.* p. 22.
[4] Webb, *op. cit.* p. 103. Jephson, *op. cit.* p. 4.
[5] Webb, *op. cit.* p. 104.

"by proper hydraulic arrangements heavy solid substances may be swept away through iron pipes."[1] The relatively cheap iron pipe itself was not so very old; and it was not anyone's fault that even well-made brick sewers were apt to be porous.

In Whitechapel, in the 'thirties, a French visitor noted "partout des mares fétides qui attestent l'absence de toute règle pour l'écoulement des eaux."[2] They called one of them the Wellington swamp. Near such a fetid pool there was a bad outbreak of fever in 1838. The local poor law authorities made appeal to the secretary of the new Poor Law Board, and Chadwick moved the Board to send down a strong committee of doctors—Arnott, Kay and Southwood Smith[3]. Their reports, especially Southwood Smith's separate report on disease and water-supply, did what Chadwick had hoped—attracted thousands of readers, startled the thinking public, and initiated systematic sanitary research. In that year also the Acts of 1837 for the registration of births, deaths and their causes, and marriages came into force (6 & 7 Wm. IV, c. 86 and 7 Wm. IV, c. 22) and Dr William Farr began his forty-two years' service in the Registrar-General's office[4]. Next year the proposal to extend the London health inquiry to the whole country was pressed resolutely by Charles Blomfield, Bishop of London. Chadwick, in old age, constantly acknowledged his, and the nation's, debt to Blomfield[5]; for Chadwick himself had not the knack of making busy and half-willing men in high places do what he wanted. As it was, the Poor Law Commissioners received their orders from Lord John Russell in August 1839, and by the end of the year the inquiry was on foot which resulted in the Report of 1842.

While the inquiry was proceeding, a House of Commons Committee on the Health of Towns was calling attention to the absence of any general laws controlling building or drainage, or enforcing "the commonest provisions for cleanliness and comfort."[6] The report anticipated, while it confirmed,

---

[1] Chadwick, *op. cit.* p. 52.

[2] Faucher, L., *Études sur l'Angleterre*, p. 22.

[3] Richardson, B. W., *The health of nations, a review of the work of Edwin Chadwick* (1887), I. xliii.

[4] As second-in-command. Chadwick failed to get Charles Babbage, the mathematician, placed at its head, as he had wished. Richardson, *op. cit.* II. xlv.

[5] He confided it "to me many times." Richardson, *op. cit.* II. liv.

[6] *S. C. on Circumstances affecting the Health...of Large Towns*, 1840 (XI), p. 13.

Chadwick's results. Before these results were ready, Peel, urged on by Lord Ashley and privately by the Prince Consort, had appointed the Royal Commission on the State of Large Towns and Populous Districts whose reports—Chadwick was behind them also—came out in 1844 and 1845. The intervening year saw the issue of Chadwick's own *Report on...the Practice of Interment in Towns*[1], with its horrible accounts of the dead kept long among the living in crowded one-room tenements, of Irish corpse wakes, and of the accumulated corruption of city churches and city graveyards; and with its thorough-going recommendation—burial in towns should be prohibited. Burial should be a national affair, duly supervised by officers of health. There should be public arrangements, "in conformity to successful examples abroad," for carrying out funerals at moderate cost. Medical officers of health should be set up: they should not be in private practice, and without their certificate no interment should take place[2].

Equally thorough-going, and just as illuminative of the conditions with which they were intended to deal, were the recommendations of Peel's Commission[3]—that sanitary control should rest with single local authorities directly under the Crown: that before any drainage scheme be carried out "a plan and survey upon a proper scale" be made: that the Crown define and extend from time to time local drainage areas: that the single local authority make all the sewers: that landlords be liable for the rates of tenement houses and cottage property: that the authority which drains do also pave: that it own all dust, ashes, and street refuse, and cleanse all cesspools and privies: that its powers to schedule nuisances, and abate nuisances summarily, be extended: that the provisions for smoke abatement already found in certain local acts be generalised: that it be imperative on the local authority to see that sufficient water for all purposes is provided: that the authority have power to raise money for street-widening and improvement: that no inhabited court be less than 20, or its entrance less than 10, feet wide: that cellars and basements be not let for human habitation unless

---

[1] 1843 (XII. 395).

[2] The Report was the occasion of a grim letter from Carlyle to Chadwick. Richardson, *op. cit.* II. lix.

[3] *Commission on the State of Large Towns and Populous Districts Report*, II. (1845), p. 13 *sqq.* The Commissioners were the Duke of Buccleuch, Prof. Owen, Lyon Playfair, Dr Reid, Capt. Denison, Robert Stephenson, Smith "of Deanston," Sir H. de la Beche and W. Cubitt.

they have fireplaces, decent windows, and proper drainage: that in all new houses suitable privies be installed: that the authority have power to insist on adequate ventilation and the compulsory cleaning of foul houses, to license lodging-houses, to appoint medical officers of health, and to raise funds for the establishment of "public walks"—since "the great towns of Liverpool, Manchester, Birmingham and Leeds, and very many others, have at present no public walks."[1]

It was hardly to be expected that so huge and difficult a matter as national sanitary reform should be tackled by parliament in 1846. But the miseries of Ireland, a return of the cholera, and the steady work of the pioneers—helped by the men of letters—forced even the apathetic mass of the public to give some attention to disease, filth, and drains. A bill based on the recommendations of the Commission was introduced in 1847 but withdrawn. Next year the Public Health Act (11 & 12 Vict. c. 63), the basis of all later sanitary law, was placed on the statute book. While it was going through parliament, the editor of the *Economist* regretted that "it had got as far as a committee without meeting the opposition it deserved." "Suffering and evil," he wrote, "are nature's admonitions; they cannot be got rid of; and the impatient attempts of benevolence to banish them from the world by legislation, before benevolence has learned their object and their end, have always been productive of more evil than good."[2] The bill of 1847 had included London: the Act of 1848 unhappily left London's formidable administrative problems for future treatment, although yet another metropolitan sanitary commission —Chadwick and Southwood Smith, of course, with three others—had in the meantime underlined their urgency. But London did get something in 1848—the establishment of the Metropolitan Commissioners of Sewers, who were given wide powers over the drainage of the whole area. In the years 1848-9 the superintendence of the new national sanitary law was given to the first Board of Health—Shaftesbury, Lord Morpeth, Chadwick and Southwood Smith. The towns had not been

---

[1] *Report*, p. 68.
[2] *Economist*, May 13, 1848. The bill referred "to a great variety of matters which we cannot even enumerate, without crowding our space with a catalogue of somewhat offensive words." But the *Economist* was right to insist that the evils legislated against were local and partial, not universal. Had they been universal the towns would have devoured population in the good old way. Above, p. 55.

made sanitary, but there was now some prospect of their becoming so[1].

The Census Commissioners of 1841 were inclined to think that the overcrowding of houses, as distinguished from that of towns, had declined a very little for the whole of England and Wales, and for many towns, since 1831, the number of houses having more than kept pace with the growth in the population[2]. This conclusion, when first put forward provisionally, Chadwick disputed, pointing out that the census of 1831 had enumerated the separate buildings whereas, in 1841, the commissioners admitted that, generally speaking, "flats, apartments and families had been reckoned as distinct houses."[3] His own evidence of increased overcrowding "from many districts" was of course trustworthy; but an inquiry such as his was less likely to hear any testimony that there may have been to decreased overcrowding, because that did not produce the sanitary evils for which his agents were looking. The Census Commissioners evidently supposed that their comparison with 1831 was reasonably valid, in spite of some slight change in method, since, when publishing it in its final form, they refused to make such a comparison for Scotland precisely because of "the peculiar difficulties attending the proper discrimination of *houses* from *tenements*" in the Scottish housing system[4].

All that even the Commissioners claimed, however, was that, for the whole of England and Wales, the number of persons per inhabited house had fallen in the decade from 5·60 to 5·40. They were right in assuming that one house one family was the normal arrangement everywhere, in spite of flats and tenements and lodgers[5]. They admitted an increase in the number of persons per inhabited house in some very important places —Liverpool for instance; they claimed no improvement in others, such as Leeds. For Manchester they did claim a slight improvement; and it is likely enough that the rapidly run up cottages on Engel's "clay hill" had eased the pressure a little on the banks of the Irk and about Old Millgate[6]. The claim

---

[1] See, for London, Jephson, *op. cit.* p. 41–4.

[2] *Census of* 1841, 1843 (XXII), p. 6, 7.

[3] *Report on Sanitary Condition*, p. 120–1.

[4] Chadwick's most telling evidence against them was Scottish, which was hardly fair.

[5] Above, p. 37.

[6] Liverpool, 1831, 6·4; 1841, 6·9. Leeds, 1831, 4·8; 1841, 4·8. Manchester, 1831, 6·0; 1841, 5·7.

made for London is interesting in this connection—that within the 1831 limits there had been a tiny increase in overcrowding (from 7·4 to 7·5) but that, taking the 1841 limits, the position was stationary, the less crowded outskirts just balancing the more crowded core.

It is very likely that the small change of method, coupled with the undoubtedly rapid growth of houses for the more comfortable classes, would about obliterate the tiny general improvement claimed for England and Wales, leaving the labouring population as a whole neither less nor more overcrowded. A general worsening is at least not demonstrable; nor do the more carefully taken returns of 1851, for which a house was exactly defined as "an isolated dwelling or a dwelling separated by party walls,"[1] reveal a worsening on 1831 or, probably, on 1841. The number of persons per inhabited house in all England and Wales was returned as 5·46 as against 5·40 in 1841, but here the definition had been stiffened; and the number of families per house—a figure not worked out in 1841—as 1·13. There had been no important change since the 'twenties, nor indeed in the century. The town with most families to a house in 1851 was Plymouth-Devonport, with 2·25. London had 1·74: in several districts two or three families to a house was the average, but some of these, like Seven Dials and the City, were districts with houses of fair size. In the towns of the South-East taken together there were 1·22 families to a house; in Bristol, the only town of the West Midlands where there was any serious excess of families over houses, 1·60; in Liverpool 1·34; in Manchester 1·22. In Leicestershire, Rutland, Lincoln, Nottingham and Derby "nearly all the families dwell in separate houses," and "the same rule" applied to Yorkshire, excepting York and Hull. Even in Hull, much the worst Yorkshire town from this point of view, the figure was only 1·16; and Hull was an ancient seaport, not yet growing very fast, with a dense core of old, fair-sized, waterside houses. The absence of any general system of tenement dwelling in most of the new industrial areas is conspicuous[2].

[1] *Census of* 1851 (1852–3, LXXXV), p. xxxvii.

[2] *Census of* 1851, as above, p. xxxviii *sqq.* In Lancashire and Cheshire over 300,000 out of 473,000 families had separate houses. Liverpool had 47,000 families in 35,000 houses, Manchester 45,000 families in 37,000 houses. North of the Tees, the "Scottish" system began to tell in the towns. Newcastle had 19,000 families in 11,000 houses.

In the insanitary and crowded towns—which, it is not to be forgotten, were less crowded than the great towns of other countries and not as a group more insanitary—and in industrialised rural districts, the money wages of labour, viewed in the mass and neglecting year to year vicissitudes, were almost stationary between 1830 and 1846–50. There were declining, improving, and stagnant trades and districts: there were trades liable to sharp wage changes and others in which standard rates were remarkably uniform; but an index number covering all shows a curious stability[1]. A great wartime rise; a post-war fall, less than the rise, often very much less; then comparative stability, is the general formula for the years 1790–1850. The building trades, untouched but not unaffected by the technical revolutions of industry, may be taken first. A London bricklayer's summer day rate, as given in builders' price books, had risen from 3s. 9d. at the end of the eighteenth century to 5s. 6d. in the dearest years of the war. It never fell again below 5s., though it rose well above 5s. during the building activity of 1822–4, and was at 5s. 3d. in 1848. The bricklayers' labourer, who was said to get 2s. 4½d. in 1786–1806, was reckoned to cost 4s. in 1811 and 3s. 6d. in 1831. This rate remained steady until beyond 1850: probably the Irish immigrants kept it down. The slightly lower figures found in other London sources of information give much the same general result—5s. reached late in the wars for skilled men of all sorts in the building trades; an abnormal rise in 1824: a fall to 4s. 6d. in 1829; then a rise to 5s. in 1844. The Manchester bricklayer, in his more competitive atmosphere, had more changes but made more progress. During the 'twenties his (weekly) wage varied from 22s. 6d. to 24s. In 1832 it was down at 18s. 6d., to rise to 23s. in 1834 and so upwards to 28s. in 1849. The Edinburgh mason, a typical Scottish building trades craftsman, had a summer weekly wage of 17s. in 1830. It was 20s. in 1840–4 and after soaring to 26s. during the railway boom of 1845–7, was back at 20s. in 1848. All these men were doing exactly the same kind of work throughout the whole period, and working their twelve hours a day in summer.[2]

[1] That constructed by G. H. Wood (see below, p. 561), which takes 1840 as the base year (100), gives 103 for 1831, 99 for 1845 and 102 for 1850.

[2] These illustrative figures are taken from Bowley, A. L., *Wages in the United Kingdom* (1900), ch. XII. See also Bowley's articles in *S.J.* 1900–1. In *The Builders' History* (1923) R. W. Postgate ignores Prof. Bowley's work but quotes (p. 455) a generalised scheme of wage movements for a 10-hours' day, according

For his own highly skilled trade, the breeches-makers—also unaffected by new invention—Francis Place stated, in 1834, that wages, rising from 22s. in 1793, had reached 36s. at the end of the wars and had never fallen since. This course of wages, though not necessarily these figures, he said was typical for a very large body of skilled metropolitan workmen[1]. The building trade figures bear him out on the whole; though they show that the war maximum was not quite maintained. So do the very complex, but very fully recorded, wages of printers[2]. Compositors' standard time wages in London, which had risen from 24s. in 1785 to 36s. in 1810, were brought down slowly after the wars to 33s., but no lower. Piece rates for "brevier" were not reduced at all, nor were the standard London rates for morning and evening newspaper work (48s. and 43s. 6d. respectively). In Edinburgh ordinary time-rates fell a few shillings from the war maximum, but piece-rates closely followed those of London. For the whole trade, the post-war reduction "was only partial," and the level thus established remained almost unchanged down to 1848 and later. The war rise, it should be noted, had not been so great as the rise in the cost of living between 1790 and 1810–15; but its approximate maintenance left the skilled tradesman relatively well off in such periods of cheap food as 1832–6, 1842–6 and, above all, 1848–50.

Between 1790 and 1839, the dearest year of the early railway age, the bare cost of living—excluding rent—had risen some 23 per cent.[3] In 1835, in 1843–6, and after 1848, it was actually lower than it had been in 1790. The least fortunate of the groups of representative craftsmen just cited had secured a wage rise of 33·3 per cent. in the interval, and some wages—as has been seen—had risen over 50 per cent.[4] Charles Kingsley wrote without complete knowledge when he argued, in 1850, that

to which carpenters, masons, bricklayers, plumbers and plasterers got 3s. a day normally in 1788–90 and 5s. a day from 1826 to 1847. In spite of this suggested rise of 66·6 per cent., which is well above any possible calculation of the rise in the cost of living in the interval, Mr Postgate says (p. 33) that "the operative builders [of the 'thirties] had fallen from respected and comfortable members of society into the position of 'ragged trousered philanthropists.'" Some evidence is given of alleged deteriorations in dress and manners. The wage figures are put in an Appendix and are not discussed.

¹ Place MSS., quoted in Bowley, op. cit. p. 60–1.
² Bowley, op. cit. p. 72 sqq., and Bowley and Wood, S.J. 1899.
³ See above, p. 128, 466, the discussions of agricultural wages and below, p. 562, the discussion of retail prices and "truck."
⁴ [Or, according to Place and the figures in Postgate, by over 60 per cent.]

competition was driving down, or would assuredly drive down, wages in all trades which were not for special reasons at a premium, like "the navigator's or engineer's."[1] Neither building, breeches-making, nor printing was a new privileged trade.

Wage problems in the revolutionised or new industries are far more difficult, because of the constant changes in the work of spinners, combers, fitters or whatever the trade may be, and the complications of woman and child labour in the textiles. The old-time all-round London millwrights, for instance, had worked up to a standard time-rate—there were no piece-rates—of 42s. about 1813[2]. They were broken by the introduction of the "engineer's economy" of specialisation and piece-rates, with individual bargains, during the next ten or fifteen years, and probably their wages fell more than the average, but the fall is not easy to trace. Fortunately figures are available for some typical engineering workers from Manchester[3], which became the chief home of the new engineering. Of these, the man whose job probably changed least from 1815 to 1848 was the iron-moulder. The highest wage recorded for him from the dear years is 34s. 8d. (1816). The maximum in 1832 is 30s. and in 1834 it is 34s. A maximum of 36s. is touched in 1845–6, but it is not maintained. He is back at 34s. in 1849. Turners' maximum wages at Manchester follow much the same course —30s. in 1813; 26s. in 1820; 30s. in 1824–34; up to 33s. in 1845 and then down again to 30s. The Manchester fitters are very near the turners. The general course of wage movements here agrees roughly with that in the building trades and the London crafts.

For the cotton manufacture the statistical difficulties are at their maximum and call for elaborate treatment. Machine is always replacing machine; women replace men and children replace women. The figures now to be given are merely illustrative of the course of the earnings of selected important groups of workers[4]. All except those of hand-loom weavers come from the Manchester district. A third-grade male spinner, turning out coarse yarn—on the jenny at first and later on the mule—made some 24s. at the close of the wars; 22s. 6d. in 1833; 21s. in 1836 and 16s. 5d. in 1839, a very bad year for his section of

---

[1] In *Cheap Clothes and Nasty*.   [2] Above, p. 206–7.

[3] Wood, G. H., in Bowley, *op. cit.* p. 122.

[4] From Bowley, *op. cit.* ch. xv, prepared in collaboration with Wood, G. H. For wage statistics generally see the series of articles by Bowley and Wood in *S.J.* 1899–1906.

the trade and a very dear year too. After further fluctuations, he made 18s. in 1849. (The effective arrival of the self-actor during the 'thirties seems to have driven wages down.) A very important class, the character of whose work probably varied less than most between 1815 and 1845, were the women throstle-spinners. Their figures are as follows: 9s. 1d. in 1810; 8s. 9d. in 1815; 9s. 1d. in 1824; a maximum of 10s. 6d. and a minimum of 7s. during the 'thirties; a maximum of 10s. and a minimum of 7s. 6d. during the 'forties[1]. The piecers, a mixed body of young men women and children, also did work of a fairly uniform character. Their average earnings are said not to have varied by 6d. from 1813 to 1833, and in 1833 they were 5s. 10d. The lowest figure recorded between 1833 and 1849 is 6s. 11d. (1839) and the highest 7s. 9d. (1846). On their lowly plane, the piecers were definitely on the upgrade—getting what some spinners were losing, so to speak.

At the other end of the scale, a first class fine spinner is credited with 44s. 6d. in 1815; 35s. 9d. in 1833; 42s. 3d. in 1839, the year when the third grade spinners were doing so badly; a minimum of 28s. 4d. (1848) and a maximum of 37s. (1849) during the 'forties. The self-actor no doubt affected these figures also, though it cannot be assumed that an improved machine will have permanent wage-depressing results. Its custodian may mind more of it, as the power-loom weavers learnt to do. A power-loom weaver, usually a woman, minding two looms made from 7s. 6d. to 10s. 6d.—probably, on an average, nearer the former than the latter—in 1824, 9s. 4d. in 1839, 10s. in 1846 and 10s. 2d. in 1849. Already in 1824, figures can be given for minders of three looms, and in 1839 for minders of four. By 1849 the former could make 13s. and the latter 16s. a week[2].

Meanwhile the cotton hand-loom weavers, except those who worked on some speciality, were being crushed out with infinite misery, as the inquiries of 1834 and 1838–41 demonstrated, had demonstration been needed of such a crying national tragedy.

---

[1] Bowley's Index Number for all cotton wages (based on the wages paid for a great number of different kinds of work) takes the 1833–4 wages as 100. The principal figures are—1815, 113; 1824, 109; 1833–4, 100; 1839, 91; 1841, 91; 1846, 97; 1846–50, 96. In spite of its special conditions, this abstract "cotton wage," which is probably fairly representative for cotton family earnings, moves very like the other wage-curves examined. The comparison of 1815 with 1833–4 is very favourable to the workers, when costs of living are considered; 1839–41 is specially gloomy; 1846–50 cheerful.

[2] The work being piece-work, there is a wide range of earnings.

The situation had been dangerous in the 'twenties, when Manchester weavers were said to be making, in a good year, 9s. a week and in a bad one 6s. 6d.[1]—if at work. The Committee of 1834 felt "deep regret at finding the sufferings of that large and valuable body of men, not only not exaggerated, but that they have for years continued to an extent and intensity scarcely to be credited or conceived, and have been borne with a degree of patience unexampled."[2] The Committee spoke helplessly of the men's schemes for central or local Boards of Trade, to regulate wages, but said that "some Legislative Enactment" was "imperatively necessary"—though what enactment other than state pensions for weavers, the prohibition of the power-loom, or the prohibition of training in hand-loom weaving, would have been of the least use it is hard to see. The Commissioners of 1841 recognised the facts and spoke politico-economically, and as it must have seemed brutally, of the problem of supply and demand—"the demand" (they had in view hand-loom weaving of all kinds, not merely of cotton) "being, in many cases, deficient, in some cases decreasing, and in still more, irregular, while the supply is, in many branches, excessive, in almost all has a tendency to increase" (by the weavers' passionate clinging to his loom and his independence; by the consequent automatic turning of weavers' children into weavers; by the terrible ease with which simple weaving was learnt; and by Irish immigration) "and does not appear in any to have a tendency to adapt itself to the irregularities of the demand."[3] How should it? How should a fourteen-hour-a-day cellar weaver (the half-mythical farmer-weaver was pretty well extinct) take up some other job when demand slackened?

The Commissioners reported—illustrations must suffice—that for plain stripes, checks, and muslins, "an adult skilled artisan on the finer qualities of the fabric," might get 7s. or 7s. 6d. a week net in the Glasgow district, "a less skilled and younger artisan on the coarser qualities" 4s. 6d. These figures applied to 28,000 looms[4]. At Blackburn twenty-eight whole weaving families averaged 9s. 6½d. per family[5]. At Ashton-under-Lyne 483 families were visited: they contained 1955 souls: the earnings recently had averaged 4s. 11¼d. per family per week. There were 213 looms idle, which shows the state

[1] Bowley's figures, from Baines and Ure.
[2] S. C. on Hand Loom Weavers' Petitions, 1834 (X), p. iii.
[3] Report, p. 124.   [4] Report, p. 5.   [5] Report, p. 4.

of trade at the time of the inquiry (1838–9)[1]. In Manchester 402 families of weavers of coarse fabrics, averaging 1¾ looms per family, made 7s. 8¼d. a week; 174 families of "first class" weavers, on high grade work, with 3 looms per family, made 16s. 4¾d.[2] Assuming one highly skilled and two less skilled members in the family, this about coincides with the Glasgow figure, and may be taken as representative of really good cotton weavers' earnings about 1840; though on a few specialities, such as fancy muslins, small groups of workers might make more[3]. The Ashton-under-Lyne average is a representative instance of extreme distress in a considerable group, though cases more pathetic and more terrible might be found.

Outside the cotton industry, hand-loom weavers on all "narrow, plain, and coarse fabrics"[4] were hard put to it. At Mirfield, 402 weavers of common narrow woollen cloth had averaged 5s. 6½d. each "per week for twelve months."[5] (As yet the power-loom had only grazed woollens.) Linen weavers at Barnsley, where few power-looms were employed, at a time when trade was good, reckoned their net weekly earnings at 7s. 8½d. At Knaresborough, for "various descriptions of linen, mostly however of the lower sorts,"[6] individual earnings were about 7s. 4d. "Good hands," i.e. able-bodied men, in the plain light trade which was "the staple linen manufacture of Scotland," made "under favourable circumstances" 7s. 6d. net[7]. In such skilled work as damask, or such heavy work as sailcloth, wages were higher. There were silk-velvet weavers in London who averaged 17s. a week net; but there were more plain silk and satin weavers at from 7s. 5d. to 5s. 11d.[8] "First hand journeymen," owning Jacquard looms at Coventry, might make 15s. 6d.; but the lowest grade of the silk industry, "single hand ribbon weavers in the villages near," made only about 5s.[9] A selected group of witnesses weaving stuffs about Bradford—stuffs were narrow and the power-loom was making

[1] *Assistant Commissioners' Reports*, v. 582–4.
[2] *Assistant Commissioners*, v. 578.
[3] As at Preston: 8s. 1½d. per *weaver*, on fancy muslins. *Ibid.* p. 588–9. It must be borne in mind that the period of this classic inquiry, 1838–41, was one of abnormally bad trade in the whole industry. Above, p. 516 *sqq.*
[4] *Report*, p. 3.
[5] *Assistant Commissioners*, v. 584.
[6] *Report*, p. 8–9.
[7] *Assistant Commissioners*, I. 188.
[8] *Assistant Commissioners*, II. 229, 232.
[9] *Assistant Commissioners*, IV. 289. *Report*, p. 7.

headway in that area—averaged 7s. 7½d. net, when in full work, in 1838[1]. On the other hand, thirty Norwich fancy stuff weavers —there were no power-looms at Norwich—averaged 14s. 5d., the highest group making 16s.; twenty-eight Leeds fine broad-cloth weavers averaged 12s. 9d., the best man making over £1 and the worst 7s. 6d.; on nearly 1000 woollen looms at Gala-shiels, Hawick and Jedburgh, "clear weekly wages" of 11s. to 16s. 6d. could be made; while, on carpet work, Scottish wages ran up to a maximum of 18s.[2]

The figures collected, and the situation revealed, in 1838–41 appear to be fairly representative for the whole period 1830–48, midway in which they fall. If a weaver could get work, these were about his earnings in the various districts and trades throughout[3]. The easier work was being transferred steadily to the power-loom. There had been 108,632 cotton, and 3082 worsted, power-looms in the country in 1835: the figures in 1850 were 249,627 and 32,617[4]. Perhaps 40,000 to 50,000 cotton hand-looms were still at work out of the 225,000 esti-mated for 1829–31. The weavers had died, or been drafted into the mills, or had taken to weaving silk and fancy goods. Fancy worsted weaving by hand could still yield a living; but worsteds were mostly woven in the mills by 1850. Woollen had moved much more slowly. From 2045 in 1835, the power-looms had grown to 9439 in 1850[5]—but abundance of hand-looms re-mained at work, and hand weavers were making their 14s. and 15s. in and about Leeds, the most mechanised district of all, during the 'fifties[6]. In silk, the 309 experimental power-looms of 1835 had only grown to 1141 by 1850[7], when there was still plenty of hand silk-weaving about Manchester, and in Maccles-field, Coventry, Spitalfields and East Anglia. Flax-weaving was in a complicated position. The power-looms had only increased from 1714 to 6092 in the fifteen years[8]. They had made less progress than might perhaps have been expected, because the plain light work could be done cheaply in Scotland and the out-lying parts of England, and still more cheaply in Ireland

---

[1] *Assistant Commissioners*, III. 562.

[2] *Report*, p. 12. *Assistant Commissioners*, III. 533; IV. 555. *Report*, p. 5.

[3] But he was less likely to get work in 1838–41 than he had previously been, and perhaps less likely than he was in 1842–6.

[4] *Report of Factory Inspectors*, Oct. 1850 (1851, XXIII. 117).   [5] *Ibid.*

[6] Baines, *Yorkshire*, II. 652–3.

[7] *Factory Inspectors' Report*, as above.

[8] *Ibid.*

—regions to which it was gravitating—while both the finer and the heavier work, in these regions and elsewhere, still required the weaver's hand.

Thanks to the ill-balance of supply and demand, hand-loom weavers suffered more than any other section of the industrial population, and the wretched cotton weavers more than other weavers, from the periodic ebb and flow of trade. When any line of cotton business was slack, the power-looms would be run if possible: the hand-looms engaged on similar fabrics could wait. With a raw material four-fifths of which now came from a single country, and that a country whose commercial relations with Britain were both dominant and unstable, with its chief markets in the ends of the earth, dependent on harvests, tariffs, monsoons and opium wars, the cotton industry went forward —as we are told that the physical universe goes[1]—by jerks. It had to bear the full accumulated effects of this blindly shifting foreign demand and of a home demand which was also particularly unstable, because the specially dear food of 1838–42 and 1846–8 reacted at once on the clothes-purchasing power of the average ill-paid consumer. So overstocked was hand-loom weaving that, even in a year of cheap food like 1834, official inquirers could write of "sufferings scarcely to be credited or conceived." Yet so confident, so justly confident, were employers of the cotton industry's expansive power, in spite of the pauses between the jerks, and of the efficiency of mechanical weaving, that power-looms were being installed at an average rate of 10,000 a year. Between 1842 and 1845, the factories in Leonard Horner's North-Western inspection area increased by 524[2]. It was fortunate that weavers' daughters and wives could earn in the loom-sheds, though it hurt the weavers' pride.

In worsted weaving the rate of introduction of power was perhaps, and in woollen linen and silk certainly, not fast enough to be dislocating. The use of worsteds was expanding, and the whole industry growing, very fast. There was room both for hand and power. Five hundred a year, the average rate of introduction of the woollen looms, would, one supposes, be a low death rate among woollen weavers; three hundred a year a very low death rate among flax weavers. Neither trade was stationary. The silk trade, which averaged only about fifty-five

---

[1] A layman's reading of the Quantum Theory.
[2] Quoted in Dolléans, E., *Le Chartisme* (1913), II. 312.

extra power-looms each year, was expanding quickly enough to be able to shelter—poorly of course—many disinherited weavers from cotton. So long as hand-loom weavers' children were turned almost automatically into hand-loom weavers, the fallings out of the older generation would not help the younger; but at some time in the early railway age—a time different no doubt for every district and almost every family—this automatic output stopped. The weavers' resistance was broken; the children went from the crowded cottages and cellars into the mills, or perhaps into other trades. It was better so. Already in 1842, Chadwick was able to report that "one effect of the attention given to the condition of the workers in the factories has been, that ventilation has been extensively introduced, and with marked effects on the condition of the workpeople."[1] He could compare the mills favourably, from the point of view of health, with many workshops and innumerable "homes."

The framework knitters, whose situation resembled in many ways that of the hand-loom weavers, had not the advantage of the factory, its ventilation, and its laws. By 1844-5, power knitting was established in Philadelphia and experiments had been made in Manchester and Loughborough[2]; but the problems of the industry were still those of an outwork trade, and the outrageously low wages seemed likely to keep them so. It was a relatively small, and a highly localised, industry. The reputed 30,000 working frames of 1812, and 33,000 of 1832, had grown only to 48,482 frames in 1844, a carefully ascertained figure which included—for the first time—the silk frames[3]. Of the 48,482, nearly 21,000 were in Leicestershire, 16,400 in Notts., nearly 7000 in Derbyshire and 2000 to 3000 in Scotland. The knitter's wages—piece rates—had fallen, without any competition from power and without any appreciable improvement in the efficiency of the frame, by about 35 per cent. in the thirty years preceding the inquiry of 1844, *i.e.* since the peak year of war wages. Contrast the bricklayer, the compositor, the iron-moulder or the woman throstle-spinner, whose standard rates in the 'forties were in no case much below, and occasionally not at all below, the highest rates recorded for the century. Like the weavers, the knitters clung to their trade.

[1] *Report on Sanitary Condition*, p. 107.
[2] *Report of the Commissioner* (R. M. Muggeridge) *appointed to inquire into the Condition of the Framework Knitters*, 1845, p. 6.
[3] *Report*, p. 2-3. Above, p. 182.

Like the weavers before the power-loom began to tell, their poverty forced them to bring up their children in it. They suffered, like the lower grade weavers, from the ease with which the work was learnt and the competition of half-skilled labour. An evil special to the knitting business—the renting out of frames by all sorts of petty capitalists as well as by true hosiers[1] —facilitated this. A novice, generally a woman or a child, could be induced to offer as high a frame rent as an expert, and was perhaps a more amenable frame tenant. Meanwhile, long breeches were shortening hose and—except in so far as a growing population provided fresh ankles to cover—were curtailing the demand for knitters' labour. Hence all the signs of an essentially unwholesome situation throughout the 'thirties and 'forties—dwellings going from bad to worse; much pawning of household stuff; avoidance of places of worship, often for lack of decent clothes; a febrile reading of the crudest revolutionary literature by a class quite unfit for revolution, whose physique was "much below the average of even the manufacturing districts of the North."[2]

All trades were subject to recurrent unemployment or smaller employment; though, of the greater trades, only hand-loom weaving—and not all sections of that—had a large and permanently redundant working force for many years. It was from the weavers that the *Northern Star* drew its illustrations when first, in 1838[3], it formulated in so many words the "Marxian" doctrine of the reserve army of labour, used by employers to beat down the pay of the regular troops. There was an element of truth in the metaphor for nearly every craft and calling; though, in spite of Marxian dogmatics, the reserve was not strong enough to do all the evil which was credited to it. Threatening many crafts of low skill stood those reserves of rural labour, only just emerging from the "redundancy" of unreformed poor law conditions, which had not yet been enrolled in railway or other work, together with the terrible hungry reserve of the poor Irish. Yet, even in weaving, the reserve—no metaphor there, but a great army of patient citizens with their regimental badge of sufferance—did not prevent the slow rise in power-loom weavers' wages.

No figures exist from which could be calculated for any trade, still less for all, what average deduction should be made from

---

[1] *Report*, p. 58, and above, p. 182.   [2] *Report*, p. 7–8.
[3] June 23, 1838. See Dolléans, *op. cit.* I. 190.

weekly or other standard earnings to arrive at yearly income. For particular groups of hand-loom weavers, such as those of Ashton-under-Lyne already quoted, the thing may be done, but as a rule only for the period covered by the extraordinarily full inquiry of 1838–41. Some very rough estimates of "normal" amounts of unemployment in such seasonal trades as painting can be found[1]. For one trade, whose importance was growing every year, that of coal-mining, a number of records of daily or weekly earnings, and certain calculations of the number of days worked per week, allow some approach to exactness in estimation; but the difficulty of interpreting miners' earnings, even with the full statistical apparatus of the twentieth century, imposes caution on the historian of the early nineteenth. Yet these earnings deserve attention, both because of the weight which mining had now acquired in the industrial balance of the country, and because of their extraordinary sensitiveness—in a steam-ruled world—to trade fluctuations[2].

Twenty years earlier, coal-mining had not been a trade of the first rank, judged by size; but by 1851 there were over 150,000 adult male colliers in Great Britain, with whom there worked 65,000 lads and young men under 20. The women and girls had been ordered out of the pits: presumably the 2650 female "coal-miners," under and over twenty years of age, reported in 1851, were "pit brow lasses" of the type which established itself in Lancashire[3].

In the 'nineties of the eighteenth century a Northumberland miner (according to Eden) made 2s. 6d. to 3s. a day, and a Scottish miner made about 3s. The latter got, or took, on an average four or five days' work a week. (Modern statistics of mine-working also suggest that $4\frac{1}{2}$ might be a safe multiplier with which to turn daily into typical weekly wages, for the late eighteenth, and early nineteenth, century[4].) A Scottish miner in the 'twenties averaged 4s. 2d. a day—making only 3s. 3d. in 1821 but 5s. 3d. in 1825, 5s. in 1826 and 4s. 3d. in 1827–30, an illustration of the close association already established

---

[1] Above, p. 165.
[2] They are in Bowley, *op. cit.* ch. XIII, with a discussion of the many difficulties in interpretation.
[3] *Census of 1851, Occupations,* I. xcvii.
[4] The average miner worked 4·54 days in the week ending June 27, 1925. An average of $4\frac{1}{2}$ days is suggested in Symons, J. C., *Arts and Artisans at Home and Abroad* (1839) for the period 1810–39. Bowley, *op. cit.* p. 14, 101.

between miners' wages and trade fluctuations[1]. The Scottish average for the 'thirties was something like 4s.—steady about 4s. 1831–5; rising to 5s. in 1837; falling to 3s. 6d. in 1839. On this curve can be placed, without much risk, figures from other districts—15s. to 20s. a week (3s. 4d. to 4s. 5d. a day) for Northumberland in 1834; an average of 4s. 3d. for the decade in Staffordshire (no doubt with a peak of over 5s. in 1837 and then a fall); 3s. 9d. a day for Durham in 1839. A reputed 25s. a week for Lancashire in 1839 sounds high; but the authority is good and it cannot be lightly rejected[2].

The 'forties were a bad time for coal-miners. During the early years of slack trade wages ran on, apparently, at or about the low 1839 level. The Ayrshire wage for 1840–5 kept near 3s. 6d. The Staffordshire wage in 1844 is 3s. 6d.; the Northumberland wage 1843–6 is given as 3s. to 4s.; the Durham wage in 1846 as 3s. 9d. An estimate made some years later puts the Yorkshire average at 3s. 6d. all the way from 1844 to 1853. The Staffordshire figures suggest most satisfactorily the curve of the 'forties, as the Scottish figures did that of the 'thirties —1844, 3s. 6d.; 1847, 5s.; 1848, 4s.; 1849, 3s. 6d. Figures from other districts confirm the low level at the close of the decade —Northumberland 1849, 3s. 6d.; Durham 1846, 3s. 9d.; South Wales 1849, 3s.; Lancashire 1849, 20s. a week as against the 25s. of ten years earlier. Putting all available colliers' wages together, the result is a fall of just over 3 per cent. between 1840 and 1850[3]. The cost of living, however, had fallen very much more than that—perhaps 30 per cent.—between these particular years.

The Handloom Weavers' Commission, when reporting in 1841 on possible remedies for weavers' distress, assigned a high place among those remedies to the repeal, or at least the fundamental revision, of the corn law. It was to "increase the exportation of the products of our own looms and to cheapen and improve the commodities which are consumed by our

---

[1] These Scottish miners also got a free house—of a sort—and free coal. So did some others.

[2] Chadwick, J., in S.J. XXIII. 1 sqq. (1860). It may perhaps include some of the allowances which for other districts are additional to the daily wage, e.g. a Scottish wage of 4s. 6d. a day in 1838 was reckoned by Symons to be worth 22s. 7d. a week with the allowances.

[3] Bowley, op. cit. p. 109, and in E.J. 1898, p. 482.

labouring population."[1] Repeal, or the low fixed duty, taken alone could have done little to cure the special ills of the weaving trade; but repeal following upon the revision of the tariff on meat, butter, cheese and other foodstuffs, between 1841 and 1846, and coinciding with the rapid extension of the railways in Great Britain and abroad, had produced—though only after 1848—those low cost of living figures, for the "labouring population" as a whole, with which the early railway age closed[2].

Before the advent of Peel there had been no close and regular connection between costs of living and Acts of parliament. The beer duty had been repealed in 1830 at a cost of £3,000,000 to the exchequer[3]. Since the duty was paid almost entirely by the "labouring people"—it worked out at 165 per cent. *ad valorem* on strong beer as against a duty of 28 per cent. *ad valorem* on claret—its repeal was, as designed, a gift of something like £1 a year to the average labouring household. There were the drawbacks noted by Sydney Smith—"everybody is drunk. Those who are not singing are sprawling. The sovereign people are in a beastly state"[4]—but £1 a year was no mean sum, even if it were all spent in more beer. With the £3,000,000 should be put a great part of the £500,000 from the excise on candles which Althorp sacrificed in 1831[5]; some little thing, too, from the reductions in the duties on sea-borne coal and from the abolition, also in 1831, of the excises on starch and tiles. What the Whigs were able to do with the paper and tea duties can hardly have swayed the balance of any labouring budget[6]; and the really cheap corn of 1832–6, which did, came by Act of God not by that of the King's advisers.

Wheat was not quite so cheap in the good years of the 'forties (1842–6) as it had been under William IV, yet costs of living were perceptibly lower. For, from 1842 onwards, Peel had first abolished all prohibitions on the entry of foodstuffs—when he came into power, cattle, sheep and swine, pork, mutton and beef, with foreign caught fish were all prohibited—and had then cut at the duties on these and other imported foods. He had touched, but barely touched, sugar, and had reduced or

---

[1] *Report*, p. 51.   [2] See the diagram on p. 128 above.
[3] Smart, *Economic Annals*, II. 537 *sqq.* The Act is 10 Geo. IV, c. 64; it had to be amended by 4 & 5 Wm. IV, c. 85. Buxton, S., *Finance and Politics*, II. 277.
[4] *Life and Correspondence*, p. 203.
[5] Buxton, *op. cit.* I. 34 n.   [6] See *Ibid.* I. 36, 39.

abolished the duties on butter and cheese and on the raw materials of clothes[1]. Railways and invention meanwhile were cheapening the clothes themselves and the fuel which rendered inferior ones more tolerable.

Driven high by the famine which, in John Bright's words, "came to the aid" of the corn law repealers, the cost of living fell precipitately after the great break in corn prices which led in the commercial crisis of 1847. Even in 1848 the figure was lower, just lower, than it had been during the happiest year of the previous decade (1835), and then came the swift closing fall to a point below anything known since before 1780. For every class of urban or industrial labour about which information is available, except—a grave exception—such dying trades as common hand-loom cotton weaving, wages had risen markedly during the intervening sixty years. For fortunate classes, such as the London bricklayers or compositors,

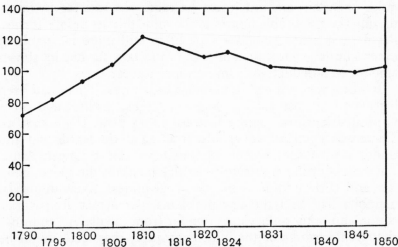

1790–1850, *The general course of industrial wages* (after Wood, *Econ. Journ.* 1899). The curve is based on figures from twenty-four towns or coalfields and over thirty industries. The wages of 1840 are taken as 100. Compare the cost of living Index in the diagram on p. 128, and see Appendix.

they had risen more than 50 per cent., and for urban and industrial workers in the mass, fortunate and unfortunate, perhaps about 40 per cent.[2] The situation in 1849–50 was relatively good; but if wages and costs of living are compared not for

[1] Above, p. 496 *sqq.*

[2] The general curve gives a rise of just over 40 per cent. (72 to 102) 1790–1850; but there are statistical difficulties, which prevent its being taken as an exact index of the course of events. See p. 549, above.

those years, but for the bad years 1838-41 and 1847, the picture is different. It was by no accident of popular psychology that Chartism was most militant and most dangerous to the established order in its earliest years. Nor was its perfect collapse after 1848 all due to the poltroonery of Feargus O'Connor and the competence of the Duke and his special constables.

Indices of wages and costs of living are always open to the criticism that retail prices, as paid by wage-earners, do not readily follow the movements of the wholesale prices upon which—until very recent years—all official and semi-official calculations have had to be based. Retail trade in the early nineteenth century was sluggish and often corrupt; but there is no proof that these defects had increased since the late eighteenth century. Probably the urban wage-earner suffered at both ends, the wartime price-rise being passed on to him quickly and subsequent price-falls slowly. Some allowance, of quite uncertain amount, must be made for this lag in interpreting the favourable figures of the mid-'thirties or late 'forties. Payment in truck provides a problem still more incapable of exact solution. How general was it and how far did its abuses amount to a deduction from nominal wages?

It was a very old evil in outwork industries. There had been legislation against paying wages in "pins, girdles, and other unprofitable wares" under Edward IV (4 Edw. IV, c. 1, s. 5). There was a general Act against truck in all the textile and iron trades, and a special Act for woollens, under Queen Anne. Later Acts of the eighteenth century mention the glove, boot, lace and cutlery trades—and also coal-mines[1]. New industrial methods had brought new problems. Coal-pits, iron-works, cotton and other mills were often far from towns. A "tommy" shop at the works or the mill, if properly managed, might be most useful. The shortage of cash and small-change during the wars might make wage-payment in goods at least convenient. Canal and railway building often depended on some sort of "colonial" organisation, as witnesses called it in the 'forties. But it was illegal—though the law could be circumvented. The old laws had been reinforced at the end of George III's reign, and at the start of the railway age by 1 & 2 Wm. IV, c. 37[2].

[1] 1 Anne, st. ii, c. 18, and 10 Anne, c. 26. See Levi, *History of British Commerce*, p. 194, for these and later Acts.

[2] See Unwin, *Samuel Oldknow and the Arkwrights*, p. 181. Ashton, *Iron and Steel in the Industrial Revolution*, p. 189. Hammond, *The Town Labourer* (with valuable H. O. matter for the period before 1830), p. 41, 65, 70. *The Skilled Labourer*, p. 161, 163. For canals and railways, above, p. 409-10.

There is no evidence of truck as a custom in the building trades or in the new engineering trades. A witness familiar with the system stated this explicitly in 1842[1]. A single bad instance of a Lancashire printer paying his men entirely in truck throws into relief the general absence of evidence for the system in what may be called the London type of skilled crafts[2]; though, at the very bottom of London industry, gross instances of criminal abuse were to be found in such sweaters' dens as those described by Charles Kingsley in *Alton Locke*. In the Sheffield trades the system had been very common, but was hit by the Act of 1831 and was dying slowly. There was still enough of it to elicit a warning to law-breakers from the Master Cutler in 1843[3]. On the railway works, as has been seen, it was both used and abused; but the best contractors discouraged it[4]. In the coal and iron industries of the 'thirties and 'forties it was still widespread, but what proportion of the workers it affected, and how adversely, is not clear. Some of the very largest concerns did not practise it. Among others, Mr Baldwin of Bilston refrained "from the systematic infractions of the law" so common among his neighbours; and the colliers on Lord Ward's estates were all paid in cash exclusively[5]. It was worse among the small coal exploiters and the "butties" of Staffordshire than in the larger collieries, and much worse in Staffordshire than in Northumberland and Durham[6]. It is recorded from collieries at Barnsley and at Bradford and, very extensively, from coal and iron works in North and South Wales, Monmouth, Lanarkshire and Scotland generally. In Merthyr itself it was not practised[7]. But, even in 1852, it was found "in twelve out of the seventeen principal iron and coal works on the hills of Monmouth and Glamorgan": the Aberdare works, under new management, had just started it[8].

Among the textile trades, the wretched framework knitters

---

[1] *S. C. on Payment of Wages*, 1842 (IX. 125), Q. 1239. Isolated cases might occur in any trade. [Mr R. W. Postgate, author of *The Builders' History* also believes that it was unknown in the building trade.]   [2] *Ibid.* Q. 1713.

[3] Lloyd, G. I. H., *The Cutlery Trades*, p. 217.   [4] Above, p. 409–10.

[5] *S. C. on Payment of Wages*, Q. 2666–7, 2713. *Report on Midland Mining* (1843), p. lxxxvi. Ant. Hill of Merthyr paid his 1500 men in gold and notes in 1833. *S. C. on Commerce and Industry*, Q. 10265.

[6] *Midland Mining*, p. ciii.

[7] *S. C. on Payment of Wages*, Q. 3306 *sqq.* (Barnsley), 190 *sqq.* (Bradford), 1524 *sqq.* (Monmouth), 1781, 2328 (S. Wales), 1467, 1668, 3399, 3448 (Scotland).

[8] *Report on the Operation of 5 and 6 Vict.* c. 99 [the coal-mines Act], 1852 (XXI. 425), p. 11–12.

probably suffered most from truck, as they always had. After
the law of 1831 it became the speciality of the middlemen and
"bagmen," just as in the nailing districts, when in bad times
decent employers could not buy, second-rate "foggers"
(factors) bought from the nailers for truck[1]. The connection
of the system with bad trade is well shown in the Yorkshire
worsted districts. There the big employers rarely practised it,
but smaller men, struggling with the depression of 1838-41
and chronically short of cash, tried to snatch the profits of
grocers' shopkeeping to balance the loss on manufacturing, or
paid their men in unsaleable worsteds[2].

In Lancashire some large, and many smaller, concerns broke
the law in one way or another in 1842, although Manchester
itself was fairly free of these breaches. So was Staleybridge.
In smaller places, just as at Bradford, bad trade had driven
manufacturers short of capital and credit to save themselves
at the expense of their workpeople, generally weavers—"to
hold the business together," as they would have said, not
altogether without justification[3]. There, as also in Staffordshire,
onlookers who cared for the poor believed that they could see
a definite loss in real wages arising from the system. McDouall,
the young Chartist doctor from Ramsbottom near Bury, said
that the difference between the workers at the Ashtons' mills,
where there was no truck, and the Grants' mills, where it
was very bad indeed, was obvious[4]. The Ashtons' people saved
and some owned their houses. He knew one worth £200 to
£300. There was none of this among the Grants' people. From
Wolverhampton, the Rev. H. Pountney drew a similar contrast between the colliers at Lord Ward's pits and those at the
neighbouring Parkside collieries[5]. A Barnsley miner said he
would rather have 17s. cash than 20s. in truck or "tommy,"
and a Monmouthshire collier went down to 15s. on a similar
calculation[6]. If the system—where practised and abused—

---

[1] *S. C. on Framework Knitters Petitions*, 1812, p. 6. *Comm. on Framework
Knitters*, 1845, p. 14, 72. *Payment of Wages* (nailers), Q. 1076 *sqq.*

[2] *S. C. on Payment of Wages*, Q. 5, 74 *sqq.* One man, with an annual wage-
bill of £4500 to £5000 said he could have got shopkeepers' profits of over £400,
but had refused to do it. Q. 612 *sqq.* Not much is heard of it in woollen.
Q. 290 (Batley)

[3] *Ibid.* Q. 946 (Manchester), 936 (Staleybridge, where however there were
abuses in connection with factory-tied houses), 1699 (Chorley), etc.

[4] *Ibid.* Q. 2052 *sqq.*   [5] *Ibid.* Q. 2173.

Ibid. Q. 3156 (Barnsley), 2290 (Monmouth).

meant only a loss of 2s. or 1s. in the pound, that would suffice amply to substantiate Pountney and McDouall's conclusions. But whether the system was abused over 5, 7½, or 10 per cent. of the British industrial field in the 'forties there is no means of determining[1].

All estimates of the welfare of the "labouring population" —industrial or agricultural—which are based only upon the earnings of the principal bread-winner are defective. But except for a few small and specially unhappy sections of the people, such as the hand-loom weavers, family earnings in the early railway age are necessarily conjectural. How early the child began to help in industries carried on at home, either as handicraft or outwork, or to earn wages from a master, is notorious. Whether the factories had lowered that age is doubtful. Factory-owning witnesses before the committee of 1816 had maintained that work began as early, and went on as long, in domestic weaving as in the mills, and that it was more laborious[2]. Nothing that is known of eighteenth-century conditions tends to invalidate at least the first contention. Out of forty-five statements as to the age at which the witness had begun regular work, or had known regular work to have begun, made before the 1832 committee on Sadler's Factory Bill[3], one said five, one "five and upwards," nine said six, twelve said seven, five said eight, five nine, seven ten, and the rest higher ages. Ten years later, the Report on the mines found five years not uncommon in Yorkshire, Lancashire, Cheshire, Derbyshire and South Wales; five and six commoner in Eastern Scotland "than in any part of England"[4]; seven or eight perhaps the representative age; and higher ages normal in a few areas such as North Staffordshire, Leicestershire, parts of Northumberland and Durham and the West of Scotland. In tin, copper, lead and zinc mining very few children under twelve went underground, and not many young people under eighteen. In 1843, the Report on child labour in the industries other than textiles and mining explained that "in general regular employment commences between seven and eight," adding that "in all cases the persons that employ mere infants and very young children are

---

[1] The minimum and maximum percentages are simply my own impressions of possibilities. I incline to a low figure for what may be called abusive truck, though most of the truck seems to have been abusive.

[2] S. C. on Children employed in...Manufactures, p. 203, 237.

[3] Report, 1832 (xv).   [4] Report, p. 18.

the parents themselves."[1] The earliest employment of all was
met with in the (domestic) machine lace trade. Here was a
recorded case of a child at work, for its mother, before it was
two, and of a four-year-old, in the same family, doing her twelve
hours a day. So it had been in the Yorkshire woollen industry
under George I: "hardly anything above four years old is
insufficient to itself. That is the reason also why we saw so few
people without doors," as Defoe wrote with frank delight[2].
The four-year-olds were doing their day's work in the staple
English "light" industry of that time.

It is probable, therefore, that when the Tory Factory Act
of 1819 (59 Geo. III, c. 66) decided that children should not
go to cotton mills before they were nine, and the Whig Act
of 1833 (3 & 4 Wm. IV, c. 103) forbade the employment of
children under nine in any textile mill, except a silk mill,
parliament was not just timidly remedying a textile abuse, but
was raising the age of entry into the mills a little above the
normal and traditional working age for the "labouring poor"
in the country as a whole—and so slightly limiting potential
family earnings—although there had been trades and districts
where, for lack of opportunity, very young children, and especially young girls, had not ordinarily been put to work. In the
Newcastle of 1816, where there were no textile and few light
trades, regular work rarely began before twelve or fourteen;
and the late entry into tin, copper, lead and zinc mining
allowed "a large majority" of the children to go to school
"commonly during some years."[3]

Typical industrial towns such as Manchester or Leeds provided opportunities for relatively considerable family earnings.
But whether the representative parent of the mill child was a
spinner, or other reasonably well-paid textile operative, or one
of the new engineers or, on the other hand, a despairing hand-
loom weaver or irregularly working Irish labourer, there is
no means of determining. Descriptions of life in the textile
towns of the 'thirties and 'forties suggest that the relatively
considerable family earnings were exceptional; but it must not
be forgotten that there were weavers, both hand and power,
and tradesmen of many other sorts, well above the despairing
class, and that a few shillings a week from the children, added
to the 15s. to 20s. and upwards of such workers, would build

---

[1] *Report*, p. 195.   [2] *Tour*, III. 101.
[3] *Report of* 1816, p. 24. *Report of* 1843, p. 203.

up a family income, certainly not adequate for the good life, yet not too hopelessly inadequate for life[1].

In the light metal, as well as in the textile, districts children found employment enough. "Many...of both sexes are engaged in almost every branch of manufacture"[2] in the Birmingham area. Women and girls were ousting men and boys from such jobs as stamping buttons and notching the heads of screws. The heavy ironmongery trades of the Wolverhampton district did not employ them—though boys went to these trades as early as to any other—but for making tin toys, nails and chains and screws, for washer-punching, and in the fast-growing japanning trade they were much used. "Since the machines have been introduced in the weaving and spinning mills, ten times as many girls come to work at nails and chains,"[3] a workman said to the Commissioners of 1843—an impressionist not a statistical estimate.

London provided less regular occupation for very young children than the manufacturing and agricultural districts. In the Census returns of 1851[4], at the close of the period, it admitted to only 155 errand boys and 58 serving girls—the largest groups in either sex—under ten years of age. On such a point the Census is liable to err, but the error is not likely to be greater in London than elsewhere. The cotton industry at the same date admitted to over 2000 boys and nearly 2000 girls under ten; woollen and worsted to nearly 3000 boys and over 2000 girls; lace—outside the factory law—to 2600 girls; and straw-plait—a small rural industry[5], also outside—to 2700 girls and 1500 boys. Factory restrictions hardly touched London; so, if there had been a tendency towards large-scale regular employment of the very young, it must have shown itself. Of irregular employment, the kind that does not appear on Census returns, there was no doubt plenty; begging, hawking and newspaper selling can be started early; but the children of the typical London wage-earners—whose wages, it will be recalled, were not of the lowest—stayed at home, or at school, until they approached, or reached, their 'teens. Then, it would seem, the "males" often took a spell as errand boys. London in 1851

---

[1] The evidence given below (p. 590) of the huge membership of Friendly Societies in the Lancashire of the 'forties suggests some margin of receipts over necessary expenditure in the typical family.

[2] *Report of* 1843, p. 16. [3] *Report*, p. 17.

[4] *Age and Occupation Returns*, as above.

[5] It employed 28,000 females and 3900 males.

had 10,500 errand boys between the ages of ten and fifteen. After that, if they had the good fortune to become tradesmen, they began to learn their trade. In 1851 there were in London 23,000 carpenters and joiners—the largest of the London crafts and a craft that had not changed perceptibly in character or traditions since 1830 or, for that matter, 1730—of whom only 270 were under fifteen, and 2000 were between fifteen and twenty[1]. There were 15,000 painters, plumbers and glaziers, of whom 200 were under fifteen and 1350 between fifteen and twenty. There were 10,000 printers—500 (the devils no doubt) under fifteen and 1800 between fifteen and twenty.

The number of town and country girls engaged in domestic service in London was extraordinary. Two figures suffice. The London of 1851 contained 115,000 "females," rich and poor, employed and unemployed, single and married, between fifteen and twenty. Of these 39,000 were paid domestic servants. How many more were unpaid in their own homes? From the same group, 10,000 were seamstresses or milliners; 1900 did laundry work; 1400 were tailoresses; 1100 were shoemakers and 1100 worked in the silk industry of the East End. About 9000 were scattered in small groups over all the other occupations of the capital—231 made straw hats and bonnets; 175 made umbrellas; and so on. The rest were school girls, homekeeping misses, or very young wives[2], who neither relieved their family of the cost of their keep, like the servant girls, nor paid cash into its weekly budget, like the seamstress girls and the silk workers.

The broad results of the Census of 1851—though not at all decisive—leave less room for the regular industrial work of married women, other than widows, in the nation as a whole, than some of the gloomier contemporary accounts of cotton mills and weavers' or nailers' cottages might suggest. Great Britain in 1851 contained 3,461,524 wives. Of these a round 2,631,000 entered themselves as wives of no specified occupation, 202,000 as the wives of farmers or graziers, 94,000 as the wives of shoemakers, 26,000 as butchers', 34,000 as innkeepers' or licensed victuallers', and 6000 as shopkeepers' wives. There were 795,590 widows of whom only 290,000 described themselves as of no specified occupation. The rest stated their

---

[1] The adults in such trades always included a large number of immigrants, who had learnt their trade in the country.

[2] Only about 3 per cent. of the London women between 15 and 20 were married.

occupations or trades. It seems unlikely therefore that many of the wives who went regularly out to work would omit to do so. It is quite likely, all things considered, that a considerable number of home-working weavers, tailoresses, nailmakers, stockingers, lacemakers and the like might get returned simply as wives[1]. It is very probable that a large number of women who did outwork of any kind intermittently in their homes might be so returned, with the wives who sometimes did a bit of charring; and there are innumerable grades between really intermittent outwork—such as that of some of the cottage glovers or straw plaiters—and work in the home which might be described as regular. The fact that the shoemakers' wives, and a few wives of shopkeepers, so described themselves suggests that they, like the farmers' butchers' and innkeepers' wives, were closely connected with the family trade—making a total of 362,000 so connected—and that, where no such description was given, no such connection existed. If most of the 2,631,000 mere wives were industrially unoccupied, or only carried on some by-employment subordinate to their domestic work, there remain, over and above the 361,000 in the five scheduled groups, some 500,000 wives who may have been regular workers in industry, trade, or agriculture. From this might have to be deducted any wives—there were probably not many—to be found among the 138,000 women returned as Independent Gentlewomen or Annuitants.

A closer examination of some of the greater women's industries bears out the general conclusion. There were certainly few mothers of families in the greatest of all, domestic service, which employed, in 1851, more than twice as many women and girls as all the chief textile industries put together[2]. "It is known by the returns, as well as from the evidence," Dr Mitchell wrote in a statistical appendix to the report of the Factory Commissioners of 1833, "that very few women work in the factories after marriage."[3] The carefully analysed returns of 1851 point in the same direction. Of 248,000 female cotton workers, 104,000 were under twenty years of age, of whom

---

[1] For the work of London tailors' wives, see above, p. 181.

[2] Domestic service, 905,000 + 128,000 farm servant girls: the chief textile industries (cotton, wool, flax, silk), about 500,000.

[3] 1834 (XIX. 261), p. 38. Note also the employers' resolution (1833, XX. 1123) "that any measure...limiting the labour of their children would compel the mothers of families to work in the mills." In hand-loom weaving families the wife almost always assisted.

67,000 were between fifteen and twenty; 51,000 were between twenty and twenty-five; 31,000 between twenty-five and thirty; 19,000 between thirty and thirty-five; and so on. The figures of a regular married woman's, or widow's, occupation—such as charwoman or washerwoman—are the exact reverse of these in character. They increase with each quinquennium up to forty or fifty. All the textile trades had a female age distribution similar to that of cotton; and so had the more domestic industries of lace making and straw plaiting. Evidently great numbers married between twenty and thirty-five and left their trades. Dr Mitchell, eighteen years earlier, said that most of them married before twenty-six, but many between twenty-six and thirty; "and even in the next five years a few."[1] In the great associated occupations of milliner, dressmaker and seamstress the fullest quinquennium was not fifteen to twenty, as in all the textiles, but twenty to twenty-five. The decline was slow to thirty and thereafter rapid. Dressmakers marry later than cotton operatives, and probably always did.

Before 1851, the most notorious, though very far from the most extensive and perhaps not the gravest, abuse of woman's labour in Britain, that in the coal mines, had been stopped. The women colliers, ten years earlier when the facts were revealed, cannot have been very many; and the married women colliers fewer still, though there were wives in the pits. The practice was local. No woman worked underground on the great Northumberland and Durham coalfield, and only a few at one old pit in Cumberland; none in Warwick, Stafford, Shropshire, Leicester or Derby; none in South Gloucestershire or North Somerset; none in North Wales, few in Western Scotland. The West Riding, Lancashire and the Eastern Scottish coalfields were the dark spots, though women went down the pits in Cheshire and South Wales and, occasionally, in the Forest of Dean. Once underground, men and women did almost identical work, except that women hewers were rare. The most wretched accounts of overwork, nakedness, and promiscuity come from parts of Lancashire and Eastern Scotland[2]. The old ripe capitalism of Tyneside was free of this

---

[1] *Loc. cit.* Note that, in 1851, only 59 per cent. of all the women in the country between 25 and 30 were wives or widows. [In 1921, 23 per cent. of female textile workers in England and Wales were married (Women in Industry, Cmd. 3508, 1930). The percentage was no doubt higher in 1851; but the general argument of the text holds.]   [2] *Report of* 1842, p. 24, 35 and *passim*.

monstrous growth, or rather inheritance from an age when such things were not looked into or caused no disgust.

When the Commissioners on Children's Employment of 1842–3 made their inquiry into the miscellaneous industries of the country, the industries which were neither mines nor "factories," as then defined by the law, they were much impressed by the vitality of apprenticeship—and by its abuses. In mines and textile mills there was no formal indenture or semi-legal subordination, though the "little piecer" or the mining lad was, in a sense, bound to his trade and was learning it under authority; but "in by far the majority of the [miscellaneous] Trades and Manufactures" apprenticeship was the rule[1]. Some children were bound apprentice legally, and for the old seven years, either before the Justices or by the Guardians of the Poor; "but the greater number are bound without any prescribed legal forms, and are required to serve their masters until the age of twenty-one, though the term of their apprenticeship may commence at the age of seven, and though there may be nothing in the manufacture deserving the name of skill to be acquired."[2] In London a large proportion of the working children were apprenticed, at fourteen in the city, at from twelve to fourteen in "the parishes." Pauper apprentices were generally bound, if boys, to shoemakers or tailors—trades in which there were plenty of small working masters to take them—if girls, to domestic service or dressmaking. In Birmingham also apprenticeship was general, but the 'prentice usually lived at home, not with his master. In the Wolverhampton area a debased form of the old residential apprenticeship prevailed. Children were more often bound illegally, by some attorney, than legally by Justices or Guardians. If bound very young they ran errands or did "dirty or household jobs" at first. Should the master die the 'prentice was treated as "part of his goods and chattels." "Whoever...may carry on the trade he is the servant of such person or persons" until his time was up, which was never before twenty-one[3].

In Sheffield boys were bound both to masters and to the half independent journeymen of the cutlery trades. "In most

[1] *Report of* 1843, p. 26.   [2] *Ibid.*

[3] P. 27. At Willenhall "sometimes a small master gets 6 or 7 and never employs a journeyman" (p. 28). [The carrying on of apprenticeship as a liability on the master's estate was part of the old law and practice, not a novel abuse.]

cases the apprentice...boards and lodges with his journeyman master." Given at first a few pence a week, at fifteen or sixteen he received a few shillings. He always served up to twenty-one. In the Potteries children were apprenticed to the better sections of the trade—usually by unstamped, and so illegal, indentures—and served from thirteen or fourteen to twenty-one. The glass industry in London, Birmingham and elsewhere, took regular "outdoor" apprentices; but in lace and hosiery and calico-printing no regular apprenticeship was found. Into the young engineering industry the commissioners did not particularly inquire[1]. The upshot of these inquiries is that personal (as opposed to factory) apprenticeship still usually accompanied handicraft and the small concern; that since the relation of 'prentice and master was now unregulated, by state municipality or gild, all the abuses with which centuries of regulation had dealt were cropping up again; that the system survived easily, or developed naturally and wholesomely, in crafts where high skill is essential, such as glass-working and all the best of the London crafts; and that the hands of the poor law authorities were not yet clean. In England they still too often apprenticed their wards as domestic drudges; from Scotland (Falkirk) is reported an abuse of the kind which had stirred Peel and Owen forty years earlier—Edinburgh pauper children bound to the proprietor of a big nailworks, and "put to most exhausting labour" from the ages of six and seven[2].

Until Lord Ashley utilised the disgust aroused by the mines report of 1842 to push through the Act which ordered women above ground (5 & 6 Vict. c. 99), the law had paid no sort of attention to the place, duration, or conditions of woman's work as such. Whatever their implications, or the desires of some of their supporters, factory acts down to the 'forties had been concerned, and often defended on the ground that they were only concerned, with parish apprentices, young children, or, latterly, "young persons." So far back as 1815, the elder Peel had suggested a ten-year-old limit and a ten hours' day for cotton factory children. From that time forward, the ten hour day had grown gradually into an ideal among the operatives of the North—ten hours for children, for women, and perhaps for men. There is a faint ten hours' agitation traceable in the

[1] *Report of* 1843, Sheffield, p. 29; the Potters' and Glass, p. 30–1; Lace, etc., p. 31.　　[2] *Report*, p. 30.

cotton towns from about 1825, at a time when "any meddling with the subject was unpopular, even amongst the masses," as one who was later to lead in the movement admitted[1]. But it was during the democratic ferment of 1830 that the organised ten hours' agitation began, in Yorkshire. The letter to the *Leeds Mercury* of September 29 from Richard Oastler, the Tory Churchman and land-agent, which marks its beginning, refers only to the "thousands of little children, both male and female, *but principally female*,"[2] who were being overdriven in the worsted mills. The banners under which working people marched their forty and fifty miles to York, eighteen months later, to demand a county meeting on the factory bill, bore such inscriptions as "For God and our Children." Choirs of ragged children only, if the narratives of the movement's early days are to be trusted, sang their factory song:

> We will have the Ten Hours Bill
> That we will—that we will.

Not until 1841 did the limitation of the hours of grown women take a place in the official programmes of the Ten Hours' party. Yet general limitation and its advantages, real ·or supposed, had been in the leaders' minds throughout[3].

Resolutions passed in the first year of the movement show this—for example: "that a restrictive Act would tend materially to equalise and extend labour, by calling into employment many male adults who...spend their time in idleness, whilst female children are compelled to labour from twelve to sixteen hours a day."[4] In 1833 it is being suggested that "adults in factories must by unions...make a Short Time Bill for themselves,"[5] and masters are explaining to the Factory Commissioners that the driving forces behind the movement are the desire to get twelve hours' pay for ten hours' work, and the hope of absorb-

---

[1] Philip Grant quoted in Hutchins and Harrison, *A History of Factory Legislation*, p. 44. The spinners and other male workers, it is to be remembered, were themselves employers of children as often as not. *Ibid.* p. 37.

[2] Quoted, among other places, in "Alfred" (S. Kydd), *The History of the Factory Movement* (1857), I. 100. The letter ends: "why should not children working in them [the worsted mills] be protected by legislative enactment, as well as those who work in cotton mills?"

[3] Alfred, *op. cit.* I. 237; II. 46. Hutchins and Harrison, *op. cit.* p. 65.

[4] Quoted in Hutchins and Harrison, *op. cit.* p. 48.

[5] Letter to Cobbett's *Weekly Register*, quoted in Hutchins and Harrison, *op. cit.* p. 56. Lord Althorp said almost the same thing to Fielden. Hammond, J. L. and B., *Lord Shaftesbury* (1923), p. 37.

ing men who are "hanging on the trade idle."[1] Next year
Oldham spinners are striking experimentally for an eight hour
day[2]. By 1837 the operatives' Short Time Committees are
prepared to *extend* young children's hours—shortened by the
Act of 1833—to ten, provided they can reduce every one else's
hours to the same figure[3].

The Act of 1833 (3 & 4 Wm. IV, c. 103) was the official
reply to the Ten Hours' bills promoted by Michael Thomas
Sadler and his parliamentary heir, Lord Ashley. It followed
on the report of the Select Committee of 1832, but was based
on the reports of the special Commissioners who, at the request
of the manufacturers and to the indignation of the Ten Hours'
party, were appointed to verify the facts of the situation, in
1833[4]. When the Act came fully into force, in 1836, no child,
under thirteen was to work more than nine hours in any day
or more than forty-eight in any week, except in silk mills,
where ten hours were permitted. No child under nine was to
work in any mill, except a silk mill. No one under eighteen
was to work at night, even in a silk mill. No young person
—between the ages of thirteen and eighteen—was to do more
than a twelve hour day or a sixty-nine hour week. The children
under thirteen were to have two hours' schooling a day, besides
their work. Four peripatetic inspectors were to see that the
Act was carried out. For this purpose they were given powers
equal to those of a Justice of the Peace.

The Commissioners explained that the inspectorate had been
recommended by "several eminent manufacturers,"[5] whose
names they did not give. These manufacturers had pressed for
resident inspectors, a policy to which the Commissioners' main
objection was that of cost. It is not to be forgotten that Yorkshire had its resident inspectors and searchers of woollen cloth
until 1821; that the statutory Worsted Committee for Yorkshire, Lancashire and Cheshire had three inspectors at this
very time; and that the better elements in the Manchester
cotton world had tried, and failed, to enforce previous laws

---

[1] *First Report* (1833, xx), p. 849.
[2] Webb, S. and B., *History of Trade Unionism* (ed. 1920), p. 151.
[3] Hutchins and Harrison, *op. cit.* p. 60.
[4] The *Reports* are in 1833, xx., xxi. and, a *Supplementary Report*, 1834,
xix. 261. For the views of the Ten Hours' party, Alfred, *op. cit.* ii. 33,
43, 47.
[5] *Report*, xx. 68.

by a committee of their own without inspectors[1]. The travelling inspectors made the new Act work, but their appointment was hardly such a novelty as has sometimes been suggested. Their regular reports to a Secretary of State, and the type of man chosen for the office, were the real administrative inventions[2].

One witness interviewed by the Commissioners of 1833 —Samuel Smith, Esq., of Leeds—begged them to widen their range and consider the collier lads, the milliners' apprentices, the shopkeepers' assistants and the school girls, particularly those at the schools called finishing schools, who, he suggested, were about as unwholesome as the factory children[3]. This they had no power to do. Seven years later, at Ashley's instigation, the Commission was appointed which drew up the reports on the labour of children and young persons in mines and manufactures; but milliners' work-rooms, shops, and school-rooms were neither, so had to wait. Meanwhile the factory act was beginning to operate, with many failures and no help from the Ten Hours' people in the North, who treated it as a shameful fraud. There were, in fact, grave difficulties in administering three different sets of hours, for children, young persons and adults, which suggested that a limitation-of-motive-power law, such as had often been talked about, was the most workable solution.

The report on the mines was only signed on April 21, 1842. On June 7 Ashley introduced his bill and, in spite of "such a display of selfishness frigidity to every human sentiment, such ready and happy self-delusion" in the Lords as he had "never seen,"[4] it was through both Houses—with some amendments inspired by the opposition under Lord Londonderry—before the end of July. "Whereas it is unfit that women and girls should be employed in any Mine or Colliery" are the opening words of 5 & 6 Vict. c. 99. The preamble runs on: "and it is expedient to make Regulations regarding the Employment of Boys in Mines and Collieries, and to make Provisions for the Safety of Persons working therein." Women are to come up, but may work at the pit-brow. Boys are not to go down before

---

[1] Above, p. 339, 343: for the Manchester Committee, *Report*, 1833, xx. 32—the attempt "has for some time been given up."

[2] Probably of Edwin Chadwick, who sat on the Commission.

[3] *Report*, xx. 577.

[4] Hodder, E., *The Life and Work of the Seventh Earl of Shaftesbury*, I. 431: quoted also in Hammond, *op. cit.* p. 80.

the age of ten. No one but a "Male of the Age of Fifteen Years and upwards" is to have charge of a winding engine. Wages are not to be paid to any mine worker whatsoever "at or within any Tavern, Public House, Beer Shop or other House of Entertainment," a clause of social expediency outside the range of the preamble. These various clauses, the mixed foundation of the subsequent mining code, were to be put in the keeping of inspectors—their number not specified—with the now well-established obligation to report to one of Her Majesty's Principal Secretaries of State.

On the report of 1843 no action was taken by government and none proposed. Two years later Ashley brought in a bill for dealing with one of the trades reported on, print-works and similar establishments. The similar establishments—bleaching dyeing and calendering—were cut out in the House, and the print-works bill became 8 & 9 Vict. c. 29. But in the year of the report, government, now regularly informed by its inspectors, had brought in a new factory bill, for the trades already regulated. The bill had to be withdrawn because of an injudicious educational clause which roused sectarian passions. Introduced again, with modifications, in 1844, it became law as 7 & 8 Vict. c. 15. During the debates the House had accepted a Ten Hours' motion from Ashley, and had gone back on it under the crack of the ministerial whip from Graham and Peel[1]. But the Act did many things for which factory reformers had worked. It provided for that fencing of machinery which the best employers had long since introduced and the inspectors desired to generalise[2]. It grouped women with young persons for all purposes of regulation. It established the half-time system for children, although it allowed them to begin their half-day's work at eight instead of nine. It took a step towards the establishment of a normal working day, by enacting that the legal mill day should begin when the first protected person came to work in the morning, and that all women and young persons should take their meals at the same time. In various ways it strengthened the hands of the inspectors.

[1] The episode occurs in most of the political biographies and in Hammond, *Shaftesbury*, p. 97.
[2] The mill at Deanston, which Smith the drainage-expert managed, and the Bannerman's mill at Aberdeen had their machinery well fenced in 1833. *Report of* 1833, xx. 16.

Encouraged by the growing friendliness of parliament, the Ten Hours' party kept at work. Ashley introduced a bill in January 1846 and the northern section started a newspaper. The bill of 1846, which passed from Ashley's keeping into that of John Fielden, the Todmorden Quaker cotton-spinner, who had worked ten hours a day in a mill at ten years of age[1], was rejected; but Fielden returned in 1847 and won, by 151 to 88 on the third reading in the Commons and even more easily, with the Bishops' aid, in the Lords. When the bill was introduced, the *Economist* wrote[2]: "the principle is precisely the same as that at issue in a Corn Law...only the particular class now to be benefitted...is professedly no longer the landlords but the factory workmen." When the bill passed, the *Economist's* leading article was headed "The Lords leagued with the Commons to prohibit Industry" and was filled with sneers at the clergy[3]. The employers—it was a bad year for trade, very bad—"believed it to be capable of proof, that the hours of factory labour cannot be reduced to ten per diem without risking and probably ensuring the entailment of this last and worst calamity ['no work at all'] upon the manufacturing operatives and all dependent on them." The Act came into force: the industry survived: cotton wages in the Manchester district were very nearly the same in 1849 as they had been in 1841[4] and the cost of living was 20 per cent. to 30 per cent. down.

In the year of the Ten Hours' bill, Ashley accepted the chairmanship of the Climbing Boys' Society to help save another group of ill-used children[5]. The Commons had, on the whole, meant well by the chimney sweeps. There had been legislation in their interest since 1788. Its failure illustrates perfectly the weakness of regulative law without the appropriate executive machinery, especially when that law applies to a small and scattered group. Attempts to prohibit the practice—the only certain cure—had failed in 1817–19. The House of Lords had thrown out the bills. A well-meant Act of 1834 (4 & 5 Will. IV, c. 35) had made the sending of a boy up a chimney on fire a misdemeanour; had prohibited apprentice-

---

[1] It was his father's mill. Alfred, *op. cit.* I. 330.
[2] February 13, 1847.   [3] May 22, 1847.
[4] Bowley, *Wages in the United Kingdom*, p. 119.
[5] See the full narratives in Hammond. J. L. and B., *The Town Labourer*, ch. IX, *Shaftesbury*, p. 218 *sqq.*

ship under ten; and had laid down rules for the construction of flues, which apparently no one obeyed[1]. These rules were re-incorporated in an Act of 1840 (3 & 4 Vict. c. 85) in the promotion of which Ashley had taken part. No person under twenty-one was to climb a chimney, which meant that no one was to climb anything but a wide factory chimney, and no boy under sixteen was to be apprenticed to a sweep. But a sweep might take an unapprenticed boy; there was no one to watch the domestic flues; and although the law was coming into force in London, and some other places, during the 'forties, Ashley's society had still a long fight ahead and Charles Kingsley wrote *The Water Babies* twenty-three years after the bill became law[2].

"The passing of the New Poor Law Amendment Act," the contemporary historian of the factory movement wrote in 1857, "did more to sour the hearts of the labouring population than did the privations consequent on all the actual poverty of the land. Rightly or wrongly...the labourers of England believed that the new poor law was a law to punish Poverty."[3] "And your petitioners are of opinion," ran a Chartist appeal to parliament of 1842, "that the Poor Law bastilles and the police stations, being co-existent have originated from the same cause, viz. the increased desire on the part of the irresponsible few to oppress and starve the many."[4] The law fell on the manufacturing districts of the North while fresh from the reputed betrayal of 1833, following close, in the opinion of the more politically minded, upon the darker betrayal of the Reform Bill. Every educated leader of the factory movement opposed it. Sadler, who died in 1835, had been an anti-Malthusian controversialist—he had suffered for it at the pen of young Mr Macaulay—and the law was as Malthusian as it dared be[5]. Oastler and "parson Bull of Bierley" thought that it was neither Christian nor constitutional, and said so with

[1] It is "An Act for the better Regulation of Chimney Sweepers and their Apprentices and for the safer Construction of Chimneys and Flues."

[2] The Census figures of 1851 fully support the literary evidence about London. The numbers and ages of chimney sweeps in all Great Britain and in London were:

	5–10	10–15	15–20	20–25
Great Britain	188	981	1009	1064
London	4	48	108	220

[3] Alfred, *op. cit.* II. 76.

[4] Quoted in Beer, *History of Socialism*, II. 132.

[5] Above, p. 350.

all the colour of popular oratory—"infidelity embodied in the accursed new Poor Law, is falsehood warring against truth; tyranny against justice; Satan against God."[1] John Fielden, who sat with Cobbett in the reformed parliament for Oldham, agreed with them. Cobbett had fought the bill in the House and, from his deathbed, in 1835, was bludgeoning "two-thousand-a-year LEWIS, penny-a-line CHADWICK and their crew," who were enforcing "this measure...intended to make the people of the midland and south of England live upon a COARSER SORT OF FOOD."[2] From Lancashire, in 1834–5, began to be heard the voice of Joseph Rayner Stephens, ejected Wesleyan minister and prophet of the people. Within a few years he was moving about the country. This is how the voice sounded at Newcastle in January 1838. "The people are not going to stand this, and I would say, that sooner than wife and husband, and father and son, should be sundered and dungeoned, and fed on 'skillee'—sooner than wife or daughter should wear the prison dress—sooner than that—Newcastle ought to be and should be—one blaze of fire with only one way to put it out, and that with the blood of all who supported this abominable measure."[3]

It is not unlikely, had the law been framed as the Poor Law Inquiry Commission originally recommended, or carried out exactly as the Executive Commissioners would have wished —that is with no outdoor relief to the able-bodied, or the least possible[4]—that blood would have been shed in the North, though perhaps not the blood of many friends of the "abominable measure," in spite of Stephens' hope that its enemies might get "every man...his firelock, his cutlass, his sword, his pair of pistols, or his pike, and every woman...her pair of scissors, and every child...its paper of pins and its box of needles."[5] Not enough had been spent on poor relief of any sort in the manufacturing districts of England; practically

[1] Oastler, in Alfred, *op. cit.* II. 76.
[2] *Political Register*, article dated Normandy, 10 June 1835. The article was dictated. He died on June 18. "Two-thousand-a-year LEWIS" is the Right Hon. T. F. Lewis, the senior Commissioner.
[3] Quoted in Gammage, R. G., *History of the Chartist Movement* (ed. 1894), p. 56.
[4] Above, p. 465.
[5] This version of the speech, in Gammage, *op. cit.* p. 57, reads more like popular oratory than that attributed to the *Northern Star* in Hovell, M., *The Chartist Movement* (1918), p. 80.

nothing for the able-bodied in those of Scotland. Only comparatively few people, hand-loom weavers, stockingers and such, had received any regular help in aid of earnings[1]. The position of the weavers was worsening in the 'thirties. The waves of trade were becoming steeper, the number of those affected by them greater, as export industrialism grew. A complete denial of temporary assistance to able-bodied, sick and aged, except under workhouse conditions, might have started that bloody revolution which Friedrich Engels still supposed to be inevitable, and very near, in 1845. Outdoor relief was, in fact, not completely denied, partly because of the way the law was framed, but partly because the industrial districts spoke their mind—their angry and rather superstitious mind—between 1836 and 1840.

Whilst the Commissioners were applying the new law to the rural districts, in 1834–5, crops were good—in 1835 magnificent—and food cheap. This greatly helped "depauperisation."[2] But when, in 1836–7, the industrial districts were taken in hand, trade was sagging, the cotton trade in particular, and living costs had got on to that upward slope which reached, in 1839, and kept, in 1840, a point higher than had been known—but for the single year 1825—since the bad post-war era ended in 1820. The Commissioners had to work amongst a people already roughly organised in protest against government[3]. In many of the huge, half-rural half-urban, parishes of Lancashire and the West Riding, cut up into "townships" and "chapelrys," and powdered over with mills mines and iron-works, as in many purely mining parishes of Northumberland or Durham, there had been a loose old-fashioned poor-law administration, without workhouse or central poor-house of any kind. Manchester had its "undeterrent" well-managed poor-house into which admission was "rather a matter of favour." Wigan had a house in which children were born to inmates. In the great well-disciplined house at Liverpool, where single men and women were severely separated, married inmates lived together[4]. So that, even where there was a

---

[1] E.g. only weavers got regular relief at Oldham. Report of 1834 (1834, xxviii), App. A, p. 918. See above, p. 364, for expenditure in manufacturing districts.

[2] Above, p. 466.

[3] Hovell, op. cit. p. 86, describes "the popular agitation" as "entirely without organisation"; but goes on to point out (p. 91) that committees sprang up, most of which "had already seen service in the Factory Act agitation."

[4] Report of 1834, App. A, xxviii. 914, 918, 922.

foundation for the principles of 1834, existing erections on it might have to be cleared away. It was not to be expected that Lancashire and Yorkshire men of that date, even if they belonged to classes favourably disposed towards the Act, would take orders readily from Somerset House. Their fathers had never been asked to take any. The Commissioners' work became very heavy in 1837–8.

At Huddersfield, Oastler's home town, the first guardians elected would not act; the second set was mobbed; not till Michaelmas 1838 did the law begin to work[1]. At Todmorden the Fieldens shut their mills to make the guardians resign. (For more than thirty years Todmorden Union had no workhouse.) There was heavy rioting in Bradford. To conciliate the factory area, the Commissioners modified their policy for thirty-one unions in Lancashire and the West Riding. Instead of issuing the famous order forbidding monetary relief "to any able-bodied male pauper who is in employment (the same not being parish work)"[2] or to his dependents, an order which had gone to all the rural unions of the South, they merely instructed the guardians to administer relief according to the Act of Elizabeth and "all other statutes relating to the relief of the poor." This left guardians free to do whatever had hitherto been done. When the Commissioners reported progress, at the end of 1839, they did not claim that the prohibition of allowances in aid of wages had been applied in Northumberland, Cumberland, Westmorland, Durham, Yorkshire or Lancashire[3]. In their eighth report (for 1841–2) they explained that there were still 132 unions, out of a total of 590, to which the general prohibitory order regulating outdoor relief had not been issued[4]. These included rural unions without sufficient workhouse accommodation, mainly in Wales; the metropolitan unions; and the unions in the manufacturing districts of Lancashire, Cheshire and the West Riding—a telling list. Even when relief actually in aid of wages was stopped, outdoor relief in general went on. Old habits, dread necessities, and easy compassion had beaten the Commissioners. In 1834, as one of them wrote—ungrammatically—"the extinction of out-door relief was reckoned upon, or at least was expected to be so far

---

[1] Nicholls, *History of the English Poor Law*, III. 250 *sqq.*, and Hovell, *op. cit.* ch. v. [Webb, S. and B., *English Poor Law History*, Part II (1929), chs. I and 2.]

[2] Nicholls, *op. cit.* III. 167.

[3] Nicholls, *op. cit.* III. 286.   [4] Nicholls, *op. cit.* III. 305–6.

reduced as to form the exception."[1] In the quarter ending Lady Day 1844, 231,000 people were relieved in the workhouses of England and Wales and 1,247,000 people outside them. For the corresponding quarter of 1848, the figures were 306,000 and 1,571,000[2].

Where the Commissioners had won they had won at a price, a price which they had calculated and faced. Nottingham was an urban area in which the refusal of outdoor relief had from the first been carried out with great determination[3]. It was a Mayor of Nottingham who wrote in 1840: "the painful and demoralising effect of refusing temporary relief, and offering the indoor test merely to get rid of the applicant, is but little known. At such times, the poor (*from dread of the House*) sell or pawn one article of clothing or furniture after another, until they have scarcely anything left...."[4] The "principle of less eligibility" was working as it was intended to work. By the later 'forties, the principle was working, less or more, almost everywhere, in spite of the failure to abolish outdoor relief. Whatever its economic merits, and however great the need for its application in pauperised rural districts, it was a permanent festering irritant in the towns.

It is fair to add that—in the then temper of the North— every act of the Commission was an irritant. Very early on, in 1834–5, they had learnt from most respectable cotton manufacturers that labouring families might with advantage be moved from the overcrowded country-side into developing industrial areas. One of their informants—Edmund Ashworth of Turton, near Bolton—told them that though Scots and Irishmen, with Northerners of all sorts, poured into Lancashire, he had himself met but one man from south of Trent[5]. The Commissioners sent a few, and then procured a full report on the past and on future prospects from Dr Kay[6], secretary of the Manchester Board of Health and one of their Assistants. Kay calculated the immigration into Lancashire for the decade 1821–31 at 17,000 a year. He had visited some of the first

---

[1] Nicholls, *op. cit.* II. 391.

[2] The increase was largely due to the influx of destitute Irish. The figures are quoted simply to illustrate the extent of the Commissioners' failure.

[3] Nicholls (*op. cit.* II. 328) praises it warmly.

[4] Roworth, W., *Observations on the administration of the Poor Law in Nottingham* (1840).

[5] Nicholls, *op. cit.* III. 215. [See Redford, A., *Labour Migrn. in Engd.* (1926), ch. VI.]   [6] Later Sir J. P. Kay-Shuttleworth.

arrivals from the South—"a more gratifying tour I never performed, as nothing could be more cheering than the gratitude
which the immigrants universally expressed for the change
which the Commissioners had accomplished in their condition."[1] Kay, although an official, was an unexceptionable
witness. The prospects seemed good. There was every reason
why a few more South-country folk should share the opportunities of Lancashire with the Irish. Some more were sent
—a few hundreds or thousands at most, drops in the flood of
migration into the cotton country[2].

Unfortunately for the Commissioners they published the
correspondence with Edmund Ashworth in their first annual
report. In one letter he had written that immigration "would
have a tendency to equalise wages, as well as prevent, in a
degree, some of the 'turns out' which have of late been so
prevalent." The anti-poor-law party fastened on the admission.
It was another of "the barbarities of such despots as the trio
of Somerset-house," this shipping of wretched paupers from
the South, to beat down wages and break "turns out" in
Lancashire, and then to fall into the misery they had helped
to make. Press and platform rang with it for years[3].

During these years, and before the Commissioners had even
begun to apply strict principles of out-relief to the factory area,
the anti-poor-law movement had merged in Chartism. Feargus
O'Connor, with a keen scent for unrest, had been sampling the
temper of the men under the "fast and grey" skies of North
England in 1836[4], before Joseph Sturge and the Birmingham
Reformers came into play or Lovett drafted the People's Charter
for the London Working Men's Association. O'Connor found
the skies of the North propitious, and his star was a *Northern
Star*. Right down to the collapse of Chartism, in 1848, the sky
of London was unfavourable. The Northern Chartists raged
against this soft metropolitan air. They had a simple, and doubtless correct, explanation. London working men "had more

---

[1] Quoted in Nicholls, III. 219.

[2] Which continued to come from adjacent areas, with Scotland and Ireland.

[3] See, among others, Alfred, *op. cit.* II. 69 *sqq.*, and the rhetorical Baxter,
G. R. W., *The Book of Bastilles* (1841). The phrase about barbarities is from
Baxter's preface, p. x. His huge volume is a compendium of newspaper extracts,
etc., for use against the Whigs, and contains many ugly facts not in Nicholls.
[Also numerous exaggerations and misstatements, as pointed out in Webb, S.
and B., *op. cit.* p. 162 *sqq.*]   [4] Hovell, *op. cit.* p. 93.

wages than the men of the North."[1] There were well paid men in the North too, but the Chartist mass was an army of misery, led by a group of sober idealists, prophets, quack prophets and demagogues, with just a sprinkling of genuine revolutionaries. The trade clubs and unions, as a whole, stood aloof; although a few, like the shoemakers, were thoroughly Chartist. When the Chartist leaders spoke of a general strike for the Charter—a Sacred Month, they called it, apparently with confused memories of the secession of the plebs to the sacred mount and the year of jubilee—there was no response from the unions; although members of clubs on strike might talk of holding out "until the Charter becomes the law of the land." Above all, the strongest and most skilled unions would never risk their funds in Chartist ventures[2]. The unfortunate and the unskilled, hand-loom weavers and framework knitters, tradesmen out of work with a few miners and other stout and rough fellows, were the typical adherents, the crowds at the mass meetings, the steady, and often deluded, purchasers of the *Northern Star*, the subscribers to the National Rent. Somehow, stockingers and weavers, who could not afford trade unions[3], found money for these things. Were they not to hasten the coming of the Charter? And was not the Charter to make the crooked straight and the rough places plain?

The course of the movement is for the social and political historian. The economist watches its flow and ebb with the vicissitudes of harvests, overseas trade, and railway building; with the changes in poor law policy; with the loss of faith in a comfortable man's parliament, and the partial recovery of faith by a people not naturally envious of good fortune or intolerant of government, when Peel—in spite of his bad record on factory legislation—began to convince some, who had doubted it, that those in power really had a care for the common man.

That trade depression of the late 'thirties and early 'forties, which furnished recruits to Chartism from all parts of industrial Britain, and delayed the full application of the amended poor

---

[1] Hovell, *op. cit.* p. 144, quoting the H. O. Papers.

[2] Webb, S. and B., *History of Trade Unionism* (ed. 1920), p. 175–8. Hovell, *op. cit.* p. 169. The strikers who spoke of holding out for the Charter only did so in 1842, when the movement was past its zenith, and then perhaps only as a rhetorical flourish. [For the strike policy see Plummer, A., "The Gen. Strike during one hundred Years," *E.J.* (*Ec. Hist.*), 1927, and Crook, W. H., *The General Strike* (Univ. of N. Carolina Press), 1931.] [3] Above, p. 211.

law in England, tried the old Scottish poor law and found it wanting[1]. Inherited unchanged from the sixteenth century, it was not applicable to Clydeside in the 'forties. The General Assembly of the Kirk had remarked in its Report for 1839 "that the situation of people destitute of employment was not to be overlooked, and that many cases might occur in which men of this class ought to obtain temporary relief in times of occasional sickness or unusual calamity, although not as a matter of right."[2] But such men got very little from the constituted authorities. In a time of grievous unemployment at Paisley, in 1819, these authorities, the heritors and Kirk session, had refused all assistance because the applicants were able-bodied; and this decision had been declared valid by the courts[3]. Between 1840 and 1843, distress in Paisley was again so grievous that a special relief committee had to be set up, which raised money both north and south of the Tweed. London sent £4715 in subscriptions and a poor law expert with a watching brief[4]. He reported that in 1841–2 Paisley itself had raised for the able-bodied—by assessment or subscription—£1227. 14s. 8d., and that from 10,000 to 13,000 people were, in that year, dependent on relief; over and above some 700 "legal" poor, who were relieved at a cost of £3682, about a normal expenditure for those described in the old Scots Law as "cruiked folk, sick folk, impotent folk, and weak folk."[5]

A Commission was appointed in January 1843 to make "a diligent and full inquiry" into the Scottish poor law system. There were those in Scotland who had long been pressing for reform[6], and Paisley provided the occasion. "The instances," the Commissioners stated in 1844, "in which...relief appears to have been afforded to able-bodied persons, on account of their inability to find employment, are of very rare occurrence."[7] Captain Miller of the Glasgow police had explained to them one normal result of this—"masons, bricklayers, slaters, etc.,

---

[1] Above, p. 365 *sqq.*

[2] Quoted in Nicholls, Sir G., *History of the Scotch Poor Law* (1856), p. 112.

[3] *Ibid.* p. 125. These were the days of the Paisley shawl, a most dangerous staple because so fashionable. It is supposed that in 1834 £1,000,000 worth were produced: then came a collapse. Blair, M., *The Paisley Shawl* (1904), p. 25.

[4] Edward Twisleton, Fellow of Balliol, an Assistant Poor Law Commissioner.

[5] *Poor Law Inquiry, Scotland,* 1844 (XIV–XX), XIV. iii. For the "legal" and "occasional" poor see above, p. 366.

[6] Such as Alison, W. P., professor of the institutes of medicine, at Edinburgh, *Remarks on the Poor Law of Scotland,* of which the fourth ed. appeared in 1844.

[7] *Report,* p. iii.

who...are frequently thrown idle in the winter season, are in some instances exposed to great privations, and have no means of obtaining relief except by public begging, to which they seldom or never resort...until every other resource has failed them."[1] Official, licensed and badged beggars, from among the "legal poor," were still found not only in the Highlands but in Perth and Kirkaldy. "Even without badges," such poor folk might be allowed to do one or two days' begging a week[2]. As the allowances to the impotent were "in general insufficient" —in Edinburgh the Town Council had for years "declined to increase the rate of assessment"[3]—begging, or worse, was essential. It was "steal or starve," said an Edinburgh minister, who asked whether this option promoted independence of character, the alleged merit of the system[4].

There was scarcely any provision for medical relief out of the poor funds. (Captain Miller mentioned that, in fever cases, the Glasgow Board of Health supplied, partially, and from private funds, soap and soda to wash the bed clothes of such as had any.) As the whole system was based on outdoor relief there was a great lack of poor law institutions. Glasgow still had nothing but the Town's Hospital. Edinburgh had three Charity Workhouses. At Perth "a house was taken by the managers in which three old women were lodged."[5] In the Barony Parish of Glasgow, "helpless paupers and children" were boarded out in four houses. In one there were sometimes eighteen children in two rooms of 14 ft. by 14 ft. In a second, fourteen inmates were well cared for in four rooms. Of one room in the third, the entry is—"maniac naked by the fire: old man ill in bed." In the fourth, "one room for males with two female idiots in it." Dundee having no poor-house, boarded out the bedridden paupers[6]. These, it will be borne in mind, were all the legal or "enrolled" poor. The "occasional poor," as the Commissioners noted, got little help anywhere.

The Commissioners were very conservative. They recommended the full recognition of medical and educational assistance as proper charges on the poor funds. They urged the establishment of more poor-houses. They were of opinion that the legal poor should receive adequate allowances. They favoured a reversion to the old practice—which had been

---

[1] *Report (Minutes of Evidence)*, Q. 5672 *sqq.*
[2] *Report*, p. xii.   [3] *Report*, p. xiv.
[4] *Report*, p. xiv.   [5] *Report*, p. x.   [6] *Report*, p. xxiii–iv.

"practically set aside"[1]—by which church collections might be used for the occasional poor. But, while noting the steady spread of assessment (rating), they were not in favour of making it compulsory. After "anxious inquiry" into relief for the able-bodied, they pointed out[2] that in the Lowland agricultural system, with its resident labourers, the problem was not pressing; that considering the Highland temperament, in the Highlands relief might be demoralising; that so long as the Scottish consumption of spirits per head was to the English as three to one, in the towns it would be dangerous. They preferred to rely on the existing law, improved, with voluntary contributions in times of emergency.

From all this Edward Twisleton, the poor law expert from South Britain, dissented because, as he asserted, it did not even insure comfort for the aged and infirm; because medical assistance was not made compulsory; because no "wards" or "houses of refuge" (casual wards, in English poor law terminology) were suggested for the able-bodied in the towns; because the building of poor-houses was not insisted on; and because there were no proposals for dealing with recurrent unemployment[3].

The resultant law (8 & 9 Vict. c. 83) cannot have satisfied Twisleton. It so far imitated the amended law of England as to create a Board of Supervision for the Relief of the Poor in Scotland—certain official members, and three members nominated by the Crown. The Board might sanction, but not as in England compel, unions of parishes for poor law work. In every burghal parish or combination of parishes, there was to be an elective board of managers of the poor. The rural boards were partly *ex officio*, partly elective, in parishes which had adopted assessment[4]; in parishes where there was no assessment the old authorities—heritors and Kirk session—became the board: they might adopt assessment with the consent of the Board of Supervision. So with poor-houses—parishes with populations above 5000 might build them if they wished; but there was no obligation. If a parish had a poor-house, it must have a properly qualified medical man to serve it. Whether it had a poor-house or not, it was bound to provide medical attendance and comforts for the sick poor "in such manner...

[1] *Report*, p. lii. [2] *Report*, p. xliv *sqq.*
[3] He signed a separate report.
[4] For these adoptions before 1830, see above, p. 367.

as may seem equitable and expedient." Parishes were encouraged to subscribe to infirmaries, dispensaries, and asylums. Every parish was to have its inspector or inspectors of the poor. Money from assessment might go to the "occasional poor" —"provided that nothing herein contained shall be held to confer a right to demand relief on able-bodied persons out of employment" (§ 68). Thus the initiative was left throughout with the parishes, as the Commission had desired, although a poor person who thought his relief inadequate might appeal to the Board of Supervision, and secure a decision that he had a just cause of action against his parish. The Act did, however, in various ways, make it easier than it had previously been for a person legally entitled to relief to secure it outside his own parish.

The law was set to work slowly and in face of grave difficulties. No centralised system for the relief of the poor could be applied at once and easily to the Lewis, Tweeddale, and industrial Glasgow. Failure of the potato crop in the Highlands and Western Isles in 1845–7 set a problem which a law framed for normal times could not hope to solve. Ireland poured casual labour into the Clyde. Medical relief was everywhere difficult to organise; in parts of the Highlands impossible. By 1848 only eight new poor-houses had been approved—not built; and the competent legal authorities had just advised the Board "that able-bodied persons accidentally or unavoidably thrown out of employment, and thereby reduced to immediate want, may be regarded as occasional poor to whom temporary relief may lawfully be given...,"[1] a fortunate if belated ruling. The Board of Supervision once said that the Act had raised "extravagant expectations" among the poor[2]. It is unlikely that the first three or four years of its working can have gratified those expectations.

The Factory Commissioners of 1833, anxious to ascertain how far the workers in British industry had been able to make provision against sickness misfortune old age and death, sent out, in a questionnaire relating to occupations wages and other matters, an inquiry about membership of Friendly Societies and sums deposited in Savings Banks. It was a complete failure. The operatives would not disclose their savings, or even the

[1] Nicholls, *op. cit.* p. 213, 219; but this advice was overruled in 1852; see Vol. II, 436.   [2] In its first report, Nicholls, *op. cit.* p. 195.

fact that they were in a position to save. As they were anxious to prove themselves under-paid, and their employers might have utilised evidence of surplus earnings in some wage controversy, their reticence, the Commissioners philosophically argued, was perfectly natural[1]. Yet, they added, the Friendly Society and Savings Bank returns show that the operatives must save, and save a good deal.

The Friendly Society movement was gathering power every year. Old societies were expanding and splitting up, new ones coming into existence. In 1832 was founded, "but whether by secession or otherwise does not appear,"[2] the Bolton Unity of Oddfellows. There would be fine spinners in that. The rather obscure and inefficient Order of Druids is said to have been reorganised in 1833. Next year, at Rochdale, the Foresters took modern form—like most societies, including the Masons, they have antique claims. In 1838 came the first of the railway Friendly Societies, that of the Great Western. The teetotal Rechabites were setting up their earliest tents (not lodges) about the same time, in the Manchester district. The Hearts of Oak date from 1841, the Nottingham Unity of Oddfellows, a product of secession, from 1843[3]. These all sprang up in a thick undergrowth of little societies, sick clubs, burial clubs, goose clubs and free-and-easies, watched by a growing force of Friendly Society statutes. By the Act of 1829 (10 Geo. IV, c. 56) a barrister had been appointed to inspect the rules of societies seeking registration from the Justices, and in 1846 (by 9 & 10 Vict. c. 27) this barrister, as Registrar of Friendly Societies, superseded the Justices altogether[4].

By 1835 it was thought "that not fewer than 1,000,000 persons in this Kingdom" were enrolled in societies of one kind or another[5]. For the year 1847 more trustworthy, but by no means complete, statistics were issued by the Registrar[6]. They dealt only with England and Wales; they included only the enrolled societies—enrolment was not compulsory—and, for lack of proper records, only those societies enrolled between

---

[1] *Supplementary Report*, 1834 (XIX. 261), p. 43.

[2] Walford, *The Insurance Cyclopaedia*, IV. 430.

[3] From the invaluable annals in Walford, *op. cit.* IV. 431 *sqq.*

[4] John Tidd Pratt, who had been the barrister, was Registrar from 1846 to 1870.

[5] Ansell, C., *A Treatise on Friendly Societies* (1835), p. 136.

[6] *Abstract of Returns respecting Friendly Societies in England and Wales*, 1852–3 (c. 109), covering the five years to December 31, 1850.

1828 and 1847 were tabulated. These numbered 10,433. On July 8, 1847, their membership was 781,722. In the preceding year, they had received from their members £693,751, and had paid out in benefits of various kinds £518,978. These figures exclude, besides many small and feeble societies, the powerful organisation of the Oddfellows, conjectured in 1845, "in its various ramifications,"[1] to have a membership of something like 400,000 and an income of well over a quarter of a million. The main body of the Oddfellows, the Manchester Unity, alone had a membership of 251,727 in January 1845, and an income for the previous year, exclusive of initiation fees, of £245,843[2]. If allowance be made for Scotland, where societies of various kinds were numerous, the total Friendly Society membership for Britain, in the late 'forties, cannot well have been much less than 1,500,000, at a time when the total male population of twenty years old and upwards was well below 5,500,000[3].

There was an extraordinary concentration of membership in Lancashire. The 1847 return gives no less than 258,000 members there, to which must be added a great body of Lancashire Oddfellows—Manchester was "the fountain head of the Unity"[4]—and presumably many smaller unenrolled societies. As there were only 538,000 males of twenty years old and upwards in the county in 1851, it is not unlikely that two-thirds of the men of Lancashire belonged to some society four years earlier. London and Middlesex together had 66,000 members in 1847; Yorkshire, 63,000; Kent, 30,000; and no other county so many. Probably the capital, with its numberless small social groups, had an abnormal proportion of little old-fashioned unenrolled societies; but that would not much affect the comparison with Lancashire, for greater London was more populous than Lancashire.

The Societies contained some bourgeois elements. The "Friend" to whom H. Mudge of Bodmin, Surgeon, addressed his sixteen letters exposing "Odd Fellowship," in 1845, was

---

[1] Neison, F. G. P., *Contributions to Vital Statistics* (1845), p. 134. The Oddfellows first came under the Friendly Societies Acts in 1851. Walford, *op. cit.* IV. 401.

[2] Neison, F. G. P., *Observations on...the Manchester Unity of the Independent Order of Oddfellows* (1846), p. 26, 38.

[3] Men often joined at 18, however, and sometimes younger.

[4] Neison, *Observations*, p. 28.

"a by no means unworthy member" of that Order[1]. But though the Oddfellows' initiation-money in the 'forties was a guinea, their weekly subscription was only 4d.; and the bulk of their membership came from among what another critic of their management called "the hard-working sons of toil."[2] Obviously this was even more true of the friendly societies in general, those of Lancashire above all. They were a working-class product as they had been from the first. They were not always well made. Actuarial mistakes constantly recurred; lodges often collapsed; fraud was not unknown. Meetings were still held in public houses, though the Rechabites had their tents. Critics from above continued to deplore the wastes of good fellowship and the inordinate expenses of management, which in one section of the Manchester Unity of Oddfellows in 1844 amounted to 150 per cent. of the expenditure on sick allowances. "The real and essential objects of the Order have been overlooked and rendered secondary to idle pomp and parade; and those funds which were meant to provide for disease and old age have been squandered away on the follies and baubles of youth."[3] But the whole movement gave remarkable proof of a growing will and a growing power to save in industrial England. It was in the factory districts that this will and this power were strongest. If too much of the savings went in banners, aprons, initiation ceremonies and liquor, there was some precedent in the history of gild pageantry, and a good defence in the failure hitherto of the new industrial society to furnish the colour, the ritual, and the cheer which men need and "hands" had not been given. There were still crowns and garters and college feasts and city dinners. How could Manchester or Leeds, without "public walks," art galleries, new buildings worth looking at or any civic splendour, expect these adult "sons of toil" never to flout sound actuarial principles, or play with "the follies and baubles of youth," when, by their own saving, they got the chance?

[1] *An Exposure of Odd Fellowship, showing that the Independent Order of Odd Fellows, Manchester Unity, is unscriptural in its Constitution; unjust in its Finance; extravagant in its Management; bankrupt in its Circumstances; deceitful in its Pretensions; dangerous in its Tendency; and immoral in its Practice.*

[2] Neison, *Observations*, p. 31. A typical London society of 1847 was composed entirely of craftsmen: none under 20. The subscription was 3s. a month: the benefits 10s. a week sick pay, 5s. superannuation pay, £7 burial money and £4 wife's burial money. *Abstract of Returns*, p. 5.

[3] Neison, *Observations*, p. 31. Ansell, *op. cit.*, was equally critical in 1835. For earlier critics see above, p. 298.

In the year in which the Factory Commissioners failed to get returns of the operatives' savings, other returns showed that the 425,000 depositors in the 408 Savings Banks of England and Wales had £14,334,000 to their credit. Two years later the Trustee Savings Bank law was introduced to Scotland (under 5 & 6 Wm. IV, c. 57) where it soon made progress in spite of the facilities offered to the small depositor by Scottish Joint-Stock Banks. By 1844, when the law was again revised (7 & 8 Vict. c. 83), the deposits in the British savings banks had risen to nearly £27,000,000, of which nearly £26,000,000 were English and Welsh, the balance Scottish[1]. There were certainly "proletarian" savings among the £27,000,000 (if a proletarian can save, and is not changed into a bourgeois in the act), but—here memory and impression must do duty for contemporary evidence—anyone familiar with the way in which Savings Banks were used, in the later nineteenth century, by Engels' "lower" and "middle" and, for that matter, by the children of his "upper bourgeoisie," may well wonder how much of the Banks' deposits actually came out of wages or handicraftsmen's earnings in 1844. The 1,012,047 depositors of that year must, from their mere number, have been in great part hand-workers. It is noticeable also that the average deposit, though still too high to be that of a typical hand-worker, had fallen since 1833, indicating a more popular *clientèle*; yet it is hard to believe that so much as half of the £27,000,000 can have come out of wages, especially when the wage-earners' contributions to Friendly Societies and trade clubs are considered.[2]

It is not easy to gauge the real importance of the trade clubs and unions in the industrial life of the 'thirties and 'forties. In the older, untouched, crafts many no doubt had continuous lives, locally at any rate, although that cannot always be proved. But an old craft in a new amorphous town might lose the club habit, or its club—even in good times—might fail to attract more than a small fraction of the workers. In all trades, but especially in the newer stormier ones, in which organisation had not the long roots that it had among hatters tailors paper-makers or millwrights[3], unions—local or general—rose and

---

[1] See article "Savings Banks" in *Dic. Pol. Econ.*
[2] Probably a good deal came from the wages of domestic servants.
[3] Above, p. 207-10.

fell with the success or failure of particular strikes, with the curve of the trade-cycle, and with the latent or active hostility of the state and the law. In a new trade, a fall might mean temporary extinction when, in an older one, it meant only loss of membership or loss of some central organisation.

It is now possible to illustrate numerically the trade union vicissitudes of an old craft, untouched by invention, from the story of the Operative Stone Masons[1]. This society, built up out of local masons' lodges in the early 'thirties, as a section of the wider and more ambitious Operative Builders' Union, is credited with 6000 members in 1833. It falls to 1678 in 1835, after the campaign of the state against the unions at the time of the trial of the Dorchester labourers, to rise again to 5590 in the good trade of 1837. By 1843, after the spell of bad trade and high prices in 1838-42, and—perhaps more important— after the London masons strike of 1841, the strike which held up the Houses of Parliament and the Nelson Column and nearly ruined the union[2], its membership is down to 2144. At the close of the decade (1848-52) it is fluctuating between 4700 and 6700. The society was English, and the Census of 1851 said that there were 66,000 "masons and paviors," of twenty years old and upwards, in England and Wales[3]. The scattering of masons in small groups and the widespread survival in the trade of handicraft masters, especially in the North-West and in Wales, help to account for the very small ratio of enrolled unionists to adult masons; but similar scattering and similar survival marked many of those old crafts in which local trade clubs, or unions based upon them, were strongest—cabinet-makers, carpenters, bricklayers, painters, bookbinders, hatters, tailors, compositors. It is unlikely, therefore, that a high percentage of workers in any trade was regularly enrolled in unions, at any time between 1830 and 1850, in spite of the strong old tradition of association among the crafts. Possibly the estimate

---

[1] Postgate, *The Builders' History* (1923), Appendix, p. 456. The figures are Mr Postgate's, the comments mine. The sections which follow are much indebted to Mr Postgate's work.   [2] Postgate, *op. cit.* p. 129-30.

[3] When Thomas Shortt became secretary, in 1838, the Masons in Union "were about 60 per cent. of the whole fraternity" (Postgate, p. 122), which, if correct, implies a "fraternity" of about 10,000. Paviors [wallers and operative masters, as Mr Postgate informs me] would not be masons to Shortt, but, when allowance is made for that and for thirteen years' increase, he seems to have had a narrow view of the "fraternity" or very imperfect information. The Census of 1831 had reported more than 35,000 masons in England and Wales.

which has been made[1], for the early 'forties, of less than 100,000 full, contributing, trade unionists, in the whole country, may be not far from the mark. But there must have been many more, especially in the building and clothing trades, hanging on to the skirts of the local clubs, frequenting houses of call, and ready for absorption into unions when they were moved to it and could afford.

Any such low figure, if accepted, throws into relief the reputed half-million and more[2] who, in a wave of popular feeling, driven by organised propaganda, joined—but so far as is known did not contribute to—the Grand National Consolidated Trades Union of 1833–4. In the 'twenties, the repeal of the combination law had set men free, or so they believed, to organise and to strike: the commercial collapse of 1825–6 had broken many strikes and wrecked much flimsy organisation. But a few far-seeing craftsmen thought they had found a way out of the wreck to rise in. In July 1827, delegates from a number of local clubs had set up in London the General Union of Carpenters and Joiners—"for the amelioration of the evils besetting our trade; the advancement of the rights and privileges of labour; the cultivation of brotherly affection and mutual regard for each other's welfare."[3] Two years later—the bare fact is known and no more[4]—the bricklayers also started a general society. Then came dearth, continental revolutions, risings in the country-side, preachings of the doctrine of "the communionists or socialists,"[5] heard at first only by the few, Cobbett's great voice sounding loud in the ears of all, and Thomas Attwood teaching from Birmingham the uses of a national Union for political ends; and after that the crowning disappointment of the Reform Bill.

Before the Reform Bill, so far as the evidence can be deciphered, the general unions of masons and bricklayers had come together with the other building crafts into a semifederal Operative Builders' Union[6]. By 1833 its membership is said to have been 40,000, and it was still growing fast, with tremendous rites of initiation. It was under Owenite influence especially in Birmingham, where its leaders—not working-men

---

[1] In Webb's *History of Trade Unionism*, p. 472, 748.
[2] Webb, *op. cit.* p. 134–5.
[3] Postgate, *op. cit.* p. 53. Webb, *op. cit.* p. 54 n.
[4] Postgate, *op. cit.* p. 54.
[5] Above, p. 315.   [6] Postgate, *op. cit.* p. 55 *sqq.*

but the partners in a firm of architects and builders, Messrs Hansom and Welsh—were in constant correspondence with the prophet. The ambition of those who inspired it was to create a Builders' Guild, in which masters were to be elective; and their special enemy was the contractor, who had no right "to barter our labour at prices fixed by" himself. This was in Birmingham. In Manchester and Liverpool masons took the lead in a similar movement, pointing out that buildings were generally "contracted for by master joiners who, while they have a just right to the privileges of their own trade, have no right to those of ours." They placarded Manchester with the demand "that no new building should be erected by contract with one person."[1] In Lancashire certainly, and perhaps in other places, many small masters were in the union—just as three hundred years earlier small masters had joined "yeomens'" societies in the more capitalistic trades of London[2]. They naturally wished to retain the old, dying, system in which the consumer of building labour made his separate contracts with the masters of the various crafts.

Contemporary with the attempt to federate the bricklayers' local lodges was John Doherty's plan for a Grand General Union of the Cotton Spinners' Societies of the United Kingdom[3], which was accepted at a conference of English, Scottish and Irish representatives in December 1829, held—where meetings of cotton operatives for other purposes have been held since—in the Isle of Man. Next year Doherty, pushing outside his own trade, is organising the Potters' Union[4], which rapidly attained a membership of 8000 and stretched from Newcastle-on-Tyne to Bristol, with its natural nucleus in Staffordshire. In Yorkshire the Leeds Clothiers' Union was fighting for the exclusion of non-unionists and a standard piece-work scale[5]. The masters replied with a proposed exclusion of unionists and a lock-out of some months' duration, in 1833.

In that year members from these and countless other unions and clubs, with multitudes who had never belonged to any organisation except perhaps some village friendly society or a Methodist class-meeting, were swept into the loosely disciplined ranks of the Grand National Trades Union. The now

[1] Postgate, *op. cit.* p. 73.
[2] Unwin, G., *Industrial Organisation in the Sixteenth and Seventeenth Centuries* (1904), p. 57 *sqq.*
[3] Webb, *op. cit.* p. 117 *sqq.*   [4] Webb, *op. cit.* p. 133 *sqq.*   [5] *Ibid.*

familiar story of that ephemeral and prophetic movement need
not be retold—its journals, its missionaries, its oaths, robes,
and figures of death painted by village carpenters, in presence
of which neophytes were initiated; or Robert Owen's attempt
to capture it for the cause of the new moral order. Its enemies
said that a London journeyman was "so overcome by the cere-
mony he went through on his admission that he died in the
agonies of raving madness"[1]; but George Loveless, the Dorset
Methodist labourer, who, with his friends, was transported for
his share in an oath of initiation at Tolpuddle, retained his sane
piety and democratic faith through worse trials. When starting
for Botany Bay, he sent his friends a poem with the lilt and
style of the poetry which he knew best, Wesley's hymns:

> God is our guide; from field, from wave,
> From plough, from anvil, and from loom
> We come our country's rights to save
> And speak a tyrant faction's doom.

The Grand National Union did not survive 1834. Local
unions and clubs and strike committees were beaten all along
the line. The violence, if not the initiation ceremonies, of some
of them had confirmed the government of the "tyrant faction"
in its fears. For safety, most of them now abandoned their
oaths and sombre pageantry. Employers called on their men
to sign "the document," abjuring unionism. Of the Operative
Builders' Union only the masons' society survived in an active
national form; and Robert Owen turned from trade unionism
to other things. But the Potters' Union kept its head above
water for a few more years. The printers', the ironfounders',
the boilermakers', the millwrights', the tailors', the glass-
makers', the paper-makers' and many other local or semi-
national unions of thoroughly skilled men, which had existed
long before the Grand National Consolidated, remained when
it had gone, even through the bad trade and high prices of
1838–41. They supplied the majority of the possible hundred
thousand trade unionists of the early 'forties.

"The history of these Unions," Engels wrote of the England
of 1844, "is a long series of defeats of the working men interrupted by a few isolated victories": they "remain powerless
against all great forces." But he admits their power "in dealing
with minor, single influences": they can prevent a manufacturer

---

[1] Quoted in Hurst, G. B., "The Dorchester Labourers, 1834," *E.H.R.*
Jan. 1925, where the whole story is reviewed.

from driving down wages at times when the general condition of the industry does not work with him: they "often bring about a more rapid increase of wages after a crisis than would otherwise follow."[1] By 1844–5 the general trade revival, after the depression of 1838–41, was very noticeable. With it had come a revival of trade union activity. Engels was specially interested, as well he might be, in the revival among the miners. Local clubs and short-lived unions had been common enough in mining districts; but in 1841 came the Miners' Association of Great Britain and Ireland with its headquarters at Wakefield, the body which, three years later, paid William Roberts, "the miners' attorney-general," £1000 a year to conduct its difficult legal business. Roberts had first served Northumberland and Durham, and had helped them to get rid of the old system of a yearly wage contract[2]. A hopeless strike in 1844 had left the North-countrymen bankrupt. They started it without resources and could not maintain it against immigrant labour, eviction from colliery cottages by the employers, and the lost monopoly of the London market which the railways had brought[3]. Nor could they any longer maintain Roberts, who transferred to headquarters and the Lancashire section of the Association. The North Country section collapsed after its eighteen weeks' strike—in which remnants of the pitmen's good furniture that Cobbett had described went to buy food and clothes[4]—but its memory lived, and the rising Lancashire and Yorkshire coal-fields kept miners' unionism alive[5].

Lancashire also helped to keep unionism alive in the building trades; but it was not more than alive. The masons, whose movable seat of government was at Liverpool in 1845, had worked their membership up to nearly 5000 in that year; but the bricklayers, whose only important centres were Manchester

---

[1] *The Condition of the Working Class*, p. 145. More orthodox economists have said much the same things since.

[2] Welbourne, E., *The Miners' Unions of Northumberland and Durham*, p. 64 *sqq.* Webb, *op. cit.* p. 181 *sqq.* The "virtual serfage" of the "yearly bond" (Webb) was popular with the older men, who liked certainty (Welbourne, *op. cit.* p. 71). For the yearly bond, above, p. 217.

[3] Welbourne and Webb, as above, and Jevons, H. S., *The British Coal Trade* (1915), p. 448 *sqq.*

[4] Above, p. 36. Previous strikes had greatly reduced the pitmen's reserves (Welbourne, *op. cit.* p. 79).

[5] The Association's membership in 1844 "rose, it is said, to at least 100,000" (Webb, *op. cit.* p. 182). As there were probably not 140,000 miners of 20 years of age and upwards in Great Britain (151,000 in 1851) this seems unlikely.

and London, are said never to have exceeded 2000, which was less than 4 per cent. of the adult bricklayers of Britain in the 'forties. The plumbers and glaziers, also with headquarters at Manchester, did rather better: their 1000 members must have formed a higher proportion of the possible total[1].

While the railway mania was in progress, the potato famine approaching, and the early railway age drawing towards its close, the formation—at Easter 1845—of the National Association of United Trades for the Protection of Labour showed that the ideals of the 'thirties were not altogether forgotten, though they were now being pursued with a judicious caution born of adversity. The scheme came from the "United Trades" of Sheffield, a kind of embryo Trades Council, and received support in its early days from similar bodies in Manchester, Hull, Norwich, Bristol and other places. Delegates were also sent by the textile and hosiery trades, the Lancashire miners —now coming to the front—and a number of the London crafts. A main object of the Association was to keep an eye on parliament and, if possible, scotch legislation inimical to labour interests. In its original prospectus and rules, it admitted the failure of "the industrious classes" to secure those ends for which unions existed: "for some years past their endeavours...have, with few exceptions, been unsuccessful." It agreed with Engels. No attempt was made to absorb existing organisations, the Association wishing rather to act as a central committee for them. Its first report did not speak of any new order of society, but of "the beneficial tendency arising from a good understanding between the employer and the employed."[2]

Although it earned an attack from *The Times*, the Association was opposed to strikes, and tried to act as a peacemaker during those of 1846–7—without much success; for, like many similar organisations in later years, it soon lost a good deal of its representative character on the workmen's side, and it was treated by employers as an irresponsible and noxious external organisation. At its conferences, people spoke of co-operative production and sometimes of agricultural communities. So far Owen and his teaching had power. There were even humble experiments with co-operative workshops, blessed by the Association and the Christian Socialists. But these had little

---

[1] Postgate, *op. cit.* p. 132 *sqq.* There were 59,000 bricklayers of 20 and upwards in 1851. Plumbers, glaziers and painters numbered 51,000 in 1851. Probably over 30,000 of these were painters.

[2] Its story is fully told in Webb, *op. cit.* p. 186 *sqq.*

national significance in their own day, nor were they to have much in the next.

The co-operative stores had significance in both[1]. In Scotland some co-operative associations of Owen's early begetting, apocalyptic associations which looked forward to the swift coming of the Day of Community, had kept up a continuous, if stagnant, life. But it is from the taking down of the shutters at the shop in Toad Lane, Rochdale, in December 1844, that the effective co-operative movement of nineteenth-century industrial Britain has always been dated, and rightly. The leaders of the Rochdale pioneers were Owenite Socialists; their followers included Socialists, Chartists and trade unionists who had just lost a strike. Whatever their dreams, and their programme looked forward both to manufacturing and agriculture on co-operative lines, they contented themselves in their early years of struggle with the supply to one another of genuine foodstuffs, the enforcement of cash payment, and the "Rochdale system" of dividing the profit on sales in proportion to the amount of purchases. They were imitated, after a couple of years, by their neighbours of the Lancashire cotton uplands —Bacup, Todmorden, Leigh, Middleton—and afterwards by groups of reformers scattered throughout most of industrial Britain. By 1851 there were something like a hundred and thirty small societies of the Rochdale type, with an aggregate membership which is not exactly known but can hardly have been more than 15,000[2]. They were all, or nearly all, in the English manufacturing North and the Scottish manufacturing Midlands. As compared with the trade unions, still more as compared with the friendly societies, the co-operators—who, as individuals, might well be both trade unionists and friendly society members—were still a feeble folk; but if creative faith, combined with sober peaceable good sense, ranks before the power to fight, in a cause however just, and before the rather obvious, if admirable, quest for good-fellowship, a little help in sickness or old age, and decent burial; then these scattered democratic stores, with simple routine and great hopes, may perhaps stand first among the self-made social institutions of British wage-earners in the bleak towns of the 'forties.

[1] Above, p. 315. For this short paragraph it is not necessary to do more than refer to Holyoake, G. J., *Self-Help, or History of the Equitable Pioneers of Rochdale*; Holyoake, G. J., *History of Co-operation*, and Potter, B. (Mrs Webb), *The Co-operative Movement in Great Britain*.

[2] The first definite figure of membership is 48,184 in 1861.

APPENDIX
PROFESSOR SILBERLING'S COST OF LIVING INDEX[1]

As this index, on which the diagram on p. 128 is based, plays a rather important part in the argument of Ch. IV and is referred to in other chapters, particularly Ch. XIII, and as it appeared in a publication accessible only in large libraries, it seems desirable to give a fuller account of it than was possible in the text or the footnotes. Professor Silberling was able to base his study of prices, of which this particular index is only a small part, on a large amount of evidence not used by Jevons in the construction of his well-known index numbers (*Investigations in Currency and Finance*). The general results do not differ greatly from those of Jevons, though there are very important differences of detail especially in the war years. It is not necessary to explain here the methods of calculation or the sources of information: it is sufficient to say that the results are a decidedly closer approximation to the truth than it was possible for Jevons to make. Professor Silberling has, in most cases, been able to base his yearly average prices on more single quotations than Jevons had at his disposal.

The cost of living index is meant to be as representative as possible of the general working-class domestic budget of the period, and the items are weighted in accordance with their assumed importance in such a budget. To food are assigned 42 points, to clothing materials 8, to fuel and light 6. The 42 points assigned to food are made up as follows: wheat 15; mutton 6; beef 6; butter 5; oats 3; sugar 3; tea 2; coffee 1; tobacco 1. The 8 points for clothing materials are made up as follows: wool 3; cotton 3; flax 1; leather 1. The fuel and light points are coal 4, tallow 2. For the average agricultural labourer's budget of the period it is probable that meat, and possible that sugar and clothing materials, are overweighted. Butter may be taken as fairly representative of cheese. Possible errors in the weighting are partly obliterated by the fact that food prices moved very much together, except in years of abnormally bad harvests, and that, in so far as the high prices of the war period were due to inflation, the operating cause acted uniformly on them all. It may be argued that in years of very bad harvests the situation of the mainly bread-and-cheese-fed labourer of South-Eastern England was somewhat worse than the comparison of the index with wage figures would suggest. This is

[1] In *British Prices and Business Cycles, 1779–1850. The Review of Economic Statistics (Harvard Economic Service)*, 1923. Norman J. Silberling.

perhaps true for such terrible years as 1800–1, 1812–13 and 1817–18; but for the purpose of the comparisons made in the text there is very little difference between Professor Silberling's index and a crude wheat index. For example, the dearest wheat years between 1820 and 1840 were 1825 and 1838–9. Taking wheat in 1790 (Professor Silberling's base year) as 100, wheat in 1825 was 126, and for 1838–9 it averaged 123. The Silberling index for 1825 is 128 and the average for 1838–9 is 120·5.

Of course these generalised national figures will not be equally applicable to all districts. There were still local prices. There are also the local dietaries to be considered. But as the main variations in diet were away from the wheat to a cheaper and less violently fluctuating basis (oats and barley prices were more stable than wheat prices), the position of the working-class consumer with a dietary different from that implied would not be worse than the figures suggest.

The series of figures on which the diagram on p. 128 is based is as follows (Col. I). They are the annual indices of the cost of living computed from the prices of the 15 articles, weighted as described (1790 = 100). [Beside them (Col. II) are now inserted the prices of the 4 lb. loaf in London in pence. They confirm the general conclusions drawn from Silberling's wholesale index: e.g. the relative comfort of the 'twenties.]

	I	II		I	II		I	II
1780	88	—	1804	140	9·7	1828	108	10·2
1781	96	—	1805	154	13·1	1829	106	11·0
1782	100	—	1806	148	11·7	1830	108	10·5
1783	93	—	1807	145	10·8	1831	111	10·4
1784	90	—	1808	159	11·6	1832	109	9·6
1785	85	—	1809	175	13·7	1833	107	8·7
1786	86	—	1810	176	14·7	1834	102	8·0
1787	93	—	1811	164	14·0	1835	99	7·0
1788	93	—	1812	180	17·0	1836	111	8·0
1789	95	—	1813	187	15·7	1837	111	8·5
1790	100	—	1814	176	11·4	1838	118	10·0
1791	98	—	1815	150	10·3	1839	123	10·0
1792	97	—	1816	135	11·7	1840	121	10·0
1793	106	—	1817	151	14·3	1841	116	9·0
1794	110	—	1818	159	11·8	1842	106	9·5
1795	130	—	1819	143	10·3	1843	94	7·5
1796	132	—	1820	132	10·2	1844	96	8·5
1797	120	—	1821	115	9·3	1845	97	7·5
1798	121	—	1822	100	8·3	1846	100	8·5
1799	143	—	1823	111	9·0	1847	116	11·5
1800	170	15·3	1824	113	10·4	1848	97	7·5
1801	174	15·5	1825	128	10·8	1849	86	7·0
1802	138	9·5	1826	111	9·2	1850	83	6·8
1803	140	8·7	1827	110	8·9			

INDEX